THE CULPABLE CORPORATE MIND

This collection examines critically, and with an eye to reform, conceptions and conditions of corporate blameworthiness in law. It draws on legal, moral, regulatory and psychological theory, as well as historical and comparative perspectives. These insights are applied across the spheres of civil, criminal and international law.

The collection also has a deliberate focus on the 'nuts and bolts' of the law: the legal, equitable and statutory principles and rules that operate to establish corporate states of mind, on which responsibility as a matter of daily legal practice commonly depends.

The collection therefore engages strongly with scholarly debates. The book also speaks, clearly and cogently, to the judges, regulators, legislators, law reform commissioners, barristers and practitioners who administer and, through their respective roles, incrementally influence the development of the law at the coalface of legal practice.

The Culpable Corporate Mind

Edited by
Elise Bant

•HART•
OXFORD • LONDON • NEW YORK • NEW DELHI • SYDNEY

HART PUBLISHING

Bloomsbury Publishing Plc

Kemp House, Chawley Park, Cumnor Hill, Oxford, OX2 9PH, UK

1385 Broadway, New York, NY 10018, USA

29 Earlsfort Terrace, Dublin 2, Ireland

First published in Great Britain 2023

A catalogue record for this book is available from the British Library.

A catalogue record for this book is available from the Library of Congress.

ISBN: HB: 978-1-50995-238-0
ePDF: 978-1-50995-240-3
ePub: 978-1-50995-239-7

Typeset by Compuscript Ltd, Shannon

FOREWORD

THE HON JUSTICE MICHELLE GORDON AC

The central purpose of this collection of essays is clear. It seeks 'to examine critically, and with an eye to reform, conceptions and conditions of corporate blameworthiness in law'.[1] In pursuit of that purpose, Professor Bant lays out the 'novel model of corporate responsibility' she has developed and calls 'Systems Intentionality'.[2] That model gives effect to the idea that 'a corporation's state of mind is manifested through its systems of conduct, policies and practices'.[3] It is proposed as an additional model for attributing corporate responsibility, not as a substitute for other models that are seen as reflected in decided cases.[4]

As the Contents of this volume shows, the authors of these essays examine notions of corporate responsibility from many different perspectives – moral responsibility, legal, economic and business history, landmark decisions, the intersections between corporate responsibility and notions like intention, knowledge, negligence, dishonesty, failure to prevent and unconscionability, and emerging issues like those presented by automated decision making. All of these different analyses combine to shed clear light on the 'conceptions and conditions of corporate blameworthiness in law'.[5] And yet, together, they show how the law has struggled, and continues to struggle, with this issue (and why the notion of Systems Intentionality may prove to be an important and valuable development).

Why has the law struggled as it has?

The limited liability company emerged in England in the middle of the nineteenth century. It was not until 1897, and *Salomon v A Salomon & Co Ltd*,[6] that the company's separate legal personality (separate that is from its corporators) was recognised. And the consequences of that decision 'for the rights of creditors and others were still being debated, and dealt with, well into the twentieth century'.[7]

[1] Bant, ch 1 of this volume, section I.
[2] ibid; Bant, ch 9 of this volume.
[3] Bant, ch 9 of this volume, section I; see also Bryan, ch 14 of this volume.
[4] Bant, ch 9 of this volume, section II.B.
[5] Bant, ch 1 of this volume, section I,; Gans, ch 13 of this volume; Carroll, ch 15 of this volume; Clough, ch 18 of this volume; and McGaughey, ch 20 of this volume.
[6] *Salomon v A Salomon & Co Ltd* [1897] AC 22.
[7] *New South Wales v The Commonwealth (Work Choices Case)* (2006) 229 CLR 1, 97 [121], citing O Kahn-Freund, 'Some Reflections on Company Law Reform' (1944) 7 *Modern Law Review* 54.

Over the decades, judges have often said that a company 'as such' cannot do anything; it must act by servants or agents. As Lord Hoffmann wrote in *Meridian Global Funds Management Asia Ltd v Securities Commission*, '[that] may seem an unexceptionable, even banal remark'.[8] But it is an observation that can complicate and obscure much of the discussion of corporate culpability and responsibility.

In *Meridian*, Lord Hoffmann said that 'a reference to a company "as such" might suggest that there is something out there called the company of which one can meaningfully say that it can or cannot do something,' but '[t]here is in fact no such thing as the company as such, no ding an sich, only the applicable rules' of attribution.[9] Is this right?

Reference to Kant's conception of 'the thing in itself' – *das ding an sich* – as opposed to the phenomenon – the thing as it appears to an observer – may serve only to obscure a basic legal proposition. A company has legal personality. It is a right- and duty-bearing entity, separate and distinct from its corporators. Its rights, duties and liabilities are different from those of its corporators, officers, employees or agents.

Thus, as several of the authors in this collection observe, 'corporations have an existence separate from, and qualitatively different from, the sum of their constituent members'.[10] Corporations are not just 'abstractions of the law' or legal 'fictions'. References to abstractions and fictions may be understood as implicitly denying the incontrovertible fact that corporations have legal personality, or, at least, may be understood as pointing towards analysing companies acquiring and holding rights or incurring liabilities by reference *only* to how natural persons do that. Neither of those conclusions is right. Each is distracting.

Yet despite companies' being distinct legal personalities, discussion of corporate culpability often focuses upon whether and when the acts or omissions of persons associated with the company can be 'attributed' to the corporation in a way that makes the company legally responsible in some way. And the discussion may proceed from the premise (sometimes express but often implicit) that corporate responsibility *depends* upon identifying one or more natural persons as the source or reason for the conclusion that the company is legally responsible.

Since at least 1915, and the House of Lords decision in *Lennard's Carrying Co Ltd v Asiatic Petroleum Co Ltd*,[11] inquiries about corporate culpability and responsibility have often been cast in terms of a search for 'the directing mind and will of the corporation, the very ego and centre of the personality of the corporation'.[12]

There may be some cases where the metaphor of directing will and mind is useful and apposite – cases where an individual's acts can readily be attributed to the company. Reading between the lines, *Lennard* may well have been such a case – Mr Lennard may well have controlled the company that owned the relevant vessel. The company's name suggested that he did. But whether he did control the company was never determined in

[8] *Meridian Global Funds Management Asia Ltd v Securities Commission* [1995] 2 AC 500, 506.

[9] ibid 506–07.

[10] Bant, ch 1 of this volume, section II.B. See also Harding, ch 2 of this volume, section II; Crofts, ch 3 of this volume, section II.A; Leow, ch 6 of this volume, section III.C; Faugno, ch 8, section II.A; Bant, ch 9 of this volume, section II.A; Dianmantis, ch 10 of this volume, section II.B; Bant, ch 11 of this volume, section I; and Derrington and Walpole, ch 16 of this volume, section IX.

[11] *Lennard's Carrying Co Ltd v Asiatic Petroleum Co Ltd* [1915] AC 705.

[12] ibid 713.

the case, because Mr Lennard did not give evidence. And the House of Lords held only that the company, as owner of the vessel, had not proved that the relevant damage had occurred without 'the actual fault or privity' of the owner.[13] It may be, then, that what was said about directing mind and will was not necessary for the decision. But the statement has since taken on a life of its own. So much so that, by 1957, Denning LJ likened a company to a human body: 'It has a brain and nerve centre which controls what it does. It also has hands which hold the tools and act in accordance with directions from the centre.'[14] Mere servants and agents are 'nothing more than hands to do the work and cannot be said to represent the mind or will … [D]irectors and managers … represent the directing mind and will of the company, and control what it does'.[15]

What has followed since *Lennard* is that too much of the subsequent discussion about corporate culpability and responsibility has proceeded by assuming a need to identify natural persons whose acts and intentions should be attributed to the corporation. And the central thrust of much of what Lord Hoffmann said in *Meridian* was framed by reference to 'rules of attribution', an expression that suggests that attributing the conduct of natural persons to the company is a step necessary to finding corporate responsibility. But as Lord Hoffmann made clear, attributing human characteristics to the corporation (by reference to 'its directing mind and will' or 'the very ego and centre of the personality of the corporation'[16]) will often distract attention from the more particular issue that must be considered.[17]

The *Lennard* case, the later House of Lords decision in *Tesco Supermarkets Ltd v Nattrass*[18] and *Meridian* all concerned the application of particular statutory provisions. *Lennard* and *Tesco* concerned exculpatory provisions; *Meridian* concerned the application of substantial shareholder provisions of securities legislation. In each case, then, there was an issue of statutory construction: did the provision apply to a company and, if it did, how did it apply? Yet what was said in *Lennard* and *Tesco* has been often read as if stating generally applicable, even universal rules.

Issues about the application of statutory provisions to corporations cannot be resolved by ritual incantation of phrases drawn from decided cases but divorced from the context in which those phrases were coined or considered. Especially is that so when the 'golden phrase' is a colourfully expressed metaphor.

Two decisions of the High Court of Australia, *Mallan v Lee*[19] and *Hamilton v Whitehead*,[20] illustrate the importance of recognising that references to directing mind and will or generalised reference to rules of attribution must not distract attention from the need to deal first with the construction and application of applicable statutory provisions. In both *Mallan* and *Hamilton*, a person who might have been seen as the directing mind and will of a corporation was charged with being an accessory to a crime committed by the corporation. In *Mallan*, the conduct of the company's public officer was itself a crime and the statute made the company vicariously responsible criminally

[13] ibid 714–16.
[14] *HL Bolton (Engineering) Co Ltd v T J Graham & Sons Ltd* [1957] 1 QB 159, 172.
[15] ibid.
[16] *Lennard* (n 11) 713.
[17] *Meridian* (n 8) 509–10.
[18] *Tesco Supermarkets Ltd v Nattrass* [1972] AC 153.
[19] *Mallan v Lee* (1949) 80 CLR 198.
[20] *Hamilton v Whitehead* (1988) 166 CLR 121.

for that guilty conduct. The Court held that to treat the public officer as an accessory to the company's offence inverted the operation of the statute.[21] By contrast, in *Hamilton*, the person who had knowledge of all the material circumstances and whose conduct constituted the commission of an offence by the company was held to be an accessory to the company's offence.[22] These conclusions depended wholly on construing the applicable statutes and, in particular, on recognising the nature of the liability incurred by the company – in *Mallan* a vicarious responsibility, in *Hamilton* liability as a principal offender.

As companies have become larger, more complex and their control and management more widely spread, any search for the directing will and mind of the company has become harder.[23] Those difficulties increase as companies use automated decision-making tools or other automated systems. Notions of will and mind do not fit easily in that context.[24]

No less importantly, more and more cases about corporate culpability concern the application of statute. In any case about the application of statutory norms, asking about a company's directing will and mind will often be irrelevant and distract attention from the need to construe and apply the relevant provisions.[25] And as Professor Bant urges, it may obscure the need to consider whether 'a corporation manifests (in both senses of revealing and instantiating) its states of mind through its systems of conduct, policies and practices'.[26]

Professor Bant says that the academy is not the sole focus of this collection of essays. Rather, she says, she has 'tried to curate a collection that will also speak, clearly and cogently, to the judges, regulators, legislators, law reform commissioners, barristers and practitioners who administer and, through their respective roles, influence incrementally the development of the law at the coalface of legal practice'.[27]

I am confident that this collection speaks clearly and cogently to all who use it. I am equally confident that it will influence the development of the law both 'at the coalface' and in the academy.

[21] *Mallan* (n 19) 215–16.

[22] *Hamilton* (n 20) 127–28.

[23] See Fisse, ch 7 of this volume.

[24] See Powles, ch 5 of this volume; Patersonn and Bant, ch 12 of this volume; and McGaughey, ch 20 of this volume. See also *Quoine Pte Ltd v B2C2 Ltd* [2020] 2 SLR 20.

[25] See Bryan, ch 14 of this volume; and Hanrahan, ch 17 of this volume.

[26] Bant, ch 1 of this volume, section I; see also Bryan, ch 14 of this volume. cf *Australian Securities and Investments Commission v Kobelt* (2019) 267 CLR 1, 77–78 [232]–[234]; *Stubbings v Jams 2 Pty Ltd* (2022) 96 ALJR 271, 286–87 [76]–[80]; 399 ALR 409, 426–27; *Crowley v Worley* (2022) 158 ACSR 505, esp at 550–51 [154]–[160].

[27] Bant, ch 1 of this volume, section I.

PREFACE

This collection arises out of, and builds upon, joint research with my good friend and colleague Professor Jeannie Marie Paterson into the regulation of misleading and unconscionable conduct at common law, in equity and under statute.[1] It also constitutes a major research outcome of my related, Future Fellowship project.[2] This seeks to examine and model reforms of the laws that currently inhibit corporate responsibility for serious civil misconduct, including the laws concerning corporate attribution. Pursuant to this project, I have proposed a novel model of liability entitled 'Systems Intentionality'. Readers will quickly appreciate how generously contributors to this collection have engaged with the model, helping me to identify and assess its strengths and weaknesses in ways that I could not have done alone. The model not only has been immeasurably improved as a result, but its legal surrounds have been closely interrogated and mapped, from a range of expert perspectives. I am enormously grateful, and proud, to have been part of such a wonderful collaborative effort. The collection stands, quite simply, as a highlight of my academic career.

The collection drafts were the subject of a delightfully collegial and effective 'blended' workshop in December 2021, hosted by the University of Western Australia Law School. My sincere thanks to my project manager at that time, Maggie Twomey, who wrangled the technology and navigated the shifting external environment with great care and priceless good cheer. I simply could not have managed without her. I also extend my heartfelt appreciation to Eloise Munro and Rachael Griffiths-Szeto for their excellent research assistance in preparing the collection for submission. Sincere thanks also go, as always, to Sasha Jawed and Tom Adams at Hart Publishing, for their longstanding and enormously helpful support. Especial and grateful mention must also be made of our outstanding copyeditor, Catherine Minahan, whose good humour and care made the production process a pleasure.

Finally, throughout this project, I have been cognisant of the striking generosity of many members of the bench and broader legal profession, who have been willing to read and critique my model in detail, with a view to its improvement. Justice Gordon's willingness to write the Foreword to this collection, and her interest in the project more generally, exemplifies this broader and essential community of support. No scholar can hope for more: I am honoured, and deeply grateful.

Elise Bant
Perth
November 2022

[1] Australia Research Council DP180100932 and DP140100767.
[2] ARC Future Fellowship FT190100475.

CONTENTS

LIST OF CONTRIBUTORS

Elise Bant is Professor of Private Law and Commercial Regulation at the University of Western Australia and Professorial Fellow at the University of Melbourne.

Michael Bryan is Emeritus Professor at the University of Melbourne.

Robyn Carroll is Professor of Law at the University of Western Australia.

Jonathan Clough is Professor of Law at Monash University.

Penny Crofts is Professor of Law at the University of Technology Sydney.

Sarah Derrington is a Judge of the Federal Court of Australia and President of the Australian Law Reform Commission.

Mihailis E Diamantis is Professor of Law at the University of Iowa.

Rebecca Faugno is Lecturer in Law at the University of Western Australia.

Brent Fisse is Honorary Professor of Law at the University of Sydney.

Jeremy Gans is Professor of Law at the University of Melbourne.

Joshua Getzler is Professor of Law and Legal History at the University of Oxford and Conjoint Professor of Law at the University of New South Wales, Sydney.

Pamela Hanrahan is Professor of Commercial Law and Regulation at the University of New South Wales, Sydney.

Matthew Harding is Professor of Law and Dean of the Melbourne Law School at the University of Melbourne.

Rachel Leow is Assistant Professor of Law at the London School of Economics and Political Science.

Fiona McGaughey is Associate Professor of Law at the University of Western Australia.

Jeannie Marie Paterson is Professor of Law and Co-Director of the Centre for Artificial Intelligence and Digital Ethics at the University of Melbourne.

Julia Powles is Associate Professor of Law and Technology and Director of the Minderoo Tech & Policy Lab at the University of Western Australia.

Samuel Walpole is Adjunct Fellow at the University of Queensland.

Lauren Willis is Professor of Law at Loyola Law School, Loyola Marymount University.

TABLE OF CASES

TABLE OF LEGISLATION

references are to page numbers

England & Wales

AUSTRALIA

Commonwealth

TABLE OF INSTRUMENTS AND OTHER MATERIALS (AUSTRALIA)

references are to page numbers

AUSTRALIAN STATE LEGISLATION

references are to page numbers

Australian Capital Territory

New South Wales

Northern Territory

Queensland

South Australia

Victoria

Western Australia

TABLE OF OTHER NATIONAL LEGISLATION

references are to page numbers

Canada

Fiji

France

Nauru

Netherlands

New Zealand

USA

California

Delaware

Montana

TABLE OF INTERNATIONAL MATERIALS

references are to page numbers

PART I

Frameworks and Contexts

1

The Culpable Corporate Mind: Taxonomy and Synthesis

ELISE BANT

I. Genesis

This collection is concerned to examine critically, and with an eye to reform, conceptions and conditions of corporate blameworthiness in law. In so doing, it draws on legal, moral, regulatory and psychological theory, as well as historical and comparative perspectives. These insights are applied across the spheres of civil, criminal and international law. However, the collection also has a deliberate focus on the legal, equitable and statutory principles and rules that operate to establish corporate states of mind, on which responsibility as a matter of daily legal practice commonly depends. Consistently, while it engages strongly with scholarly debates, the academy is not its sole focus. Rather, I have tried to curate a collection that will also speak, clearly and cogently, to the judges, regulators, legislators, law reform commissioners, barristers and practitioners who administer and, through their respective roles, influence incrementally the development of the law at the coalface of legal practice.

This practical, doctrinal emphasis reflects the genesis of the collection in two related projects, both supported by the Australian Research Council. The first project, conducted with my long-time friend and colleague, Professor Jeannie Marie Paterson, examines the regulation of misleading conduct across common law, equity and statute.[1] The second project, Future Fellowship, aims to develop principled and practical liability models, which are effective to address corporate fraud and other egregious misconduct.[2] Beyond issues of attribution and liability, it is hoped that the latter project will provide new ways to conceptualise good, proactive corporate governance and the necessary criteria for rehabilitation when corporate actors commit wrongs.

[1] Australian Research Council Discovery Projects DP180100932 and DP140100767. For the most recent publication, which records the findings of the projects, see J Sabbagh, E Bant and JM Paterson, 'Mapping Misleading Conduct: Challenges in Legislative Design' (2022) 49 *University of Western Australia Law Review* 144.

[2] Australian Research Council Future Fellowship project FT190100475 at www.uwa.edu.au/schools/research/unravelling-corporate-fraud-re-purposing-ancient-doctrines-for-modern-times.

Out of this research, I have developed a novel model of corporate responsibility entitled 'Systems Intentionality'.[3] It has been developed through a process of considering critically existing understandings of corporate responsibility, and attribution models, testing these against difficult scenarios that reflect the modern, complex and diffused corporate defendant, and building from their identified failings a more responsive and workable model. The model has then, itself, been subjected to testing and refinement.[4] This collection forms an important part of that process.

I have charted elsewhere the series of important writings and inquiries that led me, eventually, to develop the model.[5] Building, in particular, on the writings of scholars such as Peter A French[6] and contributor Brent Fisse,[7] and Australian corporate culture and statutory unconscionability reforms, I gradually realised that it was possible to align corporate systems of conduct with corporate states of mind. Put at its most simple, Systems Intentionality proposes that a corporation manifests (in both senses of revealing and instantiating) its states of mind through its systems of conduct, policies and practices. Central to its development was the realisation that systems of conduct are inherently purposive: a point so blindingly self-evident,[8] once it is made, that it has since felt like a fraud of my own to claim that it bears any novelty. Here, contributor Mihailis E Diamantis' discussion of recipes, maps and other external decision-supports[9] provided a true 'light bulb' moment, and very useful ways to explain the model, even if my interpretation of his work has led me in a slightly different, and perhaps more doctrinally technical, direction.

A key attraction of this approach was that it built on the objective, but still fault-based, concept of 'transactional neglect' developed by Rick Bigwood,[10] and supported by Paterson,[11] for justifying a finding of unconscionable conduct, and the work of

[3] E Bant, 'Culpable Corporate Minds' (2021) 48 *University of Western Australia Law Review* 352; E Bant and J M Paterson, 'Systems of Misconduct: Corporate Culpability and Statutory Unconscionability' (2021) 15 *Journal of Equity* 63; JM Paterson, E Bant and H Cooney, '*Australian Competition and Consumer Commission v Google*: Deterring Misleading Conduct in Digital Privacy Policies' (2021) 26 *Communications Law* 136; E Bant, 'Catching the Corporate Conscience: A New Model of "Systems Intentionality"' [2022] *Lloyds Maritime and Commercial Law Quarterly* 467; E Bant, 'Reforming the Laws of Corporate Attribution: "Systems Intentionality" Draft Statutory Provision' (2022) 39 *Company & Securities Law Journal* 259.

[4] The above publications all contain detailed worked examples, drawn from case law and law commission inquiries.

[5] See in particular Bant, 'Catching the Corporate Conscience' (n 3) 470–71.

[6] PA French, *Collective and Corporate Responsibility* (New York, Columbia University Press, 1984).

[7] Some of the most influential include B Fisse, 'The Social Policy of Corporate Criminal Responsibility' (1978) 6 *Adelaide Law Review* 361; B Fisse, 'Recent Developments in Corporate Criminal Law and Corporate Liability to Monetary Penalties' (1990) 13 *University of New South Wales Law Journal* 1; B Fisse, 'The Attribution of Criminal Liability to Corporations: A Statutory Model' (1991) 13 *Sydney Law Review* 277; B Fisse and J Braithwaite, *Corporations, Crime and Accountability* (Cambridge, Cambridge University Press, 1993).

[8] I am pleased to report that my hairdresser considers my model to be 'obvious' – and far easier to understand than the concept of a 'directing mind and will'. She is a captive audience and has been more helpful than she knows, both in developing my ideas and how to explain them.

[9] M Diamantis, 'The Extended Corporate Mind: When Corporations Use AI to Break the Law' (2020) 98 *North Carolina Law Review* 893.

[10] R Bigwood, *Exploitative Contracts* (Oxford, Oxford University Press, 2003); R Bigwood, '*Kakavas v Crown Melbourne* – Still Curbing Unconscionability' (2013) 37 *Melbourne University Law Review* 463.

[11] JM Paterson, 'Unconscionable Bargains in Equity and Under Statute' (2015) 9 *Journal of Equity* 188.

Paterson and Gerard Brody, in interrogating how statutory unconscionability might be understood in responding to unfair business models, rather than individual instances of misconduct.[12] However, Systems Intentionality departs from these approaches in the way in which it seeks to understand these models in terms of the specific corporate mindsets which the business models declared,[13] so tying the analysis more closely to the core role performed by state of mind in unconscionable conduct.[14]

Systems Intentionality also provided a different (but ultimately, I consider, consistent) way of appreciating Fisse's influential concept of 'reactive corporate fault'.[15] His more expansive temporal framework for assessing corporate culpability is very helpful to the systems model. Systems Intentionality encourages courts and regulators to engage in qualitative assessment of corporate conduct that goes beyond a snapshot moment taken at the point at which harm occurs. On this approach, what Fisse terms 'proactive' corporate fault encompasses the corporate choices involved in coordinating steps through a 'system of conduct' to its ultimate end point. Further, Fisse's expanded temporal lens, encompassing the corporate responses to its misconduct, has prompted me to adopt a wide 'angle of focus' to identifying and then assessing systems of conduct. On my model, systems of conduct may properly encompass not only those proactive systems that directly produce harmful outcomes, but also related audit and remedial systems. Further, again building here on Fisse, it is possible and wholly appropriate to characterise systems by reference to the wholesale *omission* of audit and remedial systems. Indeed, their omission is often a choice in system design as eloquent to corporate intention as the primary system to which any mechanisms would relate.[16] A very similar view is taken by Crofts in this volume, who argues that 'Corporate governance failings should not be considered in isolation but as part of a decision-making strategy expressed in official and unofficial, formal and informal rules.'[17] This approach addresses, I think, at least one of Diamantis' criticisms of the model of Systems Intentionality, namely, that it is inapt to address 'culpably missing systems'.[18] On the contrary, I consider this aspect of the model to be one of its strengths, disabling the common 'deficiency' narrative that has, so successfully, enabled corporations to frame misconduct in terms of negligence or mistake.

I have developed and tested the model very considerably since its inception. It has been influenced immeasurably by the generous and insightful feedback of judges, regulators, law commission officers, practitioners and eminent scholars, including

[12] JM Paterson and G Brody, '"Safety Net" Consumer Protection' (2015) 38 *Journal of Consumer Policy* 331.

[13] The relationship between the model and objection approaches to finding 'intention' in other legal contexts, such as for interpretive purposes, for example, in the context of trusts, wills, legislation, and of course contracts, must await another occasion. The concept of 'declaration' of express trusts, however, seems consistent with my use of 'manifestation' of intention by corporations, and with some discussions of the concept of parliamentary intention. It is at least plausible that Systems Intentionality is consistent with, and even reflective of, a broader principle found throughout the law.

[14] Bant and Paterson, 'Systems of Misconduct' (n 3).

[15] Fisse, ch 7 of this volume.

[16] See the analysis, in particular, in Bant, 'Catching the Corporate Conscience' (n 3) 487–90; and Bant, 'Reforming the Laws' (n 3) 16–17.

[17] Crofts, ch 3 of this volume, section II.C.

[18] Diamantis, ch 10 of this volume, section III.B.

those engaged in this collection. Paterson, as always, must come in for special thanks, for her rigorous criticisms and generous encouragement. Two particular improvements to the model arising out of this collaborative process warrant identification here. First, early articulations of the model wavered in the roles for, and nature of, systems of conduct, patterns of behaviour, policies, processes and practices. It was only in writing 'Systems Intentionality: Theory and Practice' for this volume that I worked through the distinctions between these component concepts and settled the core formula: that corporations manifest their states of mind through their 'systems of conduct, policies and practices'.[19] That chapter also provides the beginnings of the litigation roadmap promised in my original Future Fellowship grant application. It sets out the meaning of the concepts and, importantly, what kinds of evidential strategies may be utilised to establish each. My later chapter, entitled 'Modelling Corporate States of Mind through Systems Intentionally' then outlines how systems of conduct (once proven) may be understood to manifest different, paradigm mental elements.[20]

Second, in debating these chapters, I was able to confirm my tentative, original position that this process is not one of 'inference' of mental states.[21] A corporation, after all, does not have a natural mind to be inferred from its conduct. This was a concern articulated by the Law Commission of England and Wales as a reason against adopting the model, at least immediately.[22] However, this concern is, I think, misplaced. Systems Intentionality involves a process of objective characterisation of corporate mental states from the features of the proven system. Here, the point is that systems of conduct are how corporations think: how they instantiate and declare their intentions. No inference of mental states is required, or not in the same way as it might be for individual intentions. Rather, courts must assess direct evidence of the alleged system of conduct and, if the system is established, characterise what it says (reveals) about the corporate mental state it instantiates. The exercise is closer to one of 'construction' of a mental state, although I think 'characterisation' is better in capturing the essence of the task. I am not sure how much hangs on this: it seems likely that many judges will not dissect the necessarily rather messy process of fact-finding and characterisation in a pedantic way. They may well be content to treat corporate persons as for individuals in inferring mental states from conduct. And, as we shall see, Diamantis argues cogently in his chapter that there is no need to distinguish between corporate and natural persons when inferring mental states. However, given that my object is to explicate as fully as possible the doctrinal and practical applications of the model, as well as its theoretical underpinnings, it seems important to clarify this aspect of its operation. This may, in turn, spur further research into and consideration of these issues, necessary to evaluate the nature and comparative benefits of the respective approaches.

That said, it is, of course, true that a system of conduct may place an individual decision-maker at its apex, so that some inquiry into that individual's mind becomes necessary and appropriate on the model of Systems Intentionality. Indeed, as we shall

[19] Bant, ch 9 of this volume.
[20] Bant, ch 11 of this volume.
[21] Bant, 'Culpable Corporate Minds' (n 3) 382, fn 156.
[22] Law Commission, *Corporate Criminal Liability* (Options Paper, 10 June 2022) [6.34]–[6.41] ('Law Commission Options Paper').

see, in my view, some attribution rules, such as the 'Identification Doctrine',[23] are largely consistent with this sort of decision-making structure and analysis. This raises the relationship between the novel model of Systems Intentionality and other models of corporate attribution and liability. The following section critically considers this question.

II. Taxonomy and Synthesis

A. Introduction

In what follows, I aim to give a sense, necessarily brief, of the range and nature of the important contributions made by authors to this collection, which examine the conceptions and conditions of corporate responsibility. The discussion will, I hope, make clear the reasoning behind the structure of the collection, as well as connections between the chapters. But I also seek to position Systems Intentionality within those themes and inquiries, and to respond (again, in brief) to some issues very helpfully identified by the contributors. This is important given the aims of the Future Fellowship project, and the need to test critically whether the proposed model is fit for purpose.

Broadly speaking, I think the contributors' analyses endorse the view that Systems Intentionality is intuitive,[24] practically workable and proceeds on a well-supported (if not universally accepted) theoretical basis. A range of essays explore the value of the model as an additional means of holding corporations to account for serious wrongdoing, against strengths and weaknesses of other approaches. Overall, the essays demonstrate the value of a pluralistic approach to corporate regulation. This multifaceted approach to corporate regulation, however, again raises the relationship between the various approaches to corporate responsibility. Pluralism is clearly less desirable, or simply undesirable, when it merges inconsistent approaches to corporate responsibility. The following discussion therefore identifies some of the most striking intersections, as well as divergences, between leading models. In this way it seeks to develop both a taxonomy of the law and to synthesise, to the extent possible, different approaches and perspectives. It will also make apparent the very considerable further work that must be done to develop a more coherent law of corporate responsibility.[25]

B. Frameworks and Contexts

The starting point for any discussion of corporate responsibility must be with some foundational understandings of the nature of a corporation. As is well known, views can

[23] Exemplified in *Lennard's Carrying Co v Asiatic Petroleum Co Ltd* [1915] AC 705, 713 (Viscount Haldane LC) (HL); *HL Bolton (Engineering) Co Ltd v TJ Graham and Sons Ltd* [1957] 1 QB 159, 172; [1956] 3 All ER 624, 630 (Lord Denning); *Tesco Supermarkets Ltd v Nattrass* [1971] UKHL 1, [1972] AC 153, 170 (Lord Reid) (*Tesco Supermarkets*).

[24] Important, if one is to try to explain it to jurors.

[25] A key recommendation of the Australian Law Reform Commission, *Corporate Criminal Responsibility* (Report No 136, April 2020) [1.15], [1.25] Recommendation 5, [6.13]–[6.22] ('ALRC Final Report').

be roughly divided into two camps: the nominalist and realist.[26] Nominalists hold that corporations are abstractions of the law, or (even less helpfully, for liability purposes) 'fictions'. On these accounts, corporations are, in truth, collections of individuals, commonly conceived as bound together by private contractual or other consensual relationships. It follows that moral and legal responsibility for any wrongdoing rests with the individuals conducting or engaged in group activities. To speak of a corporation existing in its own right or having the qualities of a moral person, or as being capable of being legal responsible in its own right is a nonsense.[27] Corporate responsibility must always, therefore, be mediated through the fault of individual employees or agents of the company.

Realists, by contrast, consider that corporations have an existence separate from, and qualitatively different from, the sum of their constituent members. This is consistent with recognition of corporations as social facts.[28] On this account, corporate persons may manifest traits, cultures, values, choices, knowledge and intentions not solely derivatively through their employees and agents, but as entities in their own right. Their abilities mean that corporations are able properly to be considered moral and legal agents, a conclusion essential for justifying corporate criminal liability in particular.[29]

As the Australian Law Reform Commission (ALRC) has recognised in its very helpful report on *Corporate Criminal Responsibility* (references to which permeate this collection), the law's traditional attribution rules arguably straddle these views.[30] These rules identify individual employees or agents acting for and on behalf of the company, whose mind is treated, for the purposes of the law, as that of the corporation itself. The corporation is conceived as a distinctive entity with its own mind, choices, knowledge and intentions, but these are identified derivatively through specific human agents of the corporation. The same may be said of other statutory approaches that seek to cast the attribution net wider than directors and senior officers of the company.[31] This messy pragmatism does not, however, avoid the problem of trying to work out why, and how, it may be justified to treat corporations in terms of distinctively organisational blameworthiness. In particular, unless one has a decent account of the philosophical foundations of organisational responsibility, it may be premature or unjustifiable, or simply silly, to seek, for example, to develop doctrinal models of corporate culpability that are not

[26] The following does not attempt to summarise the subtle spectrum of views that may combine aspects of these, but rather to provide a rough picture of the background contexts against which the chapters may be more fully understood. For useful discussion of views, see E Colvin, 'Corporate Personality and Corporate Crime' (1995) 6 *Criminal Law Forum* 1; ME Diamantis and WS Laufer, 'Prosecutions and Punishment of Corporate Criminality' (2019) 15 *Annual Review of Law and Social Science* 453; ALRC Final Report (n 25) ch 4; E Micheler, *Company Law: A Real Entity Theory* (Oxford, Oxford University Press 2021) ch 1; Crofts, ch 3 of this volume.

[27] F Cohen, 'Transcendental Nonsense and the Functional Approach' (1935) 35 *Columbia Law Review* 809; see also J Hasnas, 'Where is Felix Cohen When You Need Him?: Transcendental Nonsense and the Morality of Corporations' (2010) 19 *Journal of Law and Policy* 55.

[28] See, eg, Harding, ch 2 of this volume, section III; Diamantis, ch 10 of this volume, section IV.B.

[29] Crofts, ch 3 of this volume, section I.

[30] ALRC Final Report (n 25) [4.32].

[31] The 'TPA model', originally contained in Trade Practices Act 1974 (Cth), s 84, is the best-known and most widely copied example: see ALRC Final Report (n 25) [3.60]–[3.63], [6.123]–[6.160].

derivative of individual fault. Rather, it is likely better to seek more effective means to hold individuals who associate to account for their wrongdoing, and to concentrate on other strategies (such as performance-based models of liability) to protect those who deal with those groups of individuals. Fortunately for me, there are, indeed, powerful and cogent 'realist' accounts of moral and legal corporate responsibility, on which I have gratefully built my doctrinal liability model. Penny Crofts' essay, in particular, provides an excellent account of these, in examining the moral agency of corporations through the lens of criminal law, to which we will return shortly. However, the fact that these provide, for me, a compelling reason to conceptualise corporations in holistic terms does not remove the importance of understanding the moral responsibilities of individuals who associate.

Given these critical issues, it is fitting that the collection commences with Matthew Harding's thoughtful and thought-provoking analysis of the moral significance of associating, in 'Associations and Moral Responsibility: Some Ground-Clearing'.[32] As Harding explains, the chapter explores the moral significance entailed in individuals' associating with others, whether it be in the context of intimate associations such as families, or those towards the other end of the spectrum of communities such as churches, corporations, charities or political organisations. Harding's basic premise is that associating with others has moral implications for an individual, offering new ways for that individual to expand her moral horizons. When an individual associates with others, she commits in some sense to the shared purposes of that group.[33] This commitment exposes her to both moral rewards and risks: the opportunity to develop wholly new ways to achieve a greater range of personal and communal goods, as well as the potential to be implicated in personal and communal wrongs of a different order and moral significance. Here, Harding identifies a range of difficult issues, including: the ambiguous quality of loyalty where that loyalty is directed towards bad associational purposes; the moral implications of just 'doing your job'; the related role of whistle-blowers, who refuse simply to do their job; and the special moral obligations senior office holders of an association bear towards those who commit to the association. Harding's characterisation of the last as raising a risk of associational abuse and betrayal of trust provides a powerful, additional lens through which to assess the sorts of repeated and longstanding governance failures discussed in his chapter, and in others, in this collection.[34]

While individuals may have less or more control over the acts of the association, Harding is clear that their commitment to it necessarily and justly involves them in some share of moral responsibility for those actions. This moral responsibility is persistent and broad-based. It does not simply track formal membership. Indeed, it is not bounded temporally (a point that might be recalled when, as too commonly occurs, directors

[32] Harding, ch 2 of this volume.

[33] The commitment might be more 'thin' and hence of marginal moral significance, such as where an individual has little economic choice but to accept an offer of employment, or more 'thick', as where a person joins the Board of a company in order expressly to promote its ends. But involuntary coordination with others, as in modern slavery, entails no commitment and 'simply underscores the grave moral wrong that is done': ibid, section II.

[34] Harding discusses Rio Tinto's destruction of the Juukan Gorge and the responsibility of the Catholic Church for child sexual abuse, amongst others. See also Crofts, ch 3 of this volume, on the Crown Casino; Powles, ch 5 of this volume, on Uber and Facebook; Bant, ch 11 of this volume, on banking misconduct.

resign to 'take responsibility for' egregious corporate misconduct under their watch, thereby seemingly also washing their hands of the whole business). Associations, after all, may retain their identity over time and through considerable changes of membership and activity.[35] Consistently, Harding explores why, and how, the act of associating attracts moral responsibility for historical associational harms. Responsibility here may extend to situations where an association has the purpose to relieve victims of another's historic wrongdoing. Harding is, however, careful to note that the individual burden of remediating this broad, persistent, shared moral responsibility might vary, both in terms of its substantive content and remedial demands.

Harding also explores a range of ways in which this moral burden might differ from legal obligations.[36] Yet, as he notes, the implications for legal accounts are both important and interesting. As we shall see, the contributions of Justice Sarah Derrington and Samuel Walpole[37] and Pamela Hanrahan[38] squarely and critically examine the justifications for and boundaries of individual legal responsibility for associating. Thus Derrington and Walpole consider the common practice of sacrificing individual scapegoats as surrogates for corporate responsibility, in the context of harms involving ships. They argue for recognition of ships as legal persons: a reminder that natural and corporate persons are hardly the sum of possibilities for attributing responsibility for harms in the law. Hanrahan examines the development of what might be called scapegoat positions, created legislatively to provide ready means to hold officers to account for sins of the corporation committed 'on their watch'.[39] Both accounts provide important additional perspectives on the difficult and delicate relationship between individual and corporate accountability at the heart of Harding's essay.

On my model, individuals embedded in corporate systems of misconduct become potentially powerful witnesses to corporate fraud, rather than necessary casualties of or substitutes for corporate responsibility.[40] However, individual accountability is by no means excluded from, or foreign to, the model of Systems Intentionality. While it is not possible to address this fully here, it will be apparent that individuals will continue to be responsible, personally,[41] through existing common law, equitable and statutory routes. These include the ongoing role for negligence and accessorial liability for directors. It is also entirely possible that lower-level managers, employees and agents may be held personally responsible for harms caused while pursuing corporate activities. However, my starting position is that individual blame must reflect, and be proportionate to, that individual's genuine, personal culpability, not merely be pursued as the necessary hook

[35] As to which, see Julia Powles' chapter, in particular on Uber's strategy of distinguishing its current from former self, and relying heavily on management renewal to that end: Powles, ch 5 of this volume, section II.A.

[36] See also Pamela Hanrahan's discussion of this distinction in ch 17 of this volume, section IV.

[37] Derrington and Walpole, ch 16 of this volume.

[38] Hanrahan, ch 17 of this volume.

[39] ibid sections I and IV.

[40] Bant, 'Catching the Corporate Conscience' (n 3) 492–95; Bant, ch 9 of this volume, section II.A. See also Powles, ch 5 of this volume, sections II.A and II.B, on the critical role of whistle-blowers in holding Big Tech to account.

[41] As opposed to being the means by which the corporation is held responsible, such as through the Identification Principle.

on which to hang corporate liability, or a means to assuage public demands for 'heads on sticks'.[42] In this respect, I think, all our accounts align.

The following essay on 'Crown Resorts and the Im/moral Corporate Form'[43] turns from a concern with the nature and bounds of individual responsibility to that of the corporation in its own right. Crofts draws on realist theory to examine the moral and legal criminal responsibility of corporations, in light of the recent Australian inquiries into the Crown Resorts group.[44] As Crofts explains, the criminal law's roots in human wrongdoing have given rise to key tenets, such as that a guilty act requires a guilty mind. Criminal law is also 'a system of blaming'.[45] This necessarily requires that the subject of the criminal law be blameworthy. It follows that, without some cogent means of understanding the moral responsibility of corporations, the criminal law will continue to struggle, and fail, to hold criminogenic corporations to account.

Here, Crofts provides an extremely helpful understanding of leading theorist Chris Chapple's three criteria for organisational blameworthiness: that corporations are distinct moral agents facing moral choices; that they have power to make those choices; and they have the capacity to exercise good judgement.[46] Mapping these on to the doctrinal requirements of the criminal law, Crofts argues that, by reference to these considerations, the Australian inquiries revealed clear evidence of criminality on the part of Crown Resorts. Her detailed analysis of why, and how, this is so explores and connects the social reality of corporate personhood with critical criminal law requirements of voluntariness, causation and intentionality. In the course of so doing, Crofts' analysis repeatedly highlights the salience of corporate culture, systems, rules, structures and procedures in establishing each of these elements. Crofts concludes that, as an (im)moral corporate agent, Crown Resorts arguably merits criminal law's denunciation and sanction. Her contribution provides a compelling case for greater involvement of the criminal law in corporate regulation. In my view, it also underscores the powerful, analytical role that may be played by systems-based conceptions of corporate responsibility, seen through a realist lens.

The following two chapters consider the strategic shifts adopted by companies to limit their liability, in response to the legal frameworks in which they operate. Joshua Getzler's chapter on 'Corporate Torts in England: Limiting Liability by Capacity' considers the historical genesis, and eventual abandonment, of the ultra vires rule in the law of torts, developed as a limitation on corporate liability.[47] The limitation responded to the risks posed by general vicarious liability on the part of a company for

[42] See, eg, ME Ziffer et al, 'Royal Commission: Damming Report: The Public was Hoping for Heads on Sticks but, Instead, we got a Grinning CEO' *The Business* (4 February 2019) at https://search.informit.org/doi/full/10.3316/tvnews.tsm201902040147, for an example of the public disappointment in the wake of publication of the Commonwealth of Australia, *Royal Commission into Misconduct in the Banking, Superannuation and Financial Services Industry* (Final Report, 1 February 2019) ('FSRC Final Report').

[43] Crofts, ch 3 of this volume.

[44] Parliament of New South Wales, *Inquiry Under Section 143 of the Casino Control Act 1992 (NSW)* (Report, 1 February 2021); State of Victoria, *Royal Commission into the Casino Operator and Licence* (The Report, October 2021) vol 1 ('VCCOL Report'); State of Western Australia, *Perth Casino Royal Commission* (Final Report, 4 March 2022).

[45] Crofts, ch 3 of this volume, section I.

[46] C Chapple, *The Moral Responsibilities of Companies* (London, Palgrave Macmillan, 2014).

[47] Getzler, ch 4 of this volume.

the acts or wrongdoing of the agents and employees through which it acted.[48] As will be apparent, this liability approach reflects an individualistic account, in which a 'corporation is incapable of acting either rightfully or wrongfully in its proper person'[49] and so must be held responsible, derivatively, through its human agents.

Before addressing the substance of his analysis, it is worthwhile noting the aptness and broader utility of Getzler's contribution for understanding some of the key themes explored in this collection. First, vicarious liability was the initial means by which corporations were held responsible as a matter of civil law for the acts or wrongdoing of their agents. Criminal law followed this lead,[50] a point underscoring the entwined development of principles of corporate responsibility across civil and criminal divides. This shared history also, arguably, supports a unified approach to any reforms of the laws relating to attribution of corporate mental states.[51] Vicarious liability has also remained an eminently useful weapon within the armoury of the law, and influenced law reform initiatives. However, as a means of holding corporations responsible for their own, organisational blameworthiness, vicarious liability suffers from the related objections that it is indirect or derivative, and hence potentially strict.[52] Thus, where it applies, the corporation is commonly understood[53] as being held responsible for another's wrongdoing. Consistently, the approach is over-inclusive, capturing without distinction the act of a rogue employee in an otherwise well-managed and ethical company, alongside that of an employee diligently carrying out instructions essential to the corporation's predatory business model. It is also under-inclusive, unable to address the significance of a predatory system of conduct coordinated across multiple employees, departments and through automated systems. In both cases, the employee's culpability need not match that of the corporation.

As Getzler explains, corporations responded to the realities of expansive vicarious liability by adopting a range of protective strategies. The justifications for these were not always sound in light of tort creditor claims. Thus asset partitioning, to restrict liability to the registered company's subscribed or guaranteed capital, might be justified for contractual liability on the dual basis that voluntary creditors can be regarded as having notice of the limit before choosing to contract, and on pragmatic commercial benefit grounds. Neither of these translates well to the context of involuntary tort creditors.

[48] It remains contentious in Australia whether vicarious liability entails that the corporation is responsible for the act of another, or the wrong of another: see *Pioneer Mortgage Services Pty Ltd v Columbus Capital Pty Ltd* [2016] FCAFC 78, (2016) 250 FCR 136, 147–49 [48]–[58] (Davies, Gleeson and Edelman JJ). If the latter, then the individual's mental state must still be established.

[49] Getzler, ch 4 of this volume, section I, citing JW Salmond, *The Law of Torts: A Treatise on the English Law of Liability for Civil Injuries*, 1st edn (London, Stevens and Haynes, 1907) 55.

[50] C Wells, *Corporations and Criminal Responsibility* (Oxford, Oxford University Press, 2001) ch 5; S Walpole, 'Criminal Responsibility as a Distinctive Form of Corporate Regulation' (2020) 35 *Australian Journal of Corporate Law* 235, 238–48.

[51] As opposed to procedural rules, which may legitimately differ: see ALRC Final Report (n 25) [4.92]–[4.142]. If the corporate state of mind is, indeed, a question of fact, it suggests that the nature of the inquiry should be the same across jurisdictions.

[52] cf the position of an 'innocent agent' knowingly ordered to commit a wrong by her principal: *White v Ridley* [1978] HCA 38, (1978) 140 CLR 342. In this case, the principal is directly responsible for the wrongdoing.

[53] But see C Tilley, 'Just Strict Liability' (2023) *Cardozo Law Review* (forthcoming), which offers an understanding of vicarious liability that reflects genuine organisational fault.

A different justification emerged for so-called 'defensive' asset partitioning: a company should not be held responsible for unauthorised acts outside the corporate purposes and business (such as conducted by the rogue employee or agent, mentioned earlier). Consistently with this understanding, the ultra vires doctrine transformed agents' misconduct outside the corporation's formal, legal capacity into unauthorised frolics for which it bore no responsibility. This shift sponsored obvious and undesirable managerial tactics, in particular of promoting a sharp liability distinction between formal and authorised activities, and the reality of the corporation's daily pursuits.

Getzler charts critically the passage of the doctrine into eventual obsolescence. Its demise is, I think, an important condition of Systems Intentionality, which is predicated on an expansive corporate capacity.[54] Here, the distinction between corporate purposes in the sense of capacity and purposes in the sense of intention is both doctrinally and practically important. Thus, suppose a corporation adopts and deploys a system of conduct that (on my account) manifests the aim of exploiting a target, vulnerable consumer group for profit. The fact that its formal 'purposes', as expressed in its published policies (or indeed constitutional instrument), might be public-spirited does not render the system of conduct void as ultra vires. Purposes here must be understood as reflecting corporate states of mind, not denying the corporation's capacity to engage in the misconduct. Through this lens, the system of conduct shows that the corporation's public face, the basis on which it seeks to attract investment, business and government privileges, has become deeply misleading or deceptive.[55] The statement of corporate purpose is a public expression of corporate values or character, but that cannot, and should not, be used to deny the reality of the corporation's daily aims, knowledge and standards. Thus, where a corporation should, as a matter of formal structure, only decide something by approval of the board, but in reality carries out its day-to-day purposes through devolved structures that are kept strictly below board-level, it would deny the insights offered by Systems Intentionality simply to say that this behaviour does not reflect the actions or intentions of the corporation. Rather, I see these cases as ones where the formal decision-making structures or systems are belied by the reality of the corporation's own embedded, instantiated systems of conduct and practices. The latter manifest the true corporate intentions.

This analysis may also help address the concern Getzler raises at the conclusion of his chapter, namely, the risk that growing calls for adoption, or imposition, of statements of ethical corporate purposes may unwittingly reinvigorate the doctrine of ultra vires.[56] Through the lens of Systems Intentionality, and seen as representations of corporate mental states rather than capacity, public-facing declarations of corporate ethics should indeed assist to hold corporations to account, but through doctrines concerned to regulate misleading conduct (including deceit). Of course, this view may serve to encourage Boards and managers to make real and effective efforts to embed and

[54] Most jurisdictions now accept that a corporation has the capacity of a natural person: see, eg, Corporations Act 2001 (Cth), s 124(1); Companies Act 2006 (UK), s 39. See also Walpole (n 50); ALRC Final Report (n 25) [4.20]–[4.45].

[55] See eg VCCOL Report (n 44) ch 8 on the huge discrepancies between Crown Casino's formal 'responsible gambling' policies and the realities of its practices.

[56] Getzler, ch 4 of this volume, section X.

audit, on an ongoing basis, formal systems, to ensure that the corporate walk matches the talk. However, if the doctrine of ultra vires were to be revived and strengthened, this might pose real challenges for my model. I can only join Getzler in hoping that the implications of so doing might prompt pause in any reforms in that direction.

The final chapter in Part I turns from an historical perspective of corporate evasive strategies to consider the frightening present and future challenges of Big Tech. In 'The Corporate Culpability of Big Tech', Julia Powles charts the hugely successful, liability-limiting strategies of leviathan organisations, which have emerged in response to and deploy new technologies.[57] Her analysis explains the destructive and well-organised conduct that operates to avoid, undermine and even destroy states' legal restrictions in the pursuit of profit. Powles explores the all-too-familiar narratives that accompany this behaviour, which cast it in terms of (trial and) error, accident, and the innocent and regretted by-product of an emergent and innovative industry.[58] She then applies the model of Systems Intentionality to two case studies: Uber and Facebook (now Meta). In her analysis, she explains how these giants' destructive business models can be understood in systems terms, yielding a compelling account of highly culpable corporate blameworthiness.

Powles observes in her concluding section that the ability for Systems Intentionality to hold Big Tech appropriately responsible for harmful business practices is significantly impacted by a range of factors, some of which are peculiar to this industry. As she notes, the introduction of licensing requirements would give regulators a prime, ex ante opportunity to consider whether Big Tech players are 'fit and proper' persons to enjoy the very significant benefits of continuing to operate in their markets. Crofts' chapter demonstrates that Systems Intentionality has proved to be a powerful regulatory tool in the casino context, where the licensing inquiry has been into the 'suitability' of corporate persons. The comparison may be particularly valuable given the size, scope for harms and facilitation of criminal activities in the tech sectors.[59] Other factors, such as the deliberate structuring of Big Tech business to avoid legal constraint, including across jurisdictions and through multiple corporate entities and intermediaries, may also be susceptible to challenge by regulators and courts willing to characterise the business strategy in systems terms. Michael Bryan's chapter, to which I return shortly, examines a good example of how this can be done. Business models will commonly combine networks of natural and corporate persons, acting in a coordinated way in pursuit of group goals.[60] There is no reason, in my view, to think Systems Intentionality cannot address these scenarios as effectively as it does the state of mind of a single corporation. Whether the cog in the system is a natural employee or an agent, or a related corporation, should make no difference to the mode of analysis. Here, I hope, Systems

[57] Powles, ch 5 of this volume.

[58] See also the FSRC Final Report (n 42) 136–57, for examples of similar strategies in Australia's banking sector: discussed in Bant, 'Culpable Corporate Minds' (n 3) and in Bant 'Catching the Corporate Conscience' (n 3) 487–90.

[59] Crofts, ch 3 of this volume; VCCOL Report (n 44) 58–69 [19]–[25], 124–27, 174–78 [87]–[102].

[60] Bryan, ch 14 of this volume, section III.B.

Intentionality may provide a real path forward for group liability, consistently with developments in England and Wales.[61]

Big Tech's ploy of distancing itself from 'historic' wrongs also must be countered. The casino inquiries provide rich instances of this form of strategy, and the ways in which it can be dismantled through re-focusing on structural and systemic change.[62] Powles' sobering, final factor is the extent to which Big Tech threatens the very rule of law on which its regulation depends. While Systems Intentionality cannot resolve this challenge, what it does, I think, is render more transparent the true level of culpability inherent in the subversive practices she identifies. One can only hope that this may enable proper and considered public and political attention to come to bear on these, most destructive, corporate practices.

C. Attribution Models

From these 'big picture' essays, the collection turns to address critically both the existing and the proposed ranges of doctrinal approaches to determining the corporate mind. In '*Meridian*, Allocated Powers and Systems Intentionality Compared',[63] Rachel Leow maps the intersections between and alignment of her ground-breaking model of 'Allocated Powers',[64] the Identification Doctrine, the context-specific *Meridian* approach[65] and the model of Systems Intentionality. She also usefully, albeit necessarily briefly, considers the concept of 'aggregation'.[66] Indeed, her chapter provides the perfect narrative thread for any reader seeking to navigate the labyrinthine intersections of the law's corporate attribution rules.

As is well known, the Identification Doctrine recognises the corporate state of mind in its 'directing mind and will', commonly limited to the Board and, perhaps, other very senior executives. Leow's model, working outwards from the Identification Doctrine, and seeking to place it on better foundations, focuses on the processes by which individuals beyond the Board and senior executives are allocated the corporation's critical decision-making powers. From the standpoint of Systems Intentionality, both the Identification Doctrine and the Allocated Powers model recognise the relevance of core systems of decision making, albeit ones that centre upon key individuals. An example, given by Leow, is the rule in a corporate constitution that 'the decisions of the board in managing the company's business shall be the decisions of the company'.[67] Such 'primary rules of attribution' represent default and core decision-making structures, without which a

[61] *Okpabi v Royal Dutch Shell Plc* [2021] UKSC 3, [2021] 1 WLR 1294; *Lungowe v Vedanta Resources plc* [2019] UKSC 20, [2020] AC 1045. cf C Witting, 'The Corporate Group: System, Design and Responsibility' (2021) 80 *Cambridge Law Journal* 581.

[62] Above n 35.

[63] Leow, ch 6 of this volume.

[64] R Leow, 'Equity's Attribution Rules' (2021) 15 *Journal of Equity* 35; R Leow, *Corporate Attribution in Private Law* (Oxford, Hart Publishing, 2022).

[65] Named after *Meridian Global Funds Management Asia Ltd v The Securities Commission Co* [1995] UKPC 26, [1995] 2 AC 500 (*Meridian*).

[66] See also Diamantis, ch 10 of this volume, section II.C; and Gans, ch 13 of this volume, section V.

[67] Leow, ch 6 of this volume, section I.A.

corporation would be largely inert.[68] The synergies between our models reflect the fact that both understand corporate mental states in terms of the decision-making structures adopted by a corporation as a matter of daily practice. Further, as Leow also notes, both models align with realist conceptions of corporate personality.

Systems Intentionality is also concerned, however, with the very many cases in which the whole point of corporate systems of conduct is to remove individual choice or judgement, and hence variability, from the equation. Examples include the use of standard operating procedures and practices.[69] Corporations often adopt these sorts of systems of conduct to promote speed, predictability and certainty in coordination of conduct to achieve corporate ends. The advantages of adopting these systems, including for consistency and quality assurance purposes, is more obvious than ever in the world of Covid-19. And, of course, the increasing trend on the part of corporations to automate key processes and activities squarely makes the point. In such cases, there may be no individual focal-point or repository of the corporate powers. The whole point is that it does not particularly matter which human is embedded in the system, nor indeed whether humans are wholly or partly replaced by automated processes. The system of conduct is objectively designed (in the sense of calculated or apt) to ensure coordinated conduct of a certain quality and, in this sense, the conduct is always and necessarily intended. Choices between conduct options are part of the system design (its 'choice architecture').[70] They are pre-programmed into the system of conduct. Recognition of this feature of systems in general is why, of course, Systems Intentionality is also able to address the significance of fully automated systems for corporate conduct, where individualistic approaches struggle.[71] The analysis is the same, whatever form the system takes.[72]

Both the Allocated Powers model and Systems Intentionality privilege the 'real' or instantiated over formal systems of conduct. Thus, on Leow's model, the critical question is the individual to whom corporate powers are allocated in practice. This may be quite different from the corporate hierarchy reflected in the formal corporate flow-charts. Similarly, on my approach, we have seen that a corporation may develop glossy policies, or (at a more granular level) standard operating procedures, post these on internal or external websites, and the Board may articulate statements consistent with those policies. However, if the corporation's daily, adopted systems of conduct and practices to which these policies and procedures supposedly relate are wholly divergent from them, it is the systems of conduct and practices as *adopted and deployed* that manifest the true

[68] Subject to general law rules about the effect, for example, of shareholders in general meeting, or other statutory rules giving corporations other decision-making organs or processes.

[69] To the extent that these are a product of persons who are allocated the company's powers, they may be accommodated within Leow's model. However, Systems Intentionality renders it unnecessary to identify an individual responsible for the design of a diffused system of misconduct, or practice, adopted or operated by a corporation. The system may be understood as manifesting directly the corporate state of mind: see Paterson and Bant, ch 12 of this volume.

[70] Paterson, Bant and Cooney (n 3).

[71] Discussed in Bant, 'Culpable Corporate Minds' (n 3) 385–87; Bant, 'Catching the Corporate Conscience' (n 3) 487–90.

[72] Again, this insight has been only possible through long discussions with Jeannie Marie Paterson, for which I remain deeply grateful.

corporate state of mind, values and aims. The formal statements of purpose, intention and values become, on this account, an instance of misleading or deceptive conduct, and thereby another means to remedy and deter corporate misbehaviour.

To the extent that it reflects a principle of statutory interpretation, both Allocated Powers and the Systems Intentionality models must accommodate the *Meridian* approach. This asks, as a matter of statutory interpretation, who the responsible decision-maker is for the purposes of a particular rule or prohibition. However, I agree with Leow that it is neither possible nor desirable to apply this model more broadly to general law fields. It requires, for a start, that we are able to determine the purpose(s) of the law's regulation in every instance, as a pre-condition to identifying the relevant person(s) for the purposes of corporate attribution. Even were this possible, as earlier observed, there seems no obvious reason why the approach to identifying corporate states of mind (as opposed to the substantive doctrinal elements of those mindsets, or the procedural rules surrounding their proof) should differ between civil and criminal law, common law and equity, or for statutes where the prohibition or rule is silent on attribution issues.[73] If the state of a corporate mind is a matter of 'fact', as we are told it is,[74] then the method of ascertaining it should be the same, whatever the context. And, frankly, even if there is a fair element of theory and policy in determining that corporations have mindsets relevant to liability, it does not follow that any inquiry into that state of mind should be determined by the relevant body of law with which a corporation is engaged. As a practical matter, this renders the inquiry, already challenging, massively more uncertain, variable and functionally unhelpful. From a corporate governance perspective, for example, do we really expect, or want, corporate officers to factor potentially highly uncertain legal doctrines into their corporate flowcharts, to ensure that the relevant person for the purposes of the law's prohibition is identified and properly trained?

Finally, Systems Intentionality was developed in light of, and to address, the common modern phenomenon of diffused corporate structures, in which individual knowledge is dispersed across individuals and corporate departments, often well below Board level.[75] This poses a particular challenge for traditional attribution rules, but also any liability approach predicated on locating an individual repository of fault from which to attribute corporate responsibility. As Leow notes, whether the *Meridian* and the Allocated Powers models are susceptible to this problem depends, in part, on their approach to aggregation.

While there are probably many versions of, and explanations for, aggregation approaches, they commonly identify and combine the subjective mental states (eg intentions, knowledge, belief) and, potentially, the normative character of individuals' states of mind (eg dishonesty, recklessness, unconscionability), adding these up to amount to a greater, corporate consciousness or culpability. This seems a pragmatic

[73] cf Law Commission, *Criminal Liability in Regulatory Contexts* (Consultation Paper 195, August 2010) [5.103]–[5.104].

[74] *Edgington v Fitzmaurice* (1885) 29 Ch D 459 (CA) 483 (Bowen LJ); *Generics (UK) v Warner-Lambert Company LLC* [2018] UKSC 56, [2018] RPC 21 [171] (Lord Briggs).

[75] B Fisse, 'Reconstructing Corporate Criminal Law: Deterrence, Retribution, Fault, and Sanctions' (1983) 56 *Southern California Law Review* 1141, 1189.

way forward. Thus Jeremy Gans proposes a model of aggregation to address what he sees as the intractable difficulties of establishing corporate dishonesty.[76] However, aggregation runs into the obvious, realist objection that a corporation is more than, and different from, the sum of its parts. Further, how can a corporation be dishonest, reckless or unconscionable by reference to an aggregation of individuals, none of whom individually is dishonest, reckless or unconscionable?[77] Nor is it clear how aggregation works when addressing blended human and automated systems, or fully automated systems.[78] That said, my own view is that aggregation may be better understood as an intuitive shift towards a Systems Intentionality approach.[79] Systems Intentionality explains who (and what, in the case of automated systems and other corporations) is relevant in any 'aggregation' inquiry, why they are relevant and how their individual roles bear on corporate responsibility. The acts of individuals are relevant, and can be combined, to the extent to which they reflect a system of conduct. Individuals' mental states may be relevant as part of this inquiry where these are critical to the system: an example is where a system culminates in an individual decision-maker. However, Systems Intentionality is no simple process of adding a succession or mass of individual mental states to ascertain the corporate mind. The critical questions are: (i) what is the system employed by the corporation; and (ii) what state of mind does the system manifest? Individuals and automated systems and corporations are only relevant to the extent to which they form relevantly part of the system.

As we have seen, Leow's chapter provides an invaluable point of reference for discussion of related issues and analyses. The following chapter arguably goes even further: it encapsulates and presents the latest findings of over 40 years of sustained scholarship into conceptions and conditions of corporate culpability.[80] In 'Reactive Corporate Fault', Brent Fisse revisits his powerful and influential concept, explaining its genesis and benefits, as well as its significant and ongoing impact on corporate regulation. Reactive corporate fault is an 'unreasonable failure by a corporation to take satisfactory preventive or corrective measures in response to the performance by the corporation of the physical elements of an offence or civil violation'.[81] As this makes clear, the model applies across civil and criminal law divides and concentrates on the significance of corporate responses to their misconduct. As Fisse explains, the model accepts that corporations can and do act intentionally in carrying out corporate policies. Reactive corporate fault is offered as an additional and alternative basis of corporate responsibility. It is not meant to replace models of proactive corporate fault. However, corporations are wont to plead accident, surprise and error in response to breaches. And most cases will involve allegations of corporate negligence, not intention. Fisse's point is that, in light of such limitations, corporate culpability on the part of a corporate wrongdoer is also and

[76] Gans, ch 13 of this volume, section V.

[77] *Commonwealth Bank of Australia v Kojic* [2016] FCAFC 186, (2016) 249 FCR 421, 449 [112] (Edelman J) (*Kojic*).

[78] See also Diamantis, ch 10 of this volume, section II.C.

[79] See also J Clough and C Mulhern, *The Prosecution of Corporations* (Oxford, Oxford University Press, 2002) 107–08, arguing that aggregation represents a clumsy attempt to construct a model of organisational blameworthiness, a view endorsed in the ALRC Final Report (n 25) 483–84.

[80] Fisse, ch 7 of this volume; and above n 7.

[81] Fisse, ch 7 of this volume, section I.

powerfully revealed by how it responds to that misconduct. Fisse points to some specific examples of criminal and civil liability, the embryonic penalty jurisprudence, as well as the use of enforceable undertaking and deferred prosecution agreements, as expressing reactive corporate fault. He concludes by proposing statutory reforms, building on the recent ALRC proposals:[82] (i) to integrate the absence of reactive corporate fault, as a mitigating factor, explicitly into corporate sentencing considerations; and (ii) to expand the ALRC attribution reform proposals to encompass reactive, as well as proactive, precautions.

Given its role as an additional responsibility model, how does the concept of reactive corporate fault fit with other approaches? Rebecca Faugno argues that the concept informed the introduction of Australia's corporate culture provisions, and agrees with Fisse that it is recognised repeatedly, albeit intuitively and in an undeveloped manner, in that jurisdiction's penalty jurisprudence.[83] Leow observes that neither the *Meridian* nor Allocated Powers models readily accommodates inquiries into reactive corporate fault.[84] This is because their time frame for assessing the corporate state of mind falls when the act of misconduct occurs. However, if the culpability inquiry is partitioned into proactive and reactive fault, it is possible, though not theoretically comfortable, for it to operate alongside more restrictive and individualistic approaches. As Fisse's proposed statutory amendments make clear, the model will provide cogent support for approaches that combine strict liability mechanisms with a 'reasonable precautions' defence.[85] Defining 'precautions' to include reactive precautions (such as remedial and disciplinary steps) would provide courts with a more explicit and principled basis for incorporating the sorts of considerations that they already do implicitly and intuitively. Finally, I have previously explained the contribution that Fisse's expanded temporal viewpoint makes to understanding the theory and practice of Systems Intentionality. Indeed, depending on the angle of focus taken to identifying the system, my model potentially encompasses and assesses in combination both proactive and reactive processes as part of a larger system of conduct. This may be particularly appropriate, for example, when dealing with 'set and forget' automated fee deduction systems, which are set in place without any mechanisms to respond to the inevitable risks of harms arising from their operation.

We have seen that reactive corporate fault is a good fit with Australian conceptions of corporate culpability. This is most evident (albeit not expressly acknowledged) in its recognition of corporate culture. As defined in section 12.3 of the Commonwealth Criminal Code 1995 (Cth) ('Criminal Code'), corporate culture means 'an attitude, policy, rule, course of conduct or practice existing within the body corporate generally, or in the part of the body corporate in which the relevant activities takes place'. This is a distinctively organisational model of blameworthiness. As Leow explains, this means that some alternative models cannot readily accommodate conceptions of corporate culture.[86] An example is *Meridian*, which focuses on the laws that apply to

[82] See ALRC Final Report (n 25) Recommendation 7, ch 6.
[83] R Faugno, 'Ideas of Corporate Culture from the Perspective of Penalties Jurisprudence', ch 8 of this volume.
[84] Leow, ch 6 of this volume, sections III.A and III.B.
[85] Clough, ch 18 of this volume; and in section II.E of this chapter.
[86] Leow, ch 6 of this volume, section II.D.

corporations, rather than the internal decision-making structures and practices of a corporation. We have seen that *Meridian* identifies the relevant person to be treated as the corporation's alter ego from the policy and purpose of the law to be enforced. This person may have no role within the decision-making structures of the corporation, although this might be expected from a rational system of regulation.[87] Even if they do, any inquiry into the decision-making structure of the corporation is only a matter of evidence, not doctrine. By contrast, the policies and practices of a corporation that encourage or authorise corporate misconduct lie at the heart of both Allocated Powers and Systems Intentionality models. Again, such a conclusion has implications for developing a rational and coherent law of attribution.

As Rebecca Faugno observes in 'Ideas of Corporate Culture from the Perspective of Penalties Jurisprudence', 'The concept of "corporate culture" has become pervasive in the Australian corporate regulatory landscape.'[88] However, this is not because it has been a success as a primary liability mechanism.[89] Rather, as a test of general blameworthiness, it has had particular traction in licensing and pecuniary penalty spheres. Her essay focuses on the latter to develop what I think is the first, detailed, doctrinal account of corporate culture.

After a brief review of the history of the corporate culture provisions, Faugno's essay interrogates their theoretical foundations through the medium of seminal scholarship, including that of Fisse. This enables her to identify common markers of corporate culture: a corporation's hierarchy and structures; its formal and de facto policies (and the gaps between them); its systems of conduct; audit and adjustment mechanisms; discipline and reward systems; training and compliance programmes; and patterns of behaviour across those parts of the corporation relevant to the wrongdoing in question. Faugno then employs those markers as reference points in her exhaustive analysis of the treatment of corporate culture considerations in the context of civil penalties jurisprudence arising in the context of statutory misleading conduct and unconscionable conduct.

As she explains, corporate culture was identified as a key sentencing consideration for both civil and criminal pecuniary penalties long before the introduction of the corporate culture provisions.[90] It may therefore be expected that courts will have developed mature understandings of the concept and its bearing on corporate culpability. What is striking from Faugno's analysis is the extent to which that expectation is disappointed. Courts generally have failed to articulate what is meant by 'corporate culture'. Consistently, they have used it as a criterion of general blameworthiness, rather than as a means to identify specific and relevant mental states. This is so notwithstanding that the 'deliberateness' and 'knowledge' with which misconduct occurs are also express factors in the sentencing process. Further, Faugno's analysis suggests that courts have preferred form over substance in assessing the significance of markers such as training programmes for sentencing purposes. Courts have, however, clearly been alive

[87] cf Hanrahan, ch 17 of this volume, section II.

[88] Faugno, ch 8 of this volume, section I.

[89] A point made colourfully and powerfully in Jeremy Gans' chapter: Gans, ch 13 of this volume. See also Law Commission Options Paper (n 22) [6.14]–[6.20].

[90] *Trade Practices Commission v CSR Limited* [1990] FCA 521, [1991] ATPR 41-076.

to the relevance of reactive corporate fault in the assessment of corporate culpability for sentencing purposes. This includes the presence of admissions of liability, cooperation with the regulator and remedial programmes. The potential significance of audit systems has been less well recognised. Finally, Faugno notes that courts have emphasised, if not consistently, the relevance of repeated prior misconduct, and systematic misconduct, as relevant to culpability. In all these respects, however, the jurisprudence remains embryonic.

Courts' reluctance to connect ideas of corporate culture to specific corporate mental states may reflect the dominant understanding of sentencing as involving an holistic assessment and 'intuitive synthesis' of a range of relevant factors, to settle an overall level of blameworthiness.[91] However, it may also reflect the view that corporate culture remains unworkable as an attribution tool. This means that it cannot effectively be used by regulators in argument, or the court in its deliberations, as a means to determine the specific mental states (such as deliberateness and knowledge) relevant to sentencing. Faugno's contribution is so valuable precisely because fundamental doubts remain over what corporate culture entails, and hence its indicia and (in turn) its manner of proof.

In that context, my following chapter, entitled 'Systems Intentionality: Theory and Practice', seeks to show how the model, which builds upon the realist insights offered by corporate culture, is, by contrast, quite workable. After introducing the model, it turns to explore and articulate more precisely the key concepts of 'systems of conduct, policies and practices'.[92] It then details how these may be proved. This includes evidential strategies and challenges. The aim is to provide the first part of a litigation roadmap for regulators, judges, practitioners and other parties seeking to use the concept, at the coalface of practice. The second part of this roadmap is contained in my later chapter on 'Modelling Corporate States of Mind through Systems Intentionality'.[93] This seeks to demonstrate how proven systems may manifest and satisfy the doctrinal requirements of specific mental elements, relevant to corporate responsibility. The analysis is supported by, and can be read in conjunction with, a range of publications that provide case studies of Systems Intentionality in practice.[94] This body of work now includes the chapter written with Paterson on 'Automated Mistakes' in this volume.[95]

Part II of the collection concludes with Diamantis' chapter on 'How to Read a Corporation's Mind'.[96] Diamantis joins Leow in offering a very helpful overview of the comparative strengths, weaknesses and relationships between a range of attribution models. In addition to his novel 'inference theory', these include 'the control group test' (a close relative of Identification Theory), '*respondeat superior*'

[91] The leading authorities and method of reasoning in the civil context are analysed in JM Paterson and E Bant, 'Intuitive Synthesis and Fidelity to Purpose? Judicial Interpretation of the Discretionary Power to Award Civil Penalties under the Australian Consumer Law' in P Vines and S Donald (eds), *Statutory Interpretation in Private Law* (Leichhardt, Federation Press, 2019) 154.

[92] Bant, ch 9 of this volume.

[93] Bant, ch 11 of this volume.

[94] Above n 3.

[95] Paterson and Bant, ch 12 of this volume.

[96] Diamantis, ch 10 of this volume.

(a form of vicarious liability), 'collective knowledge' (aggregation) and Systems Intentionality. Given the very significant influence of his work on my thinking, it is perhaps unsurprising that Diamantis considers Systems Intentionality generally to be an improvement upon the other models, particularly at the point of sentencing. However, Diamantis identifies a range of important concerns about its operation. It is worthwhile considering, albeit briefly, the nature of these concerns, before turning to discuss the form of inferential reasoning that he considers resolves these in a principled and practical way.

The issue of 'culpably missing systems' was addressed earlier.[97] Here I am reasonably confident that the answer to the problem is contained within the phrase: seen as culpable choices and in systems terms, there is no difficulty in incorporating these into the analysis, to good effect.

Another is the difficulty that Systems Intentionality may have in addressing 'out of character wrongs'.[98] I think the concern here is that Systems Intentionality is predicated on identifying some realised system of conduct, policy or practice. That is, of course, true. A corporation acting in a wholly random way will not readily accommodate this analytical model. Other routes to liability must be found. As Systems Intentionality is not an exclusive model, this remains possible. And we may question how common randomly generated harms might be, at least when dealing with larger corporations. I suspect that many 'random' harms may turn out on closer inspection to result from systems of conduct. This connects with the broader need to question corporate narratives of accident and mistake. However, I do think it is also important to emphasise that Systems Intentionality should work just as well to address the corporate fault manifested in the *first* instantiation of a corporate system as that of a well-established system. As explained in chapter 9, 'patterns of behaviour' may provide potential *evidence* of the presence of a system but they are not prerequisites.[99] Indeed, a system of conduct should be able to be the subject of injunctive and other relief *before* it has even been rolled out (for example, where a whistle-blower alerts regulators to the imminent commencement of a deceptive marketing campaign). The culpability manifested by that adopted system should also inform regulators' enforcement options, such as whether to proceed administratively, the forms of legal claims that may apply, and penalty and other ramifications. A regulator need not wait until a system of conduct is deployed, or deployed repeatedly, to act.

Two further concerns raised by Diamantis are related. These are that Systems Intentionality has an inherent tendency to shift to a strict liability approach and, consistently, is inapt to address the range of complex mental elements demanded by the law. Both to a degree respond to the fact that Systems Intentionality involves an objective assessment, and characterisation, of the pleaded system. First, there is the concern that this objective viewpoint may suggest a degree of corporate omniscience that is unfair. Diamantis poses the scenario where a corporation makes a product that is inherently harmful.[100] At T1, science is yet to discover this fact. At T2, internal

[97] Section I.
[98] Diamantis, ch 10 of this volume, section III.A.
[99] Bant, ch 9 of this volume, section III.B.
[100] Diamantis, ch 10 of this volume, section III.C.

reports circulate within the corporation identifying the risk of harm, still as yet scientifically unproven. The corporation continues production without any adjustment to the processes of production or sale. T3 marks the point at which the danger is scientifically proven beyond doubt. Diamantis' concern is that Systems Intentionality dictates that the corporation has knowledge at T1. Any other conclusion requires us to advert to the actual knowledge of individuals within the corporation. However, I do not think this is so. At T1 the corporation has (on my model) knowledge of the existence of the product: this is inherent, after all, in its deliberate production. However, the quality of the product is another matter. Dangerousness arguably is at least partly a normative assessment that must be made in light of broader, scientific evidence.[101] It is more akin to the process of assessing conduct as 'dishonest', which is a complex combination of assessments of knowledge and intention against objective standards. Further, there are different aspects of the production process that may be relevant for culpability purposes. Contrary to Diamantis' analysis, I have earlier explained that Systems Intentionality suggests that the wholesale omission of audit processes, including around safety, may be understood as a corporate choice. This choice may well manifest a reckless disregard for consumers' safety and a 'profit at any cost' attitude, consistently with Diamantis' own preferred characterisation of the corporate culpability involved. Second, there is no doubt that more work remains to be done in modelling Systems Intentionality by reference to different scenarios and mental-state elements. Precisely how the system operates, and the angle of focus that is adopted for regulatory purposes, will be important questions for regulators and prosecutors to investigate.[102] Importantly, however, as this discussion itself demonstrates, the model does not force the assessor into adopting either a strict liability or indiscriminate liability position. Further, in my view, it prompts the right, specific questions to be asked to ascertain the true nature of corporate culpability.

Diamantis' ultimate, preferred position is to employ the same, garden-variety process of inferring mental states for humans in respect of corporations. He explains the fascinating cognitive science behind inference of humans' mental states and argues that precisely the same process is routinely undertaken by natural people when considering corporate mental states. This resonates strongly with Crofts' analysis of the realist intuition and popular corporate commentary.[103] This sort of question was front of mind when first developing my basic cake-baking scenario, itself building on Diamantis' discussion of recipes, maps and notes as 'external decision supports'.[104] The scenario posits that I use a cake recipe as my cognitive aid or 'system of conduct'. The nature of the processes that I adopt manifest my purpose (to make a cake). Similarly, corporations use systems that manifest their corporate purposes. Indeed, lacking a natural mind, they cannot use anything else (hence the need for basic decision systems, such as that the decision of the Board is the decision of the corporation). This raises the question, though, whether the process of 'characterising' my intention to bake a cake from the fact of my deployment of a cake recipe is simply a process of inference? Or is something else,

[101] Gans, ch 13 of this volume, section IV.
[102] Bant, ch 9 of this volume, sections III.B and IV.A.iv.
[103] Crofts, ch 3 of this volume, section II.A.
[104] For the most recent iteration, see Bant, 'Catching the Corporate Conscience' (n 3) 472–73, 477.

or additionally, potentially going on? Ultimately, my view is that humans and corporations are relevantly different. We may properly use both inference of mental states and Systems Intentionality with natural persons. With corporations, which have no natural mental state to infer, we must characterise (or construct) that intention. As a practical matter, little might seem to hang from the question.[105] However, it does seem to me that I should be able to explain why theoretically, and how doctrinally and evidentially, we read the corporate mind on my model. And in light of my responses to Diamantis' concerns, I suspect that everyday people may be able readily to understand their intuitive processes of 'inference' in systems terms.

D. Corporate States of Mind

In Part III the collection turns to consider corporate states of mind in light of these models. The challenge here is to test how conceptions of corporate culpability translate into law in practice. Consistently, Part III commences with 'Modelling Corporate States of Mind through Systems Intentionality',[106] which starts by setting out some common judicial understandings of key mental elements, such as intention, knowledge and mistake, as well as mixed normative states such as dishonesty, recklessness and unconscionability. This discussion is not designed to provide 'best' meanings of these elements but rather prototype definitions by reference to which Systems Intentionality may be applied. Incidentally, the discussion may also help the reader, I hope, to navigate and consider Part III more generally. Chapter 11 continues by demonstrating the distinctive operation of Systems Intentionality by reference to these sample understandings. It concludes by demonstrating the process of characterisation through a worked example.

In 'Automated Mistakes: Vitiated Consent and State of Mind Culpability in Algorithmic Contracting', Paterson and I build on the analysis in the previous chapter in two major ways.[107] The first is to identify the additional challenges posed by algorithmic contracting for individualistic models of corporate attribution. The second is to explore the insights offered by Systems Intentionality in this context. The chapter does this through examining, first, the doctrinal state of mind elements required for rescission of contracts on the grounds of mistake and unconscionable conduct. It then turns to consider the algorithmic contracts the subject of the Singapore Court of Appeal decision in *Quoine Pte Ltd v B2C2 Ltd* (*Quoine*).[108] We argue that once algorithmic contracting is understood in terms of systems of conduct, it becomes possible to inquire into and characterise the salient features of the particular system that was deployed. We also explain the dangers of treating algorithms as agents: this is simply contrary to reality and leads in unprincipled and unnecessary directions. Systems Intentionality, by contrast, enables us to engage in complex and subtle characterisations of the corporate

[105] The approaches adopted by the High Court of Australia in *Stubbings v Jams 2 Pty Ltd* [2022] HCA 6, (2022) 399 ALR 409 (*Stubbings*), the subject of Michael Bryan's chapter, similarly suggest little might rest on this, as a matter of practice.

[106] Bant, ch 11 of this volume.

[107] Paterson and Bant, ch 12 of this volume.

[108] *Quoine Pte Ltd v B2C2 Ltd* (*Quoine*) [2020] 2 SLR 20.

mental states manifested through automated and machine learning systems, without doing violence to existing doctrines and principles. Its application also promotes fair trading practices and good corporate governance.

In 'Can Corporations be Dishonest?',[109] Gans charts the unhappy voyage of the prosecution's case in *R v Potter*.[110] In the course of so doing, he identifies the precise rocks against which Australia's novel corporate culture provisions foundered, and considers whether the prosecution case could have been salvaged through taking alternative liability routes. As he demonstrates, conceptions of dishonesty can be highly subtle. Whether they need always be so is a matter on which minds, courts and legislators might legitimately differ. However, it must be right that, whatever definition is adopted, a model of corporate culpability in the realist tradition must be capable of addressing its elements. Gans argues powerfully that here, the corporate culture provisions, found in section 12.3 of the Criminal Code, were doomed to failure. The provisions do not expressly mention dishonesty, for a start. That might be addressed by taking the sort of interpretive approach to dishonesty I adopt in chapter 11, by which (i) the quality of the defendant's conduct is assessed objectively (ii) in light of her knowledge and intention.[111] Both these latter states of mind are explicitly mentioned in section 12.3(1). On this approach, the section offers a modular approach to corporate culpability, in which courts may use the corporate provision to assess any mental states comprising those elements or any combination of them. Gans considers and rejects this possibility: on his account, dishonesty is, ultimately, a state of mind, but a highly complex one.[112] The objective assessment is of whatever it is that the defendant knows, believes, fears, intends, and so on, and these are not physical elements, although they will need to be assessed in light of surrounding circumstances.

This analysis leads Gans to the startling conclusion that corporations cannot be dishonest pursuant to the corporate culture provisions. It further suggests that the problem may lie in organisational models of blameworthiness, which do not sufficiently, or at all, focus on individual human fault. Gans explores this possibility by reference to other statutory liability models, as well as the ALRC's proposed options for reform to the corporate culture provisions.[113] After concluding that these also fail the workability test, particularly against the common, corporate problem of diffused knowledge, Gans proposes a way forward. Here, the reform model is the aggregation provision contained in section 12.4 of the Criminal Code, which currently applies to negligence. Gans argues that considering the various, subjective states of mind of particular individuals in the organisation is important, indeed central, to determining whether it is dishonest.[114] His model provision also emphasises the importance of both adequate management and supervision, and functioning information systems within a corporation, in assessing the question of dishonesty. Viewed through the lens of Systems

[109] Gans, ch 13 of this volume.

[110] *R v Potter & Mures Fishing Pty Ltd* (Transcript, Supreme Court of Tasmania, Blow CJ, 14 September 2015) 464.

[111] Bant, ch 11 of this volume, sections II.E and III.A.v.

[112] Gans, ch 13 of this volume, section IV.

[113] ALRC Final Report (n 25) Recommendation 7, ch 6.

[114] cf Diamantis, arguing aggregation works most cleanly with knowledge; *Kojic* (n 77).

Intentionality, these are good, if not complete, markers of systems of conduct relevant to assessing the corporate state of mind, in all its complexity.

Bryan's chapter on 'Asset-Based Lending: A Case Study in Unconscionable Systems of Conduct' provides an excellent, further doctrinal testing ground of corporate culpability.[115] It considers the most recent application by the High Court of Australia of the equitable doctrine of unconscionability to what might be justly called a predatory business model.[116] While the statutory prohibition on 'unconscionable systems of conduct' was also argued, only Kiefel J addressed its operation.

As Bryan explains, the case is striking for the readiness of all judges to strike down a business model that

> shielded lenders from any knowledge of a borrower's personal and financial circumstances. The obvious purpose of the system was to create an information barrier between lender and borrower in order to prevent the *Amadio* knowledge requirement [for the doctrine of unconscionable dealing] from being satisfied.[117]

On Bryan's analysis, the plurality judgment 'inferred' knowledge of the plaintiff's special disadvantage from two characteristics of the business model. First, the system could only apply to 'unbankable' borrowers. Second, it employed structural 'artifices' (such as the interposition of intermediaries, and the use of pro forma certificates of independent professional advice, from associates of the lender) to protect itself from knowledge of the individual borrower's particular circumstances of disadvantage. Indeed, as he identifies, the case has very significant implications for two common avoidance techniques employed by lenders. The first is the interposition of shell companies as a formal 'borrower', to bring the arrangement outside of protective consumer legislation: 'The drafting trick that enables the lender to escape the frying pan of the Code may land the lender in the fire of equity's unconscionability jurisdiction.'[118] The second is equity's willingness to examine the substance of so-called independent professional advice, including the role of the advisor within the broader lending system, over time.

As Bryan notes, viewed as a case on systemic misconduct, *Stubbings* further demonstrates that statutory 'systems of conduct' extend beyond the corporate internal structures to networks of individuals that lack any formal, group legal personality. I would also add, as previously mentioned, that it demonstrates the potential for Systems Intentionality to apply to networks of individuals and corporations, such as might operate in a corporate group.[119] While it remains necessary to identify the defendant against whom the claim can be brought, provided that it can be said that the system is one adopted or employed by the defendant, it is no barrier that the system integrates multiple actors (and automated systems) towards some end. This is wholly consistent with the very many other cases of statutory unconscionable conduct that have addressed business models that utilised third-party service providers as part of the core business.[120]

[115] Bryan, ch 14 of this volume.
[116] *Stubbings* (n 105).
[117] Bryan, ch 14 of this volume, section III.A.
[118] ibid.
[119] Section II.B.
[120] See Bant and Paterson, 'Systems of Misconduct' (n 3).

Bryan concludes that there is a strong argument for the continued relevance of equity in such scenarios, notwithstanding the broad ambit of the statutory unconscionability prohibition. I would agree, but go one step further. In my view, the plurality decision is, in substance, entirely on all fours with the form of reasoning that would be adopted through application of the model of Systems Intentionality. Even this short summary of Bryan's excellent analysis makes that clear. The separate judgment of Gordon J, which expressly considered the statutory prohibition, only serves to reinforce that point.[121] If correct, this provides significant support for the view that Systems Intentionality may readily grow from its statutory roots in corporate culture and unconscionable systems of conduct to other areas of the law. If the model can be applied readily in the field of unconscionable conduct, where courts' enquiries into defendants' mental states are extremely subtle, then there seems reason to hope that it might be put to good use elsewhere.

This conclusion is fortified by the concluding chapter in Part III. Robyn Carroll's ground-breaking assessment of 'Corporate Contrition' is, to my knowledge, the first extended treatment of the topic.[122] As she explains, contrition and remorse are, for the law's purposes, interchangeable concepts that inform a wide range of legal inquiries, in a variety of areas. Yet the phenomenon of corporate contrition is both judicially contentious and almost wholly theoretically unexplored. In her analysis, Carroll draws on social and psychological theories to examine the meaning and functions of contrition, before applying these understandings to the fields of criminal sentencing, civil and criminal pecuniary penalties, and damages awards. This enables her to identify the roles played by contrition and how courts judge its presence, or absence, in the case of individual defendants.

From that base, Carroll turns to consider corporate contrition in particular. Her analysis endorses the realist conception of the corporation. As she explains, 'genuine' corporate remorse requires a process of attribution that inevitably raises a range of difficult doctrinal and evidential questions. Carroll examines the factors that courts routinely consider when engaging in sentencing of corporate defendants. These complement, and extend, those identified by Faugno.[123] Interestingly, in this context at least, courts are alive to the ease with which corporate executives, as the directing mind and will of the defendant, may mouth empty words of contrition and apology. Courts look, therefore, to other indicia of remorse. These factors all reflect the intuitive force of Fisse's concept of reactive corporate fault:[124] they include, for example, the speed and efficiency of remedial responses, voluntary reporting of misconduct and

[121] See in particular [81]: 'It may be inferred that the system *assumed* that some borrowers and guarantors would be vulnerable in a sense capable of enlivening that jurisdiction [cf *Australian Securities and Investments Commission v National Exchange Pty Ltd* [2005] FCAFC 226, (2005) 148 FCR 132, 142–43 [43] (*ASIC v National Exchange*)]. But the lenders' system sought to "immunise" the lenders against that assumption being known to be true because knowledge of its truth would inevitably attract the court's equitable or statutory jurisdiction to set aside the transactions. That was unconscionable.' (Emphasis and authority in original.)

[122] R Carroll, ch 15 of this volume.

[123] Faugno, ch 8 of this volume, section IV.B; and section II.C of this chapter.

[124] Fisse, ch 7 of this volume.

actions taken to address the causes of the misconduct. Importantly, these will often involve introducing systemic change, such as setting up 'systems, processes, procedures or education'[125] by which a corporation manifests its intention to 'change its ways'. Carroll concludes by considering the ALRC's recent reform proposals to codify corporate sentencing factors[126] and why, contrary to those proposals, contrition should expressly be included. Her essay shows that corporate contrition can be given meaningful content and operation. It may also helpfully inform the award of proposed non-monetary penalty orders, including disclosure and corrective orders.[127]

E. Alternative Approaches

Part IV of the collection moves away from attribution models to consider alternative approaches to holding corporations responsible for serious misconduct. Again, given the traditional approach of emphasising individual responsibility for corporate wrongdoing, it makes sense to begin with chapters that probe the lure, and risks, of this approach.

As previously mentioned, Derrington and Walpole's chapter on 'Culpable Ships' is particularly concerned to identify, and reform, the practice of criminalising seafarers for maritime breaches.[128] As they note, the use of scapegoats is particularly troubling, given that many incidents arise from circumstances and factors well beyond the control, or position description, of the identified individual. After a careful introduction to the Admiralty jurisdiction and criminal procedures, the authors examine the reasons supporting the practice. These are familiar: on the one hand, there is the need to denounce and deter serious and harmful misconduct; on the other, there are the significant challenges of bringing responsibility home to the ship owner, or operator, often hidden in another jurisdiction, behind a web of corporate entities and intermediaries.

Against that background, Derrington and Walpole outline the attribution options for holding corporate ship owners and operators criminally liable, as well as alternatives such as 'failure to prevent' and 'duty-based' offences. However, the authors chiefly focus on a little-explored but time-honoured option: proceeding directly against the ship itself. They argue that ships are juristically similar to realist conceptions of corporations, and there is a long legal (and linguistic) history of treating the ship herself as both the source and limit of liability. Understanding the traditional actions in rem against the ship as reflecting the ship as legal person is also consistent with key features of the Admiralty jurisdiction, which cannot be explained if they are regarded as purely procedural devices, used to seize the vessel in order to force the owner to court. As they note, this approach also finds support in the law of civil forfeiture, itself founded in the ancient

[125] *Australian Building and Construction Commissioner v Construction, Forestry, Maritime, Mining and Energy Union* [2022] FCA 37 [81] (Banks-Smith J).
[126] ALRC Final Report (n 25) Recommendations 10 and 11, ch 8.
[127] ibid Recommendation 12.
[128] Derrington and Walpole, ch 16 of this volume.

law of 'deodand'. Thus both historical and instrumental perspectives support that the ship be held responsible for its misconduct. As they acknowledge, the aim of making this shift is to provide a means of enforcement when those who own and operate the vessel are hidden, themselves, behind legal and jurisdictional structures and strategies. Recalling Bryan's essay, it might be wondered how those structures and strategies might fare if subjected to analysis through the lens of Systems Intentionality.[129]

Hanrahan's following chapter on 'Culpable Executives' dovetails thematically with 'Culpable Ships' in considering the vexed question of how, and why, individuals should be held responsible for corporate misconduct.[130] As she says, punishing one person for the sins of the collective challenges some of the most basic tenets of liberal jurisprudence.[131] Yet there remain powerful and public calls for 'heads on sticks' when corporations break the law, particularly where those breaches are flagrant and repeated. How, then, to determine the principled boundaries of individual responsibility?

Clearly, executives who can be considered co-offenders or close accessories to the misconduct should be within the frame. Hanrahan is, by contrast, particularly concerned to address the position of executives whose main fault is that corporate law-breaking occurred on their watch. Notwithstanding being 'remote' to the wrong, the law may still seek to sanction the executive for corporate wrongdoing, in pursuit of deterrence.[132] But it is a particular type of deterrence, underpinned by what Hanrahan calls an 'enrolment' rationale.[133] This seeks to threaten or exact penalties in order to encourage the executive, and others in her position, to take steps promoting compliance, so as to 'exhibit improved risk-management behaviour'.[134] Yet, as she notes, in a corporate context, the conditions for law-breaking will often have been established 'by many hands over time'.[135] This runs the clear risk that the enrolment rationale only makes sense in addressing executives as a group. Yet it seeks to do so by encouraging individuals to use their influence to change others' behaviour.

Hanrahan focuses her analysis on role-related executive liabilities: that is, liabilities that come with the office. These can be contrasted with general liabilities, such as accessorial liability, that in theory apply to any person who satisfies the elements of the claim. Hanrahan outlines and illustrates different forms of role-related responsibilities, before turning to consider two recent Australian proposals for expanding this form of executive liability. Here, Hanrahan joins a number of the contributors in using the ALRC's recent reform recommendations as a prism through which to interrogate her topic. The ALRC's Proposals 9 and 10 were interim proposals, which were dropped from the final report.[136] They were characterised by the Commission as adopting a 'failure to prevent' model, albeit one directed at executives rather than

[129] Bryan, ch 14 of this volume; and sections II.B and II.C of this chapter.
[130] Hanrahan, ch 17 of this volume.
[131] cf Harding, ch 2 of this volume, dealing precisely with this problem.
[132] Hanrahan, ch 17 of this volume, section II.
[133] ibid sections I and III.A.
[134] ibid section I.
[135] ibid section IV.
[136] Australian Law Reform Commission, Corporate Criminal Responsibility (Discussion Paper No 87, 2019).

the corporate offender. The basic idea was that executives who were in a 'position to influence, and prevent' misconduct should be subject to a civil penalty, unless they had taken reasonable precautions to prevent the contravention. As Hanrahan observes, the concept of a person of 'influence' was too vague for this purpose. Executives might not even realise they qualify until too late. Moreover, the proposals reversed the onus of proof. While some might find this tolerable when it comes to corporations, the potentially crushing effect for natural individuals was of concern. It was therefore, perhaps, unsurprising that the proposals did not go further.

By contrast, Australia's Financial Accountability Regime (FAR) looks set to impose obligations on specified financial institutions to identify and name 'accountable persons' as part of their own accountability mapping obligation. These individuals will be registered with the Australian Prudential Regulation Authority and must comply with a series of bespoke obligations. These include taking reasonable steps in conducting their responsibilities to prevent matters arising that would result in a 'material contravention' of specified legislation.[137] Failure to meet these obligations exposes the individual to potentially serious penalties, including disqualification. Hanrahan argues that adopting this approach risks sacrificing the individual's rights and protections based on an 'enrolment' rationale, the theoretical foundations for which remain shaky. Moreover, role-related penalties are often characterised as civil or administrative in character, removing important procedural safeguards that would apply to criminal conviction.

From these individuated models of liability, we turn to consider one of the most successful reform options. 'Failure to prevent' models have been gaining traction from initially restricted fields of operation, in particular through the model adopted in section 7 of the Bribery Act 2010 (UK), to being seen as a useful, more generalised liability model. In '"Failure to Prevent" Offences: The Solution to Transnational Corporate Criminal Liability?', Jonathan Clough explains how they may offer a principled and practical step forward in the enforcement of corporate liability for transnational crimes.[138] Transnational crimes pose a particular challenge for enforcement, given the offences tend to be committed across jurisdictions and, again, often involve webs of related entities and extended supply chains, as well as intermediaries and agents. We have seen similar challenges in the context of Bryan's[139] and Derrington and Walpole's[140] chapters in particular. As Clough notes, amongst its other attractions are that the 'failure to prevent model' avoids the problem of attribution entirely. There does need to be a predicate offence (albeit not a conviction) committed by an individual or corporation that is an associate of the defendant corporation. To that extent, there may again need to be engagement with attribution principles. However, provided this is demonstrated, and the offence is one for which there is a comparable crime in the home jurisdiction, the common approach taken by 'failure to prevent' models is that the onus then falls on the defendant to show that it had 'adequate procedures' in place to prevent

[137] Financial Accountability Regime Bill 2021 (Cth), ss 10, 11.
[138] Clough, ch 18 of this volume.
[139] Bryan, ch 14 of this volume.
[140] Derrington and Walpole, ch 16 of this volume.

the commission of the offence. Clearly, these need not have been successful in order for the defence to succeed.

Clough makes the important point[141] that this form of offence is not derivative. Rather, the defendant corporation is responsible for the independent wrong of failing to prevent the nominated offence. As we have seen in Hanrahan's chapter, there are important reasons not to reverse the onus of proof where this may affect natural individuals.[142] However, Clough argues persuasively that these are far less cogent in the corporate context, and for this form of offence.[143] In particular, a corporation's systems and procedures will be within its peculiar knowledge and control. Consistently, liability reflects true organisational blameworthiness. Clough expands on this point by exploring the level of culpability reflected in this form of offence. As he notes, beyond the failure to have in place adequate procedures, which itself may be understood as a 'negative model of wickedness',[144] regard must be had to the very serious offences, and harms, resulting from the corporate failure.

Although not its chief focus, Clough's essay makes clear the justifications for assessing corporate culpability in systems terms. It is arguable that Systems Intentionality supplements this position, and the operation of the model, in two ways. The first is it provides significant guidance on how systems, policies and processes may be conceptualised and proved. The second is that it fortifies the model's intuition of culpability, by explaining how systemic 'deficiencies' can be understood in positive (active) terms. As explained earlier, a corporate decision not to have in place adequate procedures reflects just that: a choice. Systems Intentionality suggests that, depending on the angle of focus adopted when addressing harmful business models, it is not only the proactive procedures that may be core to the model but also the reactive mechanisms that monitor and remedy resultant harms as they are identified. These may manifest a corporate intention not to investigate, to turn a blind eye to obvious predatory practices, recklessness or other serious levels of culpability that are not properly labelled in the language of 'deficiency'.[145] Thus suppose a business imports and sells dirt-cheap clothing in an affluent country, which is manufactured in another jurisdiction notorious for wage exploitation. If the business has no systems in place to monitor, audit and remediate its supply chains, this absence says something very clear about the corporate values and intentions, which arguably should not be framed in terms of mere ignorance or omission. We return to this theme shortly, in relation to Fiona McGaughey's chapter.

The penultimate chapter in the collection is 'Performance-Based Consumer and Investor Protection: Corporate Responsibility without Blame' by Lauren E Willis.[146] Like the 'failure to prevent' offences, performance-based regulation seeks to avoid entirely the problems of attribution. However, it does so by focusing on the quality

[141] cf Bant, 'Catching the Corporate Conscience' (n 3), where I arguably mis-frame it as a form of vicarious liability – it is strict, but not derivative or vicarious.

[142] Hanrahan, ch 17 of this volume, sections III.A and IV.

[143] See also ALRC Final Report (n 25) [4.85]–[4.96].

[144] Clough, ch 18 of this volume, section V, citing P Crofts 'Three Recent Royal Commissions: The Failure to Prevent Harms and Attributions of Organisational Liability' (2020) 42 *Sydney Law Review* 395, 422.

[145] See section I.

[146] Willis, ch 19 of this volume.

of outcomes experienced by a business's customers, including consumers and retail investors. Willis explores in this context the novel Australian Design and Distribution Obligations,[147] as well as the UK's Consumer Duty.[148] In its report into *Corporate Criminal Responsibility*, the ALRC recently explored what it called 'duty-based liability', which seems to be a similar concept.[149] This approach is most familiar from workplace safety legislation.[150] In both cases, the approach mandates a particular standard or outcome that must be reached by businesses, leaving to them, however, how this is achieved.

A particular concern for Willis is the rise of integrated artificial intelligence (AI) within business models, which may operate to trick, manipulate and predate upon consumers and investors in new and unexpected ways. Willis rightly points to the challenges this poses for individualistic attribution approaches. Searching for the human repository of fault on whom responsibility for the harmful algorithm(s) can be settled is likely to be difficult and arbitrary. And, as Willis notes, increasingly, automated systems are being designed and distributed by other AI systems. This poses two particular challenges for attribution: first, given that the corporation's employees may not know that its systems are harming consumers, any mental-state requirements may be impossible to meet; and, second, because an AI system can produce innumerable 'personalised' versions of online or robotic interactions, it may not be possible to identify precisely the mechanism by which the corporation caused any particular consumer or investor harm. Willis identifies the second as posing a particular 'black-box' problem: the corporation's employees may not know how its machine learning algorithms are affecting the corporation's interactions with consumers.

One response to this is to say, through the lens of Systems Intentionality, that a corporate decision to deploy technology to generate maximum profit from consumers, which it has no means, or intention, of auditing, is itself highly reckless.[151] Willis rightly notes that this possibility may be dependent on the extent to which courts demand evidence that the relevant system is inherently apt to harm customers, or produce a particular form of harm.[152] This again raises the black-box problem. However, the degree of knowledge of a particular system's features need not be great for Systems Intentionality to bite. An example is where a default setting in a program is set to an option that is inherently likely to benefit the company at the expense of, or through harm to, its customers.[153] Another is where a system is programmed to explore the most profitable

[147] Treasury Laws Amendment (Design and Distribution Obligations and Product Intervention Powers) Act 2019 (Cth), incorporated into pt 7.8A of the Corporations Act 2001 (Cth).

[148] Financial Conduct Authority, Consumer Duty Instrument 2022, FCA 2022/31.

[149] ALRC Final Report (n 25) ch 7.

[150] ibid [7.178]–[7.196].

[151] Explored in Bant, 'Culpable Corporate Minds' (n 3) 385–87; Paterson, Bant and Cooney (n 3); and Bant, 'Catching the Corporate Conscience' (n 3) 487–90; as well as Bant, ch 11 of this volume, and Paterson and Bant, ch 12 of this volume.

[152] The same problem arises for the Design and Distribution Obligations and Consumer Right reforms: see Willis, ch 19 of this volume, section V.

[153] Bant, 'Culpable Corporate Minds' (n 3) 385–87; Paterson, Bant and Cooney (n 3); and Bant, 'Catching the Corporate Conscience' (n 3) 487–90; as well as Bant, ch 11 of this volume, and Paterson and Bant, ch 12 of this volume.

means of generating sales through data harvesting and direct engagement with customers, without any oversight or redress mechanisms. The corporation can be taken to know these critical features of what are, after all, its systems employed for its benefit. Regulators similarly may be able to ascertain important 'choice architecture' embedded in a digital system that renders transparent the corporate intentions. And as Willis herself notes, 'it is not credible that AI systems cannot be controlled'.[154] The choice to deploy AI without appropriate control programming is just that. If the program cannot be controlled, it should not be deployed, or should be tested and improved until it can. Here, there seems clear potential for a reinforcing effect between performance-based regulation and Systems Intentionality.

However, there is also no doubt that regulators currently lack expertise in new technologies that impede enforcement. And litigation against Big Tech, as we have seen, is notoriously difficult to prosecute with success.[155] In this context, outcome-based regulation is an important, additional avenue to hold corporations to account, and to promote good (or, at least, not bad) customer outcomes. Further, as Willis notes, performance-based regulation, Systems Intentionality and Fisse's concept of reactive corporate fault all share a common interest in the corporate responses made to the occurrence of those outcomes. These regulatory models therefore operate in a mutually reinforcing way. The same may be said for 'failure to prevent' models, although these (as explained earlier) require a predicate offence, which may itself raise attribution issues. Willis argues, however, that performance-based obligations avoid having the need in these models to assess whether executive assurances of opaque or unknowable 'reasonable precautions', or remedial 'adjustments', are genuine and effective. As Faugno notes, courts' interest to date in assessing the substance, as opposed to form, of remedial programmes, and their capacity to monitor these on an ongoing basis, are limited.[156] Willis explains that this remains a critical limitation of the new Design and Distribution Obligations and Consumer Duties, both of which demand only 'reasonable' or 'all reasonable' steps to be taken. Clearly, it is important that courts and regulators are prepared to go beyond bland executive assurances: Carroll's chapter suggests that courts have the capacity to do so, if they have the will.[157]

The final chapter in Part IV, and in this collection, really epitomises the lessons learned through the earlier essays. McGaughey's 'Regulatory Pluralism to Tackle Modern Slavery' focuses on one of the most egregious and longstanding forms of commercial misconduct.[158] Modern slavery practices tend to showcase all the worst features of corporate evasive tactics: claims of corporate (executive) ignorance, fortified through devolved corporate group structures, interposition of intermediaries and agents, spread across jurisdictions. We have seen that Clough's chapter explores the

[154] Willis, ch 19 of this volume, section VI.

[155] Powles, ch 5 of this volume.

[156] Faugno, ch 8 of this volume, section IV.B.iii. Were 'corrective' orders to become part of the courts' usual toolkit, a key question would remain the monitoring and enforcement mechanisms, such as through a 'recognisance'. An alternative would be probation orders: see ALRC Final Report (n 25) [8.64]–[8.98].

[157] Carroll, ch 15 of this volume; and section II.D of this chapter.

[158] McGaughey, ch 20 of this volume.

'failure to prevent offence' as a key to combatting this sort of egregious transnational crime.[159] As McGaughey shows, the current regulatory landscape would be boosted enormously by such a reform, and by embracing a pluralist approach. Currently, the reform mechanisms are weak, not least because of an uncoupling between criminal responsibility and business reporting requirements. Businesses are obliged to report on what they are doing to assess and address their risks of modern slavery, both with their immediate operations and in extended supply chains. But there are, in general,[160] no penalties associated with lack of compliance. This reflects both an assumption that modern slavery is endemic to supply chains, and that businesses are unaware of it. Some have suggested that there is a conundrum in both encouraging corporations to investigate and reform their supply chains and, on the other hand, potentially penalising them when they uncover slavery. 'Enforcement' is left to consumers, shareholders and broader civil society, who are assumed to be capable, and resourced, to monitor and respond to reporting failures (and reported instances of slavery practices within supply chains). The disclosure obligations in any event only apply to larger entities. Small businesses that engage in slavery practices are not subject to their requirements. Ironically, as small businesses, they are more likely to be the subject of successful prosecution on traditional attribution principles.[161] Other approaches are more promising perhaps, but require government action. Examples include import bans and public procurement and debarment regimes.[162]

Against this background, McGaughey asks whether, and how, Systems Intentionality may assist in informing a better regulatory regime. Here, she notices the potential for the analysis to capture culpable corporate groups and broader networks, mentioned earlier in relation to Bryan's chapter.[163] It also provides a means both to counter the dominant narrative of well-meaning ignorance and to understand modern slavery requirements in terms of a more 'enquiring and responsible corporate mindset'.[164] Thus corporations that apply business models that yield levels of profit only possible if slavery is present in their supply chains can be taken to understand that fact.[165] 'Ignorance' quickly takes on another, more culpable aspect. Drawing on the ALRC proposals, McGaughey identifies that 'failure to prevent' offences may be used in tandem with civil 'human rights due diligence' obligations to provide a more effective regulatory mix.[166] We have seen earlier in this section how Systems Intentionality provides a means to buttress both options.

[159] Clough, ch 18 of this volume.

[160] The new Western Australian debarment regime is an exception: see Procurement Act 2020 (WA), pt 7. Public procurement here is a potential powerful incentive to good corporate citizenship. See further F McGaughey et al, 'Public Procurement for Protecting Human Rights' (2022) 47 *Alternative Law Journal* 143; ALRC Final Report (n 25) Recommendation 15.

[161] J Gobert, 'Corporate Criminality: Four Models of Fault' (1994) 14 *Legal Studies* 393, 401.

[162] See n 159.

[163] Bryan, ch 14 of this volume; and section II.B.

[164] McGaughey, ch 20 of this volume, section IV.

[165] The case is on a par with *ASIC v National Exchange* (n 120), discussed in Bant and Paterson, 'Systems of Misconduct' (n 3) and Bant, 'Catching the Corporate Conscience' (n 3) 486–87.

[166] See particularly ALRC Final Report (n 25) [10.104]–[10.124].

III. Conclusion

In concluding this chapter, it will be apparent that the contributions to the collection add significantly to our understanding of existing conceptions of corporate culpability and the conditions for better regulatory responses to its presence and harmful consequences. Clearly, however, much remains to be done. Some work is academic: McGaughey, for example, rightly calls for 'further robust empirical, theoretical and doctrinal research on effective regulatory regimes for tackling modern slavery'.[167] Some advancements, however, will be dependent on the other legal communities identified at the outset of this chapter. My hope is that this collection will make clear the value of further, mutual collaborations, for the enduring benefit of all persons, natural and artificial alike.

[167] McGaughey, ch 20 of this volume, section IV.

2

Associations and Moral Responsibility: Some Ground-Clearing

MATTHEW HARDING

I. Introduction

My aim in this chapter is to explore some questions relating to associations and moral responsibility that I think are relevant to the theme of this collection. In a sense, my chapter steps back from that theme because I do not propose to consider in depth how law does or should handle questions of corporate action and states of mind. Instead, I want to think about questions that arise in morality, understood broadly to encompass what we owe to each other as well as how we might live good lives. In particular, I want to think about questions of moral responsibility that arise in associational settings. My hope is that a better understanding of these questions might assist in thinking through some of the legal questions with which this collection is concerned. In any event, at times I do touch on some possible points of intersection with law.

My chapter steps back from the theme of this collection in another way as well. Much of the collection will rightly dwell on the company as a legal and possibly also moral person. I want to locate my inquiry elsewhere. I want to concentrate on the position of individual human beings who associate in companies. Indeed, I want to focus more generally on the position of individual human beings who associate, and so what follows should be applicable not only in the setting of companies but also in other associational settings. Having said this, the fact that an association takes the form of a company with legal personality is relevant to the questions that I consider in this chapter, and I will return to that thought below.

In section II, I provide an outline of the morality of association, arguing that a person may change her moral horizons by making the commitments entailed in associating with others. I explore some of the limits of this proposition and also the sense in which, in the morality of association, a person's moral fortunes are tied up with those of others in ways she cannot necessarily control. In section III, I consider how the morality of association plays out in cases where members of an association share moral responsibility for associational action, suggesting that the burdens of such responsibility on individual members might not be as onerous as first appears to be the case. In section IV, I turn to the question whether the current members of an association might bear moral responsibility for harms occasioned by past associational action, and I argue that such responsibility may be accommodated squarely within the morality of association. Section IV concludes with some reflections on moral responsibility, legal liability, and the limits of private law and regulation. Finally, in section V, I look at how associations might discharge their moral responsibility, focusing on the ways in which the leaders of associations act in a representative capacity, and contrasting this with the impetus of the law of corporate attribution. Section VI concludes.

II. The Morality of Association

The concept of association has meaning in law.[1] But while the legal meaning of association overlaps with the sorts of arrangements in which I am interested in this chapter, it is not exhaustive of them. When I talk about associations, I have in mind a wide range of circumstances in which the action of individual human beings is coordinated and which are characterised in the ways I describe below. That coordination might take a form that law recognises and to which it responds in specific ways. But equally it might not. Moral thinking about associations makes sense even in circumstances where the associations in question are unknown to law.

Associations, broadly understood in this way as social phenomena, take many different forms and serve many different purposes. All of this is relevant when considering the extent to which the moral world changes for an individual when she associates with others. For the purposes of analysis, it is helpful to conceive of associations along a spectrum of involvement. At one end of this spectrum sit the rich, extensive associations of family life: a marriage, at least within conventional understandings, might be offered as an example. At the other end of the spectrum sit more localised, even transitory, engagements: a casual employee might associate with her colleagues on this basis. At different points closer to the middle of this spectrum exist the many associations that compose civil society, whether in the business world or in the not-for-profit sector, as well as the association entailed in the idea of political community. The richness and diversity of associations is such that it may be futile to try to categorise them beyond simply noting that there is this spectrum and that some associations are relatively 'thin' and others relatively 'thick'. In any event, even an inchoate sense of the spectrum of associations should suffice for present purposes.

The basic point I want to develop in this part of the chapter is that associating with others typically generates moral implications for an individual. More precisely, associating with others typically generates new moral possibilities for an individual, new ways of succeeding and failing in moral terms, new ways of proving praiseworthy or blameworthy, and new ways of being morally responsible and accountable. In this sense, I want to suggest that there is a morality of association.

[1] See, eg, the definition of an unincorporated association in *Conservative and Unionist Central Office v Burrell (Inspector of Taxes)* [1981] EWCA Civ 2, [1982] 1 WLR 522, 525 (Lawton LJ): 'two or more persons bound together for one or more common purposes, not being business purposes, by mutual undertakings, each having mutual duties and obligations, in an organisation which has rules which identify in whom control of it and its funds rests and upon what terms and which can be joined or left at will'.

Associations generate moral implications to the extent that they entail commitments on the part of the individuals concerned. The idea that commitments generate moral implications is familiar in moral theory. It is, for example, prominent in philosophical writings on the practice of promising.[2] However, the full range of commitments generating moral implications for individuals is not as fully explored in moral theory as it might be.[3] And many morally relevant commitments may be found in associational life. Of course, associations might arise out of promises: again, marriage is an excellent case in point. But most associations are not accompanied by such sharp and defined commitments. More often, becoming involved in an association might entail some commitment to pursuing a shared purpose, or discharging a particular role with certain responsibilities attached, or adhering to some set of beliefs or values. In the case of the political community, it might entail reposing a type of qualified trust in government.[4] In making these sorts of commitments, people who associate change the balance of moral reasons that apply to their circumstances, not necessarily by excluding certain reasons as is the case with promises,[5] but nonetheless in non-trivial ways.

In companies, association gives rise to commitments with moral implications just as it does in other settings. Consider, for example, shareholders who invest their capital in a company and thereby advance its purposes. The investment not only enables the advancement of those purposes. It also entails a sort of commitment to them. This is a qualified, attenuated commitment: after all, shareholders assume only limited liability in respect of the consequences of a company's actions, and their capacity to influence directors' decisions about the pursuit of the company's purposes is also limited.[6] Nonetheless, it seems clear enough that an investment of capital in a company counts as a commitment to the company's purposes. And to the extent that shareholders commit to corporate purposes, they are morally implicated in those purposes as a result.[7] Ethical investors understand this dimension of shareholding very well. In a similar way, directors assume a role with responsibilities for advancing corporate purposes and, by assuming this role, commit themselves to those purposes to that extent. Morally speaking, directors cannot then stand apart from the corporate purposes.

Interestingly, the moral dimensions of these sorts of commitments might diverge to some extent from their legal incidents. Take shareholders once again. In a legal sense,

[2] See, eg, A Ripstein, 'Kantian Perspectives on Private Law' in AS Gold et al (eds), *The Oxford Handbook of the New Private Law* (Oxford, Oxford University Press, 2020) ch 5; C Fried, *Contract as Promise: A Theory of Contractual Obligation*, 2nd edn (Oxford, Oxford University Press, 2015) ch 2.

[3] Although note the discussion of 'involvements' in D Owens, *Shaping the Normative Landscape* (Oxford, Oxford University Press, 2012) 96; and AS Gold, 'Trust and Advice' in PB Miller and M Harding (eds), *Fiduciaries and Trust: Ethics, Politics, Economics and Law* (Cambridge, Cambridge University Press, 2020) 35, 36.

[4] For a brilliant account of this qualified trust, GJ Postema, 'Trust, Distrust and the Rule of Law' in Miller and Harding (eds) (n 3) 242.

[5] On promises and exclusionary reasons, J Raz, *Practical Reason and Norms* (Oxford, Oxford University Press, 1999) 178.

[6] J Bakan, 'The Externalising Machines' in J Burchell (ed), *The Corporate Social Responsibility Reader: Context and Perspectives*, 1st edn (Abingdon, Routledge, 2008) 52 – thanks to Penny Crofts for this reference.

[7] On the nature of corporate purposes, see R Langford, 'Purpose-Based Governance' (2020) 43 *University of New South Wales Law Journal* 954.

shareholders are central to the company, and their powers and liabilities reflect this fact. In law, the association of shareholders is a critical element of the company as a legal form. In contrast, in morality, the association of shareholders might be relatively 'thin'; the association may be only peripheral to the life-plans, goals and values of individual shareholders, and shareholders themselves (for example superannuation trusts) might be institutional vehicles for individuals to pool wealth in the service of a multiplicity of goals or companies that are themselves associations of shareholders. In other cases, shareholders may invest through mechanisms such as index funds, in which case they may not even be aware of their holdings at any given point in time. Thus, for example in a large publicly listed company with a wide shareholder base or within complex corporate groups, the moral implications of the association of shareholders for any individual shareholder might be highly attenuated despite the central role the shareholders play in the corporate form.[8]

The commitments entailed in becoming a shareholder or a director seem straightforward enough to identify: in the one case, an individual 'signs up' to corporate purposes by investing capital; in the other, the individual assumes a role and thereby commits to all that is implied in that role. I now want to suggest that associating with others, whatever form that association takes, typically entails a further, more general commitment as well. This more general commitment is difficult to describe with precision but I think it is of moral significance. It is the basic commitment entailed in the very idea of association itself. To associate is, in some way, to merge one's own interests, goals, purposes and values with those of other people. Associating with others thus entails becoming morally engaged with them, putting oneself in a position where one's own moral fortunes will be determined in part by the moral fortunes of those others. In this sense, association demands a certain trust on the part of the individuals concerned, and it requires a giving up of control in moral matters. The trust and the giving up of control are a sort of commitment, and they trigger the morality of association.

In a moment I want to come back to this idea that association determines moral fortunes in ways that are not self-controlled, because I think it has interesting ramifications in corporate settings. But first I think it is important to notice that the commitment entailed in association is not always present where human action is coordinated. For example, a large number of people might all be present at the train station at 5 pm, waiting for their trains to take them home after work. There is coordination here, but the coordination is that of individuals separately pursuing their own interests, goals, purposes and values, rather than merging these in some morally interesting way.

Now consider a very different sort of situation in which coordination is unaccompanied by association. A woman who is kidnapped, sold to wealthy couple and compelled to work as their maid against her will can hardly be said to have committed to any sort of association with her captors. Indeed, her lack of commitment to that association simply underscores the grave moral wrong that is done to her.

[8] See further IB Lee, 'Corporate Criminal Responsibility as Team Member Responsibility' (2011) 31 *Oxford Journal of Legal Studies* 755, 770–71.

She is a victim and does not share in any part of the moral opprobrium rightly levelled at those who exploit and abuse her.

Thinking about corporate settings, to what extent might the position of employees of a company approximate that of the enslaved maid more than that of the shareholder and the director? There can be little doubt that some – indeed many – employees of modern business corporations have little choice or control over their work, and are in situations significantly analogous to the enslaved maid.[9] The position of many factory workers in the global South might be offered as a clear example.[10] The action of such exploited workers may be coordinated in an associational setting, but it may not entail the commitment of association even in the thinnest sense. And even if it does entail that commitment, it may generate for the workers concerned moral implications so attenuated that they are trivial. For present purposes, we may note the cases where the commitment entailed in association is in question and move on. There is no bright conceptual line to be drawn between these cases and the cases where the morality of association is triggered in a non-trivial way. All turns on a full moral appreciation of the circumstances.

Staying with the corporate setting, it seems to me that the morality of association is of interest in light of the concerns of this symposium. Becoming involved with a company, whether as a shareholder, director or employee (subject to what I have just said), typically entails the basic commitment entailed in association, viz a commitment to merging interests, goals, purposes and values with those of others, at least to some extent, and thus a commitment to the tying of one's moral fortunes to those of the others, again at least to some extent.[11] In some cases, association in corporate settings entails much more than that basic commitment – consider the position of the board of directors, the chief executive officer (CEO), or a majority shareholder for example – but in all cases corporate association entails the minimum. Thus, if a company commits crimes or engages in other morally blameworthy practices, all those who associate in the company are implicated. It will not do for the receptionist or the IT support officer to argue that she did not make or execute the relevant decisions. She is still associated with the company and to that extent implicated in its moral failings. That is how the morality of association works. We should hardly be surprised at the sweeping moral judgement expressed by the Hon Ray Finkelstein in his recent report into the Victorian casino licence holder: 'Crown Melbourne rightly deserves criticism for its past misconduct, and *no-one connected with the organisation is entitled to much sympathy*.'[12]

[9] Care is needed here, for while choice is often the vehicle by which commitment is manifested, the two are not synonymous. A nun with a strong sense of vocation may experience that vocation as a demand rather than a choice, but she nonetheless makes a significant commitment upon entering the nunnery.

[10] This is not to say that labour markets in the West are unaffected by such concerns: see, eg, D Ashiagbor, 'Race and Colonialism in the Construction of Labour Markets and Precarity' (2021) 50 *Industrial Law Journal* 506.

[11] See also Lee (n 8), arguing for a conception of corporations as 'teams' whose members share in the moral fortunes of each other. Lee seems to argue that team members are morally engaged in this way only to the extent that they subjectively identify with the team. However, it seems to me that in many circumstances commitments withstand such subjective changes of position. Promises and assumptions of social role stand as two obvious examples.

[12] State of Victoria, *Royal Commission into the Casino Operator and Licence* (The Report, October 2021) vol 1 [21] (emphasis added).

In recent work, Elise Bant and Jeannie Marie Paterson have sought to demonstrate how companies can perform actions and have states of mind of relevance to law notwithstanding their complex, diffuse, decision-making and operational structures. Bant and Paterson emphasise the operation of systems and practices within companies in arguing that corporate actions and states of mind are not only – perhaps in some cases not even – the sum of actions and states of mind of individual human beings in the association that is the company.[13] The argument is powerful and recognises that law must respond to the realities of corporate organisation and not idealised understandings of private law liability built around deontic relationships between human beings.

It might be thought that Bant and Paterson's work promises to bolster legal responses to corporate wrongdoing but at a certain moral cost. The worry might be that a focus on corporate systems and practices diverts moral attention from the individual human beings who associate in the company, and places it instead on the company as a legal – and potentially even moral – person whose systems and practices have been called into question. This might then allow individuals who should bear moral responsibility for their part in corporate wrongdoing to hide behind the legal person of the company itself and escape the moral opprobrium that should rightly be theirs.

On a proper understanding of the morality of association, this concern turns out to be unfounded. Far from diverting moral attention from the individuals who associate in the company, Bant and Paterson's approach to legal liability reminds us that, at a basic level, moral attention is rightly directed at everyone who so associates. The company whose legal liability should not, according to Bant and Paterson, be determined exhaustively by the sum of individual actions and states of mind is not only a creature of law; it is also a social and cultural construct that can, and does, act as a proxy for all those who associate in it. Understood this way, finding a company legally liable is a signal that an association of individual human beings has done something that stands to be assessed, and potentially found wanting, on the moral plane, and that to some extent the moral assessment can encompass that association as a whole.

I want to say something now about the moral possibilities that are opened up by the commitment entailed in association. To begin with, association enables individuals to prove loyal, either by 'taking the side' of members of the association or by faithfully furthering associational purposes or values.[14] As an instance of the former, consider the loyalty of members of a cricket club; as an instance of the latter, consider the loyal employee. The morality of loyalty is, of course, contingent on the character of the purposes and values for which an association stands, as the example of the loyal Nazi demonstrates. Thus, where an association pursues morally questionable purposes or stands for pseudo-values that are in fact morally worthless, loyalty must be counted a vice rather than a virtue. In this regard, it is important to emphasise that loyalty in the

[13] E Bant, 'Culpable Corporate Minds' (2021) 48 *University of Western Australia Law Review* 352; E Bant and JM Paterson, 'Systems of Misconduct: Corporate Culpability and Statutory Unconscionability' (2021) 15 *Journal of Equity* 63; Bant, ch 11 of this volume.

[14] On the two meanings of loyalty, M Harding, 'Disgorgement of Profit and Fiduciary Loyalty' in S Degeling and JNE Varuhus (eds), *Equitable Compensation and Disgorgement of Profit* (Oxford, Hart Publishing, 2017) 19, 20–23.

sense of fidelity to associational purposes and values may not require any particular affective or emotional engagement in those purposes and values. Simply 'doing your job' might suffice to demonstrate loyalty, depending on the circumstances.[15]

Against this backdrop, further moral possibilities arise. In circumstances where associational loyalty is morally questionable, individuals may exhibit virtue – may even have moral duties to act – in other ways. Voicing internal dissent and dissatisfaction might be called for.[16] In this regard, the recent Facebook papers are interesting to consider. According to a report from the *Washington Post*, they disclose internal communications of employees of Facebook in the lead-up to the failed insurrection in Washington, DC on 6 January 2021, expressing disquiet and moral concern about the extent to which Facebook was enabling the insurrectionists.[17] Those communications reflect a moral engagement on the part of employees who realised that loyalty to Facebook was morally outweighed by other priorities. The employees concerned understood well that they were implicated in Facebook's conduct in virtue of their association with Facebook. They sensed that doing nothing, and thereby demonstrating a sort of default loyalty to Facebook, was morally problematic.

It is in this light that the figure of the whistle-blower can be best understood. The whistle-blower is impelled by a sense of moral disquiet to depart from the norms of associational loyalty in potentially profound and far-reaching ways. A whistle-blower exercises the sort of voice that can make ongoing involvement in an association difficult if not impossible. It is for these reasons that the whistle-blower may need legal protection. The moral significance of a whistle-blower's actions in bringing to attention corporate crimes and other misconduct can only be fully appreciated against a baseline of associational commitment and the loyalty that this usually calls for. The whistle-blower performs a distinctive moral role in associational life, a role whose significance lies in the fact that it requires an individual to become alienated from her own commitment in the service of other moral objectives.

The morality of association is obviously much more than the moral implications of the basic commitment that association entails. For an individual involved in an association, moral success or failure, blameworthiness or praiseworthiness, responsibility and accountability will depend in large measure on a range of variables. These include the nature and incidents of the individual's role within the association, the degree of coordination and unity of purpose among members of the association generally, and the nature of the actions, states of mind and consequences about which moral questions are being asked. In a company, the CEO who presides actively over exploitative and harmful business practices is obviously more morally blameworthy than the back-office support staff. As a general rule, the board of directors is more morally engaged

[15] See further JE Penner, 'Is Loyalty a Virtue, and Even If It Is, Does It Really Help to Explain Fiduciary Loyalty?' in AS Gold and PB Miller (eds), *Philosophical Foundations of Fiduciary Law* (Oxford, Oxford University Press, 2014) 159.

[16] The full range of options have been famously conceptualised as 'exit', 'voice' or 'loyalty': AO Hirsch, *Exit, Voice and Loyalty: Responses to Decline in Firms, Organizations and States* (Cambridge, Harvard University Press, 1970).

[17] C Timberg, E Dworkin and R Albergotti, 'Inside Facebook, Jan. 6 Violence Fueled Anger, Regret over Missed Warning Signs' *Washington Post* (22 October 2021) at www.washingtonpost.com/technology/2021/10/22/jan-6-capitol-riot-facebook/.

in corporate purpose than the facilities team. The members of a close-knit team in a small business more clearly stand or fall together morally than the staff of a multinational corporation spread over numerous countries and offices. But the basic point remains: when people associate, the moral fortunes of each one of them is, even in some small way, bound up with the moral fortunes of all the others. Thus, the moral failures of the CEO or the board have ramifications for everyone in the company.

Indeed, the morality of association helps us to understand the possibility of a particular kind of moral failure on the part of those with seniority and responsibility in an association. This failure has to do with encouraging others to make the commitment entailed in association, and then knowingly exposing those others to moral opprobrium because of that commitment. This is a sort of abuse of the association itself, and it amounts to a betrayal of the trust reposed by those who associate and thereby render themselves vulnerable to the moral fortunes of others. It may provoke moral outrage on the part of those adversely affected, and efforts to sever ties with the association in question: in corporate settings, archetypes might be shareholders who divest their holdings, or employees who resign in disgust.

Before moving on, I want to address one aspect of the morality of association that is bound to cause unease in some quarters. The morality of association potentially entails the moral responsibility of members of associations for matters that are beyond their control. This engages the well-known philosophical problem known as 'moral luck' on which much has been written.[18] The worry is that if individuals bear moral responsibility for matters beyond their control, their moral agency and therefore their status as persons is undermined. However, some philosophers have argued that this has things precisely the wrong way around. Tony Honoré and, more recently, John Gardner have argued that being a person with moral agency in fact depends on bearing moral responsibility for matters beyond our control. On this view, uncontrolled moral successes and failures are a fundamental component of a person's identity over time and cannot be excluded from any account of moral responsibility that is person-centred.[19] It should be clear already that my account of the morality of association assumes the correctness of something like Honoré's and Gardner's account of moral responsibility.

III. Associations and Moral Responsibility for Actions

In this section, I want to consider the possibility that members of an association may bear moral responsibility for actions of the association. By 'moral responsibility' I have in mind a state of affairs in which a person is answerable for an action that has been called into question in light of some applicable moral norm. Moral responsibility,

[18] This literature began with two seminal works: T Nagel, 'Moral Luck' in *Mortal Questions* (Cambridge, Cambridge University Press, 1979) 24; B Williams, 'Moral Luck' in T Nagel, *Moral Luck: Philosophical Papers 1973–1980* (Cambridge, Cambridge University Press, 1981) 20.

[19] T Honoré, 'Responsibility and Luck' (1988) 104 *Law Quarterly Review* 530; J Gardner, 'Obligations and Outcomes in the Law of Torts' in J Gardner (ed), *Torts and Other Wrongs* (Oxford, Oxford University Press, 2019) 133.

thus understood, is closely connected with moral blameworthiness and also moral accountability to those who might have been harmed by the action in question.[20] Moral responsibility for an action might generate demands for further remedial or responsive actions to be taken. It might also simply call for moral disapproval, even condemnation.

Before turning to the question of moral responsibility for associational action, something should be said about associational action itself. It seems clear enough that, for moral purposes, associations can and do act, even in circumstances where they lack legal personality. Associational actions are social facts, determined by understandings, conventions and practices that may differ from one associational setting to another. Thus, for example, married couples are often understood to act jointly: when you receive an invitation to a party that my wife and I are hosting, you apprehend readily that it is *our* party and that the invitation has come from *us*. The understandings that surround the convention of viewing the actions of married couples as joint actions are not unproblematic, as feminist scholars have pointed out.[21] Nonetheless, they persist in social life.[22]

Identifying associational actions is important against the backdrop of the morality of association because it helps to clarify the range of matters in respect of which the morality of association might be activated. It does not exhaust that range – for example, members of an association might be susceptible to moral disapproval precisely because the association does not act – but it does help to constitute it in important ways. If my wife and I host a party, and our canapés give you food poisoning, we both share in the moral responsibility that is thus activated: in all likelihood, we owe you an apology, and an apology from just one of us on the basis that the other did not cook the food in question would seem odd, to say the least. *Our* action triggers *our* responsibility in the morality of association.

In civil society, including the business world, social facts about associational action are heavily influenced by law. In other words, what counts as an associational action as a matter of law largely determines what is understood socially to be associational action. In law, the actions of a company are defined with reference to the lawful exercise of powers by the board and their delegates and by the shareholders in general meeting. And that legal definition is largely carried over into social life as well. That said, associations might act socially even where they do not act legally. In recent years police forces around the world have acted in a range of ways to enforce Covid-19 pandemic restrictions. There can be little doubt that some of those actions have been unlawful.[23] They are nonetheless recognisable as the actions of *the police*, rather than the actions of individuals who happen to be wearing police uniforms.

[20] See further J Gardner, 'The Negligence Standard: Political Not Metaphysical' in Gardner (ed), *Torts and Other Wrongs* (n 19) 196.

[21] See, eg, SM Okin, *Justice, Gender and the Family* (New York, Basic Books, 1989).

[22] These social understandings are explored to hilarious effect by comedian Larry David in season 3, episode 7 of the HBO series *Curb Your Enthusiasm*.

[23] Lord Sumption, 'Government by Decree: COVID-19 and the British Constitution' (Cambridge Freshfields Annual Law Lecture, 27 October 2020) at https://resources.law.cam.ac.uk/privatelaw/Freshfields_Lecture_2020_Government_by_Decree.pdf.

In the setting of a company, the coincidence of legal and social facts about associational action means that a certain set of facts might disclose both the sort of corporate action that can trigger legal liability, and at the same time the sort of associational action that can activate the morality of association. A company might thus be liable for engaging in misleading and deceptive conduct, or unconscionable conduct, under the law,[24] and at the same time the individuals who associate in that company might share some moral responsibility in respect of the conduct in question. But what is required by way of remedy in light of the legal liability might be different from what is required in light of the moral responsibility. In law, a money award might be appropriate; in morality, it might be an apology that is required, or a sincere effort to repair or rebuild some broken relationship.

Indeed, in some circumstances a corporate action recognised in law might not attract legal liability, but the association that is the company might bear moral responsibility for the action understood as a social fact. In these circumstances, the fact that the action in question escapes legal liability will not necessarily resolve or discharge that moral responsibility. Moral remediation might still be required.

A clear example is the events surrounding the destruction of the Juukan Gorge rock shelters by the mining company Rio Tinto in May 2020. In destroying the rock shelters, Rio Tinto acted lawfully, and indeed a recent parliamentary inquiry into the matter has concluded that the legal framework in which such actions are taken should be strengthened for the future.[25] However, as the inquiry has made equally clear, the fact that Rio Tinto acted lawfully in no way diminishes the moral responsibility that the company bears for its actions. Rio Tinto has sought to discharge that moral responsibility in various ways, through issuing an apology to the Traditional Owners of the site, commitments to cultural and systemic reform, and efforts to repair and rebuild trust with the Traditional Owners.[26] It remains to be seen whether these initiatives will suffice to release Rio Tinto of the moral burden it now bears as a result of what it did in May 2020.

To be clear: when I talk about Rio Tinto's bearing moral responsibility for its actions, I mean that the individuals who associate in that company share moral responsibility for those actions in virtue of the morality of association. I make this claim quite apart from any question whether Rio Tinto can be said to be a moral as well as a legal person that can bear moral responsibility itself. Everyone associated with Rio Tinto might reasonably be called to answer for the company's actions.

Even if we accept, following Honoré and Gardner, that people can bear moral responsibility in respect of matters over which they had no control, it might still be argued that making everyone associated with Rio Tinto answerable in morality for blowing up the Juukan Gorge is placing an unreasonable burden on many of them. Surely, it might be said, those shareholders and employees who were in no way involved in the chain of

[24] See Competition and Consumer Act 2010 (Cth), sch 2, ss 18, 20–21 (ACL).

[25] Parliament of the Commonwealth of Australia, Joint Standing Committee on Northern Australia, *A Way Forward: Final Report into the Destruction of Indigenous Heritage Sites at Juukan Gorge* (October 2021) 186–204.

[26] See Rio Tinto, 'Juukan Gorge' at www.riotinto.com/en/news/inquiry-into-juukan-gorge.

events leading up to the destruction of the rock shelters are not answerable for what happened, even if they have made the basic commitment entailed in associating with Rio Tinto.

I am not so sure. For one thing, I have already alluded to the sense in which the morality of association might deliver more or less attenuated implications for different individuals depending on the character of their association. The members of an association might thus all share in moral responsibility for associational actions, but the seriousness of this for each individual member might differ in view of their different circumstances. Moreover, our moral practices already recognise ways in which those who bear moral responsibility for actions might nonetheless escape censure or blame: for instance, someone who is morally responsible for an action might offer a sufficient excuse. The moral force of an excuse presupposes an underlying moral responsibility but the existence of good reasons not to visit upon the responsible person the usual consequences (blame, punishment) that might follow from that responsibility.[27] In the case of Rio Tinto's blowing up the Juukan Gorge, it seems likely that many individuals associated with Rio Tinto are peripherally involved in that association such that moral responsibility connected with the Juukan Gorge implicates them in a relatively attenuated way. Moreover, many such individuals could offer sufficient excuses when answering for the actions of the company. In particular, it seems plausible to suggest that excuses might be available where an individual's role in Rio Tinto did not demand decisions or actions that helped to constitute the impugned corporate action, or where the individual raised concerns about, or tried to stop, that action.

In addition, we need to reflect further on what counts as answering for associational actions before we can conclude anything about the burden that moral responsibility for such actions places on members of associations. Individual members of the association that is Rio Tinto may be answerable for blowing up the Juukan Gorge. This does not necessarily mean that each individual member of Rio Tinto must now seek out Traditional Owners and offer a personal apology.[28] A collective apology issued through representative office-holders might suffice. (Indeed, this is precisely what has happened in that case.) After all, if belonging to an association entails assuming the burdens of shared moral responsibility, then it should not be surprising that it also carries with it the benefits of shared remedial action. The nature of association as a merger of interests, goals, purposes and values suggests that collective expression through representative means will often be a suitable mode of action, including in response to moral responsibility. I return to this idea in section IV when I discuss how the moral responsibility of associations might be discharged.

[27] See, eg, MN Berman, 'Justification and Excuse, Law and Morality' (2003) 53 *Duke Law Journal* 1; E Rivera-López, 'Can There Be Full Excuses for Morally Wrong Actions?' (2006) 63 *Philosophy and Phenomenological Research* 124.

[28] In some circumstances, an individual apology might be called for. Imagine that a Traditional Owner meets someone socially who works at Rio Tinto. Here, it seems to me that the Rio Tinto employee should probably attempt an apology ('I'm so sorry about what we did …').

IV. Associations and Moral Responsibility for Historic Harms

Of particular salience in any investigation of associations and moral responsibility is the question of the extent to which an association bears moral responsibility for historic harms. In Australia, the Royal Commission into the sexual abuse of children in institutional settings has brought this question very much to the surface.[29] So did the Prime Minister's 2010 apology to the Stolen Generations.[30] Elsewhere, the same question has surfaced in interesting ways: for example, in early 2021 in the United Kingdom, the National Trust was investigated by the Charity Commission for England and Wales for commissioning work exploring historic connections between the houses under its stewardship and the slave trade that sustained the English economy for many years. Presumably, the National Trust acted from a sense of moral responsibility for historic harms associated with slavery. The Charity Commission was concerned that the work was not in furtherance of the National Trust's charitable purposes, but ultimately concluded that it was consistent with those purposes.[31]

The morality of association helps to explain why the current members of an association bear moral responsibility for harms occasioned by the past actions of that association. Recall that, in associating, an individual merges her interests, goals, purposes and values with those of other people. Consequently, she is morally engaged with them and her moral fortunes are now bound up with theirs. The range of people with whom she is now morally engaged extends as far as the association extends, and there is no reason to think that this extension is temporally limited in any way. For as long as the association is identifiable over time as a matter of social fact, the morality of association is in play.[32]

In certain cases, it may be difficult to identify an association over time. For example, where there has been a political revolution, it may be hard to argue that in the new political order citizens should bear moral responsibility for state actions that took place in the old political order. Indeed, the revolution may have been triggered by the desire of citizens to distance themselves from those state actions. Revolution is a dramatic act of exit from associational life and its entailed morality. Something similar might be said of schisms in civil society associations such as churches.

On the other hand, an association may subsist over time as a matter of social fact even though its legal form changes, and even though the facts of its legal form are not well known or not known at all. As is the case with many religious associations, the Roman Catholic Church takes a variety of notoriously complex legal forms,

[29] Commonwealth of Australia, *Royal Commission into Institutional Responses to Child Sexual Abuse* (Final Report: Preface and Executive Summary, 2017) at www.childabuseroyalcommission.gov.au/sites/default/files/final_report_-_preface_and_executive_summary.pdf.

[30] For the text and a video of the apology, see Parliament of Australia, 'Apology to Australia's Indigenous Peoples' (13 February 2008) at www.aph.gov.au/Visit_Parliament/Art/Exhibitions/Custom_Media/Apology_to_Australias_Indigenous_People.

[31] See Charity Commission, 'Charity Commission Finds National Trust Did Not Breach Charity Law' (Press Release, 11 March 2021) at www.gov.uk/government/news/charity-commission-finds-national-trust-did-not-breach-charity-law.

[32] See also Lee (n 8) 774–76 discussing 'cross-temporal teams'.

and one of the challenges facing victims of child sexual abuse within the Church has been identifying defendants to sue.[33] Nonetheless, as a matter of social fact there is little doubt about what the Roman Catholic Church is, and about the fact that it has subsisted for some two thousand years. In response to the claim that members of the Church today bear moral responsibility for the past actions of the Church, it simply cannot be answered that the Church today is a different association from the Church of yesteryear.

Where an association has subsisted over time and its past actions have caused harms, it will not do for current members of the association to refuse to take moral responsibility for those actions and those harms. For those members to argue that the actions in question were someone else's actions is to misunderstand the morality of association. Many Australians will remember clearly the view of former Prime Minister John Howard in respect of an apology to the Stolen Generations: 'Australians of this generation should not be required to accept guilt and blame for past actions and policies over which they had no control.'[34] In light of the morality of association, this statement misses the point completely. Through the association of the Australian political community, Australians today share in the moral fortunes of their forebears and can be called to answer for their forebears' past acts.

Are there circumstances in which an association might bear moral responsibility in respect of historic harms that have in no sense been caused by its actions? There is a deep connection between action and moral responsibility that makes it difficult to answer this question in the affirmative. However, the fact that someone is not morally responsible for an action does not necessarily mean that she has no moral duties or reasons to act in ways that might address harms the action has caused. If my son is bullied at school, my wife and I are not morally responsible for the harms caused. Nonetheless, we have moral duties to support and care for our son in light of those harms because of a different sort of responsibility that we have towards him as parents.[35] His harms are our problem even though we are not morally responsible for them.

In a similar way, an association may assume responsibility to advance or look after the interests of some harmed group that generates moral duties or reasons to respond to harms even though the harms have been caused by someone else's action. One obvious example would be a charitable association whose purpose is to provide supports to the harmed group in question. Another, perhaps less obvious example might be a company whose operations take place in a location associated with a historically disadvantaged group and which assumes a responsibility to further the interests of that group as a result. I say nothing here about the extent to which companies that assume such responsibility in fact discharge it well or even adequately.

[33] The problem of finding a defendant to sue has been addressed by legislation in Victoria: see Legal Identity of Defendants (Organisations Child Abuse) Act 2018 (Vic).

[34] Department of Prime Minister and Cabinet, 'Transcript of the Prime Minister the Hon John Howard MP Opening Address to the Australian Reconciliation Convention: Melbourne' (PM Transcripts, 26 May 1997) at https://pmtranscripts.pmc.gov.au/release/transcript-10361.

[35] See the discussion of 'role responsibility' in HLA Hart, 'Varieties of Responsibility' (1967) 83 *Law Quarterly Review* 346, 347–48.

An association's moral responsibility for historic harms might call for different sorts of responses depending on the circumstances. These responses might be arranged roughly into two categories. On the one hand, there are responses that seek to effect a sort of corrective or remedial justice: these responses might range from an apology, to a commitment to a process of truth telling and reconciliation, to making payments with compensatory or vindicatory objectives. Such responses might overlap with remedies awarded upon findings of legal liability, but then again they might not. On the other hand, there are responses that seek to support the harmed group or to place relations between the association and the harmed group on a different footing for the future. Such responses do not necessarily seek to achieve any sort of justice but might instead be driven by other moral imperatives such as compassion or solidarity. Depending on the circumstances, the moral responsibility of an association might call for a combination of such remedial and forward-looking responses.

At this point, it is worth pausing to reflect on the ways in which moral responsibility for historic harms might demand responses that seem unavailable as a matter of private law liability. Forward-looking responses, focused on providing supports or building relationships for the future, might seem beyond the scope of private law with its focus on corrective or remedial justice. However, this assumes an account of private law and its limits that has been much contested in private law theory. One point that emerges from the critique of corrective or remedial justice accounts of private law is that courts resolving private law disputes may perform an important standard-setting and behaviour-influencing role. Indeed, in other work, Justice Chris Maxwell and I have argued that, in this forward-looking aspect, private law should strive to engage the moral sensibilities of those who manage and direct companies and other associations.[36] On this account, private law might perform useful service in orienting individuals in corporate settings towards understanding and discharging their moral responsibilities.

Moreover, the limits of private law are not typically thought to apply to regulatory approaches and techniques, and regulators might require companies to act in ways that reflect the demands of their moral responsibility for historic harms. The question of the extent to which regulators may impose such forward-looking interventions has been discussed of late in Australia. For example, the Australian Law Reform Commission considered the question in its recent report on corporate criminal responsibility. The Commission recommended changes to the Crimes Act 1914 (Cth) to enable courts to make forward-looking orders, including orders requiring companies to 'undertake activities for the benefit of the community'.[37] At the same time, Commissioner Kenneth Hayne had much to say about corporate culture in his 2019 report into abuses in the banking and financial services sector,[38] and this raises the question whether

[36] C Maxwell and M Harding, 'Private Law, Conscience and Moral Reasoning: The Role of the Judge' (2022) 46 *Melbourne University Law Review* 1.

[37] Australian Law Reform Commission, *Corporate Criminal Responsibility* (Report No 136, April 2020) 16–17, Recommendation 12.

[38] Commonwealth of Australia, Royal Commission into Misconduct in the Banking, Superannuation and Financial Services Industry (Final Report, 1 February 2019) 47–48.

Australia's corporate regulator, the Australian Securities and Investments Commission, should exercise coercive powers to require companies to take actions to improve their culture.[39] These debates are relevant to the question of the extent to which legal liability might align with the moral responsibility of companies and those who associate in them.

V. Discharging the Moral Responsibility of Associations

The University of Melbourne is an association of thousands of staff, students and others. Recently it was discovered that the University had been underpaying casual academic staff for years. Apart from any legal liability to compensate those who had been underpaid in breach of contract, as a matter of moral responsibility an apology was due. In the morality of association, the moral responsibility for wage theft lies with all those who associate in the University of Melbourne. To some extent, we (being the members of the University of Melbourne, including me) all share in the moral blameworthiness for the wage theft. Thus, in a sense, we all owe the required apology to the affected group. Nonetheless, the impracticality of every individual who associates in the University of Melbourne offering the apology in question is insurmountable. Who, then, should offer the apology? This raises the question of how best to discharge the moral responsibility of associations.

The University of Melbourne is a body corporate in law, and so in theory the moral responsibility for wage theft could have been discharged by the University itself.[40] However, the apology was not issued by the University through its governing Council. Instead, the apology was issued by the Vice-Chancellor of the University in an e-mail to all staff. In that e-mail, the Vice-Chancellor spoke for the University but in his own voice – 'I write with an apology' – as an individual with a particular role in the University and a certain authority to speak for the whole University on the question of wage theft.[41]

In a hierarchical association such as a university, where there are senior leaders who are the 'public face' of the association, looking to those senior leaders to discharge the moral responsibility of the association is commonplace. When Oxfam apologised and promised to make amends for the sexually exploitative actions of its staff in Haiti, it was the chair of the Board of Trustees who issued the apology and promised the necessary actions.[42] We expect the Pope and the senior clergy of the Roman Catholic Church to answer for the historic abuse of children.[43] Only the Australian Prime Minister could

[39] See V Comino, '"Corporate Culture" is the "New Black": Its Possibilities and Limits as a Regulatory Mechanism for Corporations and Financial Institutions' (2021) 44 *University of New South Wales Law Journal* 295. I am grateful to Elise Bant for this reference.

[40] The University of Melbourne Act 2009 (Vic), s 4 confirms that the University is a 'body politic and corporate'.

[41] E-mail from Professor Duncan Maskell to University of Melbourne staff (copy on file with the author).

[42] See C Thomson, 'Caroline's Statement in Full' at www.oxfam.org.uk/about-us/tackling-abuse-information-and-updates/carolines-statement/.

[43] See, eg, C Rousselle, 'Pope Francis' Upcoming Meeting with Indigenous Delegation a Step Toward Healing, Canadian Bishops Say' *Catholic News Agency* (10 November 2021) at www.catholicnewsagency.com/news/249552/pope-francis-canada-indigenous-meeting-vatican.

have satisfactorily delivered an apology to the Stolen Generations. In all these cases, moral responsibility rests with an association as a whole, but it is discharged by the association's leaders in order to facilitate the process of answering for pertinent actions and taking further actions necessary to achieve remedial or other morally important objectives.

There is no reason why this must be so. In theory, the shared moral responsibility of an association might be discharged in a range of ways, some of which do not depend on action through the mechanisms afforded by institutional leadership. Indeed, in circumstances where institutional leadership cannot or will not rise to the challenge of the association's moral responsibility, there may be little choice for members of the association seeking to 'do the right thing'. In the years leading up to the Australian Prime Minister's formal apology to the Stolen Generations, many Australian citizens sought to discharge their shared moral responsibility for historic harms by signing 'sorry books' in which they offered individual apologies for past actions. It is estimated that over half a million Australians signed these 'sorry books',[44] which amounts to a powerful grassroots expression of moral remorse across the Australian political community.

Yet while such grassroots options are always available in theory, they are seldom chosen in practice. Where associations have leaders, it is a social fact that associational action is often pursued through the agency of those leaders. And this is hardly surprising. Just as the CEO or the board of directors is perfectly positioned to implicate the whole association in morally questionable action, so both are well placed to discharge the moral responsibility that might arise and be borne by the whole association in respect of that action. This is because leaders are able, both legally and morally, to *represent* the associations they lead, enabling associational action to be carried out quickly and unambiguously in ways that are readily recognised socially and in law. Indeed, there seems to be a deep connection between representation and the morality of association, and this is a topic on which much more could be written.[45]

In corporate settings, the way leaders discharge the moral responsibility of associations through representative actions stands in stark contrast to the attribution of actions and states of mind that is the concern of private law. In private law, a plaintiff may seek to have the action or state of mind of an office-holder or employee attributed to the company.[46] This is understandable given the relative desirability of suing a company as opposed to the individuals who govern or work in it. Where attribution works this way in a private law setting, leading to the imposition of liability on a company, an interesting set of questions might arise about what this means for the discharge of the moral responsibility of the association that is the company.

[44] See AIATSIS, 'The Sorry Books' at https://aiatsis.gov.au/explore/sorry-books for further information on the 'sorry books' campaign.

[45] On representation, PB Miller, 'Fiduciary Representation' in EJ Criddle et al (eds), *Fiduciary Government* (Cambridge, Cambridge University Press, 2018) 21.

[46] On attribution in corporate settings, see R Leow, *Corporate Attribution in Private Law* (Oxford, Hart Publishing, 2022); and E Bant, 'Reforming the Laws of Corporate Attribution: "Systems Intentionality" Draft Statutory Provision' (2022) 39 *Company & Securities Law Journal* 259.

Attribution suggests that the moral agency of the association's leaders plays only a derivative or secondary role in the unfolding legal and moral drama. On the other hand, moral responsibility might demand some representative action from the leaders, despite the fact that their actions and states of mind are attributed to the company for the purposes of law. Where such conflicting signals are in play, it seems possible that the leaders might misunderstand what is required of them as a matter of morality, and as a result might not take the steps necessary to discharge the moral responsibility of the association in the matter at hand.

VI. Conclusion

Let me sum up by way of conclusion. First, there is a morality of association in which a member of an association is typically morally engaged in the affairs of the association. In this morality of association, someone who associates with others commits to the binding up of their moral fortunes with those of the others, at least to the extent of the association. Associations thus present individuals with circumstances in which their moral fate may lie beyond their control. Second, an association might bear shared moral responsibility for its actions (which are to be ascertained as a matter of social fact), and this moral responsibility can arise even in circumstances where legal liability does not. Third, current members of associations can bear moral responsibility for harms occasioned by past actions of the associations in question. Such associations might now have to strive for corrective or remedial justice, as well as taking forward-looking steps that seek to support and build new relationships with harmed groups. The alignment here of available legal and moral responses is an interesting and open question. Finally, an association will typically discharge its moral responsibility through the representative actions of its leaders. And given that attribution in private law typically seeks to ascribe the moral agency of the leaders of a company to the company itself, it is possible that private law attribution might complicate and even stand at odds with what is required of leaders as a matter of morality.

3

Crown Resorts and the Im/moral Corporate Form

PENNY CROFTS*

This chapter aims to contribute to a substantiation of the realist intuition as essential to attributions of culpability for certain sorts of corporate harms. Realists accept the idea of corporations as agents in their own right and argue that corporations can act and be at fault in ways that are different from the ways that their members can act and be at fault. This does not exclude ascriptions of responsibility to individuals, but it does argue that corporations can and should be regarded as moral agents in and of themselves, capable of being held criminally responsible for prohibited outcomes. Difficulties arise because criminal legal doctrine primarily engages with and privileges the ideal responsible subject as an individual human being. There is, however, some engagement with group liability under doctrines of conspiracy and accessorial liability.[1] Otherwise, group liability tends not to be considered in general criminal law texts.[2] The question of whether a corporation is a genuine agent or just a collection of individual agents is important because the answer dictates how we can explain the behaviour of corporations and whether we can and should treat them as responsible and accountable agents.[3] As I argue in section I, this question is particularly salient in criminal legal doctrine, as a central function of the criminal legal system is to establish the blameworthiness of responsible legal subjects.

* This research was funded by the Australian Government through a Discovery Early Career Researcher Award ('DECRA'), project number DE180100577, 'Rethinking Institutional Culpability: Criminal Law, Philosophy and Horror'.

[1] A Dyer, 'The "Australian Position" Concerning Criminal Complicity: Principle, Policy or Politics?' (2018) 40 *Sydney Law Review* 289; KJM Smith, *A Modern Treatise on the Law of Criminal Complicity* (Oxford, Clarendon Press, 1991).

[2] See, eg, J Horder, *Ashworth's Principles of Criminal Law*, 9th edn (Oxford, Oxford University Press, 2019). Likewise Feinberg focuses on harms caused by groups but does not consider structured forms of identity like corporations but instead random collectives like swimmers on a beach. J Feinberg, *Doing and Deserving: Essays in the Theory of Responsibility* (Princeton, NJ, Princeton University Press, 1970) 244.

[3] C List and P Pettit, *Group Agency: The Possibility, Design, and Status of Corporate Agents* (Oxford, Oxford University Press, 2011).

It is now relatively widely accepted that suitably organised collectives can be agents in their own right.[4] Christian List and Philip Pettit greatly enriched the debate on group agency, arguing that groups can meet the requirements of moral agency by virtue of the fact that they 'have representational states, motivational states, and a capacity to process them and act on their basis'.[5] Accordingly, groups can have obligations, entitlements and power relations that have hitherto gone unnoticed and that require our moral attention. However, List and Pettit's model is on groups generally and provides no more than a sketch of the core ingredients of any type of group agency. Corporations are a worthy study of group agency in and of themselves for multiple reasons, including because they are so dominant in everyday life, are capable of and have inflicted widespread systemic harms and, unlike many other groups, are structured and regulated by law. To this end, I draw upon the theorist Chris Chapple, who has modified List and Pettit's broader list to enunciate group agency requirements that are specific to corporations.[6] These three core requirements of moral agency are: the agent-choice requirement – the corporation as a distinct moral agent that faces normatively significant choices; the control requirement – the corporation has power over the choice between certain actions; and good judgement – the corporation can form and access judgements in its own right, and possesses a regulative capacity that governs the ways these intentions inform and motivate actions in a way that conforms to certain rational and epistemic standards. These fundamentals of what makes moral agents are a means of considering whether corporations can be moral agents and of analysing existing criminal legal doctrinal requirements as they apply to corporations. I consider the requirements of moral agency through the lens of criminal law and apply these insights to Crown Resorts in order to provide a concrete example. I have chosen Crown Resorts as a topic of analysis because recent independent inquiries have found multiple examples of ongoing breaches of criminal law. The New South Wales (NSW) Bergin Inquiry and Victorian Royal Commission into Casino Operator and Licence found that Crown Resorts was not a 'suitable person' to hold a casino licence.[7] These inquiries detail corporate structure, actions, decision making and harms, and accordingly provide a rich case study for the purposes of analysing corporate moral agency.

This chapter maps the philosophical requirements of moral agency onto criminal legal doctrinal categories through the case study of Crown to explore the moral and legal responsibility of corporations. Section I explores why it is important to establish the corporation as a legal agent. Section II articulates each of Chapple's requirements and applies them to criminal legal doctrine and Crown Resorts to argue that corporations can be regarded as moral agents (that can choose to act immorally).

[4] PA French, 'The Corporation as a Moral Person' (1979) 16 *American Philosophical Quarterly* 207; PA French, *Collective and Corporate Responsibility* (New York, Columbia University Press, 1984); D Tollefsen, *Groups as Agents* (Cambridge, Polity Press, 2015); List and Pettit (n 3).

[5] List and Pettit (n 3) 21.

[6] C Chapple, *The Moral Responsibilities of Companies* (London, Palgrave MacMillan, 2014).

[7] State of Victoria, *Royal Commission into the Casino Operator and Licence* (The Report, October 2021) vol 1, 3 at www.rccol.vic.gov.au/overview-recommendations (accessed 4 February 2022). Henceforth the NSW Inquiry under s 143 of the Casino Control Act 1992 (NSW) will be termed the 'Bergin Inquiry', and the Victorian Royal Commission into the Casino Operator and Licence will be termed the 'Victorian Royal Commission'.

I. Why is it Important to Establish the Corporation as a Moral Agent?

Classic positivists such as HLA Hart argue that there is no requirement to establish that corporations are moral agents, only that they are legal subjects.[8] Legislation clearly constructs corporations as legal subjects,[9] with rights and responsibilities. Corporations have the ability to own property and enter into binding contracts; they can be sued, taxed and made to fulfil obligations. For example, casino legislation requires that corporations running or associated with casinos are 'suitable persons'.[10] On this account, the concept of legal personality is 'wholly formal'.[11] For positivists, an act by a legal subject that breaches the criminal law is wrongful in and of itself.[12] There is no requirement to delve into any underlying intersection of law and morality. As such, positivists would assert that corporations are subjects of the criminal law regardless of whether they are moral agents.

Yet this response is overly simplistic and superficial, and may well leave the most interesting issues outside the carefully restricted boundaries of jurisprudence claimed by positivists such as Hart. Positivists are correct in asserting that the granting of legal personality is a constitutive role of law,[13] but it belies the fact that to a large extent corporations have been slotted into pre-existing criminal legal doctrine.[14] Of the many issues this has raised, two are of primary concern for the purposes of this chapter. First, criminal legal doctrine was constructed around the primary legal subject – the individual, biological human being. (Responsible) human beings are fundamental categories of what Steven D Smith called law's 'ontological inventories'.[15] This has resulted in difficulties in applying pre-existing categories constructed around humans to corporations. For example, a central claim of criminal legal doctrine is that a person shall not be held liable for an act unless the act was done with a guilty mind (*actus non facit reum nisi mens sit rea*).[16] Given the division of labour and decision making, this requirement

[8] HLA Hart, *Law, Liberty and Morality* (Oxford, Oxford University Press, 1963) 2.

[9] See, eg, Corporations Act 2001 (Cth), s 124; Criminal Code Act 1995 (Cth) ('Criminal Code'), pt 2.5.

[10] Casino Control Act 1992 (NSW) (Casino Control Act NSW), s 12.

[11] R Tur, 'The "Person" in Law' in AR Peacocke and G Gillet (eds), *Persons and Personality: A Contemporary Inquiry* (New York, Basil Blackwell, 1987) 121.

[12] Hart (n 8). Likewise Williams states 'a crime is an act capable of being followed by criminal proceedings having a criminal outcome, and a proceeding or its outcome is criminal if it has certain characteristics which make it criminal': G Williams, 'The Definition of Crime' (1955) 8 *Current Legal Problems* 107, 130.

[13] S Deakin et al, 'Legal Institutionalism: Capitalism and the Constitutive Role of Law' (2017) 45 *Journal of Comparative Economics* 188.

[14] Offences specific to corporations have been created, such as failure to prevent offences and industrial manslaughter, but these are regarded as tangential to criminal law proper. SF Copp and A Cronin, 'New Models of Corporate Criminality: The Development and Relative Effectiveness of "Failure to Prevent" Offences' (2018) 39 *The Company Lawyer* 104; P Crofts, 'Three Recent Royal Commissions: The Failure to Prevent Harms and Attributions of Organisational Liability' (2020) 42 *Sydney Law Review* 394; V Roper, 'The Corporate Manslaughter and Corporate Homicide Act 2007 – A 10 Year Review' (2018) 82 *The Journal of Criminal Law* 48.

[15] SD Smith, *Law's Quandary* (Cambridge, MA, Harvard University Press, 2004) 8.

[16] *Fowler v Padget* (1978) 7 Term Rep 509, (1798) 101 ER 1103. As noted in the text accompanying nn 78–81, there is legal doctrine applied to human subjects supporting the stretching of the actus reus so that mens rea is required only at some point in time during the actions and omissions of the accused. S Yeo, 'Killing a Supposed Corpse: In Search of Principle' (1998) 31 *Comparative and International Law Journal of South Africa* 350.

of temporal coincidence is almost impossible to meet in large corporations.[17] As considered below, it is also difficult to identify a corporation's mind and intent,[18] and to attribute acts and omissions to the corporation. These are practical difficulties that arise as a consequence of the historical construction of criminal legal doctrine around the 'ideal legal actor',[19] the (responsible) human being, and are frequently pointed to as an explanation for the relative dearth of criminal prosecutions of corporations for wrongdoing.[20]

Second, and relatedly, the bulk of criminal law theorists accept that the criminal law is a system of blaming.[21] The prosecution must prove the *guilt* of the accused beyond a reasonable doubt.[22] It involves and requires censure or reproof for fault, wrong, badness or wickedness.[23] The structure of criminal law seeks to establish that an accused is sufficiently blameworthy to justify punishment or sanctions. Inherent to these ideas of censure is the precondition that the accused is a moral agent, that is, a 'responsible subject'.[24] Unless a person has the capacity to freely choose to do something that they understand to be wrong, they cannot be regarded as blameworthy and should not be liable to punishment in criminal proceedings.[25] Accordingly, not all humans have legal standing, that is, the legally recognised capacity to be held responsible at law for their actions, all the time.[26] In criminal law the question of moral capacity has an impact on legal standing and is interrogated in legal doctrines such as *doli incapax*, insanity and unfitness to plead.[27] There are various ways in which we express lack of responsibility for great harms. In the modern world, we tend not to regard natural disasters as wicked,

[17] P Crofts, *Evil Corporations: Criminal Law, Horror and Philosophy* (Routledge, forthcoming).

[18] The common law solution has been to identify the 'directing mind' of the corporation: *Tesco v Nattrass* [1971] UKHL 1, [1972] AC 153 (*Tesco*).

[19] N Naffine, *Law's Meaning of Life: Philosophy, Religion, Darwin and the Legal Person* (Oxford, Hart Publishing, 2009) 67.

[20] J Clough and C Mulhern, *The Prosecution of Corporations* (Oxford, Oxford University Press, 2002); SW Buell, 'The Responsibility Gap in Corporate Crime' (2018) 12 *Criminal Law and Philosophy* 471.

[21] JB White, 'Making Sense of Criminal Law' (1978) 50 *University of Colorado Law Review* 1; G Fletcher, *Rethinking Criminal Law* (Boston, MA, Little Brown, 1978).

[22] *DPP v Woolmington* [1935] UKHL 1, [1935] AC 462.

[23] P Crofts, *Wickedness and Crime: Laws of Homicide and Malice* (Abingdon, Routledge, 2013).

[24] N Naffine, 'Our Legal Lives as Men, Women and Persons' (2004) 24 *Legal Studies* 621, 628.

[25] Sir M Hale, *History of the Pleas of the Crown* (London, Professional Books, 1736) 14–15; N Lacey, 'In Search of the Responsible Subject: History, Philosophy and Criminal Law Theory' (2001) 64 *Modern Law Review* 350, 353; V Tadros, *Criminal Responsibility* (Oxford, Oxford University Press, 2005).

[26] Legal personhood has also been based on social status. In early Roman civil law, a slave was a thing owned rather than a *persona*, and therefore did not have the right to initiate legal actions or own property. Under the doctrine of coverture, married women could not own property or be parties to contracts in their own right. D Gindis, 'Legal Personhood and the Firm: Avoiding Anthropomorphism and Equivocation' (2016) 12 *Journal of Institutional Economics* 499.

[27] P Cane, *Responsibility in Law and Morality* (Oxford, Hart Publishing, 2002). For example, the presumption of *doli incapax* is that children lack the moral and intellectual development to have the capacity to be guilty of crime. T Crofts, 'Prosecuting Child Offenders: Factors Relevant to Rebutting the Presumption of Doli Incapax' (2018) 40 *Sydney Law Review* 339. The rules of insanity under *R v M'Naghten* (1843) 8 ER 718, 722 apply when a person, at the time of the act, 'was labouring under such a defect of reason, from disease of the mind, as not to know the nature and quality of the act he was doing; or, if he did know it, that he did not know he was doing what wrong'. For a critique, see T Minkowitz, 'Rethinking Criminal Responsibility from a Critical Disability Perspective: The Abolition of Insanity/Incapacity Acquittals and Unfitness to Plead, and Beyond' (2014) 23 *Griffith Law Review* 434.

because there is nothing or no one to hold responsible.[28] There is also a tendency to use the (passive) language of accident, disaster or tragedy in response to harms where it is difficult to identify a responsible agent.[29] This is particularly the case for complex harms caused by corporations in the past and/or through governmental and regulatory failures.[30] As Scott Veitch has argued, in the production of large-scale harms the question of responsibility may not be raised at all.[31] Central to attribution of blameworthiness is that a subject can be regarded as a moral agent.

Models of culpability are contingent and have changed across time and place; but in recent centuries, the dominant model of culpability expressed in classic criminal legal doctrine is subjective, that is, the accused must have intention or knowledge in order to be at fault.[32] This was affirmed by the High Court of Australia in its statement that there is a common law presumption that every offence requires a guilty mind or subjective culpability.[33] There are necessarily difficulties in importing and applying the requirement of subjective culpability to corporations. The practical difficulties of establishing who the mind of the corporation is, what the mind was thinking at the time of offence are myriad. However, many of these practical difficulties pointed to by critics are not applicable or required in 'regulatory' offences, many of which were introduced to apply to corporations. This is because regulatory offences involve strict or absolute liability, and require only that the prosecution prove that the accused did the act, not that the prosecution establish subjective blameworthiness.[34] For example, both the Bergin Inquiry and the Victorian Royal Commission found that Crown Melbourne facilitated the laundering of millions of dollars.[35] Australia has wide-ranging anti-money-laundering criminal offences under part 10.2 of the Criminal Code Act 1995 (Cth), all with a strict liability option. Despite the relatively low evidentiary elements for the prosecution of money-laundering offences, there have been no federal prosecutions of corporations for money laundering in Australia.[36] This failure to prosecute is in part

[28] Theorists like Card have argued that responsibility can be ascribed for making the effects of disasters worse. C Card, *The Atrocity Paradigm: A Theory of Evil* (Oxford, Oxford University Press, 2002); D Tracy, 'Horrors and Horror: The Response of Tragedy' (2014) 81 *Social Research* 739. See also Neiman's discussion about the historical regard of natural disasters such as earthquakes as paradigms of natural evil visited on humans who sinned. S Neiman, *Evil in Modern Thought* (Melbourne, Scribe Publications, 2002).

[29] Rader has pointed to a tendency to a language of fate and determinism in the contemporary secular world dominated by unregulated globalisation. In tragedies, the impersonal sense of necessity always wins out. 'If forces beyond our control or comprehension are influencing our lives, what happens to choice? … How are we to conceive of ethics in a world studiously indifferent to our choices?' R Rader, 'The Fate of Humanism in Greek Tragedy' (2009) 33 *Philosophy and Literature* 442, 442.

[30] Tombs has argued that corporate harms tend not to be conceptualised as 'violence' in media or by the criminal justice system, in part because of difficulties in conceptualising who or what the authors of this violence were, and how it was generated and sustained. S Tombs, 'Home as a Site of State-Corporate Violence: Grenfell Tower, Aetiologies and Aftermaths' (2020) 59 *The Howard Journal of Crime and Justice* 120.

[31] S Veitch, *Law and Irresponsibility: On the Legitimation of Human Suffering* (Abingdon, Routledge, 2007).

[32] Fletcher (n 21).

[33] *He Kaw Teh v R* [1985] HCA 43, (1985) 157 CLR 523.

[34] Fletcher (n 21); Crofts (n 23); C Wells, 'Swatting the Subjectivist Bug' [1982] *Criminal Law Review* 209. Although there is evidence that, in many cases, even if offences do not require intention or knowledge, prosecutions will occur only if the accused had intention or knowledge. P Crofts, 'Communicating the Culpability of Illegal Dumping: Bankstown v Hanna (2014)' (2015) 2 *Australian Journal of Environmental Law* 57.

[35] Victorian Royal Commission (n 7) 2.

[36] There have been three civil penalty cases commenced by AUSTRAC against corporations – each time resulting in record-breaking penalties.

because of the perceived centrality of subjective culpability to conceptions of blameworthiness, such that regulatory offences are regarded as failing to meet the requirement of blameworthiness.[37] But this lack of prosecution may be because of a related and preceding conceptual barrier to prosecuting corporation – that is, the belief that corporations are not moral agents.

This can be seen in the governmental inquiries into Crown. Despite clear breaches of criminal law and legal duties, the inquiries have framed malfeasance at Crown Resorts as failures of corporate governance rather than criminal offences. For example, the Victorian Royal Commission notes that Crown is regulated by the Corporations Act 2001 (Cth), the ASX Listing Rules, Australian Prudential Regulation Authority (APRA) prudential standards, gambling regulation and codes, liquor controls, commercial agreements and casino control legislation in each state in which it operates (including internationally).[38] In its overview chapter on corporate governance, the Victorian Royal Commission does not include reference to criminal legislation in each state, nor does it mention anti-money-laundering and terrorism-financing legislation that should be taken into account in corporate governance. It is only in the conclusion of the chapter that it is noted that a casino operator should 'obey the law'.[39] Arguably, this reflects a tendency to conceive of corporations and corporate governance as somehow separate or aside from criminal law. Despite multiple breaches of the criminal law, the Royal Commission does not propose any criminal prosecution of Crown Resorts.[40]

II. Crown, Criminal Law and the Requirements of Moral Agency

This section maps the three requirements of moral agency onto criminal legal doctrine, and applies these requirements to Crown to argue that corporations can and should be regarded as moral agents capable of criminal legal attributions of blameworthiness.

A. Distinct Moral Agent

The first requirement, that there is a distinct moral agent that faces normatively significant choices, maps onto the criminal law requirement that an accused is a responsible

[37] Despite concerns about regulatory offences' diluting the power of the label of 'criminal', corporations expend a great deal of energy seeking to rebut or exclude it. P Crofts, 'Strategies of Denial and the Australian Royal Commission into Misconduct in the Banking, Superannuation and Financial Services' (2020) 29 *Griffith Law Review* 21.

[38] Victorian Royal Commission (n 7) ch 4.

[39] ibid [84].

[40] At the time of writing, AUSTRAC has announced that it will be commencing civil penalty proceedings against Crown for money laundering. This failure to prosecute for criminal breaches of money-laundering legislation is in accordance with the argument of this chapter on the failure to regard and regulate corporations as criminal legal subjects. For further arguments about money laundering and the lack of criminal prosecutions of corporations, see P Crofts and H van Rijswijk, 'A Case Study of State-Corporate Crime: Crown Resorts' *Current Issues in Criminal Justice* (2022), doi:10.1080/10345329.2022.2144899.

legal subject. As argued in section I, although criminal law has been constructed around the ideal legal subject – human beings – not all human beings are accorded full legal subjecthood. Legal subjecthood is not a given but rather a legal artefact that can change across time and place. With regard to corporations, in order to satisfy the agent-choice requirement, a distinct, emergent corporate state that supervenes or has a rational agent-identity over and above its individual members must be identified.[41] This question of whether or not the corporation is a distinct moral agent remains a live question in legal circles, commonly split into nominalists and realists.

Nominalists are sceptical about the idea that corporations can be moral agents. They accept, of course, that corporations have a legal identity, but this is a legal fiction serving as a nexus for contracting among individual factors of production.[42] For nominalists, the idea that a corporation can act and be blameworthy is a fiction or legal artefact. Corporations are nothing more than collectivities of individuals,[43] and corporations cannot act or intend except through individuals.[44] In contrast, realists accept the idea of corporations as agents in their own right. They argue that corporations have an existence that is independent from their members. On this account, corporations can act and be at fault in ways that are different from the ways in which their members can act and be at fault.[45]

The idea of a corporation as an agent is supported colloquially. Media reporting of the inquiries into Crown Resorts simply referred to 'Crown' or 'Crown Resorts'. The corporation was personified in reporting. Crown was 'lucky to escape [with its licence]'[46] and 'must be desperate or think we're dumb'.[47] This is likewise reflected in how the law and legal institutions conceive of and organise corporations. The various Acts regulating casinos require that operators and associates of operators are a 'suitable person'.[48] Crown is a regulated entity – 'whose privilege to hold a casino licence is dependent upon it being, at all times, a person of good character, honest and integrity'.[49] The language here is grammatically awkward. At times, Crown is personified 'whose' at others it is objectified 'its'. Crown might be singular 'it' or plural 'they'. Despite this, linguistic complications should not be regarded as justifying the failure to regard corporations as moral agents. Historically, there have been linguistic shifts in society and at law. In the late twentieth century, feminists challenged the argument that use of the pronoun *he* referred to a generic person or *man* to humanity.[50] More recently, transgender communities have

[41] Chapple (n 6).

[42] A Alchian and H Demsetz, 'Production, Information Costs, and Economic Organization' (1972) 62 *The American Economic Review* 777.

[43] PA French, *Corporate Ethics* (San Diego, CA, Harcourt Brace College Publishers, 1995).

[44] E Colvin, 'Corporate Personality and Criminal Liability' (1995) 6 *Criminal Law Forum* 1.

[45] ibid 3.

[46] D Ziffer, 'Crown lucky to escape the Victorian royal commission with its licence intact' *ABC News* (27 October 2021) at www.abc.net.au/news/2021-10-27/crown-lucky-to-survive-victorian-royal-commission-with-licence/100569696.

[47] P Martin, 'Casino operator Crown plays an old business trick – using its workers as human shields' *ABC News* (11 August 2021) at www.abc.net.au/news/2021-08-11/crown-casino-royal-commission-workers/100365220.

[48] Casino Control Act NSW (n 10), s 12.

[49] Victorian Royal Commission (n 7) [4].

[50] For example, research has shown that outcomes differ for a woman arguing a criminal defence, depending on whether juries are charged with considering her actions in relation to the reasonable man, reasonable person or reasonable woman. DA Donovan and SM Wildman, 'Is the Reasonable Man Obsolete: A Critical Perspective on Self-Defense and Provocation' (1980) 14 *Loyola of Los Angeles Law Review* 435.

pursued trans language-reform efforts.[51] These incursions highlight that language is political and constitutes, rather than reflects, specific concepts and power relations. Grammatical difficulties reflect and reinforce the complexity of imagining the corporation as an emergent legal subject.

We also express reactive attitudes to corporate wrongdoing, such as indignation and anger. The Victorian Royal Commission stated that Crown's conduct was 'disgraceful … illegal, dishonest, unethical and exploitative'.[52] Crown 'bullied' and provided the regulator with false information, and 'delayed' and did what it could to 'frustrate' the regulator's investigations. The Royal Commission ascribed emotional states to Crown, labelling it 'callous' and 'appalling'.[53] Crown 'happily assisted wealthy Chinese patrons to breach the currency laws of their country'.[54] These language choices may be of convenience or may reflect the idea of an organisation as an independent agent, with a good or bad identity, and capacity to act, have intentions and even emotional states over and above those of individual members.[55]

Corporations have a stable identity due to rules, written and unwritten, that are external and internal to the corporation. Companies have specific structures, rules and hierarchies, and are regulated in specific ways.[56] There is some complexity to Crown as an agent, to the extent that the Victorian Royal Commission devoted a chapter to enunciating its structure.[57] Crown Resorts has three operating subsidiaries: Crown Melbourne (which operates Melbourne Casino); Burswood Nominees Ltd (which operates Crown Perth); and Crown Sydney Gaming Pty Ltd (which hoped to operate Crown casino at Barangaroo). This complexity of identity frequently works in the favour of large corporations, particularly due to the corporate veil.[58] Each inquiry circumvented complexity in corporate identity by focusing on whether the subsidiary for that specific jurisdiction was a 'suitable person' to have a gaming licence, and whether Crown was a suitable person to be a close associate.[59] Crown owns all the shares in all of its subsidiaries.

Corporations codify values, goals and decision-making procedures. The rules provide a means of testing validity – are the actions those of the corporation or those of a rogue employee? The rules also mean that the behaviour of the corporation is predictable and

[51] L Zimman, 'Transgender Language Reform' (2017) 1 *Journal of Language and Discrimination* 84.
[52] Victorian Royal Commission (n 7) [10].
[53] ibid [5].
[54] ibid.
[55] See also Carroll, ch 15 of this volume, on whether corporations can feel and express remorse.
[56] P Sheehy, *The Reality of Social Groups* (Farnham, Ashgate Publishing, 2006); French (n 4).
[57] Victorian Royal Commission (n 7) ch 17.
[58] G Allan, 'To Pierce or Not to Pierce? A Doctrinal Reappraisal of Judicial Responses to Improper Exploitation of the Corporate Form' (2018) 7 *Journal of Business Law* 559; A Belcher, 'Boundaries, Corporate Decision-Making and Responsibility' (2007) 58 *Northern Ireland Legal Quarterly* 211; R Grantham, 'The Corporate Veil: An Ingenious Device' (2013) 32 *University of Queensland Law Journal* 311; S Sutherland, 'Piercing the Corporate Veil – with a Stake? Vampire Imagery in American Caselaw' in P Day (ed), *Vampires: Myths and Metaphors of Enduring Evil* (Amsterdam, Rodopi, 2006) 143.
[59] The Victorian Royal Commission (n 7) was critical of the dominance of Crown Resorts and the lack of independent management of Crown Melbourne.

regular in a way that actions of other groups may not be. It means that the corporation is independent of the specific individuals who control or work for the organisation.[60] Thus multiple employees of Crown have come and gone over the years, including the mass exodus of members of the board in the wake of the Bergin Inquiry and changing chief executive officers, yet the corporate identity of Crown continues. Corporations have a perpetual existence separate from the individual lifespans of employees or founders. Thus, although in recent times Crown has been associated strongly with the 'vision' of James Packer, Crown has assumed a life and identity of its own. With his imminent departure as dominant shareholder, Crown and its various subsidiaries endure.

Corporations are complex organisations, and members, whether as employees, managers or shareholders/owners, 'contribute to the corporate effect and are a consequence of the corporate effect'.[61] Corporations are 'an awesome social invention',[62] providing an essential means to coordinate and integrate actions of members in the right way to work towards a particular goal (usually profit) and to take advantage of market opportunities otherwise not available to individuals acting alone. Rules enable coordination and integration of individual contributions into a group judgement. Rule-based structures, whether formal or informal, shape the way that individuals think and act when on corporate business. Without these rules, different processes or outcomes might result. It is to the advantage of corporations to act as agents. There is extensive empirical evidence that there is a correlation between companies' performance in pursuit of their goals and cultural factors that support agency.[63]

One way of demonstrating how a corporation is an agent over and above its individual members is to look at when individuals working for the corporation act in ways, or support actions or omissions, with which they disagree or that they would not support or defend outside of their employment. This is in accordance with ideas about employment as a role or a 'practical identity',[64] which may exert a normative and psychologically structured influence on what features an agent is committed to displaying.[65] This idea that people may behave at work in ways that are inconsistent with beliefs they hold outside of employment is shown in relation to the way employees acted towards problem gamblers at Crown Resorts. At Crown Melbourne, hosts (employees who look after Crown loyalty programme members) acknowledged that they were 'predatory and

[60] PH Bucy, 'Corporate Ethos: A Standard for Imposing Corporate Criminal Liability' (1994) 75 *Minnesota Law Review* 1095.

[61] Singapore Government, Penal Code Review Committee, *Penal Code Review Committee Report* (Report, August 2018) 212, citing R Mays, 'Towards Corporate Fault as the Basis of Criminal Liability of Corporations' (1982) 2 *Mountbatten Journal of Legal Studies* 31, 40, 54. For the definitive critique of methodological individualism, in the context of corporate crime, see B Fisse and J Braithwaite, *Corporations, Crime and Accountability* (Cambridge, Cambridge University Press, 1993) ch 2.

[62] MK Ramirez, 'The Science Fiction of Corporate Criminal Liability: Containing the Machine through the Corporate Death Penalty' (2005) 47 *Arizona Law Review* 933.

[63] DR Denison, *Corporate Culture and Organizational Effectiveness* (New York, John Wiley & Sons Inc, 1990); DR Denison and AO Mishra, 'Towards a Theory of Organizational Culture and Effectiveness' (1995) 6 *Organization Science* 204.

[64] M Fricker, 'Can There Be Institutional Virtues?' in T Szabo Gendler and J Hawthorne (eds), *Oxford Studies in Epistemology: Social Epistemology*, vol 3 (Oxford, Oxford University Press, 2010) 235.

[65] ibid. See also P Crofts, 'The Townspeople of Derry in Stephen King's IT: Bystanders and Responsibility For Evil' in WS May (ed), *(En)Countering Pennywise: Critical Perspectives on Stephen King's IT* (University Press of Mississippi, 2022) 135.

irresponsible' in relation to problem gamblers, in order to gain revenue for Crown.[66] They would entice clients to come to the casino, would arrange gifts, would not question whether the client could afford to gamble, would rarely ask clients to take a break from gambling, would permit customers to gamble even if they owed money to Crown Resorts and would discourage gamblers from self-excluding. Other problem-gambling research has recorded the way employees at gambling venues felt about allowing or even encouraging problem gamblers to continue.[67] This facilitation of problem gambling was an informal rule, geared towards profit, which contradicted Crown's formal policies asserting world-leading approaches against problem gambling. Bant makes a similar point in relation to anti-money laundering at Crown and practices of aggregation of individual deposits that obscured what was occurring in the bank accounts. The Victorian Royal Commission accepts Bant's argument that whilst employees at Crown may have been individually honest, they were 'nonetheless cogs in a corporate process that was inherently apt to break the law'.[68]

Accordingly, corporations are recognised as agents at law and colloquially. This group agency is facilitated by (written and unwritten) rules that govern how its members act and decide, and that determine how individuals and groups behave when acting 'in' the corporation or 'for' it. Corporations have emergent properties that arise out of the various individual members and yet are novel or irreducible with respect to them.[69]

B. Control Requirement

The second requirement of moral agency is arguably akin to criminal legal doctrine actus reus requirements, that the agent has some control or power over the choice between action/omission and has some causal effect in relation to prohibited outcomes. In terms of moral agency, the emphasis is on making or facing a choice, that is, morally significant choices must be in the 'control' of the agent. To the extent that we believe individuals control and are responsible for certain actions, corporations can be handled under a similar account. Under this account, we are responsible for what is in our control – our actions and our choices. We tend to hold individuals responsible for their choices, even as we recognise that there is a range of constraints on how agents make those choices about how to act.

i. Voluntariness

Criminal law frames the question of control over action/omission in terms of voluntariness, that is, the requirement that an action is 'conscious and willed'. Criminal law theorist Peter Rush explains that voluntariness requires that 'something internal to the person must cause the conduct – such that you can say that it is the conduct of the accused'.[70] The prosecution are entitled to presume voluntariness unless and until

[66] Victorian Royal Commission (n 7) ch 8, [43].

[67] L Hancock, *Regulatory Failure? The Case of Crown Casino* (Melbourne, Australian Scholarly Publishing, 2011).

[68] Victorian Royal Commission (n 7) ch 6, [95].

[69] Chapple (n 6) 35.

[70] P Rush, *Criminal Law* (Sydney, Butterworths, 1997) 65.

the accused has satisfied the evidentiary burden.[71] Voluntariness is frequently explained through judicial analysis of involuntariness:

> [A]n act which is done by the muscles without any control of the mind, such as a spasm, a reflex action, or a convulsion; or an act done by a person who is not conscious of what he is doing, such as an act done whilst suffering from concussion or whilst sleepwalking.[72]

From this definition, a corporation might argue that its actions are 'unwilled', that it is no longer in control of its behaviour, due to the acting of various members and sections of the corporation outside of the conscious control of the 'directing mind'.

There are two related ways of considering this issue of involuntariness. First, this returns to the issue of whether a nominalist or realist conceptualisation of corporations is adopted. If a nominalist account is adopted then the actions of employees in the absence of knowledge by the directing mind might be regarded as involuntary. However, this lack of knowledge or control by the directing mind is more likely to be argued in courts as lack of mens rea rather than as involuntariness.[73] There are defined roles by which individuals can exercise certain powers,[74] which provide a means for distinguishing employees who are acting on behalf of the corporation and rogue employees. In the absence of a rogue employee, courts are dubious of corporate claims of lack of control and tend to accept that the acts or omissions of the corporation are at issue. Claims of lack of knowledge by the directing mind constitute a separate question to be dealt with under fault or mens rea requirements. For example, both inquiries established that Crown was involved in money laundering, even though the inquiries accepted the Board's claims of ignorance.

Second, the time frame in which involuntariness is considered is also significant, particularly in terms of omissions by corporations, such as the failure to comply with standards, including health and safety and protections against money laundering. The High Court has established that in cases of involuntariness, it is open to the jury to broaden the 'relevant act' under consideration.[75] For example, in the case of *Ryan*, the accused argued that he had instinctively pulled the trigger and killed the victim when the victim moved suddenly. The High Court rejected this argument and held that it was not solely the pulling of the trigger instinctively that was the 'relevant act'; rather, it was holding a loaded gun with a finger on the trigger against the head of the victim.[76] Likewise in *Jiminez*, the accused was charged with culpable driving after he fell asleep at the wheel, collided with a tree and killed one of his passengers. The High Court held:

> While he was asleep his actions were not conscious or voluntary (an act committed while unconscious is necessarily involuntary) and he could not be criminally responsible for driving the car in a manner dangerous to the public.[77]

[71] *R v Falconer* [1990] HCA 49, (1990) 171 CLR 30, 83.

[72] *Bratty v Attorney-General (Northern Ireland)* [1961] UKHL 3, [1963] AC 386, 409 (Lord Denning). See also *Falconer* (n 71) and *Ryan v R* [1967] HCA 2, (1967) 121 CLR 205, 214, 231.

[73] Involuntariness is very difficult for human individuals to argue in criminal law also. It is frequently argued for offences which do not require mens rea. See, eg *Jiminez v R* [1992] HCA 14, (1992) 173 CLR 572 (*Jiminez*); *Ugle v R* [2002] HCA 25, (2002) 211 CLR 171 (*Ugle*); *Ryan* (n 72).

[74] P French, 'Commentary' (1983) 2 *Business and Professional Ethics Journal* 89.

[75] This flexibility of temporality in criminal law is theorised by M Kelman, 'Interpretive Construction in the Substantive Criminal Law' (1980) 33 *Stanford Law Review* 591.

[76] Similar reasoning was applied in *Ugle* (n 73).

[77] *Jiminez* (n 73) 577.

However, the court applied the principles from *Ryan* and held that the period of driving immediately preceding Jiminez's falling asleep could be considered:

> It follows that for a driver to be guilty of driving in a manner dangerous to the public because of his tired or drowsy condition, that condition must be such that, as a matter of objective fact, his driving in that condition is a danger to the public. Various matters will be relevant in reaching such a conclusion. The period of driving, the lighting conditions (including whether it was night or day) and the heating or ventilation of the vehicle are all relevant considerations. And, of course, it will be necessary to consider how tired the driver was. If there was a warning as to the onset of sleep, that may be some evidence of the degree of tiredness. And the period of driving before the accident, and the amount of sleep that he had earlier had, will also bear on the degree of his tiredness. But so far as 'driving in a manner dangerous' is concerned, the issue is not whether there was or was not a warning of the onset of sleep, but whether the driver was so tired that, in the circumstances, his driving was a danger to the public.[78]

This reasoning can be applied to corporate acts and omissions. That is, rather than look at money laundering in isolation, Crown's actions – including the reduction of money-laundering compliance, the ongoing failure to heed warnings by banks, changing banks when red flags were raised and choosing to reward profit rather than protection against money laundering – demonstrate decisions and choices that were made voluntarily.

It might be argued that corporations have limited choices in how they act. Corporations act within certain constraints, such as size, capacity, law and commercial commitments, and to maximise profits. But these same arguments can be made with regard to individuals – humans have multiple constraints on the choices they make. According to criminal legal doctrine, even in cases of coercion, voluntariness is not an issue – an accused is regarded as making a choice to act, albeit under coercion. The defences of duress or necessity are raised only after the elements of offences are established. For the most part, corporations are required to achieve and maximise profit.[79] However, whilst Crown is required to achieve profit, it has a range of choices about how it goes about this, for example whether it adopts short-term easy-money or more long-term sustainable choices.[80]

Corporations have a set of decision-making rules and procedures through which courses of concerted action can be, though not necessarily are, chosen on a rational basis. If a broader time frame is adopted in accordance with existing legal doctrine and theory, these actions and omissions are conscious and willed across time.[81]

ii. Causation

The second aspect of control requires that a corporation be a controlling cause of actions in a way that may ground moral responsibility. Nominalists would argue that

[78] ibid 579.

[79] M Friedman, 'The Social Responsibility of Business Is to Increase Its Profits' *New York Times Magazine* (New York, 13 September 1970).

[80] ER Outa and S Kutubi, 'Bank Corporate Governance in Australia: Is There a Conflict between the Existing Corporate Culture and the Anglo-Saxon Model of Corporate Governance?' (2021) 32 *Journal of Corporate Accounting & Finance* 145.

[81] Kelman (n 75).

corporations can only act through individuals, and therefore it is only individuals who can be causally responsible.[82] However, realists would argue that corporations can be causally responsible in ways that transcend individual actions or omissions. Even where actions are implemented by lower-level individual members, corporations bring about actions by coordinating through processes, routines, etc to realise the goals of the company. Corporate actions feature examples where a higher-level cause, such as profit, is insensitive to the way in which it is realised. Different individuals can implement these corporation processes in different ways, provided they are working towards the relevant outcomes. If an individual did not occupy an office or a role, another would take their place and do it. For example, if an employee refused to go along with facilitating problem gambling (for which they would receive no encouragement or reward), they might lose their job or opportunities for promotion, whilst another employee would facilitate problem gambling and be rewarded. Likewise, the Royal Commission quoted Bant's argument that breaches of anti-money laundering at Crown 'were replicated over long periods, as individual employees were replaced by new employees trained in carrying out the requisite processes'.[83] On this account, a focus on individual employees fails to recognise and evaluate the corporate systems and policies that organised and systematised conduct aimed at achieving profit.

The requirement of causation in criminal law seeks to establish a connection between the accused and the prohibited consequences, that is, that an accused can only be criminally liable for harms for which they are responsible. The bar is set fairly low in Australia, requiring only that the accused was 'a substantial and operating' cause.[84] Accordingly, there can be multiple causes of a prohibited consequence. Under the Casino Control Act 1992 (WA), Crown Resorts has a duty to prevent and minimise harm from gambling.[85] Casinos are recognised as a site of risk for problem gambling. There are multiple structural ways in which Crown Resorts was a substantial and operating cause of problem gambling above and beyond the actions of individual employees. The Victorian Royal Commission Report shows that in 2018–19, 25 per cent of people who gambled at Melbourne Casino in the previous year experienced some harm from gambling, and those gambling at Melbourne Casino are more likely to have experienced at least one form of harm from gambling. It was estimated that the prevalence of problem gamblers at Melbourne Casino may be three times higher than among all Victorian adults who gamble.[86] The reasons why problem gamblers are drawn to the casino are due to organisational choices rather than the actions of specific individuals. It has long been recognised that accessibility is a major cause of problem gambling – the greater the accessibility of gambling, the greater the chance of problem gambling.[87]

[82] There is increasing recognition of the possibility of corporations acting through technology. For example, Robodebt is an example of automated generation of debt notices through problematic algorithms and an absence of human intervention. P Crofts and H van Rijswijk, *Technology: New Trajectories in Law* (Abingdon, Routledge, 2021). See also Paterson and Bant, ch 12 of this volume.

[83] Victorian Royal Commission (n 7) ch 6, [96].

[84] *Royall v R* [1991] HCA 27, (1991) 172 CLR 378.

[85] Casino Control Act 1992 (WA), s 4A(c).

[86] Victorian Royal Commission (n 7) ch 8, [10].

[87] L Nower and A Blaszczynski, 'Gambling Motivations, Money-Limiting Strategies, and Precommitment Preferences of Problem versus Non-Problem Gamblers' (2010) 26 *Journal of Gambling Studies* 361.

The casino is open 24 hours a day and has more electronic gambling machines (EGMs) than any other venue.[88] Unlike other venues in Victoria, Crown Melbourne has EGMs that are permitted to operate in 'unrestricted' mode, that is, with no maximum betting limits – another organisational (and governmental) choice.[89] The Gambling Code at Crown is out of date and focuses on external signals of distress rather than contemporary research that draws upon data collected about spending patterns (data collected for loyalty programmes but not used to fulfil problem-gambling obligations).[90] The Victorian Royal Commission found that the tools to prevent problem gambling are 'not effective' and have 'serious deficiencies'.[91] In addition, despite claiming a formal gambling code that is world-leading, staff are not adequately trained to implement the (deficient) Gambling Code. Staff who work on or near the gaming floor could not accurately describe the signs of problem gambling, nor accurately explain Crown's Play Periods Policy; they did not know what RSG (Responsible Service of Gaming) meant, and could not name the Responsible Gaming Officers at Crown and had never referred anyone to the Responsible Gaming Officers or suggested to a manager that someone be referred.[92] Crown hosts receive a bonus that is based on customer visitation, and the Royal Commission assumed a relationship between turnover and visitation. These rewards lead individual hosts to work towards increasing attendance and expenditure by clients, regardless of whether those clients are problem gamblers. The failure to prevent problem gambling, or arguably the choice to facilitate and promote problem gambling, is over and above the actions of any one individual and is in conformity with the aims of Crown Resorts to obtain profit. Through structural choices, the development of rules and policies, and corporate culture's rewarding profit over compliance with problem-gambling requirements, Crown is 'a substantial and operating cause' of problem gambling on its premises.

C. Good Judgement Requirement

The third requirement of moral agency is that of good judgement, whereby intentional acts based on the beliefs and desires of the agent are attributable to the agent.[93] This is in accordance with the ideal that a person should not be punished unless they had the capacity and a fair opportunity to obey the law.[94] For corporate moral agency, this requires that a corporation must be able to form intentions that are distinct from those of its members. Additionally, when making moral judgements about an agent's behaviour, we assume that the agent can form and access judgements in its own right and possesses a regulatory capacity that governs how these intentions inform and motivate actions in a way that conforms to rational and epistemic standards. Accordingly, in

[88] Victorian Royal Commission (n 7) ch 8, [11].
[89] Nower and Blaszczynski (n 87).
[90] Hancock (n 67).
[91] Victorian Royal Commission (n 7) ch 8, [23].
[92] ibid [25].
[93] Chapple (n 6) 112.
[94] HLA Hart, *Punishment and Responsibility* (Oxford, Clarendon Press, 1968); C Crosby, 'Gross Negligence Manslaughter Revisited: Time for a Change of Direction?' (2020) 84 *The Journal of Criminal Law* 228.

order to be regarded as capable of good judgement, a corporation must first be critically reflective, that is, have the ability to reflect and pass judgement upon its actions and the thought processes leading up to them. Second, the corporation must have a sensitivity to reasons and the ability to weigh them: this requires that evidence must be available to make decisions, even if it is not drawn upon. Third, critical reflection and reasons can make a difference to how one acts – that is, can the corporation modify its actions and intentions in response to information?[95]

The good judgement requirement has some intersections with the criminal legal doctrinal requirement of mens rea or the state of mind of the accused. In criminal law, mens rea requirements are closely associated with blameworthiness, to the extent that in some codes they are termed the 'fault elements'.[96] Mens rea requirements of offences were constructed around the privileged legal subject – the (responsible) human being. The currently dominant model of culpability in criminal legal doctrine (more honoured in the breach) is that of subjective blameworthiness, that is, intention and knowledge.[97] There are common law offences that do not require that an accused has the capacity for good judgement, but these are characterised as exceptional. This can include very serious offences, such as cases of manslaughter by criminal negligence, where the accused is measured against the objective standard of the reasonable person, as opposed to whether the accused recognised, or was even capable of recognising, that their behaviour or failure was objectively dangerous.[98] These cases have led to criticisms about the fairness of holding an accused liable for a standard that they could not meet, that is, of attributing blameworthiness when arguably the accused was not a full moral agent.[99] In addition, there are regulatory offences of strict or absolute liability with minimal or no mens rea requirements – many of which were created in order to cope with corporate wrongdoing or harms.[100] These regulatory offences have also generated a great deal of criticism from some criminal law theorists for breaching fundamental requirements of criminal legal doctrine.[101] Like the requirements of moral agency, in most criminal offences there is no requirement that an accused exercised good judgement, only that they are capable of doing so. The doctrine of unfitness to plead and defences of mental impairment and intoxication provide restricted platforms for considering the moral and mental capacity of the accused. Historically, a primary obstacle for holding corporations criminally liable stems from difficulties of establishing the mens rea of corporations.[102]

How, then, are these intersecting requirements of capacity for good judgement and the mens rea of corporations to be established? List and Pettit frame the requirement

[95] Chapple (n 6) 72.

[96] Criminal Code (n 9) div 5.

[97] Wells (n 34); Fletcher (n 21).

[98] *R v Stone and Dobinson* [1977] 1 QB 354.

[99] Crosby (n 94); L Steele and S Thomas, 'Disability at the Periphery: Legal Theory, Disability and Criminal Law' (2015) 23 *Griffith Law Review* 357.

[100] S Walpole and M Corrigan, 'Fighting the System: New Approaches to Addressing Systematic Corporate Misconduct' (2021) 43 *Sydney Law Review* 489.

[101] JD Greenberg and EC Brotman, 'Strict Vicarious Criminal Liability for Corporations and Corporate Executives: Stretching the Boundaries of Criminalization' (2014) 51 *American Criminal Law Review* 79.

[102] PH Bucy, 'Organizational Sentencing Guidelines: The Cart Before the Horse' (1993) 71 *Washington University Law Quarterly* 329.

of good judgement for group agency in terms of democratic, representational decision making.[103] But as Chapple points out, this does not accord with the hierarchical, rule-based decision making of corporations.[104] Corporate rules will set out specific procedures by which decisions are arrived at, and frequently one person will be authorised to act on behalf of the corporation.[105] Corporate hierarchies are precisely intended to place good judges in key decision-making positions. Individuals will have special roles to make decisions on behalf of the company.

Various approaches have been proposed to identify corporate intention and judgements. The dominant common law approach for ascribing corporate liability in Australia and the United Kingdom is that of identification theory, which requires proof that the 'directing mind' of the corporation has acted with the requisite fault, as set out in *Tesco v Nattrass*.[106] This approach is based on an anthropomorphic conception of the company, where only those persons invested by proper authority with managerial powers and responsibility are regarded as the head or brains of the company. The 'state of mind' of this 'directing mind' is treated by law as the state of mind of the organisation, which enables criminal liability to be imposed on a corporation for offences that require mens rea. Whilst identification theory raises problems in terms of identifying who the directing mind is, for the purposes of argument and in accordance with the bulk of doctrine I will identify the directing mind as the Board of Crown. Although not exercising good judgement, the Board meets the requirements of moral agency of the capacity to make judgements. The inquiries demonstrate evidence of the Board's capacity to be critically reflective, with the members of the Board explaining why, despite media claims of money laundering, they believed that they were the victims of a witch hunt. Evidence was available to make decisions, even if they did not draw upon that evidence. In light of media reports, directors could have asked questions and done further research, but they did not. There is also evidence that the Board members exercised (some) critical reflection and modified their actions in response to information. For example, in response to revelations of money laundering in the Riverbank and Southbank accounts, Crown introduced new policies and controls over its patron accounts.[107]

Although this satisfies the requirements of moral agency, it fails to establish any mens rea of Crown. This is because identification theory requires that the prosecution prove that the directing mind of a corporation knew of the criminal actions and possessed the necessary mens rea.[108] The problem is that in complex organisations like

[103] List and Pettit (n 3).

[104] Chapple (n 6) 77.

[105] ibid 64.

[106] *Tesco* (n 18); *Hamilton v Whitehead* [1988] HCA 65, (1998) 166 CLR 121, 127. The UK has largely reaffirmed the directing-mind approach in *Attorney-General's Reference (No 2 of 1999)* [2000] EWCA Crim 91, [2000] 3 All ER 182. The test was tempered somewhat by the Privy Council's expanding the range of people whose actions and state of mind are attributed to the company in *Meridian Global Funds Management Asia Ltd v Securities Commission* [1995] UKPC 5, [1995] 3 All ER 918.

[107] Victorian Royal Commission (n 7) ch 6.

[108] The directing mind can be more than one person acting collectively, such as a board of directors. See J Chalmers, 'Corporate Culpable Homicide: Transco Plc v HM Advocate' (2004) 8 *Edinburgh Law Review* 262. For an analysis of the common law position, see O Dixon, 'Corporate Criminal Liability: The Influence

Crown Resorts, where responsibility is diffuse and distributed, the higher up a person is, the less likely that they will have the necessary mens rea.[109] Ignorance by individual directors and Boards as a whole is a theme. In the bulk of wrongdoing at Crown, it was claimed that concerns and issues were not elevated to directors and/or the Board level by staff. The Board claimed ignorance about money laundering, problem gambling and legal issues in China. These claims are dubious, but they were accepted by the Bergin Inquiry. Accordingly, even though the Board meets the requirements of moral agency, the restrictive nature of common law identification liability effectively limits the corporation's liability for offences committed by its senior officers. This demonstrates the way in which the common law creates 'a perverse incentive for the senior management to insulate itself from the criminal activities of lower-level employees'.[110]

However, it is arguable that the courts are over-complicating the requirement of mens rea of corporations. Existing legal doctrine applied to human legal subjects points to a broader approach to establishing mens rea that could be applied to corporations. For individuals, in the absence of confession, intention is not transparent:

> As I said I think when I was directing you originally you cannot take the top of a man's head off and look into his mind and actually see what his intent was at any given moment.[111]

Why, then, do we expect intention to be transparent for corporations? Identification theory is an attempt to take the top off the corporation's head to ascertain intent at any given moment, but it relies upon records of decisions and knowledge whilst simultaneously discouraging recording and encouraging ignorance. Identification theory does not encourage directors to gain knowledge, ask questions or challenge. The classic response to allegations of wrongdoing is denial by the corporation.[112] For example, Crown continued to deny money laundering until the final days of the Bergin Inquiry, made some admissions, then withdrew these admissions for the Victorian Royal Commission.[113] In the absence of confession, criminal legal doctrine relies upon external conduct or results to ascertain the internal contents of an accused's mind.[114] This focus on manifest behaviour has strict parameters around it,[115] but, for example, in the absence of a confession or an explanation, if a person shoots into a crowd causing the deaths of multiple people, juries would be entitled to find an intention to kill or inflict grievous bodily harm. Likewise, if a person blew up a plane and confessed that they did so for the purposes of insurance, without making any mention of their intentions

of Corporate Culture' in J O'Brien and G Gilligan (eds), *Integrity, Risk and Accountability in Capital Markets: Regulating Culture* (Oxford, Hart Publishing, 2013) 251.

[109] L Campbell, 'Corporate Liability and the Criminalisation of Failure' (2018) 12 *Law and Financial Markets Review* 57, 58.

[110] R Cheung, 'Money Laundering – a New Era for Sentencing Organisations' (2017) 1 *Journal of Business Law* 23, 28.

[111] *R v Moloney* [1985] AC 905, [1985] 1 All ER 1025, 1031.

[112] Crofts (n 37).

[113] Victorian Royal Commission (n 7) ch 6.

[114] There is also recognition that intention does not necessarily equate with an outcome. For example, a golfer might always intend to get a hole in one, but the chances of this happening are minimal. This emphasis upon unsuccessful intentions is significant in the doctrine of criminal intent.

[115] See *R v Schonewille* [1998] 2 VR 625.

with regard to the passengers who died as a consequence, juries could find an intention to kill.[116] This is a complex area of law and philosophy, and would require certainty of outcome, but the latter is a form of instrumental evil, where the collateral damage was not necessarily articulated by the accused as an intended outcome but, because it was a likely certainty, the law would regard it as intentional.[117]

The Bergin Inquiry framed Crown's compliance breaches, or to put it more bluntly and accurately, Crown's crimes, as due to failure, and specifically failure of corporate governance. There are various ways to respond to this explanation for corporate wrongdoing. One approach is to emphasise and accept this narrative of 'failure' and to argue that it is in and of itself blameworthy.[118] This is in accordance with a classic negative model of wickedness and is consistent with the offence of criminal negligence.[119] This approach is reflected in crimes that have been created that are specific to corporations, such as anti-money laundering, breach of work and safety legislation, and failure to prevent offences.[120] On this approach, it is the failure to set up anti-money laundering regimes or create a safe workplace that is in itself wrongful. This approach contributes to a critique of the emphasis on subjective culpability in criminal legal doctrine, particularly as it applies to corporations. This is because it is arguable that many of the harms caused by corporations are due to failure. Accordingly, law reform in this area to criminalise corporate failure is appropriate and justified by classic theories of wickedness.

Alternatively, theoretical and legal approaches have been proposed that aim at capturing the mens rea of corporations in the absence of confessions. For example, the Model Criminal Code Officers Committee considered that corporate culture is analogous to intention.[121] Peter French argued that the Corporate Internal Decision Structure provided a means of identifying decisions and choices of the corporation:[122]

> When the corporate act is consistent with an instantiation or an implementation of established corporate policy, then it is proper to describe it as having been done for corporate reasons, as having been caused by a corporate desire coupled with a corporate belief and so, in other words, as corporate intentional.[123]

Elise Bant's theory of system of intentionality argues that a corporation's systems, policies and processes manifest its intentions.[124] The Victorian Royal Commission devoted

[116] Juries may simply not believe that an accused had not thought that blowing up a plane would cause the deaths of anyone on the plane.

[117] M Moore, 'Patrolling the Borders of Consequentialist Justifications: The Scope of Agent-Relative Restrictions' (2007) 27 *Law and Philosophy* 35; RA Duff, 'Two Models of Criminal Fault' (2019) 13 *Criminal Law and Philosophy* 643.

[118] M Midgley, *Wickedness: A Philosophical Essay* (Abingdon, Routledge, 2001).

[119] Augustine, *The Confessions of St Augustine*, tr Edward Pusey (Springfield, CO, Collier Books, 1961); Thomas Aquinas, *On Evil*, ed R Regan (Oxford, Oxford University Press, 2003); Aristotle, *The Nicomachean Ethics*, tr J Thomson (London, Penguin Books, 2004).

[120] Criminal Code (n 9), pt 10.2; Safe Work Australia, 'Law and Regulation' (2022) at www.safeworkaustralia.gov.au/law-and-regulation; Copp and Cronin (n 14); Crofts (n 14).

[121] Parliament of the Commonwealth of Australia, Model Criminal Law Officers Committee of the Standing Committee of Attorneys-General, *Model Criminal Code* (Final Report, December 1992) chs 1 and 2, 21, 107. See also Dixon (n 108). Bucy talks about the 'ethos' of an organisation – corporate identity or ethos results from the dynamic of many individuals working together toward corporate goals: Bucy (n 60).

[122] French (n 4); French (n 43).

[123] French (n 4) 214.

[124] Bant, ch 9 of this volume.

a section of its Final Report to system intentionality, labelling it a 'compelling challenge' to Crown's claims of inadvertent money laundering, quoting Bant:[125]

> Crown must be taken to understand the inherent incidents of the systems it adopts and carries out. In this case, the unchecked, intentional and longstanding aggregation process, on which the AML system depended, actively and necessarily facilitated money laundering.[126]

Bant's theory is that corporations adopt systems to enable them to make and implement decisions, and these systems constitute and reveal the corporate intention.[127]

These theories propose a more pragmatic or realistic approach to corporations that has the potential to more neatly slot corporations within pre-existing criminal legal requirements that have been modelled on the ideal responsible legal subject. This approach is consistent with the insights of Chapple about why corporations are worthy of analysis as a specific genre of group agents. Unlike many groups, corporations are legally structured, they adopt rules and policies and practices. Authority structures and the division of labour are put in place to reduce decision costs and enable the corporation to react competitively in the market.[128] The corporation programmes and prompts judgement formation; and when a person forms a judgement on behalf of the company they will be representing the company in the technical sense. The company therefore owns this intention and is committed to its consequences, as if it had been an intention of the company.

Accordingly, it is appropriate to analyse Crown's intentions in a broader time frame. Corporate governance failings should not be considered in isolation but as part of a decision-making strategy expressed in official and unofficial, formal and informal rules. The clear intention of Crown Resorts, like the majority of public corporations, is the pursuit of profit. Whilst there is some choice about how this is to be achieved, or how avidly pursued, employees are coordinated to work towards the profit of Crown even if they do not personally want Crown to profit; they may just wish to keep their jobs, or may even disagree with the decisions of the corporation. The 'failings' of corporate governance could be reshaped and rethought of instead as structural choices in the pursuit of the primary aim – that of profit. Provided profits were sustained, the Crown Board was seduced and reluctant to ask questions about any of the dubious approaches adopted. Choices were made in terms of the kind of person put in position. This extended even to choices of Board members, installing non-executive directors who were ignorant of legal requirements and the duties of casinos, and beholden in various ways to Packer. Executives were installed and rewarded who acted according to concern for short-term profitability rather than legality. Decisions were made to organise Crown to act towards the specific goal of profit, and those structures and policies that were put in place can be analysed to determine what is valued and what is not. It is absolutely clear, and accepted by the Inquiries, that Crown avidly pursued profit at the expense of legal obligations. Crown systematically and intentionally breached the

[125] Victorian Royal Commission (n 7) 174–78.
[126] ibid 177.
[127] E Bant, 'Reforming the Laws of Corporate Attribution: "Systems Intentionality" Draft Statutory Provision' (2022) 39 *Companies and Securities Law Journal* 259.
[128] Chapple (n 6) 96.

law, including tax law, anti-money-laundering law, the Casino Act and legal duties of responsible gambling, Chinese laws against gambling and border controls.

Although both Inquiries accepted that Crown did not turn a blind eye to money laundering based on the principles of identification theory,[129] in the recent case of *ASIC v Westpac* the Federal Court adopted a more practical and realist approach that is in accordance with the arguments of this chapter.[130] In that case, the Federal Court refused to accept that breaches by Westpac were not deliberate, pointing to structural decisions to under-fund and under-train the one and only compliance officer, and stated:

> The conduct was deliberate, in the sense that it was the result of a planned campaign, and was not the result of unexpected or rogue behaviour by Westpac's representatives. The compliance framework for the campaign was shown to be wholly inadequate and the individual seemingly charged with the 'front line' compliance role was not qualified to perform that role. Subsequent to the commencement of these proceedings, and even after their finalisation in the High Court, Westpac has not expressed regret for the conduct, does not appear to have taken steps to remedy the compliance deficiencies and has been tardy in progressing a remediation plan.[131]

The same arguments can be made in relation to Crown. Crown's primary intention was to achieve profit at all costs, including through breaches of the law. Despite multiple red flags, including media reporting, reports in parliament, independent research and being forewarned that casinos are sites of risk for these specific crimes, Crown demonstrated a willingness with formal and informal rules and policies to break the law to make money. These decisions were arguably rational given the relative absence and soft touch of regulators. This culture of non-compliance and criminality was reinforced by a refusal to cooperate with regulatory investigations:

> It bullied the regulator. It provided it with false or misleading information. It delayed the investigatory process. All in all, it took what steps it could to frustrate the regulator's investigations.[132]

Crown consistently refused to admit responsibility for these criminal breaches or seek to minimise harm once the breaches became apparent. As noted, Crown denied that money laundering was taking place at its premises until the final hours of the Bergin Inquiry, it then withdrew these admissions prior to the Victorian Royal Commission. Overall, Crown made clear choices to breach the law in the pursuit of profit over long periods of time.

III. Conclusion

This chapter argues that corporations can and should be conceived of as moral agents in a way that is broadly consistent with our typical accounts of moral responsibility.

[129] This was likewise mirrored in AUSTRAC civil penalty cases against corporations, where the agreed facts were that breaches that occurred over many years were 'not deliberate'.

[130] *Australian Securities and Investments Commission v Westpac Securities Administration Limited* [2021] FCA 1008, (2021) 156 ACSR 614.

[131] ibid [95] (O'Bryan J).

[132] Victorian Royal Commission (n 7) [10].

Throughout I have woven criminal legal doctrinal requirements with typical accounts of moral responsibility. If corporations are broadly consistent with our existing ideas of moral and criminal agency, this suggests that there is no need to introduce new or complex theories to explain or justify corporate responsibility. I have argued that there is a tendency to over-complicate the third requirement of moral responsibility – that of good judgement. The problem with buying into the complication of large organisations is that the larger they are, the less likely anyone or anything is to be held responsible. Instead, crimes are framed as tragic accidents or mistakes. One way of attributing culpability to Crown is to argue that failure, or lack of goodness, is blameworthy.[133] An alternative is to adopt a pragmatic, realist approach. It is clear that Crown's intention has been to pursue profit at all costs – demonstrating a willingness to undermine, override, ignore and breach criminal laws in the process of achieving this, even whilst having the capacity to draw upon legal resources that are not available to individual accused. Patterns of rule-based behaviour or corporate culture – which include written and unwritten rules – were all geared to coordinate and work towards profit. Corporations like Crown can and should be regarded as moral agents capable of making moral choices for which they can be held responsible. Although immoral in its choices and actions, these were the choices of a moral agent and, as such, blameworthiness can be attributed to Crown for its criminal actions.

[133] Midgley (n 118).

4

Corporate Torts in England: Limiting Liability by Capacity

JOSHUA GETZLER

I. The Problem of Corporate Torts

Where does legal responsibility lie where a corporation commits a tort through its agents? Clearly the agents themselves may be liable, whether directors giving orders, or servants or employees, or maybe contractors following those orders. Moreover, the corporate person may be liable for non-authorised agent or employee conduct that yet lies within the scope of the company's activities. John Salmond, in his seminal torts study of 1907, stated the basic principle as follows:

> Since a corporation is incapable of acting either rightfully or wrongfully in its proper person, the torts which the law attributes to it are in reality those of its agents and servants by whom it acts and fulfils its functions … [T]his vicarious liability of corporations is determined by the same rules which govern the liability of any other principal for the torts of his agents and servants.[1]

A common defence to this general vicarious liability is that the corporate person would be unlikely to have authorised operationally a tortious course of conduct, so that vicarious liability of a director for another corporate servant may be possible, but no such liability for the corporate person itself.[2] This is to drive a wedge between attribution based on an agency concept, whereby the corporate servant's acts, duly authorised, are the primary acts of the company, and a vicarious or strict concept, whereby responsibility is ascribed to the company as a secondary liability based on an ethic or a policy of responsibility.[3] The defence based on absence of primary authority (actually, a demurrer pleading want of cause) was used extensively in the nineteenth and early

[1] JW Salmond, *The Law of Torts: A Treatise on the English Law of Liability for Civil Injuries*, 1st edn (London, Stevens and Haynes, 1907) 55.

[2] See, eg, *Daniel v Metropolitan Railway Company* (1871) LR 5 HL 45; M Lobban, 'Daniel v Metropolitan Railway Company (1871)' in P Mitchell and C Mitchell (eds), *Landmark Cases in the Law of Tort* (Oxford, Hart Publishing, 2010) 95; RW Kostal, *Law and English Railway Capitalism 1825–1875* (Oxford, Oxford University Press, 1994) 254.

[3] See *Northern Land Council v Quall* [2020] HCA 33, (2020) 383 ALR 378 [81]–[87] (Nettle and Edelman JJ).

twentieth centuries to deny the corporate liability of the Crown for public officials' wrongdoing, leaving tort victims to shallow pockets.[4] The courts flirted with this theory for private corporations also, but eventually rejected it as a dogma unfairly blocking liability.[5] Today, the test for responsibility has moved from voluntaristic agency authorisation to a strict vicarious liability based on more flexible concepts of 'close connection' and 'control',[6] which can be used not only within the corporation to establish group liability for agent action, but also across corporate groups to establish parent liability for subsidiaries.[7]

Even with the acceptance of corporate vicarious liability for agents' conduct, there were still historical hurdles to overcome before tort victims could meaningfully recover from the corporate assets. The corporation may have organised itself to be cash poor, precisely to insulate itself from *ex lege* liabilities.[8] Or the corporation might claim a constitutional disability preventing it from committing the actions raising tort liability in the first place. Up to the late nineteenth century, jurists gave credibility to the theory that a corporation could not be made liable for either torts committed or contracts entered into by agents or servants that were ultra vires, or actions committed in the course of any business or undertaking that went beyond the limits set by law for its undertakings.[9]

A prime solution to the first problem – the capital maintenance/concealment problem – is veil piercing in order to reach into allied corporate asset pools, directors' fortunes or even shareholders' fortunes, in order to satisfy judgment debts.[10] But in the absence of fraud, such veil piercing is difficult to achieve. This is a fascinating problem but one that must be discussed on a different occasion. The solution to the second issue

[4] J McLean, *Searching for the State in British Legal Thought: Competing Conceptions of the Public Sphere* (Cambridge, Cambridge University Press, 2012) 204.

[5] Salmond (n 1) 55–58.

[6] Recent discussion in the UK Supreme Court: *Barclays Bank Plc v Various Claimants* [2020] UKSC 13, [2020] AC 973; *Various Claimants v WM Morrison Supermarkets plc* [2020] UKSC 12, [2020] AC 989; in the High Court of Australia: *Construction, Forestry, Maritime, Mining and Energy Union v Personnel Contracting Pty Ltd* [2022] HCA 1, (2022) 398 ALR 404; see further A Gray, *Vicarious Liability: Critique and Reform* (Oxford, Hart Publishing, 2021); C Beuermann, *Reconceptualising Strict Liability for the Tort of Another* (Cambridge, Cambridge University Press, 2019).

[7] *NatWest Markets plc and Mercuria Energy Europe Trading Limited v Bilta* (UK) Ltd [2021] EWCA Civ 680; *Okpabi v Royal Dutch Shell* [2021] UKSC 3, [2021] 1 WLR 1294; *Lungowe v Vedanta Resources plc* [2019] UKSC 20, [2020] AC 1045. The best modern treatment of corporate attribution of acts in tort is now R Leow, *Corporate Attribution in Private Law* (Oxford, Hart Publishing, 2022) 89–120.

[8] GP Miller, 'Das Kapital: Solvency Regulation of the American Business Enterprise', Coase-Sandor Institute for Law & Economics Working Paper No 32 (1995); LM LoPucki, 'The Death of Liability' (1996–97) 106 *Yale Law Journal* 1.

[9] Salmond (n 1) 56–58. Salmond affirmed the ultra vires rule in the next two editions of *The Law of Torts* (2nd edn, 1910; 3rd edn, 1912), citing for support JF Clerk and WHB Lindsell, *Clerk and Lindsell on Torts*, 5th edn (London, Sweet & Maxwell, 1909) 56; NL Lindley, *Lindley on Companies*, 6th edn (London, Sweet & Maxwell, 1902) i, 257–59; HSG Halsbury, *Halsbury's Laws of England*, 1st edn (London, Butterworths, 1907–) viii, s 854.

[10] See the survey articles by T Kuntz, 'Asset Partitioning, Limited Liability and Veil Piercing – Review Essay on Bainbridge/Henderson, Limited Liability' (2018) 19 *European Business Organization Law Review* 439; CH Tan, JY Wang and C Hofmann, 'Piercing the Corporate Veil: Historical, Theoretical and Comparative Perspectives' (2019) 16 *Berkeley Business Law Journal* 140; *Prest v Petrodel Resources Ltd & Ors* [2013] UKSC 34, [2013] 3 WLR 1; *Stone & Rolls Ltd v Moore Stephens (a firm)* [2009] UKHL 39, [2009] 1 AC 1391; *Hurstwood Properties (A) Ltd v Rossendale Borough Council* [2021] UKSC 16, [2022] AC 690.

of disability or want of power or capacity is to read down or eliminate the doctrine of ultra vires placing restrictions on the plenary capacities of corporations. A specific strategy is to deny that the ultra vires incapacity should ever apply to authorised but tortious and ultra vires conduct; the corporation cannot exempt itself from responsibility for its actions by hiding behind a disregard for the limits of its powers. Such a position was evoked by the United States Supreme Court in an influential decision of 1885:

> The argument is unsound that whatever is done by a corporation in excess of the corporate powers as defined by its charter is as though it was not done at all … The truth is that with the great increase in corporations in very recent times and in their extension to nearly all the business transactions of life, it has been found necessary to hold them responsible for acts not strictly within their corporate powers, but done in the corporate name and by corporate officers who were competent to exercise all the corporate powers.[11]

This argument seems to rest on a model of reliance by the community on the ostensible liability and moral responsibility of enterprises authorised by law to trade as entities. But it still begs the question – how can acts under a legally non-existent power be ascribed to a corporate entity? Observing the trend to enlarged corporate liability in 1913, Salmond abandoned his earlier position that ultra vires torts were impossible, and instead offered the argument that imposition of liability encompassed a dual analytical and a policy judgement: the company can be seen to be liable not for an act but for a default, a failure to have its servants remain within powers and perform agency tasks with due diligence to a required standard of care. The stated vires of a corporation cannot excuse culpable failures to monitor one's agents and ensure they reach a due communal standard.[12]

This artful argument points the way to a broader policy solution, which is to shave back the general operation of the ultra vires doctrine as a restraint on capacity and responsibility in all areas of private enterprise. Strikingly the latter read-down was achieved in the past 50 years in all major common law jurisdictions; but the reasons given for squeezing capacity restrictions from each system were quite varied, sometimes emphasising contractual reliance, sometimes insolvency protections, sometimes tort and regulatory convenience. This is a topic for a larger study.[13] This chapter examines the (mainly English) courts' handling of the problem of ultra vires solely in relation to the corporate person's liability in tort.

II. Why Limited Liability?

We may continue with the historical justifications commonly given for limited liability regimes for corporations, which screen the depth of recourse possible for breach

[11] *Salt Lake City v Hollister* (1885) 118 US 256, 260.

[12] JW Salmond, *Jurisprudence*, 4th edn (London, Stevens and Haynes, 1913) 287–93, 310; and see JW Salmond, *The Law of Torts: A Treatise on the English Law of Liability for Civil Injuries*, 4th edn (London, Sweet & Maxwell, 1916) 60–65. For a comparable doctrine in trusts law, see discussion in J Getzler, 'Laying the Axe to the Root of the Tree? Shielding a Co-trustee from Liability' in P Davies, S Douglas and J Goudkamp (eds), *Defences in Equity* (Oxford, Hart Publishing, 2018) 183.

[13] Note forthcoming dissertation on the full gamut of 19th- and 20th-century ultra vires law by William Moppett of Oxford University.

of contract or tortious duties.[14] Begin with contract. A company that limits its liability to the level of its subscribed or guaranteed capital through its statutory registered incorporation might claim to give notice to voluntary creditors ahead of their dealing with the company, so that they may build the legal limits of counterparty liability into their contractual assumption of risk. In other words, the asset partitions drawn by law between the internal capital of the company on the one hand, and the outside or non-corporate patrimonies of the company's agents and share owners on the other, is justified by the fair warning given to all who deal with the company, a kind of default partial-exemption clause constructed by statute. Pragmatic grounds are supplied as to why the responsibility-evading tendencies of limited liability may be tolerated: it permits ready vesting of capital in large-scale enterprises with a useful separation of ownership and control, allowing depersonalised professional management and heightened spreading of risk through joint stock trading, and protecting the arm's-length investors from risks that they cannot easily calculate or control, but without unduly shutting out creditors from recourse to enterprise assets.[15]

III. Accommodating Tort within Asset-Partitioning Models

The conventional notice justifications for asset partitioning are strained to destruction in the face of tort liability. Tort victims of corporate behaviour cannot credibly be said to agree to the exemption from damages created by the limited liability regime. Limitations of liability seem especially unfair where we are dealing with 'stranger' torts distant from voluntary transactional behaviour – though some law-and-economics theorists have bravely attempted to make just such claims, suggesting that we can each buy insurance or take added precautions to account for the non-negotiated corporate risks we all face, such that risks imposed by corporations on strangers are not really unbargained externalities. Arguably, the better justice claim goes the other way. If a tortfeasor happens to be a collective entity pursuing profits for its shareholders who have ample assets outside the corporate boundary, then shareholders' responsibility for the miscreant conduct of their collective agent might demand that those outside assets enjoy no immunity from attachment for tort damages, once the inside assets have been used up. The shareholders' culpability attaches to them personally on the ethical grounds that they failed to monitor the miscreant company that earned them profits. Such a double liability rule, binding shareholders, directors and servants for both their inside and outside assets, would give corporatised associations every incentive to avoid imposing external harm through the tort system. This is hardly a radical innovation, looking back into common law tradition; it is only to apply the partnership 'jingle' rule to corporate joint stock enterprise in the special case of torts harming involuntary creditors. Indeed, until the 1880s, lawyers and investors assumed that certain sensitive

[14] For one historian's view seeing limited liability as rent-seeking and evasion of responsibility, see P Johnson, *Making the Market: Victorian Origins of Corporate Capitalism* (Cambridge, Cambridge University Press, 2010).

[15] See further J Armour, G Hertig and H Kanda, 'Transactions with Creditors' in R Kraakman et al (eds), *The Anatomy of Corporate Law*, 3rd edn (Oxford, Oxford University Press, 2017) 109.

and high-trust forms of joint stock enterprise, such as banking and insurance, should follow a general partnership rule of full personal and solidary liability, precisely to ensure that shareholders would discipline directors and agents and curb externalities. The eventual abandonment of such solidary liability in the fiduciary financial sector was perhaps triggered by the mass insolvencies that followed the City of Glasgow Bank crash in 1878,[16] and the practical results of that relaxation of legal discipline today are not obviously salutary.[17]

The problem of tort victims of the corporation as involuntary or non-adjusting creditors was reformulated in the famous model of forward and reverse asset partitioning originally propounded by Henry Hansmann and Reinier Kraakman.[18] They argued that limited liability aimed at containing the liability of investors for the collective acts of the company, which they labelled affirmative or forward asset partitioning, was a useful but not essential element for certain forms of depersonalised joint stock activity. Partnership firms with solidary obligation and unlimited liability remained the dominant form across the nineteenth century; the subtleties of common law and equitable insolvency rules allowing contractual arrangements with creditors to create priority regimes affording sufficient protections to encourage commitment and lock-in of investment.[19] The limited liability company that arose in the mid- to late nineteenth century was rather to be explained by so-called defensive asset partitioning, dealing with the threat that agents and investors posed to the collective if they fell into debt outside the company's activities. Creditors might then be able to charge or acquire the individual debtor's share of a company capital and threaten to control or disintegrate the company stock; or, going even further, creditors of an individual agent or shareholder might be empowered to burrow deeper into solidary shares of the rest of the collective if some pooled liability could be established. Limited liability regimes locked the external creditors out of corporate capital, at least beyond the exchange value of the individual debtors' shares. The company and its membership could simply claim that an errant member's outside personal debts, such as gambling, could have nothing to do with the company's business, and hence no recourse against wider company assets should be permitted. However, such reverse or defensive asset partitioning cannot be arranged by contract but requires a statutory regime, constructing artificial legal persons to establish the necessary asset partitioning or shielding of corporate capital. Hansmann and Kraakman supplemented this model by making quite clear that forward asset partitioning should not rightly be applied to protect shareholders from the tort

[16] *Muir v City of Glasgow Bank* (1879) 4 App Cas 337; cf *Smith v Anderson* (1880) 15 Ch D 247.

[17] The leading modern study of the impact of limited liability banking is JD Turner, *Banking in Crisis: The Rise and Fall of British Banking Stability, 1800 to the Present* (Cambridge, Cambridge University Press, 2014).

[18] H Hansmann and R Kraakman, 'Toward Unlimited Shareholder Liability for Corporate Torts' (1991) 100 *Yale Law Journal* 1879; and see also H Hansmann and R Kraakman, 'The Essential Role of Organizational Law' (2000) 110 *Yale Law Journal* 387, 431.

[19] Arguments teased out in J Getzler and M Macnair, 'The Firm as an Entity Before the Companies Acts' in P Brand, K Costello and WN Osborough (eds), *Adventures of the Law: Proceedings of the Sixteenth British Legal History Conference* (Dublin, Four Courts Press, 2005) 267; followed in H Hansmann, R Kraakman and R Squire, 'Law and the Rise of the Firm' (2006) 119 *Harvard Law Review* 1333; R Harris, 'The Private Origins of the Private Company: Britain 1862–1907' (2013) 33 *Oxford Journal of Legal Studies* 339; J Morley, 'The Common Law Corporation: The Power of the Trust in Anglo-American Business History' (2016) 116 *Columbia Law Review* 2145.

liabilities of their aggregate corporation. Such a direct tort liability would positively require owners and beneficiaries of a collective enterprise to constrain externalities imposed on involuntary creditors and so not make profits unfairly at the expense of others who had no say in it.[20]

IV. Ultra Vires as a Policing Device for Authorised Action

The basic legal logic evoked by Hansmann and Kraakman of protecting the corporation from its members' actions may have proved too successful. Defensive asset partitioning served a useful purpose in isolating blatantly non-corporate activities by shareholders or agents acting in their individual capacity. There was a decent argument that the inner corporate assets should be immunised from actions wholly outside company business, that is performed non-representatively without authority to bind the company. But we then have a serious problem – what if ostensibly corporate activities are authorised by the corporate hierarchy in pursuit of corporate goals and profits, but those self-same acts are formally defined to be outwith the company business by the terms of the empowering and constitutive corporate charter, statute or memorandum and articles of association? This might even yield the obnoxious managerial tactic of seeking corporate advantage *ex ante* by promoting dealings that may be disowned *ex post* if they get the corporation into loss or strife. Here we have the nub of the problem of ultra vires.

With the rise of trading and financial corporations after 1600, English courts found themselves constantly troubled by problems of corporate ultra vires or conduct beyond powers. The doctrine of ultra vires set a boundary, a constitutional limit, to the legal capacities and powers of associations, whether formed by common law, prerogative or statute. The boundary could be set expressly by prohibition: 'thou shalt not trade abroad'; or by implication from surrounding stipulations: for example, 'thou shalt trade in England' implies not trading abroad. A classic instance was the *Ashbury Railway* case of 1875, where the House of Lords held that overseas railway contracts fell outside the stated objects of a registered commercial company formed to pursue engineering projects only, and were therefore void notwithstanding a purported ratification by the shareholders. The policy reason given was that members old and new (and perhaps creditors) had predicated their dealings with the company based on its memorandum of association, and it would breach that protection to allow the company to ratify acts in breach of the memorandum.[21] *Ashbury* opened up a long debate concerning powers of

[20] Hansmann and Kraakman, 'Toward Unlimited Shareholder Liability for Corporate Torts' (n 18); C Witting, 'Liability for Corporate Wrongs' (2009) 28 *University of Queensland Law Journal* 113; Harding, ch 2 of this volume; cf J Crowe, 'Does Control Make a Difference? The Moral Foundations of Shareholder Liability for Corporate Wrongs' (2012) 75 *Modern Law Review* 159, arguing that control must precede liability, rather than incentivising control as a response to liability.

[21] *Ashbury Railway Carriage and Iron Co v Riche* (1875) LR 7 HL 653 (*Ashbury*); *Riche v Ashbury Railway Carriage Co* (1874) LR 9 Exch 224 (*Riche v Ashbury*). The case arguably turned on the language of the specific incorporating statute; Lord Cairns in his leading speech held that since the 1862 Companies Act did not permit changes to the memorandum of association, ratification of acts in breach of the memorandum was excluded. In the later case of *Baroness Wenlock v River Dee Company* (1883) 36 Ch D 675, (1885) 10 AC 354, (1887) 19 QBD 155, Lord Blackburn, who would have found a valid ratification in *Ashbury* in any case,

ratification and *ex post* variation of memoranda of association, and the nature of third-party notice of limitations to powers. A second crucial case was *Sinclair v Brougham*,[22] decided just before the Great War, which examined how far proprietary tracing could be used to recover money paid under ultra vires dealings by a building society wrongly acting as a bank. Such cases used ultra vires to void associational activities and reverse the consequences of corporate acts. Another notorious case went the other way, ascribing added implied powers and capacities to a legal collectivity where the actors had assumed that no such powers existed. In the *Taff Vale* case of 1901, the House of Lords held that a registered trade union could as an entity commit torts through its members, and so could have its assets, including funds for mutual assistance, attached to meet its tort liabilities.[23]

Each of these great cases on group capacities caused furore and led to torrents of further litigation, to protracted bouts of statutory reform and, in the case of *Taff Vale*, to the foundation of the Parliamentary Labour Party. So the doctrine of ultra vires is important in English legal, economic and political history, well before the rise of judicial review of administrative action in the mid-twentieth century. Indeed, in 1877, shortly after *Ashbury* was decided, Mr Seward Brice, in his monumental treatise on corporate capacity, could write 'Perhaps indeed the Law of Corporations may be considered for most practical purposes as in reality only the application and development of the doctrine of *ultra vires*.'[24]

The doctrine of ultra vires was disruptive because it made for an infinite variation of legal statuses in English law. Every private and public corporation might have a different constitution limiting its capacity in a unique fashion. Hence there could be no *numerus clausus*, no standard range of types of corporate person, and this complexity of persons in turn had a profound impact on the law of things and actions. Similar problems applied to the legal categorisation of natural persons, with foreigners, married women, children, persons with physical, mental and emotional disabilities, and persons subject to undue influence each having variant capacities to own property, make contracts or commit torts and crimes; but the variations were not so infinite as with artificial persons.[25]

The position today regarding the significance of ultra vires in company law has shifted to the opposite extreme to that held in late Victorian times. Modern sentiments were summed up by the Canadian Supreme Court in 1991,[26] denouncing the operation of the ultra vires doctrine as 'a protection to no-one and a trap to the unwary'.

indicated that he would have liked to confine the strong ultra vires rule in *Ashbury* to companies incorporated under the 1862 Act, but he accepted that the case stood for a wider rule.

[22] *Sinclair v Brougham* [1914] AC 398 (HL).

[23] *Taff Vale Railway Co v Amalgamated Society of Railway Servants* [1901] AC 426 (HL). But no implied power to raise funds for political purposes could be ascribed to trade unions, according to the House of Lords in *Amalgamated Society of Railway Servants v Osborne* [1910] AC 87.

[24] S Brice, *A Treatise on the Doctrine of Ultra Vires: Being an investigation of the principles which limit the capacities, powers, and liabilities of corporations, and more especially of joint stock companies*, 2nd edn (London, Stevens, 1877) x (first published 1874).

[25] Of course slavery, ancient and modern, massively complicated the law of persons, and revulsion against slavery from the 1860s onwards led to a denial that statuses had great impact on the operation of legal systems; Henry Maine's adage 'The movement of the progressive societies has hitherto been a movement from Status to Contract' (*Ancient Law*, 1861) can be read in this light. Perhaps today the fault line lies between the citizen and the foreigner/immigrant/refugee.

[26] *Communities Economic Development Fund v Canadian Pickles Corp* [1991] 3 SCR 388.

The remedy for the mischief of the voiding of corporate acts by the ultra vires doctrine has been to render the doctrine inoperative, or at least easily surmountable, and thus irrelevant. An American code ordains 'The validity of corporate action may not be challenged on the ground that the corporation lacks or lacked power to act.'[27]

Modern English law finally grasped this position following United Kingdom's entry into the European Union (EU), as EU law required harmonised company doctrine guaranteeing security for third-party transactions with corporate entities across the single market.[28] It now goes even further and insists that corporations be treated as natural persons, including capacity to enjoy human rights, notably including freedom to move jurisdiction; and even post-Brexit, the pull of EU doctrine on English praxis remains strong. But it is the native English materials that concern us here, as these are the structuring ideas for corporate tort liabilities.

V. The History of Ultra Vires

From the time of Sir Edward Coke to the later nineteenth century, the doctrine of ultra vires evolved as the nature of corporations changed. Early corporations tended to be franchised operations pursuing public purposes, often with monopolist protection from competition, as with learned professions, trades, guilds and utilities with high sunk costs, long time horizons for realisation of profit and significant positive externalities.[29] The post-1830 corporate economy operated in more competitive factor and financial markets, and the corporation was handy to raise capital and assemble management and labour in pursuit of scale efficiencies, permitting vertical and horizontal alignments and enhanced maturity transformations.[30] The doctrine of ultra vires changed in tenor as corporations became pervasive economic players imposing heightened negative externalities on traders, customers, employees and the public, for example public and private nuisances, personal torts, market abuse.[31] Starting with the burst of railway capitalism

[27] American Law Institute, 'Model Business Corporation Act' (2006), s 3.04(a).

[28] European Communities Act 1972 (UK), s 9(1); RR Pennington, 'Reform of the Ultra Vires Rule' (1987) 8 *Company Law* 103; Department of Trade and Industry, *Reform of the Ultra Vires Rule: A DTI Consultative Document* (London, 1986), leading to partial abolition in 1989 and fuller abrogation by the Companies Act 2006 (UK), s 39: 'the validity of an act done by a company shall not be called into question on the ground of a lack of capacity by reason of anything in the company's constitution'. R Nolan draws conclusions from this story in 'Basic Corporate Plumbing' in J Armour and J Payne (eds), *Rationality in Company Law: Essays in Honour of DD Prentice* (Oxford, Hart Publishing, 2009) ch 9. For other jurisdictions: Canada Business Corporations Act 1985, s 15; Corporations Act 2001 (Cth), ss 124–125; Companies Act 1993 (NZ), ss 17–18.

[29] A Smith, 'Ultra Vires – A Problem of Sovereignty' (1946–47) 3 *Res Judicatae* 28; A Offer, *Understanding the Private-Public Divide: Markets, Governments, and Time Horizons* (Cambridge, Cambridge University Press, 2022).

[30] Some of the interplays of law, finance and corporate form are traced in J Getzler, 'The Role of Security over Future and Circulating Capital: Evidence from the British Economy circa 1850–1920' in J Getzler and J Payne (eds), *Company Charges: Spectrum and Beyond* (Oxford, Oxford University Press, 2006) 227.

[31] There was an outburst of interest in this subject in 1925–26, treated jurisprudentially rather than historically: EH Warren, 'Torts by Corporations in Ultra Vires Undertakings' (1925) 2 *Cambridge Law Journal* 180; AJ Harno, 'Privileges and Powers of a Corporation and the Doctrine of Ultra Vires' (1925) 35 *Yale Law Journal* 13; AL Goodhart, 'Corporate Liability in Tort and the Doctrine of Ultra Vires' (1926) 2 *Cambridge Law Journal* 350.

from the mid-1830s, and with the expansion of mining and heavy industry, the courts had to grapple with ascription of tort responsibilities to deep-pocketed artificial entities, where the individual responsibility of managers and owners was muted by forward asset partitioning. As limited liability and corporatisation took deeper hold at the close of the nineteenth century, spreading into the manufacturing and financial sectors, the depersonalisation of economic life intensified, and wrongful harms seemed to emanate from groups rather than individuals at all levels of the economy. David Ibbetson has suggested that this de-individualisation of fault wrought major changes to the basic liability principles in tort law, involving a shift from moral blame to social standards of care, such that corporate limited liability actually invited litigation seeking remedies against corporate assets.[32]

VI. Controlling Limited Liability

How much inhibition of liability could be tolerated in an industrialised, corporatised economy? Was it a viable position to hold that a corporation with limited legal capacity could not be held liable if its servants committed torts whilst pursuing company business yet outside the constituting purposes of the company? Distinguish the following cases. The shareholders through the corporate constitution may authorise a company to pursue acts through agents and employees that they might commit with a proper purpose but in a tortious manner. The issue is then whether the tortious performance of those acts takes them outside the authority of the agent. The law came to say there was corporate vicarious liability that was strict; the tortious quality of the act did not negate attribution of the authorised act to the company. But what if the tortious act, even if authorised by management, fell outside the corporation's formal limits of capacity? In that case the ultra vires rule dictated that those acts should be characterised not as corporate acts but as an independent enterprise, a frolic of the agent or employee outside the scope of corporate activity, and not to be ascribed to the corporation using the devices of attribution by authorisation or vicarious liability. Victims in these cases are in a difficult position, for they have no choice in being injured by an ultra vires and hence unauthorised individual tortfeasor. Should the victims nonetheless be shut out from suing the corporation with recourse to its assets, and be left to sue the directors, agents or employees as individuals who may have little fortune or insurance to meet judgment debts?

This painful ultra vires problem was long contained by the technique that originally evolved in public law and the law of trusts and partnerships, whereby individual actors attracting personal liability whilst promoting group purposes are given access to collective funds through indemnity and insurance to pay their judgment creditors. But such a solution was accidental and not to be relied upon in an emerging era of large-enterprise capitalism and mass torts. Instead of indemnity, the law searched for methods to attach the corporation itself. To understand this requires fresh historical perspectives.

[32] DJ Ibbetson, *A Historical Introduction to the Law of Obligations* (Oxford, Oxford University Press, 1999) 196–97.

VII. Defining Corporate Capacity – The Role of Charters (Prerogative Delegation) and Statutes (Legislative Creation)

We cannot investigate the historical operation of ultra vires in relation to tort without attending to the intellectual foundations of corporate capacity. The story begins with the *Case of Sutton's Hospital* (1612), where Coke found that corporations were emanations of the Crown, which was itself constituted as a 'corporation sole' by the common law, as a customary legal order defining all persons within jurisdiction.[33] In the seminal 1991 House of Lords case *Hazell v Hammersmith and Fulham London Borough Council*,[34] Lord Templeman stated that *Sutton's Hospital* case was 'largely incomprehensible' to the modern reader but still good authority. Lord Templeman explained that the case

> has been accepted as 'express authority' that at common law it is an incident to a corporation to use its common seal for the purpose of binding itself to anything to which a natural person could bind himself and to deal with its property as a natural person might deal with his own: *Riche v Ashbury Railway Carriage and Iron Co Ltd* (1874) LR 9 Ex 224, 263. The doctrine applies only to a corporation created by an exercise of the Royal Prerogative. A corporation created by or under a statute has no power except the powers granted expressly or by implication by that statute.[35]

The following doctrines emerged in the wake of *Sutton's Hospital.* Corporations could be sole or aggregate. It was a maxim of the law that 'to the existence of all corporations the King's consent is absolutely necessary'; it was tantamount to constitutional principle that such subordinate polities must be authorised by the Crown. Many of the early modern corporations would have been formed by prerogative charter, typically by grant under letters patent, and would have enjoyed the fullest capacity as a presumption of the plenitude of Crown grant. Arguably the same plenitude would have applied to those companies formed not by overt act of the Crown but by prescription, which appears to have relied on a presumption of lost grant from the Crown or even lost statute, as evidenced by long usage.[36] Many eighteenth- and nineteenth-century trading, infrastructure and finance companies were neither chartered nor registered but given a bespoke statutory incorporation by private or special legislation; these would be statutory companies and lack *Sutton's Hospital*-style full capacity. In statutory corporations (or hybrids involving a statutory regulation of a chartered entity), the extent of capacity was always a question of parliamentary intent found through the normal process of statutory interpretation.[37] To incorporation by charter, statute or prescription

[33] *Case of Sutton's Hospital* (1612) 10 Coke Reports 23a, 77 ER 960 (KB) ('before all the Judges of England') (*Sutton's Hospital*). The historical jurisprudence of early modern corporatism is explored in J Getzler, 'Frederic William Maitland – Trust and Corporation' (2016) 35 *University of Queensland Law Journal* 171; D Runciman and M Ryan (eds), *Maitland: State, Trust and Corporation* (Cambridge, Cambridge University Press, 2003); DJ Seipp, 'Formalism and Realism in Fifteenth-century English Law: Bodies Corporate and Bodies Natural' in PA Brand and J Getzler (eds), *Judges and Judging in the History of the Common Law and Civil Law* (Cambridge, Cambridge University Press, 2012) 37.

[34] *Hazell v Hammersmith and Fulham London Borough Council* [1992] 2 AC 1, [1991] 2 WLR 372, [1991] 1 All ER 545 (HL).

[35] ibid 39.

[36] See *Case of Corporations* (1597) 4 Coke Reports 77b, 76 ER 1052 (KB).

[37] *Bonanza Creek Gold Mining Co Ltd v R* [1916] 1 AC 566 (PC).

Sutton's Hospital added the fourth category of incorporation by common law, 'as the King himself',[38] by which Coke may have been asserting a political claim that the Crown as a corporation sole is created by the common law as the foundation of all legal and constitutional order – and not that the common law is the creature of the Crown's higher prerogative of justice. Such common law corporations as the Crown obviously do not need sovereign consent to exist; they just are, by fiat of customary common law.

What, then, of registered companies formed under modern companies legislation, which have comprised the great bulk of trading corporations over the past 150 years? These are created by force of a facilitating statute and hence do not fall directly under the anti-ultra vires *Sutton's Hospital* rule. If chartered and common law corporations had an inherent capacity approximating a natural person, it was equally clear that Parliament (a special law-making assembly, not itself corporate, in distinction to the Crown) enjoyed the sovereign authority expressly to limit a statutory corporation's powers and render certain acts void as beyond capacity. Two further categories of association must be added. First, partnerships, deed of settlement companies, charities, religious orders and other associations might have functional corporate qualities yet lack full legal personality. Their foundation could lie in general law principles of contract, trust and plural ownership, or in local or ecclesiastical law outside the common law. Second, municipal and borough corporations as a subset of corporations aggregate may be created by multiple *causae*, and these generated a voluminous law specifying the practical powers and capacities of local government.[39]

We now turn to the details of the *Sutton's Hospital* case. Here the existence, capacity and powers of a charitable corporation created by letters patent were challenged by two men accused of trespass on the corporation's land. The Crown charter had forbidden the foundation to alienate land save by lease; the corporation had *later* acquired land and set up a hospital with governors in a new part of England, and these acts were alleged either to be ultra vires, or else to indicate that the corporation had never properly come into existence as a land-owning foundation. The trespassers' objections were denied; it was held that the corporation could come into legal existence as a person with full incidental powers even before its governors had been appointed and its lands settled. A corporation as a *persona ficta* need not have any precise location at the time of incorporation or thereafter, and the corporation could exist with a sufficient mechanism to appoint governors before any such appointments had occurred. The nature of the corporation was stated by Coke with rhetorical flourish:

> And it is great reason that an hospital, &c. in expectancy or intendment, or nomination, should be sufficient to support the name of an incorporation when the corporation itself is only in abstracto, and rests only in intendment and consideration of the law for a corporation aggregate of many is invisible, immortal, and rests only in intendment and consideration of the law … They cannot commit treason, nor be outlawed, nor excommunicate, for they have no souls, neither can they appear in person, but by attorney … A corporation aggregate of many cannot do fealty, for an invisible body can neither be in person, nor swear, … it is not subject to imbecilities, death of the natural body, and divers other cases.[40]

[38] *Sutton's Hospital* (n 33) 29b.

[39] See further S Kyd, *A Treatise on Corporations*, 2 vols (London, Butterworths, 1793–94) i, 1–41; FW Maitland, *Township and Borough* (Cambridge, Cambridge University Press, 1898).

[40] *Sutton's Hospital* (n 33) 32b.

The chartered corporation might have a founder who had settled lands or organised an association to pursue some purpose, 'but the King alone can create or make the Corporation',[41] and can then vest powers in the founder or others to run the corporation. If the franchised powers and directions of a corporation as specified in its charter were abused or exceeded, the corporate act would have legal force, but a writ of *scire facias* lay to repeal the grant and dissolve the company. The breached direction need not expressly be a condition for repeal; any term delimiting the purpose of the franchise could supply a condition subsequent for dissolution.[42] This was always an *ex post facto* discretionary remedy for ultra vires acts, and the Attorney-General could not be forced to exercise his prosecutorial discretion if no public interest was detected in stopping the corporation's excess of powers. Thus, inaction by the Crown or Attorney-General served as a type of ratification of or acquiescence in the corporation's achieved acts. In effect, ultra vires acts were here merely voidable, and prior to any act of rescission or avoidance those acts were legally valid.

Did the natural capacity of a chartered or common law corporation extend beyond contract and property to acts amounting to torts? Earlier cases suggested not, with Sir Robert Brooke reporting a judgment in the Book of Assizes by Thorpe CJ of King's Bench around 1350 stating

> that trespass lies not against commonalities, to wit, by the name of a corporation, but against the persons who did it, by their proper names; for neither capias nor exigent lies against a commonalty.[43]

This may have been a procedural ruling pointing to difficulties in making a corporation submit to a curial remedy appropriate to trespass proper. Attachment for damages for trover and for trespass on the case were later recognised, and following this all inhibitions on attaching corporations for trespass were lost. But a more substantive principle may have informed the sense of a corporate immunity in the earlier period; for example, in a 1562 case Catesby J held that '[i]t cannot be denied that the Mayor, Sheriffs and commonalty are one entire body, which cannot be severed, and which cannot do any corporal wrong'.[44] In *The Company of Shipwrights of Redderiffe's Case* of 1614, Coke cited Manwood CB,

> as touching corporations, that they were invisible, immortall, and that they had no soule; and therefore no subpoena lieth against them because they have no conscience nor soule; a corporation, is a body aggregate, none can create soules but God, but the King creates them, and therefore they have no soules. they cannot speak, nor appear in person, but by attorney.[45]

Post-Restoration, when the basis of Crown power had shifted,[46] in *R v Mayor of London* in 1691, Holt CJ held that a *quo warranto* to take away the core powers of a

[41] ibid 34a.

[42] *The Eastern Archipelago Company v R on the Prosecution of Sir James Brooke* (1853) 2 Ellis and Blackburn 856, 118 ER 988 (Ex Ch).

[43] R Brooke, *La Graunde Abridgement* (London, Richard Tottell, 1573/6) 'Corporations' 43 c, citing 22 Ass f 100 pl 67; and see *Maund v The Monmouthshire Canal Company* (1842) 4 Manning & Granger 452, 453 c, 134 ER 186, 187–88 (CB).

[44] *Case of Norwich Corporation*, Mich 21 Eliz 4, fol 12 pl 4 (1562).

[45] *Tipling v Pexall* (1614) 2 Bulstrode 233, 80 ER 1085 (Ex).

[46] See D Kershaw, 'Revolutionary Amnesia and the Nature of Prerogative Power' (2022) *International Journal of Constitutional Law (ICON)* 1.

municipal corporation as a remedy for abuses in effect was a dissolution of the corporation by prerogative, and added that this was formally an action to be brought against the members of the corporation comprising 'the burgesses and inhabitants of the place', and not against the corporate person itself or the officers of the corporation.[47] The court doubted that any tort action associated with distress, such as replevin, could be brought directly against a corporation, though distress could be levied indirectly by action against the corporation's bailiff or agent, who might then seek indemnity or contribution.

VIII. Modern Cases on Ultra Vires

The formative modern case resolving the capacity for direct corporate tort liability was *Yarborough v Governors of Bank of England*, decided in 1812.[48] The case involved a negligent payment of stolen promissory notes, where the defendant tried to void the notes by ascribing the payor's negligence to the Bank of England. Lord Ellenborough stated:

> [T]he only question was whether an action of trover is maintainable against a body corporate; in other words, whether a corporation can be guilty of a trespass or a tort. As a corporation, they can do no act, not even affix their corporate seal to a deed, but through the instrumentality and agency of others: they cannot, as a corporation, be subject to a capias or exigent, (the process in trespass,) because the remedies which attach upon living persons cannot be applied to bodies merely politic and of an impersonal nature. But wherever they can competently do or order any act to be done on their behalf, which as by their common seal they may do, they are liable to the consequences of such act, if it be of a tortious nature and to the prejudice of others.[49]

Lord Ellenborough found many analogies in the law permitting him to attach corporations for wrongs. There were countless *mandamus* writs for false entries involving malice brought against municipal corporations, and also many counts of novel disseisin and nuisance, especially for blocking of commons. Old authority held that written instructions by the directors to commit a tort would bind the corporation, even in the absence of authorisation by common seal. The judges were unsure on this point in *R v Bigg*,[50] a 1717 case where an agent of the Bank of England had erased a receipt on a bank note using lemon juice and then fraudulently indorsed a substitute payee. If he lacked authority so to handle notes then his erasure and endorsement would be his own unauthorised act and be classed as forging and uttering, a capital felony; but if he had an implicit authority so to endorse then it would have become a fraudulent exercise of a valid power. The common law judges assembled at Serjeants' Inn to settle this important point of law, but divided on the authority question and ultimately entered a felony conviction, with a stay of execution and pardon entered on condition that Bigg

[47] *R v Mayor of London* (1691) Shower KB 274, 89 ER 569; affirmed in *Whitfield v South Eastern Railway Company* (1858) Ellis, Blackburn and Ellis 115, 120 ER 451 (QB) (*Whitfield*), a case of commercial libel against a bank.

[48] *Yarborough v Governors of Bank of England* (1812) 16 East 6, 104 ER 991 (KB).

[49] ibid 6–7, 991–92.

[50] *R v Bigg* (1717) 3 Peere Williams 419, 24 ER 1127; cf report *sub nom Dominus Rex v Bigg* (1716) 1 Strange 18, 35 ER 357.

voluntarily transport himself to Minorca. The discretionary sanction well matched the indecisive trial.

The reporter Peere Williams in the *Bigg* case was careful to note extensive arguments that a corporation aggregate could impliedly authorise its agents to act in the normal or incidental course of business, and commit torts in so doing as corporate agents, without necessarily acting under common seal or by written authority. But many of the judges agreed with the prosecution that actions putting a corporation's finances at risk required a common seal, or else were ultra vires and nullities *qua* corporate acts, and hence would fall to be characterised as a forgery by the individual. The same issue arose with some poignancy a century later in the sensational 1824 trial of Henry Fauntelroy. A flamboyant financier, he had made fraudulent transfers of trust beneficial interests and Bank of England notes in a desperate attempt to shore up a failing bank of which he was the active partner. He claimed his acts were within his ministerial powers and hence were valid if fraudulent and voidable acts; but the jury at the Old Bailey found him guilty of unauthorised acts falling within the definition of forgery.[51] The legal point continued to be debated in two further assemblies of the judges, but the forger was executed before the judges could reach a final decision. It was striking that the judges were being asked to decide whether the imprecise doctrine of corporate ultra vires should cost a man his life. Fauntelroy turned out to be the last man executed for forgery in England, and perhaps the harshness of his fate, and recoil at the legal imprecision of his trial, saved the lives of later fraudsters.

IX. Scope of Authority and Ultra Vires

Much nineteenth-century litigation concerned the methods of attribution of agents' or employees' actions to a corporation through the doctrine of vicarious liability, and here the questions concerned the scope of authority of the agent and whether the act in question was an organic act of the corporation, a vicarious act of the individual within his or her authority though committed tortiously, or a wholly unauthorised and independent action where the tort liability lay solely on the individual. Only rarely did the courts isolate the possibility of an ultra vires act that might yet be ascribed to the corporation as a tort, as this anomaly could usually be solved by holding the tortious conduct to be an independent and unauthorised act.

An example of this blurring of ultra vires with scope of authority questions was found in a string of cases concerning utilities in the early railway age. It was decided that authority to act on behalf of a corporation could be implied without formal writing, for example to distrain and collect tolls, fees and rent, where the authority implied did not vest a positive contractual authority to bind the company and did not commit its finances. In 1834, trover was successfully brought to recover the value of household furniture wrongfully distrained by a gas utility. The company, by receiving the proceeds from its agent, was held to have ratified his authority and conduct, and so made itself

[51] *Case of Henry Fauntelroy*, Proceedings of the Old Bailey, 28 October 1824, at www.oldbaileyonline.org, reference t18241028-97. I am grateful to James Edelman for alerting me to this case.

liable for the tort retrospectively.[52] In a case of 1842, the collection of rents and tolls, albeit wrongful, was said to fall within the ordinary authority of a corporate agent and so tort liability could attach to the corporation without receipt or ratification.[53]

In the important case of *R v Birmingham and Gloucester Railway Company* (1840–42),[54] a railway company was indicted for public nuisance for failing to build an adequate road and bridges to alleviate interruptions caused by its construction activities. The company was authorised by statute to acquire the land necessary to build the necessary road, but the power of acquisition had lapsed due to the company's delay. Chief Justice Denman rejected the railway company's defence that its power to remedy the default had lapsed; it remained liable as it was its own fault that the necessary statutory power was no longer available. On a further demurrer the court acknowledged the difficulties in indicting the company either through its membership or through an attorney appearing in court, but held that a distress infinite against its goods could serve as a surrogate. Justice Patteson held that despite doubts from Holt CJ in 1701,[55] there were many modern cases 'which shew that a corporation may be indicted for breach of a duty imposed upon it by law, though not for a felony, or for crimes involving personal violence, as for riots or assaults'.[56] The fact that the corporate person could not be imprisoned or arraigned for contempt was no stop on an indictment; *certiorari* could be used to remove the case to Queen's Bench, where a suitable remedy could be devised.

Once this pragmatic approach had been established in the 1840s, corporate liability for civil wrongs burgeoned, and came to embrace torts with a mental element, including malicious prosecution,[57] malicious libel[58] and false imprisonment, provided the agent or employee could be fixed with authority to act in the ordinary course of business for the corporation, as with railway employees at a station who could be taken to have authority to enforce fares.[59] The settled doctrine was stated as follows by Erle J in *Green v The London General Omnibus Company*:

> The whole course of the authorities ... shews that an action for a wrong will lie against a corporation, where the thing that is complained of is a thing done within the scope of their incorporation, and is one which would constitute an actionable wrong if committed by an individual.[60]

[52] *Smith v Birmingham and Staffordshire Gas Light Company* (1834) 1 Adolphus and Ellis 526, 110 ER 1309 (KB).

[53] *Maund v Monmouthshire Canal Company* (1842) Manning and Granger 452, 134 ER 186 (CP).

[54] *R v Birmingham and Gloucester Railway Company* (1840) 9 Carrington and Payne 469, 173 ER 915, (1841) 2 QB 47, 114 ER 21, (1842) 3 QB 223, 114 ER 492.

[55] *Anonymous* (1701) 12 Modern 559, 88 ER 1518 (KB): 'A corporation is not indictable, but the particular members of it are.'

[56] *R v Birmingham and Gloucester Railway Company* (1842) 3 QB 223, 232, 114 ER 492, 496.

[57] *Whitfield* (n 47); *Abrath v North Eastern Railway Co* (1886) 11 App Cas 247; *Cornford v Carlton Bank Ltd* [1899] 1 QB 392.

[58] *Citizens' Life Assurance Company, Limited v Brown* [1904] AC 423 (PC).

[59] *Goff v Great Northern Railway Company* (1861) 3 Ellis and Ellis 672, 121 ER 594 (QB), extensively reviewing the authorities.

[60] *Green v The London General Omnibus Company* (1859) 7 CBNS 290, 141 ER 828 (CP). Instances of this doctrinal approach can be multiplied, as with *Limpus v London General Omnibus Company* (1861) 2 Foster and Finlason 640, 175 ER 1221 (Ex, Ass), (1862) 1 Hurlstone and Coltman 526, 158 ER 993 (Ex); *Seymour v Greenwood* (1861) 6 Hurlstone and Norman 359, 158 ER 148, 7 Hurlstone and Norman 355, 158 ER 511 (Ex).

But what if the agent acted in a manner outside the power of the corporation yet within his apparent or ordinary authority? In the 1867 case of *Poulton v The London and South Western Railway Company*,[61] in the Court of Queen's Bench, a stationmaster arrested a man transporting a horse by rail on suspicion of his not having paid carriage, but the company he worked for had a statutory authority only to arrest a passenger for fare evasion, not for failing to pay for carriage of goods. Justice Blackburn held that ultra vires protected the company:

> In the present case an act was done by the station master completely out of the scope of his authority, which there can be no possible ground for supposing the railway company authorized him to do, and a thing which could never be right on the part of the company to do. *Having no power themselves, they cannot give the station master any power, to do the act.* Therefore the wrongful imprisonment is an act for which the plaintiff, if he has a remedy at all, has it against the station master personally, but not against the railway company.[62]

Justice Mellor expanded the point as follows:

> I think the distinction is clear; it limits the scope of authority, to be implied from the fact of being the station master, to such acts as the company could do themselves, and I cannot think it ever can be implied that the company authorized the station master to do that which they have no authority to do themselves: and that seems to me to be the boundary line … If the station master had made a mistake in committing an act which he was authorized to do, I think in that case the company would be liable, because it would be supposed to be done by their authority. Where the station master acts in a manner in which the company themselves would not be authorized to act, and under a mistake or misapprehension of what the law is, then I think the rule is very different; and I think that is the distinction on which the whole matter turns.[63]

Justice Shee added:

> [A]n authority cannot be implied to have been given to a servant to do an act, which, if his master were on the spot, the master would not be justified in doing, on the assumption of a particular state of facts. It is clear, from the construction of [the statute], that the company had no power to arrest this passenger because he had not paid the price for the carriage of his horse.[64]

The Court of Exchequer pursued this line of reasoning in the 1874 case of *Mill v Hawker*.[65] However, here the court split, with Kelly CB dissenting sharply (and note that it was rare for puisne justices to form a majority against the chief justice of a common law court in this time). The facts were that a highway board wrongly believed that there was a public right of way across the plaintiff's land; and after making an order for locks to be removed from an obstructing gate, it gave a written authority for the board's surveyor to remove the lock forcibly. There was no public right of way and the landowner sued the corporation's clerk and surveyor for trespass on the land and damage to property. A nonsuit was brought on the basis that this was a corporate not an

[61] *Poulton v The London and South Western Railway Company* (1866–67) LR 2 QB 534.
[62] ibid 540 (emphasis added).
[63] ibid 540–41.
[64] ibid 541.
[65] *Mill v Hawker* (1874) LR 9 Exch 309.

individual act. Baron Cleasby, with Pigott B concurring, found that there could be no such tortious corporate act displacing individual liability, and so a trial of the employees could be ordered:

> But it is equally clear that when the acts are such as the corporate body is not by law qualified to do, and the corporate body, if they pretend to do them, are acting ultra vires, then the mere fact of giving a corporate form to the act does not prevent it from being the act of those who cause it to be done. It seems plain that in such a case the individuals and not the corporation really do the act, and no authority is needed for that conclusion.[66]

Corporate employees, especially employees of public corporations, simply had to accept some individual risk of ultra vires-based liability, trusting to the good sense and proper legal advice of their corporate employer when acting. Moreover, it was said to be incorrect on policy grounds for the courts to permit or require public corporations to pay out taxpayers' money for wrongful ultra vires actions:

> The effect of holding that such a body as the highway board were competent in their corporate capacity to commit such an act of trespass as the one complained of in this case, would be that, whenever the trespass was illegal and redress was had, the persons who had really caused the trespass would not be responsible, and the damages would be paid out of funds which ought to be applied in maintaining the roads, and the persons eventually responsible would be the ratepayers, and among them, perhaps, the persons entitled to redress, and to whom the damages were to be paid. And thus the members of the highway board would acquire a power to divert and waste the funds intrusted to them for public purposes by proceedings which might originate in feelings which it would be most inconvenient to inquire into.[67]

Chief Baron Kelly, in a lengthy and reasoned dissent, held that the corporation or its board could be liable for a tort and not the employees who carried it out. First, he held that the separate corporate personality walled off the members of the highway board from individual personal liability; for this no mention of limited liability was necessary, but simply a theory of primary or organic attribution:

> I conceive it to be settled law that no action lies against the individual members of a corporation for a corporate act done by the corporation in its corporate capacity, unless the act be maliciously done by the individuals charged, and the corporate name be used as a mere colour for the malicious act, or unless the act is *ultra vires*, and is not, and cannot be in contemplation of law, a corporate act at all.[68]

Next, he held that an illegal and tortious act authorised by a corporation could arouse corporate liability, and that the ultra vires doctrine could be separated from the question of due authority in most cases of corporate wrongdoing:

> It was, indeed, once imagined, though on very technical grounds, that trespass would not lie against a corporation, and it is so stated in Comyns' Digest, Franchises, F. (19.). But, besides that many authorities are to be found in the year books to the contrary, the law is now well settled that upon any tortious act committed by a corporation, or under its authority, or by its direction, trover or trespass is maintainable … It was never suggested that … the action should have been brought against the individuals who happened to be present when the act

[66] ibid 317.
[67] ibid 319.
[68] ibid 321.

> in question was ordered to be done. I cannot doubt, therefore, that this action ought to have been brought against the board, and all these decisions are uniform to shew that it would have been maintainable. The mischief and inconvenience that would result if the contrary were held to be law is great and obvious. If judgment be recovered against these [employees] execution might issue for the whole amount of damages and costs against any one among them, and he would have no remedy for contribution against the rest, nor as it should seem, upon the facts of the case, for indemnity against the corporation. And it is at least doubtful whether the board would have a legal right to indemnify him out of the funds which come to their hands under the Act of Parliament. On the other hand, if the action had been brought against the board, and judgment obtained against them, they may pay the damages and costs out of the funds which they are enabled to provide for the various purposes of the Act …
>
> It was argued that no action could be maintained against the board on the ground that the resolution and the order to the surveyor were *ultra vires*. But I apprehend that this is a misapplication of the term *ultra vires*. If the board, by resolution or otherwise, had accepted a bill of exchange directing their clerk or other officer to write their corporate name or title across a bill drawn upon them for a debt, this would have been *ultra vires*, and no holder of the acceptance could have recovered the amount against them. It would have been void upon the face of it, and it is immaterial to consider whether the individuals who had written or authorized the acceptance would have been liable to any, and, if any, to what action at the suit of a holder for value. But it is otherwise with an act merely unlawful or unauthorized, as a trespass or the conversion of a chattel. If such an act is to be deemed *ultra vires*, and therefore no action would lie against the corporate body by whom it had been authorized, it is clear that a corporation would not be liable for any tort at all committed or authorized by them, and the decisions above cited would be contrary to law. … Poulton v London and South Western Ry Co merely shews that there is no implied authority by a railway company to their servants to do an illegal act. Here no question arises upon an implied authority, for this board have expressly authorized and commanded the surveyor to do the act complained of.[69]

Following the Chief Baron's dissent, the case was reviewed in the Court of Exchequer Chamber before six common law judges of Queen's Bench and Common Pleas.[70] Justice Blackburn led the court in holding that the servants in obeying an order that was ultra vires could not escape personal liability, and so supported the Exchequer Court majority on that point, but he also expressly refused to decide the point of whether the corporation or its board could be jointly or severally liable for authorising a tortious act ultra vires. The opinion of Cleasby B finding no corporate liability was left untouched and the question of principle evaded, precisely because it was 'one of considerable importance and great difficulty. If it were necessary to decide that question, we should require time for consideration, and possibly, when we had considered it, our decision would not be unanimous.'

Justice Blackburn's trepidation may have been exacerbated by the important decision made some seven months earlier by the Exchequer Chamber in *Riche v Ashbury Railway Carriage and Iron Co Ltd*.[71] Here the review court had split 3:3 on the question of whether a company could ratify an ultra vires act, with Blackburn J holding that it could; only four months later the House of Lords had overturned that conclusion and

[69] ibid 322–24. A similar argument against scapegoating of individual employees for corporate acts is suggested in Derrington and Walpole, ch 16 of this volume.

[70] *Mill v Hawker* (1875) LR 10 Exch 92.

[71] *Riche v Ashbury* (n 21).

insisted that the corporate objects irrevocably bound the company and voided its ultra vires acts.[72] The community of common law judges, then at their zenith of confidence and prestige, clearly found the doctrine of ultra vires flummoxing. But after exciting so much controversy, the problem faded from view. After *Poulton*, it does not seem that the tort aspects of ultra vires rule were ever litigated afterwards in a significant case, and with the intensification of vicarious liability for corporations the problem of ultra vires became moot. Salmond's conclusion that the corporation was really being attached for failures to monitor agents and prevent breach of duties, as evoked in his writings after 1913, might seem to have provided an exit.[73]

X. A Revival of Corporate Purposes Doctrine?

The historian of laws past sometimes stops to look to the history of the present, and even peer into the future. We live in an age of economic fragility, with financialisation and globalisation constantly disrupting collective economic life. Companies are no longer integrated command mechanisms with a clearly delineated hierarchy of control, but are rather a set of inputs and outputs elongated across chains of supply, arrayed into shifting form by digital communication, so abandoning the Coasean administrative theory of the firm.[74] The concept of a corporate employee and a corporate employer in a stable contractual and status relationship has become thoroughly contested legal terrain.[75] The amoral pursuit of profit by corporations with revolving management and shareholders pursuing short-term returns has been linked to environmental and social degradation across the globe. The popularity of Corporate Social Responsibility and Anti-Modern Slavery charters and Environmental, Social and Governance commitments speaks to a deep unease in the turn of the corporate economy. Scholars now speak of reviving the concept of corporate purpose and placing the idea of community-mandated and limited powers at the centre of a reconfigured corporate economy.[76] The nineteenth- and twentieth-century interaction of tort and ultra vires doctrine might have valuable lessons to teach as to how potent and disruptive collective enterprises can best be led to internalise risk and be held to account for the true social costs of their activities. We may continually pursue purposes as individuals and groups, but setting legal effect to those purposes is hardly simple.

[72] *Ashbury* (n 21).
[73] See text accompanying nn 9–13.
[74] LE Ribstein, *The Rise of the Uncorporation* (Oxford, Oxford University Press, 2009).
[75] *Uber BV v Aslam* [2021] UKSC 5, [2021] ICR 657; J Adams-Prassl, *The Concept of the Employer* (Oxford, Oxford University Press, 2015).
[76] See, eg, C Mayer, 'The Future of the Corporation and the Economics of Purpose' (2021) 58 *Journal of Management Studies* 887; cf EB Rock, 'For Whom is the Corporation Managed in 2020?: The Debate over Corporate Purpose' (2021) 76 *The Business Lawyer* 364.

5

The Corporate Culpability of Big Tech

JULIA POWLES*

I. Big Tech's Small Liabilities

Big Tech's legal liabilities have been, to date, small fry. Market leaders Google/Alphabet, Apple, Microsoft, Amazon, Facebook/Meta, Tencent and Alibaba, along with market makers such as Uber and Airbnb, all covet what is known in the industry as 'blitzscaling'[1] – the prioritisation of speed and scale of growth over everything else.[2] It is a paradigmatically reckless approach, immortalised in the early Facebook slogan 'move fast and break things',[3] and is often accompanied by a practice of barrelling apologism for everything and everyone harmed along the way,[4] inspired by the adage that 'it is easier to ask for forgiveness than to beg for permission'. Blitzscaling is a business strategy that aims for rapid and total market domination. Structurally, it has been underpinned by unprecedented investments from venture capital firms seeking 'unicorns',[5] particularly during the lengthy period of historically low interest rates since

* The author would like to thank Elise Bant and Maria Farrell for their helpful and inspiring comments, as well as Tom Loss and Heather Delfs for invaluable research assistance. This work forms part of the author's 'Big Tech Culpability' research programme at UWA Law School's Minderoo Tech & Policy Lab, which is generously supported by a donation from Frontier Technology, a Minderoo Foundation Initiative.

[1] R Hoffman and C Yeh, *Blitzscaling: The Lightning-Fast Path to Building Massively Valuable Companies* (London, HarperCollins, 2018). Recognising that Facebook sought to rebrand to Meta in 2021, its original name will be used for familiarity.

[2] M Whittaker, 'The Steep Cost of Capture' (2021) 28 *Association for Computing Machinery: Interactions* 50.

[3] S Frenkel and C King, *An Ugly Truth: Inside Facebook's Battle for Domination* (London, HarperCollins, 2021); R McNamee, *Zucked: Waking Up to the Facebook Catastrophe* (London, Penguin Press, 2019); I Hamilton, 'Mark Zuckerberg's New Values for Meta Show He Still Hasn't Let Go of "Move Fast and Break Things"' *Business Insider* (17 February 2022) at www.businessinsider.com/meta-mark-zuckerberg-new-values-move-fast-and-break-things-2022-2.

[4] K Hall, 'Public Penitence: Facebook and the Performance of Apology' (2020) 6 *Social Media + Society* 1; N Proferes, 'The Many Mea Culpas of Mark Zuckerberg' *Slate* (22 March 2018) at https://slate.com/technology/2018/03/mark-zuckerbergs-long-history-of-mea-culpas.html; AL Hoffman, 'Reckoning with a Decade of Breaking Things' *Model View Culture* (30 June 2014) at https://modelviewculture.com/pieces/reckoning-with-a-decade-of-breaking-things; Tech Transparency Project, 'Broken Promises' at https://brokenpromises.tech (last accessed 1 August 2022); J Constantine, 'Tech Giants Offer Empty Apologies Because Users Can't Quit' *TechCrunch* (26 November 2018) at https://techcrunch.com/2018/11/25/nowhere-to-go/.

[5] 'Unicorns' are companies valued at over US $1 billion. The term was coined by American VC investor Aileen Lee: A Lee, 'Welcome to the Unicorn Club: Learning From Billion-Dollar Startups' *TechCrunch* (3 November 2013) at https://techcrunch.com/2013/11/02/welcome-to-the-unicorn-club/.

the 2007–08 global financial crisis.[6] The approach has been tremendously profitable, generating the most valuable and powerful companies the world has ever seen;[7] their ascendance untroubled by the constancy of controversy, the occasional penalty, and the disgruntlement of workers and citizens.

To the extent these firms have been liable for misconduct, it has been a rap on the knuckles in confined, carefully domesticated areas – principally in privacy and data protection law, along with a sprinkling of action in competition law (antitrust), consumer law and employment law. The sheer wealth of these companies means that financial penalties as a result of misconduct are readily absorbed as the cost of doing business, especially when the numbers that matter – stock prices and 'user'[8] numbers – stay resolutely sky high, if not growing.

This chapter's overall thesis is that Big Tech's small liabilities are a paradox, given the track records of these firms, in terms both of the business they are engaged in as well as *how* they do business. The grouping 'Big Tech' unifies a group of firms offering technology-based products and services that leverage network effects and are adopted by millions or billions of people, in exchange for money, behavioural surveillance or, increasingly, both.[9] The scale of these firms is a reflection of the success of these products and services. But their commonality goes further, and also extends to *how* these firms and their associated products and services operate. Each of these firms enables practices and conditions that – for a significant number of individuals who either use them or support them (as employees, suppliers, contractors or third parties) – can be discriminatory,[10] extractive,[11]

[6] S Mallaby, *The Power Law: Venture Capital and the Art of Disruption* (London, Allen Lane, 2022).

[7] F Manjoo, 'The Rise of Big Tech May Just Be Starting' *New York Times* (16 February 2022) at www.nytimes.com/2022/02/16/opinion/big-tech-stock-market.html; M Moore and D Tambini (eds), *Digital Dominance: The Power of Google, Amazon, Facebook, and Apple* (Oxford, Oxford University Press, 2018).

[8] J McNeil, *Lurking: How a Person Became a User* (New York, MacMillan, 2020).

[9] S Zuboff, *The Age of Surveillance Capitalism: The Fight for the Future at the New Frontier of Power* (London, Profile Books, 2019); N Couldry and UA Mejias, *The Costs of Connection: How Data is Colonizing Human Life and Appropriating it for Capitalism* (Redwood City, CA, Stanford University Press, 2019); M Crain, *Profit over Privacy: How Surveillance Advertising Conquered the Internet* (Minneapolis, MN, University of Minnesota Press, 2021).

[10] SU Noble, *Algorithms of Oppression: How Search Engines Reinforce Racism* (Manhattan, NY, New York University Press, 2018); R Benjamin, *Race After Technology: Abolitionist Tools for the New Jim Code* (Cambridge, Polity, 2019); S Fowler, *Whistleblower: My Journey to Silicon Valley and Fight for Justice at Uber* (London, Penguin Books, 2020); B Edelman, M Luca and D Svirsky, 'Racial Discrimination in the Sharing Economy: Evidence from a Field Experiment' (2017) 9 *American Economic Journal: Applied Economics* 1; M Dickey, 'How Airbnb Handles Discrimination Claims' *TechCrunch* (20 November 2019) at https://techcrunch.com/2019/11/19/how-airbnb-handles-discrimination-claims/; Human Rights Watch, '"Only Men Need Apply": Gender Discrimination in Job Advertisements in China' (23 April 2018) at www.hrw.org/report/2018/04/23/only-men-need-apply/gender-discrimination-job-advertisements-china; C Gilliard, 'Caught in the Spotlight' *Urban Omnibus* (9 January 2020) at https://urbanomnibus.net/2020/01/caught-in-the-spotlight/.

[11] C Kirkham and J Dastin, 'A Look at the Intimate Details Amazon Knows About Us' *Reuters* (20 November 2021) at www.reuters.com/technology/look-intimate-details-amazon-knows-about-us-2021-11-19/; Y Eisenstat 'I Worked on Political Ads at Facebook: They Profit by Manipulating Us' *Washington Post* (4 November 2019) at www.washingtonpost.com/outlook/2019/11/04/i-worked-political-ads-facebook-they-profit-by-manipulating-us/; JC Wong, 'Revealed: The Facebook Loophole That Lets World Leaders Deceive and Harass Their Citizens' *The Guardian* (12 April 2021) at www.theguardian.com/technology/2021/apr/12/facebook-loophole-state-backed-manipulation.

abusive,[12] unsafe[13] and, in some cases, deadly.[14] The collective experience of the tech sector is that these practices have accompanied commercial success, not abated it.

How Big Tech firms operate, and the impact of their conduct on the fabric of private and public life, has been the subject of significant media and academic discourse, but has not yet been addressed through substantial legal liabilities. Instead, it is often observed that the sheer power of these firms facilitates their operation with relative impunity from nation states, laws and institutions.

The vacuum around Big Tech's legal liabilities has persisted despite evidence that they cause, and have caused over decades, individual and collective harm, including psychological illness,[15] body dysmorphia and eating disorders,[16] sexual violence,[17] human trafficking,[18]

[12] A Stewart, '"They Are Untouchable": Microsoft Employees Say "Golden Boy" Executives are Still Running Wild, 8 Years After the Company Vowed to Clean Up Its Toxic Culture' *Business Insider* (26 May 2022) at www.businessinsider.com/microsoft-toxic-culture-ceo-satya-nadella-sexual-harassment-pay-disparity-2022-5; N Martin, 'Image-Based Sexual Abuse and Deepfakes: A Survivor Turned Activist's Perspective' in A Powell, A Flynn and L Sugiura (eds), *The Palgrave Handbook of Gendered Violence and Technology* (London, Palgrave Macmillan, 2021) 55.

[13] J Murdoch, 'Apple: Human Rights Violations in Supply Chain Double in a Year, Report Reveals' *Newsweek* (3 August 2018) at www.newsweek.com/apple-human-rights-violations-supply-chain-double-year-reports-reveals-836247; J Nicas, R Zhong and D Wakabayashi, 'Censorship, Surveillance and Profits: A Hard Bargain for Apple in China' *New York Times* (17 May 2021) at www.nytimes.com/2021/05/17/technology/apple-china-censorship-data.html; M McHugh, 'Uber and Lyft Drivers Work Dangerous Jobs – But They're On Their Own' *Wired* (10 March 2016) at www.wired.com/2016/03/uber-lyft-can-much-keep-drivers-safe/; E Bartel et al, 'Stressful By Design: Exploring Health Risks of Ride-Share Work' (2019) 14 *Journal of Transport & Health* 100571; A Betts, 'Women Who Drive For Uber and Lyft Are Being Left to Fend For Themselves' *The Verge* (18 January 2022) at www.theverge.com/2022/1/18/22878214/uber-lyft-women-drivers-sexual-assault-harassment-safety.

[14] D Wakabayashi, 'Self-Driving Uber Car Kills Pedestrian in Arizona, Where Robots Roam' *New York Times* (19 March 2018) at www.nytimes.com/2018/03/19/technology/uber-driverless-fatality.html; J Whitten-Woodring et al, 'Poison If You Don't Know How to Use It: Facebook, Democracy, and Human Rights in Myanmar' (2020) 25 *The International Journal of Press/Politics* 407; M O'Brien and J Powles, 'Facebook's Meta Complicity in the Rohingya Genocide' *ABC Religion & Ethics* (2 February 2022) at www.abc.net.au/religion/facebook-complicity-in-the-rohingya-genocide/13737882; S Murphy, 'Their Teenage Children Died By Suicide. Now These Families Want to Hold Social Media Companies Accountable' *CNN* (19 April 2022) at https://edition.cnn.com/2022/04/19/tech/social-media-lawsuits-teen-suicide/index.html.

[15] ST Roberts, *Behind the Screen: Content Moderation in the Shadows of Social Media* (New Haven, CT, Yale University Press, 2019); S Levin, 'Moderators Who Had to View Child Abuse Content Sue Microsoft, Claiming PTSD' *The Guardian* (12 January 2017) at www.theguardian.com/technology/2017/jan/11/microsoft-employees-child-abuse-lawsuit-ptsd; 'Facebook to Pay $52m to Content Moderators Over PTSD' *BBC News* (13 May 2020) at www.bbc.com/news/technology-52642633; D Wiessner 'Judge Oks $85 Mln Settlement of Facebook Moderators' PTSD Claims' *Reuters* (23 July 2021) at www.reuters.com/legal/transactional/judge-oks-85-mln-settlement-facebook-moderators-ptsd-claims-2021-07-23/; D Wiessner, 'YouTube Settles Moderators' Case Over Graphic Videos for $4.3 Mln' *Reuters* (14 July 2022) at www.reuters.com/legal/transactional/youtube-settles-moderators-case-over-graphic-videos-43-mln-2022-07-13/.

[16] G Wells, J Horwitz and D Seetharaman, 'Facebook Knows Instagram is Toxic for Teenage Girls, Company Documents Show' *Wall Street Journal* (14 September 2021) at www.wsj.com/articles/facebook-knows-instagram-is-toxic-for-teen-girls-company-documents-show-11631620739.

[17] See n 12.

[18] S Sakar, 'Use of Technology in Human Trafficking Networks and Sexual Exploitation: A Cross-Sectional Multi-Country Study' (2015) 5 *Transnational Social Review* 62; O Pinnell and J Kelly, 'Slave Markets Found on Instagram and Other Apps' *BBC News* (31 October 2019) at www.bbc.com/news/technology-50228549; Polaris, 'On-Ramps, Intersections, and Exit Routes: A Roadmap for Systems and Industries to Prevent and Disrupt Human Trafficking' (July 2018) at https://polarisproject.org/wp-content/uploads/2018/08/A-Roadmap-for-Systems-and-Industries-to-Prevent-and-Disrupt-Human-Trafficking-Social-Media.pdf; J Scheck, N Purnell and J Horwitz, 'Facebook Employees Flag Drug Cartels and Human Traffickers.

hate speech,[19] fraud,[20] mis/disinformation,[21] legal and regulatory evasion,[22] political insurrection[23] and genocide,[24] all untrammelled by effective accountability. Recognising this, the chapter proposes a corrective, relying on 'systems intentionality': a model for determining organisational culpability developed by professor of private and commercial law Elise Bant,[25] including in collaboration with fellow law professor Jeannie Marie Paterson,[26] and extended in important ways in the present volume.

The core idea of systems intentionality is that firms' intentions and purposes are manifest in their systems, policies and practices. In other words, the way that we can 'know' a corporate mind is through the systems it puts in place. This clarion insight is highly generative for examining Big Tech's unchecked corporate culpability. But it has a pay-off that is larger still. Both as an overall model approach and in its component parts ('systems' and 'intentionality'), systems intentionality illuminates crucial missing pieces in the story to date of Big Tech's legal liabilities, and offers promising mechanisms to enable redress.

Systems intentionality complements the standard position that, in order to demonstrate corporate misconduct, it is generally necessary to establish misconduct by the individual directors or senior executives that constitute a company's 'directing mind and will'.[27] Recognising the reality of modern corporations, in which responsibility

The Company's Response Is Weak, Documents Show' *Wall Street Journal* (16 September 2021) at www.wsj.com/articles/facebook-drug-cartels-human-traffickers-response-is-weak-documents-11631812953.

[19] Global Witness, 'Facebook Approves Adverts Containing Hate Speech Inciting Violence and Genocide Against the Rohingya' (20 March 2022) at www.globalwitness.org/en/campaigns/digital-threats/rohingya-facebook-hate-speech/; Global Witness, '"Now is the Time to Kill": Facebook Continues to Approve Hate Speech Inciting Violence and Genocide during Civil War in Ethiopia' (9 June 2022) at www.globalwitness.org/en/campaigns/digital-threats/ethiopia-hate-speech/.

[20] C Silverman, 'How a Massive Facebook Scam Siphoned Millions of Dollars From Unsuspecting Boomers' *Buzzfeed News* (16 October 2019) at www.buzzfeednews.com/article/craigsilverman/facebook-subscription-trap-free-trial-scam-ads-inc; R Trigger and A Pancia, 'Scam Using Fake ABC News Stories About Andrew Forrest Sees Woman Fleeced of $670,000' *ABC News* (19 September 2019) at www.abc.net.au/news/2019-09-19/woman-loses-$670000-to-andrew-forrest-abc-news- scam/11529654; Meta, 'Addressing Deceptive Advertising Practices' (9 April 2020) at https://about.fb.com/news/2020/04/addressing-deceptive-ad-practices/ (last accessed 30 August 2022); E Fletcher, 'Reports Show Scammers Cashing in on Crypto Craze' *Federal Trade Commission* (3 June 2022) at www.ftc.gov/news-events/data-visualizations/data-spotlight/2022/06/reports-show-scammers-cashing-crypto-craze; A Chow, 'Here's How Shopping Scams on Facebook Are Ripping Off Thousands of Customers, With the Money Flowing Overseas' *Time* (18 December 2020) at https://time.com/5921820/facebook-shopping-scams-holidays-covid-19.

[21] Frenkel and King (n 3); J Donovan, 'Social-Media Companies Must Flatten the Curve of Misinformation' *Nature* (14 April 2020) at www.nature.com/articles/d41586-020-01107-z; I Hassan, 'Disinformation Is Undermining Democracy in West Africa' *Centre for International Governance Innovations Online* (4 July 2022) at www.cigionline.org/articles/disinformation-is-undermining-democracy-in-west-africa/; K Hao, 'How Facebook Got Addicted to Spreading Misinformation' *MIT Technology Review* (11 March 2021) at www.technologyreview.com/2021/03/11/1020600/facebook-responsible-ai-misinformation.

[22] Discussed in section II of this chapter.

[23] McNamee (n 3); S Vaidhyanathan, *Antisocial Media: How Facebook Disconnects Us and Undermines Democracy* (Oxford, Oxford University Press, 2018); Avaaz, 'Facebook: From Election to Insurrection – How Facebook Failed Voters and Nearly Set Democracy Aflame' (18 March 2021) at https://secure.avaaz.org/campaign/en/facebook_election_insurrection/.

[24] References in n 14.

[25] E Bant, 'Culpable Corporate Minds' (2021) 48 *University of Western Australia Law Review* 352.

[26] E Bant and JM Paterson, 'Systems of Misconduct: Corporate Culpability and Statutory Unconscionability' (2021) 15 *Journal of Equity* 63.

[27] *Lennard's Carrying Co Ltd v Asiatic Petroleum Co Ltd* [1915] AC 705 (HL) 713; *HL Boulton (Engineering) Co Ltd v TJ Graham and Sons Ltd* [1957] 1 QB 159, 172; *Tesco Supermarkets v Nattrass* [1972] AC 153 (HL) 170; expanded by *Meridian Global Funds Management Asia Ltd v Securities Commission* [1995] UKPC 26, [1995] 2 AC 500. See further Leow, ch 6 of this volume.

is diffused across many different people and divisions of what can be very large and complex organisations,[28] Bant argues persuasively that an exclusive focus on individual wrongdoing, in which a 'single human repository of fault' must be located,[29] provides an incomplete picture of organisational culpability. Drawing on a range of sources, from theorists of corporate behaviour to pioneering legal developments such as Australia's 'corporate culture' provisions,[30] Bant offers systems intentionality as a robust additional model for establishing distinctly *organisational* culpability.

The systems intentionality model involves assessing 'what a corporation routinely and systematically does, and what its systems are objectively apt to produce, to ascertain what it knows, intends or is reckless towards'.[31] This refreshingly direct focus on how companies actually operate on the ground powerfully augments existing legal understandings of the 'corporate mind'. As this volume attests, it is an approach specifically designed for 'massive, massively complex, multi- and trans-national corporate institutions that sit within a web of related entities'.[32] Further, it is especially well-suited to companies whose operations involve a combination of both automated and human systems,[33] as well as those engaged in systemic misconduct, such as through the use of exploitative business models and processes.[34] In short, it is a model extremely well primed for tackling the small liabilities of Big Tech, where all of these features are exemplified and magnified.

By training our attention on Big Tech's *systems*, we lay bare what is most galling about the behaviour of these firms: their routinised expectation – indeed, tolerance – of the systematic production of collateral damage, or negative externalities, as a necessary trade-off of their too-big-to-patrol products and services, their extractive business models, and their tireless hunt for scale and dominance.[35] At the same time, a focus on systems showcases these firms' highly predictable and inauthentic public-facing mechanism for responding to harm: maddening cycles of apology and promises to do better, followed by continued misconduct; a compound process characterised here as 'barrelling apologism'.[36] Less visibly, elaborate systems of jurisdictional and regulatory arbitrage bind these firms in tight layers of legal protection. Splintered across

[28] Bant and Paterson (n 26) 72–75; Bant, ch 9 of this volume.

[29] Bant (n 25) 358–60.

[30] In particular, see Criminal Code Act 1995 (Cth), s 12.3, as reviewed by the Australian Law Reform Commission, *Corporate Criminal Responsibility* (Discussion Paper No 87, November 2019), discussed in Bant (n 25) 369–74, 376–77, and Faugno, ch 8 of this volume.

[31] Bant (n 25) 383.

[32] Bant, ch 9 of this volume.

[33] Paterson and Bant, ch 12 of this volume; Willis, ch 19 of this volume; Diamantis, ch 10 of this volume. See also ME Diamantis, 'The Extended Corporate Mind: When Corporations Use AI to Break the Law' (2020) 98 *North Carolina Law Review* 89.

[34] Bant and Paterson (n 26) 79–89.

[35] Y Eisenstat and N Gilman, 'The Myth of Tech Exceptionalism' *Noema Magazine* (10 February 2022) at www.noemamag.com/the-myth-of-tech-exceptionalism/; E Morozov, *To Save Everything Click Here: The Folly of Technological Solutionism* (London, Allen Lane, 2013); Zuboff (n 9); Noble (n 10).

[36] References in n 4. See also D Lauer, 'Facebook's Ethical Failures are not Accidental; They are Part of the Business Model' (2021) 1 *AI Ethics* 395; JE Katsos and J Miklian, 'Overcoming Tech Exceptionalism: How to Improve Societal Impact by Technology Firms in Fragile and Conflict Settings' *Global Policy Journal* (9 January 2019) at www.globalpolicyjournal.com/blog/09/01/2019/overcoming-tech-exceptionalism-how-improve-societal-impact-technology-firms-fragile.

complex corporate groups,[37] crafted to both evade regulation and attract subsidies,[38] these firms evoke *sui generis* legal forms such as 'platforms',[39] and shield themselves with promises of 'disruption' and 'innovation',[40] all of which are tactics deliberately designed to evade effective regulation and oversight.[41]

Complementarily, the focus on *intentionality* allows us to unpick the conventional framing by which technology firms have been scrutinised, in particular through areas of law that are largely agnostic as to intent. Systems intentionality offers an essential tool that allows us to rip open the seams of these companies to identify new and creative avenues for potential liability. It is an approach that is so manifestly sensible that it seems obvious: at core, that a corporation's systems, policies and practices reveal corporate intent. Intent is not a relevant consideration in privacy and data protection law, by far the dominant prisms for seeking accountability in the tech sector. Nor does it feature in competition law protections against abuse of dominance, consumer law prohibitions on misleading and deceptive conduct (though intent comes into play regarding penalties), or in the machinations of employment law that lead to the classifications of different types of workers. As a result, there has been very little scrutiny of Big Tech's corporate behaviours and effects through conceptions of intent, knowledge, recklessness, dishonesty and unconscionability. A model to do so has great promise in bringing areas of law such as criminal law, tort, and a wider spectrum of equity and consumer law, firmly into view.

Engaging more deeply with causes of action in areas of law that place a spotlight on moral blameworthiness is likely to prove a productive and disarming counter-point to the tech industry's pivot to actively eliciting more regulation,[42] a move clearly conceived to reinforce familiar regulatory frames that the industry's lobbyists have successfully cabined through strong platform-level immunities and regulatory arbitrage. The beauty of the systems intentionality model is that it provides a means of naming even this

[37] A Hartmans and M Meisenzahl, 'All the Companies and Divisions under Google's Parent Company Alphabet, Which Just Made Yet Another Shakeup to its Structure' *Business Insider* (updated 12 February 2020) at www.businessinsider.com/alphabet-google-company-list-2017-4; S Bose, 'Facebook Acquisitions – The Complete List' *TechWyse* (updated 17 February 2022) at www.techwyse.com/blog/infographics/facebook-acquisitions-infographic/.

[38] ST Roberts, 'Section 230 As American Tech's "Soft Power" Secret Weapon' *Flow Journal* (28 November 2019) at www.flowjournal.org/2019/11/section-230-soft-power/; KP Thomas et al, 'Amazon.com's Hidden Worldwide Subsidies' *Good Jobs First and UNI Global Union* (January 2022) at https://uniglobalunion.org/wp-content/uploads/amazon_subsidies_final.pdf.

[39] T Gillespie, 'The Politics of 'Platforms'' (2010) 12 *New Media & Society* 347.

[40] S Leong, 'Prophets of Mass Innovation: The Gospel According to BAT' (2018) 5 *Media Industries* 69; A Daub, *What Tech Calls Thinking: An Inquiry into the Intellectual Bedrock of Silicon Valley* (New York, Farrar, Straus and Giroux, 2020).

[41] See generally, JE Cohen, *Between Truth and Power: The Legal Constructions of Informational Capitalism* (Oxford, Oxford University Press, 2019); M Moore and D Tambini (eds), *Regulating Big Tech: Policy Responses to Digital Dominance* (Oxford, Oxford University Press, 2022).

[42] See, eg, Meta, 'We Support Updated Regulations on the Internet's Most Pressing Challenges' at https://about.facebook.com/regulations/ (accessed 12 March 2022); M Zuckerberg, 'The Internet Needs New Rules: Let's Start in These Four Areas' *Washington Post* (30 March 2019) at www.washingtonpost.com/opinions/mark-zuckerberg-the-internet-needs-new-rules-lets-start-in-these-four-areas/2019/03/29/9e6f0504-521a-11e9-a3f7-78b7525a8d5f_story.html; C Duffy, 'Microsoft President Calls For Federal Regulation of Facial Recognition Technology' *CNN* (18 June 2020) at https://edition.cnn.com/2020/06/18/tech/brad-smith-microsoft-facial-recognition/index.html.

conduct as supporting a corporate strategy of prioritising profit over safety. Until now, tech firms have survived and thrived simply by weathering scandals through short-lived media and political cycles. Systems intentionality is a circuit breaker. It widens the aperture of enquiry, offering a means of harnessing and analysing a broad suite of conduct surrounding Big Tech's misbehaviour. It is an approach through which the accumulation of many consistent, repeated practices and patterns of behaviour can be sharpened into a persuasive assertion of culpability.

Big Tech will most likely defend, implicitly or explicitly, assertions founded on systems intentionality on two levels. At the macro level, tech firms consistently argue that they are exceptional because of their scale, reach, complexity and transformative effects, and so both cannot and should not be held culpable in the same way as companies in other industries.[43] At the micro level, they typically argue that publicly-known examples of harm are local or operational exceptions, and are merely the discrete and limited result of oversights, regrettable excesses and rapid scaling.[44] Additionally, their practice is to assert that any misbehaviour is contrary to internal policies, practices and organisational goals, and indeed to the desires and preferences of their well-intentioned leaders and employees.[45] In seeking to avoid the conclusion that these incidents are, in fact, the outward manifestations of core business strategy and both customary and prescribed systems, the playbook of Big Tech is to characterise misconduct as being perpetrated by rogue units or individual 'bad apples', who have now been removed or corrected.

Systems intentionality has responses equal to each of these assertions and defences. Take first the macro argument. While tech firms maintain an almost religious zeal about digitally engineering their products for universal application, this does not displace their exposure to liability nor the necessity for audit and remedial mechanisms where harm occurs. As Bant argues, the absence or ineffectiveness of these mechanisms demonstrates a reckless disregard for, if not an intention to produce, the inevitable harms.[46] This is mirrored at the micro level. If a system operates as it is designed to operate, a company cannot avail itself of the 'familiar exculpatory narrative of "systems errors"'.[47] Rather, under systems intentionality, the frequency and repetition of alleged errors, apologies and excuses only strengthens the case for culpability.[48]

Overall, systems intentionality ably rebuffs Big Tech's exceptionalism and its de-emphasising of the collateral damage occasioned by technology products and services while emphasising positive externalities. It blunts the instinct to isolate wrongdoing to discrete people or areas – misconduct must be dealt with, without pointing

[43] References in n 35.

[44] References in n 36.

[45] Eisenstat and Gilman (n 35).

[46] E Bant, 'Catching the Corporate Conscience: A New Model of "Systems Intentionality"' (2022) *Lloyd's Maritime and Commercial Law Quarterly* 467, 488–90 (addressing the example of 'fees for no services' systems adopted by financial services).

[47] Bant, ch 11 of this volume.

[48] Bant (n 46) 491: 'A corporation, like a natural person, may be honest with respect to some aspects of its activities and dishonest with respect to others. Where it is acting dishonestly, it cannot thereby avoid liability by pointing to other areas where it is compliant.' The Australian corporate culture provisions expressly recognise that culpable corporate culture may be relevantly found in part of a corporation: see further Faugno, 'Ideas of Corporate Culture', ch 8 of this volume.

elsewhere.[49] Finally, Bant is clear-eyed about the distinction between a corporation's formal policies and its customary or de facto policies, confirming that it is 'the latter that is of chief interest here from an analytical perspective'.[50] A corporation that reiterates its formal policies in spite of instantiated systems that run counter to those policies engages in misleading, and arguably deceptive, conduct.[51] In the Big Tech context, a good example is the appeal to consumers 'we care about your privacy', when it is quite clear that the de facto policies of all the tech firms involve the excessive, and only barely-authorised, surveillance, aggregation and use of personal information.

Section II characterises in broad strokes a number of key systems that underlie how Big Tech companies operate, marshalling two case studies to centre the analysis.[52] The first focuses on Uber, as the paradigm of a company that built its dominance on disregard for legal and regulatory systems, as well as the bodies of drivers and riders on which its business depends.[53] The second case study turns to Facebook, which is increasingly tarnished by its pursuit of profits while facilitating human trafficking, mis/disinformation, violence and scams.[54] These two companies are iconic flag-bearers for the way Big Tech has operated during the first two decades of the twenty-first century, along with the flagrant misconduct this has occasioned.

It is not necessary, nor is it the intent of this chapter, to prove that all Big Tech firms operate in the same fashion or carry the same specific liabilities. Rather, it is to demonstrate that Big Tech is a paragon of the problem that systems intentionality addresses – namely, the absence of a robust legal mechanism for responding to organisational blameworthiness – and that it is a sector apt for the model's solution of focusing on a company's systems, policies and practices as the manifestation of corporate intent and purpose. Most promisingly, the approach breaks essential new ground by enabling more explicit consideration of the connection between the harms occasioned by Big Tech and moral opprobrium,[55] especially through the prospect of securing criminal or tortious sanctions for particularly egregious harms – a surprisingly under-explored avenue in existing challenges to Big Tech's misconduct.[56]

The chapter concludes with some observations on practical challenges in holding Big Tech to account and identifies opportunities for future work in applying the model of systems intentionality, including issues surrounding licensure, causes of action, jurisdiction, institutional capacity, timing and defiant corporations.

[49] Bant, ch 1 of this volume; Bant (n 46) 491.

[50] Bant, ch 9 of this volume.

[51] ibid; Bant (n 46) 490–92.

[52] An exemplar case study focused on Google/Alphabet is provided in JM Paterson, E Bant and H Cooney, 'Australian Competition and Consumer Commission v Google: Deterring Misleading Conduct in Digital Privacy Policies' (2021) 26 *Communications Law* 136.

[53] Discussed in section II.A.

[54] Discussed in section II.B. See particularly J Horwitz, 'The Facebook Files: A Wall Street Journal Investigation' *Wall Street Journal* (2021–present) at www.wsj.com/articles/the-facebook-files-11631713039. A useful comparator to this conduct is *Australian Securities and Investments Commission v National Australia Bank Limited* [2020] FCA 1494.

[55] See Harding, ch 2 of this volume; Crofts, ch 3 of this volume.

[56] See N Yue, 'The "Weaponization" of Facebook in Myanmar: A Case for Corporate Criminal Liability' (2020) 71 *Hastings Law Journal* 813; J Palmieri, 'Can Social Media Corporations be Held Liable under International Law for Human Rights Atrocities?' (2022) 34 *Pace International Law Review* 135. See also n 126.

II. Big Tech's Systems

In 'Systems Intentionality: Theory and Practice',[57] Bant sets out a very helpful practical guide to identifying and proving culpable corporate systems. It comprises two main approaches. The first focuses on identifying repeated instances or patterns of externally observable events, behaviours or outcomes from which systems, policies and practices can be reliably inferred. The second approach 'attacks the presence and features of a system head-on',[58] by relying on direct evidence of internal structures, processes and methods that combine to form the alleged system that results in harmful outcomes.

Both approaches to proof are likely to be productive in applying systems intentionality to Big Tech firms. This section utilises both approaches in undertaking an initial analysis of Uber and Facebook – two instances of companies that have engaged in systems of misconduct since their founding, and to which existing legal mechanisms have been unable to respond. They are also companies where there are significant opportunities to collaborate with the emerging tech worker activist movement – including, but not limited to, whistle-blowers – as partners to source, contextualise and corroborate corporate systems, policies and practices through documentary evidence. Major caches of internal documents from both companies have been given to investigative reporters in recent years, most famously through former Facebook employee Frances Haugen to the *Wall Street Journal* in the October 2021 'Facebook Files',[59] as well as through former Uber employee Mark McGann to *The Guardian* in the July 2022 'Uber Files'.[60] As Bant notes in 'Catching the Corporate Conscience', one of the features of systems intentionality is that it transforms employees from being viewed solely as potential liability targets into important and valuable witnesses to the nature of the systems in which they are, or were, embedded.[61] This is especially the case in relation to Haugen and McGann, who have brought forward substantial evidence about the inner workings of their former employers.

A. Uber

Uber is a US ride-hailing company, founded in 2009, which has disrupted the taxi and private car-hire industry globally. The core of the service is the Uber mobile application (app), which allows passengers to request point-to-point car rides, principally by drivers who are not licensed taxi or private car-hire drivers. In turn, algorithmic or automated systems within the app match drivers with passengers, determine routing, set pricing, pay drivers, and allocate consequences to driver and passenger ratings.[62]

[57] Bant, ch 9 of this volume.
[58] ibid.
[59] Horwitz (n 54).
[60] 'The Uber Files' *The Guardian* (July 2022–ongoing) at www.theguardian.com/news/series/uber-files.
[61] Bant (n 46) 484.
[62] A Rosenblat, *Uberland: How Algorithms Are Rewriting the Rules of Work* (Oakland, CA, University of California Press, 2019).

These automated systems are optimised for Uber's priorities and operate in ways that are non-transparent for drivers, passengers and regulators.

In analysing Uber, it is useful first to explain the heart of the company's business model – its *core system*. The core system of the company, which it has practised and perfected in every city in which it now exists, is to expand the service at all costs, including by evading or breaking legal and regulatory requirements.[63] Already in 2014, Uber's strategy was to become 'too big to ban'.[64] This internal method of working is a textbook example of a 'system' in the typology of systems intentionality: it is 'inherently purposive'; 'the internal method or organised connection of elements operating to produce the conduct or outcome'.[65] Uber's core system is complemented by additional systems, policies and practices. Within Bant's typology, 'policies' and 'practices' 'may be understood as systems operating at higher levels of generality (in the case of policies) and as arising organically (in the case of practices)'.[66] Once a habitual practice has 'crossed into the realm of an adopted process', it may be characterised as a 'system'.[67]

The elephant that is Uber can of course be carved many ways. To understand the company, four systems in particular warrant attention, as foundational systems operating in conjunction with Uber's core system:

- Prioritisation of growth at the expense of driver, passenger and workplace safety.
- Financial exploitation of drivers and passengers.
- Corporate espionage and sabotage of competitors to maintain market dominance.
- Courting and manipulation of public officials to ensure governmental support.

The immediate value of identifying and elaborating these systems is two-fold. First, it dramatically alters the narrative about Uber's law-breaking, its unsafe and exploitative practices, and its volatile relationships with competitors and public officials. Rather than being accidents or errors on the path to corporate success, each of these outcomes can be seen as a clear manifestation of corporate intent. Second, the process of identification and elaboration has doctrinal relevance in considering specific liability questions. While this is not the focus of the present chapter, it is the focus of my research group in related work. One example is a project led by doctoral candidate and former litigator Helen Stamp, advancing the case that, distinct from the question of individual responsibility, Uber should bear corporate liability for reckless homicide in the now-infamous case of its autonomous test vehicle crash in Tempe, Arizona, which resulted in the death of a pedestrian.[68] Stamp's project meticulously documents

[63] M Isaac, *Super Pumped: The Battle for Uber* (New York, WW Norton & Company, 2019); J del Nido, *Taxis Vs Uber: Courts, Markets, and Technology in Buenos Aires* (Redwood City, CA, Stanford University Press, 2021).

[64] M Wohlsen, 'Uber's Brilliant Strategy to Make Itself Too Big to Ban' *Wired* (7 July 2014) at www.wired.com/2014/07/ubers-brilliant-strategy-to-make-itself-too-big-to-ban.

[65] Bant, ch 11 of this volume, section III.A.i.

[66] Bant (n 46) 472.

[67] ibid 473.

[68] See n 14.

Uber's systems, policies and practices that prioritised growth over safety and which led – inexorably, in her analysis – to that fateful crash.

Turning to Uber's *core system*, it is clear from both internal and external documents[69] that Uber's business model depends on attaining, and then retaining, a majority market share in any jurisdiction in order to be able to offer better supply and cheaper fares than its competitors. In order to facilitate this kind of market dominance, Uber has to move faster than competitors, which it can only do by flouting existing regulations surrounding the taxi or private car-hire industry. This law-breaking feature of Uber's operations is remarkable in its audacity – few, if any, international businesses would so deliberately and systematically break the law in each new market of operation. Yet, as articulated recently in the novel Australian class action of *Andrianakis*, the commission of offences 'systematically and on a large scale' is 'not a theoretical possibility' as a result of Uber's way of launching and establishing operations in a new city. Rather, it is a 'certainty' – and, indeed, 'an integral aspect of [Uber's] business model'.[70]

Uber's core system finds a useful parallel in the business model examined by the High Court of Australia in *Stubbings v Jams 2 Pty Ltd*.[71] That case involved a system of financial lending that was designed to hide, obscure and avoid the lender's knowledge of the often patent inability of guarantors to service their loans. Rather than exculpating the lender, this system of deliberately evading legal protections had the opposite effect, reinforcing the court's finding that the lender had engaged in unconscionable conduct. Uber's case is more stark again: not only do its systems deliberately evade and ignore legal protections, it has also introduced extraordinary measures to subvert law enforcement and regulators, such as by adopting a 'kill switch' to block access to its IT systems during raids,[72] and developing the notorious 'Greyball' app, which decoyed regulators seeking to impound unlicensed vehicles by having them chase fake, or 'ghost', cars.[73]

Accompanying Uber's core system is a suite of complementary systems. First is Uber's prioritisation of growth over driver, passenger and workplace safety. This encompasses the company's consistent failure to adequately enforce safety regulations,[74] lax oversight of driver and passenger safety complaints,[75] and a tentative approach to implementing safety measures,[76] despite evidence that assaults, abuse and vehicle

[69] SumOfUs, 'Why Everyone Hates Uber' at www.whyeveryonehatesuber.com/ (last accessed 1 August 2022); Uber, S-1 Filing (SEC, 11 April 2019) at www.sec.gov/Archives/edgar/data/1543151/000119312519103850/d647752ds1.htm; *Nicos Andrianakis v Uber Technologies Inc & Ors* [2022] VSC 196.

[70] *Andriankis* (n 69) [272]–[274], [277].

[71] *Stubbings v Jams 2 Pty Ltd* [2022] HCA 6; (2022) 399 ALR 409. For detailed analysis, see Bryan, ch 14 of this volume.

[72] R Davies and S Goodley, 'Uber Bosses Told Staff to Use "Kill Switch" During Raids to Stop Police Seeing Data' *The Guardian* (11 July 2022) at www.theguardian.com/news/2022/jul/10/uber-bosses-told-staff-use-kill-switch-raids-stop-police-seeing-data.

[73] R Davies and J Bhuiyan, 'Uber Used Greyball Fake App to Evade Police Across Europe, Leak Reveals' *The Guardian* (12 July 2022) at www.theguardian.com/news/2022/jul/12/uber-used-greyball-fake-app-to-evade-police-across-europe-leak-reveals; M Isaac, 'How Uber Deceives the Authorities Worldwide' *New York Times* (3 March 2017) at www.nytimes.com/2017/03/03/technology/uber-greyball-program-evade-authorities.html.

[74] SumOfUs (n 69).

[75] N Bonyhady, 'Every Day, Two Sexual Assault or Misconduct Complaints Hit Uber' *Sydney Morning Herald* (17 November 2021) at www.smh.com.au/politics/federal/every-day-two-sexual-assault-or-misconduct-complaints-hit-uber-20211115-p59901.html.

[76] Uber, 'Getting Serious about Safety' (12 April 2018) at www.uber.com/newsroom/getting-serious-safety/.

accidents are rife.[77] The company has drawn ire for misrepresenting the quality of its safety record,[78] insurance provisions[79] and driver screening methods,[80] and it has repeatedly clashed with regulators seeking more effective background checks.[81] Finally, Uber has a damning record of discrimination in its own workplace.[82]

Second, Uber systematically engages in the financial exploitation of drivers and passengers. Uber maximises profits during peak demand periods through an opaque and troublesome automated 'surge pricing' algorithm,[83] leading to investigations of 'high-tech price-gouging'[84] and 'price-fixing'.[85] Drivers have complained that similarly opaque algorithmic tools to calculate 'projected' and 'actual' fares short-change them on fare revenue,[86] with investigations of 'accounting mistakes' leading the company to repay drivers,[87] as well as consumers,[88] at scale. Most significantly, Uber has sustained a long and expensive global battle to avoid classifying drivers as workers and having to pay for minimum wages, sick leave or basic insurance.[89] Though this has not been totally successful – courts in the UK recently required Uber to provide basic working benefits to drivers[90] – it has been a considerably more profitable system than the alternative.

Third, Uber engages in a system of corporate espionage and sabotage of competitors to maintain market dominance. This has involved threatening and misleading its own drivers,[91] distorting demand through booking fake rides,[92] deploying covert operations

[77] K Browning, 'Uber Says Sexual Assaults are Down but Rate of Traffic Deaths is Up' *New York Times* (1 July 2022) at www.nytimes.com/2022/06/30/business/uber-safety-report.html; Bonyhady (n 75).

[78] Wigdor LLP, 'Uber Class Action: Wigdor LLP Files Lawsuit on behalf of Women Sexually Assaulted by Uber Drivers' (15 November 2017) at www.wigdorlaw.com/uber-class-action-sexual-assault/.

[79] C Morran, 'Judge Rejects $28.5M Uber "Safe Rides" Fee Settlement, Says Company Made $449M From These Charges' *Consumerist* (1 September 2016) https://consumerist.com/2016/09/01/judge-rejects-28-5m-uber-safe-rides-fee-settlement-says-company-made-449m-these-charges/.

[80] C Said, 'DA: Major Flaws in Uber Background Checks Allow Criminal Drivers' *San Francisco Chronicle* (19 August 2015) at www.sfchronicle.com/business/article/DA-major-flaws-in-Uber-background-checks-allow-6453865.php.

[81] A Hern, 'Uber and Lyft Pull out of Austin after Locals Vote against Self-Regulation' *The Guardian* (9 May 2016) at www.theguardian.com/technology/2016/may/09/uber-lyft-austin-vote-against-self-regulation.

[82] Fowler (n 10).

[83] C Taylor, 'Uber Kills Surge Pricing in NYC for Customers, Drivers Paid 2X Rate to Meet Post-Sandy Demand' *TechCrunch* (1 November 2012) at https://techcrunch.com/2012/10/31/uber-turns-on-surge-pricing-in-nyc-post-sandy-then-retreats-after-pr-backlash/.

[84] New York State Office of the Attorney General, 'AG Schneiderman Announces Agreement with Uber to Cap Pricing During Emergencies and Natural Disasters' (8 July 2014) at https://ag.ny.gov/press-release/2014/ag-schneiderman-announces-agreement-uber-cap-pricing-during-emergencies-and.

[85] United States District Court Southern District of New York, 'Spencer Meyer v Travis Kalanick' (1:15 Civ 9796, 16 December 2015) at https://storage.courtlistener.com/recap/gov.uscourts.nysd.451250/gov.uscourts.nysd.451250.1.0.pdf.

[86] United States District Court Northern District of California, 'Martin Dulberg v Uber Technologies, Inc, and Rasier, LLC' (21 February 2017) at https://s3.documentcloud.org/documents/3471502/Dulberg.pdf.

[87] B Carson, 'Uber is Paying its NYC Drivers "Tens of Millions" Because of an Accounting Error That Underpaid Them for Years' *Business Insider* (24 May 2017) at www.businessinsider.com/uber-paying-nyc-drivers-tens-of-millions-accounting-error-2017-5.

[88] M Mason, 'Uber Agrees to $26m Fine After ACCC Investigation' *Australian Financial Review* (26 April 2022) at www.afr.com/technology/uber-agrees-to-26m-fine-after-accc-investigation-20220426-p5ag6b.

[89] 'Exhibit A: Settlement Agreement and Mutual General Release' (13 March 2019) at www.law360.com/articles/1138858/attachments/0.

[90] *Uber BV and others v Aslam and others* [2021] UKSC 5, [2021] RTR 29.

[91] E Fink, 'Uber Threatens Drivers: Do Not Work for Lyft' *CNN Business* (5 August 2014) at https://money.cnn.com/2014/08/04/technology/uber-lyft/?iid=EL.

[92] E Fink, 'Uber's Dirty Tricks Quantified: Rival Counts 5,560 Canceled Rides' *CNN Business* (12 August 2014) at https://money.cnn.com/2014/08/11/technology/uber-fake-ride-requests-lyft/index.html.

and offering cash incentives to recruit drivers away from competitors,[93] and building elaborate spyware, in breach of US wiretapping laws.[94] Former employees and whistle-blowers have further accused the company of engaging in illegal hacking, wiretapping and espionage,[95] as well as the use of ephemeral communications to cover up such activities.[96] Uber has been investigated for bribing foreign government officials,[97] as well as for conducting covert research into potential litigants.[98]

Fourth, Uber engages in systematic courting and manipulation of public officials to ensure governmental support and avoid enforcement action. The Uber Files document how this suborning targeted high-profile figures, including Emmanuel Macron, Boris Johnson and Neelie Kroes,[99] by 'finding unofficial routes to power, applying influence through friends or intermediaries, or seeking out encounters with politicians at which aides and officials were not present'.[100] It is a stealth approach, generally comprising both a 'carrot' and a 'stick' – if inducements do not work,[101] the company will go on the attack, aggressively campaigning, marshalling the public,[102] and litigating to undermine and disempower licensing and regulatory authorities. Most of this is undeclared, defying lobbying laws. Along with the other systems described above, it fundamentally buttresses Uber's core system.

In the wake of the Uber Files, Uber's primary defence has been that it is a reformed company: 'that was the old Uber, we are the new Uber'. Uber has certainly made a

[93] C Newton, 'This is Uber's Playbook for Sabotaging Lyft' *The Verge* (26 August 2014) at www.theverge.com/2014/8/26/6067663/this-is-ubers-playbook-for-sabotaging-lyft.

[94] A Efrati, 'Uber's Top Secret "Hell" Program Exploited Lyft's Vulnerability' *The Information* (12 April 2017) at www.theinformation.com/articles/ubers-top-secret-hell-program-exploited-lyfts-vulnerability; United States District Court Northern District of California San Francisco Division, 'Michael Gonzales vs Uber Technologies, Inc' (Case No 3:17-CV-02264, 24 April 2017) at https://storage.courtlistener.com/recap/gov.uscourts.cand.310545.1.0.pdf.

[95] Scribd, 'Uber Jacobs Letter' (5 May 2017) at www.scribd.com/document/367287753/Uber-Jacobs-Letter.

[96] S Lekach and K Flynn, 'Hoo-boy! This Damning Uber Letter is a Wild Ride' *Mashable* (15 December 2017) at https://mashable.com/article/uber-damning-jacobs-letter-former-employee-waymo-trial.

[97] United States Securities and Exhange Commission, 'Form 8-K Current Report' (2 January 20220) <https://www.sec.gov/ix?doc=/Archives/edgar/data/1543151/000155278120000051/e20009_uber-8k.htm.

[98] United States District Court Southern District of New York, 'Spencer Meyer v Travis Kalanick and Uber Technologies, Inc.' (15 Civ. 9796, Opinion and Order, 25 July 2016) <https://storage.courtlistener.com/recap/gov.uscourts.nysd.451250.119.0.pdf.

[99] D Starkman and A Mustufa, 'Macron, Kroes Under Pressure as Uber Files Puts Spotlight on High Power Lobbying in Europe' *International Consortium of Investigative Journalists* (11 July 2022) at www.icij.org/investigations/uber-files/macron-kroes-under-pressure-as-uber-files-puts-spotlight-on-high-power-lobbying-in-europe/. See also Uber Files Reporting Team, 'Uber Files: Massive Leak Reveals How Top Politicians Secretly Helped Uber' *BBC News* (10 July 2022) at www.bbc.com/news/business-62057321; N Nielsen, 'EU Commission to Probe Kroes' Uber Lobbying' *EUObserver* (12 July 2022) at https://euobserver.com/eu-political/155496.

[100] H Davies et al, 'Uber Broke Laws, Duped Police and Secretly Lobbied Governments, Leak Reveals' *The Guardian* (12 July 2022) at www.theguardian.com/news/2022/jul/10/uber-files-leak-reveals-global-lobbying-campaign.

[101] 'Uber Avoids Car Pick-Up App Restrictions in London' *BBC News* (20 January 2016) at www.bbc.com/news/technology-35361153; BBC News, 'Uber Files: Tech Firm Lobbied Top Ministers at Undeclared Meetings' (11 July 2022) a www.bbc.com/news/business-62099061.

[102] 'Uber London Loses Licence to Operate' *BBC News* (22 September 2017) at www.bbc.com/news/uk-england-41358640; BBC News, 'Uber: London Mayor Sadiq Khan Backs Talks after Firm's Apology' (25 September 2017) at www.bbc.com/news/business-41384499; G Topham, 'Uber Granted London Licence as Court Rules it "No Longer Poses a Risk"' *The Guardian* (28 September 2020) at www.theguardian.com/technology/2020/sep/28/uber-keeps-london-licence-risk-tfl-safety.

significant performance of clearing house – both in terms of staffing and culture – since the ousting of chief executive Travis Kalanick and commencement of Dara Khosrowshahi in 2017. In cities around the world, Uber is making peace with taxi services and integrating them into its operating model.[103] The company is diversifying into corporate freight, food delivery and couriering, and talking a big game about sustainability and job creation. But a changing of the guard does not remove culpability, and the systems described above continue to define the company; a reflection of the vital importance of analysing corporations through a systems lens, rather than exclusively through individual fault. Misconduct warrants a legal response, regardless of its extent and its continuation. In the Victorian Royal Commission into the Casino Operator and Licence, Commissioner Finkelstein rejected a similar strategy deployed by Crown Casino.[104] Adopting the perspective of systems intentionality, he considered that widespread board and management 'renewal' was insufficient to evidence corporate rehabilitation. In light of sustained and endemic wrongdoing over many years, Crown Casino could not show it was 'suitable' to hold a casino licence without 'systemic and sustained change … as revealed through its systems, policies and processes'.[105]

The greatest challenge to securing redress for Uber's systematic wrongdoing is that its systems have been so effective that Uber no longer needs to engage in the aggressive expansion tactics detailed above; the blitzscaling has lessened a notch. The company is, by most appearances, precisely where it wants to be: at the apex of personal transit internationally, subject to broadly favourable regulatory environments, and with enormous, arguably unsurpassable advantages in terms of infrastructure, algorithms, data and brand recognition. That it reached this point by forcing its way and externalising harms, with absolute disdain for the function and sovereignty of governments, a cold and laissez-faire approach to safety and security, and countless underhanded and deceptive business practices – all underpinned by the practical impunity that comes from patient capital – is hard to prosecute, but it is the essential challenge.

The systems intentionality approach, applied to both the historic record and the revelations of the Uber Files, shows the harms of Uber's business were intentional, repeated and practised in many cities and countries. To allow Uber's dominance to remain unchallenged, simply because it has, on its own terms, won, creates significant moral hazard for other firms and their financial backers. Most importantly, failing to act now creates significant and lasting moral hazard for current and future politicians, regulators and licensing bodies who failed to resist Uber's enticements or pressure, and are currently failing to revoke its extraordinary privilege.

[103] F Siddiqui, 'Uber and Taxicabs Strike an Unlikely Partnership, Years After Ride-Hailing Destroyed the Business' *Washington Post* (24 March 2022) at www.washingtonpost.com/technology/2022/03/24/uber-taxis-nyc/.

[104] State of Victoria, *Royal Commission into the Casino Operator and Licence* (The Report, October 2021) vol 1. These included ultimately unsuccessful attempts to distance 'old Crown' from 'new Crown' at, eg, ch 5, 145 [5.70].

[105] ibid ch 6, 178 [6.101]; see also ch 18, 58–59 [18.19]–[18.25].

B. Facebook

Facebook is a US social media company, founded in 2004, which hosts one-to-one and one-to-many communications services – Facebook, WhatsApp, Instagram and Oculus – that are used by 3.65 billion monthly active users, or nearly half the global population.[106] Three of the most notable features of the company are: (i) the bulk of its revenue (more than 97 per cent)[107] comes from advertising; (ii) third parties generate everything that exists on Facebook's services apart from its architecture – that is, ads and 'content' (stories, videos, comments, etc), to follow the typical bifurcation; and (iii) as with Uber, algorithmic or automated systems underpin every aspect of how Facebook's services operate.

Facebook has interesting resonances with and differences from other tech firms. At the system level, it shares the same relentless expansionary drive and disregard for legal and regulatory requirements as Uber, with the twist that Facebook has conjured its own market – indeed, its own class – and, with it, mostly managed to define its own, unregulated legal reality. What distinguishes Facebook is its totalising ambition. This is reflected in its core system, which is focused on the outcome of embedding Facebook as *the* essential intermediary of human communication and connection. This core system rationalises the company's eye-wateringly expensive acquisitions of would-be rivals, WhatsApp and Instagram. It also rationalises the acquisition of Oculus and other virtual and augmented reality companies, as Facebook seeks to define and own the 'next computing platform' for human connection.[108] Finally, the core system helps explain the company's evolution from a college look-up directory to its expansion into ever more functions of our collective life: buying and selling goods; finding jobs or housing; social, professional and political organising; the transmission of news and information (and mis/disinformation) of all kinds. The effectiveness of Facebook's core system is facilitated by its efforts to provide a user-experience of unsurpassed convenience and reach – Facebook offers everyone a home page, a megaphone and a hypothetical audience larger than any rival. As a result, it creates dependency on its own services by choice rather than force.

There are three integral elements of Facebook's core system, all being systems in their own right:

- Self-sustenance through parasitically monetising human attention and connection.
- Prioritisation of growth over user and workplace safety.
- Regulatory evasion and insulation through novel corporate structuring.

Turning to the first system, Facebook is wedded to behavioural surveillance and targeted advertising as the quid pro quo for maintaining global services at unprecedented scale.

[106] Meta, 'Meta Reports Second Quarter 2022 Results' (27 July 2022) at https://investor.fb.com/investor-news/press-release-details/2022/Meta-Reports-Second-Quarter-2022-Results/default.aspx.

[107] Meta, 'Meta Reports Fourth Quarter and Full Year 2021 Results' (2 February 2022) at https://investor.fb.com/investor-news/press-release-details/2022/Meta-Reports-Fourth-Quarter-and-Full-Year-2021-Results/default.aspx.

[108] E Culliford, 'Facebook Sets Up New Team to Work on the 'Metaverse' *Reuters* (27 July 2021) at www.reuters.com/technology/facebook-sets-up-new-team-work-metaverse-2021-07-26/.

This means that the company is ideologically committed to monetising the human attention and connections that its services enable, that is, to being fundamentally parasitic on its own services.[109] In this it has form. Facebook has been testing the limits of what it can do with information it can extract about people since its earliest days. From the controversial 'Beacon' program, which was roundly criticised for enabling third-party surveillance of Facebook users,[110] through to the company's cooperation with project PRISM, which saw it provide access to sensitive user data to major US intelligence agencies including the NSA and FBI,[111] the company has consistently sought to capitalise on its unprecedented trove of fine-grained personal information.

Even when the company is not actively involved in harvesting its own users' data, episodes like the Cambridge Analytica revelations, which 'scraped' personal information held by Facebook and used it to generate a tool capable of micro-targeting political advertising,[112] illustrate the existential danger of Facebook's data trove.

Addressing the second system of prioritising growth over safety, Facebook's blitzscaling over nearly two decades has given rise to significant and unique challenges in terms of effective moderation of both content and ads. Given that Facebook and Instagram, in particular, have become key vectors for the distribution of mis/disinformation[113] and hate speech,[114] as well as major channels for human rights abuses,[115] effective moderation is uncontestably a matter of great social importance. However, achieving it seems all but impossible – human content moderators hired by the company to review sensitive material have succumbed to post-traumatic stress disorder in droves,[116] and attempts to supplement human reviewers with algorithmic content detection have proved woefully inadequate.[117]

Facebook typically characterises the scale of its moderation challenge as a quandary of unexpected popularity. Its systems and practices of expansion tell a different story, given the constant structural design and algorithmic optimisation to drive 'engagement' (as required by the core system and system 1); the relentless pace of growth and expansion; and the systematic exercise of starving units of resources for organisational safety functions to mitigate known and systemic harms.

[109] CBC Radio, 'Mark Zuckerberg's Former Mentor Says 'Parasitic' Facebook Threatens Our Health and Democracy' *CBC Radio* (18 January 2018) at www.cbc.ca/radio/asithappens/as-it-happens-thursday-edition-1.4493061/mark-zuckerberg-s-former-mentor-says-parasitic-facebook-threatens-our-health-and-democracy-1.4493932.

[110] B Schiffman, 'Facebook CEO Apologizes, Lets Users Turn Off Beacon' *Wired* (5 December 2007) at www.wired.com/2007/12/facebook-ceo-apologizes-lets-users-turn-off-beacon/.

[111] D Seifert, 'Secret Program gives NSA, FBI Backdoor Access to Apple, Google, Facebook, Microsoft Data' *The Verge* (6 June 2013) at www.theverge.com/2013/6/6/4403868/nsa-fbi-mine-data-apple-google-facebook-microsoft-others-prism.

[112] C Cadwalladr and E Graham-Harrison, 'Revealed: 50 Million Facebook Profiles Harvested for Cambridge Analytica in Major Data Breach' *The Guardian* (18 March 2018) at www.theguardian.com/news/2018/mar/17/cambridge-analytica-facebook-influence-us-election.

[113] See n 21.

[114] D Pierce and A Kramer, 'Here are all the Facebook Papers Stories' *Protocol* (25 October 2021) at www.protocol.com/facebook-papers.

[115] See n 18.

[116] See n 15.

[117] T Simonite, 'Facebook is Everywhere; Its Moderation is Nowhere Close' *Wired* (25 October 2021) at www.wired.com/story/facebooks-global-reach-exceeds-linguistic-grasp/.

Content moderation at global scale is extremely difficult, given the language, cultural and political differences in different countries, and how essential local knowledge and context are to determine whether social media content and contributors have broken the platform's rules. However, Facebook has repeatedly under-resourced content moderation and mistreated content moderators, employing them through third-party providers and offering paltry consideration or recompense for the significant harms they suffer. The company's highly aggressive rollout in war-torn Myanmar is illustrative:[118] the company hired only two Burmese-speaking moderators to review content for a nation of millions.[119] Only when the United Nations identified the company as having played a 'determining role' in the escalation of racially-fuelled violence in the country[120] did Facebook hire more Burmese-speaking moderators.

The starving of content moderation for 'less politically important' countries was documented by whistle-blower Sophie Zhang.[121] Her account of organisational intransigence in response to reports of systematic abuse of the platform by authoritarian regimes makes clear that what seemed like failings to a conscientious employee were simply how the system was meant to work.[122]

The final essential system that complements Facebook's core system is the novel corporate structuring that enables its regulatory evasion at scale. At the heart of this is Facebook's use of its US-based corporate entities, Facebook, Inc and Meta Platforms, Inc, to conduct its global operations, sometimes in collaboration with their related bodies corporate in Ireland. The reason for this highly unusual structure is the company's supreme confidence in the immunity granted in the US under section 230 of the Communications Decency Act of 1996,[123] which Facebook has long seen as protecting it from responsibility for either advertising or content that transits its platform. Section 230 is now the keen focus of review both legislatively and in the courts, with an express view to challenging and reversing this protection. As a result, Facebook's most trusted asset may become its weakest link.

III. Opportunities for Further Work

At least five challenges and associated questions arise in applying systems intentionality to Big Tech, all of which are likely to provide productive avenues for further work.

[118] O'Brien and Powles (n 14).

[119] S Stecklow, 'Hatebook: Inside Facebook's Myanmar Operation' *Reuters* (15 August 2018) at www.reuters.com/investigates/special-report/myanmar-facebook-hate/.

[120] 'UN Blames Facebook for Spreading Hatred against Rohingya in Myanmar' *CBS News* (13 March 2018) at www.cbsnews.com/news/facebook-un-blames-social-media-giant-for-spreading-hatred-rohingya-myanmar/.

[121] JC Wong, 'How Facebook Let Fake Engagement Distort Global Politics: A Whistleblower's Account' *The Guardian* (12 April 2021) at www.theguardian.com/technology/2021/apr/12/facebook-fake-engagement-whistleblower-sophie-zhang.

[122] ibid: 'I tried to fix this problem within Facebook … I spoke to my manager, my manager's manager, different teams, and everyone up to a company vice-president in great detail. I repeatedly tried to get people to fix things … I offered to stay on for free after they fired me, and they said no. I hoped that when I made my departure post it might convince people to change things, but it hasn't.'

[123] See s 230(c)(1) of the Communications Act of 1934 (47 USC 230): 'No provider or user of an interactive computer service shall be treated as the publisher or speaker of any information provided by another information content provider.'

First, one major difference between Big Tech and virtually every other industry – and especially financial services and casino operations, which are examined in foundational case studies of systems intentionality[124] – is that many tech firms do not require licences or other systems of registration in the markets in which they operate. Instead, the experience and practice of Big Tech is that they make the markets, and oversight is slow to catch up. This is particularly true for companies such as Facebook, Google and Amazon. But it is also the case when tech firms operate in existing markets that require licences for other operators, such as taxis and private car-hire (in the case of Uber), or hotels and short-term rentals (for Airbnb). Significantly, without systems of licensure, there are no corresponding *ex ante* obligations that a company must be a 'fit and proper person' (or similar standards, extending well beyond competence to also encompass integrity, honesty, etc) to operate a social network, or a search engine or a ride-hailing platform. Though it does not prevent assessment at the point of liability, the vacuum around licensure appears to be a significant absence for Big Tech culpability, and more work is warranted to determine whether advocating for licensure would assist in ensuring better corporate accountability.[125] The case of Uber suggests that this must be done advisedly to the fact that tech firms are very adept at working around or absorbing licensure systems that do not fundamentally disable a company's operations. Further work could also productively examine the reasons why licensing requirements have not been imposed on the broader tech ecosystem, the experience of earlier attempts at extending existing licensure models or developing new ones, and whether tech firms are truly unique in this regard.

Second, the tech sector has seen precious little exploration of causes of action with a requisite state of mind component. This is perhaps the largest conceptual challenge in using systems intentionality as a vehicle for securing better corporate accountability, though also the most exciting from the perspective of future legal developments. Once we have an operational model of organisational blameworthiness, it is of course necessary to identify causes of action to prosecute. Further work should examine potential causes of action that involve requirements of intention, knowledge or recklessness, whether there are good reasons why these have not been previously pursued in relation to tech firms' histories of harm, and any practical impediments to the application of systems intentionality within specific causes of action. In particular, it appears truly remarkable that criminal actions have been all but unexplored in relation to Big Tech firms,[126] and this is likely to be a particularly profitable opportunity for future work.[127]

[124] See Bant (n 25) 361–67, 385–87 (on financial services, drawing on the case study of 'fees for no service'); E Bant, 'Reforming the Laws of Corporate Attribution: "Systems Intentionality" Draft Statutory Provision' (2022) 39 *Companies & Securities Law Journal* 259 (on casino operations). Against this, note Paterson, Bant and Cooney (n 52), which encourages the application of systems intentionality to determining penalties in a misleading and deceptive conduct case against Google.

[125] See F Pasquale, 'Licensure as Data Governance' (Knight First Amendment Institute Symposium on Data and Democracy, 28 September 2021) at https://knightcolumbia.org/content/licensure-as-data-governance.

[126] A rare private criminal action was initiated against Facebook in 2022 in the courts of Western Australia, with the approval of the Commonwealth Attorney-General: K Ainsworth, 'Andrew "Twiggy" Forrest Launches Criminal Proceedings Against Facebook Over False Cryptocurrency Advertisements' *ABC News* (3 February 2022) at www.abc.net.au/news/2022-02-03/andrew-twiggy-forrest-launches-criminal-proceedings-facebook/100800630; AAP, 'Facebook a No-Show in Andrew Forrest Criminal Case

Third, and compounding other challenges, Big Tech companies are now more powerful than nation states, but they predominantly come from just two: the US and China. There are clearly jurisdictional issues that arise in bringing legal actions against these firms, opening up questions for future work on whether this limits the exploration of either systems of licensure or further causes of action against these firms in the many countries of the world where they operate and, in turn, how jurisdiction impacts the application of systems intentionality in practice. An additional and related issue is about institutional capacity and will to pursue causes of action against firms that are either 'too big to fail' in their own home jurisdictions, or 'too big to catch' in jurisdictions that merely consume or supply their products and services.

Fourth, there are considerations of timing. One of the ways in which tech firms have responded to accusations of misconduct is to distance their current operations from historic behaviour. Other chapters in this collection have addressed 'failure to prevent' offences and reactive corporate fault,[128] both of which expand the time horizon of potential corporate criminality. Further work could examine historic grievances in relation to starkly criminal behaviour facilitated by tech firms, such as the facilitation of human trafficking and genocide in the case of Facebook, and how the timing of legal proceedings may impact upon the prospects of successful actions.

Fifth, and finally, there is a 'meta' question of how well systems intentionality can respond to corporate conduct that threatens the very existence of institutions of law, governance and justice. It is salient to note that the tremendous power and influence of tech firms extends from untoward involvement in policymaking to shape the very rules that these firms will ultimately be required to answer,[129] to intentionally subverting democratic processes.[130] This gives rise to fundamental questions. Is corporate culpability able to deal with systems that override our very processes of lawmaking and oversight? What legal recourse is available to concerned citizens?

In closing, this chapter has argued that systems intentionality offers a corrective against the weak contours of accountability that have conditioned tech firms' behaviour, and the exceptionalism of Big Tech more broadly. Addressing this will be crucial not only to respond to the dominance and harmful effects of Big Tech, but also to dissuade other companies that are increasingly seeking to emulate 'blitzscaling' across all domains of industry and life.

Against Facebook' *The Guardian* (28 March 2022) at www.theguardian.com/australia-news/2022/mar/28/facebook-a-no-show-in-andrew-forrest-criminal-case-arguing-west-australian-court-lacks-jurisdiction.

[127] See Crofts, ch 3 of this volume.

[128] See Clough, ch 18 of this volume; Fisse, ch 7 of this volume.

[129] E Goodman and J Powles, 'Urbanism Under Google: Lessons from Sidewalk Toronto' (2019) 88 *Fordham Law Review* 457; D Gershgorn, 'A Microsoft Employee Literally Wrote Washington's Facial Recognition Law' *Medium* (3 April 2020) at https://onezero.medium.com/a-microsoft-employee-literally-wrote-washingtons-facial-recognition-legislation-aab950396927; Cohen (n 41).

[130] K Hagey, M Cherney and J Horwitz, 'Facebook Deliberately Caused Havoc in Australia to Influence New Law, Whistleblowers Say' *Wall Street Journal* (5 May 2022) at www.wsj.com/articles/facebook-deliberately-caused-havoc-in-australia-to-influence-new-law-whistleblowers-say-11651768302; J Powles and H Smith, 'Should Facebook be Criminally Liable for Interfering with Australia's Lawmaking Process?' *Rappler* (8 May 2022) at www.rappler.com/voices/thought-leaders/should-facebook-be-criminally-liable-interfering-with-australia-lawmaking-process/; D Swan, 'Facebook Executives "Hid Misconduct" Amid News Ban' *The Australian* (13 May 2022) at www.theaustralian.com.au/business/technology/facebook-executives-hid-misconduct-amid-news-ban/news-story/26a0f7ac8f50641213199eee0d8114b6.

PART II

Attribution Models

6

Meridian, Allocated Powers and Systems Intentionality Compared

RACHEL LEOW

Lord Thurlow, the Lord Chancellor between 1778–92, is reported as having once said that corporations have 'no soul to damn, no body to kick'.[1] Lacking a physical body, brain, and other characteristics of human persons, showing that companies have 'culpable minds' is a long-standing problem of considerable complexity. A company today can clearly owe and be owed duties. It may commit wrongs, albeit 'through the instrumentality and agency of others'.[2] But much of this will turn on ascertaining the state of mind of the company. Both in civil law and in the criminal law, establishing whether companies owe duties, have breached them or can be held liable will turn on proof of some state of mind. Intentions, beliefs, knowledge, recklessness, dishonesty, unconscionability and others may all be necessary ingredients of the relevant cause of action.[3]

In this chapter I compare the 'systems intentionality' model proposed by Professor Elise Bant[4] against two existing models of corporate attribution. The first is commonly regarded as stemming from the seminal decision of *Meridian Global Funds Management Asia Ltd v Securities Commission*.[5] On this account, attribution is a highly context-specific process, turning on the precise cause of action in question. An act attributed for one purpose in one cause of action may not be attributed for another.[6] While all its

[1] Attributed to Lord Thurlow: JC Coffee, '"No Soul to Damn: No Body to Kick": An Unscandalized Inquiry into the Problem of Corporate Punishment' (1981) 79 *Michigan Law Review* 386.

[2] *Yarborough v Governor and Company of the Bank of England* (1812) 16 East 6, 104 ER 991 (KB).

[3] See Bant and Paterson, ch 12 of this volume.

[4] See, eg, E Bant, 'Culpable Corporate Minds' (2021) 48 *University of Western Australia Law Review* 352; E Bant and JM Paterson, 'Systems of Misconduct: Corporate Culpability and Statutory Unconscionability' (2021) 15 *Journal of Equity* 63. See also Bant, ch 9 of this volume.

[5] *Meridian Global Funds Management Asia Ltd v Securities Commission* [1995] 2 AC 500 (PC) (*Meridian*).

[6] *Bilta (UK) Ltd (in liquidation) v Nazir* [2015] UKSC 23, [2015] 2 WLR 1168 (*Bilta*); *Singularis Holdings Ltd v Daiwa Capital Markets Europe* [2019] UKSC 50, [2020] AC 1189 (*Singularis*); *HKSAR v Luk Kin Peter Joseph* [2016] HKCFA 81, (2016) 19 HKCFAR 619. See also E Ferran, 'Corporate Attribution and the Directing Mind and Will' (2011) 127 *Law Quarterly Review* 239; E Lim, 'Attribution in Company Law' (2014) 77 *Modern Law Review* 794; J Payne, 'Corporate Attribution and the Lessons of Meridian' in PS Davies and J Pila (eds), *The Jurisprudence of Lord Hoffmann: A Festchrift for Leonard Hoffmann* (Oxford, Hart Publishing, 2015); S Worthington, 'Corporate Attribution and Agency: Back to Basics' (2017) 133 *Law Quarterly Review* 118; P Watts, 'Attribution and Limitation' (2018) 134 *Law Quarterly Review* 350.

proponents accept this basic position, there is considerable disagreement on exactly what feature(s) attribution turns on.[7] The second corporate attribution model that will be examined is the account of attribution I develop in my book, *Corporate Attribution in Private Law*.[8] On this account, attribution turns on the connection between act or state of mind, individual and the company. This connection is found in the allocation and delegation of the company's own powers to act. For short, I will call it the 'allocated powers model'.

I first set out a brief account of each of the three models in section I. In section II, I compare the three models. Do they take collective or individualist approaches? Do they apply consistently across different areas of law? What approaches do they take to corporate personality? How well do the models capture corporate culture, measures taken by the company before misconduct and measures taken by the company after misconduct? After examining the models on these points, section III considers how compatible the models are. It concludes that while systems intentionality does not sit easily with *Meridian*-type approaches, the allocated powers model generally appears to be compatible with systems intentionality. A proponent of allocated powers could consistently accept systems intentionality, though she need not do so. Whether she does may turn on a different matter: the extent to which she is willing to draw inferences about states of mind from conduct.

I. Three Models

In this section, I outline each of the three models to be considered: the context-specific approach to attribution in *Meridian*; the allocated powers model; and systems intentionality.

A. *Meridian*

Prior to the landmark case of *Meridian*, the best-known approach to corporate attribution was the 'directing mind and will' approach (sometimes also called the 'identification' approach).[9] This approach held that acts and states of mind could only be attributed to companies where they were done by or possessed by the company's 'directing mind and will'. The directing mind and will was understood to refer to a person who was so senior that he could be the embodiment of the company itself.[10] The company would simply be his 'alter ego'.[11]

[7] See all works cited in n 6.

[8] R Leow, *Corporate Attribution in Private Law* (Oxford, Hart Publishing, 2022).

[9] Best known in *Lennard's Carrying Co Ltd v Asiatic Petroleum Co Ltd* [1915] AC 705 (HL) (*Lennard's Carrying Co*).

[10] eg *Trevor Ivory Ltd v Anderson* [1992] 2 NZLR 517 (NZCA) 520 (Cooke P).

[11] Language used in different contexts, eg *Said v Butt* [1920] 3 KB 497 (inducing breach of contract). But see *Tesco Supermarkets v Nattrass* [1972] AC 153 (HL), 171–72 (Lord Reid) (*Tesco*), disapproving of that language for the very reason that 'The person who speaks and acts as the company is not alter. He is identified with the company.'

The directing mind and will approach suffered from some well-known flaws. First, on a literal reading, the directing mind and will test suggested that only the acts and states of mind of a single high-ranking individual within the company could be attributed. If correct, this would mean that it was very difficult for large organisations to be held liable in practice. In large companies, it is unlikely that such a senior person would possess the requisite mental state for the cause of action. The second criticism is connected to the first. Attuned to the dangers of the restrictive directing mind and will approach, courts often applied it loosely. In *Lennard's Carrying Co* itself, Lennard was identified as the directing mind and will because he had authority over part of the company's business, even though he did not have general decision-making authority for all of it.[12] As Hoffmann LJ (as he was then) later accepted in *El Ajou v Dollar Land Holdings plc*, '[t]he authorities show clearly that different persons may for different purposes satisfy the requirements of being the company's directing mind and will'.[13] This meant that in practice the test was so watered down as to lose most of its intuitive appeal. A third problem was that the approach was highly anthropomorphic,[14] with Lord Denning even likening persons acting for the company to parts of a human body.[15] Nearly all found this theoretically unsatisfactory, since it satisfied neither those who thought of the company as a legal fiction (fiction theorists), nor those who thought the company had a 'real' personality of its own that came into existence without the aid of the law.[16]

Against this background, *Meridian* was decided. Its facts are simple. Meridian Global Funds Management Asia Ltd (Meridian) was an investment management company. Its chief investment officer, Koo, and senior portfolio manager, Ng, were secretly embroiled in a scheme to take over a New Zealand company. They concocted a plan to raise the necessary financing by using Meridian to acquire shares in the target company, making Meridian a substantial shareholder of the target. Section 20 of the Securities Amendment Act 1988 (NZ) provided that every person who became a substantial shareholder of a public company came under a duty to disclose its substantial shareholding once it knew, or ought to know, of its substantial shareholding. No disclosure was made. The New Zealand Securities Commission then brought proceedings against Meridian for non-compliance with the Act. The key question was whether Koo and Ng's knowledge could be attributed to Meridian. The Privy Council, whose advice was given by Lord Hoffmann, held that it could.

Formulating the terminology of corporate attribution, Lord Hoffmann identified three categories of attribution rules: primary rules; general rules; and special rules of attribution.[17] Primary rules of attribution are generally found in the company's constitution or in general company law.[18] Examples include the rule that 'for the purpose of appointing members of the board, a majority vote of the shareholders shall be a decision

[12] *Lennard's Carrying Co* (n 9) 713–14.
[13] *El Ajou v Dollar Land Holdings plc* [1994] BCC 143 (CA) 159 (*El Ajou*).
[14] Ferran (n 6) 239.
[15] *HL Bolton Engineering Co Ltd v TJ Graham & Sons Ltd* [1957] 1 QB 159 (CA), 172. See also *Cassidy v Ministry of Health* [1951] 2 KB 343 (CA), 360.
[16] See Leow (n 8) ch 2.
[17] *Meridian* (n 5) 506–07.
[18] ibid.

of the company'[19] or that 'the decisions of the board in managing the company's business shall be the decisions of the company'.[20] These are supplemented with general rules of attribution – the rules of agency.[21] They are 'general' rules because they also apply equally to human persons, while the primary rules do not. In some exceptional cases, neither of these two categories provides an answer, but the court may conclude that the substantive rule of law ought to apply to companies.[22] The court must then formulate a special rule of attribution, asking 'Whose act (or knowledge, or state of mind) was *for this purpose* intended to count as the act etc of the company?'[23] In doing so, the court has to take into account the language of the rule (if it is a statute), its content and policy.[24]

On the facts of *Meridian*, there was no primary rule of attribution indicating when knowledge should be attributed, nor did the general rules appear relevant. Thus, Lord Hoffmann fashioned a special rule of attribution based on the policy of the statute, which was to compel immediate disclosure of the identity of substantial security-holders in public issuers.[25] It was the knowledge of those who acquired the securities that should be attributed.

For Lord Hoffmann, the key issue was 'one of construction rather than metaphysics'.[26] He explained the 'directing mind and will' approach was simply an example of a special rule of attribution.[27] The implication: it was not a general rule that should be applied in other contexts.

The focus on construction, particularly in the special rules, led *Meridian* to become closely associated with a highly context-specific approach to attribution. In the Hong Kong Court of Final Appeal decision of *Moulin Global Eyecare Trading Ltd v Commissioner of Inland Revenue*, Lord Walker accepted that '[o]ne of the fundamental points to be taken from *Meridian* is the importance of context … in any problem of attribution'.[28] In *Bilta v Nazir*, Lord Mance reiterated that '[a]s Lord Hoffmann made clear in *Meridian Global*, the key to any question of attribution is ultimately always to be found in considerations of context or purpose'.[29] In his view, the question is 'whose act or knowledge or state of mind is for the purpose of the relevant rule to count as the act, knowledge or state of mind of the company?'[30]

[19] See, eg, Model Articles for Public Companies, Model Art 20; Model Articles for Private Companies Limited by Shares, Model Art 17, which will apply to limited companies unless the company registers its own articles of association: Companies Act 2006 (UK), s 18.

[20] *Multinational Gas and Petrochemical Co v Multinational Gas and Petrochemical Services Ltd* [1983] Ch 258 (CA), cited in *Meridian* (n 5) 506.

[21] *Meridian* (n 5) 506–07.

[22] ibid.

[23] ibid 507.

[24] ibid.

[25] ibid 511.

[26] ibid.

[27] ibid 509.

[28] *Moulin Global Eyecare Trading Ltd v Commissioner of Inland Revenue* [2014] HKCFA 22, (2014) 17 HKCFAR 218 [41].

[29] *Bilta* (n 6) [41].

[30] ibid.

A major impetus for this move towards context-specificity was a series of difficult cases at the intersection of illegality and attribution. Directors[31] or third parties (eg the company's auditors[32] or its broker[33]) were sued by the company for breach of duty. They sought to attribute the wrongdoing of the directors of the company so that the company's claim would fail for illegality. In the first such case, *Stone & Rolls Ltd (in liquidation) v Moore Stephens*,[34] this argument succeeded before the Supreme Court, causing consternation. In the later cases of *Bilta* and *Singularis Holdings Ltd v Daiwa Capital Markets Europe*, the Supreme Court concluded that attribution turned on context, and in these cases the context was such that attribution was not available.

While all accept that attribution is context-dependent, exactly what context it turns on is controversial. In *Meridian* itself, the focus of the special rules was on the purpose and policy of the substantive rule.[35] *Bilta* and *Singularis* adopt a similar position. But others have relied on different features. One approach suggested by the distinguished agency scholar Professor Peter Watts is that attribution turns on the nature and source of the right being enforced.[36] He thus argues that where the claim concerns rights based on the intentions of the parties, attribution takes a different approach than rights that are not so based. Attribution in contractual and restitutionary claims thus differ,[37] with different sets of attribution rules used in different torts.[38] Another approach was adopted by the Singapore Court of Appeal in *Red Star Marine Consultants Pte Ltd v Personal Representatives of Satwant Kaur d/o Sardara Singh* (*Red Star*), where factors outside the cause of action were considered.[39] It was said that attribution must turn on 'both the legal and factual context' of the claim.[40] Attribution was not allowed because the company in *Red Star* was solvent and recovery under the claim could, in practice, return to the hands of the wrongdoer.[41]

B. Allocated Powers

I argue elsewhere that this context-specific approach to attribution runs into difficulty.[42] Perhaps the most serious problem is that the reasons it gives for attribution seem to miss the mark. Justifications must fit the thing to be justified.[43] Factors such as the

[31] In *Bilta* (n 6).
[32] *Stone & Rolls Ltd (a firm) v Moore Stephens* [2009] 1 AC 1391 (HL) (*Stone & Rolls Ltd (a firm)*).
[33] *Singularis* (n 6).
[34] *Stone & Rolls Ltd (a firm)* (n 32).
[35] *Meridian* (n 5) 507.
[36] eg Watts (n 6), building on his earlier work in, eg, P Watts, 'Principals' Tortious Liability for Agents' Negligent Statements – Is "Authority" Necessary?' (2012) 128 *Law Quarterly Review* 260; P Watts, 'The Acts and State of Knowledge of Agents as Factors in Principals' Restitutionary Liability' [2017] *Lloyd's Maritime and Commercial Law Quarterly* 386.
[37] Watts, 'Acts and State of Knowledge' (n 36).
[38] Watts, 'Principals' Tortious Liability' (n 36).
[39] *Red Star Marine Consultants Pte Ltd v Personal Representatives of Satwant Kaur d/o Sardara Singh* [2019] SGCA 76, [2020] 1 SLR 115 (*Red Star*).
[40] ibid [41] (emphasis removed).
[41] ibid [43].
[42] For a detailed account, see Leow (n 8) ch 2.
[43] R Stevens, 'Private Law and the Form of Reasons' in A Robertson and J Goudkamp (eds), *Form and Substance in the Law of Obligations* (Oxford, Hart Publishing, 2019) 119; B McFarlane, 'Form and Substance

purpose and policy of the substantive rule, or the nature and source of the right, might legitimately tell us something about the right or rule. But they do not appear to provide justification for attribution itself. Attribution concerns the connection between act or state of mind, individual and the company. We are looking for reasons to connect *this* act or state of mind of *this* individual with *this* company. The reasons justifying attribution should fit this structure. Factors concerned solely with the right, such as its source or the policy behind the claim enforcing the right, do not. This fundamental difficulty has led to other problems: the context-specific approach is difficult to apply; it embroils attribution in controversial questions about the purposes or policies of a claim or the source and nature of a right, it creates especial difficulty with trying to explain when attribution is unavailable in the illegality cases and creates inconsistencies in the law, risking its rationality.[44]

Instead, I argue that the necessary connection between act or state of mind, individual and the company lies in the allocation and delegation to human individuals of the company's own powers. From the date of the company's incorporation, it comes into existence as a new legal person,[45] becoming eligible to bear rights, duties and powers. Legal persons do not have a fixed set of powers,[46] so what powers the company has will depend on the company's constitution. Powers may be expressly conferred under the constitution or may be implied. 'Anything reasonably incidental to the attainment or pursuit of any of the express objects of the company will, unless expressly prohibited, be within the implied powers of the company.'[47] The modern trend is now in favour of expanding the company's purposes (or objects) and thus its powers. For instance, the Companies Act 2006 (UK) provides that unless otherwise specified, companies registered by incorporation (other than charitable companies) have unlimited powers.[48]

The company's powers will then be allocated through the company's constitution. Typically, powers are divided between the board of directors and shareholders in general meeting, though other possibilities are of course possible. From the very moment that it exists, the company comes into existence with its powers already allocated to different groups. From there they can be further delegated to other individuals. A delegated power involves giving the delegate a power to exercise the company's own powers.[49] In this sense, delegation is agency.[50] Successive rounds of delegation may occur, as where

in Equity' in Robertson and Goudkamp (eds) 197; B McFarlane and R Stevens, 'What's Special about Equity? Rights about Rights' in D Klimchuk et al (eds), *Philosophical Foundations of the Law of Equity* (Oxford, Oxford University Press, 2020) 191; T Liau, 'Standing in Private Law', DPhil thesis, University of Oxford, 2020; T Liau, 'Privity: Rights, Standing, and the Road Not Taken' (2021) 41 *Oxford Journal of Legal Studies* 803. See also EJ Weinrib, *The Idea of Private Law*, rev edn (Oxford, Oxford University Press, 2012) ch 5; EJ Weinrib, *Corrective Justice* (Oxford, Oxford University Press, 2012) 13–15, 18–20.

[44] Leow (n 8) ch 2.

[45] *Salomon v A Salomon & Co Ltd* [1897] AC 22 (HL). See now Companies Act 2006 (UK), s 16(1).

[46] *Bumper Development Corpn Ltd v Metropolitan Police Commissioner* [1991] 1 WLR 1362 (CA), 1371–72.

[47] *In re Horsley & Weight Ltd* [1982] Ch 442 (CA), 448.

[48] Companies Act 2006 (UK), s 39.

[49] R Leow, 'Understanding Agency: A Proxy Power Definition' (2019) 78 *Cambridge Law Journal* 99.

[50] cf *Northern Land Council v Quall* [2020] HCA 33, (2020) 271 CLR 394, where Nettle and Edelman JJ regarded agency and delegation as involving different concepts. In their view, while agency involves one person acting for another so that the former's acts are attributed to the latter, delegation 'in a strict or precise sense' refers to someone who acts on his own behalf and in his own name: at [77]; see also at [81]–[84]. While delegation can be used in the latter sense, it is not so clear that delegation should always be given this meaning.

the board delegates powers to manage the company's business to the chief executive officer, who further delegates finance matters to a chief financial officer, who may then delegate to senior managers, managers, employees and so on. The company's powers can thus be dispersed throughout the corporate hierarchy. This approach provides for considerable flexibility, enabling companies to adopt whatever system it chooses. It can accommodate both the one-man company[51] as well as the enormous multinational company. Some companies may choose to delegate very minimally, with most decisions being taken by a head office;[52] others may disperse powers very widely throughout the corporate hierarchy.

The task of the court is to ascertain to whom the company's powers have been allocated and delegated in practice, not simply on the books. Anyone with some experience in organisations of even moderate complexity will quickly learn that formal corporate hierarchies may not be strictly followed. A receptionist may wield very substantial power in practice. Mid-level managers may routinely be bypassed by their subordinates due to incompetence, with senior management closing an eye and endorsing the subordinates' decisions. Decision making may take place informally over dinners or long-distance cycling trips. Real-world complexities may complicate fact finding, but the underlying principles remain constant: the search is for the allocation and delegation of the company's powers.

Powers allocated or delegated can be exercised by the persons to whom they are given. Where they are exercised, the company itself acts. Those acts are the company's own. This account avoids the need to fictionally deem acts or states of mind to be the company's. It also suggests that attribution has deeper normative significance, identifying intentional acts done by the company as a 'group agent'.[53] Here, 'agency' is employed in the sense used in philosophy of action, referring to a being with the capacity for action, rather than the legal concept of agency. Such agents must be able to form intentions and goals, and act motivated by those intentions and goals.[54] The acts thereby produced are intentional ones, which may have further significance for whether companies can be held responsible for them, morally or otherwise.

In my book, I show that this analysis applies to the attribution of acts and one state of mind: knowledge. Like with the attribution of acts, attributing knowledge also turns on the allocation and delegation of the company's powers.[55] Knowledge qualifies the character of acts done, changing them from neutral or even virtuous to improper.[56] Knowledge may itself be constitutive of a wrong (as with dishonest assistance or deceit), it may put the knowledge-holder under new duties (as in the statute in *Meridian* itself) or it may qualify the knowledge-holder's rights (as with the defences of change of

[51] eg *Lee v Lee's Air Farming Ltd* [1961] AC 12 (PC).

[52] eg the insurance business carried on in *British Bank of the Middle East v Sun Life Assurance Co of Canada (UK) Ltd* [1983] 2 Lloyd's Law Rep 9 (HL), 14, 17 (Lord Brandon).

[53] See, eg, C List and P Pettit, *Group Agency: The Possibility, Design, and Status of Corporate Agents* (Oxford, Oxford University Press, 2011).

[54] See generally ibid; PA French, *Collective and Corporate Responsibility* (New York, Columbia University Press, 1984); R Tuomela, *Social Ontology: Collective Intentionality and Group Agents* (Oxford, Oxford University Press, 2013).

[55] Leow (n 8) ch 6.

[56] ibid.

position or bona fide purchase).[57] I argue that for knowledge to be attributed, it must be possessed by someone who is allocated or delegated the company's powers to act, and it must be material to the exercise of those powers (the 'materiality' test). Only such knowledge can qualify the acts done by the company.

A key implication of this model is that, unlike *Meridian*, attribution does not turn on the source or type of the right, or the purpose of the policy of the claim in question. Nor does it turn on whether the company is being sued for breach of its duties or whether the company is suing another to enforce duties owed to it. However, as we shall see later, it is still relatively individualistic in that it seeks to identify the person(s) to whom the company's powers are allocated or delegated.

C. Systems Intentionality

A third recently proposed model is that of 'systems intentionality'. It starts from the premise that existing means of establishing the corporate state of mind are inadequate and 'fraught with difficulty'.[58] This is because existing approaches are fundamentally 'human-centric'.[59] They cope poorly with the complexities of modern companies where knowledge may be highly dispersed in complicated ways throughout the corporate structure and reporting lines.[60] By contrast, the systems intentionality model seeks to identify the 'corporate mind', which is manifested through its systems, policies and practices.[61]

At the highest level of generality, companies may adopt policies that set out their corporate purposes, beliefs and instantiate their intention. For example, companies may adopt policies against using child labour in their factories or animal-testing, or 'green' policies.

Policies may then be implemented by systems that are designed to bring about certain desired effects. One might seek to implement a 'safety first' policy by instituting a system where monthly spot-checks are carried out in every factory. Policies are clearly distinct from systems, as one may have a policy but no system to implement it. But systems may also develop organically without any *ex ante* policy. Cases where senior management are alerted to potentially suspicious transactions but routinely dismiss concerns may evidence a system of disregarding potential fraud, which may be relevant to establishing the company's intentions or knowledge.[62]

A practice involves patterns of behaviour that are habitual or customary.[63] On their own, patterns of behaviour are themselves neutral to intention. It may be a practice that employees go to the café around the corner from the office building for lunch during their lunch break. However regular this may be, it seems importantly distinct from a

[57] ibid.
[58] Bant, 'Culpable Corporate Minds' (n 4) 354.
[59] ibid.
[60] ibid.
[61] ibid 355. See generally E Bant, 'Catching the Corporate Conscience: A New Model of "Systems Intentionality"' (2022) *Lloyd's Maritime and Commercial Law Quarterly* 467.
[62] For further examples, see eg Bant and Paterson (n 4).
[63] Bant, 'Catching the Corporate Conscience' (n 61).

system implemented by the company. However, if senior management stress that late returns to the office will be heavily penalised and there is no other café in the vicinity, it might then be said that there is an implicit system that strongly encourages employees to have lunch at the nearby café. Practices may thus be characterised as 'a system of conduct, where the "custom" or "habit" has crossed into the realm of an adopted process'.[64]

By stressing that the company's mind can be manifested in its systems, policies and practices of behaviour, the model thus builds on and draws support from existing work that endorses (i) the need to capture the problem of 'diffused responsibility' in large organisations;[65] (ii) the importance of taking into account what companies do or fail to do in response to harmful conduct on their behalf;[66] (iii) the importance of corporate culture;[67] and (iv) research that shows how even human persons use external systems to support decision making.[68] Not all systems, policies and practices will necessarily tell us something about the corporate state of mind. It is important to note that this model is proposed as an additional one: it does not seek to replace existing approaches but to supplement them.[69]

II. Comparing the Models

This section compares the three models on six questions. Three are more foundational: (i) Do they take individualist or collectivist approaches? (ii) How widely do they apply throughout the law? (iii) What approaches do they take to corporate personality? The remaining three ask to what extent the models can capture potentially relevant features, including (i) corporate culture, (ii) *ex ante* steps taken to prevent corporate misconduct, and (iii) *ex post* steps taken in response to corporate misconduct.

A. Individualist or Collective?

Approaches may be more individualist or collective. Individualist approaches focus on the human individual. Such approaches are sometimes motivated by 'methodological individualism', a philosophical approach to understanding social phenomena that advocates that '[t]here is no other way toward an understanding of social phenomena but through our understanding of individual actions directed toward other people and

[64] ibid.

[65] French (n 54) 41.

[66] The reactive fault idea developed by Professor Brent Fisse in, eg, B Fisse, 'Reconstructing Corporate Criminal Law: Deterrence, Retribution, Fault, and Sanctions' (1983) 56 *Southern California Law Review* 1141, 1195–2013; B Fisse, 'The Attribution of Criminal Liability to Corporations: A Statutory Model' (1991) 13 *Sydney Law Review* 277; B Fisse, 'Recent Developments in Corporate Criminal Law and Corporate Liability to Monetary Penalties' (1990) 13 *University of New South Wales Law Journal* 1; B Fisse and J Braithwaite, *Corporations, Crime and Accountability* (Cambridge, Cambridge University Press, 1993) 47–49.

[67] eg Criminal Code Act 1995 (Cth), pt 2.5.

[68] M Diamantis, 'The Extended Corporate Mind: When Corporations Use AI to Break the Law' (2020) 98 *North Carolina Law Review* 893.

[69] ibid.

guided by their expected behaviour'.[70] Others might not subscribe to methodological individualism but may believe that it is sufficient to fulfil the goals of specific areas of law to focus only on human individuals. Thus, in the criminal law, it might be thought that fit subjects of deterrence or retribution are human individuals, not companies.[71]

By contrast, collective approaches focus not on the individual but on the group. Proponents stress that acts and decisions of a collective are not reducible to the sum of their parts.[72] They argue that in both life and law, it is inaccurate to describe collectives as merely aggregates of their members.[73] Collectivists regard the nature of collective activity as significant and uncapturable by individualist approaches. In this vein, others might stress that collectives have greater political and social power than individuals do, thus requiring correspondingly greater control over them.

Perhaps the most individualist approach was the 'directing mind and will' test, which sought to equate companies to a single human person: the company was simply the human person's alter ego. But the field of options is now much wider. Of the three models here, it is probably fair to say that the systems intentionality approach appears the most overtly collective. Although it is difficult to pin down the *Meridian* context-specific approach, it is at least quite significantly individualist in flavour, subject to one caveat. The allocated powers approach probably occupies a middle ground between the other two.

The systems intentionality approach appears to take the most overtly collective approach. It accepts that 'corporations are more than the sum of their individual employees and can, and should, be treated as responsible entities on their own account'.[74] It argues that the company's state of mind is being manifested in the company's systems, policies and practices. While the acts and states of mind of individuals may be relevant to identifying systems, policies and practices, they are not necessary. Importantly, it may be possible to find that a company intended a particular outcome even if no human individual had that intention.[75]

It is less clear whether this result would be possible under either the *Meridian* or the allocated powers approaches. At least on their face, both have an individualistic focus: they search for the acts and states of mind of human persons that can then be treated as the company's. This is so whether they focus on the allocation and delegation of the company's powers under the allocated powers model, or whether they focus on the purpose or policy of the rule, or the nature of the right being enforced.

This, however, may be an over-simplification. Whether allocated powers and *Meridian* are truly so individualistic turns also on their approach to aggregation. Can the knowledge of different persons be added together to create a different state of mind?

[70] FA Hayek, *Individualism and the Economic Order* (Chicago, IL, University of Chicago Press, 1948) 6.

[71] Fisse and Braithwaite (n 66) 18.

[72] ibid 22; List and Pettit (n 53).

[73] French (n 54) ch 2; Fisse and Braithwaite (n 66) 22; List and Pettit (n 53); HLA Hart, 'Definition and Theory in Jurisprudence' in HLA Hart, *Essays in Jurisprudence and Philosophy* (Oxford, Oxford University Press, 1983) 21.

[74] Bant, 'Catching the Corporate Conscience' (n 61).

[75] See discussion of the Royal Commission into the Casino Operator and Licence, State of Victoria, *Royal Commission into the Casino Operator and Licence* (The Report, October 2021) vol 1, especially 176 (RCCOL Report).

This argument was first raised in *R v Her Majesty's Coroner for East Kent*, a case concerning the capsize of the ferry, *Herald of Free Enterprise*, when nearly 200 passengers and crew were killed.[76] The ferry had sailed with its bow doors open, leading to water's entering the ship, which quickly capsized. The evidence showed that several individuals failed to take relevant safety measures, including closing the bow doors, failing to see that the doors were closed and sailing without knowing that the doors were closed. The prosecution argued that the company was guilty of manslaughter for gross negligence even though no individual actor committed gross negligence. Bingham LJ firmly rejected the argument.[77] In his view:

> Whether the defendant is a corporation or a personal defendant, the ingredients of manslaughter must be established by proving the necessary *mens rea* and *actus reus* of manslaughter against it or him by evidence properly to be relied on against it or him.[78]

Prospects for aggregation continue to remain dim.[79] In *Stanford International Bank Ltd (in liq) v HSBC Bank plc*, Sir Geoffrey Vos MR too held that 'if dishonesty and blind eye knowledge is to be alleged against corporations, large or small, it has to be evidenced by the dishonesty of one or more natural persons'.[80] The underlying fear, identified by Vos MR, is that aggregation establishes only the company's negligence for failing to have systems in place to effectively communicate information, not dishonesty. Aggregation thus seems to be used to allow negligence in by the back door. To the extent that *Meridian* follows the current narrow approach towards aggregation, it too appears to be relatively individualist. The allocated powers account likewise endorses a narrow approach towards aggregation, though one slightly different from the current law.[81]

B. Scope of Application

How widely do these models of attribution apply to different areas of law, different causes of action and their varied goals? Proof of corporate mental states may be required across a wide range of causes of action originating from both statutory and judge-made law.[82] In civil law, it may be necessary to establish the company's beliefs (eg to establish mistake),[83] intention (eg for rectification),[84] dishonesty (eg for dishonest assistance),[85] knowledge (eg for knowing receipt)[86] or unconscionability (eg for the creation of

[76] *R v Her Majesty's Coroner for East Kent* (1987) 3 BCC 636 (QB).
[77] ibid 642.
[78] ibid.
[79] *Commonwealth Bank of Australia v Kojic* [2016] FCAFC 186, (2016) 249 FCR 421.
[80] *Stanford International Bank Ltd (in liq) v HSBC Bank plc* [2021] EWCA Civ 535 [47].
[81] Leow (n 8) ch 8.
[82] As demonstrated by the contributions in this volume by Elise Bant (ch 11), Jeannie Marie Paterson and Elise Bant (ch 12), Jeremy Gans (ch 13) and Robyn Carroll (ch 15).
[83] eg *Barclays Bank Ltd v WJ Simms Son & Cooke (Southern) Ltd* [1980] QB 677 (QB).
[84] eg *Hawksford Trustees Jersey Ltd v Stella Global UK Ltd* [2012] EWCA Civ 55.
[85] eg *Royal Brunei Airlines v Tan* [1995] 2 AC 378 (PC).
[86] eg *El Ajou* (n 13).

some constructive trusts). Statute again demonstrates a similar picture, often requiring knowledge,[87] sometimes requiring unconscionability.[88] In criminal law, mental states may play an even larger role, varying from dishonesty (eg to establish theft),[89] to intention,[90] to knowledge[91] to recklessness.[92]

On *Meridian*-based approaches, establishing a corporate mental state may plausibly depend on whether the question arises in civil or criminal law, whether it arises in a common law or equitable cause of action, or whether the action is in contract, tort or unjust enrichment. For those who think that attribution turns on the purpose and policy of the statute, it is reasonable to think that this might differ between knowing receipt, which holds the knowing recipient civilly liable to give up gains[93] or compensate the claimant for losses,[94] and a criminal statute that carries with it the stigma of conviction. Likewise, those who think that attribution turns on the nature and source of the right might also reach different conclusions in the two cases. The latter might be resolved by identifying Parliament's intention, while the former would not.

On the allocated powers and systems intentionality accounts, attribution does not change across areas of law, causes of action or their purposes. If attribution turns on the allocation and delegation of the company's powers, it does not change depending on those 'right-sided' features. An act or state of mind either is or is not the company's. If an act or state of mind can be attributed to the company for one purpose, it should also be for others. Likewise, systems intentionality tracks similar intuitions. It seeks to identify the company's state of mind from its systems, policies and practices. Again, this seems to be regardless of the nature or source of the right enforced, the jurisdictional origin of the cause of action, or the purpose and policy of the rule. The advantage of these accounts is that they provide more general answers. All other things being equal, a model that applies more generally and provides more generally applicable answers ought to be preferred to a narrower one.

C. Approaches to Corporate Personality?

Third, what approach to corporate personality do these approaches take? Debates over legal personality are long-standing, drawn across different lines. One long-standing division is between fiction theories, which see companies merely as legal fictions

[87] As in the statute in *Meridian* (n 5), the Securities Amendment Act 1988 (NZ), s 20(3). See also *Bank of India v Morris* [2005] EWCA Civ 693, [2005] BCC 739.

[88] eg Competition and Consumer Act 2010 (Cth), sch 2, ss 21–22; and see further Bant and Paterson (n 4).

[89] Theft Act 1968 (UK), s 1.

[90] eg Criminal Damage Act 1971 (UK), s 1(2); Licensing Act 2003 (UK), s 138.

[91] eg Licensing Act 2003 (UK), s 140 (allowing disorderly conduct on licensed premises), s 141 (sale of alcohol to person who is drunk), s 144 (keeping of smuggled goods).

[92] Offences against the Person Act 1861 (UK); Criminal Damage Act 1971 (UK), s 1(2). On definitions of recklessness, see eg *R v Caldwell* [1982] AC 341 (HL); *R v Lawrence* [1982] AC 510 (HL); *R v Adomako* [1995] 1 AC 171 (HL); *R v G* [2003] UKHL 50, [2004] 1 AC 1034.

[93] *Akita Holdings Ltd v AG of the Turks and Caicos Islands* [2017] UKPC 7, [2017] AC 590.

[94] eg *Ultraframe v Fielding* [2005] EWHC 1638 (Ch).

created by the law, and real theories, which see companies as having a real personality of their own. This division is often closely related to views on the role of the state. Fiction theorists generally support the view that corporate personality is a concession from the state,[95] while real theorists emphasise the company's pre-legal existence.

Approaches based on *Meridian* view the company as a fiction. *Meridian* itself amply demonstrates this.[96] Lord Hoffmann described the company as a 'persona ficta', holding that 'a company exists because there is a rule (usually in a statute) which says that a persona shall be deemed to exist and have certain of the powers, rights and duties of a natural person'.[97] Criticising those who sometimes said that companies 'as such' cannot do anything,[98] Lord Hoffmann also emphasised that 'there is in fact no such thing as the company as such, no *ding an sich*, only the applicable rules'.[99] For Lord Hoffmann, attribution rules are just necessary extensions of that fiction.[100] Other scholars following *Meridian* generally adopt similar views, with Professor Jennifer Payne accepting that 'the company cannot itself act' or 'act immaculately'.[101]

On the other hand, the allocated powers and systems intentionality models lean more heavily towards real approaches, though they do not endorse it wholly. Both accept that companies are more than the sum of their parts. Systems intentionality explicitly stresses a 'realist view that corporations are more than the sum of their individual employees'.[102] It argues that they 'can, and should, be treated as responsible entities on their own account'.[103] Both rely on philosophical work on group agency that accepts that groups can be rational agents over and above their individual members,[104] and that corporations can thus be treated as responsible agents.[105] But neither do they wholly endorse the real theory in its original form. Allocated powers, at any rate, accepts that the company's legal personality is created by statute, and that incorporation requires both 'top-down' state recognition and the 'bottom-up' efforts of incorporators voluntarily associating in business. The advantage of allocated powers and systems intentionality is that they are not wholly dependent on a particular account of corporate personality and can thus accommodate varying stances on that question. One need not endorse a particular account of corporate personality to accept either systems intentionality or allocated powers.

[95] On this version, often described as the concession theory.
[96] Leow (n 8) 28–29.
[97] *Meridian* (n 5) 506.
[98] ibid 506–07.
[99] ibid 507.
[100] Leow (n 8) ch 2.
[101] Payne (n 6) 361.
[102] See eg Bant, 'Catching the Corporate Conscience' (n 61).
[103] ibid. See further E Micheler, *Company Law: A Real Entity Theory* (Oxford, Oxford University Press, 2021).
[104] List and Pettit (n 53). See also C List and P Pettit, 'Group Agency and Supervenience' (2005) 44 *Southern Journal of Philosophy* 85; P Pettit, 'Groups with Minds of their Own' in FF Schmitt (ed), *Socializing Metaphysics: the Nature of Social Reality* (Oxford, Rowman & Littlefield, 2003) 137; P Pettit, 'Rationality, Reasoning and Group Agency' (2007) 61 *dialectica* 495; P Pettit, 'The Reality of Group Agents' in C Mantzavinos (ed), *Philosophy of the Social Sciences: Philosophical Theory and Scientific Practice* (Cambridge, Cambridge University Press, 2009) 67; C List and P Pettit, 'Group Agency and Supervenience' in J Hohwy and J Kallestrup (eds), *Being Reduced: New Essays on Reduction, Explanation, and Causation* (Oxford, Oxford University Press, 2008) 75.
[105] eg PA French, 'The Corporation as a Moral Person' (1979) 16 *American Philosophical Quarterly* 207, 210–11; List and Pettit (n 53) ch 7.

D. Relevance of Corporate Culture

Ideas of corporate culture aim to capture the important insight that there may be tacit understandings about appropriate behaviours within the company that may not be captured by looking at formal decision-making processes.[106] A company may not have formal written policies of cost-cutting at the expense of safety, but it may have a corporate culture to that effect. A good example is the Singaporean company of Stars Engineering, which manufactured fire insulation materials. A mixer exploded during the production process, killing three workers. It was discovered that the company's sole director and shareholder had purchased the machine from the Chinese online retailer, Alibaba.[107] He did not read the user guide.[108] Contrary to the instructions, he had initially filled the machine with water instead of oil for testing. After replacing the water with an insufficient amount of oil, he did not use the designated sensor to monitor the oil's temperature, assuming that it would work like a household air-fryer.[109] Workers' complaints about oil leaks, heater damage, smoke and small fires were ignored.[110] It is probably not difficult to reach the conclusion that there was a corporate culture that did not prioritise worker safety.

How well can the models capture corporate culture? Of the models, systems intentionality is best able to accommodate the insights of corporate culture. This is unsurprising; it was formulated to do so. With its focus on the company's policies, systems and practices, systems intentionality can draw on a wide range of corporate behaviour to establish corporate mental states. Companies may adopt systems that automatically accept the lowest tenders for products, adopt practices that trivialise worker safety or ignore the possible environmental impact of their factories, or create a toxic environment where employees are fearful to speak up about abuse or harassment in the workplace. The traditional difficulties were with proof of such a corporate culture, but these problems might plausibly be overcome.[111]

The allocated powers model can also accommodate corporate culture considerations. Although the company's constitution is the first port of call in determining the allocation and delegation of the company's powers, this is only a starting point. The court's task is to determine how powers have been allocated and delegated in practice, not just on paper. Individuals who hold no formal role (such as the matriarch of the founder's family) may wield enormous power in practice, with all routinely following her instructions. Incompetent managers may be bypassed, with their subordinates being the chief decision-makers in day-to-day life. Decisions may be routinely

[106] Most famously adopted in the Criminal Code Act 1995 (Cth), where it has had limited practical effect.
[107] WP Ting, 'Tuas deadly explosion: Company director who bought machine online assumed heating controls worked like they do in 'an air fryer' *Today* (24 September 2021) at www.todayonline.com/singapore/tuas-deadly-explosion-company-director-who-bought-machine-online-assumed-heating-controls-like-air-fryer.
[108] ibid.
[109] ibid.
[110] WP Ting, 'Tuas Industrial Blast Hearing: Workers raised "red flags" with bosses for 6 months before explosion claimed 3 lives' *Today* (20 September 2021, updated 30 September 2021) at www.todayonline.com/singapore/tuas-industrial-blast-hearing-workers-raised-red-flags-bosses-6-months-explosion-claimed-3.
[111] See Bant, ch 9 of this volume.

made over games of golf, cycling or dinners amongst a select cabal. These deviations from the neat reality of an organisational flowchart make it more practically difficult to ascertain the allocation and delegation of the company's powers, but they do not change the underlying principles.

Meridian-based approaches accommodate corporate culture less well, especially versions that focus on right-sided concerns, such as the nature or source of the right or the purpose or policy of the claim. As their focus is right-sided, there is little room to consider company-sided features about how the company runs in practice. There may, of course, be wider approaches associated with *Meridian*. Examples include the account advanced by Professor Jennifer Payne, who appears to accept that both right-sided and company-sided features may be relevant context. Some judicial support for similar views can also be found.[112] These approaches might regard corporate culture considerations as relevant to attribution, but only in the same way that every other factor is relevant to context. This also raises an obvious criticism of these approaches: by admitting everything into consideration, they decide nothing.

E. *Ex Ante* Measures Adopted

Ex ante measures adopted to prevent the commission of offences might be relevant to the company's fault and/or culpability for the commission of an offence. This explains the use of 'due diligence' defences, where companies have a defence if they can show that reasonable care and due diligence were exercised to prevent commission of the offence. Section 24(1)(b) of the Trade Descriptions Act 1968 (UK), the statute in question in the leading case of *Tesco Supermarkets Ltd v Nattrass*, illustrates this.[113] There the section provided that:

> If any person offering to supply any goods gives, by whatever means, any indication likely to be taken as an indication that the goods are being offered at a price less than that at which they are in fact being offered he shall, subject to the provisions of this Act, be guilty of an offence.

However, section 24(1)(b) provides a defence for the person charged, 'that he took all reasonable precautions and exercised all due diligence to avoid the commission of such an offence by himself or any person under his control'.

How *Meridian* deals with *ex ante* measures remains unclear. There are two problems. First, there is reasonable controversy as to what *Meridian*'s context-specific approach involves. Second, even if one such sub-approach is selected, it is not clear how *ex ante* measures adopted will affect the attribution of acts or states of mind. If attribution turns on the purpose and policy of a given rule, it is not evident that this purpose or policy will tell us when acts or states of mind should be affected, and what role *ex ante* measures play.

On the allocated powers model, this problem disappears. Attribution turns on the allocation and delegation of the company's powers to act. States of mind are attributable

[112] See eg *Red Star* (n 39).
[113] *Tesco* (n 11).

because they affect the exercise of those powers, qualifying it in the case of knowledge or, in the case of beliefs and intentions, providing reasons to act. *Ex ante* measures affecting the allocation and delegation of the company's powers to act in practice will thus affect which acts and states of mind can be attributed. A company that organises its internal hierarchy such that powers to enter contracts are allocated only to those at head offices thus constrains which acts and states of mind are attributable to the company. Only those with the power to contract can have their acts in contracting attributed to the company, and only those whose knowledge is material to the exercise of those powers can have their knowledge attributed. Importantly, this approach can include even *ex ante* measures that were not deliberately implemented but which have evolved informally over time.

Systems intentionality provides the greatest space to accommodate *ex ante* measures. Since it identifies the company's state of mind as that manifested in its systems, practices and policies, it can accommodate both good and bad *ex ante* measures. Good ones may include systems put in place to prevent bribery or harassment of junior employees; bad ones may include systems designed to make profits at all costs or practices where managers turn a blind eye to violations of human rights in their supply chains.

F. *Ex Post* Measures Adopted

Conversely, are *ex post* measures adopted by the company after some relevant misconduct relevant in identifying the corporate state of mind? This idea is exemplified by the concept of 'reactive corporate fault', brought to prominence by Professor Brent Fisse. This is fault by a company in failing to take satisfactory preventative or corrective measures in response to the commission of the actus reus of an offence by personnel acting on behalf of the company.[114] This proposal changes the timeframe in which corporate mens rea is to be identified to after the commission of misconduct, rather than before. As Fisse argues, reactive corporate fault seems to reflect commonly held attitudes towards companies that fail to react responsibly after having engaged in misconduct.[115]

Both *Meridian* and allocated powers likely have limited ability to accommodate measures adopted after misconduct. Under both approaches, the relevant timeframe for assessing whether states of mind should be attributed is when the act of misconduct is committed. This is assumed by the *Meridian* model. The allocated powers model explains that knowledge is attributed where it changes the character of the act done. It must thus be assessed contemporaneously with the act. Both of these approaches are incompatible with 'reactive corporate fault', which looks for the requisite mental state after the commission of the act.

Systems intentionality may be more accommodating, though it would not go as far as Fisse's original proposals. The absence of corrective measures taken by the

[114] Fisse, 'Reconstructing Corporate Criminal Law' (n 66) 1202. See also Brent Fisse's contribution to this volume (ch 7).

[115] Fisse, 'Reconstructing Corporate Criminal Law' (n 66) 1197.

company in response to misconduct may indicate that the company has an *ex ante* system of ignoring misconduct, or even that it has a general policy to permit the occurrence of that misconduct. In other words, *ex post* measures taken (or not taken) might be a source of evidence about what the company's *ex ante* measures were. Take the case of the casino operator, Crown Melbourne, which had a practice of aggregating deposit data that concealed the quantum of individual deposits and where the data entry and anti-money-laundering systems were set up and maintained separately. There was evidence that Crown was made aware of potential failures in the system but did nothing to correct it.[116] This could constitute evidence that there was a policy of ignoring 'red flags' about money laundering at the casino, which might then suggest that the company had blind-eye knowledge, was unconscionable or acted recklessly when the money-laundering acts occurred.

III. Compatibility of the Models

This section aims to examine how compatible the models are with one another. It concludes that while the allocated powers model is inconsistent with *Meridian*'s context-specific approach, it is compatible with the key decision of *Meridian* itself. Although *Meridian*-type approaches sit uneasily with systems intentionality, allocated powers appears relatively compatible with systems intentionality. A proponent of allocated powers could accept systems intentionality without much difficulty, though she is not bound to do so.

A. Allocated Powers and *Meridian*

Elsewhere, I have argued that the allocated powers account is consistent with the decision and hierarchy of attribution rules in *Meridian*.[117] It also avoids difficulties with the orthodox account of *Meridian*. This includes difficulty in justifying attribution rules, miring attribution in controversy about the purposes of a rule or the source of a right, uncertainty in application, and inconsistent answers being given in one area of the law and another. The context-specific approach was likely attractive for three reasons. First, there was significant doubt about what attribution rules applied in some areas of law or for some mental states.[118] Second, it seemed to provide easier answers to difficult cases where directors who had committed frauds or breaches of duty sought to attribute their wrongful acts and states of mind to the company where the company was enforcing its rights against those directors or some third parties.[119] Third, prevailing approaches to statutory interpretation or the interpretation of

[116] RCCOL Report (n 75) 176–77.
[117] Leow (n 8) 37–39.
[118] See eg *El Ajou* (n 13) and *Meridian* (n 5).
[119] eg *Stone & Rolls Ltd (a firm)* (n 32); *Bilta* (n 6); *Singularis* (n 6). Compare most recently *Crown Prosecution Service v Aquila Advisory Ltd* [2021] UKSC 49.

written documents may sometimes require consideration of contextual features.[120] However, these reasons do not justify adopting a general approach to attribution that turns on right-sided features. In any event, the first two sets of problems could have been addressed through alternative means.[121]

B. *Meridian* and Systems Intentionality

How compatible are systems intentionality and *Meridian*-based approaches? In theory, they could be combined, since systems intentionality does not aim to replace existing models but to supplement them. However, the two are not easy bedfellows; they appear to take largely inconsistent starting points.

The starting point of *Meridian*-based accounts is that the company is merely a legal fiction, with attribution rules a necessary extension of that fiction. The content of attribution rules does not turn on company-sided features but typically on others, whether that is the purpose and policy of the rule requiring attribution or the source and type of the right being enforced. Attribution is thus dependent on the area of law the issue arises in and the goals and purposes associated with that area of law. By contrast, systems intentionality seeks to take the company seriously as an actor, adopting the 'realist' view that it is greater than the sum of its parts. It goes beyond formal documents to look at how the company operates in practice, seeking to identify the company's state of mind from what it does. This approach does not depend on goals and purposes associated with a particular area of law. It seems implicit in systems intentionality that it seeks to identify the company's state of mind for all purposes.

While the two approaches could be combined, the resulting mix runs the risk of being incoherent. The approaches take fundamentally different approaches to corporate personality, whether answers to attribution turn on goals or purposes associated with specific areas of law, and how individualist they are. These two models differ on all these aspects, as well as on whether corporate culture, *ex ante* and *ex post* conduct of the company are relevant to assessing the corporate state of mind.

C. Allocated Powers and Systems Intentionality

Allocated powers, however, might be relatively compatible with systems intentionality. As mentioned earlier, systems intentionality was meant to supplement rather than replace existing models. Allocated powers and systems intentionality share similar starting points. They adopt relatively collective approaches to attribution, and accept that companies are more than the sum of their parts and can even be intentional actors.

[120] eg in statutory interpretation, *IRC v McGuckian* [1997] 1 WLR 991 (HL) 999: 'Where there is no obvious meaning of a statutory provision the modern emphasis is on a contextual approach designed to identify the purpose and to give effect to it.' See also *MacNiven (HM Inspector of Taxes) v Westmoreland Investments Ltd* [2001] UKHL 6, [2001] 2 WLR 377 [6]; *Barclays Mercantile Business Finance Ltd v Mawson (Inspector of Taxes)* [2004] UKHL 51, [2005] 1 AC 684 [28].

[121] Leow (n 8) ch 6 (attribution of knowledge) and ch 7 (attribution in enforcing duties owed to the company).

They look to identify general answers to attribution that are independent from the area of law in which the question arises. To varying extents, they can accommodate notions of corporate culture, and give effect to informality in how the company's affairs are organised.

Although the two also differ, these differences are not likely to lead to incompatibility. Three points can be made.

First, allocated powers focuses on legal concepts, while systems intentionality adopts a less legal approach, focusing on wider patterns of behaviour within the company. Although bearing a different focus, these approaches are consistent. Allocated powers focuses on the structure of attribution and uses legal concepts that fit this structure. It takes as its starting point the company's powers, imbued in it through the process of incorporation, and then works out how these powers may be distributed throughout the corporate hierarchy and subject to limits. This approach is relatively fine-grained, requiring the company's internal allocation of its powers to be identified. Conversely, the systems intentionality approach focuses less intensely on concepts and more on wider patterns of behaviour. If the allocated powers account involves close examination with a magnifying glass, systems intentionality takes a bird's-eye view.

Second, allocated powers and systems intentionality adopt different but compatible standpoints in assessing the corporate state of mind. Systems intentionality largely takes an external viewpoint: it assesses the conduct of people acting for the company and reaches conclusions about the corporate state of mind from these practices, systems and policies. It is not necessary to ask what those individuals knew or suspected about the patterns of behaviour. This approach is thus particularly well suited to heavily siloed companies where one cog in the wheel does not know what another is doing. Allocated powers, however, adopts a more internal approach following from its focus on the internal distribution of the company's powers and how states of mind affect the exercises of those powers. Though different, the two are not incompatible. They may even be complementary.

Third, the full implications of the allocated powers account have not been worked out for states of mind other than knowledge, while systems intentionality focuses primarily on states of mind. This lends greater credence to the possibility that the two can be combined without too much inconsistency. It is fair to say that knowledge itself will suffice to deal with many so-called states of mind in civil law, since most of those are really standards of conduct, judged against the actor's knowledge. But there will still be some that remain, as with beliefs (necessary to establish mistake) or intention (relevant for a whole host of wrongs, as well as contracting, rectification[122] and more). It is possible that this can be achieved by extending the attribution rules to knowledge to other states of mind. This does not seem implausible in the case of beliefs, and perhaps even intentions. It might be arguable that, like knowledge, beliefs and intention qualify an actor's acts, changing their character.

One final observation, however, is warranted. Allocated powers and systems intentionality appear relatively compatible, but whether systems intentionality should

[122] eg *Hawksford Trustees Jersey Ltd v Stella Global UK Ltd* [2012] EWCA Civ 55.

be adopted seems to rest on how much can be 'read in' about a company's state of mind from the actions it takes. Systems intentionality accepts that quite a lot can be. It would accept, for example, that if companies had practices where warning signs by external accountants about fraud went unnoticed, one might reasonably conclude that the company intended, or was at least reckless about, facilitating fraud. This approach bears some resemblance to (but is also importantly different from) Mihailis Diamantis's suggestion that corporate mens rea can be identified by a simple inferential approach that asks factfinders to do what they do in everyday social interactions by looking at a set of actions and their background circumstances and inferring what mental state accompanied them.[123] Strictly speaking, the allocated powers model is silent on how much can be 'read in' from the company's actions: it is consistent with a wide approach (ie systems intentionality), but also with a narrow approach. While the two are relatively consistent, acceptance of allocated powers need not lead inexorably to the acceptance of systems intentionality. The same is also true vice versa.

IV. Conclusion

Like the parable of different people grasping different parts of the same elephant and giving wholly different descriptions of it, models of corporate attribution might arguably be aiming to describe different aspects of the same phenomenon. Having contrasted systems intentionality with other accounts of corporate attribution, this chapter concludes that systems intentionality and the allocated powers account are relatively compatible. A subscriber to the allocated powers account could accept systems intentionality without much difficulty; the key question for her is not really about companies at all, but about how readily courts should draw inferences about mental states from acts done. This question goes far beyond establishing corporate states of mind. Systems intentionality may thus have wider implications than it appears.

[123] M Diamantis, 'Corporate Criminal Minds' (2016) 91 *Notre Dame Law Review* 2049, 2077–83. See later Mihailis Diamantis's contribution to this volume on 'How to Read a Corporation's Mind' (ch 10). Where Diamantis's suggestion differs from systems intentionality is that Diamantis seems to accept that the processes used to infer a human person's state of mind from its actions against the background circumstances apply equally to infer a company's state of mind, but systems intentionality appears to reject this. The latter sees its aim as identifying a distinctive organisational corporate state. The two thus differ in that Diamantis ultimately appears to advocate an approach that does not involve viewing and treating companies as different from human actors, while systems intentionality thinks the two are importantly different in identifying corporate states of mind.

7

Reactive Corporate Fault

BRENT FISSE*

I. Reactive Corporate Fault Revisited – Overview

Corporate liability for unlawful conduct traditionally has depended on proof of responsibility for causally relevant acts or omissions at or before the time the unlawful conduct occurred. Corporate criminal responsibility traditionally has depended on proof that the corporate defendant performed causally relevant acts or omissions intentionally (or knowingly or recklessly). Those approaches are based on a narrow time-frame. From another perspective, the time-frame should be extended to enable liability to be imposed on a corporation for failing to take adequate preventive or corrective action as a responsive reaction to having committed unlawful acts or omissions.[1]

This is but one of many respects in which the present law on corporate liability for wrongdoing is open to question and improvement. Two recent works highlight a wide range of concerns and advance constructive solutions to help resolve them: the Australian Law Reform Commission's *Corporate Criminal Responsibility: Final Report*[2] and John C Coffee Jr's *Corporate Crime and Punishment: The Crisis of Underenforcement*.[3] Particular mention should also be made of John Braithwaite's 'Maximal Accountability with Minimally Sufficient Punishment', a fundamental contemporary perspective on the social control of lawbreaking in modern corporate society.[4]

This chapter revisits the proposal that corporate penal responsibility be assessed on the basis of reactive corporate fault, as an additional and alternative basis of responsibility.[5]

* Thanks are due especially to John Braithwaite for his inspiration and fund of ideas on corporate crime and regulation over more than four decades. The usual disclaimers apply.

[1] On the need to reflect the corporateness of corporate action and avoid narrow legalistic conceptions of corporate responsibility, see N Lacey, 'Philosophical Foundations of the Common Law: Social Not Metaphysical' in J Horder (ed), *Oxford Essays in Jurisprudence: Fourth Series* (Oxford, Oxford University Press, 2000) 17.

[2] Australian Law Reform Commission, *Corporate Criminal Responsibility* (Report No 136, April 2020) (ALRC Final Report).

[3] JC Coffee, *Corporate Crime and Punishment: The Crisis of Underenforcement* (Oakland, CA, Berrett-Koehler Publishers, 2020).

[4] J Braithwaite, 'Maximal Accountability with Minimally Sufficient Punishment' (2021–22) 47 *Journal of Corporation Law* 911.

[5] B Fisse, 'Reconstructing Corporate Criminal Law: Deterrence, Retribution, Fault and Sanctions' (1983) 56 *Southern California Law Review* 1145, 1195–213.

Broadly, reactive corporate fault is an unreasonable failure by a corporation to take satisfactory preventive or corrective measures in response to the performance by the corporation of the physical elements of an offence or a civil violation.

The concept of reactive corporate fault seeks to address the following major known limitations of the present law in its attempt to prevent corporate lawbreaking:

- The prime goal of prevention of corporate lawbreaking implies the relevance of a reactive time-frame as well as a proactive time-frame for assessing whether or not adequate steps have been taken by a corporation to guard against repetition of unlawful conduct. The present law on the attribution of fault to corporations and the assessment of sentence or penalty does not reflect that basic implication with sufficient clarity or emphasis.
- The present law does not adequately meet the everyday expectation that a corporation that has caused a bad or harmful outcome should be held to account for failing to take action to prevent repetition of that outcome.
- Individual accountability for past corporate lawbreaking is the exception rather than the rule.[6] This is inconsistent with the commonplace understanding that individual accountability is an essential means of preventing corporate wrongdoing.
- Corporate accountability for failing to take reasonable precautions to prevent unlawful conduct almost always is limited to organisational precautions taken beforehand.[7] That is far too narrow an approach.
- Corporations typically rely on management by exception.[8] When the commission of an offence or other breach of the law emerges later as an exception to be managed, it is often easy for a corporation to deny prior fault. Excuses such as 'we were taken by surprise' or 'we delegated responsibility in good faith' are easily made and can be difficult to refute.
- Corporations can and do act intentionally in carrying out corporate policies.[9] However, in practice, the predominant form of corporate fault is more likely to be corporate negligence than corporate intention.[10] Where corporate intentionality or corporate negligence cannot be proved to exist at or before the unlawful conduct, the further question is whether or not the corporate response to that unlawful conduct is at fault.
- Enforceable undertakings, deferred prosecution agreements (DPAs) and mitigation of sentence or penalty embody reactive corporate fault implicitly. However, these forms of reactive corporate fault are embryonic, not fully developed.

[6] See B Fisse and J Braithwaite, *Corporations, Crime and Accountability* (Cambridge, Cambridge University Press, 1993).

[7] See, eg, Criminal Code Act 1995 (Cth), s 12.3(3) ('Criminal Code'); Anti-Money Laundering and Counter-Terrorism Act 2006 (Cth), s 236.

[8] LR Bittel, *Management by Exception: Systematizing and Simplifying the Managerial Job* (New York, McGraw-Hill, 1964); H Mintzberg, *The Structuring of Organizations: A Synthesis of the Research* (Englewood Cliffs, NJ, Prentice Hall, 1979) ch 21.

[9] See Fisse and Braithwaite (n 6) 26–29.

[10] ibid 29.

The limitations of the present law indicated above are discussed in more detail in section II.A of this chapter.

Reactive corporate fault is not a substitute for proactive corporate fault.[11] Lack of reactive corporate fault is not a basis for denying liability where there has been proactive corporate fault. Nor is there any suggestion that the concept of proactive corporate fault be replaced by that of reactive corporate fault.

Statutory models of corporate fault and reactive corporate fault are considered in section III, in the context of the Criminal Code Act 1995 (Cth) (Criminal Code). The options discussed are:

(1) make the absence of reactive corporate fault an explicit mitigating factor in determining a sentence for a corporate offender; and
(2) abstain from making reactive corporate fault a basis for attributing the fault element of an offence to a corporation, as under the ALRC Final Report recommendations on corporate fault; or
(3) amend section 12 of the Criminal Code by extending Option 1 and Option 2 in Recommendation 7 of the ALRC Final Report to cover reactive corporate fault.

Option (3) is commended, in combination with Option (1).

Reactive corporate fault should also be a factor to be taken into account when assessing a penalty against a corporation, as recommended in Recommendation 11 of the ALRC Final Report.

The statutory model of reactive corporate fault proposed would address the limitations of the present law outlined above and discussed further in section II.A. Statutory reform would also avoid leaving the development of the law to glacial melting at common law. A key-point summary is given in section IV.A of how Option (3) plus Option (1) would address the stated limitations of the present law.

Section IV concludes by also considering possible concerns, including the hazards of corporate dissembling, obstruction and other attempted manipulations of the administration of justice.

II. The Concept of Reactive Corporate Fault

A. Reactive Corporate Fault

Reactive corporate fault may be defined as the purposive or unreasonable corporate failure to devise and undertake satisfactory preventive or corrective measures in response to the performance of the physical elements of an offence, or a breach of a civil prohibition, by personnel acting on behalf of the organisation.[12]

[11] It has sometimes been contended that reactive corporate fault is unsatisfactory because it is an inappropriate substitute for proactive corporate fault; see, eg, Department of Justice Canada, *Corporate Criminal Liability* (Discussion Paper, March 2002) at www.justice.gc.ca/eng/rp-pr/other-autre/jhr-jdp/dp-dt/iss-ques.html. That contention is spurious because it misrepresents the concept of reactive corporate fault: reactive corporate fault is a complement, not a substitute.

[12] Fisse (n 5) 1210.

The concept of reactive corporate fault is to be contrasted with 'proactive corporate fault', which is fault accompanying or actuating the performance of the physical elements of an offence, or a breach of a civil prohibition, by personnel acting on behalf of the organisation.[13]

A cogent system of corporate penal liability will include liability based on proactive corporate fault and liability based on reactive corporate fault. Proactive corporate fault and reactive corporate fault are complements, not substitutes.[14]

The concept of reactive corporate fault seeks to address the following major limitations of the present law on corporate fault.

First, the goal of preventing corporate lawbreaking implies the relevance of a reactive time-frame as well as a proactive time-frame for assessing whether or not adequate steps have been taken by a corporation to guard against repetition of unlawful conduct. How a corporation reacts to and learns from discovering that it has engaged in lawbreaking may be no less important than what it did proactively to prevent that lawbreaking.[15] Sensible assessment of what needs to be done is not limited to what has been done or not done at the time of the unlawful conduct but extends to what is going to be done thereafter to prevent that conduct from recurring. Yet the present law on corporate liability generally locks itself onto a proactive time-frame.

Second, public responses to corporate wrongdoing typically are concerned with what a corporation does to account for the wrongdoing after the event, as well as with what it did beforehand or at the time.[16] Commonly, there is an expectation of 'responsive adjustment' by a corporation that has caused a bad or harmful outcome out of a concern that the untoward outcome not be repeated.[17] Yet the present law on corporate liability is preoccupied with the earlier time-frame and neglects the latter.[18] The expectation of responsive action is not stated explicitly as a principle of liability or sentencing or penalty assessment. There is a discontinuity between what happens in the case-by-case application of the law, on the one hand, and the focus on preventive steps that is so apparent in numerous royal commissions and coronial and other public inquiries into corporate harm causing.

Third, individual accountability for past corporate lawbreaking is far more the exception than the rule.[19] That violates the commonplace understanding that individual

[13] ME Diamantis and WS Laufer, 'Prosecution and Punishment of Corporate Criminality' (2019) 15 *Annual Review of Law and Social Science* 453, 456.

[14] See n 11.

[15] There are many examples. One is the interest shown in the response of Distillers Limited to discovering that thalidomide was causing serious deformities in babies; see M Magazanik, *Silent Shock* (Melbourne, Text Publishing, 2015). A recent example is the interest shown in the ability or otherwise of Crown Resorts, in each of Sydney, Melbourne and Perth, to resurrect itself from being unfit to hold a casino licence to being fit to do so.

[16] See, eg, the case studies in B Fisse and J Braithwaite, *The Impact of Publicity on Corporate Offenders* (Albany, NY, State University of New York Press, 1983).

[17] See PA French, *Collective and Corporate Responsibility* (New York, Columbia University Press, 1984) ch 11.

[18] For one recent study see P Gottschalk and ML Benson, 'The Evolution of Corporate Accounts of Scandals from Exposure to Investigation' (2020) 60 *British Journal of Criminology* 949. Importance generally is attached by corporations to managing public relations swiftly and effectively in the event of a crisis; see S Fink, *Crisis Management: Planning for the Inevitable*, rev edn (Bloomington, IN, iUniverse, 2000); R Campbell, *Crisis Control: Preventing and Managing Corporate Crises* (Sydney, Prentice Hall, 1999).

[19] Fisse and Braithwaite (n 6) ch 1; ALRC Final Report (n 2) ch 9; J Eisenger, *The Chickenshit Club: Why the Justice Department Fails to Prosecute Executives* (New York, Simon & Schuster, 2017).

accountability is an essential means of achieving the effective social control of corporate wrongdoing. Moreover, imposing individual accountability for past corporate lawbreaking is too narrow by itself. One reason is that those accountable may no longer be in a position of control in the same area. Another is that preventing future corporate lawbreaking depends on identifying who is responsible in the future for seeing that preventive measures are taken.[20]

Fourth, limiting corporate accountability to organisational precautions before the unlawful conduct is too narrow.[21] A frequent criticism made of the legal regulation of business is that precedent and backward-looking assessments of liability project a static model of corporate behaviour, whereas innovation and change within corporations require a more dynamic and forward-looking approach. Corporations operate in a dynamic environment. They are expected to learn from failure and to come up with a better approach for the future.

Fifth, corporations typically rely on management by exception.[22] Compliance with the law is treated as a routine matter to be delegated to and handled by employees at lower levels in corporate hierarchies unless a significant problem arises. When the commission of an offence or other breach of the law emerges later, it is easy for a corporation to deny prior fault.

Sixth, finding a genuinely corporate yet workable concept of corporate intentionality is intractable.[23] Corporations can and do act intentionally in carrying out corporate policies. One manifestation of corporate intentionality is 'systems intentionality', as proposed by Elise Bant.[24] However, in practice, the predominant form of corporate fault is more likely to be corporate negligence than corporate intention.[25] Moreover, where corporate intentionality or corporate negligence cannot be proved to exist at or before the unlawful conduct, the further question to be addressed is whether or not the corporate response to that unlawful conduct shows reactive corporate fault.

Seventh, the enforcement of corporate crime often makes criminal liability a fall-back means of social control and relies heavily on enforceable undertakings, DPAs, and mitigation of sentence by reason of preventive or other steps taken in response to prosecution.[26] Enforceable undertakings, DPAs and mitigation of sentence embody

[20] Fisse and Braithwaite (n 6) 212.

[21] ibid 211.

[22] See Bittel (n 8); Mintzberg (n 8) ch 21.

[23] Fisse (n 5) 1195–213; B Fisse, 'Penal Designs and Corporate Conduct: Test Results from Fault and Sanctions in Australian Cartel Law' (2019) 40 *Adelaide Law Review* 285, 287–92; WS Laufer, *Corporate Bodies and Guilty Minds: The Failure of Corporate Criminal Liability* (Chicago, IL, University of Chicago Press, 2006) ch 3; E Bant, 'Culpable Corporate Minds' (2021) 48 *University of Western Australia Law Review* 352; Diamantis and Laufer (n 13) 4–5; M Diamantis, 'Clockwork Corporations: A Character Theory of Corporate Punishment' (2018) 103 *Iowa Law Review* 507.

[24] Bant, ch 9 of this volume; and Bant, ch 11 of this volume.

[25] Fisse and Braithwaite (n 6) 29.

[26] See further I Ayres and J Braithwaite, *Responsive Regulation: Transcending the Deregulation Debate* (New York, Oxford University Press, 1992); C Hodges and R Steinholtz, *Ethical Business Practice and Regulation: A Behavioural and Values-Based Approach to Compliance and Enforcement* (London, Bloomsbury, 2017); K Hawkins, *Law as Last Resort* (Oxford, Oxford University Press, 2002); K Hawkins, *Environment and Enforcement* (Oxford, Clarendon Press, 1984); P Grabosky and J Braithwaite, *Of Manners Gentle: Enforcement Strategies of Australian Business Regulatory Agencies* (Oxford, Oxford University Press, 1986); JA Sigler and JE Murphy, *Interactive Corporate Compliance* (New York, Quorum Books, 1988).

reactive corporate fault implicitly. However, these forms of reactive corporate fault are embryonic, not fully developed. A useful construct for their development, as well as for locating reactive corporate fault in the enforcement scheme of things, is the pyramid of enforcement built by Ian Ayres and Braithwaite in *Responsive Regulation*.[27]

The limitations of the present law outlined above stem from the unduly narrow time-frame adopted for assessing corporate lawbreaking and determining what conduct is to be made subject to liability. The traditional time-frame adopted at common law for determining criminal or civil liability is the time when the physical elements of the offence or breach were committed, or in some circumstances when they were initiated.[28] Confining liability to conduct within that limited time-frame is arbitrary[29] and, given the practical significance of reactive corporate fault, unjustified.

B. Lineage of Reactive Corporate Fault

The common law on corporate fault has yet to live up to its general reputation for fertility. Liability as an accessory after the fact perhaps contains some trace of reactive fault DNA but is very limited in scope, as well as being designed with human offenders in mind. Contempt of court for breach of an injunction is more akin to liability based on reactive fault.[30]

The concept of reactive corporate fault is canvassed in the literature on corporate crime and corporate regulation.[31] Two signposts:

- 'Reconstructing Corporate Criminal Law' in 1983[32] set out a critique of the concepts of personal corporate fault (as under *Tesco Supermarkets Ltd v Nattrass*),[33] vicarious corporate fault and aggregated corporate fault, and advanced proposals for adopting

[27] Ayres and Braithwaite (n 26) ch 2.

[28] S Bronitt and B McSherry, *Principles of Criminal Law*, 3rd edn (Sydney, Lawbook Co, 2010) 231–34; J Horder, *Ashworth's Principles of Criminal Law*, 9th edn (Oxford, Oxford University Press, 2019) 178–80.

[29] M Kelman, 'Interpretive Construction in the Substantive Criminal Law' (1981) 33 *Stanford Law Review* 591, 593–95, 600–16.

[30] D Hanna, 'Corporate Criminal Liability' (1989) 31 *Criminal Law Quarterly* 452, 473–74.

[31] Fisse (n 5) 1195–213; B Fisse and PA French, 'Corporate Responses to Errant Behavior: Time's Arrow, Law's Target' in B Fisse and PA French (eds), *Corrigible Corporations and Unruly Law* (San Antonio, TX, Trinity University Press, 1985) 187; B Fisse, 'Reconditioning Corporate Leniency: The Possibility of Making Compliance Programmes a Condition of Immunity' in C Beaton-Wells and C Tran (eds), *Anti-Cartel Enforcement in a Contemporary Age: Leniency Religion* (Oxford, Hart Publishing, 2015) ch 10; J Braithwaite, 'Intention Versus Reactive Fault' in N Naffine, R Owens and J Williams (eds), *Intention in Law and Philosophy* (Dartmouth, Ashgate Publishing, 2001) 345; GR Sullivan, 'The Attribution of Culpability to Limited Companies' (1996) 55 *Cambridge Law Journal* 515. Reactive fault may be linked to enforced self-regulation, restorative justice and management-based regulation, as to which see especially Ayers and Braithwaite (n 26) ch 4; J Braithwaite, *Restorative Justice and Responsive Regulation* (New York, Oxford University Press, 2002); C Coglianese and J Nash (eds), *Leveraging the Private Sector: Management-Based Strategies for Improving Environmental Performance* (Washington, DC, Resources for the Future Press, 2006).

[32] See n 5.

[33] *Tesco Supermarkets Ltd v Nattrass* [1972] AC 153 (HL) (*Tesco*). The relaxation of the *Tesco* directing mind principle by the Privy Council in *Meridian Global Funds Management Asia Ltd v Securities Commission* [1995] 2 AC 500 (PC) is ill-defined and ill-related to the concept of corporate fault: see CMV Clarkson, 'Kicking Corporate Bodies and Damning their Souls' (1996) 59 *Modern Law Review* 557, 565–69; J Clough and C Mulhern, *The Prosecution of Corporations* (Oxford, Oxford University Press, 2002) 99–104.

and applying the concept of reactive corporate fault. The main proposal was that corporations be subject to liability for an offence where:

(a) the physical elements of that offence have been committed by a person for whose conduct the corporate defendant is vicariously responsible; and
(b) where the corporation has been at fault in one or other of the following ways:
  (i) by having a policy that expressly or impliedly authorises or permits the commission of the offence or an offence of the same type;
  (ii) by failing to take due precautions to prevent the commission of the offence or an offence of the same type;
  (iii) by having a policy of failing to comply with a reactive duty to take preventive measures in response to having committed the physical elements of the offence; or
  (iv) by failing to take due precautions to comply with a reactive duty to take preventive measures in response to having committed the physical elements of the offence.

Under this model, vicarious liability is imposed in relation to the physical elements of an offence but not in relation to the fault element. The fault elements are not based on the *Tesco* principle or the populist notion of 'corporate culture'[34] but on the concept of organisational fault, in the form of a corporate policy of non-compliance or a failure to take reasonable precautions and to exercise due diligence. Liability is extended to cases of reactive corporate fault, in the form of a corporate policy of unresponsive adjustment to having committed the physical elements of an offence, or a failure to take reasonable precautions or to exercise due diligence in order to prevent repetition of that conduct.

- The Accountability Model in *Corporations, Crime and Accountability* (1993)[35] is based on 20 desiderata, one of which (Desideratum 18) is a strategy based on the concept of reactive corporate fault: '*A strategy for allocating responsibility should operate with a conception of fault that is not time-bound, but copes with the dynamic nature of corporate action.*' One reason behind this strategy is to enable the law to keep pace with dynamic corporate change:

> There is ... more to the concept of reactive fault than its ability to reflect the phenomenon of corporate blameworthiness at the post-offence stage of corporate behaviour. Reactive fault also provides the key to structuring legal liability in a way that can handle dynamic changes in the corporate environment. A frequent criticism made of the legal regulation of business is that precedent and backward-looking assessments of liability project a static

[34] The concept of 'corporate culture' is problematic as a basis of liability or accountability; see C Beaton-Wells and B Fisse, *Australian Cartel Regulation* (Cambridge, Cambridge University Press, 2011) 232; J Colvin and J Argent, 'Corporate and Personal Liability for "Culture" in Corporations?' (2016) 34 *Companies and Securities Law Journal* 30; S Bronitt, 'Rethinking Corporate Prosecution: Reviving the Soul of the Modern Corporation' (2018) 42 *Criminal Law Journal* 205; ALRC Final Report (n 2) 4.79; S Crompvoets, *Bloodlust, Trust & Blame* (Melbourne, Monash University Publishing, 2021). Contrast V Comino, '"Corporate Culture" is the "New Black" – Its Possibilities and Limits as a Regulatory Tool for Corporations and Financial Institutions?' (2021) 44 *University of New South Wales Law Journal* 295; J Hill, *Legal Personhood and Liability for Flawed Corporate Cultures* (Research Paper No 19/03, Faculty of Law, The University of Sydney, February 2019) at https://ecgi.global/sites/default/files/working_papers/ documents/finalhill3.pdf.

[35] Fisse and Braithwaite (n 6).

> model of corporate behaviour, whereas innovation and change within corporations require a more dynamic and forward-looking approach. As explained below, the reactive fault element built into the Accountability Model allows the law to move in pace with changes that occur within a corporate defendant's organisation, and to insist on higher standards on a case-by-case basis, without injustice.[36]

Reactive corporate fault has yet to be adopted legislatively as a general basis for attributing fault to a corporation.[37] For instance, the concept was not adopted in part 2.5 of the Criminal Code.[38] However, statutory injunctive powers are widespread and liability for contempt where a statutory injunction is breached is in effect liability for reactive fault in the form of intentional non-compliance with a court order.

Some Commonwealth legislation imposes criminal and civil liability on executive officers of a corporation on the basis of reactive fault but, oddly, liability is limited to executive officers and does not extend to their corporate employers.[39] An example is the Environment Protection and Biodiversity Conservation Act 1999 (Cth), under sections 494–496. Section 496(1) (headed 'Did an executive officer take reasonable steps to prevent contravention?') imposes both a proactive duty and a reactive duty on an executive officer:

> (1) For the purposes of sections 494 and 495, in determining whether an executive officer of a body corporate failed to take all reasonable steps to prevent the contravention, a court is to have regard to:
>
> (a) what action (if any) the officer took directed towards ensuring the following (to the extent that the action is relevant to the contravention):
>
> (i) that the body arranges regular professional assessments of the body's compliance with this Act and the regulations;
>
> (ii) that the body implements any appropriate recommendations arising from such an assessment;
>
> (iii) that the body has an appropriate system established for managing the effects of the body's activities on the environment;
>
> (iv) that the body's employees, agents and contractors have a reasonable knowledge and understanding of the requirements to comply with this Act and the regulations, in so far as those requirements affect the employees, agents or contractors concerned; and

[36] ibid 211.

[37] The history includes the proposal by Senator Kefauver on 13 July 1961 in response to the heavy electrical equipment cases. Under that proposal: (i) the possession of knowledge or reasonable cause to believe that a corporation is engaged in or is about to engage in any violation of the penal provisions of the antitrust laws; (ii) the possession of express or implied authority vested by such corporation to stop or prevent such violation or to report such violation to a director, officer or agent empowered by such corporation to stop or prevent such violation; and (iii) the failure to exercise that authority, would constitute ratification: see AM Dershowitz, 'Increasing Community Control over Corporate Crime: A Problem in the Law of Sanctions' (1961) 71 *Yale Law Journal* 280, 303, fn 73.

[38] The background is traced in MR Goode, *Corporate Criminal Liability* (Hobart, Environmental Crime Conference, 1–3 September 1993) at http://citeseerx.ist.psu.edu/viewdoc/download?doi=10.1.1.198.2292&rep=rep1&type=pdf.

[39] The prohibitions under ss 494–495 are defined in terms of the liability of an 'executive officer', not a 'person', and hence s 498B (attribution of the conduct or fault of a director, employee or agent to a corporation) does not apply.

(b) what action (if any) the officer took when he or she became aware that the body was contravening:
  (i) this Act; or
  (ii) the regulations; or
  (iii) if the body contravened Part 3 or section 142 or 142A – any action management plan that was prepared by the body, and approved by the Minister, as required by a condition attached to an approval under Part 9 for the purposes of a provision of Part 3 of the body's taking of an action.

Reactive corporate fault is an implicit part of the structure of enforceable undertakings and DPAs.

Enforceable undertakings under section 87B of the Competition and Consumer Act 2010 (Cth) ('Competition and Consumer Act') and similar provisions in other legislation are very common. Enforceable undertakings usually require the corporation giving the undertaking to take responsive action, including the revision of compliance programmes and independent review of compliance with the undertaking.[40] Failure to take the action required is subject to the imposition of a range of possible court orders.[41]

Deferred prosecution agreements have become very common in the USA and are also used increasingly in the United Kingdom and other jurisdictions.[42] A questionable model has been proposed in Australia for a limited range of offences under Commonwealth law.[43]

Reactive corporate fault is part of the structure of DPAs.[44] Simon Bronitt has explained the connection:

> [T]he reactive fault model would prioritise the preventive purpose of DPA schemes. The model of reactive fault has profound implications for responses to alleged corporate wrongdoing. There is no need to establish that the corporate conduct was accompanied by any fault element – the corporation only need acknowledge its 'responsibility' for the prohibited acts or omissions. Consistent with the reorientation towards prevention, prosecutors need not believe there is a reasonable prospect of conviction, or, further, that the corporation must admit its guilt as a precondition of being eligible to engage in a DPA. Since this process is entirely administrative, the usual civil standard of proof on the 'balance of probabilities' would apply. Under this model, once aware of the harm caused, the corporation has a duty to take reasonable steps to engage in restorative action, but also to prevent future harms. If the corporation breaches either duty, then prosecution may be instituted in the ordinary way. At that stage, guilt is determined by assessing corporate blameworthiness before and during the alleged offences. The extent to which a corporate defendant manifested reactive fault after the alleged offence occurred would be relevant only to sentencing; for example,

[40] See, eg, the undertaking entered into by Mosaic Brands Limited: Australian Competition and Consumer Commission, 'Mosaic Brands Limited' (26 May 2021) at www.accc.gov.au/public-registers/undertakings-registers/mosaic-brands-limited.

[41] Competition and Consumer Act 2010, s 87B(4).

[42] See BL Garrett, *Too Big to Jail: How Prosecutors Compromise with Corporations* (Cambridge, Belknap Press, 2014); AS Barkow and RE Barkow (eds), *Prosecutors in the Boardroom* (New York, New York University Press, 2011); C King and N Lord, *Negotiated Justice and Corporate Crime* (London, Palgrave, 2018).

[43] Crimes Legislation Amendment (Combatting Corporate Crime) Bill 2019 (Cth). See further ALRC Final Report (n 2) 494–505; L Campbell, 'Revisiting and Re-Situating Deferred Prosecution Agreements in Australia: Lessons from England and Wales' (2021) 43 *Sydney Law Review* 187.

[44] F Mazzacuva, 'Justifications and Purposes of Negotiated Justice for Corporate Offenders: Deferred and Non-Prosecution Agreements in the UK and US Systems of Criminal Justice' (2014) 78 *Journal of Criminal Law* 249, 262.

> proof that it took steps to prevent future harm, compensate victims and cooperate with authorities may mitigate the sentence imposed in accordance with the ordinary principles of sentencing law.[45]

The main arenas where reactive corporate fault have been relevant as a factor in mitigation of sentence or penalty are civil penalties under section 76 of the Competition and Consumer Act and comparable provisions in other legislation. The statutory factors under section 76 and similar provisions have been expanded by judicial factors. Those factors include the 'French Factors',[46] the 'Heerey Factors'[47] and now the 'Beach Factors'.[48] Factor (f) in the Beach Factors relates directly to reactive corporate fault:

> The fixing of a pecuniary penalty involves the identification and balancing of all the factors relevant to the contravention and the circumstances of the defendant, and the making of a value judgment as to what is the appropriate penalty in light of the purposes and objects of a pecuniary penalty that I have just explained. Relevant factors include the following:
>
> (a) the extent to which the contravention was the result of deliberate or reckless conduct by the corporation, as opposed to negligence or carelessness;
> (b) the number of contraventions, the length of the period over which the contraventions occurred, and whether the contraventions comprised isolated conduct or were systematic;
> (c) the seniority of officers responsible for the contravention;
> (d) the capacity of the defendant to pay, but only in the sense that whilst the size of a corporation does not of itself justify a higher penalty than might otherwise be imposed, it may be relevant in determining the size of the pecuniary penalty that would operate as an effective specific deterrent;
> (e) the existence within the corporation of compliance systems, including provisions for and evidence of education and internal enforcement of such systems;
> (f) remedial and disciplinary steps taken after the contravention and directed to putting in place a compliance system or improving existing systems and disciplining officers responsible for the contravention;
> (g) whether the directors of the corporation were aware of the relevant facts and, if not, what processes were in place at the time or put in place after the contravention to ensure their awareness of such facts in the future;
> (h) any change in the composition of the board or senior managers since the contravention;
> (i) the degree of the corporation's cooperation with the regulator, including any admission of an actual or attempted contravention;
> (j) the impact or consequences of the contravention on the market or innocent third parties;
> (k) the extent of any profit or benefit derived as a result of the contravention; and
> (l) whether the corporation has been found to have engaged in similar conduct in the past.[49]

[45] S Bronitt, 'Regulatory Bargaining in the Shadows of Preventive Justice: Deferred Prosecution Agreements' in T Tulich et al (eds), *Regulating Preventive Justice* (Oxfordshire, Routledge, 2017) ch 12, 224–25.

[46] *Trade Practices Commission v CSR Ltd* [1990] FCA 521, (1991) ATPR 41-076 [42].

[47] *Australian Competition and Consumer Commission v NW Frozen Foods Pty Ltd* [1996] FCA 670, (1996) ATPR 41–515, 42, 444–45.

[48] *Chief Executive Officer of the Australian Transaction Reports and Analysis Centre v Westpac Banking Corporation* [2020] FCA 1538 [58].

[49] Credit has been given in relation to evidence that the company has instituted a compliance programme or reviewed its existing programme after a contravention has come to light: see, eg, *Australian Competition and Consumer Commission v Rural Press Ltd* [2001] FCA 1065, (2001) ATPR 41–833, 43,296 [49]; *Australian Competition and Consumer Commission v ABB Transmission and Distribution Ltd (No 2)* [2002] FCA 559,

III. Statutory Reform of Corporate Fault and Reactive Corporate Fault

A. Options for Adoption of the Concept of Reactive Corporate Fault

What statutory model, if any, would be suitable for adopting the concept of reactive corporate fault?

In the context of the Criminal Code, the main possible options appear to be:

(1) make the absence of reactive corporate fault an explicit mitigating factor in determining a sentence for a corporate offender; and
(2) abstain from making reactive corporate fault a basis for attributing the fault element of an offence to a corporation, as under the ALRC Final Report recommendations on corporate fault; or
(3) amend section 12 of the Criminal Code by extending Option 1 and Option 2 in Recommendation 7 of the ALRC Final Report to cover reactive corporate fault.

Option (3) is commended, in combination with Option (1).

Options (1), (2) and (3) are discussed in sections III.B to III.D following. Section III.E discusses the role of reactive corporate fault in the context of civil penalty prohibitions (for example, the civil cartel prohibitions in the Competition and Consumer Act).

B. Option (1) – Make the Absence of Reactive Corporate Fault an Explicit Mitigating Factor in Determining a Sentence for a Corporate Offender

The absence of reactive corporate fault is an explicit mitigating factor in determination of sentence for a corporate offender under Recommendation 10 in the ALRC Final Report:

> **Recommendation 10**
>
> The *Crimes Act 1914* (Cth) should be amended to require the court to consider the following factors when sentencing a corporation, to the extent they are relevant and known to the court:
>
> a) the type, size, and financial circumstances of the corporation;
> b) whether the corporation had a corporate culture conducive to compliance at the time of the offence;
> c) the extent to which the offence or its consequences ought to have been foreseen by the corporation;
> d) the involvement in, or tolerance of, the criminal activity by management;
> e) whether the unlawful conduct was voluntarily self-reported by the corporation;

(2002) 190 ALR 169, 183 [50]; *Schneider Electric (Australia) Pty Ltd v Australian Competition and Consumer Commission* [2003] FCAFC 2, (2003) 127 FCR 170, 182 [51]; *Australian Competition and Consumer Commission v Colgate-Palmolive Pty Ltd* [2002] FCA 619, (2002) ATPR 41–880, 45,061 [23]; *Australian Competition and Consumer Commission v ABB Transmission and Distribution Ltd* [2001] FCA 383, (2001) ATPR 41–815, 42,939 [25].

f) any advantage realised by the corporation as a result of the offence;
g) the extent of any efforts by the corporation to compensate victims and repair harm;
h) the effect of the sentence on third parties; and
i) any measures that the corporation has taken to reduce the likelihood of its committing a subsequent offence, including:
    i. internal investigations into the causes of the offence;
    ii. internal disciplinary action; and
    iii. measures to implement or improve a compliance program.

This list should be non-exhaustive and should supplement, rather than replace, the general sentencing factors, principles, and purposes when implemented in accordance with Recommendation 9.

Recommendation 10 represents an advance on the present law. However, like the Beach Factors, it takes a shopping-list approach. The factors specified should be prioritised, with much greater priority given to Factor i) than relegation to the grade of being one amongst many.

Pre-sentence reports are needed to make Recommendation 10 work. Recommendation 16 of the ALRC Final Report so recommends.[50]

C. Option (2) – Abstain from Making Reactive Corporate Fault a Basis for Attributing the Fault Element of an Offence to a Corporation

Consider the alternative recommendations on corporate fault made in the ALRC Final Report:

Recommendation 7

Option 1

Section 12.3 of the schedule to the *Criminal Code Act 1995* (Cth) should be amended to:

a) replace 'commission of the offence' with 'relevant physical element';
b) replace 'high managerial agent' with 'officer, employee, or agent of the body corporate, acting within actual or apparent authority' (with consequential amendments to s 12.3(4));
c) replace 'due diligence' with 'reasonable precautions' (with consequential amendments to s 12.5);
d) pluralise the terms 'attitude', 'policy', and 'rule' in the definition of 'corporate culture' and replace 'takes' with 'take'; and
e) repeal s 12.3(2)(d).

[50] ALRC Final Report (n 2) Recommendation 16. See also Australian Law Reform Commission, *Same Crime, Same Time: Sentencing of Federal Offenders* (Report No 103, 2006) Recommendation 14–2; New South Wales Law Reform Commission, *Sentencing: Corporate Offenders* (Report 102, 2003) Recommendation 22. See also Australian Law Reform Commission, *Compliance with the Trade Practices Act 1974* (Report No 68, 1994) [10.40].

Option 2

Section 12.3 of the schedule to the *Criminal Code Act 1995* (Cth) should be replaced with a provision to the effect that if it is necessary to establish a state of mind, other than negligence, of a body corporate in relation to a physical element of an offence, it is sufficient to show that:

a) one or more officers, employees, or agents of the body corporate, acting within actual or apparent authority, engaged in the relevant conduct, and had the relevant state of mind; or

b) one or more officers, employees, or agents of the body corporate, acting within actual or apparent authority, directed, agreed to or consented to the relevant conduct, and had the relevant state of mind.

It is a defence, if the body corporate proves that it took reasonable precautions to prevent the commission of the offence.

Neither Option 1 nor Option 2 in Recommendation 7 includes the concept of reactive corporate fault. That seems unsatisfactory. For the reasons outlined in section II of this chapter, limiting corporate liability to situations where there is proactive corporate fault is unduly narrow.

The proposed scheme for deferred prosecutions under Commonwealth law now on the table is questionable in major respects.[51] Fundamental redesign, including incorporation of reactive corporate fault as a core building block, has been urged.[52]

D. Option (3) – Amend Section 12 of the Criminal Code by Extending Option 1 and Option 2 in Recommendation 7 of the ALRC Final Report to Cover Reactive Corporate Fault

Option 1 or Option 2 in Recommendation 7 of the ALRC Final Report could well be amended to cover reactive corporate fault, as indicated below.[53]

ALRC Option 1

Extend the amendments proposed in Option 1 in the following ways:

- Amend the wording in s 12.3(3) to read: 'to prevent, and to prevent the recurrence of, the conduct, or the authorisation or permission'. This wording is intended to make it clear that the defence of reasonable precautions requires the taking of reactive precautions as well as proactive precautions.

[51] Campbell (n 43); M Lewis, 'Deterring Corporate Crime Through the Use of Deferred Prosecution Agreements: An Analysis of the Proposed Australian Deferred Prosecution Agreement Regime' (2018) 42 *Criminal Law Journal* 76.

[52] See Bronitt (n 45); S Bronitt, *Submission on Deferred Prosecution Agreement (DPA) Scheme Code of Practice* (Consultation Draft, 15 July 2018) at www.ag.gov.au/sites/default/files/2020-05/DPA-Code-Consultation-Simon%20Bronitt-Submission.PDF and the other submissions authored or co-authored by Bronitt referred to therein; B Fisse, *Improving Enforcement Options for Serious Corporate Crime: A Proposed Model for a Deferred Prosecution Agreement Scheme* (Public Consultation Paper Submission, 1 May 2017) at www.ag.gov.au/integrity/publications/submissions-received-proposed-model-deferred-prosecution-agreement-scheme-australia-consultation.

[53] Compare the more complex provisions in B Fisse, 'The Attribution of Criminal Liability to Corporations: A Statutory Model' (1991) 13 *Sydney Law Review* 277. That approach preceded the Criminal Code (n 7), with which a model proposed today needs to be aligned.

- Add a provision to s 12.3(6) along these lines: '*Reasonable precautions* include remedial and disciplinary steps taken before or after the conduct, or the authorisation or permission, and directed to putting in place a compliance system or improving existing systems and disciplining officers responsible for the conduct, or the authorisation or permission.' This wording is based on that used to express the concept of reactive corporate fault in Factor (f) of the Beach Factors.[54]

ALRC Option 2

Extend Option 2 in the following ways:

- Make it a defence if the body corporate proves that it took reasonable precautions to prevent the commission of the offence and to prevent the commission of the offence in future. It needs to be made clear that the defence of reasonable precautions requires the taking of reactive precautions as well as proactive precautions.
- Add a provision to s 12.3(6) along these lines: '*Reasonable precautions* include remedial and disciplinary steps taken before or after the commission of the offence, and directed to putting in place a compliance system or improving existing systems and disciplining officers responsible for the commission of the offence.' This suggested wording adapts that used to express the concept of reactive corporate fault in Factor (f) of the Beach Factors.[55]

Section 12.5(2) of the Criminal Code ('Mistake of fact (strict liability)') should be amended to follow the definition of 'reasonable precautions' proposed above.

E. Reactive Corporate Fault and Civil Penalty Prohibitions

In the context of civil liability for penalties, corporate reactive fault could be provided for explicitly in the provisions governing injunctions (as under section 80 of the Competition and Consumer Act), enforceable undertakings (as under section 87B of the Competition and Consumer Act) and corporate probation orders (as under section 86C of the Competition and Consumer Act).[56]

Reactive corporate fault should be a factor to be taken into account when assessing a penalty against a corporation. Reactive fault is now covered explicitly by Factor (f) of the Beach Factors. Better still, the coverage should be statutory, as recommended in Recommendation 11 of the ALRC Final Report:

Recommendation 11

To maintain principled coherence and consistency in the assessment of penalties for corporations, a statutory provision should be enacted requiring the court to consider the following factors when making a civil penalty order in respect of a corporation, to the extent they are relevant and known to the court, in addition to any other matters:

a) the nature and circumstances of the contravention;
b) the deterrent effect that any order under consideration may have on the corporation or other corporations;
c) any injury, loss, or damage resulting from the contravention;

[54] *Chief Executive Officer of the Australian Transaction Reports and Analysis Centre v Westpac Banking Corporation* [2020] FCA 1538 [58].
[55] ibid.
[56] See Beaton-Wells and Fisse (n 34) 250–53.

d) any advantage realised by the corporation as a result of the contravention;
e) the personal circumstances of any victim of the contravention;
f) the type, size, and financial circumstances of the corporation;
g) whether the corporation has previously been found to have engaged in any related or similar conduct;
h) whether the corporation had a corporate culture conducive to compliance at the time of the offence;
i) the extent to which the contravention or its consequences ought to have been foreseen by the corporation;
j) the involvement in, or tolerance of, the contravening conduct by management;
k) the degree of voluntary cooperation with the authorities, including whether the contravention was self-reported;
l) whether the corporation admitted liability for the contravention;
m) the extent of any efforts by the corporation to compensate victims and repair harm;
n) the effect of the penalty on third parties; and
o) any measures that the corporation has taken to reduce the likelihood of its committing a subsequent contravention, including:
    i. any internal investigation into the causes of the contravention;
    ii. internal disciplinary action; and
    iii. measures to implement or improve a compliance program.

See especially Factor o) above.

Like the Beach Factors, Recommendation 11 takes a shopping-list approach. The factors specified should be prioritised, with much greater priority given to Factor i) than relegation to the grade of being one amongst many.

Pre-order reports for civil penalties are needed to make Recommendation 11 work.[57] There is no recommendation in the ALRC Final Report parallel to Recommendation 16. However, an earlier report of the ALRC, *Compliance with the Trade Practices Act 1974*, recommended amending the Act so that

> the court may require a corporation that has contravened the Act to provide to the court, prior to the court assessing the need for or the amount or nature of a penalty, a report detailing what steps have been taken by the corporation since the contravention to improve the corporation's internal controls and to discipline the persons implicated in the contravention.[58]

IV. Conclusion: Advantages of Proposed Statutory Adoption of Reactive Corporate Fault and Possible Concerns

A. Advantages of Proposed Statutory Adoption of Reactive Corporate Fault

The prime advantage of the statutory adoption of the concept of reactive corporate fault would be to heed and address the limitations of the present law that stem from

[57] See further B Fisse, 'Redress Facilitation Orders as a Sanction Against Corporations' (2018) 37 *University of Queensland Law Journal* 85, 104–05.

[58] ALRC, *Compliance with the Trade Practices Act 1974* (n 50).

undue preoccupation with proactive corporate fault (see section II). Option (3) and Option (1), as set out in sections III.B, III.C and III.D, would do so basically as follows:

- The goal of prevention of corporate lawbreaking is taken to require a reactive time-frame as well as a proactive time-frame for assessing whether or not adequate steps have been taken by a corporation to guard against repetition of unlawful conduct. Option (3) explicitly adopts a reactive as well as a proactive time-frame. Option (1) makes reactive fault an explicit factor to be considered in determining sentence.
- By explicitly making reactive corporate fault relevant to liability and determination of sentence, Option (3) and Option (1) reflect the everyday expectation that a corporation that has caused a bad or harmful outcome should be held to account for failing to take action to prevent repetition of that outcome.
- Individual accountability for past corporate lawbreaking is promoted by making internal disciplinary action relevant to liability under Option (3) and to determination of sentence under Option (1). That upholds the commonplace understanding that individual accountability is an essential means of achieving the effective social control of corporate wrongdoing.
- Corporate accountability to take reasonable organisational precautions applies not only to precautions before the unlawful conduct, but also to precautions that need to be taken after the unlawful conduct to guard against repetition. The liability rules under Option (3) so provide. The sentencing factors under Option (1) include the taking or not taking of organisational precautions in response to having engaged in unlawful conduct.
- Where corporate unlawful conduct stems from management by exception, Option (3) and Option (1) make that unlawful conduct an exception that has to be managed by the corporation in a responsive way. Denial of prior fault does not get the corporation off the hook.
- A boilerplate compliance policy or adroit camouflage may enable a corporation to raise a reasonable doubt that the directors or senior managers of the corporation acted intentionally in not complying with the law. However, under Option (3) the threshold requirement is that an employee acting within his or her actual or apparent authority has acted intentionally. The corporation is then put to proving that it took reasonably proactive precautions and reasonable reactive precautions to comply with the law.
- Reactive corporate fault is made an explicit statutory sentencing factor under Option (1).

An approach parallel to Option (1) is proposed for the determination of civil penalties (see section III.E). There is also work to be done to make reactive corporate fault an explicit part of the structure of injunctions, enforceable undertakings and corporate probation orders.

B. Possible Concerns

Perhaps the main possible concern is that making reactive corporate fault relevant to liability and to sentencing and determination of penalty is a recipe for corporate cheating and evasion. Corporations typically have the resources, skills and tactical ability to have in place compliance programmes or preventive systems that look impressive on paper but have little or no substance.[59] They are also adept at advancing defences that portray them as victims of rogue activity by employees or that create other smokescreens.[60] These challenges can be met to some extent. The concept of reactive corporate fault makes it more difficult to evade responsibility, because denial of prior fault is not enough to avoid liability. Perjury and other offences relating to the administration of justice can be used to uphold the law. A pyramid of enforcement enables the enforcement response to be escalated progressively in the event of subterfuge, defiance, recalcitrance or other attempts to undermine the compliance process.[61]

Australian courts have been increasingly critical of attempts to mitigate penalty in civil penalty proceedings on the basis that the corporation had a compliance programme. There are numerous examples where compliance programmes have been examined sceptically and where it is unlikely in the extreme that the defendant could show that reasonable precautions had been taken.[62] A rightly celebrated example is *Australian Competition and Consumer Commission v Visy Industries Holdings Pty Ltd (No 3)*.[63] In this case, senior management and the founder of the business were implicated in a price-fixing and market-sharing scheme. Visy sought to mitigate the penalty to be imposed by arguing that it had a trade practices compliance programme. That plea was rejected and ridiculed by Heerey J:

> The corporate culture of Visy in relation to its obligations under the Trade Practices Act was non-existent. None of the most senior people hesitated for a moment before embarking on obviously unlawful conduct. There was in evidence a Visy document entitled 'Trade Practices Compliance Manual' dated February 1998. It was signed by Mr Pratt. It bears a distribution list, signed by Mr Debney, with the names of 50 or so personnel covering every State and Head Office. On the front cover it is said:
>
> > This is an important document. It is essential that it be read and understood by you. Visy Industries requires strict compliance with its policy on the Trade Practices Act.

[59] See Laufer (n 23) chs 4–6. See further Beaton-Wells and Fisse (n 34) ch 12; B van Rooij and D Sokol (eds), *Cambridge Handbook of Compliance* (Cambridge, Cambridge University Press, 2021).

[60] See further I Schoultz and J Flyghed, 'From "We Didn't Do It" to "We've Learned Our Lesson": Development of a Typology of Neutralizations of Corporate Crime' (2020) 28 *Critical Criminology* 739.

[61] Ayres and Braithwaite (n 26) ch 2.

[62] *Australian Competition and Consumer Commission v Australian Safeway Stores Pty Ltd (No 4)* [2006] FCA 21, (2006) ATPR 42-101, 44,830-1 [62]–[67]; *Australian Competition and Consumer Commission v George Weston Foods Ltd* [2000] FCA 690, (2000) ATPR 41-763, 40,988 [48]; *Australian Competition and Consumer Commission v Leahy Petroleum Pty Ltd (No 2)* [2005] FCA 254, (2005) 215 ALR 281, 285 [12], 293 [51]; *Australian Competition and Consumer Commission v Visy Industries Holdings Pty Ltd (No 3)* [2007] FCA 1617, (2007) 244 ALR 673, 711 [319] (*Visy Industries*). See also *Australian Securities and Investments Commission v Chemeq Ltd* [2006] FCA 936, (2006) 234 ALR 511.

[63] *Visy Industries* (n 62).

> The document includes the stem warning that price fixing and market sharing are 'strictly prohibited' and that readers of the document 'must never make (such) arrangements with a competitor'. Further, it is said Visy personnel
>
>> should avoid all contact with competitors or their employees other than contact approved by senior management or Visy Industries' Legal Counsel. All necessary contact with competitors should be conducted in formal settings.
>
> I doubt that Westerfolds Park and the Cherry Hill Tavern could be regarded as formal settings. The Visy Trade Practices Compliance Manual might have been written in Sanskrit for all the notice anybody took of it.[64]

A second concern is that the law may be interpreted and applied in too lenient a way. Consider the concern expressed by Richard Gruner that a defence of corporate due diligence could refocus the test of liability and thereby lead to unjustified acquittals:

> The punitive rationale for rejecting a due diligence defense to corporate criminal liability is that when a corporate employee commits an offense within the scope of his employment, his firm deserves punishment regardless of the surrounding efforts of firm managers to prevent that offense. A standard that immunizes firms from criminal liability based on the sufficiency of managerial efforts to control employee crimes effectively elevates the character of those preventive efforts over the quality of conduct by operating employees as the key factor determining corporate liability ... a standard limited by a due diligence defense would shift the focus of liability determinations in many cases to the merit of preventive efforts by corporate managers. The result might be that firms would escape punishment despite highly culpable conduct by operating employees that had devastating consequences.[65]

However, courts can counter this possible bias by focusing on the standard of care expected of a corporation as a baseline[66] against which to assess attempts by corporate defendants to feign virtuous compliance.

Third, part of the focus of reactive corporate fault is on internal disciplinary action as a means of increasing the extent to which individual accountability is imposed for corporate lawbreaking. This raises concerns about the risk of scapegoating and the adequacy or otherwise of protection of the rights of employees subject to internal investigations and disciplinary action. Those concerns are discussed in *Corporations, Crime and Accountability*.[67] They can and should be managed.

Fourth, objection has been raised to the placing of a persuasive burden of proof on a corporate defendant that pleads the defence precautions. The arguments and counter-arguments have been made many times. They are reviewed in the ALRC Final Report.[68] On balance, the ALRC concluded that imposing a persuasive burden of proof on corporations to establish a defence of reasonable precautions to necessary to make the law effective.

[64] ibid 711 [319].
[65] RS Gruner, *Corporate Criminal Liability and Prevention* (New York, Law Journal Press, 2008) 6–11.
[66] See Beaton-Wells and Fisse (n 34) 235.
[67] Fisse and Braithwaite (n 6) 182–87, 169–77.
[68] ALRC Final Report (n 2) 156–59, 262–65.

There is no last word on the subject of what best to do to control corporate lawbreaking. However, it is worth heeding this advice by Coffee:

> The basic default rule should be that the corporation must show us who was guilty if it itself wants to escape guilt. It is too much to argue that no one is guilty simply because the compliance plan was adequate. …
>
> The best defense against incomplete or self-serving internal investigations is a judicial power to reject them as inadequate.[69]

[69] Coffee (n 3) 152.

8

Ideas of Corporate Culture from the Perspective of Penalties Jurisprudence

REBECCA FAUGNO*

I. Introduction

The concept of 'corporate culture' has become pervasive in the Australian corporate regulatory landscape.[1] The symbiotic relationship between corporate misconduct and defective corporate culture was highlighted in the Financial Services Royal Commission[2] and has been a central focus of the series of inquiries into Crown Resorts' 'suitability' to hold casino licences in Sydney, Melbourne and Perth.[3] As those examples suggest, corporate culture is used in a swathe of contexts, ranging from a method of attribution for primary liability, to a tool for establishing defences, fashioning penalties and for regulatory and licensing inquiries.[4] Yet despite being 'the new black',[5] the concept of corporate culture remains nebulous. There is no single, accepted definition

* I would like to thank Professor Elise Bant and Dr Felicity Maher for their invaluable comments and support on earlier drafts of this chapter. All errors remain my own.

[1] As discussed in V Comino, 'Corporate Culture is the "New Black" – its Possibilities and Limits as a Regulatory Mechanism for Corporations and Financial Institutions?' (2020) 44 *University of New South Wales Law Journal* 295; E Bant, 'Culpable Corporate Minds' (2021) 48 *University of Western Australia Law Review* 352; S Burrell, 'Corporate Culture, it Seems, is "the New Black"' (2016) 68 *Governance Directions* 195; O Dixon, 'Corporate Criminal Liability: The Influence of Corporate Culture' (Sydney Law School Legal Studies Research Paper 17/14, 2017).

[2] Commonwealth of Australia, *Royal Commission into Misconduct in the Banking, Superannuation and Financial Services Industry* (Final Report, 1 February 2019) vol 1, 440–46.

[3] State of New South Wales, *Inquiry into the Barangaroo Restricted Gaming Facility Granted to Crown Sydney Gaming Pty Limited Pursuant to Section 143 of the Casino Control Act 1992* (Final Report, 1 February 2021); State of Victoria, *Royal Commission into Casino Operator and Licence* (Final Report, 15 October 2021) 124–27 (RCCOL Report). The prominence of corporate culture is now reflected in ASX Corporate Governance Council, *Corporate Governance Principles and Recommendations*, 4th edn (1 February 2019) 16–17, in particular Principle 3, which requires that a corporation should 'instil … a culture … of acting lawfully, ethically and responsibly', cited in the RCCOL Report (n 3) 120.

[4] As endorsed by the ALRC in Australian Law Reform Commission, *Corporate Criminal Responsibility* (Report No 136, April 2020) (ALRC Final Report). See, eg, ibid 232.

[5] Comino (n 1).

for 'corporate culture' in any of the many contexts in which it is invoked.[6] As a tool for determining corporate intentionality – the purpose for which 'corporate culture' was introduced into the Commonwealth Criminal Code Act 1995 (Cth) (Criminal Code) – the concept has proved to be a blunt instrument, barely used and poorly understood.[7] Nevertheless, in keeping with the arguments of Vicky Comino and others that corporate culture is capable of being used as a regulatory mechanism,[8] the Australian Law Reform Commission (ALRC), in its 2020 review of Australia's corporate criminal regime, endorsed the use of corporate culture as a method of attribution for determining primary liability, affirmed its relevance to establishing defences and recommended that courts should be able to make non-monetary orders to address systemic issues directed at corporate culture.[9]

Consistent with Olivia Dixon's suggestion that corporate culture is perhaps most useful as part of robust sentencing guidelines,[10] this chapter seeks to contribute to better understanding of the meaning of 'corporate culture' by exploring ideas of corporate culture in the context of Australian penalties jurisprudence. The analysis focuses on the rich jurisprudence on penalties arising from cases concerning misleading and unconscionable conduct under the Australian Consumer Law (schedule 2 to the Competition and Consumer Act 2010 (Cth)) (ACL) or the Australian Securities and Investments Commission Act 2001 (Cth) (ASIC Act).

In developing this analysis, the chapter begins in section II by tracing the history of the corporate culture provisions in part 2.5 of the Criminal Code (Corporate Culture Provisions), including their recent review by the ALRC. Section III considers related corporate attribution models proposed by leading scholars, and suggests a series of key markers of corporate culture identified in this scholarship. Using these markers as reference points, section IV explores ideas of corporate culture in the context of Australian penalties jurisprudence, in cases concerning misleading and unconscionable conduct under the ACL and ASIC Act. This section considers judicial articulation of the meaning of corporate culture, and seeks to assess characteristics of reasoning in civil penalties jurisprudence relevant to corporate culture.

[6] Compare RCCOL Report (n 3) 124–25, which takes a largely objective approach to the concept, to the intensely subjective inquiries into corporate employees' understandings of corporate culture the subject of Deloitte's corporate culture report, summarised at 147–49.

[7] As discussed in the ALRC Final Report (n 4), including in relation to the complexity of part 2.5: 147–48; the exclusion of part 2.5 from a broad range of legislation: 66–68, 90; its practical under-use and sidelining as an attribution model: ch 3. The UK Law Commission rejected corporate culture as a model for attribution on this basis, and also owing to the model's inability to account for states of mind other than intention and recklessness (for example, dishonesty): United Kingdom Law Commission, *Corporate Responsibility: An Options Paper* (10 June 2022) ch 6.

[8] Comino (n 1). Successive ASIC Chairmen have highlighted ASIC's 'regulatory interest in culture': J Price (Commissioner), *Book Launch: 'Managing Culture: A Good Practice Guide'* (Speech, 12 December 2017). See also J Shipton (Chair), *Keynote Address* (Melbourne, Speech, Centre for Economic Development, 27 June 2019); G Medcraft (Chairman), *Corporate Culture and Corporate Regulation* (Melbourne, Speech, Law Council of Australia BLS AGM Seminar, 20 November 2015); J Price, *Outline of ASIC's Approach to Corporate Culture* (Sydney, Speech, AICD Directors' Forum: Regulators' Insights on Risk Culture, 19 July 2017).

[9] ALRC Final Report (n 4) 232.

[10] Dixon (n 1) 16.

II. The Corporate Culture Provisions

A. Genesis of the Corporate Culture Provisions

While most jurisdictions recognise the concept of corporate criminal and civil liability,[11] the problem of how to hold corporations to account for misconduct has been described as 'one of the blackest holes in criminal law'.[12] Traditionally, courts sought to identify corporate mens rea in a single human repository, who could be identifiable as the 'directing mind and will, the very ego and centre of the personality of the corporation'.[13] This 'Identification' model of attribution[14] can be contrasted with models of vicarious liability, which hold a corporation responsible for the acts or wrongdoing[15] of an employee or agent carried out within the course of employment or within the scope of the agency agreement.[16] In a modified form of vicarious liability, the 'TPA Model',[17] originating in section 84 of the Trade Practices Act 1974 (Cth)[18] and widely adopted in Australian statutes, involves imputing to a corporation the state of mind of one or more officers, employees or agents of the body corporate, acting within actual or apparent authority.[19]

These traditional models and their offshoots have been criticised for their failure to reflect the more devolved governance frameworks of large multinational conglomerates and the reality of diffused decision making below board level.[20] The anthropomorphic approach of searching for a single human repository of fault, whose state of mind can be identified as that of the company, fails where knowledge is dispersed between individuals and across departments. It also fails to account for the possibility that a corporation may be seen to be greater than the sum of its parts.[21]

[11] Allens Linklaters, 'Corporate Criminal Liability: A Review of Law and Practice Across the Globe' (September 2016) at www.allens.com.au/pubs/pdf/ibo/CorporateCriminalLiabilityPublication_2016.pdf.

[12] B Fisse, 'The Attribution of Criminal Liability to Corporations: A Statutory Model' (1991) *Sydney Law Review* 277, 277.

[13] *Lennard's Carrying Co v Asiatic Petroleum Co* [1915] AC 705 (HL) 713; see also *Tesco Supermarkets Ltd v Nattrass* [1972] AC 153, [1971] 2 WLR 1166 (HL) (*Tesco*); *Hamilton v Whitehead* [1988] HCA 65, (1988) 166 CLR 121; discussion in ALRC Final Report (n 4), 145. Pursuant to *Meridian Global Funds Management Asia Ltd v Securities Commission* [1995] 2 AC 500, [1995] 3 WLR 413 (PC), the attribution inquiry examines and interprets the relevant rule of responsibility, liability or proscription to be applied to the corporate entity, to identify the specific human actor whose conduct or state of mind constitutes that of the corporation. For critical analysis, see Leow, ch 6 of this volume, sections I.A and II.

[14] Law Commission for England and Wales, *Corporate Criminal Liability* (Discussion Paper, June 2021) [1.7].

[15] On the debate over the proper focus of the doctrine, see *Pioneer Mortgage Services Pty Ltd v Columbus Capital Pty Ltd* [2016] FCAFC 78, (2016) 250 FCR 136 [48]–[58] (Davies, Gleeson and Edelman JJ).

[16] *New York Central & Hudson River Railroad Co v United States*, 212 US 481 (1909); *Mousell Bros v London and North-Western Railway Co* [1917] 2 KB 836; *R v Australasian Films Ltd* (1921) 29 CLR 195 (HCA) 217; *Morgan v Babcock & Wilcox* (1929) 43 CLR 163 (HCA).

[17] See discussion in ALRC Final Report (n 4) 39.

[18] Now the Competition and Consumer Act 2010 (Cth), s 84.

[19] Discussed in the ALRC Final Report (n 4) 39, 67, including in relation to the use of the TPA Model at 92–93, 219–22.

[20] ALRC Final Report (n 4) 145; J Clough and C Mulhern, *The Prosecution of Corporations* (Oxford, Oxford University Press, 2002) 90; J Gobert, 'Corporate Criminality: Four Models of Fault' (1993) 14 *Legal Studies* 393, 394; Dixon (n 1) 5–6.

[21] See, eg, Bant (n 1) 358–61; ME Diamantis, 'Corporate Criminal Minds' (2016) 91 *Notre Dame Law Review* 2049, 2070–71; and for discussion of conglomerates, aggregation and group agency, C List and P Pettit, *Group Agency: The Possibility, Design and Status of Corporate Agents* (Oxford, Oxford University Press, 2011).

Conversely, Australian courts have not found it palatable to aggregate the knowledge and state of mind of more than one individual so as to form a corporate 'superbrain'.[22] The result is that under traditional attribution models, liability is in effect detached from organisational intention and blameworthiness. The challenges to traditional corporate liability models are compounded by advances in technological systems, such as automated systems and artificial intelligence.[23]

B. The Corporate Culture Provisions

In the context of growing awareness of the deficiencies of traditional corporate attribution models, part 2.5 of the Criminal Code adopted a novel approach to attribution of corporate fault (Corporate Culture Provisions). Section 12.3(1) of the Criminal Code recognises that a state of mind of intention, knowledge or recklessness can be established where a body corporate 'expressly, tacitly or impliedly authorized or permitted the commission of the offence'. The requisite authorisation or permission may be shown by:

> (c) proving that a corporate culture existed within the body corporate that directed, encouraged, tolerated or led to non-compliance with the relevant provision; or
> (d) proving that the body corporate failed to create and maintain a corporate culture that required compliance with the relevant provision.[24]

'Corporate culture' is defined in section 12.3(6):

> '*corporate culture*' means an attitude, policy, rule, course of conduct or practice existing within the body corporate generally or in the part of the body corporate in which the relevant activities takes place.[25]

The Corporate Culture Provisions were developed by the Model Criminal Code Officers Committee (MCCOC) to incorporate principles of 'organizational blameworthiness' and to better reflect the nuanced realities of corporate function.[26] The appeal of the

[22] Compare *United States v Bank of New England*, NA, 821 F 2d 844 (1st Cir 1987); *Commonwealth Bank of Australia v Kojic* [2016] FCAFC 186, (2016) 249 FCR 421, 446 [101], 448–56 [110]–[143] (Edelman J, with whom Allsop CJ generally concurred); *R v HM Coroner for East Kent, ex parte Spooner (Herald of Free Enterprise/Zeebrugge Ferry Disaster)* (1989) 88 Cr App R 10 (QB).

[23] The challenges to regulation posed by technologies that artificial intelligence (AI) are considered, in, eg, S Chesterman, *We, the Robots? Regulating Artificial Intelligence and the Limits of the Law* (Cambridge, Cambridge University Press, 2021). Chesterman refers to 'general' or 'strong' AI as 'the creation of a system that is capable of performing any intellectual task that a human could – and raising complex questions about the nature of consciousness and self-awareness in a non-biological entity': ibid 1. See also discussion in ME Diamantis, 'The Extended Corporate Mind: When Corporations use AI to Break the Law' (2020) 98 *North Carolina Law Review* 893; Diamantis (n 21); ME Diamantis, 'Clockwork Corporations: A Character Theory of Corporate Punishment' (2018) 103 *Iowa Law Review* 507.

[24] Criminal Code, s 12.3(2). Note that in its Final Report the ALRC recommended repealing s 12.3(2)(d): ALRC Final Report (n 4) 245–46.

[25] Note the ALRC proposal to pluralise the terms 'attitude', 'policy' and 'rule', and to replace 'takes' with 'take' in ALRC Final Report (n 4) Recommendation 7 Option 1, 228.

[26] Criminal Law Officers Committee of the Standing Committee of Attorneys-General, *Model Criminal Code Chapters 1 and 2: General Principles of Criminal Responsibility* (Report, 1 December 1992) 107 (*Model Criminal Code*). See discussion in ALRC Final Report (n 4) 56–66; also discussion in J Hill, 'Corporate Criminal Liability in Australia: An Evolving Corporate Governance Technique?' (2003) 1 *Journal of Business Law* 1, 18; ALRC Final Report (n 4) 56.

provisions lies in their ability to better accommodate organisational blameworthiness and diffused responsibility, and to encourage *ex ante* steps to ensure corporate compliance. The provisions received 'overwhelming' support in submissions to the ALRC's 2020 enquiry into corporate criminal responsibility.[27] However, after more than 20 years on the statute books, the Corporate Culture Provisions have yet to be relied on in prosecution.[28] This may be due in part to the low uptake of the corporate culture model of attribution in State and Commonwealth legislation.[29] It is likely also attributable to a lack of clarity surrounding the concept of 'corporate culture'.[30] Nevertheless, the use of corporate culture as a basis for corporate attribution is supported by a significant and increasing body of scholarship, building on the seminal work of Pamela H Bucy, Brent Fisse and Peter A French.[31] Accordingly, the ALRC in its 2020 report into corporate crime recommended the Commonwealth Government choose between two reform options relating to attribution of corporate fault, both incorporating concepts of corporate culture, though at different stages of the accountability process.[32]

Option One involves a lightly amended version of the Corporate Culture Provisions, to remove a number of technical hurdles to their application.[33] These included changing the reference to 'offence' to 'the physical element', so that it clearly is unnecessary to find a single human offender whose wrongdoing (encompassing both conduct and state of mind requirements) can be attributed to the corporation.[34] It also recommends that the existing section 12.3(2)(d) be repealed, on the ground that 'it is inappropriate to require proof beyond reasonable doubt of the non-existence of a particular culture in order to attribute liability to a corporation'.[35]

Option Two involves a modified version of the TPA Model, amended to include a defence, 'if the body corporate proves that it took reasonable precautions to prevent the

[27] ALRC Final Report (n 4) 232.

[28] ibid 246; although there has been judicial consideration of the provisions in *R v Potter & Mures Shipping Pty Ltd* (Transcript, Supreme Court of Tasmania, Blow CJ, 14 September 2015). See discussion in, eg, Bant (n 1) 371–73.

[29] The ALRC noted in ALRC Final Report (n 4) that part 2.5 of the Criminal Code has not been widely adopted, and is expressly excluded by the majority of legislation reviewed by the ALRC: ALRC Final Report (n 4) 66–68.

[30] See discussion in Comino (n 1); Bant (n 1) 270–71; C Beaton-Wells and B Fisse, *Australian Cartel Regulation* (Cambridge, Cambridge University Press, 2011) 232; J Colvin and J Argent, 'Corporate and Personal Liability for "Culture" in Corporations?' (2016) 34 *Companies and Securities Law Journal* 30; GR Skupski, 'The Senior Management Mens Rea: Another Stab at a Workable Integration of Organizational Culpability into Corporate Criminal Liability' (2011) 62 *Case Western Reserve Law Review* 367, 304; WS Laufer, *Corporate Bodies and Guilty Minds* (Chicago, IL, University of Chicago Press, 2006) 58–60.

[31] PH Bucy, 'Corporate Ethos: A Standard for Imposing Corporate Criminal Liability' (1991) 75 *Minnesota Law Review* 1095; B Fisse, 'Penal Designs and Corporate Conduct: Test Results from Fault and Sanctions in Australian Cartel Law' (2019) 40 *Adelaide Law Review* 285, 285–86; B Fisse, 'Recent Developments in Corporate Criminal Law and Corporate Liability to Monetary Penalties' (1990) 13 *University of New South Wales Law Journal* 1, 3–4; B Fisse and J Braithwaite, *Corporations, Crime and Accountability* (Cambridge, Cambridge University Press, 1993); Fisse, ch 7 of this volume; R French, 'The Culture of Compliance – A Judicial Perspective' (2003) *Federal Judicial Scholarship* 1, 4; PA French, 'Integrity, Intentions and Corporations' (1996) 34 *American Business Law Journal* 141; Dixon (n 1); Bant (n 1).

[32] ALRC Final Report (n 4) Recommendation 7.

[33] ibid Recommendation 7 Option 1. These include amending the definition of corporate culture to include the plural as well as the singular and, for the avoidance of any possible confusion, replacing the idea of 'due diligence' with 'reasonable precautions'.

[34] ibid [6.56]–[6.60].

[35] ibid [6.69].

commission of the offence'.[36] As the ALRC notes, this second option does not address the diffused responsibility problem.[37] The Commonwealth Government has yet to provide its response to the ALRC recommendations or to indicate a preferred option. Either way, a clearer understanding of corporate culture is critical if the provisions are to become practically and conceptually workable tools for establishing corporate fault.

III. A Framework for Analysis of Penalties Jurisprudence

Whilst there is a dearth of judicial consideration of 'corporate culture' at the criminal attribution stage, there may be lessons to be learned from civil penalties jurisprudence. In the civil penalty field, the widespread use of corporate culture in conjunction with the 'French factors' brings the concept into judicial consideration.[38] This section seeks to establish a conceptual frame of reference for the qualitative analysis in section IV of judicial strands of reasoning relevant to the meaning of corporate culture. Consistent with the MCCOC's founding of the Corporate Culture Provisions on the work of key scholars,[39] the conceptual lens set out in this section is based on scholarly insights into corporate culture as set out in the seminal work of Bucy, Fisse and French.[40] More recently, Elise Bant has built on this work with the aim of developing a more targeted approach for corporate culture, capable of supporting findings of discrete forms of corporate states of mind.[41] The attribution models considered in this section are holistic models, founded on a rejection of vicarious liability and the Identification approach in favour of a version of fault that reflects the organisational structure and devolved decision making of contemporary corporations.[42] The aim here is not to assess the

[36] ibid Recommendation 7 Option 2, 14, 228, 233.

[37] ibid [6.126].

[38] A set of factors developed by French J (as he then was) in *Trade Practices Commission v CSR Limited* [1990] FCA 521, [1991] ATPR 41-076 (*CSR*) in order to determine the penalty to set in a particular case. The factors include whether the company has a corporate culture conducive to compliance with the Act, 'as evidenced by compliance programs and disciplinary or other corrective measures'. Note the factors are not exhaustive: *Australian Competition and Consumer Commission v Visa Inc* [2015] FCA 1020, (2015) 339 ALR 413 (*Visa*). See also discussion in, eg, CH Truong and LF Alampi, 'Increased Civil Pecuniary Penalties – The "Cost of Doing Business" or an Effective Deterrent?' (2020) 28 *Australian Journal of Competition and Consumer Law* 21. See discussion in section III.A.ii of this chapter.

[39] *Model Criminal Code* (n 26) 113, directly referencing the work of Bucy and Fisse.

[40] Bucy (n 31); Fisse, 'Penal Designs and Corporate Conduct' (n 31) 285–86; Fisse, 'Recent Developments in Corporate Criminal Law and Corporate Liability to Monetary Penalties' (n 31) 3–4; Fisse and Braithwaite (n 31); French, 'The Culture of Compliance' (n 31) 4; French, 'Integrity, Intentions and Corporations' (n 31); Dixon (n 1).

[41] Bant (n 1); E Bant and JM Paterson, 'Systems of Misconduct: Corporate Culpability and Statutory Unconscionability' (2021) 15 *Journal of Equity* 63; E Bant and JM Paterson, 'Rio Tinto and the Anatomy of Corporate Culpability' (University of Melbourne, 11 September 2020) at https://pursuit.unimelb.edu.au/articles/rio-tinto-and-the-anatomy-of-corporate-culpability; Bant, ch 1 of this volume; Bant, ch 9 of this volume; Bant, ch 11 of this volume.

[42] Fisse explores and rejects individualism as a strategy for allocating responsibility for corporate crime: B Fisse and J Braithwaite, 'The Allocation of Responsibility for Corporate Crime: Individualism, Collectivism and Accountability' (1988) 11 *Sydney Law Review* 468, 473–88. For discussion of the problems with the *Tesco* approach, see ibid 504. See also discussion in B Fisse, 'Reconstructing Corporate Criminal Law: Deterrence, Retribution, Fault, and Sanctions' (1983) 56 *Southern California Law Review* 1141, 1192–93; Fisse (n 12) 277–78.

strength or cogency of the models, but to use them to provide a theoretical context for consideration of courts' treatment of corporate culture considerations. The attribution models provide a number of useful markers of corporate culture, which are adopted in section IV of this chapter to assist in assessing the penalty cases.

A. Understanding Corporate Culture: Seminal Scholarship

i. Bucy – Corporate Ethos

Bucy proposes a corporate ethos paradigm as a conceptual and practical model for determining intent.[43] Central to Bucy's approach is the notion that a corporation has a distinctive 'ethos', separate from the personal ethos of the individuals involved.[44] Applying Bucy's corporate ethos model, '[a] corporation should be held criminally liable only when its ethos encourages criminal conduct by agents of the corporation'.[45] A corporation's ethos is shaped by a combination of formal and informal factors, and is 'identifiable, observable, and malleable'.[46]

For Bucy, determining whether a corporation's distinctive ethos *encouraged* the criminal conduct in question involves examination of the corporation's internal structure – both formal and informal. This examination is carried out by reference to factors including the structure of the corporate hierarchy; the extent to which internal procedures and lines of communications suggest an ethos of discouraging violation of the law; corporate goals as they are communicated to employees, for example through internal targets and training; the existence and calibre of internal compliance monitoring, including processes for reviewing concerns about legal compliance; the identity of the personnel involved in wrongful behaviour, whether directly or by way of reckless tolerance; and corporate reaction to past violations, including, for example, whether wrongdoers were disciplined or promoted, and the company's remuneration and benefits system. The aim of the enquiry is 'to further evaluate whether the corporation encourages or discourages illegal behaviour',[47] in order to establish whether the requisite corporate ethos exists. The factors identified by Bucy remain important indicators of corporate culture and constitute a valuable lens for examining its treatment in the penalties context.

ii. Fisse – Reactive Corporate Fault

We have seen that one of the indicators of corporate ethos identified by Bucy was corporate reactions to past misconduct. Fisse, by contrast, proposes a comprehensive

[43] Bucy recognises that concerns about the criminal prosecution of corporations are dominated by two key issues – failure to identify or prove corporate intent, and sanctions. She indicates that her model is aimed at addressing corporate intent (and by implication, not sanctions): Bucy (n 31) 1097. She seeks to address the failure to identify or prove corporate intent by proposing a 'better' resolution of corporate intent: ibid 1098.

[44] Notably, Bucy prefers the notion of 'ethos' to that of 'culture': ibid 1121.

[45] ibid.

[46] ibid 1127.

[47] ibid 1146.

and detailed reactive corporate fault model of liability, which operates as a direct means of ascertaining corporate intention. This model, developed and sustained over nearly three decades[48] and explained by Fisse in chapter 7 of this volume, is based on the view that an organisation's culture can be seen as a group of 'shared expectations', which are 'transmitted from one generation of organisational role incumbents to the next'.[49] A corporation's culture can in turn influence the corporation's reaction to wrongdoing, in that a defective culture may engender reactive corporate fault. Fisse defines 'reactive corporate fault' as 'a corporation's fault in failing to undertake satisfactory preventive or corrective measures in response to the commission of the actus reus of an offence by personnel acting on behalf of the organisation'.[50] What matters is not what a corporation's policies require but rather 'what it [a corporation] specifically proposes to do to implement a programme of internal discipline, structural reform, or compensation' following commission of the actus reus.

Under this approach, a company that is found liable for the actus reus of an offence could also be found liable for the mens rea in any of the following circumstances:

(a) 'by having a policy that expressly or impliedly authorizes or permits the commission of the offence or an offence of the same type';[51]
(b) by failing to take 'due precautions' or 'reasonable proactive steps' to prevent the commission of the offence or an offence of the same type;[52]
(c) by having a policy of 'failing to comply with a reactive duty to take preventive measures in response to having committed the external elements of the offence';[53] or
(d) by failing to take 'reasonable reactive steps to remedy the harm caused by unlawful conduct and to guard against future unlawful conduct of that type'.[54]

Similar elements are also the subject of extended examination and development in the moral philosophy of French, to which we now turn.

[48] From, eg, Fisse, 'Reconstructing Corporate Criminal Law' (n 42) to Fisse, 'Penal Designs and Corporate Conduct' (n 31).

[49] Fisse and Braithwaite (n 42) 479. Fisse supports this view with reference to psychological studies into the dynamics of group as compared to individual decision making, eg L Janis and L Mann, *Decision Making: A Psychological Analysis of Conflict, Choice and Commitment* (New York, The Free Press, 1977) 423; Fisse and Brathwaite, 'The Allocation of Responsibility for Corporate Crime' (n 42) 479.

[50] Fisse, 'Reconstructing Corporate Criminal Law' (n 42) 1195. Note a similar definition advanced in Fisse and Braithwaite (n 42) 505: 'corporate failure to devise and undertake satisfactory preventive or corrective measures in response to the commission of the actus reus of an offence by personnel acting on behalf of the organisation'; refined slightly in Fisse (n 12) 280 as 'a corporate policy of unresponsive adjustment to having committed the external elements of an offence, or a failure to take reasonable precautions or to exercise due diligence in light of having committed the external elements of an offence'.

[51] Fisse (n 12) 279.

[52] Fisse, 'Penal Designs and Corporate Conduct' (n 31) 290. Fisse proposes that the corporate culture concept in s 12.3(2)(c) and (d) of the Criminal Code should be replaced by a failure to take reasonable corporate precautions and exercise due diligence to prevent the offence: Fisse, 'Penal Designs and Corporate Conduct' (n 31) 291.

[53] Fisse (n 12) 279.

[54] ibid; Fisse, 'Penal Designs and Corporate Conduct' (n 31) 290.

iii. French – Corporate Internal Decision Structures

French's influential model for corporate intentionality stems from his development of a philosophical theory of the corporation as a moral person,[55] a conglomerate collectivity with its own identity.[56] French considers that a corporation's intentionality can be found in a Corporation's Internal Decision structure (CID Structure) or, in other words, 'the way by which [the corporation] makes decisions and converts them into actions'.[57] An act can be said to be an intentional act of a corporation if performed by a person in the employ of the corporation in implementation of its corporate policy, and in accordance with its procedural rules.[58] CID Structures comprise two critical elements: (i) organisational rules, in the form of an organisational flowchart showing corporate lines of responsibility; and (ii) policy/procedural rules that show how to recognise decisions that are corporate, as opposed to personal decisions of individual humans.[59] Policy/procedural rules are found in the basic operational documents and written policies of a company. Acceptance of these rules and policies within the corporation may be evidenced by their adoption in published sources such as annual statements, codes and policies for employees.[60]

Coupled with this conception of corporate intention is French's 'Principle of Responsive Adjustment': 'the notion that a causally responsible party for an untoward event should adopt specific courses of future action calculated to prevent repetitions'.[61] When adjustments are not made, the relevant party can be considered morally responsible for the earlier event. On this account, a past failure to take responsive corrective action may be evidence of present or future intention. In other words, a repeated wrongful action 'retrieves the previous behavior, though it does not make that behavior intentional at the time it occurred'.[62] The person who committed the act may, in French's view, be held morally responsible for the outcome on the basis of subsequent intentional acts that allow or are likely to cause repetition of the wrongful behaviour.

iv. Bant – Systems Intentionality

Finally, and building on French's philosophical approach to corporate intentionality, Bant's 'systems intentionality' model, explained in chapters 9 and 11 of this volume, considers that the corporate state of mind is manifested in its systems, policies and practices.[63] The underlying idea is that systems are inherently purposive, in that they

[55] PA French, *Collective and Corporate Responsibility* (New York, Columbia University Press, 1984) xii. French's work stems from a philosophical endeavour to build a view of the corporation as a moral person, rather than a legal endeavour to construct a model for establishing corporate criminal liability.

[56] ibid 8–18.

[57] French, 'Integrity, Intentions and Corporations' (n 31) 151.

[58] ibid 152. See also French's discussion of the example of Gulf Oil Corporation in French (n 55) ch 2.

[59] French, 'Integrity, Intentions and Corporations' (n 31) 151–52; French (n 55) 40–47.

[60] French (n 55) 53.

[61] ibid 156. See also discussion of the principle ibid 156–63.

[62] ibid 159.

[63] Bant (n 1) 355. Note the evolution of the systems intentionality model from a manifestation of the corporate state of mind through the corporation's 'systems, policy and patterns of behaviour' in Bant (n 1) 355 to the corporation's systems, policies and practices in Bant and Paterson, 'Systems of Misconduct' (n 41); see Bant, ch 1 of this volume; Bant, chs 9 and 11 of this volume.

are designed to achieve certain ends. Further, a corporation can be taken to know the main incidents of the systems it adopts or applies.[64] Corporate culpability is assessed, then, on the basis of 'the inherent design of the business system, structure or practice'.[65] This has the consequence that systemic misconduct carried out through a corporation's processes and practices cannot readily be characterised as inadvertent or a 'systems error'.[66]

Not only are corporations seen to intend the systems they have in place but, drawing on French's principle of responsive adjustment,[67] corporations can be seen to have an ability to review and adjust systems so as to ensure compliance with the law and to correct any harm resulting from those systems. The nature or omission of complaint processes, whistle-blower protections, internal and external audit functions, and so on all manifest the corporate state of mind and broader values. Thus, consistent with Fisse's concept of 'reactive corporate fault', an express or implied corporate policy to fail to take corrective measures may of itself indicate intentionality.[68] A failure to review and adjust systems – a 'set and forget' approach – can also be seen as intentional in character.[69]

In terms of its contribution to the theoretical context in which courts' treatment of corporate culture may be approached, Bant's model joins Bucy, Fisse and French in emphasising the connections between corporate policies, systems of conduct and responsive practices as being indicative of corporate culpability. It is also largely consistent with the Corporate Culture Provisions, although it aims to provide a more targeted, and practically workable, means of ascertaining distinct doctrinal mental states, again highly pertinent at the penalty phase. Finally, the model provides a means of understanding the difficult relationship between 'formal' systems, policies and practices and those that are implemented on the ground. For Bant, it is the latter that disclose the true corporate mindset. In these respects, the model proposes a way to operationalise the concept of corporate culture, so that it is readily applicable to real-life case scenarios.

v. Corporate Culture – Key Themes from the Scholarship

Analysis of the scholarship identifies a number of key themes, or markers, of corporate culture. Rather than conceiving of culture as objectively identifiable from a corporation's formal (and centralised) hierarchy, policies, training programmes and senior personnel, the holistic models considered so far suggest a more probing approach. Markers of corporate culture can be seen to include a corporation's hierarchy and structures, both centralised and decentralised; corporate policies, both formal and de facto (and the gap between them), as reflective of corporate goals, values and intentions; systems of conduct for achieving corporate purposes; audit and adjustment mechanisms; discipline and reward systems; training and compliance programmes;

[64] Bant (n 1) 18.
[65] Bant and Paterson, 'Systems of Misconduct' (n 41) 17.
[66] Bant (n 1); Bant and Paterson, 'Systems of Misconduct' (n 41); Bant, ch 9 of this volume.
[67] See discussion in section III.A.iii.
[68] See discussion in section III.A.ii; see also Bant, ch 9 of this volume.
[69] Bant (n 1) 19–21.

and patterns of behaviour, across parts of the corporate structure relevant to the wrongdoing in question. These markers can be considered both as they existed before and as they were implemented or adjusted in response to the conduct in question. With these markers in mind, our focus now turns to judicial approaches to ascertaining corporate culture.

IV. Analysis of Australian Civil Penalties Jurisprudence

The preceding section has sought to provide an understanding of scholarly conceptions of corporate culture. That understanding is used as a reference point for this section. The following analysis seeks to examine the conceptions of corporate culture articulated by courts, and to identify any core features or characteristics of judicial reasoning that may provide insights into judicial understanding of corporate culture.

A. Scope of the Analysis

i. Identification of Relevant Cases

The focus of the research is on the meaning given to corporate culture by courts at the penalties stage, in cases concerning misleading and unconscionable conduct under the ACL or the ASIC Act. This section adopts a qualitative, bottom-up approach, analysing judicial reasoning with the assistance of the analytical framework identified in section III, with a view to identifying the courts' approach to establishing corporate culture. The analysis is based around cases identified through CaseBase searches for 'corporate culture' and 'penalt*'; 'culture of compliance' and 'penalt*'; and 'French factors' and 'penalt*'. The review captures decisions delivered between 2000 and September 2021. This has resulted in a pool of approximately 180 cases for consideration. The following analysis does not seek to summarise or list the examined cases exhaustively. Rather, it seeks to identify trends of reasoning, and illustrate these where applicable from the pool of authorities.

ii. Corporate Culture, 'Intuitive Synthesis' and Civil Penalty Regimes

The civil penalty regimes under the ACL and ASIC Act allow the court, if satisfied a person has contravened certain provisions of the relevant statute, to order the person to pay 'a pecuniary penalty the court considers appropriate'.[70] In determining the penalty, the court is required to take account of 'all relevant matters', including the circumstances of the conduct, the nature and extent of the contravention and any loss or damage suffered, and any previous court findings concerning similar conduct by the person.[71]

[70] Australian Securities and Investments Commission Act 2001 (Cth), s 12GBB(3) (ASIC Act); ACL, s 224(1). The civil penalty regimes are contained in chapter 5-2 division 1 of the ACL and part 2 division 1 of the ASIC Act.

[71] ASIC Act, s 12GBB(5); ACL, s 224(2).

The courts' determination of an 'appropriate' civil penalty is 'not an exact science'[72] but is rather guided by a 'complex process of multi-factorial decision-making'[73] known as the 'intuitive' or 'instinctive' synthesis, used by courts in civil penalty and criminal sentencing determinations.[74] Intuitive synthesis has been described as 'the method by which a judge identifies all the factors relevant to penalty and, after weighing all those factors, determines the particular penalty that should be imposed'.[75] In the civil penalty context, French J in *Trade Practices Commission v CSR Limited* set out a list of factors to guide the exercise of the court's discretion in determining penalty.[76] Among other considerations, the French factors direct courts' attention to the relevance and nature of corporate culture in assessing defendant culpability and, relatedly, the appropriate level of penalty. Specifically, the French factors include 'whether the company has a corporate culture conducive to compliance with the Act, as evidenced by compliance programs and disciplinary or other corrective measures'.[77] These factors are not exhaustive[78] and have not remained stagnant. They have been augmented by further considerations, in recent years in particular.[79] However, these adjustments do not significantly affect the central role of corporate culture in the factors relevant

[72] *Australian Securities and Investment Commission v GE Capital Finance* [2014] FCA 701 [75] (Jacobson J).

[73] *Australian Competition and Consumer Commission v Reckitt-Benckiser* [2016] FCAFC 181, (2016) 340 ALR 25, 39 [44] (Jagot, Yates and Bromwich JJ) (*Reckitt-Benckiser*). See also discussion in E Bant and JM Paterson, 'Intuitive Synthesis and Fidelity to Purpose? Judicial Interpretation of the Discretionary Power to Award Civil Pecuniary Penalties under the Australian Consumer Law' in P Vines and DM Scott (eds), *Statutory Interpretation in Private Law* (Sydney, Federation Press, 2019) 154.

[74] The terminology 'intuitive synthesis' and 'instinctive synthesis' seems to be used interchangeably. See, eg, *Australian Securities and Investments Commission v Commonwealth Bank of Australia* [2020] FCA 790 (*CBA*); *Australian Competition and Consumer Commission v Murray Goulburn Co-Operative Co Ltd* [2018] FCA 1964 (using 'intuitive synthesis') and *Australian Competition and Consumer Commission v Coles Supermarkets Australia Pty Ltd* [2015] FCA 330, (2015) 327 ALR 540 (*Coles Supermarkets*); *Australian Competition and Consumer Commission v Fisher & Paykal Customer Services* Pty Ltd [2014] FCA 1393; *Australian Competition and Consumer Commission v Multimedia International Services Pty Ltd* [2016] FCA 439, 243 FCR 392 (using 'instinctive synthesis'). See also Bant and Paterson (n 73) 154.

[75] *Australian Competition & Consumer Commission v Kimberly-Clark Australia Pty Ltd* (No 2) [2021] FCA 102 [25] (Abraham J), referring to *Markarian v The Queen* [2005] HCA 25, (2005) 228 CLR 357.

[76] *CSR* (n 38) 153–54, 52 (French J). See also discussion in, eg, Truong and Alampi (n 38).

[77] *CSR* (n 38) 153–54, 52 (French J). The presence of a culture of compliance can be seen to flow from the primacy of deterrence, and might be considered to be a mitigating factor: see, eg, *Trade Practices Commission v TNT Australia Pty Ltd* (1995) 17 ATPR 40,161, 40,168 (Burchett J).

[78] *Visa* (n 38); *Australian Securities and Investments Commission v Dover Financial Advisers* [2021] FCA 170, (2021) 150 ACSR 185, 189 [11] (O'Bryan J) (*Dover*).

[79] *Singtel Optus Pty Ltd v Australian Competition and Consumer Commission* [2012] FCAFC 20, (2012) 287 ALR 249 [37] (Keane CJ, Finn and Gilmour JJ) (*Singtel Optus*); *Coles Supermarkets* (n 74) [8]; *Australian Securities and Investments Commission v Westpac Securities Administration Limited, in the matter of Westpac Securities Administration Limited* [2021] FCA 1008 [21] (O'Bryan J); *Australian Competition and Consumer Commission v Woolworths Limited* [2016] FCA 44, (2016) ATPR 42-521, 43,068 [126] (Edelman J), drawing on the relevance of profit and contrition; *Australian Securities and Investments Commission v Westpac Banking Corporation (No 3)* [2018] FCA 1701, (2018) 131 ACSR 585 [49] (Beach J) (*Westpac No 3*) and *CBA* (n 74) [68] (Beach J). Notably, Beach J's list of factors does not specifically address 'corporate culture' or a 'culture of compliance' but includes 'the existence within the corporation of compliance systems, including provisions for and evidence of education and internal enforcement of such systems': *Westpac No 3* (n 79) [49] (Beach J); *NW Frozen Foods Pty Ltd v Australian Competition and Consumer Commission* [1996] FCA 1134, (1996) 71 FCR 285, 290, 292–94 and 297 (Burchett and Kiefel JJ); *J McPhee & Son (Australia) Pty Ltd v Australian Competition and Consumer Commission* [2000] FCA 365, (2000) 172 ALR 532 [158] and [163] (Black CJ, Lee and Golding JJ) (whether the conduct was 'systematic, deliberate or covert').

to sentencing.[80] As a result, the corpus of decisions provide fertile ground from which to identify judicial markers of corporate culture.

The process of 'intuitive synthesis' takes place in the context of the broadly held view that the primary object of the civil penalty regimes is deterrence, both specific (to deter repetition by the contravener) and general (to deter similar contravening conduct by others).[81] This requires a penalty to have a requisite 'sting or burden'.[82] In other words, the penalty must be 'not such as to be regarded by [the] offender or by others as an acceptable cost of doing business'.[83]

B. Characteristics of Reasoning Related to Corporate Culture in Civil Penalties Jurisprudence

Review of the relevant cases in light of the analytical framework outlined in section III identifies a range of characteristics of reasoning in civil penalties jurisprudence related to corporate culture.

i. Express Articulation of the Meaning of Corporate Culture

It is noticeable at the outset that courts have a tendency not to expressly consider or articulate the meaning of 'corporate culture' or a 'culture of compliance'.[84] The case analysis has not revealed express judicial guidance, outside the statement of the French factors, as to how a culture of compliance should be evaluated. This is notwithstanding the oft-stated view that 'it is desirable that the instinct involved [in determining penalty] is, and is seen to be, something more than a mere "gut reaction", and that the final result is an outcome of a reasoned process'.[85] The lack of express definition is,

[80] Notably, the ALRC in its Final Report recommended enacting a statutory provision requiring the court to consider certain factors when making a civil penalty order. The recommended list of factors mirrors the 'French factors' and includes '(h) whether the corporation had a corporate culture conducive to compliance at the time of the offence': ALRC Final Report (n 4) Recommendations 11, 16.

[81] *CSR* (n 38) [40], [52], [152] (French J). See also, eg, *Australian Competition and Consumer Commission v B & K Holdings (Qld) Pty Ltd* [2021] FCA 260 (Derrington J) (*B & K Holdings*); *Reckitt-Benckiser* (n 73) [153] (Jagot, Yates and Bromwich JJ); *Australian Competition and Consumer Commission v TPG Internet Pty Ltd* [2013] HCA 54, (2013) 250 CLR 640 [64]–[66] (French CJ, Crennan, Bell and Keane JJ) (*TPG*). See discussion of 'the deterrence objective' in Bant and Paterson (n 73) 154, 164–67; Truong and Alampi (n 38) 21.

[82] *Australian Building and Construction Commissioner v Construction, Forestry, Mining and Energy Union* [2018] HCA 3, (2018) 262 CLR 157 [116]; *Australian Competition and Consumer Commission v Dodo* [2021] FCA 589 [85] (*Dodo*).

[83] *Singtel Optus* (n 79) 265 [62]–[63] (Keane CJ, Finn and Gilmour JJ), approved by the High Court in *TPG* (n 81). See also *Reckitt-Benckiser* (n 73) 39 [58] (Jagot, Yates and Bromwich JJ); *Dodo* (n 82) (Murphy J).

[84] See, eg, *Reckitt-Benckiser* (n 73) 39 [58]; *Australian Competition and Consumer Commission v Reckitt-Benckiser (Australia) Pty Ltd (No 7)* [2016] FCA 424, (2016) 343 ALR 327, 341 [59] (Edelman J) (*Reckitt-Benckiser No 7*); *Australian Competition and Consumer Commission v GlaxoSmithKline Consumer Healthcare Australia Pty Ltd (No 2)* [2020] FCA 724 (*GSK No 2*); *Australian Competition and Consumer Commission v GlaxoSmithKline Consumer Healthcare Australia Pty Ltd* [2019] FCA 676; *B & K Holdings* (n 81); *Dover* (n 78); *Singtel Optus* (n 79); *TPG* (n 81); *Dodo* (n 81); *Australian Competition and Consumer Commission v Optus Mobile Pty Limited* [2019] FCA 106 (*Optus Mobile*); *Australian Competition and Consumer Commission v Meriton Property Services Pty Ltd (No 2)* [2018] FCA 1125 (*Meriton*); *Australian Competition and Consumer Commission v Liquorland (Australia) Pty Ltd* [2005] FCA 683 (*Liquorland*).

[85] *Reckitt-Benckiser* (n 73) [175] (Jagot, Yates and Bromwich JJ).

however, consistent with Edelman J's observation that 'the courts have avoided excessive subtleties and refinements in a process which is already complicated'.[86] As noted by the Full Federal Court in *Flight Centre v Australian Competition and Consumer Commission*,

> the task [of assessing penalty] is one that is evaluative, taking into account all the circumstances of the case, not to be reached mechanically or by some illusory process of exactitude, but rather by evaluation that is articulated to a point (but no further) that is useful and meaningful.[87]

The discretionary nature of the 'intuitive synthesis' approach has resulted in a series of 'single point determinations produced by opaque intuitive synthesis',[88] which do not readily lend themselves to granular analysis on the meaning of corporate culture. Indeed, courts do not always address each of the French factors individually, or even at all.[89]

Nevertheless, though not expressly articulated, insights can be gained from consideration of the final form penalties take and the facts supporting those penalties, as well as judicial reasoning in reaching a penalty determination.

ii. Factors Bearing on Judicial Understanding of Corporate Culture – Language of the French Factors

One such insight relates to the courts' reliance on the language of the French factors as an indicator of markers of corporate culture. The courts' consideration of evidential indicia of a 'culture of compliance' tends to be limited, both expressly and through application, to the indicia specified in French J's original and seminal iteration of the French factors, being 'educational programmes and disciplinary or other corrective measures in response to an acknowledged contravention'.[90] For example, Burley J in *Australian Competition and Consumer Commission v Viagogo AG (No 3)* found a lack of compliance programmes and deficient corrective action on the part of the defendant company were 'sufficient to conclude that 'Viagogo's culture was not and is not one of proactive compliance'.[91]

[86] *Reckitt-Benckiser No 7* (n 84) [22] (Edelman J).

[87] *Flight Centre Ltd v Australian Competition and Consumer Commission (No 2)* [2018] FCAFC 53 [55] (Allsop CJ, Davies and Wigney JJ) approved in *Dodo* (n 82) [55] (Murphy J).

[88] *CBA* (n 74) [77] (Beach J).

[89] See, eg, *Australian Competition and Consumer Commission v Oscar Wylee Pty Ltd* [2020] FCA 1340; Colvin J in *Australian Competition and Consumer Commission v Geowash Pty Ltd (Subject to a Deed of Co Arrangement) (No 4)* [2020] FCA 23, (2020) 376 ALR 701 did not consider whether the defendant had a culture of compliance.

[90] *CSR* (n 38) 153–54 (French J). See, eg, *Reckitt-Benckiser* (n 73); *Reckitt-Benckiser No 7* (n 84); *B & K Holdings* (n 81); *Dover* (n 78); *Singtel Optus* (n 79); *TPG* (n 81); *Dodo* (n 82); *Optus Mobile* (n 84); *Liquorland* (n 84); *Australian Competition and Consumer Commission v Sumo Power Pty Ltd* [2021] FCA 712; *Australian Competition and Consumer Commission v Decathlon (Australia) Pty Ltd* [2021] FCA 964 (*Decathlon*); *Australian Securities and Investments Commission v Kogan Australia Pty Ltd (No 2)* [2020] FCA 1751 (*Kogan No 2*); *Australian Consumer Commission v Sony Interactive Entertainment Network Europe Limited* [2020] FCA 787; *Meriton* (n 84).

[91] *Australian Competition and Consumer Commission v Viagogo AG (No 3)* [2020] FCA 1423 [105]–[108] (Burley J) (*Viagogo*).

There are some exceptions to this, where courts have incorporated consideration of other indicia of corporate culture. For example, Murphy J in *Dodo* moved beyond the wording of the French factors in determining the existence or otherwise of a 'culture of compliance', to consider the presence in Dodo's internal structure of a 'Risk Manager and Compliance Risk Manager' who was engaged in reporting directly to the board.[92]

Justice Moshinsky, in *Australian Competition and Consumer Commission v iSelect Limited*, also looked beyond the existence of compliance programmes and corrective action, expressing a view that

> merely having in place a compliance program and going through the process of training is not sufficient. It is necessary for the relevant personnel, including senior management, to apply their minds to whether the statements made prominently on the website are truthful and accurate.[93]

A further example can be found in *Australian Securities and Investments Commission v MLC Nominees Pty Ltd*.[94] This case concerned multiple instances of misleading or deceptive conduct or false or misleading representations in relation to the charging and deduction of fees associated with superannuation funds. Justice Yates accepted that the defendant companies, MLC Nominees and NULIS, had a corporate culture conducive to compliance.[95] Though Yates J did not articulate the basis for this, it may be inferred from the defendants' submission that the culture of compliance stemmed from 'documented processes and frameworks in relation to trustee governance, risk and compliance management, and disclosure governance', as well as updates to ASIC on the progress of internal investigations and remediation following the first breach report.[96]

Finally, Jagot J, in *Australian Competition and Consumer Commission v Panthera Finance Pty Ltd*, took into account a joint statement of facts that noted that the defendant had in place 'policies and procedures … covered by an ISO quality management system standard accreditation', and that the impugned conduct was inconsistent with this system and with internal procedures.[97] Justice Jagot's approach aligns with, but

[92] *Dodo* (n 82) [94]–[95] (Murphy J). This was in addition to express consideration of the existence of compliance programmes, including training during the relevant period, and the provision of more detailed compliance training for senior staff. The parties in this case proposed agreed orders, involving payment by Dodo and iPrimus of pecuniary penalties of $1.5 million and $1 million respectively. The Court agreed with the proposed orders.

[93] *Australian Competition and Consumer Commission v iSelect Limited* [2020] FCA 1523 [59]. This case concerned representations by iSelect to consumers that the price for an available energy plan was lower than the price the consumer would, or would be likely to, pay. The parties jointly proposed orders that were considered appropriate by Moshinsky J. The orders included a pecuniary penalty of $8.5 million in respect of each act or omission constituting a contravention of ss 29(1)(g), 29(1)(i) or 34 of the ACL, together with publication by iSelect of a corrective notice on its website.

[94] *Australian Securities and Investments Commission v MLC Nominees Pty Ltd* [2020] FCA 1306 (*MLC Nominees*).

[95] ibid [224] (Yates J). Interestingly, Yates J also found that '[MLC Nominees'] systems clearly failed by not recognising that many members that were or came to be involved with the MasterKey product did not have a plan adviser'.

[96] ibid [188]–[193], [268] (Yates J). The Court ordered pecuniary penalties totalling $22.5 million, relating to multiple contraventions grouped as three courses of conduct: ibid [228].

[97] *Australian Competition and Consumer Commission v Panthera Finance Pty Ltd* [2020] FCA 340 [50] (Jagot J) (*Panthera*). Court orders in this case included pecuniary penalties totalling $500,000; a $100,000 costs order against Panthera; and a requirement that Panthera maintain a compliance programme subject to certain specifications, for a three-year period.

does not reference, French J's view in *Australian Securities and Investments Commission, in the matter of Chemeq Limited (ACN 009 136 264) v Chemeq Limited (ACN 009 135 264)*[98] that compliance programmes and practices, and the deliberateness of the conduct of a defendant company, are relevant to determining the existence of a 'culture of compliance'.[99]

Judicial consideration of these further indicia – including internal structures, systems, policies and procedures, as instantiated not merely as stated – resonates with the significance given to internal decision-making structures, systems, processes and practices in the scholarship discussed in section III. However, in the absence of express articulation of the meaning of corporate culture and of the relationship between these other markers and a culture of compliance, judicial conception of these factors and of their relationship to corporate culture remains underdeveloped. In any event, and as noted, in the vast majority of cases considered the courts' focus has been confined to those indicia specifically included in the French factors,[100] being compliance programmes and corrective measures.

iii. Compliance Programmes – Form Over Function?

Further, and relatedly, the evidential descriptors in the French factors, and correspondingly, the courts' consideration of indicia of culture, tend to be limited to objective indications of the existence of a compliance programme and of responsive adjustment measures following an 'acknowledged contravention'.[101] For example, in *Viagogo*,[102] Burley J considered that an *absence* of evidence of any compliance training or programmes for staff suggested an absence of a culture of compliance with the ACL. His Honour also considered a lack of response to the Australian Competition and Consumer Commission (ACCC) and a failure to develop compliance programmes in the wake of the liability judgment as evidence suggesting the absence of a 'culture of compliance' in Viagogo.[103]

[98] *Australian Securities and Investments Commission, in the matter of Chemeq Limited (ACN 009 136 264) v Chemeq Limited (ACN 009 135 264)* [2006] FCA 936, (2006) 234 ALR 511 (*Chemeq*).

[99] ibid [84]–[86] (French J). Justice French adopted a holistic view of compliance programmes and processes, requiring consideration of 'form and content' as well as 'the measures adopted by the corporation to ensure they are understood and applied'. Note that *Chemeq* is not discussed at length in this chapter, as that case concerned the penalty for corporate non-compliance with continuous disclosure obligations rather than a claim of misleading or deceptive conduct or unconscionable conduct under the ACLor ASIC Act.

[100] See discussion of the French factors in section IV.A.ii.

[101] This can be contrasted with the approach of French J in *Chemeq* (n 98) in the context of continuous disclosure obligations. Justice French considered that compliance programmes will only be effective if accompanied by 'a degree of awareness and sensitivity to the need to consider regulatory obligations as a routine incident of corporate decision-making': ibid [86] (French J). This requires the court to consider the form and content of company policies and procedures, as well as measures adopted by the corporation to ensure they are 'understood and applied': ibid [85] (French J).

[102] *Viagogo* (n 91).

[103] ibid [105]–[109] (Burley J). The Court ordered that Viagogo be restrained for a five-year period from making certain representations on its website in relation to the sale of tickets. The Court also ordered Viagogo to pay pecuniary penalties totalling $7 million; to establish an ACL compliance programme within 90 days, involving training for each employee or other person involved in the business and coming into contact with consumers; and to maintain and continue to implement that compliance programme for a period of three years.

Where an internal compliance programme or training is found to exist, courts tend not to go the next step to consider, for example, the quality or efficacy of any such programmes, or the taking of responsive adjustment measures following awareness of conduct that *might* constitute a contravention.[104] For example, the Full Federal Court in *Reckitt-Benckiser* did not expressly link repeated contraventions of the ACL with a lack or absence of a culture of compliance, despite finding that Reckitt had 'repeatedly contravened a basic requirement of the ACL … for nearly five years for its own commercial benefit'.[105]

Similarly, Murphy J in *Dodo* noted both a 'history of similar conduct which likely contravened … the ACL' and the apparent failure of earlier undertakings in relation to that conduct to deter the contraventions in question.[106] However, His Honour did not explicitly link this history to the efficacy or adequacy of the company's compliance programmes, or the existence (or otherwise) of a 'culture of compliance'. Courts have also declined to give weight to the costs of a defendant company's compliance programme.[107] Rather, the focus seems to be on the existence and scope of compliance training.

In this regard, it is notable that the court in *GSK No 2* stated that what is important is whether a contravening company had an 'effective compliance regime, not just one that looks good on paper',[108] and that an effective compliance programme may lessen the need for specific deterrence. This reference to efficacy strongly aligns with the scholarly framework outlined earlier and suggests a more robust, developing conception of corporate culture. Yet in considering the facts, the court in *GSK No 2* did not probe the efficacy of GSK's compliance programme or the way in which it operated in practice, but rather referred to evidence of the programme's existence. For example, the court noted evidence of GSK's competition law training programmes, including that they had been updated, that specific training had been given to staff in relation to misleading and deceptive conduct, that the company had made changes to its approval processes and 'taken a number of steps to improve its compliance', all of which were considered to suggest a 'reduced need … for a stiffer penalty to enhance specific deterrence'.[109] There is, however, no express reference to the fact that the contravening conduct occurred over an almost five-year period, or to any inferences that might be drawn from this, including inferences regarding the efficacy of the company's compliance programmes, given that they existed alongside a prolonged period of contravention.

Interestingly, at the earlier stage of assessing liability, the court in *GSK* considered that 'it was GSK's responsibility to take appropriate steps to assess its own marketing strategies and ensure compliance with the *Australian Consumer Law*'.[110] This earlier

[104] ibid [107]–[108] (Burley J).

[105] *Reckitt-Benckiser* (n 73) [160] (Jagot, Yates and Bromwich JJ).

[106] *Dodo* (n 82) [84] (Murphy J). The Court ordered agreed pecuniary penalties of $1 million and $1 million against Dodo and iPrimus respectively.

[107] *Decathlon* (n 90) [63]–[64] (Nicholas J), though note that the costs of the compliance programme in this case approximated $290,000 in a year in which annual turnover approximated $32 million. Justice Nicholas considered this cost to reflect 'the ordinary cost' of running a business of the nature of the defendant's business: ibid [64].

[108] *GSK No 2* (n 84) [55].

[109] ibid.

[110] ibid [44].

statement is suggestive of a broader view of compliance programmes as having a proactive character and needing to actually 'ensure compliance'. It is unclear why this view was not equally, if not more, apposite in the penalties context. Indeed, on the earlier analysis, it offers an important marker for assessing the level of the defendant's corporate culpability.

The approach to compliance programmes taken in the penalty judgment for *Reckitt-Benckiser No 7*, and adopted by the Full Federal Court on Appeal, was a little broader.[111] The trial judge in the penalty judgment in *Reckitt-Benckiser No 7* found that shortcomings in the company's compliance programme included the failure to specifically address the ACL and the failure to detect serious potential risks, notwithstanding obvious warnings (such as a Choice *Shonky Award* and a complaint to the Therapeutic Goods Administration).[112] These findings were unchallenged on appeal to the Full Federal Court.[113]

Similarly, O'Bryan J in *Dover*[114] and in *Australian Competition and Consumer Commission v STA Travel*[115] inquired into the adequacy and not just the existence of the defendant's compliance practices. In *STA*, O'Bryan J considered that the lack of an officer responsible for ACL compliance and the length of contravening conduct pointed to the absence of a compliance culture.[116] The defendant company's compliance in *Dover* was more rigorous. Dover had been found liable for contraventions including misleading or deceptive conduct under the ASIC Act in relation to a misleading statement contained in the company's 'Client Protection Policy'. This policy had been provided to 19,402 clients in conjunction with or incorporated into financial advice. In the penalties judgment, O'Bryan J accepted evidence about key elements of Dover's compliance practices, including that each statement of advice issued was subject to mandatory internal and external legal review; that Dover had a Compliance Committee responsible for overseeing compliance; that the Compliance Committee met quarterly until 2016 and after that monthly; that Dover provided compliance and education to its advisors and had compliance education publications on its website; that Dover had engaged numerous external law firms and compliance consultants to review its compliance processes, including the Client Protection Policy; and that Dover had a low rate of customer complaint.[117] Nevertheless, O'Bryan J found that there was 'a gap in legal compliance' and that '[n]othing in [the] evidence suggests that Dover was attentive to compliance with its obligations under the ASIC Act,

[111] *Reckitt-Benckiser* (n 73) (Jagot, Yates and Bromwich JJ); *Reckitt-Benckiser No 7* (n 84) (Edelman J).

[112] *Reckitt-Benckiser No 7* (n 84) [70], [73], [74]–[83] (Edelman J).

[113] *Reckitt-Benckiser* (n 73) [43] (Jagot, Yates and Bromwich JJ). The Full Federal Court did, however, find the $1.7 million pecuniary penalty imposed by the trial judge 'manifestly inadequate': ibid [3]. Justices Jagot, Yates and Bromwich noted that Reckitt Benckiser must have engaged in the prohibited conduct at least 5.9 million times, and imposed in lieu the pecuniary penalty of $6 million sought by the ACCC, which amount the Full Court considered to be 'at the bottom of the appropriate range for the contraventions': ibid [179].

[114] *Dover* (n 78) [82]–[88].

[115] *Australian Competition and Consumer Commission v STA Travel* [2020] FCA 723 (*STA*).

[116] ibid [1] (O'Bryan J). The Court ordered a pecuniary penalty of $14 million against STA Travel. The Court also issued a publication order, restraint order and order that STA Travel establish a compliance programme.

[117] *Dover* (n 78) [83]–[88] (O'Bryan J).

particularly the prohibition against false, misleading and deceptive conduct and other similar consumer protection obligations'.[118]

Factors referred to in support of this conclusion included that whilst there was evidence that the Client Protection Policy had been on the company's Compliance Committee agenda on four occasions, there was no record of any substantive consideration as to whether the policy might be misleading. In relation to Dover's use of external legal advisors and compliance consultants, O'Bryan J accepted that none of them had raised compliance concerns relating to the statement in question. However, His Honour found that this did not assist Dover, as the evidence showed that the company's sole director 'was generally not receptive to criticisms of the documentation being used by Dover'.[119] Justice O'Bryan's consideration of the practices and attitude of key management personnel, as well as the requirement for 'attention' to legal compliance (as opposed to merely the existence of compliance programmes), is consistent with the holistic approaches to corporate culture discussed in section III of this chapter.

Finally, Abraham J, in *Kogan No 2*,[120] took the view that 'insufficient and inadequate staff training' does not necessarily equate to 'a disregard for compliance', and that '[n]or, in so far as there have been deficiencies in the compliance programs, is that indicative of a culture of noncompliance'.[121] However, Abraham J did not elaborate as to other indicia that might be indicative of a culture of compliance or non-compliance.

iv. Corrective Measures and Reactive Fault

In keeping with the tendency to refer to indicia expressly mentioned in the French factors, courts tend to also make note of corrective action taken by a contravenor following acknowledgement of breach.[122] An interesting example is found in *CBA*,[123] which involved a range of contraventions of the ASIC Act by the CBA, including misleading or deceptive conduct through the bank's failure to provide advertised benefits on a suite of products over a 10-year period. The contraventions resulted in significant underpayments of interest and mispayment of fees, harming 8,659 customers on 131,542 occasions. Justice Beach directly addressed 'the contemporary concept of corporate culture'.[124] Justice Beach characterised the CBA's failure to provide advertised benefits on a range of products over a 10-year period as a 'systems deficiency rather than a

[118] ibid [85] (O'Bryan J).

[119] ibid [86] (O'Bryan J). The Court ordered Dover to pay a pecuniary penalty of $1.5 million, and Dover's sole director to pay a pecuniary penalty of $240,000 in respect of his knowing concern in Dover's contraventions.

[120] *Kogan No 2* (n 90) [32] (Abraham J).

[121] ibid. The Court ordered Kogan to pay a pecuniary penalty of $350,000.

[122] See, eg, *Australian Competition and Consumer Commission v Campbell (No 3)* [2021] FCA 528; *Australian Competition and Consumer Commission v Landmark Operations Limited (t/a Seednet)* [2018] FCA 1977; *Australian Competition and Consumer Commission v Launceston Superstore Pty Ltd* [2013] FCA 1315; *Australian Competition and Consumer Commission v Luv-a-Duck Pty Ltd* [2013] FCA 1136 *Australian Competition and Consumer Commission v Virgin Australian Airlines Pty Ltd (No 2)* [2017] FCA 204; *Dover* (n 78) [54] (O'Bryan J).

[123] *CBA* (n 74).

[124] ibid [122] (Beach J).

broader corporate culture problem'.[125] Justice Beach considered that the CBA's failures did not indicate a culture of non-compliance with the law but rather 'the lack of any robust systems and processes to effectuate those desires'.[126] This is despite noting a 'poor control environment', 'inadequate' complaints-handling processes, and CBA's failure to establish a business unit responsible for ensuring the CBA's package benefits were applied in accordance with the package terms and conditions. Justice Beach's narrow conception of corporate culture stands in stark contrast to the notion that systems are inherently purposive, that systemic misconduct cannot readily be characterised as 'inadvertent', and recent decisions concerning the relationship between unconscionability and state of mind.[127]

Whilst acknowledging that the CBA 'should have taken better care to ensure that its systems and processes would deliver the promised benefits', Beach J considered that 'the better measure of CBA's prevailing culture' was not its failure to deliver the promised benefits over a 10-year period but rather 'how it responded when the problem was identified'.[128] In this respect Beach J gave greater weight to the CBA's early breach notices to ASIC, its 'early self-generated' remediation programme and system changes the CBA had made.[129]

The corrective action taken by CBA can be contrasted with that in *Viagogo*, which was considered inadequate to support any mitigation at the penalties stage. *Viagogo* concerned allegations of misleading or deceptive conduct and false or misleading allegations in relation to the on-line sale of tickets. The ACCC had written to Viagogo expressing concerns about its website in March 2016 and February 2017. The court's finding that Viagogo had 'no real culture of compliance' with the ACL was based on Viagogo's failure to respond to the ACCC's March 2016 letter; its denial, in response to the ACCC's February 2017 letter, of any misleading or deceptive conduct; and a lack of evidence of any Viagogo training or compliance programme.[130] In relation to corrective action, Viagogo pointed to changes it had made to its booking website following the liability proceeding, as set out in a letter from Viagogo to the ACCC in September 2019.[131] In response to an ACCC submission that these changes were inadequate, Burley J found that the court's task in assessing penalty is 'to assess an appropriate penalty for contraventions proved during the relevant period, and not to assess penalty by reference to unpleaded conduct that has taken place subsequently'.[132] This approach seems inconsistent with principles of reactive corporate fault or responsive adjustment.[133] Nevertheless, His Honour did take into account the timing of the

[125] ibid [121] (Beach J).

[126] ibid [123] (Beach J).

[127] Including Beach J's judgment in *Australian Competition and Consumer Commission v Get Qualified Australia Pty Ltd (in liquidation) (No 2)* [2017] FCA 709; see discussion in Bant (n 1); Bant and Paterson, 'Systems of Misconduct' (n 41).

[128] *CBA* (n 74) [126] (Beach J).

[129] ibid [130], [12] (Beach J). The Court ordered a pecuniary penalty of $5 million against the CBA, and an adverse publicity notice on the CBA's website.

[130] *Viagogo* (n 91) [107] (Burley J).

[131] ibid [113] (Burley J).

[132] ibid [116] (Burley J). For the final Court order, see n 103.

[133] Discussed in section II.A of this chapter. Justice Yates in *MLC Nominees* (n 94) [290] took a similar view that in assessing pecuniary penalty, 'the focus must be the admitted contraventions' (and not, in that case, other admitted contraventions by MLC Nominees, which 'ASIC submissions tended to stray into').

website amendments, being five months after the liability judgment. This supported a view that 'Viagogo's corrective action was taken very late and for it was the legal equivalent of drawing teeth'.[134] On this basis, Viagogo's response to the contraventions was not considered to be a mitigating factor.

Whilst courts do not expressly reference concepts of reactive corporate fault or responsive adjustment, the express inclusion of corrective measures in the French factors might explain the courts' consideration of corrective measures such as remediation programmes, system changes and adjustments to compliance programmes as factors in determining the existence (or otherwise) of a 'culture of compliance'.

v. Links between 'Culture of Compliance' and Indicia of Culture Not Articulated in the French Factors

Analysis of the cases suggests that courts may be giving consideration to broader indicia of corporate culture (other than those expressly listed in the French factors) elsewhere in the penalties reasoning and/or at the stage of assessing liability, but are not linking these factors to an understanding of corporate culture or are doing so only loosely. By way of example, practices, values, beliefs and more broadly the notion of a corporate 'ethos' have not been expressly noted by the courts in assessing whether a culture of compliance exists. Yet it is possible that state of mind of the contravenor is relevant to establishing the presence or absence of a 'culture of compliance'. For example, the court in *Australian Competition and Consumer Commission v Productive Partners Pty Ltd (trading as Captain Cook College) (No 4)*[135] suggested a link between 'deliberateness of contraventions and compliance culture', but did not elaborate.[136] Similarly, Burley J in *Viagogo* considered that 'a level of deliberateness … tends in favour of the need for a significant penalty'.[137]

Another potential marker of a corporate culture of non-compliance can be found in Edelman J's view in *Reckitt-Benckiser No 7* that prior contraventions support a need for specific deterrence in the form of tougher penalties.[138] This is consistent with the ALRC's observation that repeated misconduct may warrant higher penalties, on the basis that it indicates a likelihood of greater harm.[139] In a similar vein, Anderson J in *Australian Competition and Consumer Commission v Medibank Private Ltd* grouped 'corporate culture conducive to compliance' under the same sub-heading as 'prior similar conduct'

[134] ibid.

[135] *Australian Competition and Consumer Commission v Productive Partners Pty Ltd (trading as Captain Cook College) (No 4)* [2021] FCA 752 (*Captain Cook College*).

[136] ibid [105] (Bromwich J).

[137] *Viagogo* (n 91) [99] (Burley J). Justice Burley considered that 'Viagogo's responses give it the appearance of being a company that is indifferent to the interests of Australian consumers and which prefers to elevate its own profit motives above those interests, even when on notice of the potential for harm being done.'

[138] *Reckitt-Benckiser No 7* (n 84) [89]–[90], [93] (Edelman J) referring to *Coles Supermarkets* (n 74); the finding in the penalty judgment of previous contraventions of the ACL by the defendant was unchallenged on appeal to the Full Federal Court: *Reckitt-Benckiser* (n 73) [43] (Jagot, Yates and Bromwich JJ).

[139] ALRC Final Report (n 4) 178, 294.

and discussed both in the one paragraph,[140] as did Jagot J in *Panthera*.[141] Conversely, an absence of any court findings of similar prior conduct has been found to '[weigh] in favour of' the defendant company at the stage of determining penalty.[142] Though not expressly articulated by the courts, prior contraventions might also be relevant to assessing penalty for their indication of intentionality.

Finally, some of the judgments considered draw explicit links between systematic conduct and a culture of compliance. For example, Jackson J, in *Australian Competition and Consumer Commission v Service Seeking Pty Ltd*,[143] accepted a submission that the defendant company lacked a culture of compliance with the ACL on the basis of an absence of evidence to the contrary, 'and in view of the systematic nature of the contravening conduct and the involvement of senior management in it'.[144] Similarly, McKerracher J, in *Australian Competition and Consumer Commission v Domain Name Corp Pty Ltd*,[145] accepted a submission by the ACCC 'to the effect that the "deliberate, extensive and protracted nature of the contravening conduct" further evidences a lack of a culture of compliance with the ACL'.[146] Other cases, however, do not articulate such a connection. For example, Yates J, in *MLC Nominees*, found that '[MLC Nominees'] systems clearly failed … One would have felt that alarm bells would have rung … Apparently they did not'.[147] Yet notwithstanding this system failure, Yates J was satisfied that the defendant company had a 'culture of compliance',[148] and did not draw any link between prolonged system failure and a culture of non-compliance.

V. Conclusion

This chapter has sought to explore the concept of corporate culture, from the perspective of civil penalties jurisprudence. No clear, cohesive articulation of corporate culture emerges from the analysis. Corporate culture as an analytical tool is used yet not refined. However, building on an analytical framework derived from seminal

[140] *Australian Competition and Consumer Commission v Medibank Private Ltd* [2020] FCA 1030 [84] (Anderson J).

[141] *Panthera* (n 97), though Jagot J's discussion extended to four paragraphs: ibid [113]–[116].

[142] *Viagogo* (n 91) (Burley J), though note that s 224(2)(c) requires the court to have regard to this in determining penalty.

[143] *Australian Competition and Consumer Commission v Service Seeking Pty Ltd* [2020] FCA 1040.

[144] ibid [69] (Jackson J). The Court ordered a pecuniary penalty of $600,000; an injunction restraining Service Seeking from publishing service reviews on its website without the express written consent of the person named as providing the review or the person to whom the services were provided; a corrective publication notice; and the implementation of a compliance programme.

[145] *Australian Competition and Consumer Commission v Domain Name Corp Pty Ltd* [2018] FCA 1269.

[146] ibid [51] (McKerracher J), referencing the ACCC's submission. In this case, the absence of a corporate culture of compliance had been acknowledged in a joint Statement of Agreed Facts and Admissions: ibid [51]. The two respondent companies, both having the same sole director and shareholder, were found to have issued a total of approximately 303,000 misleading and deceptive notices over the period from November 2015 to April 2017: ibid [5]–[6].

[147] *MLC Nominees* (n 94) [224] (Yates J); see discussion of the defendants' 'corporate culture conducive to compliance' at [188]–[193], [268] (Yates J).

[148] ibid [224] (Yates J). The Court ordered pecuniary penalties totalling $22.5 million, relating to multiple contraventions grouped as three courses of conduct: ibid [228].

scholarship on models of organisational liability, the chapter has sought to identify markers of corporate culture or understandings of corporate culture applied by the courts in determining penalty. Significantly, while the process of 'intuitive synthesis' tends not to encourage judicial articulation of notions of corporate culture, some strands of judicial reasoning emerge from the analysis. These include a tendency to limit express considerations of culture to those indicators included in the original iteration of the French factors, being compliance programmes – albeit for the most part in form, rather than substance – and corrective measures following an acknowledgement of contravention. This brings into consideration aspects of reactive fault. Other indicia, such as cooperation with the regulator, systematic conduct, prior similar contraventions, internal procedures and indicators of corporate 'attitude' or state of mind, are also present in penalties determinations, though for the most part they are not expressly linked to conceptions of corporate culture. Analysis of Australian civil penalties jurisprudence demonstrates both the opacity of the corporate culture concept and the potential for meaningful content for this powerful concept to be more fully developed.

9

Systems Intentionality: Theory and Practice

ELISE BANT*

I. Introduction

This chapter seeks to outline and further explain the features and operation of the model of corporate responsibility that I have developed, including in collaboration with Jeannie Paterson, in earlier work.[1] 'Systems Intentionality' is an umbrella term used to capture a broader proposition, namely that a corporation's state of mind is manifested through its systems of conduct, policies and practices. On this analysis, systems are inherently purposive: they exist to achieve certain ends. Further, those corporations that adopt and operate a system must thereby be taken to know what is necessary for the system to function. These simple insights allow us to start to piece together a more detailed understanding of the spectrum of corporate mental states required by our general law and statutory doctrines and rules, such as specific and general intention, knowledge, dishonesty, recklessness, unconscionability, mistake, and other related facts and standards.

How this is done is the subject of detailed examination in chapters 11 and 12.[2] In this chapter, the primary aim is foundational: to articulate and illustrate, with rather more precision, key concepts relevant to our enquiry, in particular the nature and features of the spectrum of behaviours signalled by the concepts of systems, policies, processes or

* This chapter builds on joint research with Professor Jeannie Marie Paterson into the regulation of misleading and unconscionable conduct, pursuant to Australian Research Council Discovery Projects DP180100932 and DP140100767. It also presents proposals developed pursuant to my ARC-supported Future Fellowship project FT190100475, which aims to examine and model reforms of the laws that currently inhibit corporate responsibility for serious misconduct. My sincere thanks to all participants for their very helpful comments and criticisms. All responsibility for errors rests with me.

[1] E Bant, 'Culpable Corporate Minds' (2021) 48 *University of Western Australia Law Review* 352; E Bant and JM Paterson, 'Systems of Misconduct: Corporate Culpability and Statutory Unconscionability' (2021) 15 *Journal of Equity* 63; E Bant, 'Catching the Corporate Conscience: A New Model of "Systems Intentionality"' (2022) *Lloyds Maritime and Commercial Law Quarterly* 467; E Bant, 'Reforming the Laws of Corporate Attribution: "Systems Intentionality" Draft Statutory Provision' (2022) 39 *Company & Securities Law Journal* 259.

[2] For early analysis of dishonesty and some discussion of knowledge and mistake, see Bant, 'Culpable Corporate Minds' (n 1) 377–85; for unconscionability, and some discussion of general intention, predatory intention, recklessness and knowledge, see Bant and Paterson, 'Systems of Misconduct' (n 1) 86–91; see also Bant, 'Catching the Corporate Conscience' (n 1) 484–89.

methods, practices and patterns of behaviour. This may allow us to identify more accurately the point at which habitual or repeated actions, for example, may take on a more purposive bent and mature into systems of conduct. The second, related aim is one of proof: how to go about establishing the existence of these varied concepts, including evidential strategies and considerations. The hope is that this combined analysis will illuminate how the model of Systems Intentionality may apply, as a matter of theory and practice, to the range of real-life scenarios that currently evade regulation through existing attribution rules.

The chapter commences by briefly outlining the genesis and features of the model of Systems Intentionality before turning to break down component elements, and the kinds of evidence (and litigation strategies) relevant to establishing each.

II. Genesis and Features of Systems Intentionality

A. Background

The genesis of the model lay in meeting twin challenges: on the one hand, the pervasive role of state-of-mind requirements in legal doctrines that seek to regulate and remedy serious corporate commercial misconduct; and on the other, the notoriously complex and yet inadequate state of the law's current approaches to identifying corporate states of mind.[3] Faced with the scale of these challenges, the proposed model draws on the insights of organisational and legal theorists, law reformers and courts regulating corporate misconduct to propose a practically workable theory of organisational culpability. The aim is for the model to enable proof of specific corporate mental states required for the application of legal doctrines, in a theoretically justified way.

As to the challenges, it is largely uncontentious (if not always fully appreciated) that assessment of the defendant's state of mind is a critical component of both general law and statutory doctrines that regulate commercial fraud. Common law and equitable doctrines include deceit, fraudulent misrepresentation, injurious falsehood, knowing receipt and assistance, and (in Australia at least) the equitable doctrine of unconscionable conduct. For example, the tort of deceit requires that the defendant has made a misrepresentation knowingly or recklessly, intending to induce reliance on the part of the victim.[4] Unconscionable conduct in equity requires the defendant to have 'taken advantage' of the plaintiff's special disadvantage: here knowledge is key to the enquiry, but courts commonly also reference defendant dishonesty, a 'predatory' intention, recklessness and deliberateness.[5]

[3] Australian Law Reform Commission (ALRC), *Corporate Criminal Responsibility* (Report No 136, 2020) ch 6.

[4] *Magill v Magill* [2006] HCA 51, (2006) 226 CLR 551.

[5] The key authorities are gathered and discussed in Bant and Paterson, 'Systems of Misconduct' (n 1), but compare *Commercial Bank of Australia v Amadio* [1983] HCA 14, (1983) 151 CLR 447, 467 (Mason J); *Kakavas v Crown Melbourne Ltd* [2013] HCA 25, (2013) 250 CLR 392, 438–39 [156]–[157], 439–40 [161] (French CJ, Hayne, Crennan, Kiefel, Bell, Gageler and Keane JJ); *Thorne v Kennedy* [2017] HCA 49, (2017) 263 CLR 85, 103 [38] (Kiefel CJ, Bell, Gageler, Keane and Edelman JJ).

In Australia, the defendant's state of mind is also invoked directly or indirectly in a number of statutory prohibitions and enforcement responses to commercial misconduct. Thus section 1041G of the Corporations Act 2001 (Cth) (Corporations Act) prohibits conduct that is dishonest; the licensing obligation imposed by section 912A of the Corporations Act is to provide financial services 'efficiently, honestly and fairly'; and a range of statutory provisions prohibit unconscionable conduct 'within the meaning of the unwritten law', alongside more expansive prohibitions on statutory unconscionable conduct.[6] These, and many others, require proof of discrete mental states. But even when a statutory prohibition is *strict*, as in the distinctive Australian prohibition of misleading conduct within trade or commerce,[7] the defendant's state of mind may play a role in remedial relief. Thus, for example, a defendant's mental state may become relevant when determining the defendant's scope of liability, apportioning loss or through defensive considerations.[8] Perhaps most importantly, as a matter of Australian regulatory practice, the ongoing relevance of culpability is particularly apparent where civil pecuniary penalties are in play. Here, drawing on the 'French factors', courts commonly look for indicia of the defendant's blameworthiness through state-of-mind criteria, such as the defendant's knowledge, intention, regret or contrition.[9]

We might also note that state-of-mind enquiries are key to much *ex ante* regulation – for example, determining whether a corporation is a 'suitable person' to hold a licence, required to conduct some regulated business activity.[10]

As I have explained elsewhere,[11] the pervasive role for state-of-mind requirements in doctrines that regulate serious commercial misconduct probably reflects the law's longstanding concern to protect natural individuals from unmerited and overly crushing personal liability. But the classic(al) market-place rogue is a far cry from the reality of the modern, commercial miscreant. In sophisticated market economies, wrongdoers

[6] Leading expressions of the statutory prohibition are found in the Competition and Consumer Act 2010 (Cth), sch 2 (ACL), s 21 and Australian Securities and Investment Commission Act 2001 (Cth), s 12CB(1) (ASIC Act), the latter of which was the subject of *ASIC v Kobelt* [2019] HCA 18, (2019) 267 CLR 1 (*Kobelt*) and is currently regarded as the leading authority on the operation of both provisions: see eg *Australian Competition and Consumer Commission v Employsure Pty Ltd* [2020] FCA 1409 [333] (Griffiths J).

[7] ACL (n 6), s 18; ASIC Act (n 6), s 12DA.

[8] See, eg, E Bant and JM Paterson, 'Limitations on Defendant Liability for Misleading or Deceptive Conduct Under Statute: Some Insights from Negligent Misstatement' in K Barker, R Grantham and W Swain (eds), *The Law of Misstatements: 50 Years on from* Hedley Byrne v Heller (Oxford, Hart Publishing, 2015) 159. See also Competition and Consumer Act 2010 (Cth), s 137B, which bars apportionment of liability between plaintiff and defendant when the plaintiff has acted fraudulently.

[9] See the 'French factors' developed in *Trade Practices Commission v CSR Ltd* [1991] ATPR para 41-076 and now authoritative: see eg *Australian Competition and Consumer Commission v Singtel Optus Pty Ltd (No 4)* [2011] FCA 761, (2011) 282 ALR 246, 250–51 [11] (Perram J); *Singtel Optus Pty Ltd v Australian Competition and Consumer Commission* [2012] FCAFC 20, (2012) 287 ALR 249, 258 [37] (Keane CJ, Finn and Gilmour JJ); *Australian Competition and Consumer Commission v Woolworths Ltd* [2016] FCA 44, (2016) ATPR para 42-521 [122]–[127] (Edelman J).

[10] eg recent inquiries into the suitability of Crown Casino corporate group members to hold casino licences: Parliament of New South Wales, *Inquiry Under Section 143 of the Casino Control Act 1992 (NSW)* (Report, 1 February 2021) (Bergin Report); State of Victoria, *Royal Commission into the Casino Operator and Licence* (The Report, October 2021) (RCCOL Report); State of Western Australia, *Perth Casino Royal Commission* (Report, 4 March 2022) (PCRC).

[11] Bant, 'Culpable Corporate Minds' (n 1) 358–61.

are far more likely to be massive, massively complex, multi- and trans-national corporate institutions that sit within a web of related entities. The law's attribution rules are poorly suited to meet this reality. Thus the traditional approach of locating the corporate 'directing mind and will' in its board and senior executives works well for small companies.[12] But, ironically, it is singularly inapt for large corporations whose harmful activities might, consequently, have far greater impact.[13] Modern, complex corporations often have devolved structures, apt to create information 'silos' and to keep relevant information concerning harmful corporate activities below board level. Knowledge about the corporation's activities will often be dispersed through its lower-level employees (the corporation's 'arms and legs') who carry out its activities. Employees may number in the thousands. And they may well have no idea of how their individual role contributes to what is, overall, unlawful conduct. They are simply doing their job. This 'diffusion of responsibility' amongst natural employees and corporate structures poses a range of challenges to the law's effective regulation of commercial misconduct.[14] The picture of complexity is only enhanced when we take into account the increasing role of automated corporate processes in which no human employee is engaged.

In searching for the (necessarily) artificial corporate state of mind, the Australian Law Reform Commission's recent report into Corporate Criminal Responsibility confirms that Australia's current rules of attribution are notoriously complex and deficient.[15] But a chief failing can be narrowed down to one simple, central feature. With the exception of the 'corporate culture' provisions (discussed in section II.B), all approaches require identification of some individual human repository of fault on which corporate culpability depends. Where knowledge and responsibility are dispersed through departments, amongst individuals and over time, these approaches all flounder. Concepts or processes of 'aggregation', which cluster the mental states of individuals to produce a greater, corporate consciousness, could go some way to addressing the diffusion problem. But these have been met with considerable judicial caution. How, paraphrasing Edelman J, then of the Federal Court of Australia, can a corporation be unconscionable, or fraudulent, (or malicious, dishonest, predatory, knowing, reckless …) when none of its employees individually hold the requisite culpable mindset?[16] This challenge becomes even greater if one accepts (as I do) that a corporation is greater than, and different from, the sum of its parts. Aggregation may be, functionally, an effective means of holding corporations to account, but it is less convincing as a means of identifying distinctively organisational blameworthiness, on a principled basis.

[12] See, eg, *Lennard's Carrying Co Ltd v Asiatic Petroleum Co Ltd* [1915] AC 705 (HL) 713; *HL Boulton (Engineering) Co Ltd v T J Graham & Sons Ltd* [1957] 1 QB 159, [1956] 3 All ER 624, 172 (Lord Denning).

[13] ALRC (n 3) [6.38]; J Gobert, 'Corporate Criminality: Four Models of Fault' (1994) 14 *Legal Studies* 393, 401.

[14] B Fisse, 'Reconstructing Corporate Criminal Law: Deterrence, Retribution, Fault, and Sanctions' (1983) 56 *Southern California Law Review* 1141, 1189.

[15] ALRC (n 3) ch 6. cf Law Commission of England and Wales, *Corporate Criminal Liability: A Discussion Paper* (2021).

[16] *Commonwealth Bank of Australia v Kojic* [2016] FCAFC 186, (2016) 249 FCR 421, 449 [112] (Edelman J). See also the discussion of aggregation in Bant, ch 1 of this volume, section II.C.

B. Systems Intentionality Outlined

Against that background, I have proposed a novel, additional model of corporate culpability. The essential proposition is that corporations *manifest* their intentions through the systems of conduct that they adopt and operate, both in the sense that any system *reveals* the corporate intention and in the sense that it *embodies* or *instantiates* that intention. Another way of putting this is to say that corporations think through their systems – and so assessment and characterisation of the system enables us to know the corporate state of mind. As will be explained, systems of conduct are key to this model because they are inherently purposive – they are objectively designed or calculated (in the sense of apt) to achieve certain ends. It follows that by adopting and implementing a system, the corporation reveals and instantiates its intention or purpose. Moreover, as Paterson and I explain elsewhere, we may justly assume that the corporation enjoys the information and knowledge required in order for the corporate system to function. From these building blocks, it becomes possible to form a clearer picture of complex mental states and standards, such as dishonesty, unconscionability and recklessness.[17]

The foundations for this model lie in the work of various scholars, reformers and courts, all concerned to meet the challenge of diffused responsibility and the conditions for organisational blameworthiness.[18] Thus it accepts the insights of Peter A French into the nature and role of 'Corporate Internal Decision' (CID) structures that go beyond the boardroom and that also reveal the corporate mindset. These include (i) the corporate lines of responsibility (the corporate 'flowchart') and (ii) corporate decision 'recognition rules' (usually found in corporate procedural rules and policies).[19] As French explains:

> [W]hen the corporate act is consistent with an instantiation or an implementation of established corporate policy, then it is proper to describe it as having been done for corporate reasons, as having been caused by a corporate desire coupled with a corporate belief and so, in other words, as corporate intentional.[20]

The model also recognises the moral force and practical utility of Brent Fisse's concept of 'reactive corporate fault',[21] the subject of extended reflection in chapter 7. This identifies organisational blameworthiness where a corporation fails to undertake reasonable corrective or remedial measures in relation to harmful conduct undertaken by personnel on its behalf.[22] Fisse has explained that where there is an express or implied corporate

[17] See in particular, Paterson and Bant, ch 12 of this volume.

[18] In addition to those discussed in this chapter, I acknowledge particular debts to the work of C Wells, *Corporations and Criminal Responsibility* (Oxford, Oxford University Press, 2001); WS Laufer, *Corporate Bodies and Guilty Minds: The Failure of Corporate Criminal Liability* (Chicago, IL, University of Chicago Press, 2006); C List and P Pettit, *Group Agency: The Possibility, Design and Status of Corporate Agents* (Oxford, Oxford University Press, 2011); and C Chapple, *The Moral Responsibilities of Companies* (London, Palgrave Macmillan, 2014).

[19] PA French, *Collective and Corporate Responsibility* (New York City, Columbia University Press, 1984) 41.

[20] ibid 44.

[21] B Fisse, 'Reconstructing Corporate Criminal Law: Deterrence, Retribution, Fault, and Sanctions' (1983) 56 *Southern California Law Review* 1141, 1195–1213.

[22] See further B Fisse, 'The Attribution of Criminal Liability to Corporations: A Statutory Model' (1991) 13 *Sydney Law Review* 277; B Fisse, 'Recent Developments in Corporate Criminal Law and Corporate Liability to Monetary Penalties' (1990) 13 *University of New South Wales Law Journal* 1; B Fisse and J Braithwaite, *Corporations, Crime and Accountability* (Cambridge, Cambridge University Press, 1993) 47–49. Arguably,

policy to fail to take preventive or corrective reactive measures, this may reflect deliberate or reckless organisational intentionality.[23] Fisse's identification of the necessity and aptness of adopting a wider timeframe for assessment of corporate culpability is particularly helpful to, and supportive of, the systems analysis offered here. I return to the significance of time and systems at the close of this chapter.

As Rebecca Faugno observes in chapter 8, Systems Intentionality expressly builds on Australia's unique 'corporate culture' provisions. Part 2.5 of the Criminal Code Act 1995 (Cth) (Criminal Code) was itself strongly influenced by the work of scholars such as Fisse and French, and constitutes strong legislative recognition of the reality of organisational blameworthiness.[24] The provisions stipulate that corporate 'intention, knowledge or recklessness' can be established by proving that a corporate culture existed within the body corporate that directed, encouraged, tolerated or led to non-compliance with the relevant provision.[25] 'Corporate culture' is defined as meaning 'an attitude, policy, rule, course of conduct or practice existing within the body corporate generally or in the part of the body corporate in which the relevant activities takes place'.[26] These provisions have failed to have their anticipated impact in practice, for a variety of reasons, discussed elsewhere.[27] For current purposes, it suffices to say that, while taking inspiration from these reforms, the model of Systems Intentionality seeks to provide a more practically workable model, capable of proving the specific doctrinal mental states required for the effective operation of common commercial rules and prohibitions.

The model also draws on Mihailis Diamantis' analysis of 'the extended mind' thesis in relation to corporations and their use of artificial intelligence (AI) systems.[28] As he explains, human use of external decision supports (like maps, recipes and notes or records) to facilitate recall and decision making parallels corporate use of AI systems. In both cases, the use of the cognitive aid or system does not alter the fact that the resultant act remains that of the human, or corporate, actor. Expanding on this analysis, Systems Intentionality proposes that, given that they lack a natural mind, corporations are necessarily and generally dependent on decision supports in the forms of systems of conduct, policies and practices, to enable and implement corporate decision making. Indeed, such corporate decision supports are essential to manage and coordinate disparate and rotating employees and other agents, who carry out corporate purposes, over time.

the concept of corporate negligence underpins the idea of corporate culture: see B Fisse, 'The Social Policy of Corporate Criminal Responsibility' (1978) 8 *Adelaide Law Review* 361, 373–76; B Fisse and J Braithwaite, *Corporations, Crime and Accountability* (Cambridge, Cambridge University Press, 1993) 29–30.

[23] Fisse (n 21) 1202.

[24] ALRC (n 3) ch 2; Criminal Law Officers Committee of the Standing Committee of Attorneys-General, Australian Government, *Model Criminal Code* (Final Report, December 1992) chs 1 and 2, at 21 and 107.

[25] Criminal Code, s 12.3(2)(c).

[26] ibid s 12.3(6).

[27] See Bant, 'Culpable Corporate Minds' (n 1) 369–74; J Clough and C Mulhern, *The Prosecution of Corporations* (Oxford, Oxford University Press, 2002) 140–47; Faugno, ch 8 of this volume. See also Law Commission of England and Wales, *Corporate Criminal Liability* Options Paper (2022) [6.3]–[6.20].

[28] M Diamantis, 'The Extended Corporate Mind: When Corporations Use AI to Break the Law' (2020) 98 *North Carolina Law Review* 893. While Diamantis' and my approaches are sympathetic, they do diverge over their role for inference and the extent to which it is legitimate to treat natural and corporate persons similarly for that purpose. On my account, any process of inference must reflect that corporations think through their systems, rather than reflect intrinsically human, cognitive processes.

This remains true even where components of a system are automated, replacing human or corporate actors.

Finally, Australian courts addressing statutory unconscionability in the context of exploitative business models and practices have been developing a rich body of jurisprudence concerning corporate systems and intentionality, which is consistent with the model. Paterson and I have examined these authorities to reveal the light they cast on the relationship between business systems and specific corporate states of mind.[29] Chapters 11 and 12 continue that work. This chapter, by contrast, returns to plumb the same authorities, this time for their lessons on the spectrum of organisational structures and behaviours that may combine to reveal a 'system' of conduct, and the difficult related question of proof.

III. Systems within the Spectrum of Behaviours

A. The Statutory Context

It should be emphasised from the outset that the statutory prohibitions on unconscionable 'systems of conduct or patterns of behaviour' do not have, as their aim, the development of a broadly applicable mechanism for corporate responsibility such as that proposed by the model of Systems Intentionality. Indeed, as will become clear, 'patterns of behaviour' are arguably neutral as to intention. Rather, on my model, patterns of behaviour constitute evidence from which systems of conduct (and hence intentionality) can be inferred. The statutory prohibitions on unconscionable patterns of behaviour may reflect a separate and legitimate policy emphasis on harmful outputs,[30] alongside the existing concern with defendant culpability, although this question has yet to be examined in the authorities. Accepting this caveat, the authorities notwithstanding provide important support and guidance for the development of Systems Intentionality as a coherent and workable liability mechanism, applicable more broadly across extant general law and statutory doctrines, rules and standards.

A very brief introduction to the prohibitions provides some context for the following discussion. The seminal case on unconscionable 'systems of conduct and patterns of behaviour' is *Australian Securities and Investments Commission v National Exchange Pty Ltd*.[31] It concerned a business model that was found to have an objective 'purpose' of exploiting anticipated disadvantage. National Exchange had sent unsolicited off-market

[29] Bant and Paterson (n 1).

[30] cf ALRC (n 3) Recommendation 8, which proposes a model offence to criminalise contraventions of certain civil penalty provisions that constitute a 'system of conduct or pattern of behaviour'. As explained in E Bant, 'Reforming the Laws of Corporate Attribution' (n 1) this is not an attribution model and remains dependent upon satisfaction of independent attribution rules. For further discussion of the proposed offence, see S Walpole and M Corrigan, 'Fighting the System: New Approaches to Fighting Systematic Corporate Misconduct' (2021) 43 *Sydney Law Review* 489.

[31] *Australian Securities and Investments Commission v National Exchange Pty Ltd* [2005] FCAFC 226, (2005) 148 FCR 132 (Tamberlin, Finn and Conti JJ) (*National Exchange*). See also *Stubbings v Jams 2 Pty Ltd* [2022] HCA 6, (2022) 399 ALR 409 [81] (Gordon J); Bryan, ch 14 of this volume; and Bant, 'The Culpable Corporate Mind' (n 16) 485–87.

offers to members of a demutualised company, Aevum Ltd, to buy shares at a price that constituted a substantial undervalue of their true worth. A Full Court of the Federal Court of Australia found that the offers reflected a predatory business strategy, aimed at anticipated members of a class. The business model was founded on the prediction (well-made, as it transpired) that, given the nature of the demutualised company, there would be a group of vulnerable and inexperienced recipients of the offer 'who would act irrationally from a purely commercial viewpoint and would accept the offer'.[32] Although traditional rules of attribution would likely have been satisfied in the case, the Court considered that the very design of the system was predatory in nature. Moreover, the defendant's knowledge of the presence of disadvantage in the class as a whole, albeit not in individual cases, was implicit in, and necessarily revealed by, the form of the business model. In short, the business model would only work and be profitable if inexperienced and, hence, commercially irrational sellers were present and likely to accept the unreasonably low offer.

Following *National Exchange*, Australia's federal consumer legislation was reformed to confirm the Federal Court's position that the statutory prohibition on unconscionable conduct 'is capable of applying to a system of conduct or pattern of behaviour, whether or not a particular individual is identified as having been disadvantaged by the conduct or behaviour'.[33] This reform has prompted a surge of litigation activity by Australia's regulators concerned to rein in unconscionable business models, and consequently very helpful judicial reflections on the nature of systems of conduct and their relationship to other, similar or related business structures and behaviours. Drawing on these authorities, the following analysis will consider, first, the relationship between systems (here incorporating more granular processes and methods) and patterns, before turning to their relationship to practices and policies. Throughout, the discussion does not seek to assert definitions as a matter of some necessary, prior truth but to offer practical and helpful ways of thinking about the graduations of structured behaviours that may be present in a corporation, and which may inform a court's deliberations on corporate states of mind. As Beach J put it in *AGM Markets*,[34] here it makes sense to talk in terms of 'connotation rather than denotation to make the obvious point that the boundaries and content of the phrase [system of conduct] or its various elements are incapable of clear or exhaustive definition'.[35]

B. Systems and Patterns

In one of the earliest cases to consider the statutory unconscionability provision, *EDirect*,[36] the alleged unconscionable conduct involved 'a high pressure sales system that was directed to an unnamed group or class of persons that could be expected to

[32] *National Exchange* (n 31) 142 [43].

[33] ACL (n 6), s 21(4)(b), introduced in 2010.

[34] *Australian Securities and Investments Commission v AGM Markets Pty Ltd (in liq) (No 3)* [2020] FCA 208, (2020) 275 FCR 57 (Beach J) (*AGM Markets*).

[35] ibid 148 [507], considering the meaning of the statutory phrase 'efficiently, honestly and fairly' in Corporations Act 2001 (Cth), s 912A. The same approach has been adopted throughout courts' discussions of systems of conduct or patterns of behaviour.

[36] *Australian Competition and Consumer Commission v EDirect Pty Ltd* [2012] FCA 1045 [72]–[73] (Reeves J) (*EDirect*).

include members who were vulnerable or susceptible to EDirect's sales process'.[37] Justice Reeves explained the relevant concept of a 'system of conduct':

> By its ordinary meaning, a system is 'an assemblage or combination of things or parts forming a complex or unitary whole; … a co-ordinated body of methods, or a complex scheme or plan of procedure': *Macquarie Dictionary*. To similar effect, Dixon CJ said of the word 'scheme' that it 'connotes a plan or purpose which is coherent and has some unity of conception': see *Australian Consolidated Press Limited v Australian Newsprint Mills Holdings Limited* (1960) 105 CLR 473 at 479.[38]

We may pause here to observe the close connection between the concept of a 'system' and those of a 'scheme', 'plan or purpose'.

In the subsequent, seminal case of *Unique*,[39] the Full Court of the Federal Court closely examined the methods of proof required to prove an unconscionable system of conduct or pattern of behaviour, to which we will return. However, in so doing, the Court articulated the key distinction between a system of conduct and pattern of behaviour in this way: 'a "system" connotes an internal method of working, a "pattern" connotes the external observation of events'.[40] In *AGM Markets*, Beach J expanded upon this distinction. Again, the purposive nature of systems is evident, while patterns are neutral as to intention: a '"system" connotes something designed or intended in its structure; contrastingly, a pattern may be manifested without any design or intentional input'.[41] A system relates to the 'internal structure, for example, internal working, of whatever it is that has produced or reflects the conduct'.[42] A '"system" also connotes an organised and connected group or set of things that can be thought of as a complex whole. The gist is organisation and connection'.[43] A pattern, by contrast, looks to 'the external manifestation of behaviour and whether it can be characterised as a pattern'.[44] His Honour considered that

> in context the meaning of pattern is most usefully expressed as 'a regular and intelligible form or sequence discernible in certain actions or situations' (Oxford English Dictionary, meaning 11(b)). So there has to be both repetition and external discernibility.[45]

Here, we may interpose to note the *Oxford English Dictionary*'s further observation (not quoted by his Honour) that 'pattern' used in this way may signify a sequence 'on which the prediction of successive or future events may be based'.[46] That is a useful expansion in this context, indicating as it does not merely ad hoc or coincidental repetition, but also a more regular recurrence, which is the hallmark of a pattern.

On this analysis, a corporation's internal structures, methods and processes may combine and connect to articulate systems that are inherently purposeful in their nature. In everyday terms, a process or method can be understood interchangeably as simply a way of doing something, according to a defined and regular plan; a mode of

[37] ibid [88].
[38] ibid [91].
[39] *Unique International College Pty Ltd v Australian Competition and Consumer Commission* [2018] FCAFC 155, (2018) 266 FCR 631 (Allsop CJ, Middleton and Mortimer JJ) (*Unique*).
[40] ibid [104].
[41] *AGM Markets* (n 34) 122–23 [389].
[42] ibid.
[43] ibid 123 [391].
[44] ibid 122 [386].
[45] ibid.
[46] *Oxford English Dictionary*, 'pattern' at www.oed.com/.

procedure in any activity or business.[47] As the Federal Court of Australia explained in *Unique*, '[a] system of conduct requires, to a degree, an abstraction of a generalisation as to method or structure of working or of approaching something'.[48] A 'system' on this account is both a generalisation and a process of characterisation or conclusion of the interactions of interrelated elements. The angle of focus required in finding a system can be correspondingly wider, or narrower. Thus a process may constitute itself a system further comprised by more granular processes and methods and, in turn, may form part of a greater whole. Systems, methods and processes are all very closely related. I do not think that it is helpful to stipulate some *a priori* difference between them: they partake of a similar character, but may be used differentially in some contexts to indicate greater, or lesser, levels of abstraction in the enquiry.

By contrast to systems of conduct, patterns of behaviour signify externally observable, repeated behaviours from which systems (and hence, on my analysis, Systems Intentionality) may be inferred. The two are closely related, albeit distinct. As Beach J observed in *AGM Markets*, a 'system of conduct' could produce a 'pattern of behaviour'. Relatedly, evidence of a 'pattern of behaviour' could enable you to infer a 'system of conduct' in some cases.[49]

On my account, this suggests that patterns are, in and of themselves, more neutral as to intentionality: they simply provide the raw materials from which (together with other factors and evidence) a system may be inferred. Of course, patterns of misconduct may be indicative of higher levels of harm than single instances of misconduct and, on that count, liable to attract greater liability.[50] But that greater liability will not necessarily be because of a greater element of intentionality associated with the conduct. By contrast, a mature system (as we have seen) is inherently purposive.

The challenge is to determine what more may be required to enable a pattern to be understood as evidencing a system. In thinking further about this relationship, two additional distinctions may be of assistance. While the concept of a 'system of conduct' is central to the model, the related concepts of 'practices' and 'policies' are analytically useful to direct courts' and regulators' (among others) attention to the ways in which systems evolve, and to the levels of generality at which they operate.

C. Practices

Again drawing on the *Oxford English Dictionary*, a 'practice' connotes:

> (a) The habitual doing or carrying on *of* something; usual, customary, or constant action or performance; conduct. Or (b) A habitual action or pattern of behaviour; an established procedure or system.[51]

The *Oxford English Dictionary* notes that, in a more obsolete form, a practice could refer to a scheme or trickery, or stratagem.

[47] ibid 'process', 'method'.

[48] *Unique* (n 39) 654 [104]. See also *Australian Competition and Consumer Commission v Productivity Partners Pty Ltd (trading as Captain Cook College) (No 3)* [2021] FCA 737 [515] (Stewart J) (*Captain Cook College*).

[49] *AGM Markets* (n 34) 123 [390].

[50] cf ALRC (n 3) Recommendation 8

[51] *Oxford English Dictionary* (n 46) 'practice'.

On these meanings, a practice offers something of a bridge between a pattern and a mature system. By definition, a practice must involve repetition and regularity, and hence must partake of the nature of a pattern. But it seems plausible that a practice may capture behaviours that go beyond a pattern, because of the key idea of its being 'habitual' or 'customary'. To go back to the idea of a pattern being more than an ad hoc coincidence of like behaviours, because of its requiring some element of regularity and predictability, a practice presents as a yet stronger form of patterned conduct. A practice is one that predictably repeats *because* it is habitual or customary: it is a default response or reaction to some recognised condition or trigger for conduct. Further, a practice may clearly be indicative of a system, where the 'custom' or 'habit' has crossed into the realm of an adopted process.

Here, however, we should be careful not to assume that, for the purposes of the idea of Systems Intentionality, only practices endorsed through a formal rule of recognition (for example, approval by a board of directors) will count. Instantiated or de facto practices that are 'passed on' through generations of employees, for example, may be precisely the sort of behaviours that may constitute or give rise to, or evidence, an adopted system. The existence of employee or agent incentives (such as bonus or commission systems, or promotions) that reward conduct consistent with the system of conduct may similarly support a finding of an adopted system.[52] As Bromwich J explained in *AIPE*,[53] 'a system of conduct or pattern of behaviour may emerge over time without having been expressly articulated. It need not have been deliberately adopted or planned.'[54] The concept of an adopted practice was, I think, used in this sense in *ASIC v Westpac*,[55] a case involving statutory unconscionable conduct. In that case, ASIC alleged that during the relevant period, Westpac traded with the sole or dominant purpose of manipulating where the Bank Bill Swap Rate was set. That purpose was said to be manifested in a 'Rate Set Trading Practice' that was 'in existence and implemented generally'.[56] The case failed for want of appropriate evidence as to the existence of the alleged practice. We return to such challenges of proof in section IV. But it seems clear that the Court accepted that, had the alleged practice been established, it could have been apposite to reveal the relevant corporate purpose.[57]

D. Policies

Patterns and practices, then, lie towards one end of the spectrum of behaviours. At the other end of the spectrum, it seems helpful to think about 'policies' as being an

[52] For example, where 'churning' practices align with and are supported by commission incentives.

[53] *Australian Competition and Consumer Commission v Australian Institute of Professional Education Pty Ltd (in liq) (No 3)* [2019] FCA 1982 (Bromwich J) (*AIPE*).

[54] ibid [174].

[55] *Australian Securities and Investments Commission v Westpac Banking Corporation (No 2)* [2018] FCA 751, (2018) 266 FCR 147 (Beach J) (*ASIC v Westpac*).

[56] ibid 158 [10]–[11].

[57] See also *Australian Competition and Consumer Commission v Geowash Pty Ltd (Subject to a Deed of Co Arrangement) (No 3)* [2019] FCA 72, (2019) 368 ALR 441, 552 [677]–[678], 553 [682] (Colvin J), upheld on appeal, *Ali v Australian Competition and Consumer Commission* [2021] FCAFC 109, (2021) 394 ALR 227 (*Ali*), a case involving a tightly directed smaller corporation, but which analysis could transfer over to larger corporate structures with more dispersed structures and lines of responsibility.

articulation of intention and therefore overtly and singularly concerned with the defendant's state of mind. Again, however, as with the relationship between systems, processes and methods, it seems that policies can be conceptualised at greater and lesser levels of abstraction or specificity. Thus French considers policies to be

> rather broad, general principles that describe what the corporation believes about its enterprise and the way it intends to operate. Policies contain basic belief and goal statements regarding both the what and the how of corporate life, but they are not detailed statements of appropriate methods.[58]

On this analysis, policies manifest or express overarching corporate purposes, belief and intentions. This is similar to, and occupies a similar level of abstraction as, the concept of 'corporate culture'. On my model, systems then instantiate or operationalise those policies at more granular and event- or conduct-specific levels. A similar conception is reflected in the *Collins English Dictionary* definition of policy: 'A policy is a set of ideas or plans that is used *as a basis* for making decisions, especially in politics, economics, or business.'[59]

We may accept that, in some cases, a policy will operate at a high level and will inform (be a 'basis'), rather than comprise, the detailed decision-making elements that we may expect to find in a system. Examples might be policy statements by a corporation around fair trade, equal opportunity and the like. While these are statements of intention or belief, we might expect related systems that reflect those high-level intentions to be far more grounded and specific in nature and to direct decisions and actions on a day-to-day basis.

Similarly, the *Cambridge Dictionary* defines a policy as

> a set of ideas or a plan of what to do in particular situations that has been agreed to officially by a group of people, a business organization, a government, or a political party.[60]

This is more specific than French's definition, as it conceives that a policy may articulate specific responses, or guide decisions with particularity, in defined scenarios. However, it seems nonetheless possible to draw a distinction here between an adopted policy that counts as a statement of intention, an 'idea' or plan, and the operationalisation of that intention, at ground level, through some implemented system. That said, the relationship between a policy and a system will, again, depend to some degree on the level of abstraction at which they are viewed. Thus, for *Merriam-Webster*, a policy is

> a definite course or method of action selected from among alternatives and in light of given conditions to guide and determine present and future decisions.[61]

This appears materially identical to my conception of a system.

Here, it may be helpful, again, to pause and consider the all-too-familiar phenomenon of 'formal' corporate policies that bear no resemblance to the systems through

[58] French (n 19) 58.

[59] *Collins English Dictionary*, 13th edn (Glasgow, HarperCollins, 2018) 'policy' (emphasis added).

[60] *Cambridge Dictionary*, 'policy' at https://dictionary.cambridge.org/dictionary/english/policy. cf *Oxford English Dictionary* (n 46) 'policy': 'A principle or course of action adopted or proposed as desirable, advantageous, or expedient; esp one formally advocated by a government, political party, etc. Also as a mass noun: method of acting on matters of principle, settled practice. (Now the usual sense.)'

[61] *Merriam-Webster Dictionary*, 'policy' at www.merriam-webster.com.

which (on my model) a corporation manifests its intentionality.[62] For my purposes, it suffices to say that we can usefully distinguish between formal and de facto (actual, real) policies. It is the latter that is of chief interest here from an analytical perspective. A corporation's true or genuine policies express or articulate its mindset as a matter of fact, albeit often at a relatively high level of generality.[63] A formal policy may be no more than a misrepresentation of the actual corporate mindset. This is not to say, however, that the fact that a corporation formally expresses its intentions in terms wholly removed from the reality of its systems of conduct is irrelevant to enquiries into corporate misconduct. The statement may constitute misleading conduct, as in cases of 'green-washing', where the corporation's professed environmental purposes are contradicted by its instantiated systems of conduct. Remembering that policies are (on this analysis) articulations, statements or expressions of intention; they can be misleading or deceptive just like any other statement. To find out what the corporation truly thinks, its core beliefs and values, one has to look behind the corporation's talk and examine its walk.

E. Synthesis

In drawing this discussion to a close, we can see that at one end of the behavioural spectrum we have policies that articulate the corporate mindset, systems that manifest them and may be comprised of more specific processes and methods of conduct that may, themselves, constitute more granular systems. Key to determining the correct frame of reference will be to ask clearly what is the required level of abstraction to meet the law's concern. This is where regulators' and private plaintiffs' litigation strategies will prove critical, in articulating the ambit of the relevant corporate system of conduct relevant to the law's enquiry.

At the other end of the spectrum lie patterns of behaviour from which it may be possible to discern the presence of a system. Patterns provide the raw material of regular and repeated actions for further analysis. As will be explained, the presence of patterns of behaviour may bolster or support a finding of a system by being consistent with it, and to evidence implementation, for example, of a policy. However, a pattern is not itself a system, though it may provide evidence of one. A practice, by contrast, displays habitual patterns of behaviour in response to certain prompts. These straddle the space between patterns and systems: the more established and articulated a practice is, the more likely it is that the practice constitutes a system, or part of a system. We can conceive of practices in this sense as combining external expressions of internal processes and methods.

[62] See, eg, the discussion in *AIPE* (n 53) [696] of the 'aspirational quality' of the defendant corporation's policies, training and induction materials, and the gulf between these and what actually occurred on the ground. See also the perceptive discussion of Google's 'Don't be evil' corporate motto in P Crofts and H Van Rijswijk in *Technology: New Trajectories in Law* (Abingdon, Routledge, 2001) ch 4.

[63] *Edgington v Fitzmaurice* (1885) 29 Ch D 459 (CA) 483 (Bowen LJ), noting that 'the state of a man's mind is as much a fact as the state of his digestion … A misrepresentation as to the state of a man's mind is, therefore, a misstatement of fact.' See also *Generics (UK) v Warner-Lambert Company LLC* [2018] UKSC 56, [2018] RPC 21, [171] (Lord Briggs): 'a person's intention is as much a matter of fact as the state of his digestion, and this is true of corporate persons as much as of individuals.'

An example of the subtle interactions that may be engaged in thinking about these concepts is *ACCC v Jayco*.[64] The Australian Competition and Consumer Commission (ACCC) alleged that in four instances, Jayco Corp prioritised resolving consumer complaints about defective recreational vehicles (RVs) under their manufacturer warranty, rather than pursuant to the more expansive statutory consumer guarantees. The ACCC alleged that this conduct was unconscionable, in that it favoured repair over replacement or refunds, contrary to consumers' statutory rights. While there were some common components of the individual instances of unconscionable conduct, the ACCC did not seek to show an unconscionable 'system of conduct'. Rather, the allegations made by the ACCC about the conduct of Jayco Corp in these specific instances were set against the background of 'circumstances of a general nature, and what were alleged to be the practices of Jayco Corp in dealing with consumer complaints'.[65] It seems, therefore, that evidence of general practices was here being used to buttress findings of individual instances of misconduct.[66] In that case, witnesses for the manufacturer and for the sales agents testified as to their complaints practices. They affirmed that there was 'no formal policy, such as any written policy' around warranty claims. Nor was there an 'informal policy' to prefer repairs to refunds or replacements. Rather there was a 'practice' to assess each case on its merits. Here, the point seems to be that the practice to assess each case on its merits meant that there was no practice of preferencing repair over replacement, and certainly no policy or 'requirement' to that effect. Importantly, those findings were part of what allowed the judge to conclude that decisions to repair rather than refund were not shown to have been made in 'conscious bad faith' or an 'objective absence of good faith' so as to support a finding of unconscionable conduct.[67] This is consistent with the approach adopted in *ASIC v Westpac* and the taxonomy suggested here.

IV. Proving Systems Intentionality

The proposition that I have been developing is that corporate systems manifest corporate intentionality, and that it is possible to understand more precisely what characteristics a system bears through reflecting on related concepts such as practices, processes or methods, policies and patterns of behaviour. How, though, does one go about establishing a system, including by reference to these related phenomena? Here, the body of cases concerned with statutory unconscionable 'systems of conduct or patterns of behaviour' is again a rich source of insights. In this section, I break the analysis into two parts: first, the approach or 'theory of the case' that may be adopted to prove the presence of a system and, through it, Systems Intentionality; and second, the kinds of evidence that may be appropriate and available to support that case.

[64] *Australian Competition and Consumer Commission v Jayco Corp Pty Ltd* [2020] FCA 1672 (Wheelahan J) (*ACCC v Jayco*).

[65] ibid [790].

[66] On this, see further section IV.A.ii–iv.

[67] *ACCC v Jayco* (n 64) [802], [820], [833], [840], [858].

A. The Theory of the Case

In the following discussion, there are interlocking issues of evidence and procedure, which I will deal with functionally, as they might arise when bringing a case. The aim here is to flesh out, as a matter of practice, how one would go about proving a system for the purpose of ascertaining corporation intentionality.

i. Pleadings: A Question of Connecting the Dots

At the outset, a striking feature of more recent cases in the Australian line of authorities addressing unconscionable 'systems of conduct or patterns of behaviour' is regulators' deliberate adoption of the 'concise statement' over the traditional statement of claim, to set out the nature of the case against the defendant company. This considered shift has been guided by courts, which have noted the narrative advantages offered by the concise statement in articulating the connected elements and purpose of the alleged system.[68] Thus in *Unique*, the Full Court commented that the regulator's statement of claim suffered from a 'certain deconstructed and particularised' character.[69] What was needed was articulation of the 'holistic interrelationship between all the factors, both as they affect the individuals and the system or pattern of behaviour'.[70]

This is the advantage afforded by the concise statement. As Allsop CJ explained in *ASIC v ANZ*:

> The question whether a body of conduct has in all the circumstances been unconscionable in the statutory sense … is not amenable to pleading 'a cause of action' constituted by 'material facts', with some distinction between them and mere 'particulars' of such. Rather, the better approach is to understand what the plaintiff says are the 'connected circumstances that ought to influence the determination of the case' … As in a bill in equity, the plaintiff should set out a well-drafted narrative of the facts and circumstances and of the wrong or grievance that constitutes the real substance of the complaint. The statement, concisely but fully expressed, should contain all the facts to be proved at the appropriate level of generality or specificity, without prolixity, as to make meaningful the grievance …[71]

The concise statement allows regulators to paint a nuanced picture of the connected elements and methods of the system as a whole, set at the correct level of abstraction for the purposes of the law in question. This can include the defendant's motive for acting. As Bromwich J explained in *AIPE*, this pleading may provide 'an important holistic dimension to [the] case'.[72] Proof of motive may 'contextualise and explain, as well as contribute to the proof of'[73] the alleged system, helping to explain, for example, 'why

[68] Led by Allsop CJ in *Australian Securities and Investments Commission v Australia and New Zealand Banking Group Limited* [2019] FCA 1284, (2019) 139 ACSR 52 (*ASIC v ANZ*). See also *AIPE* (n 53) [34], [159]–[160].

[69] *Unique* (n 39) 640 [42].

[70] ibid.

[71] *ASIC v ANZ* (n 68) 53 [2]–[3].

[72] *AIPE* (n 53) [161].

[73] ibid.

conduct or practices were carried out in a particular way or persisted with in the face of known problems'.[74]

ii. Reasoning from Particular to General and Back Again

It is, of course, not enough clearly to articulate the alleged system: it must also be proved. The concise statement cannot be used, by itself, as a 'construct to inappropriately distort the analysis'.[75] Here, our simple starting point is that misconduct that results from a system will generally recur: after all, it is in the nature of systems that they are adopted in order to regulate and promote repeated behaviours to some valued end. This is also why patterns of behaviour may be indicative of a system and why practices are similarly salient.

This means, however, that there will be two main approaches to proving a system. One starts from the observable, repeated outcomes and works backwards. This approach analyses instances of individual misconduct or harms indicating misconduct, assesses their objectively apparent common features, regularity and so on, to discern a pattern of misconduct and, through it, the potential presence of a system. Examination of repeated misconduct, with shared and salient characteristics, may indicate the presence of a pattern, itself suggestive of a practice, as a staging post on the route to finding a system. A simple hypothetical example might involve discovery of new levels of a certain kind of pollutant in a river, traceable to a pipe that leads to the defendant's factory. The fact of pollution involving a certain combination of waste being repeatedly discharged into the river is suggestive of a pattern of behaviour, which may indicate the presence of an habitual practice of dumping, which may indicate the presence of a system of conduct. Whether this is so depends on the range of available evidence and the inferences that may legitimately be drawn from the nature of the pattern supported by that evidence. Closer to the authorities on which this chapter rests, a regulator may receive a large number of complaints from vulnerable consumers about being induced to sign up for 'free' education courses by a named provider, on topics that they are ill-suited to undertake, through a combination of incentives such as free laptops or cash. If the course transpires not to be free, but rather benefits the provider through attracting significant government fees, while saddling the consumer with considerable debt, for the provision of a course they had little capacity to complete, these shared features may be suggestive of a pattern of misconduct. Through further investigation, the pattern may be found to reflect poor business practices, or even a system of misconduct supporting a predatory business model.

The other approach attacks the presence and features of a system head-on, by seeking to establish the connected internal methods, structures and processes that result in harmful outcomes. This approach will seek to identify the interacting elements of the component steps said to comprise the organised methods and processes that make up a system. The focus is on the 'structure and operation of business itself'[76] rather than

[74] ibid.

[75] *ASIC v Westpac* (n 55) 162 [25].

[76] JM Paterson and E Bant, 'Should Australia Introduce a Prohibition on Unfair Trading? Responding to Exploitative Business Systems in Person and Online' (2020) 44 *Journal of Consumer Policy* 1, 9.

on the harmful individual outcomes, although the latter may (as explained earlier) shed light on the nature of the business practices.

Each approach involves quite different litigation strategies, although (as will become apparent) combinations of the two may operate to good effect.

iii. Option 1: Proving a System through Patterns of Behaviour

We have seen that patterns of conduct involve externally observable, repeated events. In *AGM Markets*, Beach J explained that, in looking for a 'pattern', courts will be looking for 'two or more instances of identical or similar behaviour … sufficient to infer a pattern'.[77] His Honour's ensuing discussion suggests that the precise number required to show a pattern will depend on a range of factors, including the degree of similarity between individual instances, the number of similar instances, examples of counter-instances and the size of the total pool of instances. In addition, the presence of other, independent evidence as to an alleged system (to which we will return), which would be consistent with the instances being related, would also support the existence of a pattern. That is, evidence as to a system that would be consistent with the salient, shared behaviours that are alleged to constitute a pattern may confirm that these are repeated behaviours, rather than simple coincidences or behaviours that are not relevantly similar. Finally, as his Honour further observed, it is false to consider that a corporation's behaviour might fall only into a pattern or not: some parts of the corporation's conduct may exhibit a pattern and some not; a pattern may be found in some regions of a corporation's operations and not others; between some parts of a corporation, between different personnel and so on. But these divisions (or levels of abstraction) should flow naturally or truthfully from the corporation's inherent structures and operations, not be 'super-imposed artificially and retrospectively from a regulator's or litigator's perspective'.[78] This insight is particularly important when dealing with large corporations, which may have different systems operating in different departments. What is intended in one space may not be intended in another. That does not mean the purposive conduct demonstrated in one form of business dealing is any the less real and relevant.

For the purposes of proving a system through a pattern of behaviour, it is not only necessary to show that a repeated number of relevantly similar, shared behaviours has occurred. It is also necessary to show that the pattern displayed by those instances is representative of the alleged wider pattern (and through it the system). As we have seen, there may be other independent evidence of the alleged system that accords with the pattern. But in the absence of such evidence, or to bolster the cogency of the case, it may be necessary or appropriate to extrapolate from the proven repetitions of behaviour, to show that the individual instances reflected, or were consistent with, the alleged broader pattern. In *Unique*, the ACCC sought to prove an unconscionable pattern of behaviour through individual examples of unconscionable conduct. While the regulator failed, the Full Federal Court explained that this was not because a pattern cannot be proved through individual instances. Rather, the issue was that 'if one wishes to move from the

[77] *AGM Markets* (n 34) 122 [387].
[78] ibid 122 [388].

particular event to some general proposition of a system it may be necessary for some conclusions to be drawn about the representative nature or character of the particular event.'[79] This required:

> First, the selection of evidence of individual consumers through a random or representative process, with the process disclosed on the evidence. Second, the use of evidence about a reasonable number of individual consumers so that, even if intuitively, a Court could exclude hypotheses of coincidence or lack of representativeness, and could, because of the number of individual consumers about which evidence was led, safely perceive a 'pattern'.[80]

In that case, the ACCC's allegation of an unconscionable pattern of behaviour on the part of a vocational education provider largely rested on the evidence of six customers, supported by a range of broader evidence to which we will return. The consumers affected by the defendant's business numbered over 3,600. Even if these individual six cases shared common characteristics, the Court needed to have a proper basis for considering they were representative of a wider pattern of behaviour.[81] A similar problem with reasoning from single instances to (in that case) an alleged 'practice' arose in *ASIC v Westpac*. There, the learned judge rejected the financial service regulator ASIC's allegation concerning the existence of the alleged Rate Set Trading Practice, being unwilling

> to infer from the isolated instances on the specific four occasions that I have identified or from the totality of the evidence that there was a pattern or system such as to give rise to such a practice. Further, to characterise such isolated examples as in and of themselves constituting such a practice over the relevant period would be to prefer form over substance and to allow the pleader's construct to inappropriately distort the analysis.[82]

Conversely, in *Unique*, the Full Federal Court cited *IMB Group*[83] as an example of how a sample of conduct, taken randomly from a greater pool, could be seen as properly representative of a pattern of behaviour (or, indeed, disprove an alleged pattern). In *IMB Group*, the ACCC alleged that the defendant had engaged in statutory unconscionable conduct through the marketing and sale of an investment scheme, which involved the sale of investment policies to individuals. At trial, the ACCC called 15 of the 70 witnesses it originally proposed to call in support of its allegation concerning a pattern of unconscionable conduct. The respondent proposed to call another 439. A total of 3,200 policies were sold. The trial judge disallowed leave to call so many witnesses; instead, a district registrar selected 40 at random. Drawing on that evidence, the judge rejected the ACCC's case. This process of selection was endorsed by the Full Federal Court in *Unique* as one way in which a representative sample could be taken.[84]

A difficult question arises whether the use of individual instances in this way, to show a pattern of behaviour or system of conduct, constitutes the use of 'tendency' evidence and hence the subject of special procedural rules and limitations.[85] In *Unique*,

[79] *Unique* (n 39) 654 [104].

[80] ibid 655 [110]. See also *Australian Competition and Consumer Commission v Excite Mobile Pty Ltd* [2013] FCA 350 (*Excite Mobile*); *Captain Cook College* (n 48) [73].

[81] *Unique* (n 39) 672 [170].

[82] *ASIC v Westpac* (n 55) 162 [25].

[83] *Australian Competition and Consumer Commission v IMB Group Pty Ltd (in liq)* [2002] FCA 402, (2002) ATPR (Digest) para 46–221 (*IMB Group*).

[84] *Unique* (n 39) 656–67 [116]–[118].

[85] Evidence Act 1995 (Cth), s 97 (Evidence Act).

the Full Court noted[86] that the ACCC could have relied on what occurred at four sites with six particular students, all of which shared certain characteristics, as a basis to extrapolate about what occurred in respect of other sites with similar students. But the question is what material facts that evidence would be brought in order to prove. If it was brought in order to show that other individual consumers were the subject of similar unconscionable conduct, that would be an example of tendency evidence. However, if the evidence is brought in order to prove the existence of a system of conduct as the fact in issue, that will not be tendency evidence.[87] The individual examples are direct (albeit limited) evidence of the alleged system. It is going beyond an allegation of a propensity to engage in a certain type of behaviour (that is, tendency evidence), to establish a system that, if implemented, would have been consistent with the conduct evidenced in the particular case. As explained by Sackville J in *Jacara*,[88] cited with approval in *Unique*, '[t]he evidence of the system makes it more likely that the fact in issue … occurred, independently of the agent's propensity to act in a particular way'.[89] Similarly, in *AMI*,[90] the ACCC successfully argued that the use of single instances in that case, in tandem with direct evidence of the alleged system, to establish a business model was not to say that the defendant engaged in that conduct all the time, or that

> this is what you would find if you randomly sampled any instance of time during the period … We simply say, and mean, that [the defendants] did certain things generically and certain things 170 times, and that those things, taken together (or separately or in more limited combination) reflected their intention – their 'model', and therefore their attitude towards consumers.[91]

iv. *Option 2: Proving a System Directly*

The alternative approach is to bring direct evidence as to the internal structure and elements of the system. Here, the evidence of relevant individual instances can still be relevant, not as evidence of a pattern (as discussed in the previous section) but as illustrations of the operation or instantiation of the system.[92]

Recall that a pattern relates to externally observable events while a system relates to the internal structures and connections between related methods and processes. It is possible to bring evidence of a system not only through analysis of a pattern, but also through evidence of those internal policies, processes, methods and structures.[93]

[86] *Unique* (n 39) 679 [204].
[87] Evidence Act (n 85), s 94(3).
[88] *Jacara Pty Ltd v Perpetual Trustees WA Ltd* [2000] FCA 1886, (2000) 106 FCR 51.
[89] ibid 67 [67], cited in *Unique* (n 39) 679 [206].
[90] *Australian Competition and Consumer Commission v ACN 117 372 915 Pty Ltd (in liq)* [2015] FCA 368 (*AMI*).
[91] ibid [95] (North J), cited in *Unique* (n 39) 661 [130].
[92] *AIPE* (n 53) [174], where it was noted that 'it is difficult for an applicant to build a "system" case on a relatively small number of individual examples without (at least) proving how those examples were selected. But such examples may nevertheless be relevant, if only as illustrations confirming the effects of a business model.' See also *Ali* (n 57) [232].
[93] *Captain Cook College* (n 48) [76]. In that case, an overarching 'profit maximisation purpose' (on my analysis, a policy) explained the introduction of changes to an enrolment system that 'significantly weakened existing protections': ibid [523]. While corporate knowledge of this effect was established through the statutory attribution rule, it would in any event have been manifested through those system changes, on the analysis advocated here.

Thus in *Keshow* (cited in *Unique*), the regulator used individual examples of unconscionable conduct to show a pattern of behaviour, but also testimony from the natural respondent about his business model.[94] The latter is an example of evidence of the internal system – and the quite different witnesses that will become relevant. Third-party victims here may not be able to give the internal perspective required.[95] Where that is so, relevant evidence must come from the corporation itself, though its employees, documentation and so on. We will return to the range of relevant types of evidence in section IV.B.

Importantly, it may not be enough to prove the existence of system design or architecture, in order for it to manifest corporate intentionality – there must also be evidence that the system as designed was adopted, and possibly instantiated or applied. Otherwise, the system may constitute a mere 'formal', albeit particularised, policy that does not reflect the true corporate mindset. It is conceivable that there may be cases where an adopted system produces no discernible pattern of results: for example, a system may be halted by injunctive relief before it has been rolled out. But in most cases, it will be likely that both instances of externally observable events (patterns) and systems evidence will be required. This is because, unless the system can be shown to have operated in practice, it will be unclear whether it manifests the corporation's true state of mind. For example, as discussed in section IV.B.ii, a regulator may bring evidence of dishonest, predatory or unconscionable business strategies in the form of the defendant's company's sales scripts, which appear designed to be used by its sales agents or employees. However, adoption of the business strategy is not strongly evidenced through evidence of the mere existence of the scripts, which may be open to be dismissed as early drafts or discontinued models. However, if the scripts are, in fact, issued to the corporation's sales agents, the agents are trained or audited in relation to them, and the agents sufficiently follow the scripts in practice, the system as designed clearly has been adopted and instantiated. Here the corporate mindset is fully revealed.

Thus in *EDirect*, the ACCC's allegations concerned EDirect's conduct in relation to eight identified consumers. Alongside these instances of alleged individual unconscionable conduct, the ACCC also ran an 'unconscionable system of conduct' case. Aside from evidence about the transactions relating to the eight consumers, there was also evidence of the scripts of the sales component of the telemarketing calls, and there were recordings of 3,000 calls to potential customers. Reeves J said the

> fundamental issue … [is] whether the ACCC has shown that the critical features of EDirect's sales system as pleaded in its statement of claim were present *in combination* in a sufficient proportion, or number, of the recordings such that it has proved, on the balance of probabilities, that the high pressure and relentless system which is central to this issue, existed as a fact.[96]

Conversely, however, we must also understand that the fact that a system did not result in the planned result on one or more occasion does not necessarily rebut or undermine the

[94] *Australian Competition and Consumer Commission v Keshow* [2005] FCA 558 [76] (Mansfield J) (*Keshow*), cited in *Unique* (n 39) 655–56 [112]–[114]; *Captain Cook College* (n 48) [153]–[154].

[95] See the discussion of potential evidential gaps in *AIPE* (n 53) [164]–[165].

[96] *EDirect* (n 36) [107].

existence of an instantiated system. Thus a predatory business model may be applied to an intended target but fail to yield the desired outcome, for example because the victim turned out to be less vulnerable, or more protected, than anticipated. The system here must be distinguished from successful realisation of its aim or purpose. As explained in *AMI*, in the context of an unconscionable system of conduct:

> Proof of unconscionable conduct depended on what AMI and NRM did, whether or not it had an effect on the individual patient. For instance, some of the Annexure B patients did not enter into agreements at all. That did not mean that, for example, in using high-pressure selling techniques in attempting to procure contracts, AMI and NRM did not engage in unconscionable conduct.[97]

Similarly, the fact that particular features or elements of the system may vary or evolve over time, and between transactions, is not necessarily decisive against its existence and overall purpose.[98] Again, much will come down to the level of abstraction at which the system is alleged and thus sought to be proved. Here, the regulator's challenge is to ensure that the system is drawn sufficiently precisely and at the appropriate level of generality, or narrowness, to meet the law's criteria and to tailor its litigation strategy to that end.

v. Synthesis

To summarise, this section has been concerned to distinguish between two different litigation strategies, both of which aim to prove a corporation's system and, hence, its state of mind. One involves a process of inference from external patterns of behaviour; the other direct evidence of the internal structures, processes and methods that combine to form the alleged system. Regulators may, and do, usefully combine elements of both to prove adoption and operation of purposive systems of conduct. In the next section we turn to consider the kinds of evidence that may be brought in support of each approach. Of course, the range and kinds of evidence will be as varied as the systems they seek to prove. However, my thought is that by giving examples of the different kinds of evidence, and their usages, we may further understand and be in a position to realise a workable model of corporate Systems Intentionality. Again, I draw on examples from the consumer law prohibitions on unconscionable systems of conduct or patterns of behaviour, although I consider that the insights these offer may be adapted and applied more broadly.

B. Evidential Strategies

i. Patterns

When seeking to prove a pattern of behaviour, we have seen that courts look for repeated instances of conduct or outcomes that have shared characteristics or features. We have

[97] *AMI* (n 90) [939]–[942], cited in *Unique* (n 39) 661–62 [131].
[98] *AIPE* (n 53) [45]–[51]; *Ali* (n 57) [213] (Allsop CJ, Besanko and Perram JJ).

also seen that repeated conduct must be representative of the relevant class of case to which the alleged system would inherently apply. The alleged system and evidence of pattern must align.

It follows that if an alleged system operates at a high level of generality (as in one case, a sales process targeting any man suffering from impotence) then other more specific, shared features (age, level of education, literacy, race, cultural background, the circumstances or location of transacting and so on) may be largely irrelevant, or less relevant, to the enquiry.[99] In a case involving alleged manipulation of consumers to sign up for educational courses for which they are poorly suited, those personalised criteria may be far more pertinent.[100] A degree of forensic choice must therefore be exercised in discerning the relevant, shared features of the pattern of behaviour that indicate the presence of a system of conduct and hence the kind of evidence that may be appropriate. As the Court explained in *AIPE*:

> The more general or abstract the system or behaviour that is alleged and proven, the harder it may be to establish that it has the character of being unconscionable for want of necessary detail to show that is so, or that it has the necessary pervasive and proscribed character. By contrast, too granular an approach may more readily demonstrate isolated instances of contravening conduct, but may fall short of showing that any overall proscribed system or behaviour took place. That process of characterisation forms part of the evaluative exercise required to be carried out.[101]

Relevant evidence of patterns of behaviour will reflect the objective, outcomes-orientated nature of the enquiry. In the context of an alleged sales system, it could include oral testimony or other evidence of consumers' engagement with the system;[102] recordings, for example, of individual cases of sales transactions said to be consistent with, and evidence of, the alleged system in practice;[103] copies of email exchanges or web 'chat' exchanges with, or testimony from, individuals the subject of the alleged system of conduct;[104] payment records (eg receipts) issued to the consumer; unusual or distinctive features of any contracts concluded with the consumer consistent with the alleged practice;[105] incentives offered to consumers to engage in, and disincentives to disengage from, the sales process;[106] and evidence as to relevant, shared features of consumers, or of the circumstances of transacting,[107] said to be reflective of the nature of the system.

[99] *AMI* (n 90), cited in *Unique* (n 39) 662–63 [133]. See also *Ali* (n 57) [233]–[235], [283], [294] where the 'so-called "business model" was a largely consistent approach to extract money from a group of people by falsely representing to them (conformably with documents given to them) that moneys would be used in a particular way, when it was not intended to do so'. Here, the Court considered the individual attributes of the victims were less relevant, given that all were entitled to assumed a baseline of honest conduct.

[100] *Unique* (n 39) 663 [135]–[136], 666 [153], 670 [162].

[101] *AIPE* (n 53) [60].

[102] ibid [527]; *AMI* (n 90) [940].

[103] See, eg, *AMI* (n 90) [113], [360]; *EDirect* (n 36) [9], [92]–[94]; *Excite Mobile* (n 80); *AIPE* (n 53) [59], [163].

[104] *AIPE* (n 53) [60].

[105] For example, the long-term contracts in *AMI* that were without medical justification and unnecessary to protect the legitimate interests of suppliers: *AMI* (n 90) [133], [600].

[106] *Australian Securities and Investments Commission v Forex Capital Trading Pty Limited, in the matter of Forex Capital Trading Pty Limited* [2021] FCA 570 (Middleton J) (*ASIC v Forex*).

[107] *AIPE* (n 53) [60].

ii. Systems

Evidence of the internal elements of a system, by contrast, is likely to come from the corporation itself (although some external evidence may also be available where transferred to third parties – an example would be information given to a consumer about the corporate complaints process). Examples of potentially relevant categories of evidence are: testimony from employees carrying out the system as to its incidents and operation;[108] the content and delivery of employee or agent training to carry out the corporation's activities (here including scripts, guides, presentation materials and summaries) relevant to the system;[109] the conditions and nature of remuneration and incentives relating to delivery of the system;[110] payment and refund terms and any related contract terms and features;[111] complaints processes and complaints scripts;[112] the nature of automated and digital systems, such as the use of particular software;[113] and refund scripts. Careful use of expert evidence may provide a means of connecting or confirming elements of the system: for example, features of a system may take on a certain connected character when viewed in light of changes to government policy, taxation rules or the like.[114]

Regulators have had mixed success in using expert evidence to demonstrate the existence of a system of conduct. Courts are loath to stereotype, for example, residents of specific low socioeconomic communities as inherently vulnerable, and this might be suggested by bringing expert evidence of the demographic features of locations in which an allegedly exploitative system of conduct was employed.[115] In *AIPE*, an allegedly predatory business model sought to take advantage of consumers' lack of education and experience to persuade them (through cash and 'free' laptop incentives, among other strategies) to sign up for vocational education courses for which they were unsuited. Bromwich J explained the fine line that must be taken in using this form of evidence:

> [E]vidence about the demographic composition of a body of consumers is capable of founding or supporting a conclusion about how a business model was designed or how it operated. Clearly, there are considerable difficulties with a case that assumes that individual consumers are vulnerable because they are indigenous, or because they live in areas with sizeable populations of low socio-economic status. However, it cannot be controversial that there are correlations between indigeneity and low socio-economic status, on the one hand, and lack of the education and experience needed to look after one's interests on the other. Depending on the surrounding circumstances, if a business concentrates on areas of low socio-economic status or with large indigenous populations in recruiting customers, that may (at least in some cases) be taken to indicate a strategy of preferring customers who are vulnerable; and that

[108] See *AMI* (n 90) [891]. See also *AIPE* (n 53) [460] and following.

[109] *Unique* (n 39) 662 [133]; *EDirect* (n 36) [93]; *AMI* (n 90) [686]; *AIPE* (n 53) [525]–[526]; *AGM Markets* (n 34) [418]–[419], [429].

[110] *AMI* (n 90) [760]–[770], [939]; *AIPE* (n 53) [753]; *AGM Markets* (n 34) [441]; *ASIC v Forex* (n 106) [77].

[111] *AMI* (n 90) [600], [682], [939].

[112] *AIPE* (n 53) [83]–[84], [163]; *Captain Cook College* (n 48) [459]–[460].

[113] *AGM Markets* (n 34) [424].

[114] The government policy behind the ill-fated VET-FEE Help scheme is an example: see discussion in *Australian Competition and Consumer Commission v Cornerstone Investment Aust Pty Ltd (in liq) (No 4)* [2018] FCA 1408 [7] (Gleeson J) and AIPE (n 53) [72]–[93] (Bromwich J).

[115] *Unique* (n 39) 656 [115], endorsing the views of Mansfield J in *Keshow* (n 94) [87].

> may be an ingredient of unconscionability. At least, the presence of disadvantaged or vulnerable people in the target audience makes it more important for recruitment to be conducted consistently with proper notions of consumer protection.[116]

The use of 'summaries of evidence'[117] and other statistical tools in support of allegations of systems or patterns of conduct must also be carefully designed and deployed. In *EDirect*, we have seen that the ACCC alleged that the defendant conducted a 'high pressure sales' system. It put into evidence sales scripts that, on their face, gave a degree of support to the alleged system, for example by presenting 'choices' to the customer that both involved the customer's signing up. But these scripts needed to be coupled with recordings to demonstrate that the scripts were applied, or at least evidence from a sufficient sample of customers consistent with the application of the scripts.[118] Further, on their face, the scripts could not establish other elements of the pleaded system, such as that salesmen spoke over customers, avoided answering direct questions, and kept customers on the phone for unreasonable periods of time so as to create a sense of overall urgency and pressure.[119] The recordings that were available to the Court to assess these elements were limited. Officers of the ACCC had reviewed more samples of recordings and purported to summarise their features for the Court. But the assessment criteria were very subjective, involving 'value judgments such as: "speed", "avoid direct answers" or, most significantly, "urgency/pressure"'.[120] These went beyond summaries of evidence and were better characterised as submissions. These opinion-based documents, which seek to present a conclusion based on an exercise of judgement, applied to primary evidence, can be contrasted with use of information summaries, such as simple application of arithmetical formula.[121] The review also failed to show that the identified factors suggesting pressure were sufficiently shared, or characteristic of the sales calls, to reveal a system of pressure marketing.

iii. Timing and Inference

Finally, in drawing this discussion to a close, the issue of timing must be addressed. We have seen that it is possible for a practice to develop that, over time, evolves into an adopted system of conduct. It is in the nature of such a system that it might have no clear starting date, compared to a system that is actively designed and rolled out through (for example) issuing instructions and training to employees in the steps and processes of the system. And it may be that there is not always contemporaneous and continuous evidence of the system in operation.

Australian courts, addressing this challenge in the context of unconscionable systems of conduct, have taken a practical approach.[122] Thus in *AIPE*, witnesses gave evidence

[116] *AIPE* (n 53) [174].
[117] Evidence Act (n 85), s 50. See also *Captain Cook College* (n 48) [461], [469]–[471].
[118] *EDirect* (n 36) [93].
[119] ibid [95].
[120] ibid [103]. See further *Idylic Solutions Pty Ltd & ors – Australian Securities and Investments Commission v Hobbs* [2012] NSWSC 568, 24 [63] (Ward J) (*Idylic*).
[121] *Idylic* (n 121) 29–30 [78].
[122] See also *Captain Cook College* (n 48) [524], [534].

of the alleged system by reference to their practices and activities while employed by the defendant. The defendant asserted that the Court could draw no conclusions as to the existence of the system prior to their employment. Justice Bromwich rejected the argument, noting that this

> way of viewing organisational change may be seen to be far removed from ordinary human experience and the repetitive nature of tasks related to such things as marketing and enrolment. This is not tendency or coincidence evidence, but direct evidence able to support inferences about a system.[123]

Given that systems are embedded and repeat, it may be legitimate to infer that an extant system was representative of conduct at an earlier point in time, and also after the departure of relevant employee witnesses.[124] Evidence that a corporation is slow to review or audit processes, evidence of complaint responses and so on may bolster that inference, in the usual way.

V. Conclusion

This chapter had two aims: to clarify the nature and meaning of the essential concepts of 'systems of conduct, policies and practices' that underpin Systems Intentionality; and to explicate, as a matter of legal practice, how these may be proved. As will be clear, beyond being a discussion of academic interest, I hope that the chapter may provide a useful road map for practitioners, barristers, regulators and the judiciary seeking guidance on the operation of the model of Systems Intentionality in litigation practice. This reflects my longstanding project aim to develop a theoretically sound and practically workable model that is 'fit for purpose' as a means to call corporations to account for highly culpable misconduct. How it may be employed to address the specific doctrinal mental states required for the effective operation of common commercial rules and prohibitions is the subject of chapter 11.

[123] *AIPE* (n 53) [465].
[124] ibid [465]–[466].

10

How to Read a Corporation's Mind

MIHAILIS E DIAMANTIS

The heart dwells in the sea of blood which surges back and forth, where especially is what is called thought by men.

Empedocles of Acragas[1]

The governing faculty is in the brain.

Alcmaeon of Croton[2]

I. Discerning the Corporate Mind, From Where to How

Influenced by Egyptian wisdom, the Ancient Greek philosopher Empedocles believed that human cognition resides in the heart. The blood vessels all flow to that central muscle, positioning it as an obvious candidate for governing the entire organism. His contemporary, Alcmaeon, conducted several dissections and was more impressed by the network of nerves he observed stretching throughout the body. He concluded that the brain must house human thought. Many centuries later, medical science proved Alcmaeon right.

What was at stake in the contest between the cardio- and cephalocentrists? Clearly there was a medical angle to the dispute. Because we now know what organ carries out cognition, doctors can identify when physical trauma and genetic abnormalities might interfere. Sometimes, treatments even restore lost function.

Outside of medicine, there are fewer reasons to care about where the mind is located. It makes little difference to our social, moral or cultural understanding of ourselves whether the mind is in the heart or the brain. There is no evidence that cardiocentrists and cephalocentrists related to their fellow humans differently, or made different judgements about whom to befriend, whom to idolise or whom to shun. Nor is there any sign that they judged each other's mental lives differently – whom they identified with

[1] H Diels (ed), *Die Fragmente der Vorsokratiker*, 6th edn, rev with additions and index by Walther Kranz, 3 vols (Berlin, Weidmannche Verlagsbuchhandlung, 1952).

[2] H Diels, *Doxographi Graeci* (Editio Iterata, Lipsiae, G Reimer, 1879) 407.

good or ill intent, whom they deemed knowledgeable or ignorant, whom they thought cautious or reckless.

Alcmaeon won the ancient debate about the human mind, but fundamental controversies about the corporate mind remain undecided. Understanding the corporate mind is important for regulating corporations.[3] To hold corporations liable for most significant harms, the law needs a mechanism for attributing mental states like purpose and knowledge.[4] These mental states serve as proxies for corporate fault that distinguish, for example, an unavoidable death from a criminal homicide. Implementing effective doctrines of corporate liability turns on the law's ability to get the corporate mind right. Overly narrow doctrines are manipulable because corporate strategists can put distance between any part of the corporation and the drivers of corporate misbehaviour. Overly broad doctrines are socially wasteful because they force corporations to implement unnecessary layers of expensive compliance. Even moderate doctrines will backfire if they are not meaningfully calibrated to a sensible measure of corporate fault.

The standard policy puzzle frames itself as an inquiry about where corporate mental states reside. Like Empedocles and Alcmaeon, scholars debating the nature of the corporate mind focus on where it might be among the various parts of the body corporate. Pinpointing the corporate mind has proved difficult because it is hard to know where to start looking. Unlike humans, corporations have no 'hearts' or 'brains'. They vary dramatically in composition, size and form. They lack a stable or predictable structure.

Current law typically locates corporate cognition in the mental lives of individual employees (section II). Roughly speaking, corporations think what their employees think. Most commentators agree that this approach is too limiting. It overlooks emergent psychological phenomena – like cultural dispositions and collective knowledge – that can be the real force behind corporate malfeasance. These sorts of corporate fault arise from interactions between employees, rather than in single employees' heads.

An emerging proposal – systems intentionality – holds promise because it untethers the corporate mind from the biological minds of employees (section III). It supplements traditional doctrine by allowing that the corporate mind may inhere in stable corporate systems too. This systems approach is a marked improvement over current law, but it does not go far enough. Like current law, it frames the basic inquiry in positional terms that are inherently limiting. By circumscribing where the corporate mind might appear, systems intentionality cannot account for corporate fault that arises elsewhere.

This chapter argues that the law and its critics should abandon their effort to locate the corporate mind.[5] Just as for human minds, it does not matter *where* the corporate mind is. What matters is *how* the corporate mind, wherever located, influences behaviour (section IV). Rather than looking for the vessel that contains the corporate mind, we should start with a more basic question: What should count as evidence that

[3] ME Diamantis, 'Corporate Criminal Minds' (2016) 91 *Notre Dame Law Review* 2049.

[4] 'The law' throughout this chapter refers to US law. Many of the observations below should resonate for readers from other (particularly common law) jurisdictions.

[5] The chapter has nothing to say about the liability of individuals within corporations. They should be held to account to the extent they are responsible. See Hanrahan, ch 17 of this volume. Individual responsibility in corporate settings remains undertheorised. See Harding, ch 2 of this volume.

a corporation has a mental state? Drawing on cognitive science and social psychology, this chapter suggests that relevant evidence includes any corporate behaviour, whatever its causal source, whether an individual employee, a corporate system or something else entirely.

Were courts to draw on this evidence, they would not need to rummage around inside corporations to *find* mental states. They could instead *infer* corporate mental states from externally observable corporate behaviour. This 'inference theory' starts with what matters most to the law in regulating corporate behaviour – the troubling behaviour itself. By inferring corporate mental states from relevant evidence rather than looking for corporate mental states in pre-determined corporate structures, the law could develop a more nuanced and inclusive notion of corporate fault.

Even under an inference-based approach, the task of locating culpable corporate mental states in corporate systems would still be important, but not at the liability phase (section V). Like a surgeon who removes a tumour, sentencing courts must know where corporate misbehaviour originates in order to fix it.

II. A Tradition of Looking for Corporate Mental States

The law has bound itself to a perspective that assumes corporations possess mental states. When the law first recognised corporate entities, it needed a way to fit them into the vast pre-existing framework of civil and criminal liability. Lawmakers did this by extending the definition of 'person' (the legal object of such liability) to include business organisations.[6] Liability typically requires some measure of fault, and culpable mental states – like purpose or recklessness – are the law's entrenched proxy for fault. So, regardless of whether the concept of corporate personhood is a pragmatic pretence or a sincere effort to mirror moral reality,[7] the law must have some mechanism to attribute mental states to corporations.[8]

Lawmakers have displayed a profound lack of creativity in designing doctrines for attributing corporate mental states. Current law traces its roots to ancient rules that governed a much simpler economic relationship. Under Roman law, the owner of a slave could be liable for the slave's misdeeds.[9] In that dyadic scenario, there is little question about where the culpable mental state had to be – if not in the slaveholder then in the slave. The remainder of this section traces the threads of this Roman law to lawmakers' present-day efforts to locate corporate mental states in the much more complicated nexus of relationships that makes up the modern corporation.

[6] Dictionary Act, 1 *United States Code*, s 1 (2018) (defining 'person').

[7] *International Shoe Co v Office of Unemployment Compensation & Placement* 326 US 310 (1945) ('[T]he corporate personality is a fiction, although a fiction intended to be acted upon as though it were a fact.').

[8] In a similar vein, Robyn Carroll observes that '[t]he law attributes remorse and contrition to a culpable corporation through consideration of various forms of evidence'. See Carroll, ch 15 of this volume, section II. Justice Sarah Derrington and Samuel Walpole offer a nice application of this pragmatic perspective when they consider the advisability of holding ships criminally liable: see Derrington and Walpole, ch 16 of this volume.

[9] WP Keeton, *Prosser and Keeton on Torts*, 5th edn (Eagan, West Group Publishing, 1984) 499–508.

A. The Control Group Test

The most restrictive existing doctrine for attributing mental states to corporations is the control group test. It locates culpable corporate mental states in the heads of high-level corporate officers and managers. While federal courts have considered and ultimately rejected control group tests,[10] many State legislatures embrace some version of it.[11]

The control group test has intuitive appeal. It views directors and officers as alter egos of the corporation they work for. These high-level officials, the thinking goes, ultimately control their subordinates' conduct. Courts and commentators often describe directors and officers as the 'brains' of a corporation that cause the rest of the corporate hierarchy – the 'hands' – to move.[12] If the hands happen to move on their own, without any directing influence from the brain, the body corporate as a whole cannot be at fault.

The failings of the control group test are well known. The analogy between corporate officials and the brains of a corporation is often misplaced. Legally speaking, directors and officers have ultimate authority and control over a corporation, but the reality of corporate operations, especially for large corporations, can be very different.[13] Directors and officers can be distant from day-to-day business functions, where misconduct most often occurs. Indeed, data show mid-level managers commit most violations within corporations.[14]

This dynamic provides corporations with an opportunity to game their civil and criminal liabilities.[15] By strategically insulating officers and directors from higher-risk corporate operations, corporations can immunise themselves from potential liability when harm results.[16] Simple information management can do the trick. It is a well-tested informal rule of corporate governance that bad news does not flow up. Valuable mid-level managers know what information to pass up the chain of command and, as importantly, what not to pass up; what to put in writing and what to deliver by oral report. If officers and directors have plausible deniability of any involvement, the corporations they work for are off the hook under the control group test.

B. *Respondeat Superior*

Respondeat superior is the predominant doctrine in US federal law for attributing mental states to corporations. Like the control group test, it locates corporate mental states

[10] *CIT Corp v United States* 150 F 2d 85 [89] (9th Cir 1945); *Standard Oil Co v United States* 307 F 2d 120 [127] (5th Cir 1962); *Riss & Co v United States* 262 F 2d 245 [250] (8th Cir 1958); *United States v Armour & Co*, 168 F 2d 342 (3rd Cir 1948) 343–44.

[11] *Model Penal Code*, s 2.07(1)(c).

[12] HW Edgerton, 'Corporate Criminal Responsibility' (1927) 36 *The Yale Law Journal* 827, 840–41.

[13] *Commonwealth v Beneficial Financial Co* 275 NE 2d 33 (1971) ('Employees who are in the lower echelon of the corporate hierarchy often exercise more responsibility in the everyday operations of the corporation than the directors or officers.')

[14] G Gilchrist, 'Individual Accountability for Corporate Crime' (2018) 34 *Georgia State University Law Review* 365.

[15] ME Diamantis, 'Functional Corporate Knowledge' (2019) 61 *William & Mary Law Review* 319.

[16] DK Brown, 'The Problematic and Faintly Promising Dynamics of Corporate Crime Enforcement' (2004) 1 *Ohio State Journal of Criminal Law* 521, 546 ('Firms with information control are likely sometimes to be able to "push liability downward" to mid-level employees who responded to corporate incentives rather than acted as pure renegades.').

in the heads of natural people. However, *respondeat superior* is much more permissive about which natural people count.[17] Rather than limiting its scope to directors and officers, *respondeat superior* extends to every individual corporate employee.[18]

Since *respondeat superior* locates corporate mental states throughout the corporate hierarchy, it ameliorates some of the pathologies of the control group test. A corporation gains nothing under *respondeat superior* simply by distancing its directors and officers from misconduct occurring elsewhere in the body corporate. The organisation can be liable for that misconduct regardless of which employee carries it out or who knows about it. This incentivises corporations to be more proactive about monitoring and training all employees.

The intuition behind *respondeat superior* – that collective fault must reside with individual members of the collective – may serve well enough for simple groups. It was with such groups in mind that lawmakers originally developed the doctrine. *Respondeat superior* – or 'let the master answer' – is the true modern successor to the Roman law that held slaveholders liable for the violations of their slaves. Today, *respondeat superior* is a pitiful anachronism.[19] Modern, capitalist corporate behemoths bear no resemblance to ancient, feudal slaveholding. Not a single US scholar fully endorses *respondeat superior* as an appropriate mechanism for measuring corporate fault or attributing corporate mental states.

Because *respondeat superior* still purports to tell courts where to find corporate mental states, it necessarily overlooks cases when corporate fault resides elsewhere. For complex groups like modern corporations, collective fault often arises in the interstices between group members.[20] That is to say, the organisation itself, the structures it has in place or those it lacks, can be the ultimate drivers of misconduct.[21] For example, a corporation may have one employee who knows about a mandatory reporting requirement and another who knows about a triggering event.[22] If the communication channel between them is broken (or was never established in the first place), the corporation will violate the requirement though no employee will be in a position to know it. As organisational scientists widely recognise, collective action is more than the sum of its parts.[23] Even well-intentioned members in a dysfunctional organisation may end up engaging in behaviour that, in aggregate, is indistinguishable from civil or criminal harm.[24]

To make matters worse, *respondeat superior* gives corporations perverse incentives that exacerbate corporate harm. *Respondeat superior* encourages corporations to

[17] There are intermediate positions between the control group test (just high-level personnel can think for a corporation) and *respondeat superior* (any employee can think for a corporation). Rachel Leow's allocated powers model is one intriguing example. See Leow, ch 6 of this volume.

[18] *Restatement (Third) of Agency*, s 7.07 (2006).

[19] WR Thomas, 'When and How Corporations Became (and Remain) Persons under the Criminal Law' (2018) 45 *Florida State University Law Review* 479.

[20] ME Diamantis, 'The Law's Missing Account of Corporate Character' (2019) 17 *Georgetown Journal of Law & Public Policy* 865, 876–79.

[21] ME Diamantis, 'Successor Identity' (2019) 36 *Yale Journal on Regulation* 1, 21–26.

[22] These are the facts of *United States v Bank of New England* 821 F2d 844 (1st Cir 1987).

[23] E Lederman, 'Models for Imposing Corporate Criminal Liability: From Adaptation and Imitation Toward Aggregation and the Search for Self-Identity' (2000) 4 *Buffalo Criminal Law Review* 641, 688. This goes in the other direction too. Sometimes collective action can be *less* than the sum of its parts. ME Diamantis, 'The Corporate Insanity Defense' (2021) 111 *The Journal of Criminal Law and Criminology* 1.

[24] For related observations, see Gans, ch 13 of this volume.

disperse responsibilities across employees and discourages oversight.[25] These measures increase the chance that corporate harm will occur but simultaneously mitigate corporate liability because individual employees are less likely to acquire culpable knowledge. Furthermore, *respondeat superior* strongly incentivises corporations to refrain from appointing anyone to look into the adequacy of existing compliance mechanisms and information channels.[26] In the course of that inquiry, that employee could gain a mental state (eg knowledge about how risky business operations really are) that the corporation, for liability purposes under *respondeat superior*, would rather avoid.

C. Collective Knowledge

In partial response to *respondeat superior*'s deficiencies with respect to diffused responsibility, one Circuit in the United States adopted the collective knowledge doctrine.[27] Under it, courts must still locate culpable corporate knowledge in the heads of employees, but they need not locate the totality of relevant knowledge in a single employee. Rather, the collective knowledge doctrine allows courts to aggregate bits of knowledge from different employees, and then attribute the lot to the corporation. Individual employees in a corporation may each have only innocent items of knowledge (eg 'that X must be reported' or 'that X occurred') that, when aggregated, can trigger liability.

The collective knowledge doctrine improves *respondeat superior* in cases where liability requires culpable knowledge but that knowledge is divided across multiple employees. This negates some of the immunity corporations can gain by dispersing responsibilities across employees, and provides some incentive to implement and maintain channels of communication.[28] If a corporation expects to be held to account for aggregate knowledge, it will probably want a mechanism in place to proactively aggregate and assess that knowledge.

Yet the collective knowledge doctrine is a very limited improvement. By its own terms, it only applies to knowledge. It is harder or impossible to aggregate other sorts of mental states. For example, there is no easy equation for summing recklessness if some employees are rash and others prudent. Aggregating corporate purpose raises an even more formidable challenge. Individual employees may have conflicting purposes that are impossible to fuse into a single collective purpose.[29]

The more relevant shortcoming of the collective knowledge doctrine is that it still purports to locate corporate mental states. It expands the set of points where corporate knowledge can reside – from individual employees to groups of employees – but still ties corporate mental states to employees' heads. As a consequence, it necessarily overlooks corporate fault – even knowledge-based fault – that arises elsewhere in the corporate

[25] Diamantis (n 15).

[26] J Arlen, 'The Failure of the Organizational Sentencing Guidelines' (2012) 66 *University of Miami Law Review* 321, 325.

[27] *United States v Bank of New England* [1987] 821 F2d 844, 856 (1st Cir); *United States v TIME-DC, Inc* 381 F Supp 730 (WD Va 1974), 738.

[28] Diamantis (n 15).

[29] ME Diamantis 'Corporate Identity' in K Tobia (ed), *Experimental Philosophy of Identity and the Self* (New York, Bloomsbury, 2022) 203.

structure. For example, an automated computer algorithm (eg a loan approval system) that carries out business operations (eg approving loans) may have access to information (eg the race of applicants) that no human employee knows.[30] If the algorithm utilises that information to cause harm (eg discriminating against applicants), victims may deserve a remedy and the corporation may need an external incentive to improve.[31] The collective knowledge doctrine, however, would not help hold the corporation liable. As discussed in section III, algorithms are just one example of non-employee corporate systems that may house corporate fault.

III. Systems Intentionality

An exciting new approach to attributing corporate mental state is emerging in both law and legal scholarship. Elise Bant calls it 'systems intentionality', and she has collaborated with her colleague Jeannie Marie Paterson to flesh out its details.[32] Systems intentionality takes the criticism of the three previously discussed doctrines – all of which locate corporate mental states in the heads of employees – as its starting point: '[H]uman-centric mode[s] fail[ ] to address the complexities of dealing with modern corporate defendants, where the corporation has no natural "mind" and the knowledge of its human agents is often dissipated through complex, decentralised structures.'[33] Drawing inspiration from section 12.3 of Australia's Criminal Code, systems intentionality liberates the search for corporate mental states from the confines of employee grey matter. The Criminal Code contemplates that corporate fault may reside in a corporate culture that 'direct[s], encourage[s], tolerate[s], or [leads] to non-compliance', even though no individual employee can embody a corporation's culture. In an effort to 'operationalise' this provision,[34] Bant and Paterson maintain that a corporation's mental states may be manifested in its 'systems of conduct, policies and practices'.[35]

Like each of the approaches successively discussed above, systems intentionality represents a distinct improvement over its predecessors. It seeks to expand the set of legally recognised locations 'where the corporate mind naturally and necessarily resides'.[36] This can help judges, plaintiffs and prosecutors find 'the elusive corporate state of mind', even when no identifiable employees instantiate it.[37] Victims would

[30] ME Diamantis, 'The Extended Corporate Mind: When Corporations Use AI To Break the Law' (2020) 98 *North Carolina Law Review* 893; Paterson and Bant, ch 12 of this volume.

[31] ME Diamantis, 'Algorithms Acting Badly: A Solution from Corporate Law' (2021) 89 *Georgetown Washington Law Review* 801; ME Diamantis, 'Employed Algorithms: A Labor Model of Corporate Liability for AI' (2023) 72 *Duke Law Journal* (forthcoming); ME Diamantis, 'Vicarious Liability for AI' in K Johnson and C Reyes (eds), *Handbook of Law and AI* (Cambridge, Cambridge University Press 2023) (forthcoming).

[32] E Bant, 'Culpable Corporate Minds' (2021) 48 *University of Western Australia Law Review* 352; E Bant and JM Paterson, 'Systems of Misconduct: Corporate Culpability and Statutory Unconscionability' (2021) 15 *Journal of Equity* 63.

[33] Bant, 'Culpable Corporate Minds' (n 32) 358.

[34] ibid 378.

[35] Bant and Paterson, 'Systems of Misconduct' (n 32) 76.

[36] ibid 79.

[37] ibid 65.

have recourse in more circumstances of palpably improper corporation behaviour. The prospect of systems liability would incentivise corporations to attend to criminogenic internal systems, even when those systems do not culpably implicate individual employees. Such systems are often the persistent drivers of corporate harm: '[S]taff routinely leave, are transferred to other roles, are fired, promoted or resign. What remains constant are the company's structures, polices and processes that dictate how the next round of employees should act when engaged in the corporation's activities.'[38]

Systems intentionality is still in its infancy. Its adherents (I consider myself a fellow traveller) will no doubt refine and extend the approach in the years to come. There is some indication that systems intentionality has relatively modest ambitions – to improve upon, but not necessarily to perfect, the law's understanding of corporate mental states. By that measure, systems intentionality unquestionably succeeds. Lawmakers should take it seriously and implement some version of the expanded notion of corporate fault that it represents.

As the remainder of this chapter argues, though, lawmakers should enact systems intentionality but not stop with it. Systems intentionality is a continuation of the trend identified in the previous section. Each successor theory improves upon the deficiencies of its predecessor by expanding the possible set of corporate structures where corporate mental states may reside. Though proponents of systems intentionality sometimes speak of a corporation's mental states being 'manifested *through* its corporate systems',[39] their predominant language is less adverbial and more spatial: corporate mental states 'are manifested *in* the system itself',[40] 'are *found* … *in* the broader Corporate Internal Decision Structure'[41] and '[are] manifested … *where* [a corporation] adopts a system'.[42] Ultimately, little turns on the adverbial or spatial formulation – systems intentionality, like its predecessors, is incomplete because it places undue limits on how courts can discern corporate fault. If the law is to rid itself of doctrines that 'disproportionately protect[ ] [corporations] from the full legal consequences of their misconduct', it needs a fundamentally different framework for discerning corporate mental states.[43] The sections that follow focus on intuitive examples and modes of corporate fault that escape the purview even of systems intentionality's expanded conception of the corporate fault.

A. Out-of-Character Wrongs

Systems intentionality is an attempt to operationalise the notion that corporate fault can be embedded in corporate culture. Culture is, by its nature, a relatively stable and enduring social phenomenon. True to its inspiration, systems intentionality looks to stable corporate features for evidence of fault: 'what a corporation routinely and

[38] Bant, 'Culpable Corporate Minds' (n 32) 371.
[39] ibid 355 (emphasis added).
[40] Bant and Paterson, 'Systems of Misconduct' (n 32) 84.
[41] ibid 76.
[42] Bant, 'Culpable Corporate Minds' (n 32) 382 (emphasis added).
[43] ibid 360.

systematically does'[44] or its 'system of conduct or pattern of behaviour'.[45] In earlier work, I have described such stable corporate behavioural dispositions as corporate 'character traits'.[46] Systems intentionality supplements existing 'human-centric' models of corporate mental states, which look exclusively to employees' mental lives for evidence of corporate mental states, by allowing evidence of corporate character traits to count too.

One concern with using corporate character as a measure of fault is that, just as people can act out of character, so can corporations. Acting out of character does not ordinarily negate fault. Indeed, in criminal trials, character evidence is usually excluded.[47] While a defendant's patterns of behaviour may be relevant at sentencing, he cannot defend simply by claiming that he committed the crime in an uncharacteristic moment of weakness. Since systems intentionality references stable corporate structures, it overlooks corporate fault that does not manifest in an enduring system or pattern of behaviour. Imagine, for example, that a large utility company fails to adequately maintain some isolated electric wires but that no identifiable employee is to blame. Until the utility establishes a system or pattern of such failures, a liability model premised on systems intentionality will have difficulty intervening, even after the wires start a fire.

This is not a fleeting or trivial drawback. For every eventual pattern of corporate misconduct, there will always be initial instances that, at the time they occur, do not yet suffice to establish a pattern. By requiring a stable system or pattern before liability attaches, systems intentionality leaves the first victims without recourse. It also encourages corporations to adopt a 'wait and see' approach: test out a business practice, see whether it hurts anyone and then respond as necessary with revisions. We should ultimately hope for a system of corporate liability that gives even initial victims an opportunity to find justice and incentivises corporations to be more proactive in assessing risky operations from the get-go.

B. Culpably Missing Systems

The central premise of systems intentionality is that corporations can be at fault for having systems in place that produce corporate wrongs, even when there is no identifiable culpable employee. However, the *absence* of corporate systems can generate wrongs too. The corporate culture provisions of the Australian Criminal Code acknowledge as much: corporate culpability can be established by demonstrating 'that the body corporate failed to create and maintain a corporate culture that required compliance'.[48]

Imagine, for example, that a corporation has several consumer-facing employees but performs no background checks before hiring them and does nothing to train them. Or imagine a corporation lacks crucial information channels for ensuring that it complies with mandatory reporting to authorities. Such a corporation would likely generate a

[44] ibid 383.
[45] ibid 382.
[46] ME Diamantis, 'Clockwork Corporations: A Character Theory of Corporate Punishment' (2018) 103 *Iowa Law Review* 507, 539–40 ('[C]haracter is just a disposition to behave in a certain way.').
[47] Federal Rules of Evidence, r 404(a)(1).
[48] Criminal Code Act 1995 (Cth), pt 2.5, div 12.3 (Australia).

diverse range of harms, but it is not clear that systems intentionality would have the tools to hold it liable. The harms the corporation generates may not be uniform enough to constitute a system or pattern. Nor is it clear if (or precisely when) the absence of a system could itself qualify as a system that would trigger liability under systems intentionality. The advocates of systems intentionality may eventually be able to provide an answer, but it will require some heavy metaphysical lifting that will necessarily be theoretically controversial.

C. Turning Towards Strict Liability

Systems intentionality offers a mechanism for telling courts how to recognise when culpable corporate mental states inhere in corporate systems. Unlike the human-centred approaches discussed in section II, systems intentionality is not a model that points directly to pre-existing mental states for onward corporate attribution. Rather, systems intentionality has only two variables to mediate the translation: the presence of a corporate system (or practice) and its aptness to cause harm. It then needs a rule for pairing these variables with mental states. The effort to translate just two non-mental phenomena into the full range of fault-bearing mental states risks veering towards a strict liability.

Indeed, the language utilised by advocates of systems intentionality to link corporate systems to corporate fault often sounds in strict liability:

- To establish fault, systems intentionality 'look[s] to what a … corporation['s] systems are objectively apt to produce'.[49]
- A product 'may be intrinsically and necessarily misleading'.[50]
- '[S]ome ruse or deception [may be] inherent in the business practices'.[51]
- '[T]he very design of [a] system [may be] predatory'.[52]
- '[A corporate] defendant's business model could itself generate disadvantage and be relevantly exploitative'.[53]

On the systems intentionality approach, simply having a system in place that causes harmful conduct can be sufficient to establish fault: 'a corporation's state of mind is manifested … where it adopts a system of conduct or pattern of behaviour *that results in a contravention, or is apt to … contravene, the conduct element* of some … prohibition'.[54]

A simple example helps to establish the point. Suppose a corporation makes a product (eg asbestos, opioids, cigarettes) that, when used as directed, has a high likelihood of killing the user. If the manufacture is accompanied by a culpable mental state – like intent to kill, knowledge that the product would kill, or recklessness with respect to

[49] Bant, 'Culpable Corporate Minds' (n 32) 383.
[50] Bant and Paterson, 'Systems of Misconduct' (n 32) 80.
[51] ibid 80.
[52] ibid 82.
[53] ibid 84.
[54] Bant, 'Culpable Corporate Minds' (n 32) 382.

the risk that the product would kill – the corporation would likely be guilty of a crime. Now consider three points in time. At time T1, the corporation makes and distributes the product, but there is no indication it might be dangerous. Science has not established that fact, and no human being has any reason to suspect it. Several years later, at time T2, some internal reports circulate within the corporation noting potential (though unproven) dangers of the product, but the corporation continues to sell the product unmodified and without warning. Several years after that, T3, further study in the scientific community establishes the dangers of the product definitively; yet the corporation maintains its course.

At what point does the corporation have a culpable mental state? Intuitively, one might say T2 or T3, after the corporation was (or should have been) on notice that the product kills people. To hold the corporation criminally liable at T1 would smack of strict liability, because culpability would be premised on facts that were not even scientifically available. Yet systems intentionality seems to demand precisely that result. The product did not become dangerous after its toxicity was discovered; it was dangerous all along. At T1, the only two variables in the systems intentionality picture point very strongly toward a culpable mens rea: the corporation had in place a system (manufacturing a product) that was apt to cause harm (killing consumers). There is no way, internal to systems intentionality, to avoid that result. The obvious response might be something like, 'Oh, come on, it's clear the corporation didn't know. No one knew!' But recall, the whole point of systems intentionality is to get beyond reliance on such 'human-centric' models of corporate mental states.

This possible shift toward strict liability is subtle, but it is something advocates of systems intentionality probably want to avoid. After all, systems intentionality is supposed to be a mechanism to help courts better discern culpable corporate mental states. Strict liability undermines that ambition by reading culpable mental states out of the picture. It would also transform the current system of corporate liability – with all of its nuanced attention to fault – into a very different system. According to the advocates of systems intentionality, consistency with the current legal framework is meant to be one of its leading advantages.[55]

D. Distinguishing Mental States

Corporate liability is currently calibrated to a broad range of fine-grained culpable mental states. In US federal criminal law alone, there are more than 100 different types of mens rea.[56] They include the familiar modern states, like purpose, knowledge and recklessness, as well as many more obscure common law fault elements, like malice, dishonesty and wilfulness. The line between innocence and guilt can turn on which if any of these mental states a corporation satisfies, as can the line between different degrees of liability (and how severe any penalties will be).

Though systems intentionality can help discern whether a corporation is at fault or not, it is not clear that the model has tools to distinguish the various mental states

[55] ibid 77–78.
[56] WS Laufer, 'Culpability and the Sentencing of Corporations' (1992) 71 *Nebraska Law Review* 1049, 1064.

that mark finer-grained differences between levels of fault. Advocates of systems intentionality are aware of this challenge. A year ago, they noted that '[i]t is unclear how the concept of a corporate culture bears on specific forms of state of mind'.[57] They observed that 'the various "state of mind" enquiries vary widely', but at the time found it 'only possible to note the nature of this challenge and to identify … the sorts of circumstances in which they arise'.[58] Today, in this volume, Bant and Paterson take up the task.[59] No doubt, given time, systems intentionality theorists will eventually have much more to say on the matter. This section measures the extent of the challenge that remains.

Can systems intentionality as presently articulated and supplemented discriminate between the full range of mental states relevant to assessing corporate liability? Because, like its predecessors, systems intentionality attempts to locate corporate states of mind in a limited domain – corporate systems (plus whatever prior doctrines allowed) – systems intentionality has its work cut out for it. Recall that according to system's intentionality, finders of fact assess corporate mental states by evaluating whether the corporation undertook 'a system of conduct or pattern of behaviour that results in contravention, or is apt to … contravene, the conduct element of some … prohibition'.[60] The only non-binary variable implicit in that mechanism is how apt a system is to produce harm. While degrees of likelihood of harm may be a good measure of how reckless a corporation was in adopting a system, it is difficult to see how to move from recklessness to other mental states. When is the aptness of a corporate system to produce harm so great that it amounts to knowledge or purpose? And what distinguishes either of these last two from corporate malice under the systems intentionality model? As an initial matter, it seems that the model would need to incorporate more variables to distinguish between all the legally relevant corporate mental states.

Consider once again the example in section III.C of the corporation that manufactured the harmful product. Though there is certainly room for disagreement about what culpable mental states the corporation had at which times, one intuitive account would be: at T1, none; at T2, recklessness with respect to killing; at T3, knowledge that death would result. On the systems intentionality approach, the answer must be that the corporation had the same mental state from start to finish. The manufacturing system and its aptness to cause harm were the same at all times. Given the close connection between the product and extreme harm to customers, systems intentionality seems like it would take a rather stark stance. Among available mental states, systems intentionality seems likely to regard the corporation as having had from the very beginning a mental state that is intuitively absent even at the end: *intent* to cause death. 'Where the system is apt to … produce some outcome, and does always or usually produce that outcome, it is specifically intended.'[61] Yet it would be counterintuitive to say the manufacturer ever intended to kill its customers.

Unless it acknowledges additional variables, systems intentionality risks flattening some of the existing fault-based texture of the corporate liability inquiry. Currently,

[57] Bant, 'Culpable Corporate Minds' (n 32) 352, 381.
[58] ibid 378.
[59] Bant, ch 11 of this volume.
[60] Bant (n 32) 382.
[61] Bant, ch 11 of this volume, section III.A.ii.

human-centric doctrines for attributing mental states to corporations can capture and distinguish a range of applicable mental states. They simply direct finders of fact to identify a mental state in a human employee and then, under the right conditions, to attribute that mental state to the corporation. To identify mental states in human employees, finders of fact inevitably draw on the same implicit sophisticated folk psychology that we all use to understand each other's mental lives. That folk psychology readily distinguishes between the various possible mental states articulated in the law. If systems intentionality does not have the same level of nuance as folk psychology, it will erase important distinctions in the context of corporate liability. The advocates of systems intentionality say the doctrine would 'sit alongside and support other general law and statutory attribution … approaches'.[62] But presumably it would have primacy of place, capable of overriding human-centric attribution mechanisms where they conflict with what systems intentionality would dictate. After all, systems intentionality is meant to be a doctrine that measures corporate fault even where all individual employees may be acting reasonably and in good faith. But if systems intentionality overrides the human-centric doctrines, it may also erase some of their nuance in measuring corporate fault.

Advocates of systems intentionality have made some admirable progress towards distinguishing a few corporate mental states. Their general strategy has been to reduce the subjective component of various mental states to intent and knowledge. For example, Bant breaks dishonesty down to two parts, 'the quality of the defendant's conduct in light of the defendant's actual intention and knowledge'.[63] While this reductive strategy may be persuasive for the six mental states advocates of systems intentionality have tackled so far – intent, knowledge, recklessness, negligence, dishonesty, unconscionability – it is an open question whether it would succeed for mental states like malice, wickedness, wantonness, wilfulness, corruptness, circumspection, premeditation and the hundred or so other mental states that appear in US federal criminal law alone.

The strategy of tying all corporate mental states to intention and knowledge also has its risks. The accounts of all other mental states would inherit any weaknesses of the accounts of those two. On the systems intentionality account, any stable corporate system that has '[t]he general capacity … to prompt a certain kind of choice' from employees inherently 'express[es] a choice as to how to direct conduct'.[64] Because systems intentionality wants to locate mental states in corporations' systems, it needs each system's purposes to be internal to the system itself – 'the nature of a "system" … is inherently purposive'.[65] But maintaining that internalist stance proves difficult. The advocates of systems intentionality often talk about systems as being 'designed to' or 'calculated to' produce some outcome. For example, its supporters say that 'in some cases, there can be no other explanation for a system of conduct than that it was designed to achieve a certain outcome'.[66] The quoted language directs attention to an external vantage from which the system's actual purpose is to be ascertained. That external vantage does

[62] Bant (n 32) 377.
[63] Bant, ch 11 of this volume, section II.E (emphasis omitted).
[64] ibid section III.A.ii.
[65] ibid section III.A.iii.
[66] ibid section III.A.ii.

substantive work separating innocence and guilt on the systems intentionality framework. According to systems intentionality theorists, a corporate system may produce an outcome that deviates from the system's design. For example, suppose 'an individual employee presses a button that puts into operation a system in circumstances for which it was not designed'.[67] Such deviant outcomes, we are told, are akin to innocent mistakes that the corporation did not intend.

This line of thought begs the question 'Whose "design" for a corporate system matters?' Given the focus on corporate mental states, the answer that calls out is 'The corporation's!' Yet that answer leads to circularity: the whole point of systems intentionality was to explain corporate mental states. Relying on corporate mental states in accounting for them would leave the whole unexplained. A different approach might point instead to the intended design of some employee. But the advocates of systems intentionality will likely find that answer unappealing too. The view's ambition was to move past human-centrism. If not the corporation or its employees, it is unclear whose designing mind to look to.

IV. Inferring Minds, Natural and Corporate

The doctrines for attributing corporate mental states that have been considered up to this point have one thing in common – they purport to locate corporate mental life in increasingly wider sets of corporate phenomena. Each existing doctrine struggles to recognise corporate fault when it arises somewhere outside the set it embraces. The natural culmination of this trend would be to abandon the effort to locate corporate mental states by acknowledging that corporate fault could reside anywhere in a corporation.[68] As suggested at the start of this chapter, we would not necessarily lose anything of evaluative significance – the location of an actor's mind is irrelevant to assessing the actor's conduct.

This section offers a different approach to corporate fault that starts with the premise that the location of corporate mental states does not matter. The approach is grounded in cognitive science and has, or so I argue, ready responses to hurdles that systems intentionality faces.

A. The Science of Reading Each Other's Minds

While 'mind reading' might sound like a mentalist magic trick, for cognitive scientists it refers to the very pedestrian capacity we all have for figuring out what another human being is thinking.[69] In some sense, it *is* a remarkable ability. Other people's minds are

[67] ibid section III.A.iii.

[68] Or one could go in the opposite direction and say that fault may sometimes reside nowhere, but the corporation should still be accountable on a strict-liability model. Lauren Willis proposes such an approach for some algorithmic harms. See Willis, ch 19 of this volume.

[69] S Nichols and SP Stich, *Mindreading: An Integrated Account of Pretense, Self-Awareness, and Understanding Other Minds* (Oxford, Clarendon Press 2003).

opaque to us, so we cannot observe them directly. And yet, when someone walks toward the water fountain on a hot day, we know she wants a drink. When someone yelps after stubbing her toe, we know she feels pain. When someone aims an arrow at a target, we know she intends to hit it. We take in observable data about a person and infer something about her unobservable mental life.

Cognitive scientists know quite a bit about how mind reading works. We are not born with the ability. It normally develops in very early childhood through social and biological mechanisms.[70] Cognitive scientists see evidence of mind reading in children as young as 4 years old. For example, in a 'false belief' test, experimenters have a child watch an adult put a toy in a box.[71] Then, after the adult leaves the room, a puppet enters the scene, removes the toy, and places it in a different box. Using eye-tracking technology, the experimenters gauge where the child expects the adult to look for the toy after returning to the room. If the child expects the adult to look in the original box, even though the child knows the toy is actually in the new box, then the child understands something about the adult's mental life and how it differs from reality – the adult has a false belief about where the toy is.

There is nothing clairvoyant about mind reading. In day-to-day life, it usually happens automatically and effortlessly. There are some situations that give us pause where we become more reflective. Perhaps we encounter a tricky scenario where multiple mental states could be appropriate – 'Does Hamlet really love Ophelia?' – or perhaps the stakes are high so we want to be confident in our conclusion – 'Did he know the gun was loaded?' Whatever the occasion, mind reading is not magic. It is an ordinary, inference-based mental practice. All normally developed and socialised adults share a common practice of mind reading that they apply to fellow human beings. We gather two types of observable information – what a person did and the circumstances in which he did it – and triangulate to the person's unobservable mental states.[72]

The mental states we attribute through mind reading include those that are central to our ethical evaluation of each other – what people intend, know, feel, experience, etc. Whether we praise or blame each other depends in significant part on the mental states we attribute. When fact finders in a court of law attribute mental states to a defendant – for example figure out whether he intended to permanently deprive the victim of her property – they engage their mind-reading capacities.[73] Mind reading is not usually statutorily prescribed or detailed in any procedural code.[74] Rather, it is a bedrock

[70] S Baron-Cohen, M Lombardo and H Tager-Flusberg, *Understanding Other Minds: Perspectives from Developmental Social Neuroscience* (Oxford, Oxford University Press, 2013).

[71] H Wimmer and J Perner, 'Beliefs about Beliefs: Representation and Constraining Function of Wrong Beliefs in Young Children's Understanding of Deception' (1983) 13(1) *Cognition* 103.

[72] BF Malle and J Knobe, 'The Folk Concept of Intentionality' (1997) 33(2) *Journal of Experimental Social Psychology* 101; BF Malle, *How the Mind Explains Behaviour: Folk Explanation, Meaning, and Social Interaction* (Cambridge, Bradford Publishing Company, 2004).

[73] *People v Conley* 543 NE2d 138 (Ill App Ct 1989) ('[T]he surrounding circumstances, the use of a bottle, the absence of warning and the force of the blow are facts from which the jury could reasonably infer the intent to cause permanent injury.')

[74] Though sometimes it is! *Montana Code Annotated*, s 45-2-103(3) (1993) ('The existence of a mental state may be inferred from the acts of the accused and the facts and circumstances connected with the offense.'); *Delaware Code Annotated* tit 11, s 307(a) (1987) ('The defendant's intention, recklessness, knowledge or belief at the time of the offense for which he is charged may be inferred by the jury from circumstances surrounding the act he is alleged to have done.')

psychological phenomenon on which the law implicitly relies. When the law says the case against an individual turns on whether he possessed a specified mental state, it assumes that finders of fact will activate their normal capacity to attribute mental states when deciding the case. That capacity is mind reading.

B. Reading Corporate Minds

Even though there is nothing remarkable about reading each other's minds, attributing mental states to corporations may seem exceptional, mysterious or arbitrary. We cannot observe human minds, but we do know (or at least think we know) there is some underlying neurological fact of the matter about what is going on. The same is not true of corporations. Corporate theorists disagree about how to discern what mental states corporations have, where corporate mental states might reside and whether corporations can have mental states at all. So, it may seem that talk of corporate mental states, let alone any particular approach to attributing corporate mental states, carries a special, perhaps unsurmountable, burden. 'The challenge to understand defendants' states of mind for the purposes of satisfying these difficult and volatile elements becomes exponentially greater when dealing with modern, devolved and complex corporate wrongdoers to which the same elements apply.'[75]

As it happens, reading corporate minds is no more mysterious or complicated than reading natural minds. Cognitive scientists have confirmed what any Google search of corporate news would immediately reveal: we attribute mental states to corporations without hesitation.[76] While academicians in university hallways debate whether corporations truly have mental states and what they might be, when they go home at night they once more become normal people and find they have more overlapping than divergent intuitions. Whether or not it is a 'truism that corporations do not possess natural or innate states of mind',[77] we are all naturally inclined to think, talk, respond and act as though corporations do.[78]

As with reading human minds, cognitive scientists have discovered there is nothing magical about how we read corporate minds. Indeed, all evidence suggests that we use the same underlying cognitive mechanisms for attributing mental states to corporations and to humans.[79] Due to their internal cohesion, corporations are an example of what cognitive scientists call entitive groups.[80] We represent such entitive groups in our cognitive economy as though they were unified agents, like natural people.[81]

[75] Bant, ch 11 of this volume, section I.

[76] J Knobe and J Prinz, 'Intuitions About Consciousness: Experimental Studies' (2008) 7 *Phenomenology and the Cognitive Sciences* 67; MJ O'Laughlin and BF Malle, 'How People Explain Actions Performed by Groups and Individuals' (2002) 82 *Journal of Personality and Social Psychology* 33.

[77] Bant, 'Culpable Corporate Minds' (n 32) 378.

[78] Crofts, ch 3 of this volume.

[79] BF Malle, 'The Social and Moral Cognition of Group Agents' (2010) 19 *Journal of Law and Policy* 95, 132.

[80] B Lickel et al, 'Varieties of Groups and the Perception of Group Entitativity' (2000) 78 *Journal of Personality and Social Psychology* 223, 259; SJ Sherman and EJ Percy, 'The Psychology of Collective Responsibility: When and Why Collective Entities are Likely to be Held Responsible for the Misdeeds of Individual Members' (2010) 19 *Journal of Law and Policy* 127, 150.

[81] AL Johnson and S Queller, 'The Mental Representations of High and Low Entitativity Groups' (2003) 21 *Social Cognition* 101.

Cognitive scientists have run studies in which they present participants with scenarios that describe corporations and individuals undertaking similar courses of action. Through targeted questions, the scientists elicit participants' propensity to ascribe mental states to the characters in the scenarios. The results show that we are equally likely to attribute mental states to natural and corporate people, and that in relevantly similar scenarios, we are inclined to attribute *the same mental states to both*. Cognitive scientists deduce that we use the same psychological mechanisms to read both corporate and natural minds: we triangulate from behaviours and circumstances to motivating mental states.

This inferential characterisation of corporate mind reading carries over to morally charged settings. Our assessments of corporate fault are mediated by attributions of the same mental states that are morally salient when we evaluate individual fault. Our practice of blaming corporations is 'psychologically sensible and sustainable' because we use the same mechanisms for inferring corporate and human mental states.[82]

C. Inferring Corporate Mental States in the Courtroom

The science of mind reading suggests a straightforward approach for fixing corporate mental states. Rather than theorise about where corporate mental states reside (I confess my scepticism that there is any real answer), we might let jurors attribute mental states to corporations in the courtroom as they naturally would out of the courtroom. This is implicitly what courts already do with individual criminal defendants. Courts set aside philosophical debates about what intentions are or how knowledge works. They do not tell jurors what neuroscience says about which brain regions carry out what thought processes, or when people are likely to have one mental state or another. Rather, judges just assume jurors will engage their ordinary practices for inferring from available evidence what was going on in the defendant's mind. The pervasive familiarity of the practice renders it invisible and banishes any mystery surrounding it. Since we all have an equally robust, shared psychological mechanism for inferring corporate mental states too, courts could treat corporate defendants similarly.

This 'inference theory' would mark a significant break with existing legal doctrine and proposals for reform, but a break in favour of common sense. For centuries, lawmakers and scholars have tried to develop special doctrines for telling jurors where to find the corporate mind. As discussed at the start of this chapter, the biological location of an agent's mind is irrelevant to our assessment of his thoughts and behaviour. Under an approach informed by inference theory, jurors would need no special instructions. Courts could leave jurors to approach corporate cases as they do individual cases: 'Weigh the evidence and infer what was going on in the defendant's mind as you ordinarily would.' The law does not need its own theory for attributing corporate mental states because finders of fact naturally bring their own.

In practice, inference theory would induce attorneys to approach corporate cases much as they do individual cases. Just as for individual defendants, jurors would infer corporate defendants' mental states by triangulating from actions and circumstances.

[82] Sherman and Percy (n 80).

Perhaps channelling the intuition behind inference theory, an Australian judge recently remarked that '[t]he ethical quality of a corporation's behaviour must be assessed by reference to the actions of the corporation itself'.[83] As with individual defendants, every corporate action and surrounding circumstance would be potentially admissible at trial, subject to applicable rules of evidence.[84] This does not mean that factfinding devolves into an aimless free-for-all. As in cases with individual defendants, inundating jurors with extraneous facts would dilute one's case. Skilled attorneys need to be selective. They need to identify which actions and circumstances to emphasise, and portray competing narratives that raise the salience of their preferred mental state inference. Jurors then weigh the plausibility of each narrative and decide which mental state to attribute. Under inference theory, this same dynamic would play out for corporate defendants. Importantly, jurors never have to consider the question that is at the centre of current disputes over corporate fault: *where* precisely the culpable corporate mental state arose.

D. Evaluating Inference Theory

There are several immediate benefits to inference theory. To begin with, it levels the playing field between corporations and individual defendants.[85] Current law and available proposals all start by assuming some form of corporate exceptionalism; they then then offer special doctrines for attributing mental states to corporations. By contrast, inference theory promotes parity of treatment across natural and artificial defendants because it leverages the exact same psychological mechanism for attributing culpable mental states to both.

Inference theory also excels with respect to basic goals of corporate liability like retribution and prevention. The most reliable path to realising criminal law's retributive aims is to align it with intuitive assessments of fault. Inference theory does precisely this because it grounds the law of corporate mens rea in the psychological reality of how people ordinarily decide whether a corporation has a culpable mental state. Furthermore, by focusing on factors external to the corporate structure – corporate acts and circumstances – rather than a limited number of structures within corporations, inference theory can deter pernicious corporate dynamics wherever they might arise. This incentivises corporations to be proactive about assessing the entirety of their operations and rooting out or reforming potentially harmful elements.

Each of these above-mentioned benefits is also an advantage that systems intentionality has relative to existing law for attributing corporate mental states. By untethering the inquiry from location-based considerations, inference theory pushes these benefits further, and in so doing avoids some of the challenges raised in section III that systems intentionality must still address:

- *Out-of-character wrongs.* Since systems intentionality looks to stable corporate systems or patterns of harm, it is an awkward fit for evaluating corporate fault for

[83] *PT Ltd v Spuds Surf Chatswood Pty Ltd* [2013] NSWCA 446.

[84] Admissible acts and circumstances could even include those that arise after the instance of misconduct under consideration. See Fisse, ch 7 of this volume.

[85] Bant, 'Culpable Corporate Minds' (n 32) 360.

one-off or first-time harms. Inference theory does not have this limitation. It permits attribution of mental states to corporations regardless of whether a stable system, an individual employee or some other mechanism altogether produced the corporate behaviour. While a pattern of behaviour may be a helpful contextual datapoint for evaluating the mental state behind any given instance of behaviour, it is not a prerequisite under inference theory. We commonly recognise that people – corporate and natural – can act out of character. In the right circumstances, a sequence of actions can motivate an inference that the actions were taken with intent or knowledge or malice, even if the actions were unlikely ever to recur.

- *Culpably missing systems*. Systems intentionality is also an awkward fit for situations where a corporation engages in harmful behaviour because it *lacks* a system. Since inference theory looks directly to corporate behaviour, it can recognise corporate fault irrespective of the presence or absence of an internal corporate mechanism that generated (or failed to prevent)[86] the behaviour.
- *Turning towards strict liability*. Because systems intentionality attempts to pair just two non-mental variables – the presence of a system and its aptness to produce harm – with culpable mental states, it risks sliding into a strict liability regime. Recall the example of a corporation that sold a product that science had not yet discovered was harmful. Since the corporation engaged in a pattern of harmful behaviour, systems intentionality seems counterintuitively committed to saying the corporation knowingly harmed its customers. Inference theory can avoid that result, since the variables from which it allows finders of fact to infer corporate fault include the key circumstance – that nobody could possibly have known at the time that the product was harmful. Since inference theory mirrors the implicit default standard for inferring fault in the rest of criminal law, there is no risk of its setting a stricter standard than presently applies to individual defendants.
- *Distinguishing mental states*. Systems intentionality presently struggles to distinguish the full range of mens rea that appears in criminal law. This is because there can only be so many ways to pair mental states with the two variables in systems intentionality: the presence of a system and its aptness to produce harm. In the example of the corporation that sold the harmful product, the corporation's system and its harms remained the same all times, even as people's understanding of the product's harms evolved. Inference theory easily addresses the full panoply of available mental states. It directly incorporates the intuition that, as the circumstances surrounding the manufacture of a harmful product evolve, so too may the mental state of the manufacturer. When internal corporate reports about possible harms of the product being to circulate, the inference to corporate recklessness becomes stronger. When the wider scientific community begins to acknowledge the harms, the inference to corporate knowledge becomes more salient. Inference theory's ability to distinguish mental states should be unsurprising. If a mental state is one people ordinarily attribute to corporations outside of the courtroom, inference theory would allow finders of fact to attribute it within the courtroom too.

[86] Jonathan Clough offers a similarly wide-ranging approach to evaluating corporate liability for failure to prevent offences. See Clough, ch 18 of this volume.

V. Systems Intentionality at Sentencing

As a doctrine for establishing corporate fault, systems intentionality has clear advantages over current law. It closes a liability loophole by recognising that culpable corporate mental states sometimes reside in broken corporate systems, rather than just in the heads of employees. Lawmakers should adopt some version of it. Yet they should also not end the process of legal reform there. Systems intentionality does not purport to be a comprehensive theory of corporate fault. In at least one respect, systems intentionality is continuous with current doctrine – it is an effort to locate culpable corporate mental states in a restricted set of corporate phenomena. Any approach that places limits on where corporate fault can arise will overlook corporate fault that arises elsewhere.

Inference theory, the approach advanced here, would break with the tradition of trying to *locate* corporate fault by acknowledging it could reside anywhere within the corporate structure. Inference theory grounds itself in the science behind people's ordinary judgements about corporate fault. Rather than forcing fact finders to identify some internal mechanism behind harmful corporate behaviour, it allows them to consider the harmful behaviour in context and directly infer whether the corporation had a culpable mental state. By casting off the effort to pinpoint corporate fault, inference theory allows for a wider-ranging, more natural evaluation of corporate accountability. In so doing, it has ready answers to several challenges that systems liability must still face, like holding corporations accountable for non-systemic harms and distinguishing the full range of corporate mens rea.

Even if inference theory is a preferable doctrine for establishing corporate liability, it would be a mistake for the lawmakers to overlook systems intentionality.[87] Adopting inference theory outright would be a politically heavy lift. Systems intentionality could be a salutary intermediary step in the right direction. Additionally, systems intentionality has advantages that extend beyond establishing liability. While locating the corporate mind may not be relevant for assessing corporate fault, judges at sentencing must channel the dispute between Empedocles and Alcmaeon. Locating the source of culpable corporate mens rea is a critical first step to devising sanctions that will cure corporate fault and prevent future harm. Insights from systems of intentionality should guide that inquiry.[88] There is all the difference in the world between isolated misconduct that traces to a single rogue employee and sustained patterns of misconduct that issue from corporate systems that are 'objectively apt to produce' harm.[89] Each requires its own treatment approach. Simply firing rogue employees may sometimes be sufficient. However, more embedded mechanisms will require courts, regulators and any appointed monitors to step in for a more extended programme of reform.[90]

[87] Diamantis (n 46) (offering a virtue ethical approach to corporate punishment that focuses exclusively on reform).

[88] See Faugno, ch 8 of this volume.

[89] Bant and Paterson, 'Systems of Misconduct' (n 32) 77. This may, in part, explain why the US Organizational Sentencing Guidelines tell sentencing judges to assess internal factors like how pervasive misconduct was within the corporation or whether the corporation had an effective compliance programme, considerations that are absent from US law on liability: *2016 US Sentencing Guidelines Manual*, ch 8.

[90] ME Diamantis, 'Monitorships: An Academic Perspective' in AS Barkow, N Barofsky and TJ Perrelli (eds), *Global Investigations Review – Guide to Monitorships* (London, Law Business Research Ltd, 2019) 91.

PART III

Corporate States of Mind

11

Modelling Corporate States of Mind through Systems Intentionality

ELISE BANT*

I. Introduction

Lord Justice Bowen famously observed that 'the state of a man's mind is as much a fact as the state of his digestion'.[1] That said, it is no easy task to identify and characterise, let alone prove,[2] the mental states of a natural person relevant for the purposes of the law. For centuries, courts have grappled with, and wavered over, the nature of core concepts such as intention, knowledge and mistake that underpin a vast swathe of statutory and general law rules. The relationship between these mental states and normative standards, such as dishonesty, unconscionability and recklessness, has been correspondingly opaque and unstable. The law's requirements for state of mind elements often differ not merely between national and state jurisdictions, but between civil and criminal law, and between general law and statutory doctrines within the one jurisdiction. They are also prone to remarkable shifts over time.

The challenge to understand defendants' states of mind for the purposes of satisfying these difficult and volatile elements becomes exponentially greater when dealing with modern, devolved and complex corporate wrongdoers to which the same elements apply.[3] A corporation has no natural mind. The traditional strategy of identifying the

* This chapter builds on joint research with Professor Jeannie Marie Paterson into the regulation of misleading and unconscionable conduct, pursuant to Australian Research Council Discovery Projects DP180100932 and DP140100767. It also presents proposals developed pursuant to my ARC-supported Future Fellowship project FT190100475, which aims to examine and model reforms of the laws that currently inhibit corporate responsibility for serious misconduct. My sincere thanks to all participants for their very helpful comments and criticisms, and to Penny Crofts, Mihailis Diamantis and, of course, Jeannie Marie Paterson for their generous, ongoing discussions. All responsibility for errors rests with me.

[1] *Edgington v Fitzmaurice* (1885) 29 Ch D 459 (CA) 483 (Bowen LJ); *Generics (UK) v Warner-Lambert Company LLC* [2018] UKSC 56, [2018] RPC 21, [171] (Lord Briggs): 'a person's intention is as much a matter of fact as the state of his digestion, and this is true of corporate persons as much as of individuals'.

[2] The question of how to prove 'systems, policies and practices', relevant to the model of Systems Intentionality, is the subject of Bant, ch 9 of this volume.

[3] I do not attempt to address here more radical options of adopting distinctively corporate liability regimes, such as strict liability strategies through outcome- or performance-based, or 'failure to prevent' approaches: see Clough, ch 18 of this volume; Willis, ch 19 of this volume. However, I do note the Australian experience

corporate mind with those of its directors, or with other employees or agents through more expansive attribution rules, remains stubbornly anchored to identification of the corporate mind with specific individuals.[4] How, then, is a court to ascertain the complex mental states necessary to satisfy elements of doctrines such as deceit or unconscionable dealing, for example when addressing a corporation comprising potentially many thousands of employees, fragmenting tasks and knowledge across dozens of semi-autonomous departments, and making increasing use of automated processes? The problem further magnifies if one accepts, as I do, the realist view that corporations are more than the sum of their human, corporate and automated parts.[5] If we are to work with the law and corporations as we find them, we need a model that permits assessments of the spectrum of required mental elements demanded across common law, equity and statute, in terms of corporations' distinctively organisational blameworthiness.

This chapter seeks to address that challenge, using the model of Systems Intentionality introduced in chapter 9.[6] It does so, first, by identifying 'test' definitions of key mental states commonly demanded by the law, including as elements of normative standards; and, second, by modelling how Systems Intentionality may be used to identify those mental elements existing in a corporation. To this end, the chapter proceeds by settling plausible 'test' definitions of general and specific intention, knowledge and mistake, and marking out their potential relationship to mixed conceptions of recklessness, dishonesty and unconscionability. As other contributors to this collection well demonstrate, these are often highly contested and evolving concepts, the meanings of which have varied, and no doubt will continue to vary, within and between jurisdictions, legal areas and across time.[7] This chapter will not seek to resolve these debates: it stays strictly agnostic as to the 'best' meanings of these ideas. However, the discussion is reasonably detailed, in order to make clear the nature and boundaries of the test definitions, including from alternative definitions, as well as from each other. The chapter then seeks

that state-of-mind elements remain stubbornly persistent, even in strict liability contexts, for example through remedial, defensive and sentencing considerations: see, eg, E Bant, 'Culpable Corporate Minds' (2021) 48 *University of Western Australia Law Review* 352, 353–54, 356–58; JM Paterson and E Bant, 'Intuitive Synthesis and Fidelity to Purpose? Judicial Interpretation of the Discretionary Power to Award Civil Penalties under the Australian Consumer Law' in P Vines and MS Donald (eds), *Statutory Interpretation in Private Law* (Sydney, Federation Press, 2019) 154. See also Crofts, ch 3 of this volume.

[4] Explored in Leow, ch 6 of this volume. Compare, eg, *Lennard's Carrying Co v Asiatic Petroleum Co Ltd* [1915] AC 705 (HL), 713 (Viscount Haldane LC); *Meridian Global Funds Management Asia Ltd v The Securities Commission Co* [1995] UKPC 26, [1995] 2 AC 500 (*Meridian*); Australian Law Reform Commission, *Corporate Criminal Responsibility* (Report No 136, 2020) [6.153], [6.159], discussing the iterations of the Australian 'TPA models', which combine an expansive vicarious liability approach to conduct with a state-of-mind component that deems the intention of employees and agents acting for the company to be that of the company.

[5] See Crofts, ch 3 of this volume for a powerful and rigorous defence of this position.

[6] This will, it is hoped, go some way to addressing the Law Commission's concerns: see Law Commission of England and Wales, *Corporate Criminal Liability* (Options Paper, 2022) [6.42]–[6.46]. See also Bant, 'Culpable Corporate Minds' (n 3); E Bant and JM Paterson, 'Systems of Misconduct: Corporate Culpability and Statutory Unconscionability' (2021) 15 *Journal of Equity* 63; E Bant, 'Catching the Corporate Conscience: A New Model of "Systems Intentionality"' (2022) *Lloyds Maritime and Commercial Law Quarterly* 467; E Bant, 'Reforming the Laws of Corporate Attribution: "Systems Intentionality" Draft Statutory Provision' (2022) 39 *Company and Securities Law Journal* 259.

[7] Gans, ch 13 of this volume in particular; but see also Carroll, ch 15 of this volume and Bryan, ch 14 of this volume.

to show how Systems Intentionality may apply to meet these test definitions. This is done in order to illustrate the operation of the model and its capacity to respond to the spectrum of legal, equitable and statutory mental states and related normative standards, which may (as noted) be prone to change. Even should wholly different definitions apply, or different mental states be in issue, my aim is that this modelling should provide a solid foundation for understanding the application of Systems Intentionality to the doctrinal requirements of the law, as, when and where they are found.

II. A Spectrum of Mental States and Related Norms of Conduct

A. Intention (and Mistake, as 'Vitiated' Intention)

It is generally accepted that the concept of 'intention' is core to many forms of liability, and conceptions of culpability, across the full ambit of the law. In the words of John Finnis:

> Intention is a tough, sophisticated, and serviceable concept, well worthy of its central role in moral and legal assessment, because it picks out the central realities of deliberation and choice: the linking of means and ends in a plan or proposal for action adopted by choice in preference to alternative proposals (including to do nothing).[8]

That being (beautifully) said, as a matter of legal doctrine, there is no settled meaning of intention, which will depend on jurisdiction and context, including the terms of any statutory provision.[9] Nonetheless, a helpful starting point for unpacking this concept for current, pragmatic purposes is the sense that 'intention' involves a 'directing of the mind, having a purpose or design'.[10] A classic, lay definition is that given in by Connelly J in *R v Willmot (No 2)*: '[t]he ordinary and natural meaning of the word "intends" is to mean, to have in mind'.[11] More fulsomely, Peter A French has explained that 'saying "someone did *y* intentionally" is to describe an event as the upshot of that person's having had a reason for doing *y* which was the cause of his or her doing it'.[12] Intention in this sense connotes purpose that goes beyond mere knowledge of the nature of the act

[8] J Finnis, 'Intention in Tort Law' in J Finnis, *Intention and Identity: Collected Essays*, vol II (Oxford, Oxford University Press, 2011) 198, 198.

[9] See, eg, *SZTAL v Minister for Immigration and Border Protection* [2017] HCA 34, (2017) 262 CLR 362, 369 [18] (Kiefel CJ, Nettle and Gordon JJ), 389–92, [84]–[89] (Edelman J).

[10] ibid 367, 368–69 [9], [15] (Kiefel CJ, Nettle and Gordon JJ) endorsing *Zaburoni v The Queen* [2016] HCA 12, (2016) 256 CLR 482, 489 [11] (Kiefel, Bell and Keane JJ) citing *R v Reid* [2007] 1 Qd R 64, (2006) 162 A Crim R 377, 93 [93] (Chesterman J). See also *Zaburoni* 501 [55] (Gageler J). See also *SZTAL* (n 9) 397 [101] (Edelman J).

[11] *R v Willmot (No 2)* [1985] 2 Qd R 413, (1985) 18 A Crim R 42, 418 (Connolly J), endorsed in *Zaburoni* (n 10) 488 [8] (Kiefel, Bell and Keane JJ) and *SZTAL* (n 9) 367 [9] (Kiefel CJ, Nettle and Gordon JJ), 397 [101] (Edelman J).

[12] PA French, *Collective and Corporate Responsibility* (New York, Columbia University Press, 1984) 40. See also V Tadros, 'The Significance of Intentions' in V Tadros, *Criminal Responsibility* (Oxford, Oxford University Press, 2007) 212, 216: 'Acting intentionally is acting for a reason.'

and its likely consequence. I return to the relationship between intention in this sense and conceptions of knowledge and foresight in section II.B.

We might usefully note here that French's approach provides a useful way of understanding ideas of mistake that may operate to vitiate or impair a person's intention.[13] Although courts have avoided attempting a comprehensive definition of mistake,[14] one conception is that 'a mistake is made when a person's decision is based on incorrect data'.[15] That is, adapting French's account, one of the 'reasons' for action is vitiated or impaired because it does not accord with reality. Courts have also considered that mistakes may include 'sheer ignorance' of a fact or matter relevant to the transaction. Here, in order for 'ignorance' to count, the fact or matter must relate to one of the 'reasons' for the decision. It is not enough that, had the party been aware of the existence of that fact or matter, they would (or might or could) have incorporated that fact or matter as a reason for decision.[16]

I have here adopted a definition of mistake that is connected to decision making, and hence to conduct, through causation.[17] However, it remains possible to have a passive mistake, in which the party's subjective belief on some fact or matter does not accord with reality. It may be that passive mistakes will more rarely be relevant to a defendant's culpability.[18]

Returning to my conception of intention, we have seen that on one approach, intention involves a choice directed towards some end. This is sometimes expressed in terms of desire. However, here we need to be careful. Some scholars have argued that it is possible to intend something without desiring it (or, perhaps more accurately, without finding it desirable).[19] Justice Edelman has considered that, for that reason, we need to distinguish between volitional desire (necessary for intention) and emotional desire: 'A person can desire a consequence in the sense of volitionally choosing it. Or a person can desire a consequence in the sense of emotionally wanting it.'[20] On balance, it seems plausible that the law need not require a person to desire something in an emotional sense in order to intend it in a legal sense. I proceed here on that basis.

[13] The following discussion adopts and builds on that in J Edelman and E Bant, *Unjust Enrichment* (Oxford, Hart Publishing, 2016) ch 8.

[14] *Barrow v Isaacs & Son* [1891] 1 QB 417 (CA) 425 (*Barrow*) (Kay LJ): 'Very wisely, as I presume to think, the Courts have abstained from giving any general definition of what amounts to mistake.'

[15] Edelman and Bant (n 13) 172. See also *Great Peace Shipping Ltd v Tsavliris Salvage (International) Ltd* [2002] EWCA Civ 1407, [2003] QB 679, 696 [28] (Lord Phillips MR): 'an erroneous belief'; *Roles v Pascall & Sons* [1911] 1 KB 982 (CA) 987 (Buckley LJ): '[a] mistake exists when a person erroneously thinks that one state of facts exists when, in reality, another state of facts exists'; *Barrow* (n 14) 420 (Lord Esher MR): '[thinking] that one thing was in existence, whereas something else was in existence'; *Westpac Banking Corporation v Hilliard* [2006] VSC 470, [211] (Hansen J): 'a positive belief in the existence of something which does not exist but also may include sheer ignorance of something relevant to the transaction in hand', approved on appeal in *Hilliard v Westpac Banking Corporation* [2009] VSCA 211, (2009) 25 VR 139, 155 [68] (Maxwell P, Dodds-Streeton JA and Osborn AJA).

[16] *Pitt v Holt* [2013] UKSC 26, [2013] 2 AC 108, [105]–[108], [114] (Lord Walker, delivering the judgment of the Court), excluding 'mere causative ignorance' from actionable mistake.

[17] On the relevant test of causation for decision making, see E Bant and JM Paterson, 'Statutory Causation in Cases of Misleading Conduct: Lessons from and for the Common Law' (2017) 24 *Torts Law Journal* 1; Edelman and Bant (n 13) 190–94.

[18] For a potential example, see the discussion in section II.B regarding reckless inadvertence.

[19] M Moore, *Placing Blame* (Oxford, Oxford University Press, 1997) 451.

[20] *SZTAL* (n 9) 394–95 [97] (Edelman J), citing Finnis (n 8) 205.

In discussing intention in tort law, Peter Cane draws a further, helpful distinction for the current discussion, between intention in relation to conduct and intention in relation to outcome or consequences:

> [T]he most widely accepted account of the 'core' of the concept of intention in relation to conduct is based on the idea of choice; and in relation to consequences, on the concepts of aim, purpose, and objective.[21]

Similarly, I find it helpful to distinguish between the situation where a person has a 'general' intention to engage in conduct and a 'specific' intention to achieve some outcome through that conduct. Thus in the criminal law context, the High Court of Australia explained in *He Kaw Teh v The Queen*, 'General or basic intent relates to the doing of the act involved in an offence; special or specific intent relates to the results caused by the act done.'[22] A similarly honed conception of specific intention can be seen in *Zaburoni v The Queen*,[23] endorsed by the plurality in *SZTAL v Minister for Immigration and Border Protection*: 'a person intends a result when they have the result in question as their purpose.'[24]

B. Recklessness

Cane distinguishes these forms of general and specific intention from recklessness, which 'in its core sense is commonly conceptualized in terms of a risk that certain consequences will result from conduct, and indifference to that risk.'[25] While (as discussed immediately below) courts and commentators have vacillated over both the meaning of recklessness and its relationship to intention, it seems that recklessness can sensibly be understood as a complex, multifaceted concept that draws together mental states and normative judgements. Drawing on the earlier distinctions concerning intention, a plausible conception of recklessness, for current forensic purposes, combines:

(a) a general intention to engage in some conduct;
(b) knowledge or 'foresight' of the outcome that the conduct is apt to produce (often described as a 'risk' of harm); and
(c) the application of a normative standard that a decision to proceed with the conduct in light of that known risk is unreasonable.

On the first element, as Cane says:

> While the frame of mind of the intentional agent is different from that of the reckless agent in relation to the consequences of their conduct, their frame of mind in relation to the conduct

[21] P Cane, 'Mens Rea in Tort Law' (2000) 20 *Oxford Journal of Legal Studies* 533, 534. See also E Farnsworth, 'Alleviating Mistakes' (Oxford, Oxford University Press, 2004) 87, distinguishing between '"action-intent" – the intent to take the action that has resulted in harm to another person and … "consequence-intent" – the intent not merely to take the action that has resulted in the harm to another person but the intent to produce that harm as a consequence'.

[22] *He Kaw Teh v The Queen* [1985] HCA 43, (1985) 157 CLR 523, 569 (Brennan J).

[23] *Zaburoni* (n 10).

[24] *SZTAL* (n 9) 372 [26] (Kiefel CJ, Nettle and Gordon JJ); see also ibid 397 [101] (Edelman J).

[25] Cane (n 21) 535.

> itself is the same – both set out to engage in the conduct, the reckless person regardless of the risk of the consequence, and the intentional person in order to produce that consequence.[26]

Perhaps due in part to this commonality in terms of general intention, in some jurisdictions, during some periods, for some purposes, recklessness has been equated with specific intention.[27] This has seemed particularly attractive where the intended course of conduct is patently likely, or certain, to produce the result that in fact occurred. Thus, Gageler J, dissenting in *SZTAL*, considered that for the purposes of the statutory provision there under consideration, 'intention' encompasses both

> where the perpetrator means to engage in conduct meaning to bring about the result adverse to the victim; and where the perpetrator means to engage in conduct aware that the result adverse to the victim will occur in the ordinary course of events.[28]

Consistently, conceptions of recklessness have sometimes been termed 'oblique intention', on the basis that a person 'must be taken' to intend the certain or highly probable consequences of his actions.[29] An example of this approach is found in section 5.2(3) of the Criminal Code Act 1995 (Cth) (Criminal Code) (emphasis added):

> **5.2 Intention**
>
> (1) A person has intention with respect to conduct if he or she means to engage in that conduct.
>
> (2) A person has intention with respect to a circumstance if he or she believes that it exists or will exist.
>
> (3) A person has intention with respect to a result if he or she means to bring it about *or is aware that it will occur in the ordinary course of events.*

Again, I am neutral as to the 'best' meaning of recklessness. My purpose is to identify a test conception appropriate for modelling the operation of Systems Intentionality. However, in Australia at least, the current trend of judicial reasoning is to eschew 'oblique intention' as a general, 'natural' or ordinary meaning of specific intention, on the grounds that it entails a false equivalence.[30] Rather, the fact that a plaintiff knows or predicts that, in the ordinary course of events, harm will result from her (intended) actions will provide evidence from which specific intention to achieve the result may be inferred.[31] The more certain she is about the result, the stronger the inference. However, on current authority, foresight is not considered the same as specific intention. Thus, Edelman J

[26] ibid.

[27] *Vallance v The Queen* [1961] HCA 42, (1961) 108 CLR 56, 59 (Dixon CJ) citing C Kenny, *Outlines of Criminal Law* (Cambridge, Cambridge University Press, 1902) 148. See also *Peters v The Queen* [1998] HCA 7, (1998) 192 CLR 493, 522 [68] (McHugh J); M Briggs, 'Criminal Intention Revisited' (2013) *New Zealand Law Journal* 153, discussing *Police v K CA* [2011] NZCA 533 (Stevens, Roland Young and Andrews JJ).

[28] *SZTAL* (n 9) 378 [47] (Gageler J).

[29] G Williams, 'Oblique Intention' (1987) 46 *Cambridge Law Journal* 417. Examples in the authorities include *Hyam v Director of Public Prosecutions* [1975] AC 55 (HL) (Lords Hailsham, Diplock, Cross and Kilbrandon, Viscount Dilhorne); *Peters* (n 27) (McHugh J).

[30] eg A Kenny, 'Intention and Purpose' (1966) 63 *Journal of Philosophy* 642, critically analysing the 'presumption in law that a man intends the natural consequences of his acts'; Finnis (n 8) 212; *SZTAL* (n 9) 382 [61]–[62], 392–98 [93]–[103] (Edelman J).

[31] *SZTAL* (n 9) 372 [26]–[27] (Kiefel CJ, Nettle and Gordon JJ); *R v Moloney* [1985] AC 905 (HL) (Lords Hailsham, Fraser, Edmund-Davies, Keith and Bridge); *R v Hancock; R v Shankland* [1986] AC 455 (HL) (Lords Scarman, Keith, Roskill, Brightman and Griffiths).

in *SZTAL*, agreeing with the majority plurality,[32] stated that 'to prove an intention to produce a particular result, by the ordinary meaning of intention, it is necessary to establish that the accused meant to produce that result by his or her conduct'.[33] 'Oblique intention' by contrast, 'is not intention at all'.[34] Engaging in conduct with foresight of consequence is not the same as having those consequences in mind as the purpose or aim of the conduct, and hence it is better labelled in terms of recklessness.[35]

Harking back to the idea of intention as acting for a reason, another way of putting this (as Victor Tadros has done) is to observe that 'an agent may perform an action, knowing that it will have a certain consequence, but that consequence does not provide [a] reason for the action'.[36]

Consistently with this analysis, Edelman J has recently suggested that a principled definition of recklessness would be: (i) that the accused person foresaw the possibility of harm but proceeded nonetheless to take that risk; and (ii) that the risk was unreasonable in the circumstances known to the accused.[37] Similarly, the Criminal Law Reform Committee of the Law Commission of England and Wales proposed that recklessness arose where: (i) the accused foresaw that their act might cause the particular result; and (ii) the risk of causing that result which they knew they were taking was, on an objective assessment, an unreasonable risk to take in the circumstances known to the accused.[38]

Similarly, the current definition of recklessness in section 5.4 of the Criminal Code states:

> (1) A person is reckless with respect to a circumstance if:
> (a) he or she is aware of a substantial risk that the circumstance exists or will exist; and
> (b) having regard to the circumstances known to him or her, it is unjustifiable to take the risk.

[32] *SZTAL* (n 9) 372 [27] (Kiefel CJ, Nettle and Gordon JJ), citing *Zaburoni* (n 10) 490 [14]–[15] (Kiefel, Bell and Keane JJ).

[33] *SZTAL* (n 9) 397 [101] (Edelman J).

[34] ibid 383–84 [67], 397–98 [103] (Edelman J).

[35] ibid 383–84 [67] (Edelman J).

[36] Tadros (n 12) 217. Notwithstanding this distinction, Tadros considered that where a person intentionally acts, knowing that it is virtually certain that the act will result in another's death, this should satisfy murder, albeit as an 'alternative' to intention: see ibid 217, 230. This echoes the idea of a spectrum of culpability in relation to recklessness.

[37] *Director of Public Prosecutions Reference No 1 of 2019* [2021] HCA 26, (2021) 96 ALJR 741, 757–59 [64], [69] (Edelman J), drawing on *Aubrey v The Queen* [2017] HCA 18, (2017) 260 CLR 305, 327–29 [43]–[47], [49] (Kiefel CJ, Keane, Nettle and Edelman JJ). See also *R v G* [2003] UKHL 50, [2004] 1 AC 1034 (Lords Bingham, Browne-Wilkinson, Steyn, Hutton and Rodger). The reference before the High Court concerned whether the accused needed to foresee the probability, rather than possibility, of the harm to the victim: thus in *R v Campbell* [1997] 2 VR 585 (VSCA) (Hayne JA and Crockett AJA, Phillips CJ dissenting), the Victorian Supreme Court of Appeal (following *R v Nuri* [1990] VR 641 (VicCCA) 643 (Young CJ, Crockett and Nathan JJ)) had adopted a construction of the element of recklessness for the offence of recklessly causing serious injury under s 17 of the Crimes Act 1914 (Cth) that an accused must have foresight of the *probability and not the possibility* of relevant consequences. In dissent, Kiefel CJ, Keane and Gleeson JJ considered that the reason for the higher test of 'probability' used in definitions of recklessness in the case of common law murder 'is the near moral equivalence of intention to kill or cause grievous bodily harm and the foresight of the probability of death or grievous bodily harm'. Their Honours considered it should be limited to that context. The majority, while not disagreeing with that view, considered that subsequent legislative reforms to s 17 had proceeded on the basis of the 'probability' test, precluding use of the 'possibility' formulation. Interestingly, Edelman J considered express recognition of the element of reasonableness would diminish the difference between the two formulations, a view that seems plausible.

[38] Criminal Law Revision Committee, *Fourteenth Report: Offences against the Person* (1980) 5 [12].

(2) A person is reckless with respect to a result if:
  (a) he or she is aware of a substantial risk that the result will occur; and
  (b) having regard to the circumstances known to him or her, it is unjustifiable to take the risk.

(3) The question whether taking a risk is unjustifiable is one of fact.

(4) If recklessness is a fault element for a physical element of an offence, proof of intention, knowledge or recklessness will satisfy that fault element.

Here, the concept of 'unjustifiable' risk points to the application of an objective standard of reasonableness, assessed in light of the defendant's knowledge.[39]

I have thus far considered characteristics relevant to (a) and (c) of the 'test' concept of recklessness proposed at the commencement of this section. A further subtlety is what it is that the accused must have foreseen or known. Again, it seems that here a plausible distinction can be drawn between the conduct in which the accused must have acted intentionally and the result of that conduct. For the purposes of recklessness as postulated here, it will be the *result* that must have been the subject of knowledge or foresight, although again the specificity of the anticipated harm (ie to this victim, or to a category of persons to whom the victim belonged) may be the subject of further debate and will be influenced in reality by, among other matters, the terms of any applicable statutory provision on the prohibited conduct.[40] In some cases, for example, it is recklessness as to the state of mind of another person, at the time of engaging in intentional conduct, that is the gist of the prohibition.[41]

Finally, we may note that, at some points in time, and for some purposes,[42] it has been argued that recklessness should comprise, or more closely align to, a wholly objective standard of conduct. This is best exemplified in the line of House of Lords cases that considered that a person may be reckless both where that person takes a known risk and where she should have foreseen some clear risk but did not turn her mind to it.[43] The latter form relatively quickly, however, led to further, difficult enquiries, into, for example, whether the person's inadvertence to the obvious risk was itself culpable or not: here ideas of mistake, for example, might operate to mitigate her fault.[44] For present purposes, it suffices to note that states of mind appear almost inexorably to inform the assessment of the extent to which a person's conduct fails the required

[39] See, eg *R v G* (n 37).

[40] *Banditt v The Queen* [2005] HCA 80, (2005) 224 CLR 262 (Gummow, Hayne, Callinan, Heydon JJ).

[41] *Castle v R* [2016] NSWCCA 148, (2016) 92 NSWLR 17, 28 [34] (Bathurst CJ), addressing a kidnapping offence where the victim's lack of consent is a key element.

[42] See, eg, *Director of Public Prosecutions v Morgan* [1976] AC 182 (HL) 215 (Lord Hailsham), where Lord Hailsham described the mens rea for rape as 'the intention to commit that act, or the equivalent intention of having intercourse willy-nilly not caring whether the victim consents or no'; cf, eg, K Amirthalingam, 'Caldwell Reckless is Dead, Long Live Mens Rea's Fecklessness' (2004) 67 *Modern Law Review* 491, on the desirability of separating the fact of the mental state from its blameworthiness.

[43] *Director of Public Prosecutions v Smith* [1961] AC 290 (HL) (Viscount Kilmuir LC, Lords Goddard, Tucker, Denning and Parker); *Metropolitan Police Commissioner v Caldwell* [1982] AC 341 (HL) (Lords Wilberforce, Diplock, Edmund-Davies, Keith and Roskill); *R v Lawrence* [1982] AC 510 (HL) (Lords Hailsham, Diplock, Fraser, Roskill and Bridge).

[44] *R v Reid* [1992] 1 WLR 793 (HL) (Lords Keith, Roskill, Ackner, Goff and Browne-Wilkinson).

normative standard. We shall see that the same phenomenon is apparent in both unconscionability and dishonesty. This is not to say that it would not be impossible to untether these standards from state-of-mind requirements, as we shall see occurs in negligence. This might be a very useful approach for corporate culpability. However, the point is that courts are commonly concerned, where issues of serious culpability are in question, to ensure that the defendant's conduct warrants the censure and consequences that characterisation entails.[45] And it appears that here, a culpable mental state is regularly perceived as important. Given this, it is appropriate that our test definition reflects the state-of-mind components that pose a particular challenge for corporate regulation.

C. Knowledge

We have seen that some conceptions of recklessness have occupied an overlapping sphere of operation with those of intention. Likewise, it is apparent that recklessness has sometimes been equated with knowledge. The seminal classification of knowledge types for the purposes of civil liability is found in *Baden Delvaux & Lecuit v Société Générale pour Favoriser le Développement du Commerce et de l'Industrie en France SA*.[46] In that case, Peter Gibson J classified knowledge as falling into five categories:

(1) actual knowledge;
(2) wilfully shutting one's eyes to the obvious;
(3) wilfully and recklessly failing to undertake such inquiries as an honest and reasonable person would undertake;
(4) knowledge of circumstances that would indicate the facts to an honest and reasonable person; and
(5) knowledge of circumstances that would put an honest and reasonable person on inquiry.

Putting, again, to one side what is the 'best' understanding of knowledge and its graduations, we may observe that these categories rather freely combine mental states and standards.[47] Categories (1)–(3) are generally treated by courts as constituting 'actual' knowledge. Category (1) actual knowledge may be understood as a subjective belief concerning some fact or matter held by a person and which is objectively correct. In French's terms, it is a 'reason' concerning some fact or matter that accords with reality. Some philosophers have argued that this belief must be 'justified' to count as knowledge. This would, I think, bring in some sort of standard-based assessment, as we saw

[45] Bant, 'Culpable Corporate Minds' (n 3) 354.

[46] *Baden Delvaux & Lecuit v Société Générale pour Favoriser le Développement du Commerce et de l'Industrie en France SA* [1993] 1 WLR 509, [1992] 4 All ER 161, 235, 242–43 (Peter Gibson J) (*Baden Delvaux*), condemned as 'best forgotten' by Lord Nicholls in *Royal Brunei Airlines v Tan* [1995] 2 AC 378 (PC) 392 (Lord Nicholls), but alive and well in practice.

[47] *The Bell Group Ltd (in liq) v Westpac Banking Corporation (No 9)* [2008] WASC 239, (2008) 39 WAR 1, 135 [931]–[933] (Owen J); *Bank of Credit and Commerce International (Overseas) Ltd v Akindele* [2001] Ch 437, 454 (Nourse LJ); *Farah Constructions Pty Ltd v Say-Dee Pty Ltd* [2007] HCA 22, (2009) 230 CLR 89, 162–54 [171]–[178] (Gleeson CJ, Gummow, Callinan, Heydon and Crennan JJ) (*Farah*).

for recklessness, and seems an unnecessary complication for our current, taxonomical purposes.

A characterisation of category (2) as involving actual knowledge may be accepted on the basis of an inference, from a person's conduct and the broader context, that the person knows in substance the truth of the matter but tries to avoid explicit or detailed knowledge.[48] But in category (3), it is far more likely that the person does not actually know, but is acting in such a culpable way that she fails to attain the standard of honest and reasonable conduct required by law.[49] This is, in effect, an elision of knowledge with concepts of dishonesty and recklessness, echoing the elision discussed earlier in relation to the some-time treatment of recklessness as equivalent to intention. While we may be prepared in such circumstances to 'deem' the person to know the relevant fact or matter, we should be aware that this is not the same as actual knowledge, as defined for current forensic purposes.[50]

By contrast, categories (4) and (5) are broadly accepted not to constitute actual knowledge. Category (4) is commonly understood to involve 'constructive knowledge': as the label indicates, here we are clear that the person does not actually know of the relevant fact or matter but is being treated 'as if' she knew. This is, presumably, for policy reasons relevant to the particular doctrine, or because the defendant was under some obligation to make enquiries that would have revealed the true fact or matter. Finally, category (5) constitutes 'constructive notice', the most attenuated form of knowledge on the *Baden Delvaux* scale.[51] This is far removed from actual knowledge, being a circumstance where the party clearly did not know the relevant fact or matter. Here, the most that can be said was that the person was negligent in failing to enquire into known circumstances that, if she had undertaken enquiries, would have resulted in actual knowledge. We may now turn to consider rather more closely the nature of negligence.

D. Negligence

We have seen that ideas of recklessness have historically permeated understandings of both intention and knowledge, although recklessness retains distinctive, normative

[48] See, eg, *Stubbings v Jams 2 Pty Ltd* [2022] HCA 6 [27], [29]–[30], [47]–[49] (Kiefel CJ, Keane and Gleeson JJ), [145]–[146], [167]–[168] (Steward J). A similar conception appears to be entailed in 'blind-eye knowledge': see *Manifest Shipping Company Limited v Uni-Polaris Shipping Company Limited and Others* [2001] UKHL 1, [2001] 1 All ER 743, [2001] 2 WLR 170, 173 [3] (Lord Clyde): 'Blind-eye knowledge in my judgment requires a conscious reason for blinding the eye. There must be at least a suspicion of a truth about which you do not want to know and which you refuse to investigate.' See also the careful discussion ibid 178–79 [23]–[26] (Lord Hobhouse) discussing *The Eurysthenes* [1977] QB 49, 207–08 [112] (Lord Scott) ('Nelson at the battle of Copenhagen made a deliberate decision to place the telescope to his blind eye in order to avoid seeing what he knew he would see if he placed it to his good eye') and further at 209 [116] (Lord Scott). For further discussion of this concept and its relationship to dishonesty, see Australian Law Reform Commission, *Review of the Marine Insurance Act 1909* (Final Report, No 91, 30 May 2001) 169 [9.162]; *Group Seven Ltd v Notable Services LLP* [2019] EWCA Civ 614, [2020] Ch 129, [59]–[61], discussed in *Natwest Markets Plc v Bilta UK Ltd (in Liquidation)* [2021] EWCA Civ 680, [130]–[133] (Asplin, Andrews and Birss LJJ).

[49] *Stubbings* (n 48) [59], [80]–[81], [91]–[92], [94] (Gordon J), [160]–[163] (Steward J).

[50] R Bigwood, *Exploitative Contracts* (Oxford, Oxford University Press, 2003); T Duggan, 'Unconscientious Dealing' in P Parkinson (ed), *The Principles of Equity*, 2nd edn (Sydney, Lawbook Company, 2003) 127.

[51] Bigwood (n 50).

characteristics that mark it as a separate category of concept. In its role as a legal standard, the boundary between recklessness and negligence has been similarly unstable, in part, again, because of the unclear roles and influence of ideas of intention and knowledge.

Thus, for some jurisdictions, at some points in legal history, negligence has been understood as involving 'inadvertent' conduct that breaches a standard of care, while recklessness involves 'advertent' conduct. In the words of a leading Canadian text, 'the difference between recklessness and negligence is the difference between advertence and inadvertence: they are opposed and it is a logical fallacy to suggest that recklessness is a degree of negligence'.[52] However, even without tackling the meaning of 'advertent' (commonly understood to involve 'intentional, deliberate, conscious'[53] conduct), it cannot be thought that this distinction currently reflects the state of the law in Australia.[54] Employers' failures to provide safe systems of work may often be deliberate, in the sense of reflecting a choice to engage in conduct that 'cuts corners', in contravention of a legal standard of reasonable care, in order to save money or generate additional revenue. It would be very odd for that conduct to be incapable of regulation through the law of negligence, merely because it was conduct engaged in deliberately and conscious of the risk thereby posed to workers.

Indeed, in Australia at least, it seems quite possible and acceptable for negligence to be engaged where not only the conduct was intended but also the result. Thus, in *Gray v Motor Accident Commission*, exemplary damages were considered in theory available in a case of negligence, where the defendant had driven deliberately at the plaintiff and his companions, resulting in severe injury to the plaintiff.[55] Again, there seems little reason as a matter of principle or practicality to deny the operation of the law of negligence in this context. Negligence is a standard that may apply to conduct and, indeed, to states of mind. Consistently, a person may breach that same standard through conduct so as to attract liability in negligence without any mental state at all. Advertent or inadvertent conduct may both count as negligent: the main focus of the law is on whether the defendant's conduct breached the required standard.

It seems appropriate, on this account, to adopt test conceptions of both recklessness and negligence that involve breach of a legal standard. However, my test conception of recklessness engages an additional, required baseline form of mental state, in the sense that the defendant must have chosen to engage in the conduct. This, in turn, may be contrasted with the scenario where the defendant chooses to act so as to achieve some purpose through that conduct, which we have seen may constitute specific intention.

[52] Kenny (n 27), cited in *O'Grady v Sparling* (1960), 128 CCC 1, 13; 33 CR 293, 296 [1960] SCR 804 (Kerwin CJ, Taschereau, Locke, Cartwright, Fauteux, Abbott, Martland, Judson and Ritchie JJ), discussed in M Eisen, 'Recklessness' (1989) 31 *Criminal Law Quarterly* 347, 349.

[53] *Oxford English Dictionary*, 'advertent' at www.oed.com/.

[54] See P Handford, 'Intentional Negligence: A Contradiction in Terms?' (2010) 32 *Sydney Law Review* 29, discussing the clear trend in Australian law to this conclusion, the foundations of which are laid in English cases.

[55] *Gray v Motor Accidents Commission* [1998] HCA 70, (1998) 196 CLR 1, 9–10 [21]–[24] (Gleeson CJ, McHugh, Gummow and Hayne JJ).

E. Dishonesty

In the final two subsections of this section, I consider two leading norms that frequently engage with questions as to the defendant's state of mind.[56] As with the other concepts outlined so far, the nature of dishonesty has been contested and variable over time and jurisdictions, including whether it should, indeed, vary at all.[57] For a long time, dishonesty in criminal law (and for a period, for some purposes, in civil law) in both England and Australia largely followed the *Ghosh* test.[58] This adoption extended to prohibitions under statutory prohibitions such as section 1041G(2) of the Corporations Act 2001 (Cth) (Corporations Act). According to the dual test adopted in *Ghosh*, the acts in question must be dishonest according to current standards of ordinary decent people *and* the accused must have realised that they were dishonest by those standards. The second limb of the *Ghosh* test was rejected by the High Court of Australia in *Peters v The Queen*,[59] a position that it has repeatedly affirmed.[60] The test has also now been authoritatively abandoned in England as a wrong turn in the law.[61]

Similarly, courts applying civil law doctrines in which dishonesty forms a component have refused to adopt the second limb.[62] Thus the New South Wales Court of Appeal in *Hasler v Singtel Optus Pty Ltd* stated:

> Dishonesty amounts to a transgression of ordinary standards of honest behaviour. It is not necessary to say anything else by way of elaboration, save to confirm that it is not necessary to demonstrate that the person thought about what those standards were.[63]

[56] The following analysis replicates in substance that contained in Bant, 'Culpable Corporate Minds' (n 3) on dishonesty and Bant and Paterson, 'Systems of Misconduct' (n 6) on unconscionability; cf Gans, ch 13 of this volume.

[57] cf *Ivey v Genting Casinos (UK) Ltd* [2017] UKSC 67, [2018] AC 391, 411–12 [63] (Lord Hughes, with whom Lord Neuberger, Lady Hale, Lord Kerr and Lord Thomas agreed); D Lusty, 'The Meaning of Dishonesty in Australia' (2012) 36 *Criminal Law Journal* 282; J Gans, 'Submission to Legal and Constitutional Affairs Legislation Committee of the Commonwealth of Australia', *Inquiry into the Crimes Legislation Amendment (Combatting Corporate Crime) Bill 2019* (12 December 2019).

[58] Named after *R v Ghosh* [1982] QB 1053, [1982] 2 All ER 689 (Lords Layne CJ, Lloyd and Eastham JJ).

[59] *Peters* (n 27).

[60] *Spies v The Queen* [2000] HCA 43, (2000) 201 CLR 603, 630–31 [79]–[81] (Gaudron, McHugh, Gummow and Hayne JJ); *McCann v Switzerland Insurance Australia Ltd* [2000] HCA 56, (2000) 203 CLR 579, 596 [55], 608 [89] (Kirby J), 617–18 [120]–[121] (Hayne J); *Macleod v The Queen* [2003] HCA 24, (2003) 214 CLR 230, 241–43 [35]–[39], 245 [46] (Gleeson CJ, Gummow and Hayne JJ), 256 [99]–[101] (McHugh J), 264–65 [130] (Callinan J); *Polyaire Pty Ltd v K-Aire Pty Ltd* [2005] HCA 41, (2005) 221 CLR 287, 295–96 [17]–[18] (McHugh, Gummow, Hayne, Callinan and Heydon JJ); *Farah* (n 47) 126 [73]; *Marcolongo v Chen* [2011] HCA 3, (2011) 242 CLR 546, 559 [33] (French CJ, Gummow, Crennan and Bell JJ). This has been welcomed by commentators: see, eg, M Gleeson, 'Australia's Contribution to the Common Law' (2008) 82 *Australian Law Journal* 247, 249; Lusty (n 57).

[61] *Ivey* (n 57) 416–17 [74]–[75]; *R v Barton* [2020] EWCA Crim 575, [1] (Lord Burnett CJ). See also *Group Seven Ltd v Notable Services LLP* [2019] EWCA Civ 614, [2020] Ch 129 [52]–[58] (Henderson, Peter Jackson, Asplin LJJ).

[62] For a stark example in the context of the English doctrine of 'dishonest assistance', see *Royal Brunei Airlines* (n 46) 389 (Lord Nicholls), re-interpreted in *Twinsectra v Yardley* [2002] UKHL 12, [2002] 2 AC 164, 174 [35]–[36] (Lord Hutton), rectified in *Barlow Clowes International Ltd (in liq) v Eurotrust International Ltd* [2005] UKPC 37, [2006] 1 All ER 333, [2006] 1 WLR 1476, 1479–80 [10] (Lord Hoffmann), and then endorsed in *Ivey* (n 57) 416–17 [74]–[75], and reiterated in *Group Seven* (n 61) [58]. In Australia, see *Farah* (n 47) 126 [73].

[63] *Hasler v Singtel Optus Pty Ltd* [2014] NSWCA 266, (2014) 87 NSWLR 609, 636 [124] (Leeming JA, Barrett and Gleeson JJA concurring).

Likewise in *Ancient Order of Foresters in Victoria Friendly Society Limited v Lifeplan Australia Friendly Society Limited*, Kiefel CJ, Keane and Edelman JJ stated (in the context of an equitable claim of knowing assistance in a breach of fiduciary duty):

> [P]articipation in a dishonest and fraudulent breach of fiduciary duty includes knowingly assisting the fiduciary in the execution of a 'dishonest and fraudulent design' on the part of the fiduciary to engage in the conduct that is in breach of fiduciary duty. The requisite element of dishonesty and fraud on the part of the fiduciary is met where the conduct which constitutes the breach transgresses ordinary standards of honest behaviour [citing *Hasler*].[64]

This shift to a more objective standpoint is reflected in the recent amendment to the definition of 'dishonest' in section 9 of the Corporations Act, by which 'dishonest means dishonest according to the standards of ordinary people'.

This trend of reasoning might suggest that dishonesty is a wholly objective standard of conduct, similar to the Australian overarching norm against 'misleading conduct'.[65] It would be entirely possible to take that approach, particular when dealing with corporate actors, so as to obviate inquiry for liability purposes into the corporate state of mind.[66] However, on the existing state of authorities, it remains necessary to assess objectively the quality of the defendant's conduct *in light of the defendant's* actual intention and knowledge.[67] For example, the conduct in question must have been intentional rather than accidental or inadvertent. As the High Court of Australia explained in *Peters*, 'ordinary, honest persons determine whether a person's act is dishonest by reference to that person's knowledge or belief as to some fact relevant to the act in question or the intention with which the act was done'.[68] I accordingly adopt this approach for my modelling purposes.

F. Unconscionability

Finally, I consider the ubiquitous and powerful Australian conceptions of unconscionability. In its modern, Australian form, the equitable doctrine of unconscionable dealing has two main elements. First, the plaintiff must be subject to some 'special' disadvantage that 'must seriously affect their ability to make a judgment about their own interests'.[69]

[64] *Ancient Order of Foresters in Victoria Friendly Society Limited v Lifeplan Australia Friendly Society Limited* [2018] HCA 43, (2018) 265 CLR 1, 31 [71] (Gageler J).

[65] Competition and Consumer Act 2010 (Cth), sch 2 (ACL), s 18. See also *Parkdale Custom Built Furniture Pty Ltd v Puxu Pty Ltd* [1982] HCA 44, (1982) 149 CLR 191, 197 (Gibbs CJ).

[66] E Bant, 'Submission No 21 to Australian Law Reform Commission', *Corporate Criminal Responsibility* (28 January 2020).

[67] *Ivey* (n 57) 416–17 [74]; *Barton* (n 61) [84], [107]–[108]; *Group Seven* (n 61). This notably contradicts the recent statement in *Australian Securities and Investments Commission v MLC Nominees Pty Ltd* [2020] FCA 1306, (2020) ACSR 266, 276 [51] (Yates J) that dishonesty 'does not rely on any proof or finding of intent' and is wholly determined by reference to objective circumstances.

[68] *Peters* (n 27) 503 [15] (Toohey and Gummow JJ).

[69] *Australian Securities and Investments Commission v Kobelt* [2019] HCA 18, (2019) 267 CLR 1, 95–96 [282] (Edelman J).

Second, the defendant must exploit or take advantage of that special disadvantage.[70] The defendant's state of knowledge is key to the second element of advantage taking:

> It is the defendant's knowledge of the special disadvantage of the plaintiff and, in the face of this knowledge, the defendant's failure to take any steps to protect the interests of the plaintiff, which taints the conscience of the defendant so as to justify the court setting aside the transaction.[71]

We can therefore see that, like dishonesty, unconscionability combines normative and state-of-mind inquiries. And as we have also seen, the concept of 'knowledge' itself spans a spectrum of states. Consistently, courts assessing unconscionable dealing have variously emphasised and endorsed the spectrum of possibilities, from actual knowledge (here including wilful ignorance)[72] to defendant awareness of 'facts that would raise that possibility in the mind of any reasonable person'.[73] In *Kakavas v Crown Melbourne Limited*, the High Court of Australia introduced what appeared to be an additional requirement for the equitable doctrine that the defendant be shown to have acted with a 'predatory state of mind', at least in 'an arm's length commercial transaction'.[74] While the status of this requirement is highly uncertain,[75] if it exists, it may point to a specific intention on the part of the defendant to harm the victim.[76]

Given its ubiquity, a brief mention of the statutory prohibition on unconscionable conduct is warranted, to underscore the similar combination of normative standard and state-of-mind inquiry.[77] In its core form,[78] this prohibits conduct that is 'in all the circumstances' unconscionable, and provides a set of interpretive principles to guide

[70] ibid. See also *Australian Competition & Consumer Commission v Radio Rentals Ltd* [2005] FCA 1133, (2005) 146 FCR 292, 297–98 [19] (Finn J) (*Radio Rentals*).

[71] Bant and Paterson, 'Systems of Misconduct' (n 6) 66; Bigwood (n 50) 249; Duggan (n 50) 146–48. cf the leading Canadian authority of *Uber Technologies Inc v Heller*, 2020 SCC 16, [85] (Abella and Rowe JJ), the majority reasoning of which has been criticised (including by the minority judges: see ibid [164]–[167] (Brown J) [287]–[288] (Côté J) for abandoning a knowledge requirement: see also C Hunt, 'Unconscionability in the Supreme Court of Canada: *Uber Technologies Inc v Heller*' (2021) 80 *Cambridge Law Journal* 25. This aspect of the Court's reasoning, however, does avoid the difficult questions addressed here, an important matter given the parties to the disputed services 'contract of adhesion' were the driver and Uber subsidiaries incorporated in the Netherlands with offices in Amsterdam. It may be, however, that even on those facts, on the proposed Systems Intentionality approach discussed in section III, the necessary state of mind would be disclosed by the Uber business model and standard terms. See also Powles, ch 5 of this volume and Bant, ch 1 of this volume, section II.C.

[72] *Kakavas v Crown Melbourne Limited* [2013] HCA 25, (2015) 250 CLR 392, 438–39 [156]–[157] (French CJ, Hayne, Crennan, Kiefel, Bell, Gageler and Keane JJ).

[73] *Commercial Bank of Australia v Amadio* [1983] HCA 14, (1983) 151 CLR 447, 467 (Mason J); cf *Amadio* (n 73) 474 (Deane J); *Thorne v Kennedy* [2017] HCA 49, (2017) 263 CLR 85, 103 [38] (Kiefel CJ, Bell, Gageler, Keane and Edelman JJ).

[74] *Kakavas* (n 72) 439–40 [161] (French CJ, Hayne, Crennan, Kiefel, Bell, Gageler and Keane JJ).

[75] See, eg, *Thorne* (n 73); *Kobelt* (n 69) 17–18 [15] (Kiefel CJ and Bell J), 48 [118] (Keane J), 95–96 [282] (Edelman J); *Kobelt* (n 69) 36 [81] (Gageler J) 'exploitation' is sufficient, 84–85 [258] (Nettle and Gordon JJ) affirming passive exploitation; and now *Nitopi v Nitopi* [2022] NSWCA 162, discussing the trend of High Court authority. See also JM Paterson, E Bant and M Clare, 'Doctrine, policy, culture and choice in assessing unconscionable conduct under statute: *ASIC v Kobelt*' (2019) 13 *Journal of Equity* 81, 96.

[76] *Bodapati v Westpac Banking Corporation* [2015] QCA 7 [75] (Peter Lyons J, Holmes and Gotterson JJA agreeing).

[77] This discussion draws on Bant and Paterson, 'Systems of Misconduct' (n 6).

[78] See, eg, ACL (n 65) s 20; Australian Securities and Investments Commission Act 2001 (Cth) s 12CB (ASIC Act).

courts in assessing impugned conduct. Importantly for current purposes, these include that the statutory prohibition 'is capable of applying to a system of conduct or pattern of behaviour, whether or not a particular individual is identified as having been disadvantaged by the conduct or behaviour'.[79] The interpretive principles also include a list of factors to which the court may have regard in deciding if conduct is unconscionable.[80] These include whether the defendant acted 'in good faith', thereby potentially engaging an inquiry into the defendant's state of mind, as well as an objective standard. In assessing the statutory standard, courts commonly consider a range of further factors that relate to the defendant's mindset, including whether the impugned conduct was deliberate,[81] dishonest,[82] predatory,[83] or undertaken with sufficient knowledge of relevant disadvantage or vulnerability.[84]

Again, the precise degree of knowledge or kind of intention need not detain us here. What we can observe is that the concept combines a normative standard, which is assessed by reference to the defendant's state of mind. So, however framed, the state-of-mind component must be capable of being established with reference to corporate defendants.

III. Systems Intentionality and Mental States

A. States of Mind and Norms

i. A Recap of Systems Intentionality

We are now, finally, in a position to model the operation of Systems Intentionality in respect of each of the main test forms of mental state and associated standard. To recap, Systems Intentionality conceptualises the corporate state of mind as manifested in its systems of conduct, policies and practices. Chapter 9 explains that a 'system of conduct' is the internal method or organised connection of elements operating to produce the conduct or outcome. It is a plan of procedure, or coherent set of steps that combine in a coordinated way in order to achieve some aim (whether conduct or, additionally, result). A 'practice' involves patterns of behaviour that are habitual or customary in nature. A practice may cross over into a system, where the 'custom' or 'habit' has become an embedded process or method of conduct. Finally, corporate 'policies' partake of the same nature of systems, but can be understood as generally operating at a higher level of generality. These manifest overarching and high-level purposes, beliefs and values.

[79] ACL (n 65) s 21(4); ASIC Act (n 78) s 12CB(4).

[80] ACL (n 65) s 22; ASIC Act (n 78) s 12CC.

[81] See, eg, *Violet Home Loans Pty Ltd v Schmidt* [2013] VSCA 56, (2013) 44 VR 202, 221 [62] (Warren CJ, Cavanough and Ferguson AJJA).

[82] *Kobelt* (n 69) 30–31 [59]–[60] (Kiefel CJ and Bell J).

[83] ibid 47–49 [116]–[120] (Keane J).

[84] See, eg, *Tonto Home Loans Australia Pty Ltd v Tavares* [2011] NSWCA 389, (2011) 15 BPR 29, 699 (Campbell JA); *Colin R Price & Associates Pty Ltd v Four Oaks Pty Ltd* [2017] FCAFC 75, (2017) 251 FCR 404 (Rares, Murphy and Davies JJ).

They embody and reveal the overall corporate mindset, which is then instantiated or operationalised through corporate systems at more granular and event- or conduct-specific levels.

In what follows, it is important to recall that the inquiry is not a process of 'inference' of the corporation's mental state, in the same way as might apply to an individual: after all, the corporation lacks a natural mind. Rather, it involves *characterising* through an objective process of evaluation the systems of conduct through which the corporation pursues its purposes. The particular corporate state of mind will be hugely dependent, therefore, on the nature of the system, policy or practice the subject of the inquiry. However, the necessarily generalised discussion should help illustrate the kinds of features and inquiries that will bear on the existence of specified corporate mental states, by reference to the model of Systems Intentionality.

ii. General and Specific Intention

Turning, therefore, to its practical application to the specific, doctrinal mental states discussed earlier, we may commence with the central conception of 'intention'. Here, the distinction drawn earlier between intention as choice of *conduct* and intention in terms of chosen conduct *directed to certain results* is very helpful when thinking about Systems Intentionality. As to the first, some systems are rigid and direct actions to a predefined outcome: for example, pay $*x* on date *y*. Other systems may allow those acting within the system a degree of choice. But even here, the system may deploy a 'choice architecture': the design or features of the choices that are available.[85] These kinds of systems allow a degree of participant choice, but though default settings and other strategies nudge participants into making predetermined choices.

I suggest that both of these kinds of systems, and indeed the combinations in between, manifest general intention – the systems express a choice as to how to direct conduct. And a system can be said to do this even if a person performing some part of, or role within, the system can at times decide to act in a different way, or can decide to perform their allocated task for a variety of reasons.[86] The general capacity of the system to prompt a certain kind of choice should be sufficient for this purpose of finding intention. As French expresses it (albeit in terms of higher-level policies):

> When the corporate act is consistent with an instantiation or an implementation of established corporate policy, then it is proper to describe it as having been done for corporate reasons, as having been caused by a corporate desire coupled with a corporate belief and so, in other words, as corporate intentional.[87]

Where the system choices are coordinated so as to produce some specific outcome, or a likelihood of a specific outcome, I consider that the system manifests specific intentionality. The design of the system is necessarily assessed objectively, by reference to its elements and the outputs that are determined, or strongly influenced, by

[85] JM Paterson, E Bant and H Cooney, '*Australian Competition and Consumer Commission v Google*: Deterring Misleading Conduct in Digital Privacy Policies' (2021) 26 *Communications Law* 136.
[86] French (n 12) 44.
[87] ibid.

the coordination of those elements as part of the system.[88] Where the system is apt to (calculated to, designed to, of a nature to) produce some outcome, and does always or usually produce that outcome, it is specifically intended.

Here, the analysis may seem to elide specific intention and foresight, contrary to the previous analysis. We saw earlier that 'oblique' intention has been used both in general law and under statute to capture cases where a natural person's (generally intended) course of conduct is patently likely, or certain, to produce the result that in fact occurred. The High Court of Australia has explained that, in this case, the better analysis is that the course of conduct is evidence from which intention can be inferred. Adapting this approach for a corporate context, where only one (or effectively one) output can be, and was in fact, produced from the corporation's deliberate system of conduct, it is reasonable to characterise the system as geared, or organised, to produce that outcome. Another way of putting this, in terms more redolent of purpose, is to say that, in some cases, there can be no other explanation for the system of conduct than that it was designed to achieve a certain outcome.[89]

Where the system of conduct is apt to produce a range of outcomes, only one of which is harmful, is the harmful outcome also specifically intended? It seems plausible that a system of conduct may be designed (of a nature, calculated) to achieve a range of consequences or results. Again, to recall French, 'saying "someone did *y* intentionally" is to describe an event as the upshot of that person's having had a reason for doing *y* which was the cause of his or her doing it'.[90] Where the system of conduct was a reason for producing the harmful result, this suggests that corporate intention to produce that result may be present. This conclusion may be strengthened where the system was apt to produce the harmful outcome it produced, and the achievement of that outcome was consistent with corporate policy (eg a delinquent policy of 'profit over compliance').[91] The result may not be 'desired' but it is 'intended'. However, I consider (following Brent Fisse) that this conclusion will be fortified where the harmful result is repeated through the system of conduct and, notwithstanding having capacity to address the harm, no steps are taken to prevent that result.[92] It may also be the case that where a system is introduced that is intended to operate over a long period of time, and which necessarily entails repeated acts that will inevitably (if not always) result in significant harm, the omission of responsible audit and adjustment mechanisms may form part of the system 'as designed'. That is, the omission of adjustment mechanisms that are integral to

[88] To look for some human designer on whom to hang corporate intention for the system would be to replicate the problematic approach this model seeks to avoid: see further Paterson and Bant, ch 12 of this volume.

[89] Examples, in my view, include the branding marketing campaigns in the Nurofen and Voltaren cases, which could have no other purpose than to deceive customers into paying a premium for what is, in truth, a product no different from the generic, and much cheaper, product: see *Australian Competition and Consumer Commission v Reckitt Benckiser (Australia) Pty Ltd* [2016] FCAFC 181, (2016) 340 ALR 25 (Jagot, Yates and Bromwich JJ); *Australian Competition and Consumer Commission v GlaxoSmithKline Consumer Healthcare Australia Pty Ltd (No 2)* [2020] FCA 724 (Bromwich J).

[90] French (n 12) 40.

[91] Said to be the 'corporate culture' at play in the Crown Casino group of companies, in the Victorian Royal Commission: see State of Victoria, *Royal Commission into the Casino Operator and Licence* (The Report October 2021) vol 1, 142–54 [52]–[113].

[92] B Fisse, 'Reconstructing Corporate Criminal Law: Deterrence, Retribution, Fault, and Sanctions' (1983) 56 *Southern California Law Review* 1141, 1195–202.

avoiding identified harms signal that the corporation intends to implement a system in which some inevitable outcomes will not be prevented, as a matter of choice.

iii. Mistake

We have seen that, on the foregoing analysis, a system of conduct will always and necessarily manifest 'general' intentionality. That is the nature of a 'system' – it is inherently purposive. Given this, the starting position when addressing instantiated systems of conduct is that they are not manifesting 'accidental' or 'mistaken' conduct. If a system is operated according to its terms then it manifests, on the face of it, a clear choice of conduct. This runs contrary to the familiar exculpatory narrative of 'systems errors' often (at least in the Australian context) surrounding long-standing systems of misconduct (including, but not limited to, 'set and forget' automated systems).[93]

In some cases, corporations may claim that the outcome of a system of conduct (as opposed to the conduct itself) was 'unintended' or a 'mistake'. These sorts of claims must be treated with some caution. As for the law of unjust enrichment, a claimed 'misprediction' (that is, where a person is in possession of all the correct, current data but predicts incorrectly what will happen in the future) is not necessarily an exculpatory or vitiating factor: it may simply indicate that the party proceeded with conduct in the face of known risks about the outcome of that conduct.[94] This suggests that claimed 'mispredictions' should rarely operate as a get-out-of-jail-free card. In any event, I consider that ideas of 'misprediction' are better avoided in the context of Systems Intentionality, because these may encourage a search for subjective understandings of individual employees associated with the system, rather than to understand the inherent incidents of the system itself.

Finally, Paterson and I have suggested that there is an emerging and growing body of authority supporting the view that where a system is of a nature or patently likely (and in that limited sense objectively 'predictable') to produce certain conduct, or the conduct is recurrent, and no positive steps are taken to avoid harm resulting from the conduct, the system manifests recklessness.[95] Indeed, we saw in the previous section that, in some cases, a failure to correct repeated harm may, over time, support a finding of specific intention. The fact that a harm is not desired does not mean that it was not relevantly intended, or the result of corporate recklessness.

Importantly, it will not necessarily be exculpatory for the purposes of mistake for a company to demonstrate that, for example, directors were individually 'ignorant of' the existence and nature of some adopted and deployed corporate system. It is well established in the law of unjust enrichment in both Australia and England that, in order for ignorance to give rise to a mistake, it must have informed a positive but incorrect assumption on which a decision was based. It is not enough to claim that 'but for' being

[93] Commonwealth of Australia, *Royal Commission into Misconduct in the Banking, Superannuation and Financial Services Industry* (Final Report, February 2019) vol 1, 154–57, discussed in Bant, 'Culpable Corporate Minds' (n 3) 385–87; E Bant, 'Catching the Corporate Conscience' (2022) *Lloyd's Maritime and Commercial Law Quarterly* 467, 487–90.

[94] Edelman and Bant (n 13) 174–79.

[95] Bant and Paterson, 'Systems of Misconduct' (n 6).

ignorant of some fact or matter, a different course of action would have been adopted. Mere causative ignorance does not count.[96] Moreover, on the Systems Intentionality approach, we are wholly justified in rejecting directors' claims that their ignorance can shield the corporation from knowledge of what are, after all, *its own embedded practices, or longstanding systems of conduct*, often performed in accordance with a real-life corporate policy of profit over compliance.

What, then, does a genuine mistake look like from the perspective of Systems Intentionality? In essence, the preceding analysis suggests that a genuine 'systems error' may arise where the system operated by the company is not deployed correctly or implemented correctly, including in the sense that one of its component steps is omitted or fails (an error 'in the system'). An example of a systems error in deployment may be where an individual employee presses a button that puts into operation a system in circumstances for which it was not designed.[97] An example of an error 'in the system' may be where some components of a system fail due to external factors, such as a labour strike or electricity shortage. An example of an internal error 'in the system' might be where a rogue employee substitutes one step in the system for another. Again, however, we need to be careful. As chapter 9 explains, a single employee's practice of omitting, for example, some step in a formal system (for example, a 'standard operating procedure') may develop into a widespread practice that simply changes the nature of the corporate system *as implemented*. It is the operated or instantiated system that manifests the corporation's intentionality. As this suggests, systems audit and maintenance is an intrinsic part of corporate responsibility for the systems it intentionally deploys.

iv. Knowledge

Given this approach to mistake, how is corporate 'knowledge' revealed in the context of a system of conduct? On the foregoing analysis, actual corporate knowledge (*Baden Delvaux* Category (1)) of some facts will be implicit in, and revealed by, the features of the system that it operates. Given a system of conduct is, by definition, intended, a corporation will know at least its broad outline and the key features required for it to be deployed. This means that the starting point for any inquiry is that corporations know the nature of the conduct in which they are engaged through those systems.

Will a corporation always have knowledge of the outcomes produced by its systems? This will depend, I think, on the nature of the system. Where a system is designed to produce a specific sort of outcome (for example, a cheap but defective product), so that the outcome is specifically intended, knowledge of that outcome produced from operating the system of conduct is implicit in the system. Further, where the company has engaged in a specific transaction with a particular client or party through its system of conduct, knowledge of the occurrence of that transaction (albeit not necessarily

[96] Edelman and Bant (n 13) 173–74.

[97] E Snodgrass, 'The University of Kentucky Accidentally Sent 500,000 Acceptances to a Program that Usually Only Accepts 35 Students' *Insider* (9 April 2021) at www.insider.com/university-of-kentucky-sends-500000-accidental-acceptances-2021-4 (accessed 1 September 2021). My thanks to Rachel Leow for drawing this case to my attention.

the identity of the particular client) must be implicit in the application of the system. Knowledge of some features of specific parties transacting with the corporation may be implicit in the system of conduct. Thus, where a predatory business model depends on and anticipates the existence of a class of consumer that shares particular vulnerabilities, likely to fall prey to the scheme, it is open to find corporate knowledge of both the existence of that target group sharing those characteristics, and the fact of its transacting with vulnerable customers sharing those characteristics through its system of conduct.[98]

However, where there is a variety of outcomes likely to be produced from a system, the corporation's form of knowledge may range down the *Baden Delvaux* scale. We have seen there that these tend to combine state-of-mind inquiries (such as knowledge of certain facts and general and specific intention) with concepts of dishonesty, recklessness and negligence. In this respect, while negligence is a squarely objective standard, we have seen that dishonesty and recklessness involve a further combination of state-of-mind elements and an objective, normative assessment.

v. Recklessness, Dishonesty and Unconscionability

Turning to this final category, we have seen that recklessness, dishonesty and unconscionability combine various conceptions or elements of intention and knowledge with objective norms or standards of conduct. Although these are complex and layered inquiries, armed with the foregoing analysis, it becomes possible to break the mental elements and normative components into analytically distinct stages.

Thus, I suggested earlier that a plausible, working definition of recklessness may be understood to combine:

(a) a general intention to engage in some conduct;
(b) knowledge or 'foresight' of the outcome that the conduct is apt to produce (often described as a 'risk' of harm); and
(c) the application of a normative standard that a decision to proceed with the conduct in light of that known risk is unreasonable.

Where there is a system of conduct, (a) is established. Further, corporate knowledge of key aspects of the system are implicit from its deployment, as we have seen. Consistently, it is possible, and appropriate, to assess corporate 'foresight' from the objectively obvious (patent) risks of outcomes arising from the known and intended system of conduct, or from repeated instances of harmful outcomes arising from application of the known and intended system, where there are no audit or remedial steps taken to respond to the materialised harm. An unreasonable decision to proceed in light of those known risks, or repeated harm, manifests recklessness.

[98] *Australian Securities and Investments Commission v National Exchange Pty Ltd* [2005] FCAFC 226, (2005) 148 FCR 132 [33], 142–43 [43], discussed in Bant and Paterson, 'Systems of Misconduct' (n 6) 81–82. A consistent analysis is contained in *Stubbings* (n 48) [81] (Gordon J). See also *Australian Securities and Investments Commission v Westpac Securities Administration Limited* [2021] FCA 1008, (2021) 156 ACSR 614 (*Westpac Securities*) [39], [47] (O'Bryan J), analysed in Bant, 'Reforming the Laws of Attribution' (n 6).

Dishonesty assesses the quality of conduct against the standard of honest people, seen in light of the defendant's knowledge and intention. Unconscionability also combines application of (variously) equitable and statutory norms of conduct in light of the defendant's knowledge and intention. This inquiry tends to be heavily dependent on the particular facts of the case. However, some examples of how this assessment may be undertaken conclude the next subsection of this chapter.

vi. A Case Study

Here, I seek to give a necessarily brief but, it is hoped, meaningful analysis of how Systems Intentionality may shed light on state-of-mind inquiries, through a worked example.[99]

In *Australian Securities and Investments Commission v National Australia Bank Limited*,[100] National Australia Bank Limited (NAB) introduced a programme whereby

> unlicensed 'Introducers' would 'spot' prospective customers and 'refer' them to bankers; if the bank then advanced a loan, the Introducers were rewarded by a payment – the bigger the loan, the bigger the reward.[101]

For most of its 19 years' lifespan, the programme had no quality assurance (for example, Introducer or banker training) or audit processes, and visited no consequences on those engaged in carrying out its programme for non-compliance with the law.[102] The programme resulted in huge benefits to the bank in the form of increased loan business and associated profits,[103] as well as widespread examples of unlawful practices on the part of individual Introducers, as they scrambled to generate commissions. This individual misconduct included forgery, inclusion of false information in loan application documents and conflicts of interests. NAB's formal compliance policies were routinely honoured in the breach.[104] The conduct was only 'detected' by NAB when whistleblowers spoke up.[105]

Notwithstanding the scale of the problem, the Australian Securities and Investments Commission (ASIC) only brought proceedings in relation to 25 of the thousands of Introducers the subject of the programme. NAB admitted a range of the alleged contraventions of the prohibition under section 31 of the National Consumer Credit Protection Act 2009 (Cth) on a holder of Australian Credit Licence from conducting business with an unlicensed person, as well as the licensing obligation under section 47(1)(a) and (d) to do all things necessary to ensure authorised credit activities are engaged in 'efficiently, honestly and fairly'. In settling a civil pecuniary penalty of $15 million for the

[99] For further, worked examples of real cases, see Bant, 'Culpable Corporate Minds' (n 3); Bant and Paterson, 'Systems of Misconduct' (n 6); Paterson, Bant and Cooney, '*Australian Competition and Consumer Commission v Google*' (n 85); Bant, 'Catching the Corporate Conscience' (n 93); Bant, 'Reforming the Laws of Corporate Attribution' (n 6).

[100] *Australian Securities and Investments Commission v National Australia Bank Limited* [2020] FCA 1494.

[101] ibid [1] (Lee J).

[102] ibid [51].

[103] ibid [150].

[104] On this, see Bant, ch 9 of this volume.

[105] *National Australia Bank* (n 100) [148].

misconduct, Lee J expressed concern about the limited scope of ASIC's enforcement action. His Honour further stated:

> The conduct engaged in by NAB as a corporate entity was not deliberate. But this means that the deterrence needs to be such as to motivate changes to the *systems* underlying the contravening conduct. By that I mean compliance reporting, governance structures and systems integrations. While there was no evidence of the involvement of senior members of the organisation participating in or having knowledge of the contravening conduct, it is also not the case that proactive steps were put in place, such as adequate training or systems, to prevent the conduct from occurring in the first place.[106]

Here, the Systems Intentionality analysis points to a significantly different enforcement approach and, consequently, a different assessment of the nature and degree of culpability manifested by NAB through the programme.[107] On this approach, the point is not that compliance systems needed overhaul, although this certainly was the case. Rather, Systems Intentionality identifies the 'Introducer programme' *itself* as a system of misconduct that reflects a deliberate corporate strategy or method of generating loan business and, indeed, profits.[108] Importantly, proof of corporate culpability through this mechanism does not require proof on the part of ASIC of the thousands of Introducers, their individual knowledge, intentions and misconduct. Rather, its focus is on the proving the system of misconduct itself, which was abundantly clear on the materials before Lee J.[109] Nor does the apparent, personal ignorance of NAB's directors and senior officers of the programme and Introducer misconduct operate as a factor reducing corporate blameworthiness. NAB did not (and could not) deny that the Introducer programme was its programme and operated to its benefit. The programme was its system of conduct. And its system of conduct manifested its corporate values, intention and state of mind.

Turning to the specific mental states manifested by the programme, it can be accepted on the Systems Intentionality approach that the particular instances of Introducer misconduct may not have been the aim of the programme: in this sense, it may be that NAB held no *specific* intention to produce the resultant Introducer misconduct. However, the conduct of the programme itself, including its problematic features, certainly was deliberate or 'generally' intended. Consistently, on this analysis, the corporation must have been aware of the broad nature of its longstanding system of conduct, namely a commission-based use of unlicensed and untrained 'spotters' to generate loan business. Without these critical features, the programme could not be deployed successfully to the benefit of NAB. Further, this programme necessarily generated a very high risk of unlawful outcomes, which were realised repeatedly, yet NAB continued with it for 19 years, without any effective audit or compliance programme. Here, omission of audit and compliance mechanisms seems reflective of a design choice – at the very least, a decision not to care about the inevitable harm that would result to some customers through being engaged in loan products for which they were unsuited or did not need.

[106] ibid [152].

[107] An important contrasting case, and reasoning, is found in *Westpac Securities* (n 98), examined in Bant, 'Reforming the Laws of Corporate Attribution' (n 6).

[108] *Westpac Securities* (n 98) [150].

[109] See Bant, ch 9 of this volume.

On the foregoing analysis, general intention and actual, corporate knowledge of the key features of the system are established. Further, the system of conduct arguably manifests 'recklessness' as previously defined. It manifested:

(a) a general intention to engage in the programme;
(b) knowledge or 'foresight' of the patent risk of Introducer misconduct, repeatedly realised, with no audit or compliance mechanisms to address that risk or repeatedly realised harm; and
(c) application of a normative standard suggests that NAB's decision to proceed with the conduct in light of that known risk was wholly unreasonable. Here, the applicable standard is that of an honest, expert bank.

On this account, NAB is clearly open to be adjudged reckless. It is further open to being assessed as having failed to perform its services 'honestly' as required by section 912A,[110] and as having engaged in statutory unconscionable conduct. On the latter, and to adopt the words of Bromwich J in *Australian Competition and Consumer Commission v Australian Institute of Professional Education Pty Ltd (in liq) (No 3)*:

> The conclusion that the conduct overall was unconscionable would be more readily reached if such an outcome was either *intentional or sufficiently predictable or recurrent to require overt steps to be taken to minimise the chance of it* occurring.[111]

It is plausible to consider that for an expert bank to adopt and maintain a programme for profit that contains a patent risk of repeated and widespread harm to customers, and unlawful conduct, is to fall well below the standards of honest and fair conduct that underpin our financial system.

IV. Conclusion

Chapter 9 examined the theoretical concepts of systems of conduct, policies and practices that underpin Systems Intentionality and how these may be proved as a matter of litigation practice. This chapter has, in turn, sought to show how Systems Intentionality may then apply to meet a range of plausible test definitions of corporate mental states. This analysis further demonstrates, I consider, the practical utility of the approach and its capacity to respond in a nuanced and principled way to the spectrum of doctrinal state-of-mind formulations that appear across common law, equity and statute. Chapter 12 demonstrates that this utility extends to automated and algorithmic contexts. While I have, throughout, focused on the role of Systems Intentionality as a liability mechanism, there seems no reason, in principle, why similar analytical and evidential methods cannot apply successfully to address corporate mental states wherever they arise: as elements of corporate plaintiff claims (such as for the recovery of mistaken payments), in defensive and remedial contexts, or as part of ex ante regulation.

[110] cf *Australian Securities and Investments Commission v Australia and New Zealand Banking Group Ltd (No 3)* [2020] FCA 1421 [62], characterising misconduct as not honest, rather than dishonest.
[111] *Australian Competition and Consumer Commission v Australian Institute of Professional Education Pty Ltd (in liq) (No 3)* [2019] FCA 1982 [80] (Bromwich J) (emphasis added).

12

Automated Mistakes: Vitiated Consent and State of Mind Culpability in Algorithmic Contracting

JEANNIE MARIE PATERSON AND ELISE BANT*

I. Introduction

In this chapter, we consider the application of the doctrines of unilateral mistake and unconscionable conduct to relieve against plaintiff mistakes in what are sometimes termed 'algorithmic contracts': contracts for which formation and/or performance are automated through computer software. Current and emerging uses of computer software allow contracts to be made, processed and performed more quickly, in response to more variables and with greater accuracy than if done by human hand. This trend of algorithmic contracts seems likely to continue.[1] As software become more sophisticated, the contracting processes they may inform and operate will become more complex, and the involvement of humans in the transaction more attenuated. Humans will determine the design, development and deployment of the automated process. However, there may be no direct human involvement or intention applying to any particular transaction.[2]

It seems reasonably clear that automation does not preclude effective contract formation.[3] This is because in deciding whether the parties have made a legally binding

* This chapter builds on joint research into the regulation of misleading and unconscionable conduct, pursuant to Australian Research Council Discovery Projects DP180100932 and DP140100767. It also presents proposals developed pursuant to Elise Bant's ARC-supported Future Fellowship project FT190100475, which aims to examine and model reforms of the laws that currently inhibit corporate responsibility for serious misconduct. Our sincere thanks to participants in the workshop for their very helpful comments and criticisms. Responsibility for all remaining errors rests with us.

[1] See LH Scholz, 'Algorithmic Contracts' (2017) 20 *Stanford Technology Law Review* 128; M Rizzi and N Skead, 'Algorithmic Contracts and the Equitable Doctrine of Undue Influence: Adapting Old Rules to a New Legal Landscape' (2020) 14 *Journal of Equity* 301. See also AJ Casey and A Niblett, 'Self-Driving Contracts' (2017) 43 *Journal of Corporation Law* 1.

[2] cf *Quoine Pte Ltd v B2C2 Ltd* [2020] 2 SLR 20 [1] (Menon CJ, Phang and Prakash JJA and French IJ agreeing).

[3] E Mik, 'From Automation to Autonomy: Some Non-Existent Problems in Contract Law' (2020) 36 *Journal of Contract Law* 205.

contract and determining the scope of that contract, the law looks to the objective or inferred intentions of the parties, not whether a specific individual actually applied their mind to the transaction in question.[4] There is more uncertainty about how contractual vitiating factors apply, if at all, to such transactions. Plaintiff mistake is a factor that may vitiate contractual consent under both general law and statute. Relief in such circumstances may be premised on misrepresentation, unilateral mistake or unconscionable conduct, depending on the source of the mistake and the conduct of the defendant. For relief on grounds of unilateral mistake or unconscionable conduct, courts look to the culpability of the defendant, which commonly involves requirements of deliberateness or knowledge.

It is well understood that these concepts can have an awkward fit when dealing with transactions involving corporations. Where one party is a company, which has no natural state of mind, the mental element required to establish culpability must be found in its agents and officers or, as we have also argued, its systems, policies and practices.[5] Similar challenges are posed by developments in the field of algorithmic contracts.[6] What do ideas of consent, mistake and culpability mean when the contracting process is informed by instructions to computers? In these contracts there may be minimal direct human involvement, and so how is a culpable human or corporate mind identified? Certainly automation through software adds elements of complexity and opacity that may make the task of attributing fault when things go wrong more difficult.[7] We suggest, however, the problem is not insurmountable.

We prefer an approach that treats algorithms used in contracting as tools or, more accurately, systems of conduct. Attribution of state of mind flows from this characterisation. This approach means that the likelihood of a successful claim for unilateral mistake in algorithmic contracts is low. Relief for unilateral mistake requires the non-mistaken party to have knowledge of the other party's mistake. It is unlikely that this will be the case in a transaction that is automated to deal with many different counterparties. Moreover, in our view, it would be artificial, and indeed inconsistent with the defining character of algorithmic contracts, to somehow attribute knowledge of the circumstances of the transaction to the non-mistaken party each time a contract is entered into. This conclusion does not mean, however, that relief based on vitiating factors is necessarily precluded. It should be possible to consider the design and operation of the system that is being used to automate the transaction. If that system is by design or effect likely to take advantage of mistaken or otherwise vulnerable contracting partners, then relief on grounds of unilateral mistake or unconscionable conduct may be available on that basis.

[4] *Quoine* (n 2) [96]. See also V Ooi, 'Contracts formed by software: an approach from the law of mistake' [2022] 2 *Journal of Business Law* 97.

[5] E Bant and JM Paterson, 'Systems of Misconduct: Corporate Culpability and Statutory Unconscionability' (2021) 15 *Journal of Equity* 63.

[6] See also J Fu, 'Algorithmic Contracts: Who is to Blame?' (2020) 12 *Singapore Law Review Juris Illuminae* at www.singaporelawreview.com/juris-illuminae-entries/2020/algorithmic-contracts (accessed 19 November 2021).

[7] Noting that in many if not most cases, algorithmic contracts are expressions of coded rules determined by humans, which may perform at rapid speed but do not show the black-box hurdle to understanding their outputs found in more complex machine-learning systems. See, eg, *Quoine* (n 2).

We begin our discussion by outlining the nature of algorithmic contracts. We then turn to the conundrum of unilateral mistake in algorithmic contracting raised by the decision of the Singapore Court of Appeal in *Quoine Pte Ltd v B2C2 Ltd* (*Quoine*).[8] We consider the doctrinal elements of these claims, focusing on the requirements of defendant state-of-mind culpability, before turning back to the application of these doctrines to algorithmic contracts, starting with *Quoine* and then considering other possible scenarios where a claim to rescission on the basis of vitiated consent to automated contracting processes may arise.

II. Algorithmic Contracts

Digital technology is quickly transforming legal practice. Parties may already make use of commercial products using software to assist with contract preparation,[9] contract review,[10] due diligence,[11] contract management[12] and legal compliance.[13] The very entry into and performance of contracts is also being automated.[14] Automated contracts are not new. Early examples are vending and ticketing machines.[15] Parties have for some time used software automating aspects of contract performance, such as sending notices and making payments. The programs used in these systems rely on relatively simple commands, such as a direction to pay $X to Y on the occurrence of Z event. Contracting parties are increasingly making use of more sophisticated computing techniques for automating aspects of contract preparation, negotiation and performance. These contracts are sometimes termed 'algorithmic contracts' to distinguish them from more straightforward automated systems.[16] Parties make use of algorithmic contracts

[8] ibid.

[9] See, eg, Contract Express at https://legal.thomsonreuters.com/en/products/contract-express (accessed 19 November 2021); Donna Legal, at www.donna.legal (accessed 19 November 2021); Legal Zoom at www.legalzoom.com/country/au (accessed 19 November 2021); Neota Logic at www.neotalogic.com (accessed 19 November 2021); Docusign at www.seal-software.com (accessed 19 November 2021).

[10] See, eg, eBrevia at www.dfinsolutions.com/products/ebrevia#overview (accessed 19 November 2021); Contract Probe at www.contractprobe.com/index.php/fronts/how_its_works (accessed 19 November 2021); Kira at https://kirasystems.com/how-it-works/contract-analysis (accessed 19 November 2021); ThoughtRiver at www.thoughtriver.com (accessed 19 November 2021); Docusign (n 9).

[11] See, eg, eBrevia (n 10); Luminence at www.luminance.com (accessed 19 November 2021); Docusign (n 9).

[12] See, eg, Neota (n 9); Docusign (n 9).

[13] See, eg, Kira (n 10); Neota: (n 9).

[14] See *Quoine* (n 2) [79], [95].

[15] Often discussed as the early exemplar of the smart contract: N Szabo, 'Formalizing and Securing Relationships on Public Networks' (1997) 2 *First Monday* at https://journals.uic.edu/ojs/index.php/fm/article/view/548 (accessed 19 November 2021). For a legal analysis of vending machines, see *Thornton v Shoe Lane Parking Ltd* [1970] EWCA Civ 2, [1971] QB 163.

[16] 'Algorithmic contracts are contracts in which one or more parties use an algorithm to determine whether to be bound or how to be bound': Scholz (n 1) 134. On the sociotechnical use of the phrase 'algorithmic', see also K Yeung, 'Algorithmic Regulation: A Critical Interrogation' (2018) 12 *Regulation & Governance* 505, 506, 'social scientists typically use the term [algorithmic] as an adjective to describe the *sociotechnical assemblage* that includes not just algorithms but also the computational networks in which they function, the people who design and operate them, the data (and users) on which they act, and the institutions that provide these services, all connected to a broader social endeavour and constituting part of a family of authoritative systems for knowledge production'.

to speed up transactions, and also to aid in making more accurate decisions about whether to contract and on what terms or at what price. Algorithmic contracts of this kind are being used in high-frequency share trading[17] to buy or sell rapidly on favourable market terms, and similarly in insurance broking.[18] Algorithmic contracts are also used in online sales, including consumer transactions, utilising dynamic pricing.[19] In the context of smart contracts linked to blockchain technology, algorithmic contracts are also used in applications such as capital and derivative markets,[20] trade finance,[21] insurance[22] and shipping.[23]

Algorithmic contracts may vary in their degree of complexity. Typically, they are based on pre-programmed instructions determined by humans.[24] These kinds of algorithmic contracts may respond to a significant number of variables, perhaps programmed as expert systems or decision trees. Algorithmic contracts may also use models derived from machine-learning applications, which inform contracting decisions about pricing or terms.[25] Algorithmic contracts informed by machine learning are typically determinative – that is, working on fixed models or static data sets – rather than adaptive, in the sense of being able to vary their responses as more data are gathered.[26]

Notwithstanding their advantages in speed, volume and accuracy, algorithmic contracts may also produce adverse outcomes for one or other of the parties. There may be mistakes in the programming, bias in the data used as the basis for decisions, or unforeseen outcomes due to changes in the events that trigger performance.[27] In some

[17] See, eg, *Quoine* (n 2).

[18] See, eg, *Software Solutions Partners Ltd v HM Customs and Excise* [2007] EWHC 971 (Admin), [2007] All ER (D) 80 (May) (*Software Solutions*).

[19] See J Paterson, G Bush and T Miller, 'Transparency to Contest Differential Pricing' (2021) 93 *Computers & Law* 49.

[20] See, eg, R Clements, 'Evaluating the Costs and Benefits of a Smart Contract Blockchain Framework for Credit Default Swaps' (2019) 10 *William & Mary Business Law Review* 369. See also Australian Stock Exchange, 'About CHESS Replacement' at www.asx.com.au/services/chess-replacement.htm (accessed 19 November 2021); ISDA, 'Digital Asset and ISDA Introduce Tool to Help Drive Adoption of ISDA CDM' (Press Release, April 9 2019) at www.isda.org/2019/04/09/digital-asset-and-isda-introduce-tool-to-help-drive-adoption-of-isda-cdm/ (accessed 19 November 2021); M del Castillo, 'Citi, Goldman Sachs Conduct First Blockchain Equity Swap On Ethereum-Inspired Platform' *Forbes* (6 February 2020) at www.forbes.com/sites/michaeldelcastillo/2020/02/06/citi-goldman-sachs-conduct-first-blockchain-equity-swap-on-ethereum-inspired-platform/?sh=7816b3563694 (accessed 19 November 2021).

[21] See, eg, Deloitte, 'How Blockchain Can Reshape Trade Finance' at www2.deloitte.com/content/dam/Deloitte/global/Documents/grid/trade-finance-placemat.pdf (accessed 19 November 2021).

[22] PwC, 'Blockchain: A Catalyst for New Approaches in Insurance' (Report) at www.pwc.com.au/publications/pwc-blockchain.pdf (accessed 12 October 2020); B3i, 'Major Re/Insurers and Brokers Complete Complex Placements on B3is Blockchain Platform' (Media Release, 12 February 2020) at https://b3i.tech/news-reader/major-re-insurers-and-brokers-complete-complex-placements-on-b3is-blockchain-platform.html (accessed 19 November 2021).

[23] See, eg, J Herd, '"Blocks of Lading": Distributed Ledger Technology and the Disruption of Sea Carriage Regulation' (2018) 18 *Queensland University of Technology Law Review* 306.

[24] See, eg, *Software Solutions* (n 18).

[25] See, eg, Paterson, Bush and Miller (n 19) 49–53. See also J Meehan and E Gruyaert, '6 Disruptive Trends in Pricing' *Wall Street Journal* (2 March 2018) at https://deloitte.wsj.com/articles/6-disruptive-trends-in-pricing-1519966937 (accessed 19 November 2021).

[26] On adaptive systems, cf The Alan Turing Institute at www.turing.ac.uk/research/research-projects/adaptive-machine-learning-changing-environments (accessed 19 November 2021).

[27] cf E Snodgrass, 'The University of Kentucky Accidentally Sent 500,000 Acceptances to a Program that Usually Only Accepts 35 Students' *Insider* (9 April 2021) at www.insider.com/university-of-kentucky-sends-500000-accidental-acceptances-2021-4 (accessed 19 November 2021).

cases, these events might produce a breach of contract. In others, the complaint may be that one or other of the parties' consent to the transaction should be regarded as vitiated, such as on the basis of factors including unilateral mistake or unconscionable conduct. The essential difficulty, as we shall see in the next section, is that these kinds of doctrines require some form of culpability on the part of the defendant – typically a state of mind such as knowledge – to ground the action. The challenge raised is in how this may be attributed in an algorithmic contracting process where there may be no human or corporate mind directly involved in making or performing the contract.

Certainly, humans will make decisions about the design of the software within which an algorithmic contract operates, and the kinds of algorithms that are used. Humans may further determine the data that will inform any outcomes derived from machine learning. However, once algorithmic contracts are up and running, humans may not be directly involved in entry into the contract or its performance outputs. The humans utilising the systems may not even understand how the processes work or how the outcomes are reached. These factors have led to increased attention on governance and regulatory strategies for ensuring that both public bodies and private companies are accountable for their use of algorithmic decision making.[28] The discussion has primarily focused on risks of bias,[29] as well as technical mechanisms for ensuring the transparency, reliability and contestability of automated processes.[30] Our focus is different. We are interested in what reliance on algorithmic contracts means in analysing circumstances where the plaintiff claims their consent to contract is vitiated and the contract should be set aside on the basis of some wrongful conduct by the defendant. It is to the legal basis for such relief that we now turn.

III. Plaintiff Mistakes and Defendant Culpability

Mistake is the paradigm vitiating factor in the law of unjust enrichment, and the mistaken payment is the core case where, absent defences or other bars to recovery, the plaintiff will be entitled to restitution of the benefit.[31] However, if the parties have entered into a contract, any enrichment of the non-mistaken party is 'justified' by the contract. The contract entitles the defendant to retain the benefit. It follows from this that the contract must be set aside, or found to be void or otherwise 'negated', before the

[28] See, eg, Yeung (n 16). See also European Commission, 'On Artificial Intelligence: A European Approach to Excellence and Trust' (White Paper, February 2020); Select Committee on Artificial Intelligence, *AI in the UK: Ready, Willing and Able?* (HL 2017–19, 100).

[29] See, eg, Australian Human Rights Commission, *Human Rights and Technology* (Final Report, 2021) 105; E Jillson 'Aiming for Truth, Fairness, and Equity in your Company's Use of AI' (US Federal Trade Commission, April 2021) at www.ftc.gov/news-events/blogs/business-blog/2021/04/aiming-truth-fairness-equity-your-companys-use-ai (accessed 15 October 2021).

[30] See, eg, D Dawson et al, 'AI Ethics Framework' (Australian Government Department of Industry, Innovation and Science, 2019) at www.industry.gov.au/data-and-publications/australias-artificial-intelligence-ethics-framework (accessed 15 October 2021); Proposal for a Regulation of the European Parliament and of the Council (EU) COM(2021) 206 final laying down harmonised rules on artificial intelligence (artificial intelligence act) and amending certain union legislative acts.

[31] See generally J Edelman and E Bant, *Unjust Enrichment*, 2nd edn (Oxford, Hart Publishing, 2016) chs 7 and 8.

plaintiff is entitled to restitution of benefits transferred pursuant to the contract. This may occur where the mistake has been induced by the defendant, or where the defendant knows of and encourages, or at least fails to clarify, the mistake. In doctrinal terms, the relevant kinds of claim are potentially for misrepresentation, unilateral mistake and unconscionable dealing.

A. Unilateral Mistake

Unilateral mistake operates where, viewed in terms of their subjective state of mind, the parties are not in agreement but one party's view accords with the objective interpretation of the contract.[32] Given the objective approach to consent in contract, unilateral subjective errors on the part of the plaintiff will not normally be enough to set aside a contract and obtain restitution of benefits transferred pursuant to it. Were it otherwise, the law of unjust enrichment would contradict the law of contract. So, something more than a subjective unilateral error is required to ensure that bargains objectively struck between parties are not unduly undermined.

Relief setting aside a contract on grounds of unilateral mistake may be granted in law and in equity. In law, relief may be granted where the non-mistaken party has actual knowledge that the other party is mistaken.[33] This set of cases is sometimes described as involving 'snapping up' a bargain. In these cases, a lack of consensus (unilateral mistake) is typically inferred from the non-mistaken party's acceptance of an offer that is patently 'too good to be true'.[34] To the extent that unilateral mistake at common law results in the contract's being void, the doctrine would not seem to be recognised in Australia.[35] Rather, unilateral mistake operates to render the objectively agreed contract voidable, consistently with the equitable doctrine.

In equity, relief for unilateral mistake requires that the mistaken party be able to point to facts demonstrating it would be unconscionable to hold the parties to the contract. The parameters of the doctrine, being factually dependent, are still being developed.[36] In Australia, this required element of unconscionability will be shown where the non-mistaken party is aware of circumstances that indicate that a mistake has been made and, possibly, deliberately sets out to ensure that the non-mistaken party does not become aware of the mistake.[37] In *Taylor v Johnson*, Mason ACJ, Murphy and Deane JJ explained:

> [A] party who has entered into a written contract under a serious mistake about its contents in relation to a fundamental term will be entitled in equity to an order rescinding the contract

[32] See generally A Robertson and J Paterson, *Contract: Cases and Materials*, 14th edn (Pyrmont, Lawbook Co, 2020) ch 31.

[33] *Chwee Kin Keong v Digilandmall.com Pte Ltd* [2005] SGCA 2, [2005] 1 SLR(R) 502 (*Digilandmall*).

[34] ibid [53] (Chao JA, Kan J and Yong CJ agreeing). See also *Hartog v Colin & Shields* [1939] 3 All ER 566, 568.

[35] Edelman and Bant (n 31) 146–47; N Seddon, R Bigwood and MP Ellinghaus, *Cheshire & Fifoot Law of Contract*, 10th edn (Chatswood, Butterworths, 2012) 12 [12.48].

[36] *Reilly v Australia and New Zealand Banking Group Limited (No 2)* [2020] FCA 1502 [143] (O'Bryan J).

[37] *Taylor v Johnson* [1983] HCA 5, (1983) 151 CLR 422 (*Taylor*).

> if the other party is aware that circumstances exist which indicate that the first party is entering the contract under some serious mistake or misapprehension about either the content or subject matter of that term and deliberately sets out to ensure that the first party does not become aware of the existence of his mistake or misapprehension.[38]

Subsequently, it has been suggested that this statement was not intended as a comprehensive description of the doctrine.[39] On this view, if the non-mistaken party knows of the mistake and omits to clarify the situation, that may be sufficient to ground relief in equity for unilateral mistake.[40] It has further been suggested that in equity it may be sufficient to show that the non-mistaken party suspected that the other party was mistaken or ought reasonably to have been aware of it.[41] In Singapore, constructive knowledge may be enough for relief to be granted in equity.[42]

Knowledge, like any other state of mind, is generally inferred from the circumstances, including from admissions, inferences from the evidence and judicial notice of notorious facts. In *Digilandmall*, knowledge of a mistake as to pricing was inferred from an obvious mistake on the part of the seller and the speed with which the buyer acted to 'snap up' the mispriced product and the volume of purchases made.[43] How would such knowledge be inferred in a process that relies on an algorithmic contract – in which contracting decisions rely on automated systems? The speed at which a contract is concluded will not be conclusive given that this is one of the purposes of automation. An overreaching response to a patently mispriced product will also not necessarily be conclusive where one of the instructions to the automated system is to 'buy' at a price less than $X. In such cases there must be some further basis for attributing knowledge of the mistake to the firm using the automated system. This kind of inquiry was raised in *Quoine*, which we shall shortly consider. First, however, we need to address the related doctrine of unconscionable dealing.

B. Unconscionable Systems and Patterns of Conduct

Unconscionable conduct 'within the meaning of the unwritten law' is recognised in equity and also in section 20 of the Australian Consumer Law (ACL).[44] The key elements of the equitable wrong is that a defendant takes unconscionable advantage of a plaintiff's special disadvantage.[45] Section 21 of the ACL contains a broader prohibition,

[38] ibid 432.

[39] See, eg, *Tutt v Doyle* (1997) 42 NSWLR 10, 14; *Blackley Investments Pty Ltd v Burnie City Council (No 2)* [2010] TASSC 48 [64]; *Chwee Kin Keong v Digilandmall.com Pte Ltd* [2004] SGHC 71, [2004] 2 SLR 594 [73].

[40] *Smith v Smith* [2004] NSWSC 663, (2004) 12 BPR 23,051 [50]. Another recent decision of the New South Wales Supreme Court held that failure to inform appears to have sufficed to satisfy the requirement that the non-mistaken party deliberately set out to ensure that the mistaken party did not become aware of the mistake: see *Moobi Pty Ltd v Les Gunn Properties Pty Ltd* [2008] NSWSC 719, (2008) 14 BPR 27,035 [55].

[41] *Taylor* (n 37) 432.

[42] *Digilandmall* (n 33) [53] (Chao JA, Kan J and Yong CJ agreeing).

[43] See generally ibid.

[44] Competition and Consumer Act 2010 (Cth), sch 2 (ACL). Note that s 20 does not apply where s 21 is applicable, and so its scope is now limited.

[45] *Thorne v Kennedy* [2017] HCA 49, (2017) 263 CLR 85.

with which this chapter is chiefly concerned. In its current form, section 21 prohibits conduct 'in trade or commerce' that is, 'in all the circumstances, unconscionable'.[46] The meaning and operation of the prohibition in section 21 of the ACL have always been contentious.[47] In 2012, section 21 was amended to introduce a set of interpretative principles to guide courts in their application of the prohibition. These interpretative principles confirm that the statutory prohibition on unconscionable conduct is not confined by the doctrine of unconscionable dealing developed in equity.[48] The principles also confirm that the 'section is capable of applying to a system of conduct or pattern of behaviour, whether or not a particular individual is identified as having been disadvantaged by the conduct or behaviour'.[49] Section 21 is supplemented by section 22, which contains a list of factors to which the court may have regard in deciding if conduct is unconscionable contrary to the statute.

Different views have been expressed by courts as to the scope of the statutory prohibition. As described by Allsop J, the statutory prohibition on unconscionable conduct requires an evaluation of

> the deep and abiding requirement of honesty in behaviour; a rejection of trickery or sharp practice; fairness when dealing with consumers; the central importance of the faithful performance of bargains and promises freely made; the protection of those whose vulnerability as to the protection of their own interests places them in a position that calls for a just legal system to respond for their protection, especially from those who would victimise, predate or take advantage; a recognition that inequality of bargaining power can (but not always) be used in a way that is contrary to fair dealing or conscience …[50]

This statement brings out the dual focus of the doctrine – in most forms it considers the element of disadvantage or vulnerability in the plaintiff that makes them unable to protect their own best interests in the transaction, and an element of culpability in the defendant that looks to take advantage of those in the position of disadvantage. It is here that unilateral mistake starts to merge with unconscionable conduct. The focus is not only on plaintiffs' mistakes but also, particularly under statute, on plaintiffs' inability to protect their own interests in the transaction.

In its most straightforward form, the prohibition on unconscionable conduct may be enlivened where one party takes advantage of another party's mistake, disadvantaged position or inexperience in the transaction. This advantage taking may be established by showing that the firm knew of the other party's position of disadvantage but proceeded with the transaction in any event, without providing the assistance that was needed to support the weaker party's decision.[51] Unconscionable conduct may also be established

[46] ACL (n 44) s 21.

[47] See AJ Duggan, 'Some Reflections on Consumer Protections and the Law Reform Process' (1991) 17 *Monash University Law Review* 252.

[48] ACL (n 44) s 21(4)(a).

[49] ibid s 21(4)(b).

[50] *Paciocco v Australia and New Zealand Banking Group Ltd* [2015] FCAFC 50, (2015) 236 FCR 199, 274 [296] (Allsop CJ), cited in JM Paterson, E Bant and M Clare, 'Doctrine, Policy, Culture and Choice in Assessing Unconscionable Conduct Under Statute: *ASIC v Kobelt*' (2019) 13 *Journal of Equity* 81, 93.

[51] *Australian Competition and Consumer Commission v Australian Institute of Professional Education Pty Ltd (in liq) (No 3)* [2019] FCA 1982 [80], [84] (Bromwich J); *Australian Competition and Consumer Commission v Cornerstone Investment Aust Pty Ltd (in liq) (No 4)* [2018] FCA 1408 [750], [751] (Gleeson J).

where the advantage taking arose 'by design', in the sense of being the kind of conduct that would only ever impact on those unable to protect their own interests or who misunderstood the transaction. *National Exchange* was essentially an example of this kind of concern.[52] There, the central complaint made was that the form of the offer to buy was set out in such a way that it was only likely to be accepted by people who misunderstood or were mistaken about its impact.

IV. Algorithmic Contracts and Plaintiff Mistakes

The challenge in applying doctrines of unilateral mistake or unconscionability to algorithmic contracts arises from the absence of direct human involvement in the contract at hand. In both unilateral mistake and unconscionability, the element of knowledge, or at least deliberate design, is central to relief. Where the stronger party has made use of an automated system or algorithmic contracting systems, it is not readily apparent how these elements are established. Entry into the contract and the terms of the contract will have been determined by computer software. An exemplar of the challenges in applying doctrines of mistake and unconscionability to algorithmic contracts is found in the decision of the Singapore Court of Appeal in *Quoine*.[53]

A. Mistake and Algorithmic Trading

In *Quoine*, the appellant, Quoine, was the operator of a cryptocurrency exchange platform. Quoine also functioned as a market-maker on the platform by placing buy and sell orders to create liquidity. The respondent, B2C2, was a trader on the platform and also a market-maker, which traded using its own automated trading software, developed by its director. Built into B2C2's trading software was a fail-safe 'deep price' of 10 Bitcoin (BTC) to 1 Ethereum (ETH), which would be invoked should input data from the platform be unavailable. In 2017, Quoine mistakenly failed to make necessary updates to the platform's critical operating systems. The failure meant that the platform could not access market information about prices and, using this information, generate new orders to keep liquidity within the trading system. This led to a failure to generate new orders. B2C2's trading software accordingly defaulted to the deep price and conducted 13 trades at a rate approximately 250 times the then going rate in the market of around 0.04 BTC for 1 ETH.

When Quoine became aware of these trades the next day, it unilaterally cancelled them and reversed the settlement transactions on the basis that the trades were concluded at highly abnormal rates. B2C2 commenced proceedings against Quoine, alleging that its unilateral cancellation of the disputed trades and reversal of the settlement transactions

[52] cf *Australian Securities and Investments Commission v National Exchange Pty Ltd* [2003] FCA 955, (2003) 202 ALR 24.

[53] *Quoine* (n 2).

were in breach of contract or breach of trust. Importantly, for our purposes, Quoine argued that the traders it represented had contracted under a unilateral mistake. At first instance B2C2's claims were allowed. Quoine appealed against the whole of the Judge's decision. The Singapore Court of Appeal (Sundaresh Menon CJ, Andrew Phang JA, Judith Prakash JA, Robert French IJ; Jonathan Mance IJ dissenting) found that the conduct was inconsistent with Quoine's own terms and conditions, and that a term that Quoine argued authorised this behaviour was not incorporated into the contract.[54] The Court of Appeal rejected Quoine's defences of unilateral mistake at common law and in equity.

Identifying the relevant mistake is not without difficulty in this scenario. In unilateral mistake, the operative kinds of mistake are usually errors as to a 'fundamental term' of the contract,[55] which may include pricing errors.[56] An operative mistake for the purposes of the doctrine in law or equity does not include a 'mistaken assumption about the circumstances under which the contract was or would be concluded'.[57] Also, mistakes as to the quality or value of the subject matter of the contract are typically not within the doctrine.[58] This is because mistakes as to quality are founded in an active exercise of judgement in which risk of error is always a key consideration. If parties wish to protect against that risk, typically the law takes the view that they should do so through a contractual warranty. More broadly, the authorities sometimes refuse relief where the plaintiff is said to have 'assumed' the risk of error or mistake.[59] Classic examples include when a plaintiff decides to pay some benefit to the defendant to settle a dispute, knowing that there is a risk that the plaintiff would have won the case; or where a plaintiff is told that they might be mistaken or doubts the fact or matter on which they are acting, and proceeds nonetheless without making further enquiries.[60]

In *Quoine*, the problem arose from Quoine's own error, in failing properly to update software. Somewhat oddly, Quoine argued that the operative mistake was between the parties on the platform and B2C2, a characterisation accepted by the court for the purpose of the appeal.[61] Even on this approach, there remains a question as to whether the alleged mistake was one that could give rise to relief. The court considered it did not. The mistake was not as to the terms of the contracts but the 'premise on which the buy orders were placed'.[62] In other words, the counterparties' mistake was over the operation of the trading platform,[63] which controlled the liquidity of the market, and through this the trading price. Software or coding errors seem an inherent risk of algorithmic

[54] ibid [66].

[55] ibid [80] (Menon CJ, Phang and Prakash JJA and French IJ agreeing), citing *Digilandmall* (n 33) [34] and [80] (Chao JA, Kan J and Yong CJ agreeing); *Statoil ASA v Louis Dreyfus Energy Services LP* [2008] EWHC 2257 (Comm) [2008] 2 Lloyd's Rep 685.

[56] See *Taylor* (n 37); *Quoine* (n 2) [91] (Menon CJ, Phang and Prakash JJA and French IJ agreeing).

[57] *Quoine* (n 2) [82] (Menon CJ, Phang and Prakash JJA and French IJ agreeing). See also *Smith v Hughes* (1871) LR 6 QB 597, 606–07 (Cockburn CJ, Blackburn J agreeing), 611 (Hannen J).

[58] But cf *Quoine* (n 2) [169] (Mance IJ).

[59] Edelman and Bant (n 31) 176–79.

[60] *Lahoud v Lahoud* [2010] NSWSC 1297 [180] (Ward J); *Salib v Gakas* [2010] NSWSC 505 [333] (Ward J).

[61] *Quoine* (n 2) [78] (Menon CJ, Phang and Prakash JJA and French IJ agreeing).

[62] ibid [114].

[63] ibid.

contracting, akin to a mistake as to quality, and something that should be allocated under the contracts with the platform.[64]

However, the question with which we are concerned here is less around the scope of the doctrine than its required elements of culpability when applied to algorithmic contracts. As we have seen, relief for unilateral mistake requires the non-mistaken party to know of the mistake. In the case of an algorithmic contract where the human involvement or oversight may occur in the design and deployment of the system, whose knowledge and what the nature of this intention might require are far from straightforward. Returning to the case of *Quoine*, where the problem arose in a failure of the Quoine trading platform to set a viable base price and the subsequent fortuitous trades of B2C2, how should this state of mind be attributed? The platform was trading at a rapid rate. Where might it realistically be said that a state of mind, such as knowledge, would lie?

B. Algorithms as Tools

On one approach to algorithmic accountability – that is, responsibility for decisions that are determined by software – algorithms are treated as mere tools of the firm that deploys them[65] or, in our framework of systems intentionality, a system or process.[66] Knowledge for the purpose of determining culpability then turns on two questions: Whose knowledge is considered? And at what point of time in the transaction? In *Quoine*, the majority judges identified the person holding the relevant knowledge as the 'programmer' or 'person running the algorithm'.[67] In *Quoine*, the programmer and the CEO of the company in question were the same and so looking to the programmer's state of mind was appropriate. In other cases, this divide between programmer and the firm developing or using the algorithmic contracting tool may, as Low and Mike point out, be somewhat of a distraction. It may sometimes be that the knowledge of the programmer or, more accurately, the team of programmers will be central to the design and operation of the system. In other or perhaps most instances, programmers will possess little insight into the overall operations of the program they produce, and even less of a decision-making role with respect to how the program is deployed or governed. But in both scenarios, responsibility and oversight will rest with the firm that has chosen to adopt an automated system, and it is here that the requisite knowledge of mistake must be found. In other words, accountability on this approach – including for our purposes, accountability that depends on a certain state of mind – rests with the person or firm that deploys the algorithm.[68]

[64] See also Mik (n 3) 226.

[65] 'Irrespective of their technological complexity, computers must be regarded as tools': ibid 222; cf as critical of this approach Scholz (n 1) 132, 134.

[66] cf ME Diamantis, 'The Extended Corporate Mind: When Corporations Use AI to Break the Law' (2020) 97 *North Carolina Law Review* 893, advocating a theory of extended mind.

[67] *Quoine* (n 2) [97]–[99] (Menon CJ, Phang and Prakash JJA and French IJ agreeing).

[68] See K Low and E Mik, 'Lost in Transmission: Unilateral Mistakes in Automated Contracts' (2020) 136 *Law Quarterly Review* 563.

The court in *Quoine* held that the relevant time for considering what was known by the programmer/user firm was from the time of programming the automated process and up until the time the contract was concluded.[69] The relevant knowledge was not specific knowledge of the mistake at the time of concluding each individual contract. This was because the very purpose of the system was to enter into and conclude contracts without human oversight or right of review.[70] Hence, the contracting parties would not know beforehand they were going to contract and on what terms.[71] Rather, the court said the kind of the knowledge that needed to be held by the programmer was knowledge such that, in the kind of circumstances that occurred, a contracting partner would only ever contract if acting under a mistake. Thus, the court explained that the relevant question in establishing unilateral mistake was:

> When programming the algorithm, was the programmer doing so with actual or constructive knowledge of the fact that the relevant offer would only ever be accepted by a party operating under a mistake and was the programmer acting to take advantage of such a mistake?[72]

We return in section V to an alternative approach to understanding knowledge of mistake, derived from the inherent features or design of the automated process. For current purposes, it suffices to note that the court's reference to 'constructive knowledge' appears to point, consistently with our analysis, to an assessment of the inherent or patent incidents of the system. Where counterparty mistake is a necessary part of a system's design, the programmer may be taken to have knowledge of it.

We might also note that in the Australian context, as referred to earlier, it has been questioned whether the second element of deliberate advantage taking is really necessary in equity. The argument is that knowledge of the mistake, and proceeding with that contract without addressing that concern, is sufficient to establish the element of unconscionability required for relief.[73] Consistent with this approach, the court in *Quoine* considered that relief for unilateral mistake may be available where the programmer subsequently learnt of the relevant mistake and 'yet allowed the algorithm to continue running, intending thereby to take advantage of the mistake'.[74] This approach is also consistent with the approach to 'systems intentionality', whereby the ongoing tolerance of a system that generates harm may become intentional even if it was not at the outset.[75]

The court rejected Quoine's defences of unilateral mistake at common law and in equity. It concluded that when B2C2 programmed its trading software, there was no evidence it intended to take advantage of errors on the part of Quoine. B2C2 was not aware of the terms of the margin contracts that might result in opportunities for exploitation of illiquidity in the platform.[76] The court accepted the trial judge's finding that B2C2's purpose in programming the pricing strategy for the trading software was to

[69] *Quoine* (n 2) [99] (Menon CJ, Phang and Prakash JJA and French IJ agreeing).
[70] ibid [104] (Menon CJ, Phang and Prakash JJA and French IJ agreeing).
[71] ibid.
[72] ibid [103] (Menon CJ, Phang and Prakash JJA and French IJ agreeing).
[73] ibid [171] (Mance IJ), discussing unconscionability for unilateral mistake arising from 'standing by'.
[74] ibid [99] (Menon CJ, Phang and Prakash JJA and French IJ agreeing). See also ibid [125].
[75] See Bant, ch 11 of this volume.
[76] *Quoine* (n 2) [119] (Menon CJ, Phang and Prakash JJA and French IJ agreeing).

protect itself against adverse consequences.[77] Accordingly, the ground of unilateral mistake was not made out. The decision appears correct to us,[78] but it is worth exploring the alternative analysis.

C. Algorithmic Agents

A different approach to accountability for decisions informed by algorithms treats the algorithm as an agent of the person who deploys it.[79] Lauren Scholtz explains that '[m]achine learning enables sophisticated algorithms to be more similar in function to a human employee with a task to achieve than a tool'.[80] The algorithmic contract in *Quoine* was, as the court stressed, 'deterministic',[81] which meant it performed precisely as programmed and did not 'have the capacity to develop its own responses to varying conditions'.[82] Nonetheless, the dissenting judgment of Mance IJ demonstrates an approach that is closer to treating algorithms as agents rather than as tools or systems.[83]

International Judge Mance justified taking a different approach from the majority on the ground that that '[t]he law should be adapted to the new world of algorithmic programmes and artificial intelligence, in a way which gives rise to the results that reason and justice would lead one to expect'.[84] International Judge Mance considered that the doctrine of unilateral mistake should not be interpreted to ignore the 'obvious' malfunctioning of a computer program.[85] This was important, because Mance IJ thought that computers should be treated as 'outworkers not overlords to whose operations parties can be taken to have submitted unconditionally in circumstances as out of ordinary as the present'.[86] Thus, Mance IJ held that relief on grounds of unilateral mistake should depend on what a person in the position of B2C2 would have 'known or perceived' if they had knowledge of the circumstances that actually occurred.[87] From this perspective, relief should be available if it would at once have been perceived by an honest and reasonable trader, given knowledge of the specific circumstances, that some fundamental error had occurred.[88] International Judge Mance justified this approach as consistent with the realities of algorithmic programs and artificial intelligence.[89] In this

[77] ibid [120] (Menon CJ, Phang and Prakash JJA and French IJ agreeing).

[78] cf Low and Mik (n 68).

[79] See especially S Chopra and LF White, *A Legal Theory for Autonomous Artificial Agents* (Ann Arbor, MI, The University of Michigan Press, 2011) 6. See also M Diamantis, 'Algorithms as Employees: Holding Corporations Accountable for Their Digital Workforce' (19 October 2021) at https://ssrn.com/abstract=3945882 (accessed 19 November 2021): 'If a corporation employs an algorithm that causes criminal or civil harm, the corporation should be liable just as if the algorithm were a human employee.'

[80] Scholz (n 1) 133.

[81] *Quoine* (n 2) [15], [97], [98], [114] (Menon CJ, Phang and Prakash JJA and French IJ agreeing).

[82] ibid [15] (Menon CJ, Phang and Prakash JJA and French IJ agreeing).

[83] This kind of approach may or may not advocate attributing legal personality to algorithms, but doctrinally the two questions are distinct.

[84] *Quoine* (n 2) [193].

[85] ibid [193].

[86] ibid; see also ibid [200].

[87] ibid [194].

[88] ibid; see also ibid [198] (Mance IJ).

[89] ibid [193].

case, Mance IJ considered it could not be said the parties had accepted the risk of error in or affecting the computer programs making the contracts.[90]

The difference between these approaches to algorithmic contracts, and with that the issue of intention or knowledge of the parties, is significant and goes beyond the immediate dispute. The approach taken by Mance IJ effectively assimilates the algorithm to a worker or employee. This allows the court to treat the algorithm as operating in a manner akin a human agent, for which an intention can be inferred, and then attributed to the person or firm deploying it.

We agree with the majority that such an approach is 'wholly artificial' in the circumstances.[91] It assumes that the operations of an algorithmic system can be substituted with those of a person, so that a person would hypothetically be dropped into the transaction at a certain point to determine how they would have viewed the scenario. But the operations of computer software are nothing like a person.[92] Algorithms follow pre-coded instructions at high speed, including in some instances to complete or use statistical methods over high volumes of data. They do not act 'like' an agent in law: algorithms are simply instructions to a computer chosen by a human, and it is these instructions that determine the operation of the automated system.[93]

The approach suggested by Mance IJ, of considering the knowledge of a hypothetical reasonable person in the circumstances that occurred, is also in our opinion inconsistent with the core defining characteristic of an algorithmic contracting system, which is to allow a series of rapid, accurate and uniform transactions. It disrupts their intended allocation of risk. As a factual matter, the parties have chosen not to scrutinise each transaction, prioritising speed and predictability instead. To open the circumstances of each contract's formation to review undermines their intention to prefer efficiency over accuracy. By having entered into the arrangement, both parties are taken to have accepted the risks associated with the occurrence of an error in the course of performance that cannot be corrected within the time allowed. As the majority stated in the case, the parties' use of algorithmic contracting simply does not accommodate 'the court artificially (or 'equitably') interposing another last look at the proposed terms immediately prior to the algorithms concluding the contract and, for that matter, still less after'.[94]

D. Does Machine Learning Change the Analysis?

In *Quoine*, both the majority and dissenting judges emphasised that their decisions applied to a deterministic system – namely, one where the outcome was determined

[90] ibid; see also ibid [196].

[91] ibid [39] and [97], quoting the view of the trial judge. See also Mik (n 3).

[92] L Kostopoulos, *Decoupling Human Characteristics from Algorithmic Capabilities* (IEEE Standards Association, 2021) 1: 'The prevalence of attributing human traits to Artificial Intelligence-Systems in efforts to describe its capabilities and use-cases does not adequately represent the technology in a sufficient way to allow for decision makers to fully engage with the ethical questions they are accountable for.'

[93] See also DKB Seng and CH Tan, 'Artificial Intelligence and Agents' (2021) NUS Centre for Technology, Robotics, Artificial Intelligence & the Law Working Paper 21/02, at https://ssrn.com/abstract=3935446 (accessed 19 November 2021); Mik (n 3) 210.

[94] *Quoine* (n 2) [104].

exactly by the programmer's instructions.[95] The contrast is presumably with algorithmic contracting that relies on a model derived from machine learning. It is here that the black-box effect of complex machine-learning systems might be raised as a hurdle to firm responsibility. With machine learning, the decision to contract, and on what terms, may be based on models derived from correlations and patterns identified in large data sets. These models may even change over time if the system is adaptive in the sense of 'learning' from its new data. This may make algorithmic-contracting systems more opaque and difficult to scrutinise. Indeed, the officers of a firm may not understand precisely how the algorithmic-contracting system works. Nonetheless, in our view this should not make a difference in attributing responsibility or culpability for the outputs of the system.[96]

Treating an algorithmic-contracting system as deploying some form of machine learning as an agent commonly overestimates the system's capabilities. While complex, automated systems – including those that that are premised on predictions derived from machine learning, and even those that are in some way adaptive – do not exercise autonomous decision-making capacity or agency as understood by lawyers or philosophers.[97] The firm deploying the algorithmic-contracting system, acting through programmers, will determine the objectives of the system and the contexts in which it operates, as well as exercising oversight of the outputs.

Moreover, to treat the system as the equivalent to the agent of the firm means that the firm may be absolved of responsibility for unforeseen or unexpected outcomes.[98] To the contrary, we suggest that this is precisely the responsibility that is assumed in deciding to deploy such a system in the market. Moreover, as we discuss in section V, in some scenarios the firm's use of algorithmic systems will be the basis for attributing culpability for harmful outcomes.

V. Algorithmic Contracts and Systematic Wrongdoing

Like the majority in *Quoine*, we suggest that in looking for intention or other related states of mind in algorithmic processes, the requisite inquiry should be into what was known at the time of programming. The concern with this approach may be that contracting parties are left unprotected in circumstances where they make a mistake about the terms of the contract.[99] However, in any circumstance, unilateral mistake is a narrowly defined doctrine with only a few successful cases. This is largely because parties are expected to scrutinise carefully the terms of contracts they enter into, and conversely because of the fact that it is, in any event, often difficult to attribute knowledge of a mistake to a contracting counterparty due to the scale of contracting processes

[95] ibid [98] (Menon CJ, Phang and Prakash JJA and French IJ agreeing), [152] (Mance IJ).

[96] Mik (n 3) 221–22.

[97] See also Seng and Tan (n 93).

[98] Scholz (n 1) 155: 'In agency law, principal is not always bound by the actions of their agents; the agents might act in a way that goes directly contrary to the stated goals and interests of the principles [*sic*].' See also Mik (n 3) 212–13, which criticises this approach.

[99] Compare also the analysis in Ooi (n 4).

in modern times. Notably, however, we suggest that there are other perspectives that may assist: these move away from a narrow focus on knowledge of a particular mistake, towards an inquiry into the design and governance of the system being scrutinised.

In particular, different considerations will apply where a firm has designed its algorithmic contracting process specifically to create, or capitalise upon, a mistaken belief by the counterparty. In some cases, like *National Exchange* discussed earlier, the very operation of the system is premised on the existence of a mistake by the counterparty. In other cases, the very design of the system may be directed to generating counterparty mistakes for profit.[100] In both scenarios, knowledge of the mistake on the part of the firm deploying the system is readily found, without requiring identification of some natural individual, such as a programmer (or teams of programmers) bearing the requisite knowledge. In these cases, unconscionability will likely also be established, again because the system is geared to take advantage of the known error.

Consistently, relief for misrepresentation, or unconscionable conduct, for example, may lie where one party has misled the other into thinking the dealing involves an exchange between humans, who will be informed by relational values and committed to not capitalising on each other's mistakes. As recognised by the court in *Quoine*, there is scope for applying unilateral mistake in a case where the firm responsible for the algorithmic contracting system knew that a relevant offer would only ever be accepted by a party operating under a mistake, and designed its system to take advantage of that error.[101] In such circumstances, unless that other party wantonly disregarded the risk of error in these circumstances, the resultant contract may be capable of being set aside on grounds of fraud or mistake.

Similarly, consider the use of predictive algorithms to identify consumers likely to sell below market value or buy at inflated prices. In some instances, such conduct may move beyond market research to more objectionable and unconscionable conduct, such as where the sale is pursued at a grossly disproportionate price or accompanied by the digital equivalent of hectoring conduct. Where an automated system is designed for the purpose of targeting counterparties who are vulnerable to mistake or unable to protect their own interests in the transaction, the very design of the system evidences a deliberateness that establishes culpability.[102]

The element of culpability may be less evident in algorithmic-contracting processes that were not designed for deliberate advantage taking but nonetheless have the effect of targeting parties acting under some element of disadvantage. In these scenarios it may be difficult to know whether the system is systematically targeting disadvantaged parties, or whether this is an outlier effect that is unfortunate but not necessarily unconscionable. Here there is potentially relief for systematic predatory contracts through recognising the possibility of unconscionable 'systems of conduct or patterns of behaviour'.[103] At some point where the operation of a firm's algorithmic-contracting

[100] JM Paterson, E Bant and H Coone, 'Australian Competition and Consumer Commission v Google: Deterring misleading conduct in digital privacy policies' (2021) 26 *Communications Law – Journal of Computer, Media and Telecommunications Law* 136.

[101] *Quoine* (n 2) [103] (Menon CJ, Phang and Prakash JJA and French IJ agreeing).

[102] Bant and Paterson (n 5) 82–83, 89.

[103] ibid 81–91.

processes consistently impacts unfairly on the other parties to the transaction, this becomes a pattern of behaviour. The failure of a firm to respond to this pattern of advantage taking at some point becomes purposive and culpable. In such situations, responsibility for that system may be attributed to the firm, without the necessity of finding a natural person who holds a deliberate intention or even direct knowledge of this occurrence.

Another possible scenario is where the algorithmic contracting system has 'learned' to target vulnerable parties, such as through high-price, low-value contracts in order to increase sales. Here it might be objected that the firm did not design or intend such an outcome. Yet it might be argued that culpability for the purposes of unconscionable conduct may for these purposes rest on omission of governance. This might be a lack of oversight or a failure to respond when a problem was identified. A firm that implements an algorithmic process knowing of its complexity should put in place processes for reviewing its operation, auditing outcomes and responding to complaints or concerns. A firm that puts these processes in place and fails to respond to defined problems has essentially decided to sanction those outcomes. A firm that fails to put these protective mechanisms in place should not be in any better position through turning a blind eye to the risk of harm caused by algorithmic-contracting process engaging in predatory conduct.

VI. Conclusion

Contract law and associated equitable doctrines have proved remarkably resilient in responding to new technologies. Provided we do not get carried away in attributing anthropomorphic superpowers to algorithmic contracts, the challenge may lie in the technical practicalities of oversight rather than the application of the law to curb excessive self-interested and predatory behaviour by a party with stronger bargaining power.

13

Can Corporations be Dishonest?

JEREMY GANS

I. Introduction: A Rock and a Hard Place

> **Article 1**
>
> La Nouvelle-Calédonie comprend:
>
> La Grande-Terre, l'île des Pins, l'archipel des Bélep, Huon et Surprise, les îles Chesterfield et *les récifs Bellone* ...[1]

In 1793, the British merchantman *Bellona* – sometime between Tuesday, 19 February, when it left Sydney (having deposited a mostly spoiled cargo, 17 female convicts and the continent's first non-Indigenous free settler families), and when it reached Penang on Thursday, 16 May (en route to China and England)[2] – passed through a South Pacific reef system. Captain Matthew Boyd bestowed his ship's name on the reef, including its southernmost point: a cluster of atolls at 22 degrees south and 159 degrees east, now known as South Bellona.[3]

In 1878, the French warship *La Seudre* – sometime between Saturday, 8 June, when it left Noumea (having been alerted by a British trader about a plan to appropriate various Coral Sea islands for their guano), and its return on Wednesday, 19 June (having granted that same trader a guano licence with taxes payable to France) – spent several days at Long Island, one-tenth of a square kilometre of sandy rock at 20 degrees south and 158 degrees east, the largest body of land in the Chesterfield Isles. On the final Saturday of the trip, Captain Louis Adolphe Gudon planted a French flag, claiming, on behalf of New Caledonia's Governor Jean Baptiste Léon Olry, the entire archipelago, including *les récifs Bellone*.[4]

In 2010, the Australian boat *Diana* – sometime between early June, when it left Brisbane (bearing a high-seas fishing permit and equipment for demersal long-line fishing), and when it returned on Wednesday, 28 July (where skipper Russell Potter was met by

[1] 'Loi organique n° 99–209 du 19 mars 1999 relative à la Nouvelle-Calédonie' (Version consolidée au 21 décembre 2017) at www.drom-com.fr/medias/org-411/shared/loi-organique-n---99-209-du-19-mars-1999-version-consolidee.pdf (emphasis added).

[2] J Willets, 'Convict Ship Bellona' at www.freesettlerorfelon.com/convict_ship_bellona_1793.htm (accessed 15 November 2021).

[3] J Cumpston, *Shipping Arrivals & Departures, Sydney, 1788–1925*, 1st edn (Canberra, Roebuck Society, 1963) 28.

[4] B Fuligni, *Tour du Monde des Terres Françaises Oubliées* (Paris, Éditions du Trésor, 2016) 20–38.

Australian Fisheries Management Authority (AFMA) officers) – worked the Capel Bank, an area of the Coral Sea between 24 and 25 degrees south and 159 and 160 degrees east. On the final Saturday of the trip, a pilot from Australia's Customs Service flew over the 72-foot vessel and noted its position, which was within 200 nautical miles of South Bellona.[5]

These three events, spanning four centuries and degrees of latitude, prompted criminal charges. The most obvious – laid because, as the officers told Potter, 'We believe you are fishing in New Caledonia waters' – was under the Fisheries Management Act 1991 (Cth):[6]

105C Australian-flagged boat fishing in foreign waters

(1) A person is guilty of an offence if:

(a) the person intentionally uses an Australian-flagged boat for fishing; and
(b) the boat is in the exclusive economic zone, territorial sea, archipelagic waters (as defined in the United Nations Convention on the Law of the Sea) or internal waters of a foreign country and the person is reckless as to that fact; and
(c) the law of the country requires the person to have an authorisation (however described) given under the law of the of the country for the fishing and the person is reckless as to that fact.

(2) The offence is punishable on conviction by a fine not more than 500 penalty units.[7]

But this charge was complicated by two esoteric details of the law of the sea. France didn't deposit charts setting out its South Pacific exclusive economic zone (EEZ) claim until nearly a year after *Diana*'s 2010 expedition;[8] and, anyway, it was not clear whether barren South Bellona was an 'island' (which could delimit the 200km exclusive economic zone of whoever claimed it) or a 'rock' (which couldn't).[9]

That is presumably why Potter and his employer, Mures Fishing Pty Ltd, each eventually faced 60 counts under a quite different provision, in the Criminal Code Act 1995 (Cth):

135.1 General dishonesty

(7) A person is guilty of an offence if:

(a) the person does anything with the intention of dishonestly influencing a public official in the exercise of the official's duties as a public official; and
(b) the public official is a Commonwealth public official; and
(c) the duties are duties as a Commonwealth public official.

Penalty: Imprisonment for 5 years.[10]

[5] See at www.un.org/depts/los/LEGISLATIONANDTREATIES/PDFFILES/MAPS/FRA_MZN81_2011_00200.jpg; described at www.un.org/depts/los/LEGISLATIONANDTREATIES/STATEFILES/FRA_Deposit_MZN81.htm.

[6] See Derrington and Walpole, ch 16 of this volume, on whether *Diana* could have been prosecuted for this offence. As they note in section X, the usual reason to do so – because the ship's owners would otherwise be out of jurisdiction – does not arise here. Also, the language of s 105C(1)(a) of the Fisheries Management Act 1991 (Cth) is hard to square with a prosecution of a ship.

[7] Fisheries Management Act 1991 (Cth), s 105C(1)–(2).

[8] See United Nations, 'Circular Communications from the Division for Ocean Affairs and the Law of the Sea Office of Legal Affairs' (MZN 81.2011.LOS of 3 May 2011) at www.un.org/depts/los/LEGISLATIONANDTREATIES/STATEFILES/FRA.htm.

[9] Convention on the Law of the Sea, opened for signature 10 December 1982, 1833 UNTS 3 (entered into force 16 November 1994) Art 121.

[10] Criminal Code Act 1995 (Cth), sch, s 135.1(7) ('Criminal Code').

Figure 13.1 France, 'Submission in compliance with the deposit obligations pursuant to the United Nations Convention of the Law of the Sea (UNCLOTS): Chart No 7321 (INT636) – "Des Récifs Bampton à l'île Hunter Nouvelle-Calédonie Vanuatu", Scale 1:1,500,000'

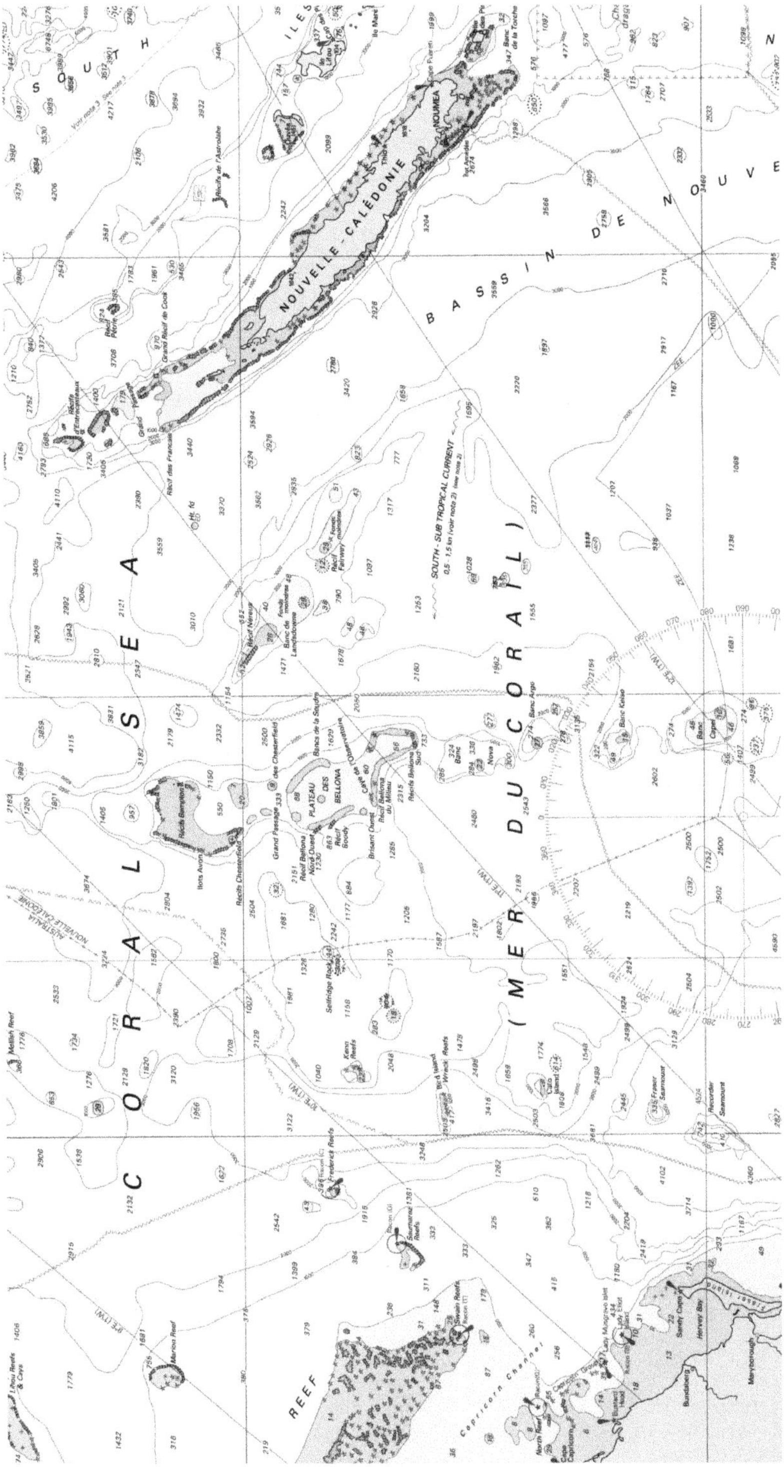

But this charge was complicated by two esoteric details of federal criminal law: Potter's prosecutors needed to prove that the skipper was 'dishonest' and Mures Fishing's prosecutors needed to satisfy a novel test for corporate criminal responsibility in section 12.3 of the Criminal Code.

This chapter first sets out how the prosecutors failed to surmount either of these obstacles, reprising territory familiar to criminal lawyers: the complexities of both dishonesty and corporate responsibility. The chapter then examines the unpublished ruling from Tasmania's Chief Justice to the effect that no federal prosecutor could ever surmount both obstacles simultaneously. It explores the cogency and effect of this dictum, which goes well beyond fishing regulation, and indeed federal criminal law. The chapter concludes by outlining an alternative option for defining corporate dishonesty in criminal trials.

These are uncharted waters in two senses: the *Diana* trial seems to be the only Australian case where a judge has expressly grappled with these combined questions; and the key rulings are unpublished. That's why I've opted for a deep dive, using university funds to purchase Blow CJ's key mid-trial extempore reasons and also – because they were already transcribed – the closing jury arguments from both sides.[11] That being said, because obtaining full transcripts was too expensive and pursuing other sources of information would require ethical clearance, there are doubtless further depths I haven't plumbed.

II. Criminal Dishonesty: Lies, Damned Lies and Logistics

> And these figures here are the lats and longs that represent where the shot started and where it's finished, is that correct? **It's – yes.**
>
> Is that right? **Yeah, I'm probably not always spot on with it but –**
>
> When you say you are not always spot on, what do you mean by that? **Well, sometimes I might not get it perfectly right but it should be pretty much within the area.**[12]

In his interview with AFMA's officers, Potter admitted that *Diana*'s logbooks weren't always right when it came to the ship's position at the start and end of its fishing shots. The officers already knew that: they had compared earlier logbooks submitted to AFMA with data from *Diana*'s automated GPS system records, and confirmed the data via the Customs flyover. But that didn't prove Potter's guilt of any crime.

Falsehoods are only sometimes illegal. It's legal to overstate the size of the fish you caught last week, at least to your buddies. And you can lawfully lie to more important people too, like your lover (but not to get money or sex) and your boss, your colleagues, a pesky journalist, your constituents and so on (though, again, not for money or sex.) But lies to government are a different matter. It can be illegal to write wrong things in a government form, especially if that form warns you that false or misleading statements

[11] *R v Potter & Mures Fishing Pty Ltd* (Transcript, Supreme Court of Tasmania, Blow CJ) 464–29 (14 September 2015), 530–44 (15 September 2015) (Transcript).

[12] ibid 522–23.

are a serious offence.[13] Potter's logbooks, which he was required to keep by statute and under *Diana*'s licence, included such a warning.[14]

But even when falsehoods are illegal, not all such falsehoods will see you found guilty in a criminal trial. Fraud (lying for money) is illegal, but the criminal law doesn't punish generally accepted types of lies for money, such as the exchange of lies during haggling (eg 'a special price for you', 'this is my final offer'). Likewise, only some lies for sex are an offence. And even writing falsehoods (or, um, misleadinghoods) on government forms that warn you not to do so isn't always criminal. Rather, those wrong statements have to be both 'knowing' (and not, say, 'sometimes I might not get it perfectly right') and 'material' (and not, say, 'pretty much in the area'). So, depending on some (admittedly difficult) questions of degree, Potter's wrong logbook entries, at least on his version of events, were not sufficiently bad to merit punishment in and of themselves.

Instead, Potter and Mures Fishing's prosecutors opted to make a different allegation of criminality: that he made the wrong logbook entries 'with the intention of dishonestly influencing a public official in the exercise of the official's duties as a public official'. The relevant 'public official', according to the prosecution, was Heidi Prislan, AFMA's licensing manager, and her relevant duties were checking that licensees complied with their licences and the federal fisheries statute. The prosecution argued, and the trial judge, Blow CJ, agreed, that it didn't matter if Potter knew who Prislan was, so long as he knew there was someone like that doing something like that somewhere in some government. It also didn't matter whether Prislan, or anyone else, actually read *Diana*'s logbooks, much less believed them or was affected by them in any way. Instead, all that mattered was what Potter wanted to achieve by being 'probably not always spot on' in recording his ship's position and, crucially, whether acting on that hope was 'dishonest'.

The element of dishonesty plays two overlapping roles in criminal law. One is to check whether typically bad conduct (such as lying for money or taking someone else's property without asking) is actually acceptable conduct in a particular instance, and accordingly decriminalising honest scenarios (such as haggling or pocketing abandoned coins). The other is to identify when typically good conduct (such as receiving money from the government or trying to persuade an official about something) is actually unacceptable in a particular instance, and accordingly criminalising dishonest scenarios (such as fooling or bribing an official.) Either way, it's defined in the Criminal Code in a circular way to mean:

(a) dishonest according to the standards of ordinary people; and
(b) known by the defendant to be dishonest according to the standards of ordinary people.[15]

This definition doesn't so much define dishonesty as spell out whose view of dishonesty counts. The answer (for most offences) is that dishonesty is whatever ordinary people think is dishonest and (for some offences, including, for now, those in the Criminal Code) what the accused thinks ordinary people think.

[13] Criminal Code (n 9), ss 137.1, 137.2.
[14] Transcript (n 10) 501.
[15] Criminal Code (n 9), s 130.3.

Although dishonesty looks like (and indeed is) a 'know it when you see it' concept, senior courts assure us that actual disagreements about what is and isn't dishonest are rare and that most disputes about dishonesty are about what the accused was really thinking:

> [P]utting to one side the exceptional case where it is in issue, it is sufficient for a trial judge simply to instruct the jury that they must be satisfied beyond reasonable doubt as to the knowledge, belief or intent alleged by the prosecution before they can convict.[16]

The *Diana* case was not exceptional. Chief Justice Blow, rejecting an argument by Potter and Mures Fishing, ruled that it didn't matter whether *Diana* actually fished in France's exclusive economic zone, or even if that zone extended into the Capel Bank or existed at all.[17] Instead, rejecting an argument by the prosecutor, he ruled that it was crucial that the prosecution convinced the jury that Potter believed that France's zone *could* extend into Capel Bank.[18] That belief was a necessary part of the prosecution's claim that Potter's goal when he filled out the logbooks was to reduce the chances that someone like Prislan would look into *Diana*'s possible breach of maritime boundaries.

Potter's prosecutors failed to meet the test Blow CJ set for them. As the defence pointed out, none of the chain of possibilities the prosecution had to establish – Potter making *possible* logbooking errors to avoid Prislan *possibly* detecting *Diana's possible* fishing in France's *possible* waters – was especially likely on even the *prosecution's* evidence. It wasn't clear that Potter's logbooks were especially wrong, rather than mainly just the infelicities that come from the logistics of demersal fishing; boats that fish the ocean bottom use lines that are a mile long, making it hard to pin down (and, hence, to log) exactly where and when the fishing occurs. And Potter had little reason to think his logbook entries would actually fool AFMA, given that AFMA had ready access to his ship's automated GPS records and had sometimes placed its officers on the deck while it fished the Capel Bank. Also, not all of Potter's recordkeeping errors were one-way (specifically, away from South Bellona); some put *Diana* closer to or within France's possible waters, or somewhere ridiculous like central Australia, fooling no one. Finally, there was no reason for Potter to think he was anywhere near a relevant maritime boundary; he claimed that AFMA itself had told his boss he could fish anywhere in the Capel Bank, and that was backed up by AFMA's own maps, which didn't include France's purported claim.

In short, Potter's *possibly dishonest* logbooking was never more than that. Rather, most of the prosecution's own evidence backed up what *Diana*'s skipper had told AFMA's investigators on the Wednesday they boarded his ship: he was simply slipshod when it came to filling in the ship's log. Whatever else that may be, it is not dishonesty or any other serious crime. Unsurprisingly, Potter's jury speedily acquitted him.[19]

[16] *Peters v R* [1998] HCA 7, (1998) 192 CLR 493, 508 [28] (Toohey and Gaudron JJ).

[17] *R v Potter* [2015] TASSC 44, (2015) 25 Tas R 213.

[18] Transcript (n 10) 494.

[19] D Abbey, 'Mures and skipper found not guilty' *The Mercury* (16 September 2015) at www.themercury.com.au/news/scales-of-justice/mures-and-skipper-found-not-guilty/news-story/67335772fdf2b7ecf08c8d87858e503b.

III. Corporate Culture: Longitudes and Attitudes

> Mr Mure said that when The Diana was at sea on a fishing trip he would speak to the skipper daily, that he did not discuss the location of the vessel except in general terms, that there was no training regime in place, that he didn't check the completed log books but just stored them and that there was no process for checking on the locations where the vessel had been other than daily conversations.[20]

Will and Sarah Mure inherited their parents' restaurant and fishing business when George Mure died in 2003, with Will running the fishing side and his sister running the restaurant. After he and his wife bought out his sister and her husband, Mure mused to *Restaurant and Catering* about why Tasmania's fishing scene was thriving:

> Will points to the Australian Fishery Management Authority, which is responsible for the efficient and sustainable management of Commonwealth fish resources, as one of the reasons why the country, especially Tasmania, has such an excellent reputation. 'Back in the old days, trolling [sic] was bad because there were no restrictions. Nowadays, it's completely different. It's well-managed by the Australian fishing industry and people only fish in areas they have always fished, so there's no further damage to the habitat. It's come a long way since the days we first started.'[21]

He was speaking just months before his company's and his skipper's trial on 60 counts of general dishonesty, and years after AFMA officers interviewed him about the warmer waters *Diana* (named after his grandmother) trawled in Tasmania's off-season.

When AFMA officials first spoke with Mure, they likely were exploring a possible prosecution under the Fisheries Management Act 1991 (Cth), which included this provision on corporate criminal responsibility:

> **164 Conduct of directors, servants and agents**
>
> (1) Where, in proceedings for an offence against this Act it is necessary to establish the state of mind of a body corporate in relation to particular conduct, it is sufficient to show:
>
> (a) that the conduct was engaged in by a director, servant or agent of the body corporate within the scope of his or her actual or apparent authority; and
>
> (b) that the director, servant or agent had the state of mind.
>
> (2) Any conduct engaged in on behalf of a body corporate by a director, servant or agent of the body corporate within the scope of his or her actual or apparent authority is taken, for the purposes of a prosecution for an offence against this Act, to have been engaged in also by the body corporate unless the body corporate establishes that the body corporate took reasonable precautions and exercised due diligence to avoid the conduct.[22]

This is what the Australian Law Reform Commission (ALRC), in its recent report on corporate criminal responsibility, dubbed the 'TPA model' of corporate criminal responsibility. The model, named after a provision in Australia's trade practices statute,[23] makes a company vicariously liable for its employees' crimes, unless the company can prove

[20] Transcript (n 10) 466.

[21] 'The Man and the Sea' *Restaurant and Catering* (2 June 2015).

[22] Fisheries Management Act 1991 (Cth), s 164.

[23] Competition and Consumer Act 2010 (Cth), s 84. This statute was previously named the Trade Practices Act 1974 (Cth).

that it took sufficient steps – here, both 'reasonable precautions' and 'due diligence' – to stop the employee's conduct. In short, AFMA may have assumed that Mures Fishing's criminal responsibility for Russell Potter's actions in the Coral Sea would be something the accused company would have to disprove, as per the closing words of section 164(2).

Mures Fishing would have struggled to prove that it exercised reasonable precautions or due diligence in relation to where Potter took *Diana*. Will Mure, in his interview, 'said that he made big picture strategic decisions as to where to fish, but that where Mr Potter fished within the big picture was up to him'.[24] That is, he pretty much admitted (on behalf of his company) that he (and, seemingly, the rest of his company) had done little to check whether or not Potter was fishing in France's (or anyone else's) EEZ. But, as already noted, France's EEZ was written in water (or at least was in 2008 to 2010), making it hard for prosecutors to prove that any 'conduct engaged in by' Potter in sailing around the Capel Bank was a crime under the fisheries statute, much less that his 'state of mind' satisfied any corresponding mental element. When Mures Fishing entered a not guilty plea to 41 counts under that offence (which would have required proof that Potter was aware of a 'substantial risk' that *Diana* was fishing in France's EEZ), the prosecution offered no evidence and Blow CJ dismissed the charges.[25]

However, the other offence Mures Fishing faced – general dishonesty – differs not only in its elements, but also in the applicable rule for corporate criminal responsibility, which is in section 12.3(1) of the Criminal Code:

> If intention, knowledge or recklessness is a fault element in relation to a physical element of an offence, that fault element must be attributed to a body corporate that expressly, tacitly or impliedly authorised or permitted the commission of the offence.

This test of corporate fault, contained in part 2.5 of chapter 2 of the Criminal Code (and also the criminal codes of the Australian Capital Territory, Northern Territory, Fiji and Nauru),[26] applies to the hundreds of offences in the remaining chapters of the Criminal Code (including the offences of false statements in government documents and general dishonesty), and in many other parts of federal, territory and overseas statute books. However, as is well known, part 2.5 is also excluded from many key federal regulatory schemes. The ALRC reported that the fisheries legislation was among the first to be so amended, to ensure that that statute 'would operate in the same way' as it always had, a decision a parliamentary committee characterised as 'a decision not to take advantage of the improvements contained in the *Criminal Code*'.[27]

Many federal enforcement agencies, and perhaps also the ALRC, don't see part 2.5 as an 'improvement' over the TPA model. The *Diana* case demonstrates how part 2.5 can disadvantage prosecutors. In contrast to the TPA model, it never deems a corporation to be criminally responsible for anyone else's actions, either by vicarious liability or a reverse onus, let alone both. Instead, Mures Fishing's prosecutors could only succeed if

[24] Transcript (n 10) 466.

[25] D Killick, 'Mures' fish case dropped' *The Mercury* (12 February 2016).

[26] Criminal Code 2002 (ACT), s 51; Criminal Code Act 1983 (NT), sch 1, s 43BM; Crimes Decree 2009 (Fiji); Crimes Act 2016 (Nauru), s 39.

[27] Australian Law Reform Commission, *Corporate Criminal Responsibility* (Report No 136, April 2020) [2.80] (ALRC Final Report), citing Scrutiny of Bills Committee, *Agriculture, Fisheries and Forestry Legislation Amendment (Application of Criminal Code) Bill 2001 Bills Digest* (Digest No 20 of 2001–02) 34.

they proved that the corporation 'expressly, tacitly or impliedly authorised or permitted' whatever Potter did. That requirement transforms Mure's statement about his hands-off approach to *Diana*'s navigation from an apparent admission under the TPA model (specifically that Mures Fishing didn't take reasonable precautions or exercise due diligence about anything Potter did with the logbook entries) to an apparent rebuttal of the prosecution's charge under the Code scheme (specifically that Mures Fishing didn't authorise or permit whatever Potter did with those entries).

Or does it? The Criminal Code sets out four (non-exhaustive) ways for prosecutors to prove that a corporation authorised or permitted an offence.[28] The first two equate roughly to the common law's attribution model:

> (a) proving that the body corporate's board of directors intentionally, knowingly or recklessly carried out the relevant conduct, or expressly, tacitly or impliedly authorised or permitted the commission of the offence; or
> (b) proving that a high managerial agent of the body corporate intentionally, knowingly or recklessly engaged in the relevant conduct, or expressly, tacitly or impliedly authorised or permitted the commission of the offence …

These tests are often criticised as too narrow to capture large corporations where key decisions are made by middle managers, but that isn't a problem when it comes to prosecuting a small family company like Mures Fishing. Rather, the problem in the *Diana* case is that the prosecutors lacked evidence that anyone with any say at all at Mures Fishing – Mure or his sister or their spouses or anyone else who would fit these categories – had any involvement with Potter's logbooking. There's every reason to think they were all as hands-off as Will Mure told AFMA that he was. In any case, the prosecution did not claim otherwise.

Rather, the prosecution of Mures Fishing rested entirely on the other two specified ways that a corporation's authorisation or permission of an offence can be established under the Criminal Code:

> (c) proving that a corporate culture existed within the body corporate that directed, encouraged, tolerated or led to non-compliance with the relevant provision; or
> (d) proving that the body corporate failed to create and maintain a corporate culture that required compliance with the relevant provision.

These much-loved (by academics at least) but little-used (in courts at least) provisions allow prosecutors to look beyond, or even around, the minds of any of the corporation's employees, high or low. The Criminal Code defines 'corporate culture' to mean:

> an attitude, policy, rule, course of conduct or practice existing within the body corporate generally or in the part of the body corporate in which the relevant activities takes place.[29]

Chief Justice Blow criticised this definition, not just for its grammar – seemingly single-handedly prompting an ALRC corrective recommendation – but its breadth: '[O]ne rule amounts to corporate culture. One policy amounts to corporate culture.'[30] Such breadth is, of course, good news for federal prosecutors.

[28] See Criminal Code (n 9), s 12.3(3).
[29] ibid s 12.3(6).
[30] Transcript (n 10) 466.

And yet the Chief Justice refused to even leave the question of Mures Fishing's alleged dishonest corporate culture to the jury. Instead, he found that the company's prosecutors had offered almost no evidence either way on that topic:

> [I]n this case, there is no evidence as to any aspect of corporate culture within the company generally, the interview – the assertions in the interview were limited to comments about the relationship between Mr Mure and Mr Potter, except for one perhaps general comment that there wasn't a training regime, but that – it's not clear – it's not clear how wide that comment was meant to be.[31]

He added that the same was true about Mures Fishing's alleged missing honest corporate culture:

> The interview with Mr Mure did not thoroughly explore what attitudes, policies, rules, course of conduct or practices there were in relation to the lodgement of daily logs or dishonest influencing of officials. The – it must follow, on my view, that the jury – that it's not reasonably open to the jury to infer that the body corporate failed to do anything that required compliance with the section about intentions to dishonestly influence Commonwealth officials. We – the evidence establishes that some things were not done. It doesn't follow that nothing was done and reading 12.2(d) together with the definition in my view requires the Crown to establish that nothing was done.[32]

These findings are surely overstated. There was clearly evidence of some 'aspects' of Mures Fishing's culture, specifically of at least one 'attitude' or 'course of conduct' or 'practice' of Will Mure: his hands-off approach when it came to Potter's logbooking, and specifically a lack of training about or checking of those logbooks. There's no doubt that the AFMA officers could have asked a lot more about those practices (and perhaps didn't because they were anticipating Mures Fishing bearing the onus of proof). But that failure is a matter for the prosecutor and jury, not the trial judge.

However, Blow CJ went on to specify a more particular gap in the evidence: AFMA had not explored how anything Will Mure (or anyone else in his company) did 'led to' Potter trying to influence AFMA:

> Now, as to the – the body corporate generally, in my view, there is no reasonable basis for an inference that any aspect of Mures' corporate culture directed or encouraged the dishonest influencing of any officials or involved tolerating any such offence, or led to any such offence being committed. There's almost no evidence in relation to – or there's little or no evidence as to the corporate culture features of the corporation generally. I take the words 'led to' as relating to causation, and there's so little evidence as to any aspect of the corporate culture of the company generally that there's, in my view, no rational basis for an inference adverse to the company in relation to any corporate culture, attitude, policy, rule, course of conduct or practice existing within the body corporate generally ...[33]

Here, the Chief Justice is on stronger ground, albeit still one where reasonable minds can differ. Like most issues of criminal fault, the question of whether an attitude or course of conduct or a practice 'led to' (or 'tolerated' or 'encouraged') another's behaviour turns

[31] ibid.
[32] ibid 467–68.
[33] ibid 467.

on an assessment of circumstantial evidence. The question of whether Mure's hands-off approach to Potter's actions on the Coral Sea 'led to' the skipper deliberately making incorrect entries in his logbook or at least 'tolerated' that happening is, surely, one for a jury (and an appeal court reviewing the safety of a jury's verdict), not a trial judge.

The Chief Justice took the same stance when it came to Mures Fishing's alleged lack of a pro-compliance culture:

> In my view even if one looks at corporate culture generally rather than taking the literal approach that the section would seem to compel the evidence only goes so far as to establish a lack of a formal training regime at least for skippers and the fact that Mr Mure didn't check on latitude and longitude entries in the daily logs. That falls a very long way short of what would be needed for a jury to be satisfied beyond reasonable doubt of a lack of a corporate culture as to honesty and trustworthiness. There may be scintillas of evidence that support the Crown case but a scintilla of evidence does not amount to a prima facie case ...[34]

Again, this is a stronger basis for Blow CJ's ruling, but still not an overwhelming one. Why couldn't the prosecution seek to convince the jury that management's lack of training, checking and discussion about the details of *Diana*'s voyages meant that Mures Fishing's culture didn't 'require compliance' with big things like federal dishonesty laws?

On balance, I think that the Chief Justice should have left these matters to the jury (and if they convicted, an appeal court) to sort out. Nevertheless, his reasoning accurately sets out the steep uphill battle the prosecutors would have faced had the trial of Mures Fishing proceeded to a non-directed verdict. It's very hard to prosecute a corporation for having a dishonest culture (or lacking an honest one) when you have little evidence of either dishonesty or culture. And yet, even that wasn't the biggest problem this prosecution faced.

IV. Corporate Dishonesty: Neither Fish nor Foul

> HIS HONOUR: Now, you've got a question, Mr Foreman?
>
> MR FOREMAN: Yes thanks, your Honour. The question was how long might the trial continue for?
>
> HIS HONOUR: I think it will finish tomorrow. You'll begin to see why in a moment.[35]

The jurors were obviously frustrated, having sat through two weeks of hearings and 11 prosecution witnesses testifying about fishing regulations, and then being kept out of the courtroom for a day while the 'legal issues' were sorted. Potter and Will Mure, on the other hand, must have sensed that the cloud of criminal charges hanging over them for years was about to clear. The thoughts of the prosecutor, David Staehli, or the then Commonwealth Director of Public Prosecutions, Robert Bromwich, are harder to guess, but it's possible they were in shock.

[34] ibid 468.
[35] ibid 477.

'Take a seat,' Blow CJ had told the trial lawyers that morning, before ruling:

> The opening [words] of s12.3(1) aren't satisfied. The section only applies if intention, knowledge or recklessness is a fault element. In this case, or in the case of s135.1(7), it's dishonesty, not intention, knowledge or recklessness that is, in substance, the fault element. And the – given that's the Crown have particularised the charge against Mures Fishing Pty Ltd so as to – so that it depends on criminal liability under s12.3(1), it follows that the company has no case to answer.[36]

This ruling has nothing to do with *Diana*, the logbooks or anyone's *Zone Économique Exclusive* or any of the evidence against Potter and Mures Fishing, or with anyone's corporate culture. Rather, it is a ruling that no corporation could ever be convicted of the federal crime of general dishonesty. The prosecution of Mures Fishing was doomed from the start.

And so – if Blow CJ's ruling is followed in other federal criminal trials and appeals – are all other federal prosecutions of corporations for general dishonesty. Mures Fishing Pty Ltd can't be prosecuted for general dishonesty in the future. Nor could any other corporation. Indeed, no such prosecutions, much less convictions, should ever have happened. That includes, for example, the conviction of a company called Wood Grain Pty Ltd's on 67 charges under section 135.1(7), resulting in a $680,000 fine, three months before Mures Fishing was acquitted;[37] according to Blow CJ, Wood Grain pleaded guilty to a crime that it couldn't have committed.[38]

And there's (much) more. The Tasmanian Chief Justice's ruling would seem to hold equally for other federal offences that require proof of dishonesty in regimes that are subject to section 12.3 of the Criminal Code.[39] If persuasive in the territory or overseas courts, it will also cover all or most dishonesty offences in the Australian Capital Territory, the Northern Territory and Fiji.

But much depends on whether Blow CJ's ruling is correct, and also why. His ruling that section 12.3(1) doesn't apply to section 135.1(7) rests on a polysyllogism:

- Section 12.3(1) only applies to the fault elements of intent, knowledge or recklessness.
- Section 135.1(7)'s fault element is dishonesty.
- Dishonesty isn't intent, knowledge or recklessness.

The complication is that there are counter-arguments to each of these steps.

[36] ibid 465. (The transcript actually begins 'So, the opening word of section 12.3(1) aren't satisfied.')

[37] See Australian Law Reform Commission, *Corporate Criminal Responsibility* (Discussion Paper No 87, 15 November 2019) [3.60] (ALRC Discussion Paper).

[38] The basis of the guilty plea is not clear. A media report at the time attributes the criminal conduct to a contractor working for the company: 'Commonwealth prosecutor Peter Callaghan SC told the court a pest contractor had signed blank fumigation certificates for the company, which submitted the documents with false information between 2007 and 2009. The pest contractor concerned received a similar sentence after pleading guilty before Toowoomba District Court in October 2012 to his role in the offending.' See J Taylor, 'Grain company and director Thomas Dudley Woods guilty of lying about fumigating chickpea shipment to India' *ABC* (31 July 2015). The media report also suggests that the company's director may simultaneously have pleaded guilty on the basis of complicity in the company's crime: 'Judge Brendan Butler found the fraudulent scheme was initiated by someone other than Woods, but the director of the family-owned company later helped conceal the crimes. "Very likely it was to protect the company, the family and perhaps your brother in circumstances where the scheme had already commenced and you became aware of it," the judge said. "In that time as a director of the company and operations manager it was your duty to ensure the company complied … and continued to act lawfully."' If that's right, then Woods may have pleaded guilty (and received an 18-month sentence) for complicity in a corporate non-crime.

[39] In 2013, a company called Sarai Holdings pleaded guilty to a different general dishonesty offence and was fined $60,000. See ALRC Discussion Paper (n 36) [3.60].

For section 12.3(1), the counter-argument is that there are clear textual and structural indications that the Criminal Code is supposed to provide for corporate responsibility for all fault elements, not just some of them. Part 2.5, which governs corporate criminal responsibility, opens with two general principles: 'This Code applies to bodies corporate in the same way as it applies to individuals' and 'a body corporate may be found guilty of any offence'.[40] Its remaining sections track the structure of part 2.2, which is the Criminal Code's core part on how all federal offences are structured and construed:

12.2 Physical elements
12.3 Fault elements other than negligence
12.4 Negligence
12.5 Mistake of fact (strict liability)
12.6 Intervening conduct of event

In particular, section 12.3's heading expressly excludes only negligence (dealt with in section 12.4) from its coverage of fault elements, reflecting similar rules elsewhere in chapter 2.[41]

But there is a clear rejoinder to that counter-argument: unlike other similar provisions of the Criminal Code, the text of section 12.3(1) only refers to intent, knowledge and recklessness, and that seems likely to be by design. Section 12.3's origins date to a 1992 report by an ad hoc law reform body, the Criminal Law Officers' Committee (later the Model Criminal Code Officers' Committee (MCCOC)). In its 'discussion draft' on the proposed general principles of criminal responsibility, the Committee devised two provisions for corporate criminal responsibility – one for intent and knowledge, the other for recklessness:

> 501.3 If intention or knowledge is a required fault element of an offence, that fault element exists on the part of a body corporate that expressly, tacitly or impliedly authorised or permitted the commission of the offence …
>
> 501.4 If recklessness is a required fault element of an offence, that fault element may exist on the part of a body corporate if a servant, agent, employee or officer of the body corporate acting within the scope of his or her employment or his or her actual authority has that fault element. But that element cannot be attributed to the body corporate if it was aware that there was a substantial risk of the commission of the offence and it took measures that resulted in it not being unjustifiable to take that risk.[42]

This pair of provisions clearly didn't cover any other fault elements. Later that year, the final text of what became section 12.3 appeared in the Committee's final report, which explained its decision to combine the two early provisions into one:

> This section deals with offences requiring proof of intent, knowledge or recklessness. The Discussion Draft had a separate provision for offences based on recklessness but, on reflection the Committee concluded that it was inconsistent and impractical to have different mechanisms for intent and recklessness.[43]

[40] Criminal Code (n 9), s 12.1.
[41] See ibid ss 8.2, 8.3, 9.1.
[42] Criminal Law Officers' Committee, *General Principles of Criminal Responsibility* (Discussion Draft, July 1992) 94, 96. The Committee's annotation states at 101 'The corporate definition of recklessness follows the separate decision of the Committee to define the general concept of "criminal recklessness" in terms of substantial risk rather than probable or possible risk, and in terms of taking "unjustifiable risk".'
[43] Criminal Law Officers' Committee, *General Principles of Criminal Responsibility* (Report, December 1992) 111.

While the combined provision could plausibly suit a one-size-fits-(almost)-all approach to corporate criminal responsibility for all fault elements, there is no sign that that's what the Committee intended; rather, all signs are that the Committee only sought to cover the same territory that the previous two draft provisions had. The upshot is that, while it's far from clear how MCCOC wanted fault elements other than intent, knowledge or recklessness treated when it comes to corporate criminal responsibility, it seems likely that part 2.5 was never meant to set out how corporate criminal responsibility works for offences that contain other sorts of fault elements. This includes the Criminal Code's offence of general dishonesty.

Or does it? The counter-argument is that the actual offence Mures Fishing was charged with, section 135.1(7), has a fault element that is clearly covered by section 12.3 (emphasis added):

> A person is guilty of an offence if:
>
> (a) the person does anything *with the intention* of dishonestly influencing a public official in the exercise of the official's duties as a public official; and
> (b) the public official is a Commonwealth public official; and
> (c) the duties are duties as a Commonwealth public official.
>
> Penalty: Imprisonment for 5 years.

The Chief Justice expressly addressed this detail, but declared it a red herring:

> Although the adverb 'dishonestly' is used to modify the word – influencing, and although the adverb dishonestly is used to qualify the word 'intention', if one considers the ingredients of the offence from a – if one considers the ingredients of the offence and what has to happen in order for the offence to be committed, it's clear that the subsection is intended to prohibit dishonest conduct not a dishonest result. So although the subsection has been worded as though dishonesty has something to do with influencing, it's really the conduct of the – the offender that needs to be dishonest in order for the offence to be committed.[44]

Squinting a bit – well, a lot – his point is that the adverb 'dishonestly' really modifies the offence's conduct element ('does anything') and not the additional intention set out in much of paragraph (a). That is an unusual but plausible reading – one of the other three general dishonesty offences in section 135.1 is expressly drafted so as to work that way,[45] and there is no reason to think the four offences were meant to work differently from each other; indeed, most dishonesty offences work the way Blow CJ described.

But the Chief Justice added a further, more compelling rejoinder:

> There's nothing inherently improper about influencing a commonwealth public official or intending to influence a commonwealth public official. The subsection is directed at criminalising the doing of an act dishonestly with an intention of influencing a commonwealth public official. And that leads me to conclude that the fault element in a s135.1(7) offence is dishonesty not intention to influence or any other sort of intention, and the fault element certainly isn't knowledge or recklessness.[46]

[44] Transcript (n 10) 464–65.
[45] Criminal Code (n 9), s 135.1(5).
[46] Transcript (n 10) 465.

His point is that 'dishonestly' is the only word in section 135.1(7) that involves any wrongdoing at all, so it should be the key one in determining criminal responsibility, including corporate criminal responsibility. And dishonesty isn't one of the fault elements provided for in part 2.5.

Or is it? The counter-argument is that the element of dishonesty has, well, elements of the elements that part 2.5 does provide for. Throughout the Criminal Code (for now), dishonesty is defined to mean:

(a) dishonest according to the standards of ordinary people; and
(b) known by the defendant to be dishonest according to the standards of ordinary people.[47]

Obviously, paragraph (b) of this definition is just a knowledge requirement, and knowledge requirements are expressly covered by section 12.3. So, that leaves paragraph (a), whatever it is. One possible answer is that paragraph (a) isn't a fault element at all, but rather a physical element – a description of someone's conduct (much like other 'standards' like indecency or offensiveness or dangerousness that can be used to characterise the defendant's conduct), or maybe a circumstance in which that conduct occurs (the same way a substance or a document or a victim of crime can have a particular legal character).[48] On that approach, section 12.2 (on physical elements) is the rule for attributing paragraph (a) to a corporation and section 12.3 (on knowledge et al) is the rule for attributing paragraph (b), and that leaves corporate dishonesty fully covered by part 2.5.

But the rejoinder to this argument is that paragraph (a) isn't really a physical element. Rather, the main thing ordinary people assess when working out whether someone is honest or dishonest is that person's mind. Was Potter trying his best to fill in the logbook correctly? Did he figure part of the French EEZ might be in the Capel Bank? Did he worry he could sometimes stray into it? Did he fear that someone would give him grief about it? Did he hope sloppy logbooking would stop or hamper such a reckoning? Did he think about these things a lot, a little or not at all? All of those things affect whether Potter was dishonest, but none of them sound remotely like physical elements. Rather, they sound like the various states of mind that can readily count as fault elements, even if they differ from the terms of art in part 2.2 like recklessness or negligence.

That doesn't make paragraph (a) a fault element, though, because there are also other things – fishing practices, regulatory practices, logbooking practices, commercial practices, broader societal notions of good fishermanship or good business or good citizenship – that are relevant to whether or not someone's conduct was dishonest; some of those sound like physical elements, others like something else altogether. In short, paragraph (a) is neither a physical nor fault element, but a complex or third category of element.

The upshot is that Blow CJ's startling ruling that corporations can't be dishonest under the Criminal Code and similar statutes elsewhere … appears to hold water! The Criminal Code only seems to provide for corporate criminal responsibility for offences

[47] Criminal Code (n 9) s 130.3. But see Crimes Amendment (Combating Corporate Crime) Bill 2019 (Cth), sch 3.

[48] See A Steel, 'Describing Dishonest Means: The Implications of Seeing "Dishonesty" as a Course of Conduct or Mental Element and the Parallels with Indecency' (2010) 31 *Adelaide Law Review* 7.

of intent, recklessness and knowledge, and not for offences that are effectively about whether particular behaviour was honest or not.

Is this another tale of the Criminal Code's clumsiness (whether in its original drafting, or in its implementation by the federal parliament)? Perhaps. But (like many other supposed failings of the Criminal Code) it may just reveal a deeper problem in modern criminal law, specifically the entire project of attributing criminal responsibility to corporations via some sort of organisational, rather than human, notion of fault.

To see what I mean, consider again the TPA model of corporate criminal responsibility contained in the current Fisheries Management Act 1991 (Cth):

> **164 Conduct of directors, employees and agents**
>
> (1) Where, in proceedings for an offence against this Act it is necessary to establish the state of mind of a body corporate in relation to particular conduct, it is sufficient to show:
>
> (a) that the conduct was engaged in by a director, employee or agent of the body corporate; and
>
> (b) that the director, employee or agent had the state of mind.
>
> (2) Any conduct engaged in by a director, employee or agent of a body corporate is taken, for the purposes of a prosecution for an offence against this Act, to have been engaged in also by the body corporate unless the body corporate establishes that the body corporate took reasonable precautions and exercised due diligence to prevent the conduct.[49]

As is typical, this doesn't expressly provide for vicarious liability for a particular employee's crimes. Rather, it provides, arguably separately, for the attribution to the corporation of the state of mind of an employee and the conduct of a (possibly different) employee, a similar division to sections 12.3 and 12.2 of part 2.5 of the Criminal Code.

The obvious difference is that, while section 12.3 only expressly provides for attribution of an employee's intent, knowledge or recklessness, the TPA model provides for attribution of any employee's 'state of mind'. In its 2019 discussion paper, the ALRC thought that that broader term sufficed to overcome the problem raised by the *Diana* case.[50] After all, not only is 'state of mind' more general than the three section 12.3 fault elements, but – again, as is typical of the TPA model – there is an express provision that the term includes:

> (a) the knowledge, intention, opinion, belief or purpose of the person; and
>
> (b) the person's reasons for the intention, opinion, belief or purpose.

This is, and is clearly intended to be, broad. But it is surely at least questionable whether it is broad enough to include dishonesty, which is a different kettle of fish. As the ALRC later acknowledged, albeit a bit cryptically:

> [U]nder the Criminal Code, dishonesty is not a state of mind itself; rather, 'dishonesty' is a character given to the fault element (knowledge) in a particular circumstance.[51]

[49] Fisheries Management Act 1991 (Cth), s 164.

[50] ALRC Discussion Paper (n 36) [6.22]–[6.23]. But it omitted this change without an express explanation for one of the two proposed reforms to s 12.3 – the one that largely retains the existing s 12.3 – in its final report: see ALRC Final Report (n 26) Recommendation 7 – Option 1, 228.

[51] ALRC Final Report (n 26) [6.64], citing S Odgers, *Principles of Federal Criminal Law*, 4th edn (Pyrmont, Lawbook Co, 2019) [5.1.170].

The upshot is that it's at least possible that the TPA model suffers the same deficiency as section 12.3 when it comes to attributing responsibility for a complex element like dishonesty.

It so happens that there are no dishonesty offences in the Fisheries Management Act 1991 (Cth) or in most of the many federal regulatory schemes that displaced part 2.5 in favour of the TPA model. Indeed, of the hundred or so federal dishonesty offences, just five are subject to the TPA model:

- inducing persons to deal in financial services by dishonest concealment of material facts;
- general dishonesty in financial services businesses;
- corrupting unions or their employees;
- speech calculated to dishonestly influence a deportation commissioner; and
- dishonestly contravening a superannuation civil penalty provision.[52]

The ALRC was sanguine about the prospect of these offences not being applied to corporations, declaring that 'it will be rare for a corporation to be prosecuted for a dishonesty offence, as these are more directed to human conduct' and citing the lack of corporate prosecutions to date for general dishonesty in financial services businesses.[53] But it is hard to see why such prosecutions ought to be rare, especially as several may well be particularly likely to be committed by corporate employees.

The same potential problem also arises in non-criminal code jurisdictions that also use something like a TPA model. I haven't attempted a survey, but consider a recent prominent example that, while deviating in some respects from the TPA model, is also quite a significant instance of the potential difficulty Blow CJ's ruling may cause. In 2020, the Victorian parliament enacted a landmark new law providing for an offence of 'wage theft':

> **Dishonest withholding of employee entitlements**
>
> (1) An employer must not *dishonestly*—
>
> (a) withhold the whole or part of an employee entitlement owed by the employer to an employee; or
>
> (b) authorise or permit, expressly or impliedly, another person to withhold the whole or part of an employee entitlement owed by the employer to an employee and that other person does so.
>
> Penalty: In the case of a body corporate, 6000 penalty units;
>
> In any other case, level 5 imprisonment (10 years maximum).[54]

Unlike the offence Mures Fishing was charged with, dishonesty is not central to this offence. Rather, it is only included to exclude some arguably acceptable scenarios – accidental

[52] Corporations Act 2001 (Cth), ss 1041F, 1041G (Corporations Act); Fair Work Act 2009 (Cth), s 536D; Migration Regulations 1994 (Cth), reg 5.12(d); Superannuation Industry (Supervision) Act 1993 (Cth), s 202.
[53] ALRC Final Report (n 26) [6.63].
[54] Wage Theft Act 2020 (Vic), s 6(1) (emphasis added).

withholdings, or brief changes to manage a cash-flow difficulty or the like – from this new form of criminality. But the prosecution nevertheless still have to prove the element of dishonesty, including where, as will often be the case, the employer is a corporation.

Unsurprisingly, there's a detailed provision in the new law for corporate criminal responsibility for employee behaviour:

> **11 Attribution to body corporate of conduct, knowledge, intention and belief of officers and associates**
>
> ...
>
> (2) For the purposes of a proceeding against a body corporate for an employee entitlement offence—
>
> (a) relevant conduct engaged in by an associate of the body corporate must also be attributed to the body corporate if—
>
> (i) an officer of the body corporate or the board of directors of the body corporate authorised or permitted the relevant conduct to be carried out, whether expressly or impliedly; or
>
> (ii) a corporate culture existed within the body corporate that directed, encouraged, tolerated or led to the relevant conduct being carried out; and
>
> (b) knowledge or intention of, or a belief held by, an associate of the body corporate must also be attributed to the body corporate if a corporate culture existed within the body corporate that directed, encouraged, tolerated or led to the acquisition of the knowledge or the formation of that intention or belief.
>
> (3) It is not necessary that each element of an employee entitlement offence that is attributed to a body corporate by force of this section be supplied by the same … associate of the body corporate.[55]

This isn't your average TPA model. Indeed, it very closely resembles what the ALRC has proposed as a modification of section 12.3 to include some features of the TPA model, notably allowing direct attribution of employees' states of minds to the corporation, alongside the Criminal Code's corporate culture options. The offences in the Act also contain their own due diligence defences, which is the other key part of the ALRC proposal.

But eagle-eyed readers will quickly spy a catch: like section 12.3 of the Criminal Code (and also like the ALRC's proposal for modifying that section), the Wage Theft Act 2020 (Vic) corporate responsibility regime only provides for attributing the 'knowledge or intention of, or a belief held by,' an employee. Not an employee's dishonesty. In short, unless an alternative statutory provision for vicarious liability for the crimes of 'officers' (not other employees) applies,[56] or Blow CJ's approach is distinguished or discarded in Victoria's courts, a corporation can't be prosecuted for wage theft in Victoria. That would, of course, be an astonishing gap in the State's landmark new law.

[55] ibid s 11. An 'associate' is defined to include 'an employee or agent of the body corporate to the extent that the person is acting within the actual or apparent scope of the person's employment or within the person's actual or apparent authority': ibid s 3(1).

[56] ibid s 10, which includes a 'defence to the charge for the body corporate to prove that it exercised due diligence to prevent the commission of the offence by the officer.' An 'officer' is 'an officer of the corporation within the meaning of section 9 of' the Corporations Act (n 51) s 3(1).

V. Conclusion: Can Corporations be Honest?

> A single statutory method will improve simplicity and certainty for corporations (and their directors and officers), as well as regulators and prosecutors.[57]

On Tuesday, 18 September 2001, *HMAS Manoora* (bearing 600 asylum seekers from the *MV Tampa*) arrived at Nauru (21 square kilometres of largely arid land surrounded by coral cliffs, home to 10,000 and, at 32 degrees south and 166 degrees east, nearly as far north of Capel Bank as Hobart is south of it), improvising the Pacific Solution. Nearly 15 years later, in an effort to accommodate some of the legal complexities of being one of Australia's offshore detention centres, the micronation became the most recent, and possibly last, jurisdiction to enact Australia's Model Criminal Code. However, there was at least one difference:

> **39 Application of fault elements to bodies corporate**
>
> (1) If there is a *fault element* in relation to a physical element of an offence, that fault element must be attributed to a corporation if the corporation expressly, tacitly or impliedly authorised or permitted the commission of the offence.[58]

Perhaps because it was enacted after the *Diana* case unravelled, the new law provides for corporate criminal responsibility for *all* fault elements (including negligence), rather than just intent, knowledge and recklessness.

Does this solve the problem raised by Blow CJ? I doubt it. One problem is that it is still not clear that dishonesty is a 'fault element', as opposed to a physical element or some other thing altogether. Another is that, even if it is a fault element, it's not clear that it's a fault element 'in relation to a physical element'. (Section 135.1(7)'s fault element appears to be what's commonly called a 'hanging' fault element, sitting outside of the Criminal Code's preferred offence design of fault elements that are expressly about a corresponding physical element.) And a third, running in the background of all parts of the *Diana* case, is that it has never been clear what it means to authorise or permit 'the commission of the offence'. What exactly did Mures Fishing (or its board, high managerial agents or culture) have to authorise or permit (or lead to, encourage, tolerate or fail to prevent) about what Potter allegedly did? Did Mures Fishing have to authorise Potter's entire alleged plan to fool AFMA about possible breaches of maritime fishing rules? Or only the shoddy bookkeeping that was alleged to have been the means to that end?

According to the ALRC, the latter ought to suffice in future, at least for offences structured like section 135.1(7). The ALRC's proposed revision of section 12.3 of the Criminal Code involves replacing 'the commission of the offence' with 'relevant physical element',[59] meaning that a corporation could be convicted of a crime even if it only

[57] ALRC Discussion Paper (n 36) [6.4].

[58] Crimes Act 2016 (Nauru), s 39 (emphasis added).

[59] ALRC Final Reporrt (n 26) [6.50]; Recommendation 7 – Option 1(a).

authorised or permitted an employee's conduct, whether or not it authorised whatever thoughts accompanied those actions to make them criminal. Because section 135.1(7)'s physical element is simply 'doing anything', the ALRC's proposed model would have made Mures Fishing criminally responsible for merely permitting Potter's shoddy book-keeping, whether or not the corporation – or even Potter himself – had any dishonest intention.

The TPA model the ALRC largely favours has always generally worked that way, by providing a due diligence or reasonable precautions defence for the attribution of an employee's conduct, not his or her state of mind, although the ALRC's own recommended model is not expressed so precisely. But this all strikes me as unsound, at least for offences (like most dishonesty offences) whose physical elements are innocuous absent the accompanying fault (or other) elements. For example, why should Mures Fishing be deemed guilty of 'general dishonesty' for permitting or not preventing Potter's shoddy logbooking, even though there was even less evidence that Mures Fishing hoped to trick AFMA with imprecise records than there was that Potter wished to do so? Such an approach leaves few options for corporations to be, like Potter most likely was, imperfect but still honest.

That being said, it's not clear that the other extreme – requiring proof Mures Fishing permitted everything Potter did or thought that made him dishonest – is apt either. For starters, that would bar corporate dishonesty unless a particular employee was dishonest too. But the likelihood that Potter wasn't dishonest – perhaps because he didn't know about the risk that he was fishing in France's EEZ – doesn't necessarily mean that Mures Fishing also wasn't. For instance, it might be enough if one of Mures's directors knew of the possible crossing of maritime boundaries and deliberately chose not to check the skipper's logbooks for that reason. Or it may suffice that one or other of the Mures saw a broad advantage in muddying the waters about *Diana*'s Coral Sea activities so as to keep regulators off their back, or that they were aware (say) that Potter was willing to break the rules if he thought he could get away with it, even though they didn't know most, many or even any of the finer details about logbooks or EEZs. That is, the knowledge or intentions that can amount to criminal dishonesty can be spread throughout an organisation, in a way that leaves the organisation as a whole dishonest even though no one individual is.

The middle approach that I am describing here demands very careful attention to the components of criminal dishonesty. Dishonesty could arise at the macro-level – an overall willingness to do things that ordinary people would think of as the wrong thing, including a business cutting record-keeping corners to muddy law enforcement. Or it could arise at the micro-level – the managers being aware of a specific risk of rule-breaking (such as crossing into forbidden waters) and eschewing the kind of risk management that ordinary people would expect. What exactly would suffice would also vary depending on how dishonesty is defined, for example incorporating a requirement like the one in paragraph (b) of section 130.3 of the Criminal Code – knowledge of what ordinary people would think – into either the business's culture or what the managers know of the lines their employees were willing to cross.

This sounds complex, and it is, but that doesn't necessarily have to flow through to legislative complexity. Indeed, it seems to me that we already have a simple legislative model to deal with organisational responsibility for multi-faceted and multi-level notions of criminal responsibility:

> **12.4 Negligence**
>
> (2) If:
>
> (a) negligence is a fault element in relation to a physical element of an offence; and
> (b) no individual employee, agent or officer of the body corporate has that fault element;
>
> that fault element may exist on the part of the body corporate if the body corporate's conduct is negligent when viewed as a whole (that is, by aggregating the conduct of any number of its employees, agents or officers).[60]

This provision only covers negligence, which doesn't easily fit into the usual 'state of mind' type of fault elements dealt with in section 12.3 and the TPA model. But it could be easily expanded to cover other fault elements of that sort, including dishonesty.

The ALRC didn't propose any changes to section 12.4 of the Criminal Code, and its proposed TPA option wouldn't cover negligence either.[61] By contrast, Nauru dropped section 12.4 from its new crime legislation, opting to instead fold it in together with all other fault elements in its expanded version of section 12.3. In both instances, these reforms seem to have missed a potential trick: expanding section 12.4 to include dishonesty within the concept of aggregated fault.

To be sure, aggregate fault has its own problems, especially when it comes to dealing with conflicting states of mind within a company, and it remains every bit as untested as the Criminal Code's corporate culture provisions. And the current terms of section 12.4(2) are overly focused on conduct, which is inadequate when it comes to how both negligence and dishonesty capture particular types of criminal wrongs. But these, it seems to me, are problems that can be readily overcome, in ways that do not require forcing the element of dishonesty (in its many varieties) into a framework that is designed for simpler fault elements. For example:

> **12.4A Dishonesty**
>
> If:
>
> (a) dishonesty is a fault element in relation to a physical element of an offence; and
> (b) no individual employee, agent or officer of the body corporate has that fault element;
>
> that fault element may exist on the part of the body corporate when viewed as a whole (that is, by aggregating the conduct and state of mind of any number of its employees, agents or officers).

Indeed, an aggregate responsibility model can be readily used in non-criminal code jurisdictions, and indeed non-common law ones (which don't rely on element analysis at all).

[60] Criminal Code (n 9), s 12.4.
[61] ALRC Final Report (n 26) [6.194].

The current section 12.4(3) readily shows how organisational, or systemic, or cultural or maritime[62] notions of liability can readily be part of – perhaps a big part of – the assessment of corporate criminal responsibility:

> (3) Negligence may be evidenced by the fact that the prohibited conduct was substantially attributable to:
>
> (a) inadequate corporate management, control or supervision of the conduct of one or more of its employees, agents or officers; or
>
> (b) failure to provide adequate systems for conveying relevant information to relevant persons in the body corporate.

However, the aggregation model differs from organisational notions of fault because it leaves open a role, perhaps a central one, for the various states of mind of particular individuals in an organisation, whether they are the corporation's captains or its ships' skippers. I suggest, for example:

> Dishonesty may be evidenced by the fact that the prohibited conduct or state of mind was substantially attributable to:
>
> (a) inadequate corporate management, control or supervision of one or more of its employees, agents or officers; or
>
> (b) failure to provide adequate systems for conveying relevant information to relevant persons in the body corporate.

That is important, and likely crucial, when it comes to the particular features of criminal dishonesty.

When Blow CJ told Mures Fishing's jury on the last Monday of the trial that they should acquit the company of general dishonesty, he did not describe his ruling that federal criminal law seemingly doesn't allow any corporation to be convicted of a dishonesty offence. Instead, he explained the difference between a dishonest company and a merely imperfect one:

> If the attitude of the company was tell lies to AFMA, we want as much fish as possible and if you need to pull the wool over their eyes you do that, if that was the attitude within the company, for example, then the company would have to take the blame for anything that an employee did, but if you look at what evidence there is in relation to attitudes within the company, or policies or rules or anything like that within the company, all that we really know is what Mr Mure said in his interview, and all that Mr Mure said that might in any way be used against him was he didn't have training regimes in place.[63]

It is unlikely that Blow CJ or the jury would have reached a different verdict if they were required to consider not *either* Mures Fishing's culture *or* the acts and thoughts of Will Mure *or* the acts and thoughts of Russell Potter, but instead all of those together in the aggregate. But it seems to me that this consideration would have produced a clearer answer, either way, on the question of whether this particular family fishing business was a dishonest one for the purposes of the criminal law.

[62] See Derrington and Walpole, ch 16 of this volume.
[63] Transcript (n 10) 480.

14

Asset-Based Lending: A Case Study in Unconscionable Systems of Conduct

MICHAEL BRYAN

I. Conscience and Corporations

Courts of equity have overseen the activities of corporations for centuries. The imposition of fiduciary obligations on company directors in order to deter abuse of position is an obvious example. Fiduciary duties primarily concern the activities of directors, managers and employees within an organisation, although the voluminous *Barnes v Addy*[1] jurisprudence illustrates how external parties can also be held accountable for their involvement in internal wrongdoing. Other equitable doctrines directed at setting aside flawed transactions, such as relief against unconscientious bargains, mistake or misrepresentation, are relevant to contracts between corporations and parties with whom they do business, typically clients and service providers. They come into play when the consent of the party dealing with a corporation has not been freely given. The corporation, acting through its directors or other agents, may have been responsible for the defective consent. Alternatively, the defect may have arisen from circumstances surrounding the making of the contract, which the corporation advantageously exploited.

The deficiencies of equity in cases of corporate malfeasance are well known. Some are doctrinal, such as the doubtful availability of compensatory damages as a remedy in equity (as opposed to under statute) for unconscionable conduct.[2] Others raise 'access to justice' considerations, such as the 'asymmetry in civil law matters'[3] favouring the well-resourced corporate defendant in private law litigation brought by an individual,

[1] *Barnes v Addy* (1874) LR 9 Ch App 244.

[2] On one view, compensation is only available in equity for unconscionability as a restitutionary (but not compensatory) remedy where rescission is unavailable: *Paroz v Paroz* [2010] QSC 41 [133]. But, following the English Court of Appeal decision in *Mahoney v Purnell* [1996] 3 All ER 61, compensatory orders have been made in some Australian unconscionability decisions where no statutory claim for damages has been brought: *Smith v Glegg* [2004] QSC 443, [2005] 1 Qd R 561 [64]; *McFarlane v McFarlane* [2021] VSC 197.

[3] R Cranston, *Legal Foundations of the Welfare State* (London, Weidenfeld & Nicolson, 1985) 55.

and which is not entirely offset by the adoption of class action procedures.[4] The contemporary response to the inadequacies of equitable (or, for that matter, common law) doctrine has been to enact legislation enlarging the field of civil liability while simultaneously conferring powers of intervention on regulators who are better resourced than a private individual to challenge systemic wrongdoing.

Legislative regimes do not prevent victims of corporate wrongdoing from pursuing equitable relief. The legal databases reveal a steady flow of cases in which relief from unconscionable transactions is sought in equity instead of, or in addition to, the award of a statutory remedy. The resilience of equitable relief in the domain of statute poses a question going to the function of equitable doctrine. What purpose is served by the retention of equitable relief if the conduct proscribed by equity is also prohibited by legislation? Any justification for equitable intervention must overcome the obvious rejoinder that legislative remedial regimes are generally more extensive than the relief available in equity.[5] Indeed, it might be argued that the whole point of enacting statutory proscriptions of unconscionable conduct is to broaden the remedies available to a victim of exploitation. Some tentative answers to this question will be proposed at the end of this chapter.

Neither equitable doctrine nor the economic forces that shape capitalist activity are static. The relevant law is a law of moving parts. The equitable principles for setting aside unconscientious transactions must respond not only to economic opportunism, but also to the protean legal structures commercial lawyers put in place to facilitate opportunism. Commercial lawyers in turn respond to doctrinal evolution, particularly when it constrains freedom of contract, or is otherwise perceived as inhibiting economic activity.[6] This is an example of what Hugh Collins has termed the story of recursivity in the law.[7] 'Not only does the legal system observe the behaviour of social actors, but they [the social actors] also respond to the legal system.'[8]

This chapter is a case study of recursivity in the law of unconscientious transactions. Its focus is on the practice of 'asset-based' lending, an established commercial lending practice that becomes controversial when the borrower is a consumer. The stimulus for

[4] R Mulheron, *The Class Action in Common Law Legal Systems: A Comparative Perspective* (Oxford, Hart Publishing, 2004) 52–57.

[5] The statutory menu of remedies does not typically include accounting for profits, except under intellectual property legislation, such as the Copyright Act 1968 (Cth), s 115(2). Relinquishment orders under s 12GBCC of the Australian Securities and Investments Commission Act 2001 (Cth) (ASIC Act) share some of the characteristics of an account of profits insofar as they permit a court to order the defendant to pay an amount assessed as the benefit derived from unconscionable conduct, but the amount assessed is payable to the Commonwealth, and not to the complainant.

[6] Examples of recursivity drawn from other areas of equity include: (i) (in England) the adaptations to lending practice made by banks in response to the steps prescribed by the House of Lords in *Barclays Bank plc v O'Brien* [1994] 1 AC 180, [1993] 3 WLR 786 in order to avoid being fixed with knowledge of undue influence exercised in family guarantee cases, the adaptations necessitating further judicial interventions in *Royal Bank of Scotland v Etridge (No 2)* [2001] UKHL 44, [2002] 2 AC 773; (ii) (in Australia) responses of banks to the decision of the High Court in *Andrews v Australia and New Zealand Banking Group Ltd* [2012] HCA 30, (2012) 247 CLR 205 that a breach of contract was not a precondition to the application of the penalties doctrine.

[7] H Collins, 'Legal Classifications as the Production of Knowledge Systems' in P Birks (ed), *The Classification of Obligations* (Oxford, Clarendon, 1997) 57.

[8] ibid 66.

writing the chapter is the recent High Court of Australia decision in *Stubbings v Jams 2 Pty Ltd* (*Stubbings*).[9] The arrangement put in place by the lenders' solicitor in *Stubbings* demonstrates how, recursively, lending practice responds to case law and regulatory developments, and also how, in turn, the judiciary responds to drafting ingenuity. The aim of the chapter is to explain the persistence of the equitable unconscionability doctrine in an area perceived as enjoying ample and effective statutory coverage.

II. Asset-Based Lending and the Law

As Jeannie Marie Paterson remarked in a path-breaking article, asset-based lending 'is not necessarily problematic'.[10] It is an accepted commercial lending practice. Lawyers routinely advertise to business clients their willingness to draft loan agreements that do not depend on the lender's assessment of the borrower's ability to repay from income, if the capital security available to the lender in the event of default is sufficient. Asset-based loan contracts are commonly entered into by borrowers with cyclical or seasonal businesses that rely on their working capital facilities when cash flow is limited. The loan agreements will usually not require financial covenant compliance. There have been suggestions that the implementation of the Personal Property Securities Act 2009 (Cth) (PPSA) has facilitated asset-based lending, since different kinds of personal property, for example shareholdings, inventory and receivables, as well as chattels of various descriptions, can be bundled together easily and then registered as a security interest on the PPS Register. This avoids the complex multiple registrations required before the PPSA was brought into force. The enactment of the PPSA enables practitioners and courts to draw on the experience of other personal property security jurisdictions in facilitating asset-based lending, namely Canada and New Zealand, as well as the jurisprudence of article 9 of the United States Uniform Commercial Code on creating and enforcing personal property security interests.

Asset-based lending is designed to serve business, not consumers. There is an obvious difference between a company taking out an asset-based loan to overcome a temporary liquidity problem, and a consumer with no income (or no reliable source of income) taking a loan that is forensically described as 'doomed to fail'. The latter is liable to be set aside in equity as an unconscientious transaction. Relief on the ground of unconscionability evolved from a miscellany of eighteenth- and nineteenth-century cases concerning the mortgaging of the interests of expectant heirs,[11] the dissipation of sailors' prize money,[12] and others where judicial intervention had a flavour of 'class protection', into a general equitable principle relieving against different kinds of individual vulnerability. Poverty has long been recognised as a ground of disadvantage

[9] *Stubbings v Jams 2 Pty Ltd* [2022] HCA 6, (2022) 399 ALR 409 (*Stubbings*), on appeal from *Jams 2 Pty Ltd v Stubbings* [2020] VSCA 200, reversing *Jams 2 Pty Ltd v Stubbings (No 3)* [2019] VSC 150.

[10] JM Paterson, 'Knowledge and Neglect in Asset-Based Lending: When is it Unconscionable or Unjust to Lend to a Borrower Who Cannot Repay?' (2009) 20 *Journal of Banking & Finance Law & Practice* 18.

[11] *Earl of Aylesford v Morris* (1873) 8 Ch App 484; C MacMillan, 'Earl of Aylesford v Morris' in C Mitchell and P Mitchell (eds), *Landmark Cases in Equity* (Oxford, Hart Publishing, 2012) 329.

[12] *Baldwin and Alder v Rochford* (1748) 95 ER 589; *Taylour v Rochfort* (1751) 28 ER 182; PS Atiyah, *The Rise and Fall of Freedom of Contract* (Oxford, Oxford University Press, 1979) 171–72.

justifying relief in cases of exploitation.[13] Australian equity developed an organising conceptual framework for analysing cases of unconscionability, based on judicial identification of a 'special disability or disadvantage', amounting to something more than inadequacy of consideration, and proof that the party against whom relief has been sought was aware of the disability or disadvantage. To these is added the requirement that the stronger party must have exploited the weaker party. Until recently it was uncertain whether exploitation (or victimisation)[14] was a discrete element that must be proved, or whether it was implicit in any equitable claim based on knowledge of the plaintiff's special disadvantage. Recent judicial restatements favour the former analysis.[15] The conceptual framework was formulated and applied by the High Court in *Commercial Bank of Australia v Amadio.*[16]

Legislation also prohibits unconscionable asset-based lending practices and renders the lender liable to civil penalties. The lender may be in breach of the responsible lending conduct provisions of the National Consumer Credit Protection Act 2009 (Cth) by making a loan that cannot be repaid out of income resources.[17] The practice may also constitute unconscionable conduct in connection with financial services under section 12CB of the ASIC Act, which proscribes conduct that is, in all the circumstances, unconscionable in the supply of financial services.[18]

Liability under these various heads is not absolute. A finding of unconscionability in equity is dependent on proof that the lender had knowledge of the borrower's position of special disadvantage. The equitable doctrine of constructive notice does not constitute knowledge for this purpose, although 'constructive knowledge', in the sense of knowing facts from which it can be concluded that a person ought to have known that another person was under a special disadvantage, is sufficient to establish liability.[19] Moreover, a contract will not be rescinded in equity if the lender can show that it was 'fair, just and reasonable'.[20] The receipt of independent legal and financial advice is relevant either

[13] *Clark v Malpas* (1862) 45 ER 1238. cf *Blomley v Ryan* (1956) 99 CLR 362 (HCA) 405 (Fullagar J): 'poverty and need of any kind …'.

[14] *Kakavas v Crown Melbourne Ltd* [2013] HCA 25, (2013) 250 CLR 392, 403 [26] (*Kakavas*).

[15] cf *Stubbings* (n 9) 13 [39] (Kiefel CJ, Keane and Glesson JJ). But see *Nitopi v Nitopi* [2022] NSWCA 162 [41], Bell CJ expressing 'the provisional view that the existence of a predatory state of mind may be presumed once it is established that the gift was made by a person suffering under a special disadvantage in the *Amadio* or *Blomley* sense and the recipient of that gift had actual knowledge of that special disadvantage'. President Ward, on the other hand, stated (ibid [105]) that exploitation must be established as a condition of granting relief.

[16] *Commercial Bank of Australia v Amadio* [1983] HCA 14, (1983) 151 CLR 447 (*Amadio*). Other common law jurisdictions have developed different paradigms constructed from the same equitable materials: Canada (*Harry v Kreutziger* (1978) 95 DLR(3d) 231)); New Zealand (*Nichols v Jessup* [1986] 1 NZLR 226); Singapore (*BOM v BOK* [2019] 1 SLR 349).

[17] National Consumer Credit Protection Act 2009 (Cth), ch 3 (NCCP Act). See, in particular, s 118(2)(a), providing that 'the contract will be unsuitable for the consumer' if 'the consumer will be unable to comply with the consumer's financial obligations under the contract, or could only comply with substantial hardship'.

[18] ASIC Act (n 5) s 12CC(1) lists matters to which the court may have regard including '(l) the extent to which the supplier and the service recipient acted in good faith'. State legislation is also relevant, such as the Contracts Review Act 1980 (NSW) applied in *Elkofairi v Permanent Trustee Co Ltd* [2002] NSWCA 413, (2002) 11 BPR 20,841 (*Elkofairi*), but will not be discussed in this chapter.

[19] *Amadio* (n 16) 447 (Mason J), 479 (Deane J); *Kakavas* (n 14) 443–50; *Nitopi* (n 15) [6] (Bell CJ), [121] (Ward P), [199] (White JA).

[20] *Amadio* (n 16) 479 (Deane J).

(negatively) to show that the lender has not exploited the borrower's position of disadvantage or (affirmatively) to substantiate the fairness of the agreement. As Anthony J Duggan notes, the issue in the case of the provision of advice 'is not so much what the adviser actually said to [the borrower], as to what [the lender] is entitled to assume was said'.[21] Proof that the borrower received inadequate advice will not be fatal to the validity of the loan contract, provided the lender was unaware of its inadequacy.

The National Credit Code (the Code) intrudes more deeply than equity into lending practice. Credit assistance providers are subject to an affirmative duty to undertake a preliminary inquiry into the suitability of the credit contract, with special reference to the borrower's requirements and financial situation.[22] But the scope of the Code is restricted in critical respects. The borrower must be a natural person[23] and the credit must be provided, or intended to be provided, for personal, domestic or household purposes.[24] Given how easy it is to form a shell corporation, it is surprising that the legislature has selected the legal personality of the borrower as a principal ground of differentiation between consumer and commercial lending. The limitation of the Code to natural persons has not gone unnoticed by drafters of asset-lending contracts, as the facts of *Stubbings* illustrate.

If a question arises as to whether a loan was taken out for personal purposes, the lender is aided by a statutory presumption that a loan has not been taken out for a personal purpose if the debtor declares, before entering into the contract, that the credit is being wholly or predominantly provided for a non-Code purpose.[25] The presumption arguably entrenches form (namely, the borrower's formal declaration that the credit has not been obtained for a Code purpose) over substance if the borrower in fact applies the loan for personal or domestic purposes. Indeed, the statute's preference for form over substance in this respect has been exploited by some creators of lending systems, who require borrowers to sign declarations that the loan is being taken out for a business purpose. But form will not prevail if the lender 'knew or had reason to believe' that the loan was going to be applied for personal or domestic purposes.[26] The burden rests on the borrower to rebut the statutory presumption by showing that the lender knew, or had reason to believe, that the loan was made for purposes covered by the Code.

The scope of section 12CB of the ASIC Act is also broader than equitable liability in important respects. Section 12CB(4)(a) explicitly states that the section 'is not limited by the unwritten law of the States and Territories [ie equitable doctrine] relating to unconscionable conduct'. Furthermore, section 12CB(4)(b) states that the section

[21] AJ Duggan, 'Unconscientious Dealing' in P Parkinson (ed) *The Principles of Equity*, 2nd edn (Sydney, Lawbook Co, 2003) 150. See also M Sneddon, 'Unfair Conduct in Taking Guarantees and the Role of Independent Advice' (1990) 13 *University of New South Wales Law Journal* 302. Negligent advice will be the subject of a separate claim. See the claim brought against the accountant providing financial advice in *Jams 2 Pty Ltd v Stubbings (No 3)* (n 9) [329]–[339].

[22] NCCP Act (n 17) ch 3, div 4.

[23] ibid sch 1, s 5(1)(a). The Code also applies to strata corporations.

[24] ibid sch 1, s 5(1)(b). The Code also covers loans made to purchase, renovate or improve residential property for investment purposes.

[25] ibid sch 1, s 13(2).

[26] ibid. The declaration will also be ineffective if the lender would have known, or had reason to believe, had reasonable inquiries about the purpose for which the loan was to be applied been made.

'is capable of applying to a system of conduct or pattern of behaviour, whether or not a particular individual is identified as having been disadvantaged by the conduct or behaviour'. A court is therefore entitled to take a holistic view of a system of conduct, without the necessity of determining whether equity's concept of 'special disadvantage' applies to any given individual. A system can be proscribed as unconscionable, even though the borrower is in no sense vulnerable, provided that it fails to meet a normative standard identified by reference to a range of statutory considerations set out in section 12CC of the Act.[27]

In spite of being untethered from equitable restrictions, the application of section 12CB is not completely straightforward. First, the relevance and weight to be accorded to the criteria listed in section 12CC can in practice be hard to assess. As tends to be the case with open-textured legislation, 'there is no clear baseline moral standard for what constitutes "unconscionable conduct" within s 12CB of the ASIC Act'.[28] The decision containing this dictum, *Australian Securities and Investments Commission v Kobelt*,[29] highlights the problems of applying discretionary mandates of this kind. The High Court split four to three in deciding that section 12CB did not apply to the supply of goods to Anangu Indigenous customers under the 'book-up' system practised by a storekeeper. The system involved deferral of payment for goods in return for the customer providing the storekeeper with the key card and PIN linked to the account into which the customer's wages or Centrelink payments were credited. It was unchallenged that the customers lacked financial literacy. The division in judicial opinion was said to illustrate the principle that '[h]ard cases test and sometimes strain legal principle' and 'do not always lend themselves to elucidation of legal principle in a way that can be predicted to provide precedential guidance of the systemic usefulness generally to be expected from a decision of an ultimate court of appeal'.[30] The process of fixing the moral standard appropriate to the facts of a given case is contentious, often generates appeals and later judicial clarifications, and is costly for litigants.[31]

Second, courts have recognised that under section 12CB, as in equity, the concept of unconscionability imports some kind of knowledge on the part of the party acting unconscientiously. This is because 'A conscience is the moral force that acts upon an individual with knowledge'.[32] A finding that conduct contravenes notions of commercially acceptable conduct assumes, first, that the party in contravention has sufficient agency to make a choice whether or not to engage in that conduct and, second, making that choice presupposes some cognition of the consequences of making it.[33] But, as experience with other areas of law has shown, knowledge tests raise a variety of litigious issues. The answers to two knowledge-based questions are relevant to the imposition

[27] *Australian Competition and Consumer Commission v Quantum Housing Group Pty Ltd* [2021] FCAFC 40, (2021) 285 FCR 133 [53]–[54] (*Quantum*), citing *Australian Securities and Investments Commission v Kobelt* [2019] HCA 18, (2019) 267 CLR 1 [84] (Gageler J) (*Kobelt*).

[28] *Kobelt* (n 27) [295] (Edelman J).

[29] ibid.

[30] ibid [95] (Gageler J).

[31] cf the 'clarification' of *Kobelt* in *Quantum* (n 27) [37]–[79], discussed in section III.B.

[32] *Kobelt* (n 27) [280] (Edelman J), cf [208]–[210] (Nettle and Gordon JJ).

[33] *Tonto Home Loans Australia Pty Ltd v Tavares* [2011] NSWCA 389, (2011) 15 BPR 29,699 [292]–[293] (Allsop P) (*Tonto Home Loans*).

of statutory liability.[34] The first is the content question: what facts must the defendant know in order to be held accountable? The second question is the cognizance question: how must the facts be known? Is liability grounded solely on the defendant's actual knowledge of the facts? Or is proof that the defendant chose not to know facts, or not to institute inquiries based on known facts, sufficient to justify a finding of unconscionable conduct?

Turning to the content question, knowledge under section 12CB is not limited, as it is in equity, to awareness of the borrower's disability or disadvantage. This is because liability under the section does not depend on proof of disability or disadvantage. Liability is instead based on the financial provider's knowledge of the impact, or potential impact, of its conduct on the financial circumstances of those who have been, or are likely to be, adversely affected by that conduct. Some precision in applying this test is necessary when ascertaining the identity of affected persons. In *Kobelt*, the relevant knowledge possessed by the defendant was held to be of the circumstances of the 117 recipients of book-up services identified as part of ASIC's case, and not of the Anangu people or of Indigenous communities generally.[35]

As far as the cognizance question is concerned, statutory liability does not depend on proof that a provider of financial services had actual knowledge of the impact of its conduct. Conduct will be unconscionable if the provider shut its eyes to the possibility of harmful economic impact, or recklessly failed to investigate the possibility that its conduct might cause economic harm, in spite of knowing facts that called for further inquiry.[36] Extending liability beyond actual knowledge will be critical if the basis of the unconscionability inquiry is a system of conduct established by the financial service provider or by the provider's agent. A feature of many systems are organisational structures designed to shield the provider from any actual knowledge of the consequences of its own conduct.[37] A provider whose system is found to be offensive to community norms will not be permitted to argue that it was ignorant of its offensive operation if the system was expressly designed to keep the provider in a state of ignorance.

It follows *a fortiori* that a financial services provider should also not be allowed to plead ignorance of community standards of business behaviour relevant to his or her sphere of activity. The provision of responsible lending or other financial activities presupposes an understanding of commercial standards applicable to the activity in question. To allow ignorance of relevant commercial morality to be raised as a defence would render section 12CB toothless.

Relevant knowledge of the impact of the financial provider's conduct includes knowledge obtained by the lender's, but not the borrower's, agent.[38] Courts have

[34] Liability under ASIC Act (n 5) s 12CB3(a) is limited to circumstances that were reasonably foreseeable at the time of the alleged contravention. This is a conceptually distinct remoteness limitation, but it may be relevant in some cases to defining the facts that the financial services provider ought to have known.

[35] *Kobelt* (n 27) [218] (Nettle and Gordon JJ).

[36] *Elkofairi* (n 18), where the fact that the borrower did not fill in the income section of the loan application form should have resulted in the lender's making further inquiries.

[37] See also *Commonwealth Bank of Australia v Kojic* [2016] FCAFC 186, (2016) 341 ALR 572. Justice Edelman suggested obiter at [153] that a corporation will be liable if it puts in place procedures intended to ensure that no particular individual had the requisite knowledge, or was reckless about serious consequences.

[38] *Tonto Home Loans* (n 33) [192]–[194] (Allsop P). See Paterson (n 10) 25–26 for discussion of the agency issues.

emphasised the consensual, but not necessarily contractual, relationship between principal and agent, and the consequent attribution of the agent's knowledge to the principal within that relationship. But where there is no direct consensual relationship between the parties, as can occur in multipartite lending systems, it has been held that knowledge gained by one participant cannot be attributed to the lender. Any approach to agency that 'elevates the organisational or enterprise structure of the relevant business and activity as a key factor in determining agency' is incompatible with fundamental principles of agency law.[39] There has so far been no judicial inclination, at least in cases where agency principles are in play, to develop a theory of enterprise liability as a substitute for agency, along the lines of the imposition of enterprise vicarious liability in tort.[40]

Consumer lending raises issues as to the lender's knowledge of the borrower's personal circumstances and financial literacy at several points in the lending process. A principal aim of the responsible lending provisions of the Code is to ensure that lenders are pro-active in obtaining this knowledge. It was previously noticed, however, that drafting ingenuity has succeeded in negating these provisions in some cases, for example by interposing a shell company as the borrower, so that the real borrower becomes the guarantor of the company's indebtedness, rather than the principal debtor.

Another 'knowledge avoidance' device concerns the requirement that borrowers obtain professional advice before signing the loan contract. Judicial insistence that borrowers receive legal advice has a long history in equity jurisprudence. As Brereton J remarked, the concept of 'independent legal advice … long predates financial planners and financial advice'.[41] Since the *Amadio* decision, the provision of certificated legal and other professional advice to prospective borrowers has become a routine step in consumer lending, promoted by successive editions of the *Banking Code of Practice*.[42] The certificates record that the legal and financial risks involved in taking out the loan agreement have been fully explained. The practice is designed to negate an unconscionability argument based on an allegation that insufficient information was provided to the borrower. As in the equity cases, the critical concern under section 12CB is not so much the quality of the advice (though that issue will be central to any later negligence claim brought against the professional adviser) but the knowledge of that advice possessed by the lender.[43] Some lending systems have exploited certification as an information barrier to the lender's acquiring knowledge of a borrower's financial illiteracy. This is achieved by establishing a process of certification undertaken by an adviser, often recommended to the borrower by the lender and remunerated out of the proceeds of

[39] *Tonto Home Loans* (n 33) [192] (Allsop P). The borrower's agent may nonetheless incur contractual or tort liability to the borrower for failure to advise the borrower of the systemic risks known to the agent.

[40] A Gray, 'The Enterprise Risk Theory of Vicarious Liability' (2018) 46 *Australian Business Law Review* 178.

[41] *Riz v Perpetual Trustee Australia Ltd* [2007] NSWSC 1153 [116] (*Riz*).

[42] Australian Banking Association, *Banking Code of Practice* (revised 5 October 2021) pts 5–7.

[43] *Elkofairi* (n 18) [56] (Beazley JA); *Tonto Home Loans* (n 33) [292] (Allsop P). In *Jams 2 Pty Ltd v Stubbings* (n 9), the Court of Appeal applied the *Baden Delvaux* scale of knowledge (cf *Baden v Société Générale pour Favoriser le Développement du Commerce et de l'Industrie en France SA* [1992] 4 All ER 161, [1993] 1 WLR 509, 575–76 [250] (*Baden Delvaux*)), approved, for the purpose of imposing liability for knowingly assisting a breach of fiduciary duty, in *Farah Constructions Pty Ltd v Say-Dee Pty Ltd* [2007] HCA 22, (2007) 230 CLR 89 [171]–[178], but also criticised for excessive refinement in *Grimaldi v Chameleon Mining NL (No 2)* [2012] FCAFC 6, (2012) 287 ALR 22 [260].

the loan. The certificate itself is couched in 'bland boilerplate language',[44] confirming that the nature and effect of the loan agreement have been explained to the borrower, and that the borrower appeared to understand both its terms and the financial risks to which the borrower was exposed. The provision of advice on boilerplate terms raises a 'form versus substance' question. That question lay at the heart of the *Stubbings* litigation, discussed in the next section.

To summarise the analysis up to this point, statute provides a more robust basis for setting aside an unconscionable asset-based lending agreement than the equitable principles governing unconscientious bargains. But the legislation poses its own challenges for the judges who must interpret it. Jurisdictional limitations (in the case of the Code) may encourage drafting workarounds by ingenious lawyers; there may be uncertainty as to where the 'moral baseline' of statutory unconscionability is located (illustrated by the division of High Court judicial opinion in *Kobelt*); and the knowledge inquiry is as complex under section 12CB as it is in equity, and potentially just as open to manipulation by system designers.

III. *Stubbings v Jams 2 Pty Ltd*

The issues identified in the previous section were essentially those considered by the High Court in *Stubbings.*[45] The case concerned an unemployed borrower, financially illiterate and of low general intelligence, whose only income was derived from mowing lawns and mending taps. He owned two properties occupied by members of his family. When he found another property that he wished to buy as his own residence, his application to obtain a loan was predictably rejected by a regular bank because of his lack of income. He approached a broker, who undertook to obtain finance for the purchase. The broker contacted a solicitor whose principal activity was arranging for his clients to lend on mortgage. Three clients of the solicitor were willing to fund the borrower's acquisition. The security for the clients' loans were the two properties already owned by the borrower, as well as the property to be purchased with the loans. The loan contract was for a minimum term of six months (during which time the borrower had to keep up interest payments) and for a maximum of 12 months. Leaving aside the unlikely possibility of refinancing the loan before the expiry of 12 months, the loan could only have been repaid from the proceeds of the sale of the properties.

The solicitor employed a lending system designed to prevent the possible invalidation of the loan contract on the grounds on the grounds of statutory and equitable unconscionability. He never met a prospective borrower in person but communicated solely with the borrower's broker or other agent. His clients never lent their money directly to the borrower but to a shell company (in this case, the Victorian Boat Clinic Pty Ltd) formed by the borrower, the borrower guaranteeing the company's repayment obligations. Apart from expressing a view on the valuation of the proposed security, the solicitor did not advise his clients to make a loan but left the decision to their exercise

[44] *Stubbings* (n 9) [49] (Kiefel CJ, Keane and Gleeson JJ).
[45] ibid.

of judgement. Finally, he prepared formal certificates, to be signed by the borrower in the presence of another solicitor and an accountant. The identity of each adviser was suggested, but not insisted upon, to the borrower's broker by the lenders' solicitor. The certificates confirmed that the borrower understood the legal and financial consequences of taking out the loan. The advisers were paid out of the proceeds of sale. The loan agreement itself provided that the proceeds were not to be used for personal, household or domestic purposes but were to be applied solely for business purposes.

After settlement the borrower repaid two interest instalments before default. The company to which the loan had been made stored some hulls on the property but never undertook any business. Moreover, the property purchased with the loan was not zoned for business activity.

The lenders sought possession of the property. The primary judge declined to make a possession order, instead holding that the loan contract was unconscionable in equity, as well as under section 12CB of the ASIC Act. The contract was rescinded on terms, the borrower being required to account on an unsecured basis to the lenders for $109,315 that he had been paid prior to rescission.

The Court of Appeal allowed the lenders' appeal. The Court agreed with the primary judge that the system created by their solicitor, involving lending to a shell corporation while the 'real' borrower guaranteed the performance of the corporation's repayment obligations, successfully removed the case from the ambit of the Code.[46] But the Court disagreed with the primary judge's holding that the arrangement was unconscionable. Liability required proof that the lenders, through their solicitor, had knowledge of the borrower's financial position. Whereas the primary judge had found that the lenders' solicitor had recklessly failed to make inquiries into the state of the borrower's finances, the Court of Appeal was not satisfied that he had either recklessly failed to make inquiries or possessed knowledge of circumstances that would have put an honest and reasonable lender on inquiry.[47] In reaching this conclusion the Court found that it was reasonable for the lenders' solicitor to rely on the certificates, particularly the accountant's certificate, in refraining from inquiry into how the borrower proposed to service the loans.[48] In the opinion of the Court, 'The [primary] judge's adverse view of the system of lending – in substance an adverse view of asset-based lending as a concept – overwhelmed … his determination of the unconscionability issue.'[49]

A further appeal to the High Court was unanimously allowed. The plurality (Kiefel CJ, Keane and Gleeson JJ) held that the solicitor's conduct, in the steps he took in

[46] A different conclusion on this point might have been reached if the court had concluded that, in spite of the guarantee, the borrower was in substance the primary debtor. A borrower cannot be both a debtor and a guarantor of the same debt: *Jowitt v Callaghan* (1938) 38 SR (NSW) 512. See *Integrated Securities No 3 Pty Ltd v Creatrix Web Development & Online Marketing Solutions Pty Ltd* [2021] NSWSC 596 (*Integrated Securities No 3*), where a borrower, described as 'debtor' and 'guarantor' in different parts of the loan agreement, was found to be primarily liable in the capacity of debtor. *Jams 2 Pty Ltd v Stubbings (No 3)* (n 9) was distinguished on this ground at [86]. At [121], Rein J directed that a copy of the reasons in the case be sent to ASIC in order to draw attention to the interposition of companies into loan agreements and to consider 'whether steps should be taken to seek to have the legislation extended to cases where a company borrows for no purpose genuinely connected with its normal business'.

[47] *Jams 2 Pty Ltd v Stubbings* (n 9) [130].

[48] ibid [133].

[49] ibid [126].

the capacity of the lenders' agent, amounted in equity to the unconscientious exploitation of the borrower's special disadvantage. Justice Steward reached the same conclusion in a separate judgment. Neither judgment considered it necessary to determine whether the borrower's claim would have succeeded under section 12CB of the ASIC Act. Justice Gordon, agreeing with the plurality on the analysis of the equitable claim, also held that the lending system employed was contrary to section 12CB.

The decision in *Stubbings* raises some intriguing questions. They concern both the application of the equitable unconscionability doctrine to asset-based lending systems and the relationship between the equitable and statutory approaches to relieving against unconscientious transactions.

A. Equity and Asset-Based Lending Systems

The High Court emphasised that the practice of asset-based lending was not inherently unconscionable.[50] On the contrary, it was the application of specific equitable criteria to the facts of the case that supported the primary judge's finding that the loan agreement was unconscionable. Importantly, the plurality emphasised that the trifecta of *Amadio* criteria – the 'special disadvantage' of the weaker party, knowledge of that disadvantage by the stronger party, and unconscientious exploitation by the stronger party – were not to be analysed in isolation from one another. '[T]hese considerations should not be understood as if they were to be addressed separately as if they were separate elements of a cause of action in tort.'[51] The interconnectedness of the elements of an *Amadio* claim are essential to understanding the result reached in *Stubbings*.

The finding that Mr Stubbings was under a 'special disadvantage' in negotiating the contract of loan was not controversial. He was unable to perform simple calculations, still less to understand the risks involved in signing the loan agreement. His financial circumstances were described as 'bleak'.[52] It was also a simple matter to conclude, on the facts, that the loan contract was exploitative, since 'The inevitable outcome of the transaction was, objectively speaking, that [Mr Stubbings's] equity in his properties would be taken by the [lenders] by way of interest payments, including at default interest rates.'[53]

The critical question was whether the solicitor, acting as the lenders' agent, knew of Mr Stubbings's special disadvantage, given the lengths to which the solicitor had gone to design a lending system that shielded lenders from any knowledge of a borrower's personal and financial circumstances. The obvious purpose of the system was to create an information barrier between lender and borrower in order to prevent the *Amadio* knowledge requirement from being satisfied. The plurality judgment linked the knowledge requirement to the finding of exploitation. Knowledge of the borrower's 'special disadvantage' could be inferred from the creation of a lending system that made loans only to borrowers who could not obtain finance from regular banks, and on terms that

[50] *Stubbings* (n 9) [51] (Kiefel CJ, Keane and Gleeson JJ), [152] (Steward J).
[51] ibid [39].
[52] ibid [41] (Kiefel CJ, Keane and Gleeson JJ), [81] (Gordon J), [157]–[159] (Steward J).
[53] ibid [43] (Kiefel CJ, Keane and Gleeson JJ), [91] (Gordon J), [169] (Steward J).

would inevitably result in the borrower's default. The inference of 'knowledge' was drawn by the plurality from the characteristics of the system employed by the lender:

> [O]ne might regard the deployment of such artifices in a context where the lender or its agent deliberately distances itself from evidence that must confirm the dangerous nature of the transaction for the borrower or its guarantor as evidence pointing to an exploitative state of mind on the part of the lender.[54]

The conclusion demonstrates the adaptability of equity in not allowing its doctrines to be subverted by the creation of systems designed to prevent the application of its criteria for relief. Over-ingenious drafting will be self-defeating if its transparent aim is to prevent equitable scrutiny of the substance of a transaction. The plurality's willingness to infer knowledge from the deliberate creation of information barriers designed to prevent actual knowledge of a 'special disadvantage' has important implications for two systemic techniques employed in drafting loan contracts. The first is the insertion, for no legitimate commercial reason, of a shell company as the primary borrower, the 'real' borrower acting as guarantor of that company's indebtedness. We have seen that this device is currently effective to exclude the operation of the 'responsible lending' provisions of the Code.[55] But adoption of the device may well justify the inference that the lender had knowledge of any 'special disadvantage' affecting the borrower, or at least was wilfully blind to the possibility that a special disadvantage existed. The drafting trick that enables the lender to escape the frying pan of the Code may land the lender in the fire of equity's unconscionability jurisdiction.

The second systemic aspect of consumer lending to which the plurality's analysis of inferred knowledge is relevant concerns the requirement of providing certificated advice to borrowers. Following the *Amadio* decision, the provision of independent and objective professional advice has become an essential pillar of consumer lending. We previously observed that the courts have been concerned to ensure that apparently responsible advice has been given. The quality of the advice is immaterial unless the lender is aware of its defects, or there are circumstances that should have made the lender aware of its defects.[56] The significance of the plurality judgment in *Stubbings* on this point lies in its willingness to go beyond the form of the certificates and to determine, as a matter of substance, whether genuine advice has been given. The judgment referred to 'the bland boilerplate language of the certificates' and to the inference that could be drawn that the certificates were 'mere window dressing' and were 'a precautionary artifice designed to prevent an inference that the [lenders] were wilfully blind to the obvious danger to the [borrower]'.[57]

What is relevant for the purpose of an unconscionability inquiry is, as previously observed, not so much the quality of the advice (which will be the principal consideration in a negligence claim)[58] but whether independent and objective advice was in fact given.

[54] ibid [49] (Kiefel CJ, Keane and Gleeson JJ), [161]–[162] (Steward J). Justice Steward alternatively found at [165]–[168] that the agent was wilfully blind to the borrower's disadvantage.

[55] See text at n 23 and n 45.

[56] See text at n 21.

[57] *Stubbings* (n 9) [49] (Kiefel CJ, Keane and Gleeson JJ).

[58] *Jams 2 Pty Ltd v Stubbings (No 3)* (n 9) [329]–[339], holding that the advice given by the accountant was negligent.

This holistic inquiry includes, among other relevant factors, whether the lender or the lender's agent influenced the borrower in the selection of adviser, whether the adviser was paid from the proceeds of the loan, and (if the stated purpose of the loan is to assist the borrower to pursue a business) whether the advice was directed to the attainment of the borrower's business aims.[59] In respect of all these matters the exercise of systemic ingenuity in the certification process will be self-defeating. A process designed to ensure the lender's ignorance of the advice, beyond the bland certificated confirmation that advice was given and apparently understood, may of itself justify an inference that the lender knew of, or at least strongly suspected, the borrower's special disadvantage.

B. Statute and Asset-Based Lending Systems

The judgments of the plurality and Steward J in *Stubbings* upheld the primary judge's decision that the asset-based loan agreement challenged by Mr Stubbings was unconscionable in equity. Neither judgment considered it necessary to determine whether the agreement was unconscionable under section 12CB of the ASIC Act. Claims had been brought both in equity and under section 12CB, and the primary judge had not distinguished between the two jurisdictions in finding the lending agreement to be unconscionable. At a subsequent hearing, however, the remedial orders were made in the exercise of the Court's equitable jurisdiction, applying the equitable authorities on rescission.[60]

The judgment of Gordon J is of particular interest, because her Honour agreed with the other members of the Court that the loan agreement was unconscionable in equity but also held that it was invalid under section 12CB of the ASIC Act. The judgment emphasised two statutory provisions applicable to the facts of *Stubbings*.[61] The first was section 12CB(4)(b), enacting that the section can apply 'to a system of conduct or pattern of behaviour, whether or not a particular individual is identified as having been disadvantaged by the conduct or behaviour'. A 'system of conduct' is distinguishable from a 'pattern of behaviour' in that the former 'connotes an internal method of working', whereas the latter 'connotes the external observation of events'.[62] Second, since statutory liability is not limited to the unwritten (equitable) law of the States and Territories, it was relevant to a 'systems' case such as *Stubbings* that proof of an individual's 'special disadvantage' is not required. A 'system of conduct' or 'pattern of behaviour' can be unconscientious even though no specific individual is identified as disadvantaged.[63]

[59] *Stubbings* (n 9) [50] (Kiefel CJ, Keane and Gleeson JJ) approving *Jams 2 Pty Ltd v Stubbings (No 3)* (n 9) [314] (Robson J). See also *Stubbings* (n 9) [93] (Gordon J) and [172] (Steward J) emphasising the finding that the advice had been provided to the shell company and not to Mr Stubbings in the capacity of the company's guarantor.

[60] *Jams 2 Pty Ltd v Stubbings (No 4)* [2019] VSC 482 [3] (Robson J). The Court of Appeal would have modified the terms on which rescission had been granted, had it upheld the finding of unconscionability: *Jams 2 Pty Ltd v Stubbings* (n 9) [135].

[61] See text at n 27.

[62] *Stubbings* (n 9) [55] (Gordon J); *Kobelt* (n 27) (Nettle and Gordon JJ), citing *Unique International College Pty Ltd v Australian Competition and Consumer Commission* [2018] FCAFC 155, (2018) 266 FCR 631, 654 [104].

[63] *Stubbings* (n 9) [55] (Gordon J).

Applying the statutory considerations set out in section 12CC to the lending system developed by the lenders' agent, Gordon J concluded that the system was 'outside the societal norms of acceptable behaviour so as to warrant condemnation as offensive to conscience. It does not reflect values that can be recognised by a court to prevail within contemporary Australian society.'[64]

Viewed as a case on systemic misconduct, *Stubbings* is valuable because it demonstrates that the systems attracting the application of section 12CB are not confined to the organisational structures and practices of corporations.[65] The system put in place by the lenders' solicitor involved a network of individual lenders and professional advisers, established for the purpose of ensuring that the form, though not the substance, of the *Amadio* requirements were satisfied. The scheme illustrates how a cynical and exploitative 'culture' can permeate a network, which has no legal personality, just as much as it can actuate the unconscionable conduct of a corporation that, as a legal person, is directly amenable to statutory and equitable relief.[66]

The judgment of Gordon J highlights the significance of section 12CB as an independent head of liability, and helpfully provides a template, for the benefit of practitioners, of how a claim under this provision should be pleaded. For the purpose of establishing statutory liability, it was unnecessary for Mr Stubbings to prove that he was subject to a 'special disability' recognised in equity. What had to be shown, and was in fact proved, was that the system was intended to apply to vulnerable borrowers whose lack of income deprived them of access to regular bank loans.[67] This is an illustration of the proposition that the statutory inquiry under section 12CB focuses on how a lending system affects an identified class of borrowers, whereas the equitable inquiry focuses on the exploitation of the personal or economic weakness of an individual borrower.

The judgment also rejects, albeit by implication, a post-*Kobelt* argument that there are two distinct types of section 12CB case, one dependent on proof of the exploitation of individual 'special disability' and the other proscribed because the defendant's conduct is 'offensive to conscience'.[68] The recognition of two analytical frameworks for assessing section 12CB claims would be an unfortunate over-elaboration of the statutory unconscionability regime. The boundary between the two types of case is unclear, and its very existence would encourage sterile litigation as to the correct choice of framework. Not the least of the merits of Gordon J's judgment is the confirmation that there is only one basal test to determine whether conduct is unconscionable for the purpose of the provision, namely, whether, having regard to the considerations enumerated in section 12CC, the conduct is 'outside societal norms of acceptable commercial behaviour so as to warrant condemnation as conduct that is offensive to conscience'.[69] There are section 12CB cases, of which *Kobelt* may be one, involving alleged exploitation of a 'special disadvantage', the disadvantage either being individual or common

[64] ibid [84] (Gordon J).

[65] cf E Bant and JM Paterson, 'Systems of Misconduct: Corporate Culpability and Statutory Unconscionability' (2021) 15 *Journal of Equity* 63.

[66] ibid 76–78.

[67] *Stubbings* (n 9) [82]–[83] (Gordon J).

[68] *Quantum* (n 27) [39], suggesting that *Kobelt* (n 27) was a 'special disadvantage' case, 'not merely as some forensic choice, but as a natural consequence of the facts and circumstances as they presented themselves'.

[69] *Stubbings* (n 9) [58] (Gordon J) citing *Kobelt* (n 27) [92].

to members of a class of the community, but these cases can easily be accommodated within social norms test restated by Gordon J.

Justice Gordon's conclusion that the lenders' conduct was unconscionable within section 12CB must be correct. Her Honour's concurrence with the plurality judgment makes clear that the conduct was unconscionable *both* under the statute *and* in equity. But if section 12CB and its counterparts in other federal, State and Territory legislation adequately cover the territory of commercially unacceptable behaviour, an obvious follow-up question suggests itself: has statutory unconscionability rendered the equitable unconscionability doctrine redundant, at least in practice, if not in law?

IV. The Survival of Equitable Unconscionability?

A conclusion that statutory unconscionability has replaced the *Amadio* doctrine over its entire field of operation would be surprising. Neither the legislation nor the parliamentary materials envisage anything as dramatic as the extinction of equitable doctrine.[70] Indeed, the survival of equitable unconscionability is assumed by section 12CA, which provides:

> A person must not, in trade or commerce, engage in conduct in relation to financial services if the conduct is unconscionable within the meaning of the unwritten law, from time to time, of the States and Territories.

Moreover, liability under section 12CB is defined negatively by reference to the 'unwritten' (essentially equitable) law in section 12CB(4)(a) providing that liability under section 12CB is not 'limited' by that (presumably extant) law. As 'textbook law', the *Amadio* doctrine undoubtedly endures, even in the arena of financial services. The harder question is whether it survives as 'law in action' in that arena. As a practical matter, a case could be made that section 12CB and equivalent or near-equivalent Commonwealth, State and Territory legislation nowadays cover most of the ground formerly inhabited by equitable doctrine.[71] Though still extant, the argument might run, the 'unwritten law' has been largely superseded by legislation that is not restricted to the notion of exploitation of an individual's 'special disadvantage'.

Legislation expressly designed to counteract systemic unconscionability is, self-evidently, more likely to be more effective in neutralising systemic wrongdoing than individualistic private law doctrine, especially when the legislation confers powers on a regulator to promote enforcement. But it would be premature to write the obituary of the *Amadio* doctrine, even in a field such as the provision of financial services, where extensive consumer protection legislation has been enacted. A number of considerations point to the continued vitality of the *Amadio* doctrine in asset-based lending cases, and more generally where individual weakness has been exploited in the provision of financial services.

[70] Wholesale abolition of equitable doctrine is rare, but see Law of Property (Miscellaneous Provisions) Act 1989 (Eng) abolishing the doctrine of part performance.

[71] Competition and Consumer Act 2010 (Cth), sch 2, s 21 and State and Territory Laws applying s 21, eg Australian Consumer Law and Fair Trading Act 2012 (Vic), s 8; Contracts Review Act 1980 (NSW), s 7.

An obvious reason for retaining the *Amadio* doctrine is that some unconscionable practices may escape legislative sanction for jurisdictional reasons. Loan contracts will often be drafted with the express aim of avoiding the long arm of statutory invalidation, by well-informed lawyers responding recursively to judicial decisions on the scope of the legislation. The practice of lending to shell corporations, repayment being guaranteed by the de facto individual debtor, was identified earlier as a currently effective mode of removing asset-lending from the ambit of the NCCP Act.[72] Equity may afford relief in some of these cases. This reason may appear less compelling in the context of the statutory unconscionability provisions where federal, State and Territory laws interact to provide comprehensive jurisdictional coverage.[73] But if doubt exists, for example, as to whether a facility is a 'financial product' under section 12BAA of the ASIC Act, it may be prudent for the plaintiff to claim relief in equity, as well as under section 12CB. Equity, in this type of case, performs its historic 'gap filling' function of reinforcing a statutory provision. Provided that the criteria of the *Amadio* doctrine are strictly observed, there can be no objection based on judicial overreach to the application of equity to overcome jurisdictional limitations.

A second argument for the continued relevance of the equitable unconscionability doctrine relates to the application of equitable principles in awarding relief. *Stubbings* conveniently illustrates this point. Like other consumer welfare legislation, the ASIC Act enacts various criminal and civil remedies that can be awarded upon proof of unconscionable conduct, the latter including awards of damages and injunctions.[74] But the statutory smorgasbord is far from comprehensive. Recall that Mr Stubbings's aim was to prevent loss of his properties by resisting the possession order sought by the lenders.[75] Unconscionability was pleaded as a defence to the claim to possession. The orders made by the primary judge, which were upheld by the High Court, consisted of a declaration that the loan agreement was invalid, together with rescission in equity, fashioned 'to ensure Mr Stubbings does not make a windfall gain and that due consideration is given to other lenders'.[76] The judge proceeded to apply the well-known equitable principles for rescinding a contract on terms that achieve 'practical justice'.[77] The terms of relief required Mr Stubbings to account for $109,315 due to the lenders.[78] The orders were made in the exercise of the Court's equity jurisdiction, not simply because the loan was found to be unconscionable in equity but because the ASIC Act makes no provision for rescission of loan contracts that contravene section 12CB.[79] What in practice occurs at the remedy stage of the inquiry, unless the statutory remedies are sufficient to achieve

[72] In addition to *Jams 2 Pty Ltd v Stubbings (No 3)* (n 9), this lacuna was noted in *Equititrust Ltd v SLM* [2010] NSWSC 1059; *Devon v Thirteenth Kaysan Pty Ltd* [2016] FCA 357; *Commercial Funds Pty Ltd v Fraval* [2020] VCC 1787; *Integrated Securities No 3* (n 46); and see n 40.

[73] See, eg, Australian Consumer Law and Fair Trading Act 2012 (Vic), s 12.

[74] ASIC Act (n 5) pt 2, div 2, sub-div G.

[75] *Jams 2 Pty Ltd v Stubbings (No 3)* (n 9) [218].

[76] *Jams 2 Pty Ltd v Stubbings (No 4)* (n 60) [3].

[77] *Alati v Kruger* [1955] HCA 64, (1955) 94 CLR 216; *Maguire v Makaronis* [1997] HCA 23, (1997) 188 CLR 449.

[78] No security for payment was imposed because the lenders' obtaining of security under the mortgage was part of the imposition and exploitation of the defendant by the unconscionable conduct: *Jams 2 Pty v Stubbings (No 4)* (n 60) [20]–[26], applying *Perpetual Trustees Victoria Ltd v Burns* [2015] WASC 234.

[79] ASIC Act (n 5) s 12GND empowers a court to make a declaration that a term of a consumer contract is unfair; but even under this provision, rescissionary terms of relief will be equitable.

full justice, is that equity acts in support of statutory rights. Section 12CB establishes the invalidity of the loan contract on the ground of unconscionability, but equity will often, as in *Stubbings*, determine the consequences of invalidity.

Rescission on equitable terms is an application of unjust enrichment principles, having regard to the policy of preventing the unjust enrichment of the plaintiff, as well as of the defendant.[80] Effect is given to that policy in fashioning the terms of relief. Fine tuning the terms of relief in order to achieve justice for both parties is an established equitable technique that can be invoked to supplement statutory remedies. The latter are typically claimant-centred, being directed at preventing the continuation or repetition of wrongdoing, and at compensating for losses caused by the defendant's conduct. Equity comes into its own when regard must be had to the interests of both parties in awarding relief.

A third reason for the persistence of equitable relief for unconscionability concerns the character of private law claims to relief. The plaintiff's claim in many unconscionability cases is focused exclusively on the transaction from which she is trying to escape. Her sole concern will be to demonstrate that a debt, or a guarantee of repayment of a debt, should be set aside, or that a threatened possession order should not be made. Unlike a regulator, the plaintiff will usually have no interest in establishing the relevant community norms or the extent of departure from those norms. But she will want to convince the court that she was unable, by reason of financial illiteracy or other vulnerability, of assessing the financial risks she incurred in signing the loan contract. As the judgment of Gordon J demonstrates, proof of the elements of the equitable claim can also establish the existence of a 'system of conduct' that brings the facts within the scope of section 12CB of the ASIC Act. Nevertheless, the fact that section 12CB can apply to a system of conduct 'whether or not a particular individual is identified as having been disadvantaged by the conduct or behaviour', is of no special value to a litigant whose claim is explicitly premised on the exploitation of her own financial illiteracy or other vulnerability.

Mr Stubbings's sole interest was in resisting the lenders' claim to possession of the property he had bought and in obtaining favourable terms for repayment of the debts he owed under the rescinded mortgages. To that end, the evidence was directed to proof of the lenders' exploitation of his own impecuniosity and inability to assess financial risk. The implications for other borrowers of the asset-based lending scheme put in place by the lenders were irrelevant to the attainment of his personal litigation objectives. In private law litigation not brought as class actions, and where there is no intervention by a regulator interested in bringing public interest considerations to the attention of the court, equity's emphasis on the exploitation of an individual's special disadvantage is likely to prevail.

A final argument for the continued relevance of equity in the age of statutory unconscionability is that the accumulated experience of courts applying the equitable concept of unconscionability remains relevant to the application of the statutory regime. Even though the section 12CB conception of unconscionability is broader than its equitable

[80] *Equuscorp Pty Ltd v Haxton* [2012] HCA 7, (2012) 246 CLR 498.

counterpart, and notwithstanding that the considerations to which a court must have regard under section 12CC include some that do not typically figure in an equitable inquiry, 'the appropriation of the terminology of equity'[81] assumes that the equity authorities continue to be relevant to determining whether conduct is unconscionable under the statute. One example of equity's continuing relevance to the imposition of statutory liability concerns the provision of legal or other professional advice to a contracting party in a case where improper pressure is alleged. Not only the necessity for advice but also its sufficiency in overcoming potential unconscionability or undue influence is a topic that has attracted significant judicial analysis over the years. The advice 'must be both independent and effective'.[82] The certificated 'advice' provided to Mr Stubbings fell so far below the standards of independence and effectiveness that no citation of authority was required to establish its inadequacy. Nevertheless, the equity authorities on the provision of independent professional advice may well provide valuable guidance in other cases on the nature and quality of advice that satisfies community norms for advice to borrowers.[83] Section 12CB is not a clean slate from which prior judicial analysis of recurring legal problems is wiped away.

V. Conclusion

Asset-based lending is neither good nor bad in itself. As elsewhere in the law, everything depends on context. Applied to corporations with fluctuating income cashflow, perhaps because of the seasonal nature of the corporation's business, the practice has commercial utility. Applied to consumers, on the other hand, lending without regard to the borrower's ability to repay out of income may well be exploitative, since it is apt to be the last resort of income-poor borrowers who are cut off from access to regular banks. When the validity of an asset-based loan is challenged, the court's role, applying statute and equitable doctrine, is to distinguish between acceptable and objectionable lending practice. The Court of Appeal in *Stubbings* rejected the primary judge's unconscionability ruling in that case as being 'a bridge too far'. The fear underlying the Court's judgment was that, by stigmatising *this* asset-lending system as unconscionable, the primary judge had cast a shadow of uncertainty over asset-lending practices *generally* that were commercially legitimate.[84] The High Court decision, reversing the Court of Appeal, demonstrated that the fear was groundless: equitable and statutory unconscionable principles are effective to counteract exploitative asset-based lending without disturbing settled commercial lending practice.

[81] *Kobelt* (n 27) [90] (Gageler J).

[82] *Riz* (n 41) [119].

[83] See *Inch Noriah v Shaik Allie Bin Omar* [1929] AC 127, [1928] All ER Rep 189 (PC); *Perpetual Trustee Co of New South Wales Ltd v Bridgewater* [1936] 3 All ER 501 (PC); *Bester v Perpetual Trustee Co Ltd* [1970] 3 NSWR 30 (NSWSC); *Stivactas v Michaletos (No 2)* (NSWCA, 31 August 1993); *Riz* (n 41) [116]–[119]. See also P Young, C Croft and M Smith, *On Equity* (Sydney, Thomson Reuters, 2009) [5.280] on the different roles independent legal advice plays in undue influence and unconscionability.

[84] *Jams 2 Pty Ltd v Stubbings* (n 9) [126].

In *Kobelt*, Gageler J observed that '"Unconscionable" is an obscure English word which centuries of use by courts administering equity have transformed into a legal term of art.'[85] The ASIC Act gives statutory expression to the term of art in section 12CA, together with an enhanced catalogue of remedies. Section 12CB does 'something more'[86] than the equitable unconscionability doctrine since it is not limited to the unwritten law of the States and Territories. Deciding precisely what is, or is not, that 'something more' remains judicial work in progress. The only point this chapter makes is that 'something more' does not mean the wholesale exclusion of equitable principles from the territory covered by statutory unconscionability. On the contrary, the statutory proscription of unconscientious conduct requires the continued involvement of equitable doctrine and remedies if the aims of the legislation are to be fully achieved in relieving against unconscionability. Statute and equity are cooperative, not antagonistic.

[85] *Stubbings* (n 9) [81].
[86] *Kobelt* (n 27) [83] (Gageler J).

15

Corporate Contrition

ROBYN CARROLL*

I. Introduction

In September 2021, the Federal Court of Australia imposed a penalty of $10.5 million on Westpac for its 'egregious' conduct in misleading superannuation customers in contravention of provisions in chapter 7 of the Corporations Act 2001 (Cth) (Corporations Act).[1] In determining the civil penalty to be paid by the bank for its contravening conduct O'Bryan J took into account that Westpac had made 'no expression of contrition or remorse', that it had not sent any correspondence to the affected members, nor had any correspondence containing any apology to those individuals been proposed, despite the passage of more than six months since the High Court of Australia handed down its decision affirming Westpac's contraventions of the Corporations Act.[2] In determining a penalty 'at the highest levels permitted by the Act' O'Bryan J emphasised that Westpac 'has not expressed regret for the conduct, does not appear to have taken steps to remedy the compliance deficiencies and has been tardy in progressing a remediation plan'.[3]

Cases like *ASIC v Westpac* and other cases discussed in this chapter invite us to consider whether a corporation can experience remorse or contrition and, if so, how this is expressed. Why does the law consider remorse and contrition, how do courts judge whether a corporation can be attributed with being remorseful or contrite and for what purposes? Is an apology ever sufficient and always necessary? The aim of the chapter is to answer these and other questions that arise when we consider corporate remorse and contrition.[4]

* I acknowledge with thanks the excellent research assistance of Katherine Swann for my preparation of this chapter.

[1] *Australian Securities and Investments Commission (ASIC) v Westpac Securities Administration Limited, in the matter of Westpac Securities Administration Limited* [2021] FCA 1008, (2021) 156 ACSR 614 [45] (*ASIC v Westpac*); M Pelly, 'Judge blasts "no regrets" Westpac over super bungles' *Australian Financial Review* (13 September 2021).

[2] *Westpac Securities Administration Ltd v ASIC* [2021] HCA 3, (2021) 270 CLR 118, (2021) 387 ALR 1 (*Westpac v ASIC*), affirming the decision of the Full Court of the Federal Court in *ASIC v Westpac Securities Administration Ltd* [2019] FCAFC 187, (2019) 272 FCR 170 (*ASIC v Westpac Securities*).

[3] *ASIC v Westpac* (n 1) [95].

[4] The discussion in the chapter is based on Australian legislation and case law. To the extent that remorse and contrition are relevant to decision making about the consequences of corporate misconduct in other jurisdictions, we might expect the principles and guidelines discussed here to be relevant in jurisdictions where the objects of the law and functions of remorse and contrition are the same or similar.

Section II of the chapter identifies the challenge of attributing the emotional state of remorse and contrition to a corporation, and identifies in broad terms the ways courts deal with this challenge. Section III discusses the meaning of remorse and contrition. Section IV identifies the objects of criminal law and civil penalty regimes and the functions that remorse and contrition serve in the law. With these objects and functions in mind, section V discusses what courts regard as evidence of remorse and contrition and what factors influence the weight given to that evidence. Section VI discusses the circumstances that courts identify as evidence of genuine corporate contrition and remorse. This is followed in section VII by an exploratory discussion of the merits of recognising contrition as a corporate 'state of mind', and what having regard to corporate systems as well as corporate words and actions brings to this inquiry. The chapter concludes that despite the difficulties of attributing remorse and contrition as a state of mind to a corporation, this inquiry is consistent with long-standing approaches and principles in the law and supports the law's goals of corporate compliance and regulation.

II. Corporate Remorse and Contrition: A Challenging Concept

In the introduction to their interdisciplinary study of remorse, Michael Proeve and Steven Tudor describe remorse as a 'fundamentally important moral emotion'.[5] As they explain, while remorse, as a type of emotion, is of interest to psychologists, it is also of interest to philosophers and lawyers because of its moral aspects and its role in the law, particularly criminal law.[6] This chapter considers the circumstances in which this 'moral emotion' plays a role in the law in sentencing corporations and in determining civil penalties for contraventions of the law by corporations. The concept of a corporation experiencing human feelings and emotions that might accompany wrongdoing and its aftermath, including guilt, shame, remorse and regret, obviously is challenged by the artificial legal personality of a corporation. Leaving to one side the capacity of the natural persons who constitute the organs of a corporation or are its agents and employees to feel these emotions, we are left with the question whether a corporation can be attributed in some way with the 'fundamentally important' moral emotions of contrition and remorse. Courts express scepticism at times that contrition can be attributed to a corporation, particularly in the context of civil penalties regimes. In *ACE Insurance Ltd v Trifunovski (No 2)* (*Trifunovski*), Pellam J stated:

> It is not clear to me how an artificial construct such as a corporation can experience the complex human emotion of contrition made up, as it is, of an amalgam of distinctly human emotions such as regret, shame and sympathy. I do not doubt that a corporation may exhibit signs of regret but it is too much to expect that such an artificial construct can be meaningfully contrite.

[5] M Proeve and S Tudor, *Remorse: Psychological and Jurisprudential Perspectives* (Farnham, Ashgate, 2010), 1. While the focus of their work is remorse, the words 'remorse' and 'contrition' are used interchangeably in the law, as will be seen in section III.

[6] ibid. The authors note that remorse is generally viewed as a significant emotion in restorative justice, much more so than in traditional criminal justice. This chapter raises for consideration the role of remorse in regulatory proceedings, where arguably there are similar public interest concerns in punishing and deterring anti-competitive behaviour and protection of consumers.

> For civil penalty cases involving corporations it would be more coherent to ask only whether the corporation has changed its behaviour. Nothing more can be expected; a person who does not literally or physically exist may not wear sackcloth.[7]

Other judges have referred to there being 'some conceptual difficulty in the notion of a corporation expressing "contrition"'.[8] Similar scepticism is also evident in law reform recommendations. In discussing what factors should be provided for sentencing a corporation in its Criminal Corporate Responsibility Report (2020 Report), the Australian Law Reform Commission (ALRC) expressed doubts about the utility of considering corporate contrition as a factor.[9] Referring to the sentencing factors in section 16A of the Crimes Act 1914 (Cth) (Crimes Act), which includes the factor in section 16A(2)(f), namely 'the degree to which the person has shown contrition for the offence', the Commission refers to the focus on 'contrition' as being 'less cogent for corporate offenders'[10] than for natural persons.

Notwithstanding the reservations expressed in the context of corporate wrongdoing, courts express judicial pragmatism in other cases. This pragmatism is informed no doubt by the fact that criminal sentencing policy considerations currently are applied to natural and corporate defendants. For example, in sentencing a corporation in *Ampol Ltd v Environment Protection Authority*,[11] Grove J states that '[w]hilst "contrition" is perhaps an inappropriate attribute for a corporation, it should be deemed to possess the equivalent'.[12] The same pragmatism is evident in civil penalty regimes aimed at deterring corporate wrongdoing. It is also evident from civil cases in which evidence of contrition is admissible as a factor relevant to the assessment of compensatory and exemplary damages for some torts, including where the defendant is a corporation.[13]

Besides pragmatism, there are indications that courts consider that having regard to expressions of contrition and remorse by corporations furthers the law's objects, notwithstanding the conceptual challenge of their being an artificial construct. In *Construction, Forestry, Mining and Energy Union (CFMEU) v Pilbara Iron Co (Services) Pty Ltd (No 4)*,[14] for example, while accepting the force of Pellam J's comments in *Trifunovski* noted above, Katzman J considered that 'more can be expected of a corporation than that it has changed its behaviour'.[15] There are multiple ways that a corporation can express contrition and in doing so demonstrate 'consciousness of the seriousness of the contravening conduct that may be relevant to penalty'[16] and an intention to make

[7] *ACE Insurance Ltd v Trifunovski (No 2)* [2012] FCA 793 (*Trifunovski*). In this case Perram J concludes that 'for civil penalty cases involving corporations it would be more coherent to ask only whether the corporation has changed it behaviour': ibid [113]–[114].

[8] *Comcare v John Holland Pty Ltd* [2014] FCA 1191 [101] (*Comcare*).

[9] Australian Law Reform Commission (ALRC), *Corporate Criminal Responsibility* (Report No 136, April 2020) Ch 8 (ALRC Final Report).

[10] ibid [8.40] note 42.

[11] *Ampol Ltd v Environment Protection Authority*, No 60139/1995 (NSWCCA, 26 October 1995) (*Ampol*) (Grove, Newman and Dunford JJ agreeing). See also *Morrison v Powercoal Pty Ltd & Anor (No 3)* [2005] NSWIRComm 61, (2005) 147 IR 117 [111] (*Morrison*).

[12] *Ampol* (n 11) 12.

[13] See section IV.D.ii.

[14] *Construction, Forestry, Mining and Energy Union (CFMEU) v Pilbara Iron Co (Services) Pty Ltd (No 4)* [2012] FCA 894, (2012) 225 IR 113 (*Pilbara Iron Co*).

[15] ibid [34].

[16] *Director of Consumer Affairs Victoria v Gibson (No 3)* [2017] FCA 1148 [50] (*Gibson*).

amends for their wrongdoing (or not) and other states of mind relevant to culpability notwithstanding that it is an artificial construct.[17]

The law attributes remorse and contrition to a culpable corporation through consideration of various forms of evidence that are discussed in section VI. I use 'attributes' here in a broad sense to mean ways in which the law has regard to consciousness and intention on the part of a corporation. These forms of evidence include words and actions of corporations consistent with existing general law and statutory attribution rules,[18] and 'systems intentionality' by which a corporation's state of mind is manifested through its systems, policies and practices.[19]

Questions whether a corporation can 'feel' remorse or contrition and has moral obligations beyond obligations imposed by the law invite inquiries into corporate culpability beyond the scope of this chapter: some of these are undertaken ably by the authors of other chapters in this book, who provide philosophical and jurisprudential reasons for attributing moral and legal responsibility to a corporation.[20] Ultimately, whether 'being' remorseful or contrite is described as a state of emotion ('feeling' contrite) or a state of mind ('thinking' contritely) makes little or no difference for the purposes of the analysis of corporate contrition. In attributing contrition and remorse to a corporation in sentencing and imposing a civil penalty and elsewhere in the law, courts take a pragmatic approach to the corporation as a legal construct in order to further the objects of the law.

III. Meaning of Remorse and Contrition

This section identifies the meaning attributed to remorse and contrition in leading dictionaries, social and psychological accounts, and the law. The functions of remorse and contrition and how courts judge whether a person expresses these emotions are discussed in subsequent sections of the chapter in light of the discussion in this section.

A. Dictionary Definitions of Remorse and Contrition

The *Australian Oxford Dictionary* defines remorse as 'deep regret for a wrong committed', and contrition as 'the state of being contrite; thorough penitence'.[21] The *Oxford English Dictionary* (OED) definition of 'remorse' refers to:

> deep regret or guilt for doing something morally wrong; the fact or state of feeling sorrow for committing a sin; repentance or compunction … an attack of deep regret or guilt.[22]

[17] For analysis of limitations of traditional methods of attributing mental states to corporations, see E Bant, 'Culpable Corporate Minds' (2021) 48 *University of Western Australia Law Review* 352, 354; E Bant, 'Catching the Corporate Conscience: A New Model of "Systems Intentionality"' (2022) *Lloyd's Maritime and Commercial Law Quarterly* 467, 468–71 and sources cited therein; Bant, ch 9 of this volume; M Diamantis, 'Functional Corporate Knowledge' (2019) 61 *William & Mary Law Review* 319; Diamantis, ch 10 of this volume.

[18] Generally, see R Leow, *Corporate Attribution in Private Law* (Oxford, Hart Publishing, 2022); Leow, ch 6 of this volume.

[19] Bant, 'Catching the Corporate Conscience' (n 17).

[20] See Harding, ch 2 of this volume; Crofts, ch 3 of this volume.

[21] *Australian Oxford Dictionary*, 2nd edn (Melbourne, Oxford University Press ANZ,2004) 'remorse'.

[22] *Oxford English Dictionary* at www.oed.com/, 'remorse'.

The OED definition of 'contrition' is:

> the condition of being bruised in heart; sorrow or affliction of mind for some fault or injury done; spec penitence for sin.[23]

The *Encyclopaedic Australian Legal Dictionary* defines 'remorse' as 'contrition or shame' but does not provide a separate definition of 'contrition'.[24]

B. Social and Psychological Accounts of Remorse

Proeve and Tudor provide a detailed psychological account of remorse and the related emotions of regret, guilt and shame.[25] From a philosophical perspective, remorse is one of the 'retractive emotions', in that 'the remorseful person retracts or withdraws from something which is seen as part of or associated with oneself'.[26] Other retractive emotions include guilt, shame, regret, compunction, contrition and repentance. From a psychological perspective, the central constitutive thought of regret is 'the wish that things were otherwise than they actually are'.[27] Regret, Proeve and Tudor explain, will generally include remorse, guilt and shame,

> each as types of 'agent regret', as opposed to 'spectator regret'. The distinction between remorse and guilt is not always easy to draw; both involve a sense that one has done wrong. The main way to distinguish between the two, however, is in terms of their object: generally, guilt is more focussed on oneself as guilty of having transgressed some authoritative rule or command, while remorse is more focussed on one's deeds and its consequences. Shame is also closely related to remorse (and guilt), but involves a greater sense of oneself as flawed, disgraced or discredited, and characteristically involves a desire to cover one's flaw, to hide or withdraw.[28]

Remorse is an emotion in which the remorseful person's behaviour towards others, through apologies and making amends by repairing damage, plays a central role.[29] Responses of others to a remorseful person are also a key part of the interpersonal nature of remorse. These responses include judgment and punishment (in both formal and informal settings). There is also the possibility 'that a person's remorse can serve as an indicator of changed behaviour in the future'.[30] Proeve and Tudor present a working definition of remorse that includes several characteristics, such as

> recognition that one has caused harm, an acceptance of responsibility for causing that harm, an associated internal strife, a desire to atone or make things right, a desire to be forgiven and perhaps some actions in furtherance of atonement and reparation.[31]

[23] ibid 'contrition'.
[24] *Encyclopaedic Australian Legal Dictionary – Online* (Sydney, Butterworths, 2002) 'remorse'. Interestingly, this Encyclopaedia entry for 'remorse' cites the Crimes Act (n 24), s 16A(2)(f), which refers to 'contrition' not 'remorse'. See section III.C.
[25] Proeve and Tudor (n 5).
[26] ibid 2.
[27] ibid.
[28] ibid 2–3.
[29] ibid 3.
[30] ibid. I discuss the functions of remorse in the law in more detail in section IV, and how it is judged in section V.
[31] Proeve and Tudor (n 5) 48. See also S Bandes, 'Remorse and Criminal Justice' (2016) 8 *Emotion Review* 14, 15.

Many of these characteristics are reflected in what the law says is evidence of contrition and remorse for sentencing and imposing civil penalties, including evidence of corporate remorse and contrition, as we see in section VI.

C. Meaning of Remorse and Contrition in the Law

There is a long history in criminal law of courts' taking into account whether an accused is genuinely remorseful for having committed the offence as a mitigating factor.[32] There is legislation throughout Australia and case law that confirms the common law principle that genuine remorse and contrition are relevant to sentencing. The words 'remorse' and 'contrition' are not defined in the legislation. The meaning of remorse, explains Adams J in *Georgopolous v The Queen*,[33] 'is a commonsense one – as shown by all the dictionary definitions – it is regret or sorrow for the wrongdoing'.[34] In discussing the meaning of remorse, the New South Wales Court of Criminal Appeal states in *Alvares v The Queen*:

> [R]emorse in this context means regret for the wrongdoing which the offender's actions have caused because it can be safely assumed that an offender will always regret the fact that he or she has been apprehended. Remorse is but one feature of post-offence conduct upon which an offender may seek to rely as a matter which has the potential to mitigate penalty. The manner in which the issue of remorse is approached is not unique to either the sentencing process or to the courtroom. Indeed, it is a common feature of everyday existence.[35]

An offender's expression of remorse or contrition is distinct from a sense of regret.[36] As noted in *Alvares*, courts distinguish between general regret as a result of the offence and genuine contrition for having committed the offence.[37] There can be no real remorse without an acceptance of responsibility.[38] In criminal proceedings the extent to which remorse may be inferred from a plea of guilty will depend in large measure upon the motivation of the person entering the plea. The court asks the question 'does the plea reflect genuine remorse, or is it simply a recognition of the inevitable?'[39] Where there is a strong case against the accused, a denial of responsibility may demonstrate an absence of remorse.

i. Sentencing Legislation

State and federal legislation set out multiple factors for courts to take into account in sentencing a defendant. In the federal jurisdiction, section 16A(1) of the Crimes Act

[32] See, eg, *Neal v The Queen* [1982] HCA 55, (1982) 149 CLR 305, 315; *R v Cameron* [2002] HCA 6, (2002) 209 CLR 339 [65] (*Cameron*); Crimes Act (n 24), s 16A(2)(f); Crimes (Sentencing Procedure) Act 1999 (NSW), s 21A(3)(i); Criminal Law (Sentencing) Act 1988 (SA), s 10(1)(g).

[33] *Georgopolous v The Queen* [2010] NSWCCA 246 (*Georgopolous*).

[34] ibid [11].

[35] *Alvares v The Queen* [2011] NSWCCA 33, (2011) 209 A Crim R 297 [44] (*Alvares*).

[36] *R v Hargraves* [2010] QSC 188 [45]. In *R v Alqudsi* [2016] NSWSC 1227 [106], for example, where the offender was convicted of offences contrary to the Crimes (Foreign Incursions and Recruitment) Act 1978 (Cth), the Court found that while expressing regret, the conduct of the offender did not amount to contrition.

[37] *R v Loiterton* [2005] NSWSC 905 [182].

[38] *R v Hall (No 2)* [2005] NSWSC 890 [112].

[39] ibid [109], citing *R v Winchester* (1992) 58 A Crim R 345, 350.

provides that in determining the sentence to be passed, or the order to be made, in respect of any person for a federal offence, a court must impose a sentence or make an order that is of a severity appropriate in all the circumstances of the offence.[40] In addition, section 16A(2) states that a court must take into account a number of other matters as are relevant and known to the court, and which include:

> (f) the degree to which the person has shown *contrition* for the offence:
>
> (i) by taking action to make reparation for any injury, loss or damage resulting from the offence; or
>
> (ii) in any other manner. [emphasis added]

Section 16A was introduced into the Crimes Act in 1990 and refers to 'contrition' rather than remorse.[41] It appears from the cases that section 16A(2) was intended to reflect the existing common law and general law sentencing considerations at the time the section was introduced.

There do not appear to be any cases that consider the specific meanings of 'contrition' in the statutory context of section 16A(2) of the Crimes Act.[42] The cases do not indicate any significance difference between the meaning of 'contrition' and 'remorse' for sentencing purposes under this section, and a number of cases indicate that 'contrition' and 'remorse' are used interchangeably by courts.[43] For example, in *Director of Public Prosecutions v Goldberg*,[44] where Vincent JA (Winneke P and Batt JA agreeing) considered whether contrition is distinguishable from remorse, his Honour concludes:

> Whether or not a distinction that is of practical significance can be made, or was intended to be made by the legislature, between the notions of remorse and contrition under Section 16A, I have serious doubts. The section, it is to be noted, contains no reference to remorse as a sentencing consideration. Apart from what I would anticipate would be the difficulty in attributing different meanings to the words contrition and remorse which would be capable of useful application on a day to day basis, I consider that it is highly unlikely that when setting out an extensive list of factors which a sentencer was required to take into account, the presence of remorse was deliberately omitted.[45]

[40] Section 16A was introduced into the Crimes Act (n 24) by the Crimes Legislation Amendment Act (No 2) 1989 (Cth) (No 4 of 1990) (Amending Act). Section 16A came into effect on 17 July 1990. The intention of the Amending Act was to streamline the principles applicable to sentencing offenders in Commonwealth and State jurisdictions, Second Reading Speech. Section 16A was based on s 10 of the (now repealed) Criminal Law (Sentencing) Act 1988 (SA) (CLS Act). The CLS Act was replaced by the Sentencing Act 2017 (SA), which uses the term 'remorse' and not 'contrition'.

[41] The Crimes Act (n 24) was amended by the Crimes Legislation Amendment Act (No 2) 1989 (Cth) (Amending Act) and came into effect on 17 July 1990.The Amending Act was introduced in response to Australian Law Reform Commission, *Sentencing* (Report No 44, March 1988), which was tabled in Parliament in 1988. See also ALRC, *Same Crime, Same Time: Sentencing of Federal Offenders* (Report No 103, 2006) (ALRC Report No 103). The ALRC recommended wholesale reforms of s 16A, including for the common law principles of sentencing to be codified in federal sentencing legislation.

[42] National Judicial College of Australia, Commonwealth Sentencing Database, 'Contrition and Reparation' at https://csd.njca.com.au/principles-practice/general_sentencing_principles/s16a_specific_relevant_factors/contrition/ (accessed 2 August 2022) (Commonwealth Sentencing Database).

[43] ibid, citing *Director of Public Prosecutions v Goldberg* [2001] VSCA 107 [41] (Vincent JA, Winneke P and Batt JA agreeing) (*Goldberg*). See also *Alvares* (n 35).

[44] *Goldberg* (n 43).

[45] ibid [41].

Further, in *Alvares*,[46] Buddin J (McClellan CJ at CL and Schmit J agreeing) did 'not detect any meaningful distinction between' the two terms 'remorse' and 'contrition'.[47] This is consistent with the use of both terms interchangeably in criminal and civil penalty case law.[48]

ii. Civil Penalties Regimes

Contrition and remorse are recognised by the courts as factors to be taken into account in determining the civil penalty to be imposed under a considerable number of statutes enacted in Australia since 1974 that create civil penalties and regulate corporate activities, including banking, commercial activities, occupational health and safety, and industrial law.[49] The words 'remorse' and 'contrition' are not defined by the legislation. The meaning given to these words is consistent with their meaning in the common law, which, historically, is drawn from criminal law outlined in the previous section. The words 'contrition' and 'remorse' are used interchangeably in both federal and State civil penalty cases.[50]

iii. Civil Actions

In tort cases, which arise primarily under State law in Australia, courts generally refer in their judgments to acts of 'contrition' using its common law meaning. For example, in defamation cases, courts may inquire whether a 'contrite apology' was offered.[51] Use of the word 'contrition' rather than reference to 'remorse' in civil actions may be an attempt to articulate the importance of genuine sorrow and regret as a mitigating factor in civil actions, in a way that is distinct from criminal law, where 'remorse' is a well-established factor in State sentencing legislation. Other than that possible explanation, there is nothing to suggest that remorse and contrition have any different meaning in this context.

iv. Summary

A review of Australian legislation and case law reveals that the words 'remorse' and 'contrition' are used interchangeably as having the same or similar meaning. A person is described as being in a contrite state or remorseful when they show regret and other emotions for their actions, that they accept responsibility for their actions and

[46] *Alvares* (n 35).

[47] ibid [38].

[48] *Director of Public Prosecutions v Thomas* [2016] VSCA 237, (2016) 347 ALR 275 [13] confirms that all of the 'matters specified in s 16A(2) to which the Court must have regard, with the exception of (p) have been conventionally regarded as matters which sentencing courts took into account at common law prior to the amending legislation'. (Section 16A(2)(p) provides for 'the probable effect that any sentence or order under consideration would have on any of the person's family or dependants'.)

[49] *Commonwealth v Director, Fair Work Building Industry Inspectorate* [2015] HCA 46, (2015) 258 CLR 482 (*Agreed Penalties Case*), providing examples to support this at fn 17.

[50] For example, in *Gibson* (n 16) [50], Mortimer J refers to 'remorse or contrition' as relevant to penalty; cases referred to in section IV.C.ii.

[51] For example, *Pedavoli v Fairfax Media Publications Pty Ltd* [2014] NSWSC 1674, (2014) 324 ALR 166 [99] (McCallum J) (*Pedavoli*).

the harm they have caused, and they acknowledge their wrongdoing and the injury it has caused, or take action to make reparation or both. No distinction appears to be made between the meaning of these words in the context of individual or corporate defendants, notwithstanding the conceptual difficulty identified in section I of attributing emotions to a corporation. There is no indication in the statutes or case law in Australia that the words 'contrition' or 'remorse' have distinct and different meanings as factors in sentencing, in civil penalty regimes or in civil actions. It might be preferable for the word 'contrition' to be used in civil actions given the long association of 'remorse' with sentencing principles. At the same time, it might also be preferable, in cases that arise in the federal jurisdiction in Australia, to inquire into the presence or absence of 'contrition' rather than 'remorse' when dealing with a culpable corporation in view of the reference to 'contrition' in section 16A(2)(f) of the Crimes Act. In the end, nothing appears to turn on which word is used.[52]

IV. Functions of Remorse and Contrition

The law has regard to remorse or contrition as a mitigating factor when a defendant is being punished for a crime, when a penalty is being imposed to deter contraventions of the law outside the criminal law and where an act of contrition is relevant in civil claims to damages. Evidence that a defendant is remorseful or contrite is one of many factors that can be taken into account in the holistic approach taken in each of these situations. While the primary objects of criminal law, civil penalties regimes and civil claims differ, there is an overlap in the objects of punishment and deterrence. This section begins with reference to theoretical accounts of the functions of remorse, then examines the objects of criminal law, civil penalties regimes and civil actions and the functions of remorse and contrition in each.

A. Theoretical Accounts of the Function of Remorse and Contrition

Proeve and Tudor explain that there are a number of theories in the criminal law context that account for the function of remorse, and which help to explain why the law takes remorse and contrition into account in determining the consequences of wrongdoing.[53] They refer to three accounts. First, equity theory, according to which punishment restores some sense of equity between a victim and offender. A lesser degree of punishment will be needed to restore equity in the case of an offender who is remorseful than an offender who is unremorseful. A second account emphasises the communicative function of remorse. Erving Goffman and Aaron Lazare suggest that remorse communicates support for community values, while a lack of remorse communicates rejection of those values, which leads to the concern that an offender is likely to reoffend. A third

[52] Accordingly, it is of no consequences that I refer sometimes to remorse *and* contrition and at other times to remorse *or* contrition in this chapter.

[53] Proeve and Tudor (n 5) ch 4.

account, Affect Control Theory, regards emotions such as remorse as signals about a person's character. In this way, 'evaluations of one's identity by others is enhanced by showing negative emotions after negative behaviours and positive emotions after positive behaviours'.[54] Proeve and Tudor explain the last theory is consistent with meta-analysis showing that an expression of remorse can lead to a more positive judgment about an offender and lower punishment than where there is no expression of remorse. These theories contribute to our understanding of these emotions, and why the law recognises remorse as a mitigating factor in determining the legal consequences of crimes and civil wrongs.

Proeve and Tudor identify a number of rationales for treating remorse as a mitigating factor in sentencing, favouring the rationale 'that mitigation is a way of recognising the offender in his remorse, and so is a way of honouring remorse as a good. This rationale builds on a communicative approach to sentencing.'[55] This analysis raises for consideration the rationale for treating contrition and remorse as a factor in sentencing corporations, when imposing civil penalties as distinct from criminal sentencing, and whether remorse and contrition is a 'good' in itself in the corporate context, a question to which we return in section VII.

Despite doubts that have been expressed about whether judges can reliably ascertain an offender's remorse, and consequently whether such an uncertain factor should be given any role in sentencing, Proeve and Tudor conclude that judges and juries are likely to remain 'deeply interested in whether or not an offender is remorseful' because:

> Remorse is a sign of the possibility of redemption, a deep theme in our legal system. It serves as a key point of agreement between the accused and their accusers: the court denounces the actions of the accused person, and the accused reciprocates by remorsefully repudiating their actions in turn.[56]

This assessment of the law's interest in remorse is borne out by legislation and case law principles in Australia referred to in the next section.

B. Criminal Law and Remorse and Contrition in Sentencing

i. Objects of the Criminal Law

The purposes of criminal punishment are various; they include the protection of society, deterrence of the offender and of others who might be tempted to offend, retribution and reform. The High Court in *Veen v The Queen (No 2)* explains that these purpose overlap and that

> none of them can be considered in isolation from the others when determining what is an appropriate sentence in a particular case. They are guideposts to the appropriate sentence but sometimes they point in different directions.[57]

[54] ibid 208.

[55] ibid 210.

[56] K Rossmanith, S Tudor and M Proeve, 'Courtroom Contrition: How do Judges Know?' (2018) 27 *Griffith Law Review* 366, 367.

[57] *Veen v The Queen (No 2)* [1988] HCA 14, (1988) 164 CLR 465, 476 (Mason CJ, Brennan, Dawson and Toohey JJ).

In giving effect to the retributive and other purposes of the criminal law the courts apply a fundamental principle of sentencing law, which is proportionality.[58] The principle of proportionality requires the judge

> to make a judgment concerning the relationship of the penalty to the facts. This is a value judgment, based on experience and instinct, derived after taking into account all the facts and circumstances of the case.[59]

In general, a sentencing court will, after weighing all of the relevant factors, reach a conclusion that a particular penalty is the one that should be imposed.[60] In weighing these factors the court applies what is referred to as an 'instinctive synthesis approach', which recognises that there must be a synthesising of the relevant factors in the process of which 'greater and lesser weight will be allocated to some factors depending on their relevance to the person convicted and his or her crime'.[61]

ii. Functions of Remorse in Sentencing Laws

The factors considered in sentencing include factors in mitigation. Evidence of genuine contrition may indicate the offender has reasonable prospects of rehabilitation,[62] which may work to reduce the sentence otherwise imposed.[63] As Adams J explains in *Georgopolous*, remorse 'will often be relevant to a greater or lesser extent to the assessment of the prospects of rehabilitation'.[64] This is because, as stated by the Victorian Court of Appeal in *Barbaro v The Queen*:

> If there is evidence of remorse, and if that remorse is genuine, it is a very important element in the exercise of the sentencing discretion. Remorse of this kind enhances prospects of rehabilitation and reduces the need for specific deterrence. An offender who pleads guilty because he or she has an accurate appreciation of the wrongfulness of his or her offending, and of its impact upon its victim or victims, and who desires to do what reasonably can be done to repair the damage and to clear his or her conscience, is someone to whom mercy – in the form of a material reduction in what would otherwise be an appropriate sentence – is very likely due.[65]

The law's approach to remorse in sentencing and mitigating factors reflects the principle of proportionality. It also speaks to a reduced need for specific deterrence where there is a good prospect of rehabilitation.[66] In *R v Zhu*,[67] Hall J held that as a result of the genuine contrition displayed by the offender, less weight was to be given in that case to the

[58] *Hoare v The Queen* [1989] HCA 33, (1989) 167 CLR 348, 354 (Mason CJ, Deane, Dawson, Toohey and McHugh JJ); ALRC Report No 103 (n 41) 150 [5.3]; *Australian Building and Construction Commissioner v Pattinson* [2022] HCA 13 [89]–[90] (Edelman J) (*Pattinson*).

[59] *Markarian v The Queen* [2005] HCA 25, (2005) 228 CLR 357, 385 [69] (McHugh J).

[60] ibid 373 [37] (Gleeson CJ, Gummow, Hayne and Callinan JJ).

[61] ibid 387 [73] (McHugh J).

[62] Commonwealth Sentencing Database (n 42) '6. Interaction with other sentencing purposes'.

[63] *Georgopolous* (n 33) [11]–[14].

[64] ibid.

[65] *Barbaro v The Queen* [2012] VSCA 288 [39] (*Barbaro*). This passage is also stated in *R v Phillips* [2012] VSCA 140, (2012) 37 VR 594.

[66] *Cameron* (n 32) [65].

[67] *R v Zhu* [2013] NSWSC 127.

need for the penalty to achieve specific deterrence.[68] In *Cameron v The Queen*,[69] Kirby J also suggested that evidence of genuine contrition may indicate less emphasis needs to be placed on general deterrence.[70] The extent to which contrition is relevant to general and specific deterrence is significant not only to the imposition of a criminal sentence which aims to punish, it also speaks to the law's aim to deter reoffending and to deter others more generally.

C. Civil Penalty Regimes and Civil Penalties

i. Objects of Civil Penalty Regimes

In essence, 'civil penalty provisions are included as part of a statutory regime involving a specialist industry or activity regulator or a department or Minister of State of the Commonwealth ("the regulator")'.[71] Whereas criminal penalties import notions of retribution and rehabilitation, the purpose of a civil penalty, as French J explained in *Trade Practices Commission v CSR Ltd*,[72] is 'primarily if not wholly protective in promoting the public interest in compliance'.[73] In *CFMEU v Australian Building and Construction Commissioner*,[74] the Full Court of the Federal Court cited the decision of French J in *CSR Ltd*[75] and the reasons of the plurality in *Commonwealth v Director, Fair Work Building Industry Inspectorate* (*Agreed Penalties Case*)[76] as establishing that deterrence is the 'principal and indeed only object of the imposition of a civil penalty, concluding '[r]etribution, denunciation and rehabilitation have no part to play'.[77] Most recently, in *Pattinson*, the High Court confirmed that the purpose of civil penalty regimes created by legislation 'is primarily, if not solely, the promotion of the public interest in compliance with the provisions of the Act by the deterrence of further contraventions of the Act'.[78]

As in criminal law, the court considers both general and specific deterrence. The need for specific deterrence is informed by the attitude of the contravener to the contraventions, both during the course of the contravening conduct and throughout any civil penalty proceedings.[79] By analogy with criminal sentencing, contrition and remorse conventionally give some comfort to a court that reoffending is unlikely and therefore specific deterrence less important.[80]

[68] ibid [221].
[69] *Cameron* (n 32).
[70] ibid [65].
[71] *Agreed Penalties Case* (n 49) [24].
[72] *Trade Practices Commission v CSR Ltd* [1990] FCA 521, (1991) ATPR 41-076, 52, 152 (*CSR Ltd*).
[73] *Agreed Penalties Case* (n 49) [55] (French CJ, Kiefel Bell, Nettle and Gordon JJ), [110] (Keane J). See also *Australian Competition and Consumer Commission (ACCC) v TPG Internet Pty Ltd* [2013] HCA 54, (2013) 250 CLR 640 (*ACCC v TPG*) [65] (French CJ, Crennan, Bell and Keane JJ.)
[74] *CFMEU v Australian Building and Construction Commissioner* [2018] FCAFC 97, (2018) 264 FCR 155.
[75] *CSR Ltd* (n 72).
[76] *Agreed Penalties Case* (n 49).
[77] ibid [19].
[78] *Pattinson* (n 58) [9]. In a separate judgment, Edelman J reasons that while deterrence is the primary principle of justice in imposing civil penalties, other manifestations of the primary principle of justice, 'totality, consistency, and course of conduct', still apply. The continued recognition of these manifestations of the concept of 'desert' means that although deterrence might be the principal purpose, it cannot be the only purpose for the imposition of civil penalties: ibid [103]–[104].
[79] *ACCC v Reckitt Benckiser (Australia) Pty Ltd* [2016] FCAFC 181 [159] (*Reckitt Benckiser*).
[80] ibid.

ii. *Functions of Remorse and Contrition in Determining Civil Penalties*

In fixing the amount of a civil penalty, courts have regard to a list of factors developed by the courts to give effect to the purpose of the civil penalty provisions. The list of factors originates in those identified by French J in *CSR Ltd* (the 'French Factors') and a similar list identified by Santow J in *Australian Securities and Investments Commission (ASIC) v Adler*.[81] The factors and consideration may be broadly grouped into two categories: those factors and considerations relating to the objective nature and seriousness of the offending conduct, and those relating to the particular circumstances of the contravenor.[82]

In *Australian Competition and Consumer Commission (ACCC) v Woolworths Ltd*, Edelman J surveyed the factors described in previous cases that will commonly be relevant in considering deterrence and included 'the extent of contrition for the conduct' as a factor relating to the particular circumstances of the contravenor.[83] This factor has been referred to in subsequent Federal Court and Full Federal Court decisions as a factor relevant to the need for a penalty to achieve specific deterrence.[84] In *Pattinson*, the High Court referred to 'remorse' as a factor that may be taken into account in determining a civil penalty, as a factor of the kind adverted to by French J in *CSR Ltd*.[85]

The approach taken by the courts to fixing a civil penalty, while seeking only to determine what penalty is needed to achieve deterrence, is much the same as the sentencing decision-making process. In *ASIC v Westpac*, O'Bryan J summarised the way the courts apply these factors:

> These factors are neither exhaustive of potentially relevant matters to be considered nor 'a rigid catalogue or checklist of matters to be applied in each case': *Australian Building and Construction Commissioner v Construction, Forestry, Mining and Energy Union* (2017) 254 FCR 68 at [101]. The process of fixing an appropriate civil penalty may, to an extent, be likened to the 'instinctive synthesis' method involved in the criminal sentencing process: *Westpac BIO case* at [261]; *Australian Competition and Consumer Commission v Reckitt Benckiser (Australia) Pty Ltd* [2016] FCAFC 181; 340 ALR 25 (*Reckitt Benckiser*) at [44]. This involves addressing each relevant matter and, without expressly giving a weighting to those matters, instinctively synthesising them to apply a value judgment and arrive at an ultimate penalty that is proportionate to the contraventions at issue.[86]

[81] *Australian Securities and Investments Commission (ASIC) v Adler* [2002] NSWSC 483, 42 ACSR 80. See also a list of factors identified by Perram J in *ACCC v Singtel Optus Pty Ltd (No 4)* [2011] FCA 761, (2011) 282 ALR 246, 250–51 [11], referred to without objection on appeal: *Singtel Optus Pty Ltd v ACCC* [2012] FCAFC 20, (2012) 287 ALR 249, 258 [37] (the Court).

[82] *Australian Building and Construction Commissioner v Construction, Forestry, Mining and Energy Union* [2017] FCAFC 113, (2017) 254 FCR 68 [102] (Dowsett, Greenwood and Wigney JJ) (*Queensland Infrastructure Case*); *Australian Securities and Investments Commission v Westpac Banking Corp* [2019] FCA 2147 (*Westpac BIO* case) [256]–[260] (Wigney J).

[83] *ACCC v Woolworths Ltd* [2016] FCA 44 [126] (*Woolworths*).

[84] *ACCC v Reckitt Benckiser (Australia) Pty Ltd (No 7)* [2016] FCA 424, (2016) 343 ALR 327 (Edelman J) (*Reckitt Benckiser No 7*), applied by the Full Court of the Federal Court as a factor on appeal in *Reckitt Benckiser* (n 79) [159]; *ACCC v Superfone Pty Ltd* [2021] FCA 278 [84] (Murphy J) (*Superfone*); *Gibson* (n 16) [50] (Mortimer J), referring to 'remorse and contrition'; *ASIC v Westpac* (n 1) [22] (O'Bryan J), 'remorse and contrition'.

[85] *Pattinson* (n 58) [47] (Kiefel CJ, Gageler, Keane, Gordon, Steward, Gleeson JJ).

[86] *ASIC v Westpac* (n 1) [23].

The extent of contrition of a contravenor is considered, therefore, in a holistic assessment of the penalty to be imposed. In the event that the need for specific deterrence does not arise in the circumstances of the case, lack of contrition for the wrongful conduct will be of no particular relevance to the assessment of penalty.[87]

D. Civil Actions

i. The Objects of Damage Awards in Civil Actions

The primary object of awarding damages for wrongdoing is to compensate the victim of a tort or breach of contract, with the aim, so far as possible, of putting a party who suffers loss or damage in the same position she would have been in had the tort or breach of contract not occurred.[88] The payment of money is awarded as 'a substitute for that which is generally more important than money: it is the best that a court can do'.[89] In contrast, exemplary damages are available in some areas of the law and are awarded 'to punish the defendant, and presumably to serve one or more of the object of punishment – moral retribution or deterrence'.[90] Exemplary damages are awarded for conduct that is 'conscious wrongdoing in contumelious disregard of another's rights'.[91] The assessment of exemplary damages is at the discretion of the judge or jury, and the considerations that enter into the assessment of exemplary damages are quite different from the considerations that govern the assessment of compensatory damages.[92] In view of the purposes of exemplary damages, all conduct aggravating or mitigating the circumstances will be taken into account.[93]

ii. Functions of Remorse and Contrition in the Assessment of Damages

To achieve the compensatory purpose of damages, the law looks to the plaintiff's loss or damage rather than to the defendant's conduct in response to the wrong. Contrition and remorse have, therefore, a very limited role to play in the law of torts and other civil actions. In actions where damages are available for torts that protect reputation, dignity and feelings, however, the common law has long recognised the significance of contrition by a defendant in mitigation of damages. For example, in defamation, a suitable and sufficient correction and apology, or the lack thereof, is a factor in mitigation[94]

[87] *ASIC v Dover Financial Advisers Pty Ltd (No 3)* [2021] FCA 170 [141] (O'Bryan J).

[88] *Livingstone v Rawyards Coal Co* (1880) 5 App Cas 25, 39 (HL) (torts); *Robinson v Harman* (1838) 1 Ex 850, 154 ER 363 (breach of contract).

[89] H McGregor, *McGregor on Damages*, 19th edn (London, Sweet & Maxwell, 2014) 13 at [2-001], cited by Edelman J in *Woolworths* (n 83) [166].

[90] *Uren v John Fairfax & Sons Ltd* [1966] HCA 40, (1966) 117 CLR 118, 149 (Windeyer J) (*Uren*).

[91] *Whitfeld v De Lauret & Co Ltd* [1920] HCA 75, (1920) 29 CLR 71, approved in *Uren* (n 90) 154 (Windeyer J).

[92] *XL Petroleum (NSW) Pty Ltd v Caltex Oil (Australia) Pty Ltd* [1984] HCA 12, (1985) 155 CLR 448 [203].

[93] *Fontin v Katapodis* [1962] HCA 63, (1962) 108 CLR 177 [187] (HCA) (Owen J). See also *Pattinson* (n 58).

[94] *Cassell & Co Ltd v Broome* [1972] AC 1027, 1071 (HL). As Michael Tilbury notes, 'mitigation is used "in a peculiar sense" in defamation, false imprisonment and malicious prosecution actions to show that the plaintiff's loss is less than, at first blush, it appears to be': M Tilbury, *Civil Remedies*, vol II: *Principles of Civil Remedies* (Sydney, Butterworths, 1993) [11027].

or aggravation[95] of loss.[96] In this respect, the publication of a reasonable correction combined with 'a contrite apology' can mitigate the damage to the plaintiff's reputation and feelings and reduce the damages payable by the defendant[97] or the amount of monetary compensation required for an offer to make amends to be reasonable.[98] To be significant as a mitigating factor, the apology must be an expression of regret for the plaintiff's hurt and embarrassment[99] and accept responsibility for the inaccuracy.[100] Apologies are also relevant to the assessment of exemplary damages.[101]

V. Judging Remorse and Contrition

The law regards the presence of these emotions as significant to the justice system where they provide evidence of mitigation, of the potential for rehabilitation of the defendant and of deterrence, general and specific. The approach to judging remorse and contrition is similar in sentencing and determining civil penalties, even though the objects of sentencing are broader than civil penalties. Judging remorse and other emotions such as regret and sorrow is a judicial exercise informed by the facts and circumstances of each case. The extent of those emotions will determine the extent of remorse and, hence (within limits), the extent of mitigation.[102] It is for the defendant, or respondent, to satisfy the court that there is 'genuine penitence and contrition and a desire to atone'[103] by putting evidence of remorse or contrition before the primary judge as 'a circumstance of mitigation'.[104] This section discusses in general terms the nature of the evidence to which courts have regard in assessing contrition. Section VI discusses specifically what courts consider as evidence of contrition when the defendant is a corporation.

A. Guilty Pleas, Admissions and Cooperation are Discrete Mitigating Factors Relevant to Judging Remorse

In sentencing a defendant, the law differentiates between a guilty plea as a mitigating factor in sentencing and a plea of guilty as evidence of remorse or contrition. This is despite the fact that in many cases, perhaps, the plea of guilty will be motivated or

[95] *Rookes v Barnard* [1964] AC 1129 (HL); *Carson v John Fairfax & Sons Ltd* [1993] HCA 31, (1993) 178 CLR 44.

[96] Exemplary damages were previously but no longer are available in Australia for defamation: Defamation Act 2005 (NSW), s 33 and equivalent Defamation Act provisions in other States and Territories.

[97] ibid s 38.

[98] *Pedavoli* (n 51) [99].

[99] *Uren* (n 90) 141 (Menzies J).

[100] *Pedavoli* (n 51) [99] (McCallum J).

[101] *Uren* (n 90).

[102] *Georgopolous* (n 33) (Adams J).

[103] *Barbaro* (n 65) [38] (Maxwell P, Harper JA and T Forrest AJA).

[104] *Reckitt Benckiser* (n 79) (Jagot, Yates and Bromwich JJ) [161]–[162], citing *Barbaro* (n 65) [38] (Maxwell P, Harper JA and T Forrest AJA) in the criminal context and *National Tertiary Education Industry Union v Swinburne University of Technology (No 2)* [2015] FCA 1080 [109] (Mortimer J) in the civil penalty context.

at least accompanied by regret for the crime that has been committed.[105] A court has regard to a guilty plea that brings the criminal proceedings to an end without a trial of the charges as a separate factor under section 16A(2)(g) of the Crimes Act: a guilty plea is regarded as having utilitarian value because it saves time and the expense of prosecution and a trial. In *Xiao v R*,[106] for example, the Court was considering whether the utilitarian value of a guilty plea should be taken into account under the separate provision in section 16A(2)(g) of the Crimes Act in addition to contrition under section 16A(2)(f). In relation to paragraph (g), the Court concluded that contrition and a guilty plea should both be taken into account, saying:

> It is important to bear in mind that if the utilitarian value of the plea could not be taken into account it would leave s 16A(2)(g) with very little work to do. Contrition and remorse are factors that are separately required to be taken into account under s 16A(2)(f). The fact that the various factors in s 16A(2) will from time to time overlap, does not lessen the force of this consideration.[107]

Similarly, as the cases discussed in section VI.B.i show, contrition or remorse as a mitigating factor can play an overlapping role with admissions of contraventions and cooperation with regulators in civil penalty regimes.

B. Judicial Consideration of Contrition and Remorse Raises Multiple Issues

As Ian Freckleton reminds us, there are many issues in the criminal law concerning remorse that arise at the point of sentencing an offender. These issues concern the means of assessing the genuineness or otherwise of asserted remorse, the amount of significance that should be given when it is found, and dealing with the risk of double counting in reducing a sentence for the interrelated factors of an offender's remorse, good prospects of rehabilitation and a finding as a result that they are unlikely to reoffend.[108] Many of the same issues arise when fixing the amount of a civil penalty to achieve the objectives of that regime, including the need to consider different forms of evidence of remorse, to avoid double counting between factors and to assess whether or not the expression of remorse is genuine.

C. Evidence of Contrition and Remorse Takes Many Forms

The law is not prescriptive about what can constitute evidence of remorse, generally leaving this as an open-ended inquiry that looks to evidence that shows that a defendant feels regret or other emotions as a result of their actions, that they accept responsibility for

[105] *Georgopolous* (n 33) [11]–[14] (Adams J).
[106] *Xiao v R* [2018] NSWCCA 4, (2018) 96 NSWLR 1.
[107] ibid [272].
[108] I Freckleton, 'Book Review: Remorse: Psychological and Jurisprudential Perspectives, by M Proeve and S Tudor' (2011) 18 *Psychiatry, Psychology and Law* 315, 318.

their actions and the harm it has caused, acknowledge their wrongdoing and the injury it has caused, or take action to make reparation or both. In many instances, however, 'the most compelling evidence of this will come from testimony by the offender'.[109] At the same time, it is commonly understood that 'remorse that results in actions and not only words is plainly more significant'.[110] Some legislation makes express reference to how contrition can be shown; for example, section 16A of the Crimes Act expressly refers to 'taking action to make reparation … or in any other manner'.[111] Other sentencing legislation is more prescriptive, stipulating the evidence that must be provided if remorse is to be considered as a mitigating factor. For instance, section 21A(3)(i) of the Crimes (Sentencing Procedure) Act 1999 (NSW) provides that remorse may only be considered as a mitigating factor if the offender has provided evidence that they have accepted responsibility for their actions and have acknowledged the injury, loss or damage caused by their actions or made reparation for such injury, loss or damage (or both).[112]

D. Empirical Insight into what Courts Consider when Judging Remorse

Proeve and Tudor's research on remorse in the legal system includes a study with Kate Rossmanith of how judges know about remorse.[113] Courtrooms can serve as 'theatres of remorse, and of remorselessness'.[114] In many instances, however, courts will look for evidence of remorse outside the courtroom. In a study published in 2018, the authors interviewed 20 magistrates and judges in New South Wales, exploring how judges themselves understand their own ways of knowing about remorse. They report that many judges want to see remorse in the courtroom and are confident that they know it when they see it. At the same time, they consider it important to have regard to evidence of an offender's remorse outside the courtroom, from the moment the offence was committed up until the sentencing hearing (which is often over a period of several years). The authors conclude, based on the interview data, that 'Although in-court displays of remorse can be highly significant, perhaps the most remorse-indicative behaviours are those that occur outside the courtroom.'[115]

It is clear from the factors applied by the courts in civil penalty proceedings that evidence of contrition outside the courtroom is also highly important in these proceedings, not only in criminal proceedings.

[109] *Barbaro* (n 65) [38] (Maxwell P, Harper JA and T Forrest AJA).
[110] *Georgopolous* (n 33) [11]–[14] (Adams J).
[111] Commonwealth Sentencing Database (n 42).
[112] See also Sentencing Act 2017 (SA), s 11.
[113] Rossmanith, Tudor and Proeve (n 56). The authors cite previous studies published in recent years, involving formal and informal interviews with sentencing judges in relation to remorse: ibid fn 19.
[114] ibid 367.
[115] ibid 378.

E. Genuineness of Remorse and Contrition

The many challenges associated with judging the genuineness of remorse and contrition and the role of remorse in the justice system are well known to the law and to scholars from many disciplines.[116] Assessments of the genuineness of remorse, regret and sorrow are not confined to the justice system; indeed, this is acknowledged in *Alvares* as 'a common feature of everyday existence'.[117] Individuals and the public also judge the sincerity and value of expressions of remorse and contrition in the form of apologies on a daily basis.[118] Research and scholarship on apologies by philosophers, sociologists, criminologists, psychologists, lawyers and others offer many valuable insights into the meanings of apologies and the components of an apology that will usually be necessary for an apology to be judged as genuine. This body of literature in turn deepens our understanding of how remorse and contrition are expressed.[119]

Nick Smith and others[120] attribute meaning to apologies by reference to component parts, which in turn are important to understanding the meaning of what is variously described as a full, meaningful, genuine, 'categorical' or 'good enough' apology.[121] There is consensus that a full apology incorporates an expression of heartfelt regret and remorse for what has happened, sympathy for the victim and acknowledges the wrongdoer's transgression.[122] For some, the apology must also offer some form of recompense and a commitment to change in the future.[123] The presence of these core components is consistent with the ways of showing genuine remorse in society and in the law. Another insight from apology scholarship for judging remorse concerns the importance of identifying the moral community by whom the offender is being judged.[124] In the justice system, judges reflect legal and societal expectations in their judgments, which include civil norms about how wrongdoers respond to their conduct and the harmful

[116] Leading works include Proeve and Tudor (n 5) and N Smith, *Justice Through Apologies: Remorse, Reform and Punishment* (New York, Cambridge University Press, 2014).

[117] *Alvares* (n 35) [44].

[118] Psychological research tells us that what constitutes an apology for the recipient in any particular situation and context is a highly unique and subjective experience; see A Allan and R Carroll, 'Apologies in a Legal Setting: Insights from Research into Injured Parties' Experiences of Apologies after an Adverse Event' (2016) 24 *Psychiatry, Psychology and the Law* 1, 10.

[119] N Smith, *I Was Wrong: The Meanings of Apology* (New York, Cambridge University Press, 2008); N Tavuchis, *Mea Culpa: A Sociology of Apology and Reconciliation* (Stanford, CA, Stanford University Press, 1991); A Lazare, *On Apology* (Oxford, Oxford University Press, 2004); K Gill, 'Moral Functions of Apology' (2000) 31 *Philosophical Forum* 11; J Gardner, *From Personal Life to Private Law* (Oxford, Oxford University Press, 2018) ch 4; A Allan, 'Functional Apologies in Law' (2008) 15 *Psychiatry, Psychology and Law* 369; P Vines, 'The Power of Apology: Mercy, Forgiveness or Corrective Justice in the Civil Liability Arena?' (2007) 1 *The Journal of Law and Social Justice* 1.

[120] Smith (n 119); Lazare (n 119); D Slocum, A Allan and M Allan, 'An Emerging Theory of Apology' (2011) 62 *Australian Journal of Psychology* 83.

[121] Smith (n 119) 'categorical'; Slocum, Allan and Allan (n 120) 'good enough'.

[122] A Allan, 'Apology in Civil Law: A Psycho-Legal Perspective' (2007) 14 *Psychiatry, Psychology and Law* 5.

[123] ibid. See also C Petrucci, 'Apology in the Criminal Justice Setting: Evidence for Including Apology as an Additional Component in the Legal System' (2002) 20 *Behavioral Sciences & the Law* 337, 341; C Petrucci, 'Apology in the Criminal Justice Setting: An Update' (2017) 7 *Oñati Socio-Legal Series* 437.

[124] P Vines 'The Value of Apologising within a Moral Community: Making Apologies Work' (2017) 7 *Oñati Socio-Legal Studies* 370.

consequences of their actions on others. Corporations are also commonly judged by consumers and markets on how they respond to corporate wrongdoing and harm.[125]

Notwithstanding the difficulties of judging remorse and contrition, judges regularly undertake this exercise. Genuineness of remorse is important in sentencing, as explained by Simpson J in *Mariam v R*:

> [A]lthough it is well established that remorse may be taken into account as a mitigating factor in sentencing, some attention needs to be paid to the logic of doing so. Genuine remorse may be an indicator of the unlikelihood of further offending, in which case it may have significant relevance. If it is not indicative of that likelihood, I see little relevance in such evidence.[126]

Questions persist about the ability to judge whether an offender's remorse is genuine.[127] In particular, it may be difficult to differentiate a corporation's genuine remorse or contrition from mere lip service. Notwithstanding, courts have accepted that it is possible to assess the genuineness of corporate remorse, for example, in occupational health and safety matters. In *WorkCover Authority of New South Wales (Insp Mulder) v Yass Shire Council*, Wright J states:

> Although some commentators have pointed out that it is impossible for a judge accurately to estimate the sincerity of remorse or contrition (Ashworth, Sentencing and Criminal Justice, London, 1994 at 130, as cited by Mack and Anleu, Pleading Guilty: Issues and Practices, Australian Institute of Judicial Administration, 1995 at 161), experience in occupational health and safety matters indicates that in many cases it is possible for an employer charged under the Act to provide tangible confirmation of contrition by support and assistance rendered to injured employees or to the families of victims of fatal accidents.[128]

Courts make assessments of genuineness in determining what weight, if any, to give to a defendant's expression of remorse or contrition. It is clear that this exercise takes on further complexity when the defendant is a corporation. Given that courts deem corporations capable of possessing the equivalent of contrition attributed to a natural offender,[129] it is unsurprising that the process of judging essentially is the same, notwithstanding the need for attribution based on principles applicable to an artificial construct.

[125] See, eg, K Vinayagamoorthy, 'Apologies in the Market Place' (2013) 33 *Pace Law Review* 1081; R Carroll, C To and M Unger, 'Apology Legislation and its Implications for International Dispute Resolution Practitioners' (2015) 9 *Dispute Resolution International* 115. For an analysis of issues specific to collective apologies, including corporations, see Smith (n 119) ch 10.

[126] *Mariam v R* [2013] NSWCCA 338 [64] (Simpson J, Price and RA Hulme JJ agreeing).

[127] Contrast the situation in facilitated resolution of disputes, where it is for the parties to judge the meaning and value of an apology, not a judge, and implications of this for the parties involved: Allan and Carroll (n 118).

[128] *WorkCover Authority of New South Wales (Insp Mulder) v Yass Shire Council* [2000] NSWIRComm 57, (2000) 99 IR 284 [35], where his Honour cites in support of his conclusion the decision in *WorkCover New South Wales (Inspector Page) v Walco Hoist Rentals Pty Ltd (No 2)* [2000] NSWIRComm 39, 43; *WorkCover Authority (Inspector Tyler) v Abigroup Contractors Pty Ltd* [2000] NSWIRComm 40, 29; *Corinthian Industries (Sydney) Pty Ltd v WorkCover Authority of New South Wales* [2000] NSWIR Comm 46, (2000) 99 IR 159.

[129] *Ampol* (n 11). See also *Morrison* (n 11) [111].

VI. Corporate Contrition and Remorse

Sentencing and civil penalties legislation in Australia does not make specific provision for corporate defendants, despite ALRC calls for reform in this regard. The cases make clear that the corporate nature of the defendant does not prevent an inquiry into whether a corporation shows contrition for crimes and corporate misconduct, and provide guidance on what evidence is relevant. This section considers how contrition and remorse are attributed to a corporation and what forms of evidence the courts consider show genuine remorse.

A. Attribution of Contrition or Remorse to a Corporation

The ways in which a corporation can express remorse or contrition include the ways in which a natural person can express these emotions, except that in the case of a corporation, courts look to establish the state of mind of the corporation by considering evidence of remorse and contrition provided by the board, by directors, officers and employees of the corporation, and by corporate systems. While individuals can express remorse and contrition, the inquiry here concerns how contrition is expressed for the purposes of being attributed to the corporation as a distinct entity.[130]

Analysis of the case law reveals that the courts have regard to at least four forms of evidence to judge corporate remorse and contrition, in addition to and aside from admissions of guilt or to contraventions of the law. Admitting to a contravention and submitting to a penalty shows willingness on the part of the defendant 'to accept responsibility for its actions and to facilitate the course of justice',[131] which bears on the need for a penalty to specifically deter future contraventions.

B. Forms of Evidence Showing Corporate Contrition and Remorse

In *Environmental Protection Authority v Waste Recycling and Processing Corporation*,[132] Preston CJ identified four forms of action underlying genuine contrition and remorse that may justify a reduction in the context of a prosecution for environmental damage, which may be summarised as:

(1) the speed and efficiency of action to rectify any harm caused or likely to continue to be caused by the commission of the offence is the clearest indication of contrition and remorse;

[130] For discussion and critique, see Bant, 'Catching the Corporate Conscience' (n 17) and sources cited therein for theories and judicial approaches to attributing corporate culpability and other states of mind, including contrition and remorse, to corporations.

[131] *Queensland Infrastructure Case* (n 82) [163].

[132] *Environmental Protection Authority v Waste Recycling and Processing Corporation* [2006] NSWLEC 419, (2006) 148 LGERA 299 (*Waste Recycling and Processing Corporation*). For an example of where these principles have been applied, see *Secretary, Department of Planning and Environment v Shoalhaven Starches Pty Ltd* [2018] NSWLEC 23 (*Shoalhaven Starches*).

(2) voluntarily reporting the commission of the offence and any concomitant environmental harm to relevant authorities indicates a genuine desire to act responsibly;
(3) taking action to address the causes of the offence, such as designing and installing improved pollution prevention and control systems indicates a genuine desire to act responsibly; and
(4) the personal appearance of corporate executives in court and their personal evidence outlining the company's genuine regret and stating future plans to avoid repetition of such offences is an indication of genuine corporate contrition.[133]

Although these 'well-founded'[134] principles are identified in the context of a prosecution for environmental damage, they can be applied to other corporate sentencing contexts.[135] They are also consistent with the approach by courts in civil penalty regime cases when considering contrition and remorse as a mitigating factor. We saw in section I the damning comments by O'Bryan J about the absence of remorse shown by Westpac for contravening the Corporations Act.[136] O'Bryan J took into account in determining a penalty 'at the highest levels permitted by the Act' that Westpac had made 'no expression of contrition or remorse'. This finding was based on the absence of any or any proposed correspondence containing any apology to affected clients, that the Bank had not expressed regret for the conduct, did not appear to have taken steps to remedy the compliance deficiencies and had been tardy in progressing a remediation plan.[137] Had it been otherwise, the presence of evidence of some or all of these ways of showing remorse would have been considered.

Similarly, in the earlier case of *Pilbara Iron Co*,[138] Katzman J considered as evidence of remorse in addition to changing its behaviour, that a corporation might admit its wrongdoing and spare the other parties the costs of prosecuting the case. It might offer recompense, it might apologise and it might introduce precautions to guard against the risk of reoffending.[139]

It appears from some cases that acceptance of responsibility by a corporation, recognition of the consequences of the wrongdoing and any apologies are regarded as separate mitigating factors from contrition and remorse.[140] This suggests some confusion about what it means for a corporation to be remorseful or contrite, and the role of

[133] *Waste Recycling and Processing Corporation* (n 132) [204]–[214].

[134] See *Chief Executive, Office of Environment and Heritage v Ausgrid* [2013] NSWLEC 51, (2013) 199 LGERA 1 [80] (Pepper J) (*Ausgrid*); *Environment Protection Authority v Moolarben Coal Operations Pty Ltd* [2012] NSWLEC 65 [85]–[89]; *Environment Protection Authority v Moolarben Coal Operations Pty Ltd (No 2)* [2012] NSWLEC 80 [101].

[135] Decisions concerning occupational health and safety prosecutions of corporations confirm that remorse or contrition can be demonstrated by a variety, or combination, of factors and are relevant to mitigation of penalty, eg: *Inspector Patton v Western Freight Management Pty Ltd (No 2)* [2009] NSWIRComm 124 [76] (Boland J); *Inspector Christensen v Lend Lease Engineering Pty Ltd (formerly Abigroup Contractors Pty Ltd)* [2014] NSWIRComm 42 [55] (Walton J, President).

[136] *Westpac v ASIC* (n 2) affirming the decision of the Full Court of the Federal Court in *ASIC v Westpac Securities* (n 2).

[137] *ASIC v Westpac* (n 2) [95].

[138] *Pilbara Iron Co* (n 14).

[139] ibid [34].

[140] See reference to the ASIC submission in *ASIC v Mayfair Wealth Partners Pty Ltd* [2021] FCA 1630 [237] relating to Australian Securities and Investments Commission Act 2001 (Cth) and Corporations Act 2001 (Cth), s 1041H relating to false, misleading or deceptive conduct. Significant pecuniary penalty ordered in respect of all defendants.

apologies as evidence of being in this state rather than as a separate mitigating factor. The following analysis identifies the multiple forms of evidence that can show genuine contrition and remorse. The four categories are indicative of contrition and remorse, they are not prescriptive. The words and actions that fall within these categories can serve as evidence relating to one or more of the factors and considerations a court takes into account in sentencing and civil penalty regimes. A court may conclude that an aspect of contrition is present, for example by admitting the contravention and submitting to a penalty even though there was no apology, where the court accepts that an apology was not particularly appropriate to the circumstances of the contravention.[141]

i. Acknowledgement and Voluntary Reporting of the Offence or Contravention and Cooperating with Prosecutors and Regulators

As discussed earlier in the chapter, entering a guilty plea is a mitigating factor in sentencing legislation, which also can show a defendant's remorse and contrition. Relatedly, voluntarily reporting the commission of an offence or contravention also can be evidence of genuine remorse.[142] Cooperation with authorities in the course of investigations and subsequent proceedings is regarded as a mitigating factor that will almost certainly reduce the penalty that would otherwise be imposed, and reflects the fact that such cooperation is evidence of contrition.[143] In civil penalty regimes, cooperation and assistance with the relevant regulatory authority is a factor concerning the particular circumstances of a corporate contravenor.[144] Cooperation is also regarded separately as evidence of contrition and remorse by a corporation for its contraventions, although cooperation does not necessarily evidence remorse, as it might 'reflect nothing more than an acceptance of the inevitable'.[145]

In *Woolworths*,[146] Edelman J considered that Woolworths' cooperation with the ACCC should provide a significant discount from the penalty his Honour otherwise would have awarded in that case. Woolworths were found to have engaged in conduct in their commercial operations that involved multiple contraventions of the Australian Consumer Law. Justice Edelman found that Woolworths' substantial cooperation included assistance with the ACCC investigation, undertaking to the ACCC that Woolworths would address its concerns, and engaging with the ACCC on Woolworths' new product-quality framework and other new initiatives, initiating settlement discussions and reaching agreement on contraventions with the ACCC, including the appropriate relief (other than as to penalty) to be recommended to the Court. The agreement on contraventions meant that 'the parties and the Court were spared the substantial cost of a trial'.[147]

[141] *Australian Federation of Air Pilots v HNZ Australia Pty Ltd* [2015] FCA 755 [43], referred to in *Australian Building and Construction Commissioner v Construction, Forestry, Maritime, Mining and Energy Union* [2022] FCA 37 (*NEXT DC P2 Project Case*).

[142] *Waste Recycling and Processing Corporation* (n 132).

[143] See *Commissioner of Taxation v Arnold (No 2)* [2015] FCA 34, (2015) 324 ALR 59 [189] for cases cited for authority on this point and a discussion of authorities more generally on cooperation as mitigation.

[144] *CSR Ltd* (n 72) 52, 152.

[145] *Queensland Infrastructure Case* (n 82) (Dowsey, Greenwood and Digney JJ) [164]; *NEXT DC P2 Project Case* (n 141) [80].

[146] *Woolworths* (n 83).

[147] ibid [162]

His Honour considered Woolworths' actions of cooperation were evidence of a desire to redress their failings, leading his Honour to comment that 'Woolworth's cooperation is also evidence of contrition for its contraventions'.[148] Further evidence of contrition in this case was found in Woolworths' offers and payments of compensation and their apologies to affected consumers.

ii. Rectification, Reparation and Other Forms of Recompense

Rectification of harm, past and future, can be undertaken in various ways, including repair, reparation and recompense. Reparations are a way of showing contrition, for example when sentencing a defendant pursuant to section 16A(2)(f) of the Crimes Act. Reparation payments made by a corporate wrongdoer will constitute evidence of contrition where the wrongdoer had no obligation to make a payment in reparation.[149] In criminal proceedings in *ACCC v Santo Pennisi*,[150] the corporation was found on its plea of guilty to have made false or misleading representations contrary to section 75AZC(1)(A) of the Trade Practices Act 1974 (Cth) by its mixing petroleum fuel types. In relation to contrition, Logan J had regard to a donation to a local charity made in circumstances where the defendant was under no obligation to make any such donation. In his Honour's view, the donation evidenced contrition and 'was in a sense a form of reparation to the community' in that, whilst it is not readily possible to identify particular consumers by name affected by the conduct, 'the type of donation made at least can be seen to have the ability to benefit the motoring public through the better training of drivers or at least the enabling of a charity to undertake that task'.[151]

Another example of the importance of reparation in conjunction with other acts of contrition is provided by the decision in *Director of Public Prosecutions v Hazelwood Power Corp Pty Ltd (Sentence)*,[152] in which a corporate defendant was found guilty of occupational health and safety offences in relation to fires at its mining operations. Justice Keogh accepted the defendant corporation's submission that it demonstrated remorse in a number of ways, including by the provision of $100 gift cards to each of the 6,700 households in the local community affected by the fires, to be spent in local business (costing a total of approximately $650,000). This accompanied a $100,000 contribution to a local council's community clean-up initiative; a $50,000 donation to the Gippsland Emergency Relief Fund; and making $500,000 available to the Community Social Capital Committee (which comprised local organisations such as rotary clubs and church associations), and other community sponsorship.[153]

Reparation payments will not necessarily be afforded much or any weight as evidence of contrition. For example, in determining the civil penalty to be applied in

[148] ibid [163].

[149] See *Director of Public Prosecutions v Hazelwood Power Corp Pty Ltd (Sentence)* [2020] VSC 278 [163] (*Hazelwood Power Corp*).

[150] *ACCC v Santo Pennisi* [2007] FCA 2100.

[151] ibid [47]. One might question whether the donation was sufficiently directed to the harm the provision is intended to prevent and to which the penalty was directed, so as to justify a reduction in penalty on the ground of deterrence in this case.

[152] *Hazelwood Power Corp* (n 153).

[153] ibid [167].

an occupational health and safety case following the death of an employee in *Comcare v John Holland Pty Ltd*,[154] Siopis J considered that little weight could be attached to financial and other contributions to community projects in the context of an Act directed towards one specific aspect of the way in which the employer conducts its business operations, 'namely, the employer's conduct in relation to protecting the safety of its employees at the workplace. It is that specific aspect of an employer's conduct which forms the focus of attention in relation to the imposition of a civil penalty.'[155]

It some contexts, action taken, including payment of compensation that a defendant is legally obliged to make, can be evidence of contrition. In civil penalty cases, for example those resulting from contraventions of consumer protection and corporate regulation provisions, a corporation may be obliged to compensate consumers, members and other people who have suffered loss or damage as a result of the contravention. Can a willingness to pay compensation in these circumstances demonstrate contrition or remorse? Payment of compensation for breach of a common law or statutory obligation may be regarded as evidence of contrition in some circumstances in at least two ways. First, the voluntariness and speed with which action is taken or offers and payments are made may show contrition.[156] Second, when offered in conjunction with an apology, the promise to make good the harm in this way may show that the apology is sincere and meaningful. The first aspect was significant in *Woolworths*. In that case, Edelman J had regard to Woolworths' offers and payments of compensation (and their apologies) to affected consumers as evidence of contrition, noting:

> Woolworths' offers of compensation were not cynical offers made on the eve of litigation. Compensation was paid to some consumers even before this litigation was commenced. All those who sought compensation were compensated.[157]

Subsequently, in *ACCC v Superfone Pty Ltd*,[158] Murphy J cited Edelman J in *Woolworths* on compensation's being evidence of contrition in support of his conclusion that Superfone showed remorse by accepting responsibility and apologising for contravening provisions of the Australian Consumer Law and, further, by consenting to consumer redress orders.[159]

iii. Corporate Expressions of Regret and Apologies

Apologies and expressions of regret are further ways in which a corporation can express contrition and remorse in mitigation of sentence or penalty.[160] The cases discussed in

[154] *Comcare* (n 8) [97] (Siopis J).
[155] ibid.
[156] *Woolworths* (n 83) [163]; *Waste Recycling and Processing Corporation* (n 132) [204]–[212].
[157] *Woolworths* (n 83) [163].
[158] *Superfone* (n 84).
[159] ibid [84].
[160] The authorities indicate that any lack of contrition or remorse, and the absence of an apology, is not an aggravating circumstance such as might increase the penalty, although evidence of contrition can operate to reduce a penalty: *BHP Steel (AIS) Pty Ltd v Construction, Forestry, Mining and Energy Union* [2001] FCA 336 (Kiefel J); *Cahill v Construction, Forestry, Mining and Energy Union (No 4)* [2009] FCA 1040, (2009) 189 IR 304 [87] (Kenny J); *Automotive, Food, Metals, Engineering, Printing and Kindred Industries Union v Visy Packaging Pty Ltd (No 4)* [2013] FCA 930 (Murphy J).

this subsection show that judges assess the genuineness of a corporate apology and its value in mitigation by reference to many factors, which include timing, fullness and voluntariness: this is consistent with psychological research into what makes an apology meaningful.[161]

A corporate apology raises at least two additional issues: attribution of remorse or contrition as a state of mind, and the mitigating value of a corporate apology. The first issue relates to how a corporation can express regret or offer an apology. There must be some basis for attributing remorse or contrition to a corporate offender based on words offered by the corporation, for example through a resolution of the board of directors, or a public apology on behalf of the corporation, for example by the chief executive officer or other senior executives. In *Chief Executive, Office of Environment and Heritage v Ausgrid*,[162] for example, the defendant corporation was found to have expressed contrition and remorse through affidavit and in-court oral evidence of the company's Chief Operating Officer, whereby he unreservedly apologised on behalf of the company for the commission of the offence and the harm caused to an Indigenous community by damage to a rock engraving attributed to the company's excavation.

More generally, while words of apology by corporate executives and officers will be considered, it is clear that evidence of contrition and remorse is more readily accepted through a corporate defendant's actions. Courts have said in a number of cases that corporate contrition cannot be demonstrated through the evidence of the personal feelings of remorse of senior officers of a company.[163] The personal evidence of senior officers as to the company's contrition, however, and the company's steps taken to ensure wrongdoing never occurs again, is relevant.[164] The following two cases, both involving criminal proceedings, show that evidence of genuine remorse of senior officers of a corporation is not the only way to attribute this state of mind to the company, and that the genuineness of corporate remorse may be ascertained through the content of its submissions and legal arguments proffered at trial.

In *Secretary, Department of Planning and Environment v Shoalhaven Starches Pty Ltd*,[165] a company failed on five occasions to disclose political donations as required by law. Justice Moore considered whether the company had shown remorse for the offence as required by section 21A(3)(i) of the Crimes (Sentencing Procedure Act) 1999 (NSW). The Company Secretary filed an affidavit 'on behalf of the defendant' that included an apology. The prosecution sought to diminish the weight of this as evidencing contrition because the directors more senior to the Secretary gave no such evidence. Justice Moore rejected this submission (as the evidence was not challenged in cross-examination) and held that an affidavit and statement of apology, both of which were stated to have been made 'on behalf of' the company, were valid statements that demonstrated the company's remorse as to the wrongdoing.'[166]

[161] This research is discussed in Allan and Carroll (n 118).

[162] *Ausgrid* (n 135).

[163] See *Director of Public Prosecutions v Esso Australia Pty Ltd* [2001] VSC 263, (2001) 124 A Crim R 200 (*Esso*); *Waste Recycling and Processing Corporation* (n 132).

[164] See *Ausgrid* (n 135) [80] (Pepper J).

[165] *Shoalhaven Starches* (n 132).

[166] ibid [77].

In *Director of Public Prosecutions v Esso Australia Pty Ltd* (*Esso*),[167] two workers were killed and others were injured in an explosion at one of Esso's three Longford gas-processing plants. The court had to decide the sentence for Esso's criminal offences committed under the Occupational Health and Safety Act 1985 (Vic). The Chairman and Managing Director were found to have exhibited genuine remorse. However, those personal expressions of remorse of the senior officers were not translated into corporate remorse for three reasons. First, Esso was found to have treated its employees in a litigious matter. This was evidenced through the content of the submissions put forward by Esso's lawyers. For instance, Esso made submissions that an employee had the requisite information to protect himself from harm, when in fact it was found that 'there was only one entity responsible … Esso' and it was only the corporation who was found to have committed the wrong. Second, although Esso was found to limit the issues in trial and make admissions, its defence at trial was described by the court as 'obfuscation – designed not to clarify, but to obscure', whereby 'Esso sought to make it appear that the identification of the hazard, risk and cause was impossibly difficult'.[168] Third, and significantly in this case, Esso failed to accept responsibility for what happened at the plant. This was seen in qualifying comments by the counsel for Esso in face of its defence, for example, 'Whilst Esso does not accept the accuracy or correctness necessarily of each of the criticisms levelled …'[169]

The Court in *Esso* also said, in relation to acceptance of responsibility:

> Normally in sentencing, a failure to accept responsibility sounds in the matter of specific deterrence. This is not so here, because Esso has demonstrated by its subsequent operational reforms that it has acted responsibly to remedy past deficiency. But its lack of acceptance of responsibility has a relevance in my not accepting that Esso's expression of remorse is practical and operational. Esso's failure to still accept responsibility for these tragic events is a serious deficiency.[170]

The important message this case signals is that 'expressions of remorse need to be translated into reality',[171] including in the way that a trial is conducted. It is not uncommon for legal representatives to offer apologies on behalf of their corporate client. While a corporation can show genuine contrition and remorse through apologies by its executives and representatives, Preston CJ eloquently explains that this 'is more readily demonstrated by an offender "taking actions" rather than offering "smooth apologies" through legal representatives'.[172]

A second issue concerns the assessment of an apology and the weight given to words of this nature as evidence of contrition. Even when a court does accept an expression of regret and contrition as genuine, whether by a natural person or a corporation, its value in mitigation will be diminished, for example, by attempts to attribute responsibility for the conduct to the provocative conduct of others, and when the expressions

[167] *Esso* (n 163).
[168] ibid [45].
[169] ibid [46].
[170] ibid [48].
[171] ibid [43] (Cummins J).
[172] *Waste Recycling and Processing Corporation* (n 132) [203].

were belated.[173] Further issues arise in the case of a corporate apology that shows genuineness, for example, by including an undertaking to operate differently in the future, when the value of that undertaking might be doubted because the make-up of the board of directors or individual executives and officers has changed since the wrongdoing, or will inevitably change in the future.

iv. Taking Action to Address the Causes of the Offence or Harm

In *Waste Recycling and Processing Corporation*,[174] the defendant pleaded guilty to polluting waters in breach of section 120(1) of the Protection of the Environment Operations Act 1997 (NSW), when toxins from its landfill waste disposal site entered nearby creek waters. In sentencing the defendant, Preston CJ said that 'taking action to address the causes of the offence, such as designing and installing improved pollution prevention and control systems' to ensure that the type of incident did not happen again, indicated a genuine desire to act responsibly and showed the genuine contrition and remorse of the defendant.[175] This category of evidence looks to the prevention of ongoing loss or harm and in the future, in other ways than the previous categories.[176]

There are many forms that action showing remorse and contrition might take, including taking steps to remedy compliance deficiencies and developing and implementing a remediation plan. Actions undertaken by a corporation for the purpose of preventing future contraventions of the law and to avoid potential loss and damage in the future are of much interest to scholars, regulators and courts.[177] Changes in behaviour of this nature provide insight into the state of mind of a corporation that supports theories of corporate accountability[178] and informs decision making by regulators in deciding what remedial and other actions to take.[179] Evidence of contrition may be relevant to the decision to accept an enforceable undertaking from a corporation, for example, and whether

[173] For example, *Construction, Forestry, Maritime, Mining and Energy Union v Kyren Pty Ltd* [2020] FCA 1356 [74]–[75].

[174] *Waste Recycling and Processing Corporation* (n 132). For an example of where these principles have been applied, see *Shoalhaven Starches* (n 132).

[175] *Waste Recycling and Processing Corporation* (n 132) [212], citing *Camilleri's Stock Feeds Pty Ltd v Environment Protection Authority* (1993) 32 NSWLR 683 at 700–01.

[176] In contrast to undertakings and promises to change behaviours and systems of operations in the future incorporated, for example, in an apology, this category focuses on actions taken subsequent to the offence or contravention to make the change.

[177] Actions of this nature undertaken by a corporation and that show insight, regret and contrition can be relevant for purposes other than mitigation of sentence and penalties. They may be relevant, eg, to a corporation's fitness to hold a licence and operate regulated business. Examples of conduct, culture and insights relevant to operating a casino are provided in State of Western Australia, *Perth Casino Royal Commission*' (Final Report, 4 March 2022) ch 17, 'Assessment of Crown Suitability and Path Forward'.

[178] Brent Fisse for example, promotes 'reactive corporate fault' as way to attribute culpability to a corporation and as a factor in mitigation in sentencing and regulatory decision making; see B Fisse, 'Reconstructing Corporate Criminal Law: Deterrence, Retribution, Fault, and Sanctions' (1983) 56 *Southern California Law* Review 1141; B Fisse and J Braithwaite, *Corporations, Crime and Accountability* (Cambridge, Cambridge University Press, 1993); Fisse, ch 7 of this volume.

[179] See Bant, 'Catching the Corporate Conscience' (n 17) 470, fnn 24 et seq, where Bant acknowledges scholars whose work informs theories of corporate liability and 'systems intentionality' as a model of corporate responsibility.

to commence civil penalty proceedings.[180] Bant makes the important point that 'as a matter of regulatory practice, the defendant's state of mind influences the enforcement strategy deployed by the regulator'.[181] Evidence that a corporation has taken measures to reduce the likelihood of its committing a subsequent offence is also relevant in criminal law to punishment, rehabilitation and deterrence. Similarly, in civil penalty cases, it is relevant to deterrence if a corporation shows an intention (or not) to 'change its ways'.[182]

Examples of action taken for this purpose were noticeably absent in the *ASIC v Westpac* case referred to in section I. Other examples of corporate misconduct in the banking industry were identified in the Royal Commission into Misconduct in the Banking, Superannuation and Financial Services Industry in 2019.[183] The 'fees for no service' cases involving AMP, in which bank customers were charged fees for services without authority after they died through automated fee deduction systems, are one such example.[184] Bant uses this misconduct of the AMP group companies as an example of where 'the absence of any effective system for overseeing and auditing outcomes arguably itself reflects an intentional decision not to "care" about the accuracy of payments'.[185] According to Bant, in the event that a corporation is notified of a continuing contravention through an automated system and yet continues to run its system, an 'inference of specific intention in cases where the unlawful takings occurred becomes irresistible'.[186] Similarly, a corporation's continuing to run its system in these circumstances could allow a court to draw inferences as to the corporation's remorseful or contrite state of mind.

There are other ways in which a corporation can demonstrate contrition or remorse by undertaking preventive action in the future. In the *NEXT DC P2 Project Case*,[187] Banks-Smith J considered that a corporate defendant could demonstrate that it intended

[180] The ACCC, for example, has broad authority to accept written undertakings in the exercise of its powers under the Competition and Consumer Act 2010 (Cth) (CCA). These enforceable undertakings have, in the past, included provisions for a party to undertake corrective advertising, refunds and education programmes. In some instances, undertakings include voluntarily issuing a public apology: see, eg, ACCC, 'Advanced Lifestyle International Retail Pty Ltd – s.87B Undertaking' (1 September 2011) at www.accc.gov.au/public-registers/undertakings-registers/s87b-undertakings-register/advanced-lifestyle-international-retail-pty-ltd-s87b-undertaking; and ACCC, 'Harris Scarfe Admits Sale Prices May have Misled, Issues Public Apology' (4 November 2004) at www.accc.gov.au/media-release/harris-scarfe-admits-sale-prices-may-have-misled-issues-public-apology>. Section 87B of the CCA empowers the ACCC to accept written undertakings in the exercise of its powers under the CCA (other than pt X). It also allows for the enforcement of such undertakings in the Federal Court of Australia. Where an undertaking is accepted by the ACCC, litigation and the imposition of penalties may be avoided.

[181] Bant, 'Culpable Corporate Minds' (n 17) 357. In support, Bant references ASIC, 'ASIC Corporate Plan: 2019–23' (August 2019) at https://download.asic.gov.au/media/5248811/corporate-plan-2019-23-published-28-august-2019.pdf (ASIC Corporate Plan).

[182] *NEXT DC P2 Project Case* (n 141) [81]; *Queensland Infrastructure Case* (n 82) [164] (Dowsett, Greenwood and Wigney JJ).

[183] Commonwealth of Australia, *Royal Commission into Misconduct in the Banking, Superannuation and Financial Services Industry* (Final Report, 1 February 2019).

[184] See ASIC, 'Concise Statement' (*Australian Securities and Investments Commission v AMP Financial Planning Pty Ltd*, VID420/2021, 29 July 2021) at https://asic.gov.au/media/f0rim31a/concise-statement-asic-v-amp-financial-planning-pty-ltd.pdf; *Australian Securities and Investments Commission v Australia and New Zealand Banking Group Ltd (No 3)* [2020] FCA 1421 (Allsop CJ), discussed in Bant, 'Catching the Corporate Conscience' (n 17) 488–89.

[185] Bant, 'Catching the Corporate Conscience' (n 17) 489.

[186] ibid.

[187] *NEXT DC P2 Project Case* (n 141).

to change its ways by setting up 'systems, processes, procedures or education to ensure that its officers did not encourage unlawful conduct in the future'.[188] In that case, the Court imposed a pecuniary penalty after making a declaration with the consent of the parties that the respondent contravened section 500 of the Fair Work Act 2009 (Cth). The contravention was the result of the improper conduct of the respondent Union's official, who was present on a building and construction site for a period without escort and who failed to comply with a request to move. An order was also made by consent for the Union at its cost to arrange for each of relevant permit-holding officials to attend stipulated training. In determining the appropriate penalty, her Honour referred to one of the real issues between the parties as being 'whether by the Union's conduct is has expressed contrition'.[189] Justice Banks-Smith discounted the penalty by taking into account the Union's cooperation and an element of contrition on the basis that 'however described, the fact that the Union consented to an order that it implement the third party training program (at its cost) indicates a willingness to "change its ways"'.[190]

Contrast the decision in *Automotive, Food, Metals, Engineering, Printing and Kindred Industries Union v Visy Packaging Pty Ltd (No 4)*.[191] In this case, Murphy J also took account of arrangements made by the company for compliance training of employees and for future advice to be provided regarding employees' rights to raise relevant concerns. His Honour regarded these as corrective action that tends to reduce future loss and damage, however, and as a factor tending to mitigate a civil penalty in a Fair Work Act, but not as evidence of contrition. I suggest the better view is that corrective action of this nature can also be evidence of contrition if it shows that a corporation is remorseful for its conduct in the past and intends to make changes to its operations in order to comply with the law in the future.

Another example of a corporation 'changing its ways' is provided by *Chief Executive Officer of the Australian Transaction Reports and Analysis Centre v Commonwealth Bank of Australia Ltd*.[192] In this case, Yates J referred to the defendant Bank's contrition and remorse in respect to its money-laundering contraventions, as evidenced by its acknowledgement of the seriousness of its contraventions and by undertaking significant steps to address the underlying deficiencies that led to the contraventions.

VII. Corporate Remorse and Contrition: Future Directions

In this final section of the chapter, I explore two related issues that emerge from the case law and the ALRC's 2020 report on *Corporate Criminal Responsibility*.[193] The first issue

[188] ibid [81]. Contrast the conclusion on the facts in *Queensland Infrastructure Case* (n 82) [102], [164] (Dowsett, Greenwood and Wigney JJ).

[189] *NEXT DC P2 Project Case* (n 141) [57].

[190] ibid [81].

[191] *Automotive, Food, Metals, Engineering, Printing and Kindred Industries Union v Visy Packaging Pty Ltd (No 4)* [2013] FCA 930 (Murphy J).

[192] *Chief Executive Officer of the Australian Transaction Reports and Analysis Centre v Commonwealth Bank of Australia Ltd* [2018] FCA 930 [43].

[193] ALRC Final Report (n 9).

is whether there is a place for contrition as a discrete factor in any future codification of the factors to be considered when sentencing a corporation and determining civil penalties. The second and related issue is whether sentencing and civil penalty factors ought only to include factors relating to a corporation's behaviour, rather than a state of mind, namely, contrition.

A. Codification of Corporate Sentencing Factors

In the *Same Time, Same Crime: Sentencing of Federal Offenders Report*[194] in 2006, the ALRC recommended wholesale reforms to section 16A of the Crimes Act, including for common law principles of sentencing corporations to be codified in federal sentencing legislation. In its subsequent 2020 Report, the ALRC reiterated its recommendation for its 2006 recommendations to be implemented. The ALRC notes that the courts have drawn on the case law relating to imposing civil penalties on corporations to fill the gaps in section 16A(2) for corporate offenders. It cites as an example *Director of Public Prosecutions (Cth) v Nippon Yusen Kabushiki Kaisha*, where Wigney J observed that the factors that have emerged from civil penalty cases will generally be relevant to sentencing corporations for criminal offences, in addition to the section 16A(2) factors from the Crimes Act.[195]

Recommendation 10 in the ALRC's 2020 Report is that the Crimes Act to be amended to require a court to consider stated factors when sentencing a corporation (as distinct from a natural person).[196] The factors set out by the ALRC in Recommendation 10 do not include remorse or contrition. The Commission refers to contrition as 'less cogent for corporate offenders'.[197] Recommendation 10 includes a number of factors the cases discussed in section VI indicate could provide evidence of expression of remorse or contrition, in particular:

(e) whether the unlawful conduct was voluntarily self-reported by the corporation;

…

(g) the extent of any efforts by the corporation to compensate victims and repair harm;

…

(i) any measures that the corporation has taken to reduce the likelihood of its committing a subsequent offence, including:
   i. internal investigations into the causes of the offence;
   ii. internal disciplinary action; and
   iii. measures to implement or improve a compliance program.

[194] ALRC Report No 103 (n 41).

[195] Section 16A(2)(f) refers to the degree to which the person has shown contrition for the offence (i) by taking action to make reparation for any injury, loss or damage resulting from the offence; or (ii) in any other manner. See ALRC Final Report (n 9) [8.30]; *Commonwealth Director of Public Prosecutions v Nippon Yusen Kabushiki Kaisha* [2017] FCA 876, (2017) 254 FCR 235 [220] (*Nippon Yusen Kabushiki Kaisha*).

[196] Neither federal nor State legislation includes factors specific to corporations.

[197] ALRC Final Report (n 9) [8.40]. As we have seen earlier in this chapter, the courts do refer to contrition in the context of corporate wrongdoing. See, eg, *Woolworths* (n 83) [161]–[167]; *Nippon Yusen Kabushiki Kaisha* (n 194) [253]–[254].

Each of these factors concerns actions taken after the wrongful conduct, which reflects an acknowledgement by the corporation of its wrongdoing, an intention to make amends in some way and to prevent subsequent offences.[198]

The ALRC recommends its proposed statutory guidance on sentencing corporations in its Report on the basis that it would

> highlight the relevance of certain factors that have not consistently been cited in the case law, namely, whether the company has undertaken any internal investigations or disciplinary action; any advantage realised by the corporation; and the effect of the sentence on third parties.[199]

Specifically, the explicit inclusion as mandatory considerations of 'measures that the corporation has taken to reduce the likelihood of its committing a subsequent offence' and 'the extent of any efforts by the corporation to compensate victims and repair harm' may incentivise good corporate behaviour in response to offences.[200] The ALRC suggests there is a policy argument for specifically spelling out the relevance of voluntary self-reporting in respect of corporate offenders, given its particular importance in the corporate crime context, and equally a policy argument for specifically providing for 'the extent of any efforts by the corporation to compensate victims and repair harm' (in factor (g)). The Recommendation is for these specific factors to apply to corporations, rather than relying on section 16A(2)(f) of the Crimes Act.

The Recommendation 10 factors indicate a preference for evidence of actions rather than words of contrition or evidence of this corporate state of mind. This argument appears to be based on the conceptual challenge of attributing a human emotion and feelings of contrition to a corporation.

There is merit in codifying factors relevant to corporations that might not be captured by current sentencing factors applicable to natural persons, or which are not applied consistently in the case law. Recommendation 10 is for a non-exhaustive list of factors to supplement, rather than replace, the general sentencing factors, principles and purposes when implemented with the 2006 recommendations. There is scope to argue, therefore, that contrition remains a relevant factor. In the event of reform, however, and notwithstanding the ALRC's reasons for not expressly including this factor, I advocate that corporate contrition or remorse be expressly included as a separate factor on a number of grounds.

First, as seen in section VI, the factors that currently apply under sentencing legislation allow for both behaviours and evidence of a contrite corporate state of mind to be considered in giving effect to the objects of the criminal law. There is an established body of case law to guide decision making about whether a corporation has expressed

[198] The primary object of compensation in the law is corrective justice rather than retribution or deterrence, and for this reason it serves a purpose different from reparations and other non-monetary forms of redress by which a defendant offers to make amends for wrongdoing independently of any liability to pay compensatory damages. As discussed in section VI, this does not preclude the act of offering compensation as being capable of showing contrition.

[199] ALRC Final Report (n 9) [8.34].

[200] ibid [8.40]. Arguably, some of the factors included in Recommendation 10 are captured by the existing (or amended) list of general factors that apply to any defendant. In particular, factor (e) – voluntary self-reporting – overlaps with Crimes Act (n 24), s 16A(2)(h) – cooperation with law enforcement agencies in the investigation of the offence.

contrition or remorse for crimes and contravention of civil penalty provisions, and how much weight ought to be given to that corporate state of mind. Courts are experienced in avoiding double counting when applying factors that overlap; this could include distinguishing evidence of behaviour and as to state of mind. An assessment of contrition as state of mind (or absence thereof) that takes into account evidence of past and future behaviours attributable to a corporation through the words and actions of its board of directors and senior officers, and by reference to systems intentionality, potentially informs a court and regulators more holistically whether a company has mended or intends to mend its ways than would limiting the inquiry only to behaviours such as voluntarily cooperating with a regulator, making repair and restoration, and taking steps to prevent a reoccurrence of harm in the future. Systems intentionality, which looks beyond words and actions of the corporate officers and the directing mind and will of the corporation, captures more fully the evidence of intention that a court needs to give effect to the objects of the law in imposing sentences and civil penalties.

Second, retaining contrition as a mitigating factor in sentencing a corporation recognises and honours remorse and contrition as a societal 'good' (to use Proeve and Tudor's words[201]) significant to both natural and corporate defendants. This social 'good' is an interest of the law in the reference to 'the public interest' in the words of Kirby J in *Cameron*:

> Where genuine remorse is established to the satisfaction of the sentencing judge, it may be in the public interest to mitigate punishment further as a reinforcement for the prisoner's resolve to avoid repetition of such conduct in the future and as an example to others.[202]

Recognition of genuine remorse and contrition communicates the value society places on these emotional states for punishment and deterrence. By taking account of contrition amongst other factors when imposing civil penalties, the law looks for evidence of corporate remorse or contrition, or which otherwise indicates 'consciousness of the seriousness of the contravening conduct that may be relevant to penalty'.[203] In doing so, the law provides incentives for corporations and other defendants to comply with the law in the future and to take responsibility for their actions. This is consistent with the comment of the High Court in *Pattinson* that an expression of genuine remorse by those responsible for a contravention might justify only a modest penalty, 'because no more would be necessary to incentivise the contravenors to remain mindful of their remorse and their public expressions of that remorse to the court'.[204]

Third, the law already takes into consideration evidence of corporate contrition in awarding compensatory and exemplary damages in some tort cases, notwithstanding the inability of a corporation to 'feel' contrite. Although the purpose of attributing contrition to a corporation in assessing tort damages primarily is to compensate rather than punish and deter, the latter are objects of civil damages in some cases and, where available, the approach to judging contrition is much the same.

[201] Proeve and Tudor (n 5) 210.
[202] *Cameron* (n 32) [65].
[203] *Gibson* (n 16) [50] (Mortimer J). See also *Superfone* (n 84) [20] (Murphy J).
[204] *Pattinson* (n 58) [47].

Finally, legal personality and the privileges that attach to that status provide a defensible basis on which to impose moral and legal obligations for culpable behaviour, as a number of the authors of chapters in this collection demonstrate.[205] Conceptualising the corporation as a legal and moral agent whose conduct makes it culpable and accountable in law justifies legally and morally the attribution of contrition and remorse to the corporation to inform decisions on mitigation of sentences and penalties.

B. Two Further Matters

There are further matters arising from the ALRC's 2020 recommendations that warrant consideration beyond the scope of this chapter, but which are worth noting here. The first matter concerns the potential function of contrition and remorse in the event that the ALRC's 2020 Report Recommendation 12 were implemented.[206] This proposed amendment to the Crimes Act would give a court sentencing a corporation the power to make a number of non-monetary penalty orders, including publicity or disclose orders and corrective orders. The presence or absence of contrition could be a relevant factor in this decision making.

The second matter concerns whether contrition should be codified as a statutory factor not only in sentencing corporations but also in determining civil penalties. Evidence of remorse and contrition is relevant to decision making in civil penalty regimes at two points in time at least. First, when a regulator is deciding what action to take when a corporation has contravened the law. Evidence of contrition may be highly relevant to the decision to accept an enforceable undertaking from a corporation, for example, and whether to commence proceedings for the imposition of a civil penalty.[207] Second, evidence of a corporation's state of mind is particularly relevant when a regulator commences proceedings for a civil penalty to be imposed. Here, as Bant explains, courts commonly look for indicia of the defendant's blameworthiness through factors including state-of-mind criteria, such as the defendant's knowledge, intention, regret or contrition.[208] The clear rationale for taking evidence of contrition into account when determining a civil penalty is that where a wrongdoer is contrite, the object of deterrence can be achieved by a lesser penalty than might otherwise be the case.[209]

The ALRC recommends the enactment of a statutory list of factors to be considered by a court when making a civil penalty order in respect of a corporation, to maintain 'principled coherence and consistency in the assessment of penalties for corporations'.[210]

[205] Harding, ch 2 of this volume; Crofts, ch 3 of this volume.

[206] ALRC Final Report (n 9) ch 8, 347.

[207] See section VI.B.iv.

[208] Bant, 'Catching the Corporate Conscience' (n 17) 483.

[209] Paterson and Bant argue that the fact that courts routinely take into account considerations of defendant culpability, contrition and cooperation in assessing the proper level of a civil penalty for contraventions of the Australian Consumer Law 'inherently reflects concepts of retributive justice and "just deserts"', not just deterrence: JM Paterson and E Bant, 'Intuitive Synthesis and Fidelity to Purpose? Judicial Interpretation of the Discretionary Power to Award Civil Penalties under the Australian Consumer Law' in P Vines and MS McDonald (eds), *Statutory Interpretation in Private Law* (Leichhardt, Federation Press, 2019) 154, 171. Support for this view is provided by *Pattinson* (n 58) [103]–[104] (Edelman J).

[210] ALRC Final Report (n 9) Recommendation 11, ch 8, 337.

The factors, listed in Recommendation 11, would apply 'to the extent that they are relevant and known to the court', and would apply 'in addition to any other matters'.[211] Unlike the case law factors that include contrition and remorse, but consistent with the sentencing factors listed in Recommendation 10, there is no express reference in Recommendation 11 to remorse or contrition. Contrition should be included as a factor if the civil penalty factors are codified, for the reasons advanced in section VII.A in respect of sentencing factors. This would guide corporate decisions, systems, policies and practices, decisions by regulators and determinations of civil penalties by the courts.

VIII. Conclusions

A person is described as being in a contrite state or remorseful when they show regret and other emotions for their actions, that they accept responsibility for their actions and the harm it has caused, and acknowledge their wrongdoing and the injury it has caused or take action to make reparation, or both. Although apologies and statements made in court are a significant way to express remorse, more is expected than 'smooth words', even when an apology is offered with sincerity. The law takes genuine remorse into account as a mitigating factor in sentencing a person, including a corporation, because it is considered just to impose a lesser penalty when remorse or contrition is shown. The punishment and deterrent functions of criminal law are served even though the sentence is reduced, because the offender has experienced remorse and expressed support for community values, which lessens concern about reoffending. When a civil penalty is imposed, the court looks to what is necessary to achieve general and specific deterrence.

What purpose does remorse and contrition serve, and how does a court judge corporate contrition? Corporate contrition is a factor in the assessment of sentences and civil penalties. Evidence of contrition is found in words that express regret, remorse and sorrow, and that acknowledge wrongdoing and its impact on others. This includes personal evidence of corporate executives expressing the company's genuine regret. A corporation can also express contrition in more tangible ways through its actions by rectifying past and potential future harm, cooperating with regulators, and through stating plans or taking actions to address the cause of the offence and avoid its repetition offence in the future. The inquiry into a corporation's state of mind judged by its actions to date and its intention to 'mend its ways' is conducted by considering many forms of evidence, including words, actions and corporate systems, policies and practices. In this way actions, not just words, and what action is taken, guide judgments as to whether a corporation is genuinely contrite.

[211] ibid.

PART IV

Alternative Approaches

16

Culpable Ships

SARAH DERRINGTON AND SAMUEL WALPOLE

I. Introduction

Ships are different – or are they? So posited Lord Mustill in 1993 when writing of the international limitation of liability regime that protects shipowners from what would otherwise be crippling awards of damages for civil claims in the event of major shipping casualties.[1] Corporate shipowners, operators and charterers are, however, not immune from increasing regulation by government regulators, often with criminal sanctions attached, for breaches of laws implementing international conventions designed to protect the safety of seafarers, ships and the marine environment. As the concept of 'organisational blameworthiness' has developed, there is increasingly little to distinguish between the legal personality accorded to corporations and ships. A corporation can sue and be sued in its own name, as can a ship. A corporation can be charged with a criminal offence and be sentenced for that crime, as can a ship. Is there any need to go beyond the ship itself when the criminal law is transgressed? In what circumstances might it be necessary to bring criminal proceedings against the corporate shipowner, rather than the ship?

The use of corporate criminal liability as a mechanism of corporate regulation has, in recent decades, attracted sustained attention from policymakers, scholars and legal practitioners. This reflects, in part, the continuing theoretical and practical challenges involved in securing the criminal responsibility of corporations in a normatively justifiable way, while having regard to the realities of corporate action. It also reflects the occurrence of many prominent examples of corporate misconduct in recent history,[2] and the growth in regulation generally to seek to ensure that such events do not occur.

The maritime sector is no exception. Over the course of the twentieth century, the international community, through a series of international conventions and other mechanisms, developed a framework for the regulation of international shipping, particularly in relation to safety and protection of the environment. While those instruments,

[1] MJ Mustill, 'Ships Are Different – Or Are They?' [1993] *Lloyd's Maritime and Commercial Law Quarterly* 490.

[2] See generally, Commonwealth of Australia, *Royal Commission into Misconduct in the Banking, Superannuation and Financial Services Industry* (Final Report, 1 February 2019) vol 1.

enacted in domestic law, provide a detailed and effective body of substantive maritime regulatory law, recent history is replete with examples of maritime casualties that have involved contravention of those regulations. In many of these cases, responsibility lies with corporations that own or operate these vessels, but truly effective enforcement of these laws through proper utilisation of principles of corporate criminal liability has yet to be realised. Much of the difficulty in using corporate criminal liability effectively in a maritime context stems from the international nature of the industry, and the complex webs of corporate ownership and responsibility involved.

This chapter seeks to address these enforcement issues. The focus of this chapter is whether and, if so, how a foreign shipowner can be prosecuted and appropriately sanctioned by an Australian court consequent upon the commission of an offence under Australian law, or alternatively, and somewhat more radically, whether criminal liability can and should attach to the ship itself.

II. The Origin of Criminal Admiralty Jurisdiction

The origin of the Admiralty jurisdiction, as it now exists in the twenty-first century, can be traced back, albeit dimly, to the medieval period. Based on ordinances, some writers posit its existence at least to the reign of Edward I (1272–1307), or even during the reign of Henry I (1100–1135).[3] For others, like Blackstone, Admiralty jurisdiction emerged during the time of Edward III (1327–1377).[4] Various common law and statutory texts from the fourteenth and fifteenth centuries have survived, including the *Black Book*.[5] These early maritime laws were mainly concerned with criminal matters, in particular, piracy and murder, with evidence from 1361 establishing that the Admiral was authorised to try a case of piracy and murder according to the maritime law.[6] The surviving records of the Admiral's court start with the early Tudor reorganisation of the court, with extant records being warrants from 1515, libel files from 1519, act books from 1524, and examinations from 1536.[7]

It was during the Tudor period that the court of Admiralty came to assume a greater role, especially following the accession of Henry VIII (1509–1547), who was conscious of the expansion of foreign trade and the increase in exploration and discovery throughout the sixteenth century.[8] The patents issued by Henry VIII to his Admirals made clear that he intended to enhance and expand the jurisdiction of the Admiral and his court, containing as they did a *non obstante* clause, which was intended to override the effect of the statutes enacted in the reign of Richard II (1377–1399). By statutes of 1389 and 1391,[9]

[3] LH Laing, 'Historic Origins of Admiralty Jurisdiction in England' (1946) 45 *Michigan Law Review* 163, 163.

[4] ibid. Laing concedes that it is not possible 'to fix with certainty the date of the establishment of' the Admiralty jurisdiction: ibid 164.

[5] MJ Prichard and DEC Yale (eds), *Hale and Fleetwood on Admiralty Jurisdiction* (London, Selden Society, 1993) xxix.

[6] ibid xxx.

[7] ibid xxix.

[8] W Holdsworth, *A History of English Law*, vol I (London, Methuen, 1909–66) 546; HJ Bourguignon, *Sir William Scott, Lord Stowell* (Cambridge, Cambridge University Press, 1987) 5.

[9] 13 Rich II c.5; 15 Rich II c.3.

Parliament had sought to restrain the Admiral from meddling 'henceforth of anything done within the realm, but only of a thing done upon the Sea', and declared that the Admiral's court had no jurisdiction over 'all manner of contracts, pleas, and quarrels, and all other things rising within the bodies of counties, as well by land as by water, and also of wreck of the sea'.[10] However, during Henry VIII's reign, the criminal jurisdiction of the Admiralty court was reformed by a statute of 1536, the Offences at Sea Act 1536 (UK), and was identifiable with that of the commissioners of oyer and terminer, appointed under 27 Henry VIII c.4 and 28 Henry VIII c.15, gaining jurisdiction. These were High Court judges on circuit authorised to hear and determine at the assizes all indicted cases of treason, felony or misdemeanour committed in the county. In 1540, jurisdiction was given to the Admiral in matters of freight and damage to cargo.[11] Between 1536 and 1834, the commissioners exercised this jurisdiction in place of the Admiral acting solely under his patent and by his lieutenant, the Judge of the Court of Admiralty.[12] The commissioners came to be known as the Justices of the Admiralty and their sittings acquired the title of Admiralty Sessions. These continued until 1834, when the Central Criminal Court was established and was empowered to try offences committed within the jurisdiction of the Admiralty.[13] The Offences at Sea Act 1799 (UK) extended the 1536 Act (in relation to the trial of offences in England) to all offences on the high seas out of the body of a county.[14] This Act has been interpreted as having ambulatory effect in that it picks up new offences as they are created by the UK Parliament and applies them to acts within the Admiral's authority.[15] The Admiral's jurisdiction was also confirmed in relation to acts of piracy by the Piracy Act 1698 (UK); in relation to murder by the Offences at Sea Act 1806 (UK); and in relation to certain murders and manslaughters committed on land in certain overseas settlements by the Murders Abroad Act 1817 (UK). Furthermore, jurisdiction was conferred on the High Court of Admiralty over forfeitures imposed as part of the penalty for certain offences committed at sea, in particular piracy,[16] assisting a foreign state at war with a friendly state,[17] and using or fitting out a vessel for the slave trade.[18]

III. Criminal Admiralty Jurisdiction in Australia

On settlement of the British penal colony in New South Wales in 1788, English law applied within the colony and to all subsequently established colonies. A Court of Vice-Admiralty was established in New South Wales by Letters Patent.[19] Vice-Admiralty

[10] Holdsworth (n 8) 548; Bourguignon (n 8) 4.

[11] 32 Hen VIII c.14, s 10.

[12] Prichard and Yale (eds) (n 5) cxxxvii.

[13] ibid.

[14] Australian Law Reform Commission (ALRC), *Reference on Admiralty Jurisdiction – Criminal Admiralty Jurisdiction* (Research Paper No 4, 1988) 5.

[15] *Oteri v R* [1976] UKPC 25, [1976] 1 WLR 1272, 1277.

[16] Piracy Act 1850 (UK).

[17] Foreign Enlistment Act 1870 (UK).

[18] Slave Trade Act 1873 (UK).

[19] J Allsop, *Admiralty Jurisdiction and Marine Insurance* (Admiralty & Marine Insurance Lecture, New South Wales Bar Association, 24 September 2003) [38].

courts were later established in all of the Australian colonies.[20] The Vice-Admiralty courts were separate from the other courts established in the colony – they were examples of 'an Imperial Court', with judges 'holding office by virtue of an appointment from the British Admiralty'.[21] The Colonial Courts of Admiralty Act 1890 (UK) abolished, from 1890, the separate existence of Vice-Admiralty courts in Australia in all colonies except New South Wales and Victoria, and instead conferred Admiralty jurisdiction on the Supreme Courts of those colonies.[22] The 1890 Act did not come into force in New South Wales and Victoria until 1911.[23]

The Offences at Sea Act 1799 (UK) conferred jurisdiction upon Australian courts in regard to offences aboard British ships committed at sea between the low water mark of the colony out to the coast of any foreign country. Other statutes conferred jurisdiction over specified areas, vessels and persons: the Australian Courts Act 1828 (UK), the Admiralty Offences (Colonial) Act 1849 (UK), the Courts (Colonial) Jurisdiction Act 1874 (UK), the Territorial Waters Jurisdiction Act 1878 (UK) and the Merchant Shipping Act 1894 (UK).[24]

After Federation, Australia began to enact its own laws, and gradually the British statutes ceased to have application. The first statute of significance in the context of the Admiralty jurisdiction was the Crimes Act 1914 (Cth), which applied, alongside existing State criminal laws, to crimes committed in those areas acquired by the Commonwealth after Federation. Subsequently, several more specific statutes have been promulgated, including the Crimes at Sea Act 2000 (Cth) (which repealed the 1979 Act of the same name and which creates a cooperative scheme to apply the criminal laws of the States extraterritorially in the areas adjacent to the Australian coast). Further specific offences, directed at individuals, were created by the Crimes (Hostages) Act 1989 (Cth), the Crimes (Ships and Fixed Platforms) Act 1992 (Cth) and the Maritime Powers Act 2013 (Cth).

A further suite of legislation has been enacted over the past several decades that imposes criminal liability on both individual persons and bodies corporate within the maritime context. These statutes are principally directed to the regulation of shipping. Examples include the Protection of the Sea (Prevention of Pollution from Ships) Act 1983 (Cth), the Fisheries Management Act 1991 (Cth), the Maritime Transport and Offshore Facilities Security Act 2003 (Cth) and the Navigation Act 2012 (Cth). There are State and Territory analogues of many of the offence provisions contained in the Commonwealth statutes. Many of these offences are derived from international conventions.[25]

[20] ibid.
[21] ibid.
[22] ibid [40].
[23] ibid.
[24] ALRC (n 14) 8.
[25] For example, the Protection of the Sea (Prevention of Pollution from Ships) Act 1983 (Cth) gives effect to the International Convention for the Prevention of Pollution from Ships, opened for signature 2 November 1973 (entered into force 2 October 1983) (MARPOL). Different parts of the Act give effect to different annexes of MARPOL, each of which is concerned with distinct types of pollution arising from vessels.

IV. Modern Maritime Criminal Proceedings

By way of illustration, in 2009, the master and the corporate owners of the ship *MV Pacific Adventurer* were charged with committing the offence of discharging oil from the ship into Queensland coastal waters contrary to section 26(1)(a) of the Transport Operations (Marine Pollution) Act 1995 (Qld).[26]

The *MV Pacific Adventurer* was loaded with cargo, including some 50 containers stowed on deck and secured with lashings, in Newcastle. She set sail northwards, aware of developing severe tropical cyclone Hamish. The master complied with the passage-planning advice provided by an independent weather consultant in order to take a safe passage to Brisbane. He ordered additional lashings to be applied to the container before the vessel set sail because of the looming cyclone. On 11 March 2009, 31 containers collapsed and were lost overboard. Some of the containers impacted the hull of the ship and holed or punctured the hull in two places on both the port and starboard sides where the fuel tanks were located. In all, approximately 270.79 tonnes of oil leaked from the ship and entered Queensland coastal waters.

The owners were aware that the container-lashing gear was substandard and of the consequences that might have for the ship. In 2011, the owners, Bluewind Shipping Ltd and Swire Navigation Company Ltd, each pleaded guilty to the charges. The sentencing judge found that the master had acted reasonably both in the preliminary steps he took and in controlling the ship after the holing of the hull had occurred. The owners were fined $1.2 million and were ordered to make a public apology, but the charges against the master were not dropped until after the sentencing of the owners, two and half years after they were originally laid.

Had the shipowners not pleaded guilty, it would have been necessary for the prosecution to attribute the necessary mens rea to each shipowner through one or more individuals using an applicable attribution method. It would appear that, in the absence of an applicable statutory method of attribution under the Queensland legislation, the common law approach in *Meridian* would apply.[27]

Seafarers are increasingly subject to criminal prosecution after incidents of this type. Examples of criminal action being taken against seafarers in the aftermath of maritime accidents, particularly those that involve marine pollution, include the criminal charges laid against the masters of the *Exxon Valdez*,[28] *Nissos Amorgas*,[29] the *Erika*,[30] the *Tasman Spirit*,[31] the *Prestige*,[32] the *Hebei Spirit*[33] and the *Full City*.[34]

[26] *R v Santos, Bluewind Shipping Ltd and Ors* [2011] QDC 254.
[27] See *Meridian Global Funds Management Asia Ltd v Securities Commission* [1995] UKPC 5, [1995] 2 AC 500, approved in *Director of Public Prosecutions (DPP) (Vic) (Reference No 1 of 1996)* [1998] 3 VR 352, (1997) 96 A Crim R 513 (VSCA); *ABC Developmental Learning Centres Pty Ltd v Joanne Wallace* [2006] VSC 171, (2006) 161 A Crim R 250. See Leow, ch 6 of this volume, section I.A.
[28] Grounding of a tanker on a reef off the coast of Alaska, 1989.
[29] Grounding of a tanker off the coast of Venezuela, 1997.
[30] Breaking in two of tanker off the coast of Brittany, 1999.
[31] Grounding of a tanker at the entrance to Karachi Port, 2003.
[32] Breaking in two of tanker off the coast of La Caruña after being refused port of refuge, 2002.
[33] Oil spill in South Korea at anchorage after being hit by a crane barge, 2009.
[34] Grounding after loss of power off Norway, 2011.

In the *First Report of the CMI International Working Group on the Fair Treatment of Seafarers* in 2006, Professor Edgar Gold summarised the then current problems facing seafarers as including:

(a) criminal prosecution of seafarers involved in maritime accidents that have been beyond their control;
(b) criminal prosecution of seafarers involved in maritime accidents due to negligence, despite the fact that negligence has rarely, if ever, been considered a criminal offence in the maritime context;
(c) lengthy delays in the administration of the criminal law process following maritime accidents, resulting in seafarers' being required to remain within the jurisdiction of the relevant state for long periods;
(d) cases where the relevant seafarers have not been found at fault but they are, nevertheless, held under criminal law provisions as 'material witnesses'; and
(e) seafarers held in custody without criminal conviction; denied access to legal counsel and assistance.[35]

On 27 April 2006, the International Maritime Organisation (IMO) adopted the *Guidelines on Fair Treatment of Seafarers in the Event of a Maritime Accident* (Guidelines).[36] The IMO observed that:

> The objective of these Guidelines is to ensure that seafarers are treated fairly following a maritime accident and during any investigation and detention by public authorities and that detention is for no longer than necessary.[37]

The Guidelines are detailed and include guidance for port or coastal states, flag states, seafarer states, shipowners and seafarers. The principles contained in the Guidelines include, but are not limited to, the following:

- that port or coastal states should conduct investigations into maritime accidents 'in a fair and expeditious matter';
- that port or coastal states should treat seafarers 'in a manner which preserves their basic human dignity at all times';
- that port or coastal states are to 'ensure that due process protections are provided to all seafarers in a non-discriminatory manner';[38] and
- that flag states should 'assist in ensuring that shipowners honour obligations to seafarers involved in a maritime accident or any investigation'.[39]

Significantly, the Guidelines state that '[w]ith regard to investigations, shipowners have an overriding duty to protect the rights of seafarers employed or engaged, including the right to avoid self-incrimination and to take steps to ensure their fair treatment'.[40]

[35] E Gold, *First Report of the CMI International Working Group on Fair Treatment of Seafarers* (CMI Yearbook, 2005–2006) 180.
[36] Legal Committee of the International Maritime Organisation Resolution, 'Adoption of Guidelines on Fair Treatment of Seafairers in the Event of a Maritime Accident' (Resolution LEG.3(91), 27 April 2006).
[37] ibid 3.
[38] ibid 4.
[39] ibid 6.
[40] ibid 8.

Despite the adoption of the Guidelines in 2006, the problems referred to by Gold remain. In May 2020, the master of the *APL England* was charged with discharging garbage into the sea, contrary to section 26F of the Protection of the Sea (Prevention of Pollution from Ships) Act 1983 (Cth), and failing to ensure that the vessel did not cause pollution or damage to the marine environment, contrary to section 141 of the Navigation Act 2012 (Cth), after the ship lost approximately 40 containers overboard when her propulsion failed, and pitched and rolled heavily. After several weeks, the master was granted bail on a $60,000 surety and was permitted to return to Malaysia to continue working. He has, however, been required to return to Australia for trial. The ship itself was permitted to return to its shipyard in China after the Australian Maritime Safety Authority (AMSA) received a formal written undertaking from the ship's insurer, Steamship Mutual, that it will pay fines and other amounts agreed or imposed by a court for an amount up to $22.5 million.[41]

As Gold observed, seafarers may be charged with causing the relevant marine accident despite the fact that there is rarely any directly attributable responsibility for such accidents, which may result from circumstances quite beyond the operational responsibility or competence of those charged.[42]

V. Why Criminalise Seafarers?

One reason for laying criminal charges against individual seafarers is to ensure that there is appropriate denunciation and condemnation of the conduct constituting the offence, and when the circumstances are such as to require an appropriate degree of deterrence. Criminal charges are often also justified by the level of potential harm that may occur as a consequence of the conduct. Marine pollution incidents are notorious for the harm that may be caused not just to the marine environment, but also to the livelihoods of those who depend on that environment for their economic sustainability. When dealing with the aftermath of the *APL England*, AMSA said that the decision to lay charges against the ship's master was not taken lightly:

> This and other incidents remind us of the important role the ship's Master has in ensuring the ships that ply our waters are operated safely and do not damage our marine environment.
>
> Today's actions should not detract from the responsibility of the ship owner APL Singapore, insurer Steamship Mutual, and operator ANL who remain accountable for remediation of any impacts of this incident.[43]

[41] Australian Maritime Safety Authority, 'APL England Container Loss' (10 July 2020) at www.amsa.gov.au/news-community/campaigns/apl-england-container-loss. Section 27A of the Protection of the Sea (Prevention of Pollution from Ships) Act 1983 (Cth) permits AMSA to detain a foreign ship in connection with pollution breaches. By s 27A(3), a ship is to be immediately released if security is provided in accordance with s 27A(4).

[42] ibid.

[43] Al Schwartz, AMSA General Manager Operations, quoted in Australian Maritime and Safety Authority, 'APL England Shipping Container Loss – Update 5' (29 May 2020) at www.amsa.gov.au/news-community/news-and-media-releases/apl-england-shipping-container-loss-update-5.

Another reason for the practice of criminalising seafarers is the difficulty of establishing the requisite degree of criminal responsibility on the part of the shipowner. Not all will plead guilty, as did the owners of the *Pacific Adventurer*. As observed by Sarah Kirby, shipowners are often 'shielded from accountability for pollution incidents through tangled corporate ownership webs'.[44] She quotes from an editorial published in the English newspaper, *The Observer*, shortly after the sinking of the *Prestige*:

> The Prestige was not just a garbage ship. It has exposed the international framework of maritime regulation and attitudes of many shipping companies as garbage as well. This was a vessel chartered by the Swiss-based subsidiary of a Russian conglomerate registered in the Bahamas, owned by a Greek through Liberia and given a certificate of seaworthiness by the Americans. When it refueled, it stood off the port of Gibraltar to avoid the chance of inspection. Every aspect of its operation was calculated to avoid tax, ownership obligations and regulatory scrutiny.[45]

These ownership structures are facilitated by the widespread use of 'flags of convenience'.[46] Under the United Nations Convention on the Law of the Sea, 'Ships have the nationality of the State whose flag they are entitled to fly'.[47] In 2019, more than 70 per cent of global merchant shipping fleet by tonnage flew a flag foreign to that of its actual owner.[48] While Greece, Japan and China are the most significant shipowning economies, the most significant flags of registration in terms of tonnage are Panama, Marshall Islands and Liberia, then Hong Kong and Singapore.[49] Panama, the Marshall Islands and Liberia are described as 'open registries' due to the 'relative lack of requirements' imposed for vessels that fly such a flag.[50] Importantly, open registries permit vessels under foreign ownership and control to be registered under commercially attractive terms.[51]

The complexity and opacity of the corporate structures of the international maritime industry do not stop there. As Gold identifies, 'ship operations may be delegated to operating companies' and 'these may hand over actual day-to-day operations to management companies who may also not be aware who the real owners are'.[52] Vessels may be the subject of a bareboat charter to a further company, who may then time charter the vessel to another who may then enter into a voyage charter with yet another company. All of these companies may have different nationalities, and their nationalities are unlikely to be that of the ship itself. The commercial maritime environment results in a uniquely difficult web for regulators to unpick.

[44] SM Kirby, 'The Continuing Criminalization of Seafarers' in A Chircop et al (eds), *The Regulation of International Shipping: International and Comparative Perspectives – Essays in Honor of Edgar Gold* (Leiden, Brill Nijhoff, 2012) 443, 462.

[45] ibid.

[46] For an overview, see NP Ready, 'Nationality, Registration, and Ownership of Ships' in DJ Attard et al (eds), *The IMLI Manual on International Maritime Law*, vol II: *Shipping Law* (Oxford, Oxford University Press, 2016) 19.

[47] Convention on the Law of the Sea, opened for signature 10 December 1982, 1833 UNTS 3 (entered into force 16 November 1994), Art 91(1).

[48] United Nations Conference on Trade and Development, *Review of Maritime Transport* (2019) 36.

[49] United Nations Conference on Trade and Development, *Handbook of Statistics* (2020) 77.

[50] HE Anderson, 'The Nationality of Ships and Flags of Convenience: Economics, Politics, and Alternatives' (1996) 21 *Tulane Maritime Law Journal* 139, 140.

[51] See Ready (n 46) 32–35.

[52] E Gold, 'Bloodhounds, Scapegoats and Fatcats: Criminal Action, Professional Duty and Corporate Responsibility in the Maritime Menagerie' (2005) 24 *University of Queensland Law Journal* 251, 253.

When the circumstances of a maritime casualty or incident are such that criminal culpability should properly rest with a corporate shipowner or operator, how can such a corporation be found liable for criminal offences? In the maritime context, matters are complicated by the types of corporate structures and arrangements referred to above. There is no universally accepted understanding of how criminal liability can, or should, attach to a corporation.

VI. Corporate Attribution

Under Commonwealth criminal law in Australia, criminal offences generally apply to corporations because offences typically apply to corporations in the same way as they apply to individuals. This is made explicit by section 12.1 of the Criminal Code Act 1995 (Cth) (Criminal Code), which provides:

> **12.1 General principles**
>
> (1) This Code applies to bodies corporate in the same way as it applies to individuals. It so applies with such modifications as are set out in this Part, and with such other modifications as are set out in this Part. And with such other modifications as are made necessary by the fact that criminal liability is being imposed on bodies corporate rather than individuals.
>
> (2) A body corporate may be found guilty of any offence including one punishable by imprisonment.[53]

In addition, the Acts Interpretation Act 1901 (Cth) provides, in section 2C(1), that under any Commonwealth Act, unless the contrary intention appears:

> expressions used to denote persons generally (such as a 'person', 'party', 'someone', 'anyone', 'no-one', 'one', 'another' and 'whoever') include a body politic or corporate as well as an individual.

Whilst it is relatively straightforward to conceptualise the application of criminal offences to corporations in a theoretical sense, the reality is that the application of the criminal law to a corporation itself remains controversial.[54] The Australian Law Reform Commission (ALRC) has recently observed that, given the law recognises the corporation as an entity, the question that then arises is whether the application of criminal law can be justified having regard to the nature of a corporation. It concluded that there are two key reasons why the existence of a capacity for a corporation to be criminally responsible is justified.[55] The first is that it is possible to develop models of corporate fault or blameworthiness, having regard to corporate sociology and behaviour, that would justify the capacity of a corporation to be responsible for a crime that can properly be said to have been committed *by the corporation*.[56] The second reason places greater

[53] For an analysis of the effect of a statutory provision similar to s 12.1 in a State context, see *Presidential Security Services of Australia Pty Ltd v Brilley* [2008] NSWCA 204, (2008) 73 NSWLR 241 [1]–[26], which considers s 10(1) of the Criminal Procedure Act 1986 (NSW).

[54] Australian Law Reform Commission, *Corporate Criminal Responsibility* (Report No 136, April 2020), para 4.1.

[55] ibid para 4.33.

[56] ibid para 4.34.

emphasis on the juristic nature of the corporation,[57] agreeing with Robert Thomas that the decision that corporations may be criminally responsible can be justified by 'fairness norms' – as a corollary of the conferral of legal personhood upon the corporation.[58]

The more difficult question concerns the appropriate method of corporate attribution in the context of the criminal law. Different methods of attribution of corporate responsibility, in relation to both civil and criminal liability, have developed over the past century. Each of these models conceptualises the capacity of the corporation to be criminally responsible in different ways. The more traditional methods of attribution conceptualise corporate fault in a narrow way with reference to particular individual actors.[59]

Nonetheless, those traditional methods of attribution model corporate fault differently. One approach, vicarious liability, makes a corporation responsible for the acts and mental states of its agents – through making the corporation liable either for the agent's conduct or for the agent's own liability.[60] Corporate criminal responsibility is established derivatively under such a model.[61] Identification theory, on the other hand, ascribes the conduct and states of mind of particular individuals to the corporation itself.[62] The conduct and states of mind of those individuals are considered by the law to be those of the corporation.[63]

Under Commonwealth criminal law, the most widely used method of attribution of responsibility in Australia is based on a method that first appeared in section 84 of the Trade Practices Act 1974 (Cth) (the TPA Model).[64] Under that method of attribution, corporations are responsible for both criminal offences and contraventions of civil penalty provisions based on the state of mind of a director, employee or agent. Although attribution founded on this model predominates across the Commonwealth statute book, it is by no means a uniform approach, there being many variants of the TPA Model.[65]

More holistic approaches to criminal responsibility have emerged in recent decades. These approaches focus on 'organisational blameworthiness', which interrogates the issue of corporate fault in relation to the corporation itself. While identification theory also does this in a sense (through providing for the direct liability of a corporation), under organisational models corporate criminal responsibility does not need to be mediated through particular individual actors. The corporation has a 'distinct and identifiable

[57] ibid para 4.42.

[58] WR Thomas, 'How and Why Corporations Became (and Remain) Persons under the Criminal Law' (2018) 45 *Florida State University Law Review* 479, 504.

[59] M Wilkinson, 'Corporate Criminal Liability: The Move towards Recognising Genuine Corporate Fault' (2003) 9 *Canterbury Law Review* 142, 145.

[60] See *Pioneer Mortgage Services Pty Ltd v Columbus Capital Pty Ltd* [2016] FCAFC 78, (2016) 250 FCR 136, 147–49 [48]–[58] (Davies, Gleeson and Edelman JJ).

[61] *New York Central and Hudson River Railroad Company v United States*, 212 US 481 (1909); *Mousell Brothers Ltd v London v North-Western Railway Co* [1917] 2 KB 836; *R v Australasian Films Ltd* [1921] HCA 11, (1921) 29 CLR 195.

[62] *Lennard's Carrying Co Ltd v Asiatic Petroleum Co Ltd* [1915] AC 705, [1914–15] All ER Rep 280 (HL); *HL Bolton (Engineering) Co Ltd v TJ Graham & Sons Ltd* [1957] 1 QB 159, [1956] 3 WLR 804; *Tesco Supermarkets Ltd v Nattrass* [1972] AC 153, [1971] 2 WLR 1166 (HL); *Hamilton v Whitehead* [1988] HCA 65, (1988) 166 CLR 121; *Meridian Global Funds Management Asia Ltd v Securities Commission* [1995] UKPC 5, [1995] 2 AC 500; *ABC Developmental Learning Centres Pty Ltd v Joanne Wallace* [2006] VSC 171, (2006) 161 A Crim R 250.

[63] ALRC (n 54) para 4.48.

[64] The Trade Practices Act 1974 (Cth) was renamed the Competition and Consumer Act (2010) (Cth). The relevant provision is now s 84 of the latter Act.

[65] ALRC (n 54) para 3.63.

personality independent of specific individuals'.[66] An example of such an approach is found in part 2.5 of the Criminal Code. Part 2.5 sets out the legal tests for attributing the physical and fault elements of an offence to corporations. The most innovative aspects of part 2.5 are located in section 12.3(2), which permits the fault elements of intention, knowledge and recklessness to be attributed through a corporation's board of directors, a high managerial agent or its corporate culture.

Despite the novel approach to attribution contained in part 2.5,[67] it has not been widely adopted across Commonwealth legislation, and indeed is expressly excluded from some of the most important statutes in the maritime sphere, including the Fisheries Management Act 1991 (Cth) and the Protection of the Sea (Prevention of Pollution from Ships) Act 1983 (Cth). Where part 2.5 is excluded, it is most usual to find the TPA Model used as the method of attribution.[68] By way of example, the Fisheries Management Act 1991 (Cth) provides:

> **164 Conduct of directors, employees and agents**
>
> (1) Where, in proceedings for an offence against this Act it is necessary to establish the state of mind of a body corporate in relation to particular conduct, it is sufficient to show:
>
> (a) that the conduct was engaged in by a director, employee or agent of the body corporate; and
>
> (b) that the director, employee or agent had the state of mind.
>
> (2) Any conduct engaged in by a director, employee or agent of a body corporate is taken, for the purposes of a prosecution for an offence against this Act, to have been engaged in also by the body corporate unless the body corporate establishes that the body corporate took reasonable precautions and exercised due diligence to prevent the conduct.
>
> (2A) For the purposes of subsection (2), in determining whether a body corporate took reasonable precautions and exercised due diligence to prevent conduct engaged in by a director, employee or agent of the body corporate, the matters to which regard is to be had include:
>
> (a) any action the body corporate took to inform the director, employee or agent of the legal obligations of the body corporate, director, employee or agent, in relation to the conduct; and
>
> (b) any action the body corporate took to ensure that those obligations were understood and complied with by the director, employee or agent; and
>
> (c) when any such action was taken; and
>
> (d) whether there were any other actions that the body corporate could reasonably have taken that may have prevented the conduct.
>
> …
>
> (10) Part 2.5 of the *Criminal Code* does not apply to an offence against this Act.

While part 2.5 is excluded from most Commonwealth maritime regulatory legislation, one of the few cases to consider the operation of the corporate culture provisions in

[66] O Dixon, 'Corporate Criminal Liability: The Influence of Corporate Culture' (Sydney Law School Legal Studies Research Paper No 17/14, University of Sydney, February 2017) 3.

[67] Amendments to pt 2.5 also continue to be proposed: see ALRC (n 54) Recommendations 5–7; E Bant, 'Reforming the Laws of Corporate Attribution' (2022) 39 *Company and Security Law Journal* 259; E Bant, 'Catching the corporate conscience: a new model of "systems intentionality"' [2022] *Lloyd's Maritime and Commercial Law Quarterly* 468; Fisse, ch 7 of this volume.

[68] ALRC (n 54) para 2.82.

part 2.5, *R v Potter & Mures Fishing Pty Ltd*, arose in a maritime context. It is a case that demonstrates the complexity of the Criminal Code.[69]

VII. Alternatives to Liability Based upon Corporate Attribution

An increasing number of offences are being framed so as to apply only to corporations, rather than relying on attribution methods to adapt general offences to a corporate context. These offences recognise the capacity of a corporation to act uniquely as a corporate entity, comprised of, but greater than, a mere combination of individuals. Such offences might be framed as 'failure to prevent' offences, particularly in the context of transnational crimes, for example the failure to prevent foreign bribery,[70] or as 'duty-based' offences, such as are frequently found in work health and safety legislation.

In its report on *Corporate Criminal Responsibility*, the ALRC envisaged the development of an additional type of specific offence. It recommended that, where appropriate, the Australian Government should introduce offences that criminalise contraventions of prescribed civil penalty provisions that constitute a system of conduct or pattern of behaviour by a corporation.[71] Such an offence is designed to focus on systemic misconduct.[72]

In the shipping sector, many of the international conventions agreed under the auspices of the IMO give an express right to states for the enforcement of their provisions under port state control (PSC), a system of inspection of ships that come into their ports.[73] In Australia, the responsibility for this system lies with AMSA. From 2013 onwards, ships and operators with a record of poor performance can be refused access to Australian ports through a direction issued under section 246 of the Navigation Act 2012 (Cth).[74] This power is used only when a systemic failure has been identified. Through an internationally agreed system of PSC, and the reporting on the performance of each flag in accordance with a policy agreed by the first regional PSC agreement (the Paris Memorandum of Understanding (MoU) 1982),[75] systemic failures of particular ships and/or systemic misconduct or patterns of behaviour exhibited by particular ship-owners are relatively easy to identify.

[69] As discussed in Gans, ch 13 of this volume.

[70] See Clough, ch 18 of this volume.

[71] ALRC (n 54) Recommendation 8.

[72] Criminalisation of systemic misconduct has received significant attention following the ALRC Report, either in the context of an additional type of corporate offence, or as an alternative model of attribution: see, eg, S Walpole and M Corrigan, 'Fighting the System: New Approaches to Addressing Systematic Misconduct' (2021) 43 *Sydney Law Review* 489; E Bant, 'Culpable Corporate Minds' (2021) 48 *University of Western Australia Law Review* 352; Bant, ch 11 of this volume; Bant (n 67).

[73] See P Boisson, 'Law of Maritime Safety' in DJ Attard et al (eds), *The IMLI Manual on International Maritime Law*, vol II: *Shipping Law* (Oxford, Oxford University Press, 2016) 180.

[74] In 2020, AMSA refused access to five ships for periods ranging between three to 12 months for significant breaches of the Maritime Labour Convention: Australian Government, 'Port State Control' (Annual Report, Australian Maritime and Safety Authority, 4 June 2021).

[75] The other regional regimes are encompassed by the Tokyo MoU, Acuerdo de Viña del Mare, Caribbean MoU, Abuja MoU, Blac Sea MoU, Mediterranean MoU, Indian Ocean MoU, Riyadh MoU and the United States Coast Guard MoU.

By way of example, in 2018, AMSA banned the Philippines-flagged cargo ship *Thorco Luna* after it was detained by PSC inspectors for the third time that year.[76] The ship had been issued with 34 deficiencies over a six-month period, including for violations of the Safety of Life at Sea Convention (SOLAS).[77] Circumstances such as these, involving a pattern of multiple breaches of civil penalty provisions over a sustained period, provide an example of circumstances that might be susceptible to criminal prosecution for an offence of the type recommended by the ALRC.

VIII. The Juristic Entities Compared – Corporations and Ships

As the concept of 'organisational blameworthiness' has developed, there is increasingly little to distinguish between the legal personality accorded to corporations and ships. A corporation can sue and be sued in its own name, as can a ship. A corporation can be charged with a criminal offence and be sentenced for that crime, as can a ship. Is there any need to go beyond the ship itself when the criminal law is transgressed? In what circumstances might it be necessary to bring criminal proceedings against the corporate shipowner, rather than the ship?

The common law did not originally recognise the capacity of a corporation to be criminally responsible. The classic historical statement of the principle that a corporation itself could not be criminally responsible is that of Sir Edward Coke in the *Case of Sutton's Hospital* in 1612:

> [T]he corporation itself is only in abstracto, and rests only in intendment and consideration of the law; for a corporate aggregate of many is invisible, immortal, and rests only in intendment and consideration of the law … They cannot commit treason, nor be outlawed, nor excommunicated, for they have no souls, neither can they appear in person, but by attorney … A corporation aggregate of many cannot do fealty, for an invisible body can neither be in person, nor swear …[78]

A similar view continued to prevail two centuries later in the United States, when Marshall CJ said:

> A corporation is an artificial being, invisible, intangible, and existing only in contemplation of law. Being the mere creature of law, it possesses only those properties which the charter of its creation confers upon it, either expressly or as incidental to its very existence. These are such as are supposed best calculated to effect the object for which it was created. Among the most important are immortality, and, if the expression may be allowed, individuality; properties, by which a perpetual succession of many persons are considered as the same, and may act as a single individual.[79]

[76] Australian Maritime Safety Authority, 'Cargo Ship Thorco Luna Banned from Australian Ports' (8 June 2018) at www.amsa.gov.au/news-community/news-and-media-releases/cargo-ship-thorco-luna-banned-australian-ports.

[77] SOLAS is implemented in Australia by the Navigation Act 2012 (Cth).

[78] *Case of Sutton's Hospital* (1612) 10 Co Rep 23a, 77 ER 960, 973.

[79] *Trustees of Dartmouth College v Woodward* 17 US 518, 636 (1819).

Nonetheless, Marshall CJ appeared to be more comfortable with the nature of the 'being' that is a ship when, in that same year, he held in *United States v The Schooner Little Charles*:

> This is not a proceeding against the owner, it is a proceeding against the vessel for an offence committed by the vessel, which is not the less an offence, and does not the less subject her to forfeiture because it was committed without the authority and against the will of the owner. It is true that inanimate matter can commit no offence. But this body is animated and put in action by the crew, who are guided by the master.[80]

One can see the parallels with organisational theories of the corporation within this passage from Marshall CJ's opinion.

Over time, judicial resistance to the idea that corporations had the capacity to be criminally responsible receded. As Day J famously stated in *New York Central & Hudson River Railroad Co v United States*:

> If, for example, the invisible, intangible essence of air, which we term a corporation, can level mountains, fill up valleys, lay down iron tracks, and run railroad cars on them, it can intend to do it, and can act therein as well viciously as virtuously.[81]

The better view of the earlier denial of corporate criminal liability is not that the law denied the existence of a corporation as an entity (albeit one constructed by law), but rather that the law did not consider that this type of juristic entity had the *capacity* to be criminally responsible.[82] Ultimately, the law came to recognise such capacity in corporate entities. It was then necessary for the law to construct the scope of such capacity to be criminally responsible – the different conceptualisations of corporate fault reflected in the various methods of corporate attribution are manifestations of this.[83]

By the time of Coke, the action *in rem* was already well established in the Admiralty jurisdiction. The action is *in rem* in the sense that, from beginning to end, it needs no defendant other than the *res* (most usually the ship) and the liability is *in rem* in that it follows the *res* into whoever's hand it comes. As the judgment is *in rem*, it has a binding effect on persons who are not parties to the action and can bind third parties.

The characteristic incidents of an action *in rem* include:

(1) Once a claim form *in rem* has been issued, a change in ownership in the vessel will be ineffective to prevent the action proceeding against it, an effect known colloquially as the 'statutory lien';
(2) In the absence of statutory permission, an action *in rem* lies only against the vessel in connection with which the claim arises;
(3) If the owners of the ship appear and defend the action (or at any rate submit to the jurisdiction of the court) the action proceeds thereafter as if it had also been commenced *in personam*, with the result that if the *res* itself proves insufficient to meet the claimant's claim, the owners' other assets will be available for enforcement purposes;
(4) Conversely, if the owners do not appear, the claimant is limited to such of the realizable value of the *res* which is available once those whose claims rank in priority have been satisfied. Any balance may be recovered in a subsequent action *in personam*;

[80] *United States v The Schooner Little Charles* 1 Brock Rep (1819) 347, 354.
[81] *New York Central & Hudson River Railroad Co v United States*, 212 US 481, 493 (1909).
[82] For discussion, see S Walpole, 'Criminal Responsibility as a Distinctive Form of Corporate Regulation' (2020) 35 *Australian Journal of Corporate Law* 235.
[83] ibid 236–37, 248, 251–52.

(5) Participation in *in rem* proceedings is not confined to the claimants and to the owners of the *res*; others may intervene in the proceedings in order to assert or protect their own rights or the priority accorded to them. Such participation neither requires nor brings with it any personal liability to the claimant;
(6) A cause of action in rem does not merge in a judgment *in personam*;
(7) The claimant in an action *in rem* may procure the issue of a warrant of arrest after judgment as well as before judgment; and
(8) Once arrested, the ship may be sold by the court, in which event all outstanding claims which could be brought by action *in rem* against her are transferred to the fund in court.[84]

The authors of *Hale and Fleetwood on Admiralty Jurisdiction* consider that the action *in rem*, as it developed in the fifteenth and sixteenth centuries, was derived from a process that was available in the Middle Ages.[85] That process was not dependent on the existence of a right *in rem* or a proprietary claim in the nature of a lien or hypothèque, but on the notion of contumacy evinced by the defendant's refusal to appear before the court and participate in the litigation. The authors posit that the ambivalent character that the Admiralty process *in rem* had developed, by at least the sixteenth century, enabled the process to encompass claims that, in modern times, are regarded as purely *in personam* and at the same time to foster the notion that the process rendered the ship, or other *res*, directly liable.[86]

Two competing theories attempt to explain the basis of the modern action *in rem* and, in particular, the conclusion that the action *in rem* is against the ship. According to Lord Steyn, the 'personification theory' was developed 'as a means of defending and extending the jurisdiction of the High Court of Admiralty, in the days before the *Admiralty Court Act of 1840*, against the encroachments of the common law courts and their writs of prohibition'.[87] As formulated by Lord Steyn, this theory would seem to hold that the vessel is a quasi-juristic person since 'The ship was regarded as both the source and limit of liability. The ship herself was the "wrongdoer"'.[88]

This accords with the fact that, by the sixteenth century, there is evidence that a transaction may be intended to bind the ship and not merely the parties to the transaction.[89] There is also acceptance of the idea that the action is against the ship and may be pursued against it without the interposition of any human defendant.[90] It follows, according to this theory, that the action is independent of any action against the owner and that it is based on a substantive claim against the thing. As Professor David Jackson notes, there are eighteenth-century (and earlier) cases stressing the liability of the ship, as distinct from the owners.[91]

[84] SC Derrington and JM Turner, *The Law and Practice of Admiralty Matters*, 2nd edn (Oxford, Oxford University Press, 2016) para 2.07.
[85] Prichard and Yale (eds) (n 5) xxxix.
[86] ibid xl.
[87] *The Indian Grace (No 2)* [1997] UKHL 40, [1998] AC 878, 907.
[88] ibid; Derrington and Turner (n 84) para 2.27.
[89] *Austen v Castelyn* (1541) *Select Pleas*, I, 107; *Cogley v Taylor* (1548) *Select Pleas*, II, 7, cited in Prichard and Yale (eds) (n 5) xliv, fn 6.
[90] Prichard and Yale (eds) (n 5) xlv.
[91] DC Jackson, *Enforcement of Maritime Claims*, 4th edn (London, Informa, 2005) para 10.9.

Against those authorities, however, are cases expressing the opposing view. In *The Druid*, Dr Lushington said (expressing an opinion he later recanted[92]):

> In all causes of action which may arise from circumstances occurring during the ownership of the person whose ship is proceeded against, I apprehend that no suit could ever be maintained against a ship where the owners were not themselves personally liable, or where personal liability had not been given up, as in bottomry bonds, by taking a lien on the vessel. The liability of the ship and the responsibility of the owners in such cases are convertible terms; the ship is not liable if the owners are not responsible, and vice versa, no responsibility can attach upon the owners if the ship is exempt and not liable to be proceeded against.[93]

The personification theory prevails in the United States, where it was famously explained in *Tucker v Alexandroff*:

> Prior to her launching she is mere congeries of wood and iron – an ordinary piece of personal property … In the baptism of launching she receives her name, and from the moment her keel touches the water she is transformed, and becomes a subject of admiralty jurisdiction. She acquires a personality of her own; becomes competent to contract, and is individually liable for her obligations, upon which she may sue in the name of her owner, and be sued in her name.[94]

The personification theory is countered by the procedural theory, which posits that an action *in rem* is not based upon the wrongdoing of the ship personified as an offender but is simply a means of bringing the owner of the ship to meet his personal liability by seizing his property. The difficulty with the characterisation of the action *in rem* as a purely procedural device is that it stumbles when one seeks to explain various features of the Admiralty jurisdiction, such as how some maritime liens could be enforced against an owner and bona fide purchaser despite the lack of personal liability in the owner, or that a cause of action *in rem* does not merge with a judgment *in personam*.[95]

In Australia, the Full Court of the Federal Court has held that the action *in rem*, at least prior to the unconditional appearance of a relevant person, is an action against the ship, not the owner or demise charterer of the ship. After the appearance, it continues as an action *in rem* and also as if it were an action *in personam* against the relevant person who appears.[96]

IX. Criminal Liability against a Ship

If the law is prepared to visit civil liability on a ship by the action *in rem*, whether or not action is taken against the owner *in personam*, there seems no compelling reason why criminal liability should not also attach to a culpable ship, thereby avoiding the need to

[92] *The Ticonderoga* (1856) Swab 215, 166 ER 1103; *The Ruby Queen* (1861) Lush 266, 167 ER 119; *The Edwin* (1864) B&L 281, 167 ER 365.

[93] *The Druid* (1842) 1 W Rob 391, 399, 166 ER 619, 622; and to the same effect see *The Parlement Belge* (1880) 5 PD 197, 218.

[94] *Tucker v Alexandroff*, 183 US 424, 438 (1902).

[95] See Derrington and Turner (n 84) para 2.33; and see *Tecoil Shipping Ltd v Neptune EHF* [2021] EWHC 1582 (Admlty).

[96] *Comandate Marine Corp v Pan Australia Shipping Pty Ltd* [2006] FCAFC 192, (2006) 157 FCR 45 [128].

consider various methods of corporate attribution. The corporate structures through which the ship was owned and operated would be irrelevant; so too, at least for the purposes of the proceedings against the ship, would be the state of mind of any director, employee or agent of the corporation.

Such an approach would be consistent with civil forfeiture, which has at its base the so-called 'legal fiction' that the government is acting against the property itself, rather than against the owner. The remedy finds its origin in the law of deodand (literally 'to give to God'), whereby an inanimate object that caused a death was deemed to be 'guilty' of a crime and therefore was offered to God through forfeiture to the King.[97] The law of deodand can be traced back to the Middle Ages (or earlier),[98] and significantly it appears to have been irrelevant whether or not the owner of the offending object was guilty.[99] Oliver Wendell Holmes Jr observed that the deodand actions were not based on the fault of the owner – 'the action followed the guilty thing into whosever hands it came'.[100]

In *Austin v United States* in 1993, Blackmun J, in whose judgment White, Stevens, O'Connor and Souter JJ joined, said:

> Three kinds of forfeiture were established in England at the time the Eighth Amendment was ratified in the United States: deodand, forfeiture upon conviction for a felony or treason, and statutory forfeiture. See *Calero-Toledo*, 416 US, at 680–683. Each was understood, at least in part, as imposing punishment.
>
> > 'At common law the value of an inanimate object directly or indirectly causing the accidental death of a King's subject was forfeited to the Crown as a deodand. The origins of the deodand are traceable to Biblical and pre-Judeo-Christian practices, which reflected the view that the instrument of death was accused and that religious expiation was required. See O Holmes, The Common Law, c. 1 (1881). The value of the instrument was forfeited to the King, in the belief that the King would provide the money for Masses to be said for the good of the dead man's soul, or insure that the deodand was put to charitable uses. 1 W Blackstone, Commentaries 300. When application of the deodand to religious or eleemosynary purposes ceased, and the deodand became a source of Crown revenue, the institution was justified as a penalty for carelessness'. *Id*, at 680–681 (footnotes omitted).
>
> …
>
> Third, 'English law provided for statutory forfeitures of offending objects used in violation of the customs and revenue laws.' *Calero-Toledo*, 416 US, at 682. The most notable of these were the Navigation Acts of 1660 that required the shipping of most commodities in English vessels. Violation of the Acts resulted in the forfeiture of the illegally carried goods as well as the ship that transported them … The statute was construed so that the act of an individual seaman, undertaken without the knowledge of the master or owner, could result in forfeiture of the entire ship … Blackstone considered such forfeiture statutes 'penal'.[101]

[97] P Berman, 'An Anthropological Approach to Modern Forfeiture Law: The Symbolic Function of Legal Actions against Objects' (1999) 11 *Yale Journal of Law and Humanities* 1.

[98] OW Holmes Jr, *The Common Law* (Boston, MA, Little, Brown and Co, 1881) 7–8. Beyond the common law, forfeiture has been said to be 'as old as the Mosaic Code': JJ Guthrie Jr, 'Rum Running, Property Rights and Prohibition Enforcement in Florida, 1921–1930' (1997) 5 *Journal of Southern Legal History* 99, 99.

[99] Berman (n 97) 5.

[100] Holmes (n 98) 9.

[101] *Austin v United States*, 509 US 602, 611–12 (1993).

The concept of deodand has been criticised.[102] Relatedly, Professor Albert Alschuler has argued that some contemporary justifications of corporate criminal liability simply involve treating a corporation as a deodand.[103] The position is not that simple, however, both in respect of corporations and in Admiralty. In both cases, the law's focus is upon a juristic person – a construct, constructed by law – and about the liability that the law confers upon it. In Admiralty, the action *in rem*, dependent upon the juristic entity of the ship, confers significant instrumental advantages that are facilitative of global trade. In regard to the corporation, the existence of corporate criminal liability is reflective of the recognition of corporate existence in law and, from an instrumental perspective, provides for the establishment of liability based upon the realities of corporate action; that is, the fact that a corporation can act in ways that are greater than the sum of its parts.

In early Vice-Admiralty courts, ships were treated as if endowed with personality and prosecutions were initiated against vessels by name. Holmes identifies this as the 'most remarkable transformation of this [the liability of inanimate things] principle'.[104] He wrote:

> A ship is the most living of inanimate things. Servants sometimes say 'she' of a clock, but everyone gives a gender to vessels. And we need not be surprised, therefore, to find a mode of dealing which has shown such extraordinary vitality in the criminal law applied with even more striking thoroughness in the Admiralty. It is only by supposing the ship to have been endowed with personality, that the arbitrary seeming peculiarities of the maritime law can be made intelligible, and on that supposition they at once become consistent and logical.[105]

The characteristic of the action *in rem* – that once a claim has been issued, it attaches to the ship and therefore survives a change in ownership – resonates with one justification for the modern recognition of the forfeiture tradition. The Supreme Court of the United States has recognised the difficulty in certain circumstances of tracking down the owner of an object that has caused harm and to determine whether the owner actually knew about the illegal activity.[106] In *Bennis v Michigan*, decided in 1996, the Supreme Court affirmed that forfeiture of an object, in this case a car, does not depend on proof that the owner knew or agreed that the object would be used in a proscribed manner. Chief Justice Rehnquist, delivering the judgment of the majority, held that 'a long and unbroken line of cases holds that an owner's interest in property may be forfeited by reason of the use to which the property is put even though the owner did not know that it was to be put to such use'.[107]

That line of cases commences with *The Palmyra*, itself an Admiralty matter, in which the ship had been commissioned as a privateer by the King of Spain and was ultimately

[102] See, eg, JH Baker, *An Introduction to English Legal History*, 4th edn (Oxford, Oxford University Press, 2007) 387.

[103] See AW Alschuler, 'Two Ways to Think about the Punishment of Corporations' (2009) 49 *American Criminal Law Review* 1359.

[104] Holmes (n 98) 25.

[105] ibid 26–27. See also, however, Holmes CJ's (as he then was) critique of personification doctrine: *Tyler v Judges of the Court of Registration*, 175 Mass 71 (1900).

[106] *Bennis v Michigan*, 516 US 442, 472 (1996); see also *Austin* (n 101) 616; *United States v Ursery*, 518 US 267, 275–76 (1996).

[107] *Bennis* (n 106) 446.

captured by a US warship. The Court rejected the owner's contention that the vessel could not be forfeited until he was convicted for the privateering. In delivering the judgment of the Court, Story J held:

> It is well known, that at the common law, in many cases of felonies … that in every case where the crown sought to recover such goods and chattels, it was indispensable to establish its right by producing the record of the judgment of conviction. In the contemplation of the common law, the offender's right was not devested until the conviction. But this doctrine never was applied to seizures and forfeitures, created by statute, *in rem*, cognizable on the revenue side of the Exchequer. *The thing here is primarily considered as the offender or rather, the offence is attached primarily to the thing*; and this whether the offence be *malum prohibitum* or *malum in se*. *The same principle applies to proceedings* in rem, *on seizures in Admiralty*. Many cases exist where the forfeiture for acts done attaches solely *in rem*, and there is no accompanying penalty *in personam*. Many cases exist where there is both a forfeiture in rem and a personal penalty. But in neither class of cases has it ever been decided that the prosecutions were dependent upon each other.[108]

Similarly, in *Harmony v United States*, a case concerned with forfeiture of the vessel and cargo on charges of piracy, Story J held:

> It is not an uncommon course in the admiralty, acting under the law of nations, to treat the vessel in which or by which, or by the master or crew thereof, a wrong or offence has been done as the offender, without any regard whatsoever to the personal misconduct or responsibility of the owner thereof … In short, the acts of the master and crew, in cases of this sort, bind the interest of the owner of the ship, whether he be innocent or guilty; and he impliedly submits to whatever the law denounces as a forfeiture attached to the ship by reason of their unlawful or wanton wrongs.[109]

X. Criminal Liability of Ships – To What End?

The history of both the civil and criminal Admiralty law suggests that not only is it possible but also entirely consistent with the development of the action *in rem* and the laws of forfeiture for the ship to be a proper defendant in circumstances where the ship is guilty of the offending conduct – for example, causing marine pollution or environmental damage,[110] or engaging in illegal fishing.[111]

If the owners of the offending ship are not amenable to the criminal jurisdiction of the courts, there should be no difficulty in prosecuting the ship itself and, upon conviction, its being forfeited to the crown *bona vacantia*. Indeed, a 1766 English case, *Mitchell qui tam v Torup*, proposed the prevention of the 'perpetual evasion' of the statute as the rationale for providing for the forfeiture of the ship without proof of the 'privity or consent of the master, mate or owners' in relation to a customs offence.[112]

[108] *The Palmyra*, 25 US (12 Wheat) 1, 14–15 (1827) (emphasis added).

[109] *Harmony v United States*, 2 How 210, 43 US (1844) 210, 233–34.

[110] Protection of the Sea (Prevention of Pollution from Ships) Act 1983 (Cth); Navigation Act 2012 (Cth).

[111] Fisheries Management Act 1991 (Cth) pt 6, div 6. See, eg, *Olbers v Commonwealth (No 4)* [2004] FCA 229, (2004) 136 FCR 67; *Director of Public Prosecutions (Cth), ex parte Lawler* [1994] HCA 10, (1994) 179 CLR 270; *Australian Fisheries Management Authority v Su* [2009] FCAFC 56, (2009) 176 FCR 95.

[112] *Mitchell qui tam v Torup* (1766) 145 ER 764, 766.

Therein lies the real function of being able to proceed in Admiralty against the ship itself – providing a mechanism for enforcement where the controllers of the vessel are otherwise beyond the jurisdiction. It is more about overcoming challenges with enforcement posed by corporate structures and the fact that the corporate owner is outside of the jurisdiction,[113] rather than the limitations of corporate attribution alone. In such circumstances, long-standing principles of Admiralty law provide a conceptual basis for proceeding against the vessel.

Concerns about effective enforcement have long been understood to underpin the rationale for the action *in rem* (and the concept of ship arrest) in civil Admiralty jurisdiction. More recently, Rares J described how

> [t]he *Admiralty Act* reflects long established principles of international maritime law developed by sea trading nations over millennia, to protect the interests of those who trade or have encounters with a peripatetic ship and those interested in her which may never again call in a port of the creditor's own jurisdiction.[114]

Accordingly, recognising the ability to proceed against a ship for criminal liabilities would not only be consistent with the history and theory of Admiralty, but would also be entirely consistent with the rationale for the processes of Admiralty jurisdiction and practice.

The remedy of forfeiture of the vessel is already provided for in legislation dealing with customs and excise, environmental pollution and port state control. The Fisheries Management Act 1991 (Cth), for example, provides that a court may order the forfeiture of a vessel used in the commission of an offence under that Act. A similar power is also available under the Migration Act 1958 (Cth) in relation to contraventions of that Act.[115]

So far as the recovery of any monetary fine or penalty is concerned, it is likely that the only feasible way to compel the appearance of a foreign owner who wished to have its ship released would be through the mechanism provided by the civil Admiralty jurisdiction. In the UK, section 20(2)(s) of the Senior Courts Act 1981 (UK) provides that an action *in rem* may be brought against the ship or property that relates to any claim for the forfeiture or condemnation of a ship or goods that are being or have been carried, or have been attempted to be carried, in a ship, or for the restoration of a ship or any such goods after seizure, or for droits of Admiralty. The Admiralty Act 1988 (Cth) does not have an equivalent to section 20(2)(s) of the Senior Courts Act. There may also be scope, with the necessary legislative amendments, to proceed by recourse to the detention power given to AMSA under some of the legislation that it administers.[116]

[113] The problems posed by defendants located outside of the jurisdiction have recently been the subject of substantial exploration in a civil context in several parent company liability cases in England: *Okpabi & Ors v Royal Dutch Shell Plc & Anor* [2021] UKSC 3, [2021] 1 WLR 1294; *Lungowe v Vedanta Resources plc* [2019] UKSC 20, [2020] AC 1045. Another example is *Begum v Maran (UK) Limited* [2021] EWCA Civ 326, which concerned whether an English ship manager that sold a ship for breaking up in Bangladesh could owe a duty of care to a worker killed during the shipbreaking.

[114] *Kim v Daebo International Shipping Co Ltd* [2015] FCA 684, (2015) 232 FCR 275 [14].

[115] Migration Act 1958 (Cth), s 261A. See, eg, *Saric v Commonwealth* [2018] FCA 1620, (2018) 266 FCR 469.

[116] See, eg, Navigation Act 2012 (Cth), ch 8, pt 3; Protection of the Sea (Prevention of Pollution from Ships) Act 1983 (Cth), s 27A.

It would seem that just as criminal prosecutions are not brought against deceased persons, neither should they subsist when a ship has been lost and become 'wreck'. Notorious examples of such circumstances include the *Torrey Canyon* (1967), the *Amoco Cadiz* (1978), the *Exxon Valdez* (1989), the *Erika* (1999) and the *Prestige* (2002). In cases such as these, unless the shipowner is amenable to the relevant criminal jurisdiction, it is unlikely that any criminal proceedings could be brought, regardless of the culpability of the shipowning corporation or the ship. In the first place, this would seem to be because once a 'wreck', a vessel is no longer a 'ship'.[117] Once a ship is wrecked – and no longer of value as a ship – the basis for proceeding against the vessel rather than the corporate owner recedes. Second, the consequences of wreck are subject to their own bespoke regulatory regimes, and it is not immediately clear how criminal liability as it is proposed in this chapter would cohere with those regimes.[118] Under Australian law, the 'registered owner' of a ship that is wrecked is liable for locating, marking and removing the wreck.[119] There are a number of distinct maritime and regulatory imperatives associated with wreck that might, potentially, be seen as superseding the public interest in prosecuting a vessel for crimes committed.

So, just as with corporations generally, there is no single solution to seeking appropriate redress in circumstances where a shipowner, manager or operator fails in the duties imposed upon them to ensure the safety of the vessel and the crew and to avoid pollution and damage to the environment. The consequences of such failures can seldom be avoided, even by a competent master and crew. The weight of denunciation and condemnation of the conduct constituting the offence should not be borne by the 'scapegoats for actions over which they have no or only very limited control'.[120] That weight should be borne by the culpable corporations, and, if the law cannot reach them, by the ship itself – consistent with the history and practice of the Admiralty jurisdiction over the centuries.

[117] For discussion of the meaning of 'wreck' in maritime law, see C Forrest and N Gaskell, *The Law of Wreck* (London, Informa, 2019) 211–13.

[118] In an international context, the Nairobi International Convention on the Removal of Wrecks, opened for signature 18 May 2007 (entered into force 15 April 2015) (Nairobi Wreck Removal Convention). Australia is not, at time of writing, a state party to the Nairobi Wreck Removal Convention.

[119] Navigation Act 2012 (Cth), s 232. If the Nairobi Wreck Removal Convention were to be implemented in Australia, AMSA would acquire a right to proceed against the insurer of a shipowner (including foreign shipowners) in respect of wreck-removal costs: see N Gaskell and C Forrest, *Australia's Accession to the Nairobi International Convention on the Removal of Wrecks 2007* (Submission, September 2020) 4.

[120] Gold (n 52) 252–53.

17

Culpable Executives

PAMELA HANRAHAN

I. Introduction

Lawmakers have always struggled with the problem of how to attribute fault to a large corporation when blameworthiness for its unlawful conduct is dispersed across the many systems, norms, practices and people that comprise the corporate actor.

The same conceptual difficulty gets in the way of holding individual executives to account in connection with corporate lawbreaking. When lawbreaking is an emergent property of a large business corporation, rather than the linear consequence of an act or choice of an identifiable individual, punishing one (human) person for the sins of the collective runs into some of the most basic concerns of liberal jurisprudence. The problem of what to do when all are complicit and none are directly responsible is hardly new,[1] nor confined to the corporate sphere.[2] But the perceived accountability deficit in relation to corporate executives has been the subject of renewed debate since the financial crisis of 2008, and is now an important area of focus for legislatures and law-reform bodies around the world, including the Australian Law Reform Commission (ALRC) on whose work parts of this analysis builds.[3]

[1] The literature is extensive. A useful place to start with is with B Fisse and J Braithwaite, 'The Allocation of Responsibility for Corporate Crime: Individualism, Collectivism and Accountability' (1988) 11 *Sydney Law Review* 468. Recent contributions include L Freeburn and I Ramsay, 'The Recent Australian Debate About Individual Liability for the Criminal Misconduct of Corporations' (2021) 42 *Business Law Review* 214; M Lewis, 'Corporate and Individual Accountability for Foreign Bribery – An Analysis of Diverging Enforcement Approaches' (2022) 37 *Australian Journal of Corporate Law* 114.

[2] Similar issues arise in other institutional settings, for example in the military. For a discussion of the problem of culpability in the chain of command in international criminal law, see eg D Robinson, 'How Command Responsibility Got So Complicated: A Culpability Contradiction, Its Obfuscation, and a Simple Solution' (2012) 13 *Melbourne Journal of International Law* 1; JL Root, 'Some Other Men's Rea: The Nature of Command Responsibility in the Rome Statute' (2013–4) 23 *Journal of Transnational Law and Policy* 119. See n 70 and the accompanying text.

[3] See Australian Law Reform Commission, *Principled Regulation: Federal Civil & Administrative Penalties in Australia* (Report No 95, 2002) (ALRC Report No 95); Australian Law Reform Commission, *Traditional Rights and Freedoms – Encroachments by Commonwealth Laws* (Report No 129, 2016) (ALRC Report No 129); Australian Law Reform Commission, *Corporate Criminal Responsibility* (Report No 136, April 2020) (ALRC Report No 136). In the United Kingdom (UK) in 2013, the Parliamentary Commission on Banking Standards concluded that senior executives in banks operated in an environment of 'insufficient personal responsibility'

At a hearing of the United States (US) Senate Banking Committee into the cross-selling scandal at Wells Fargo & Company in 2016, Senator Elizabeth Warren challenged its then Chairman and Chief Executive Officer (CEO) on his lack of accountability, concluding:

> The only way that Wall Street will change is if executives face jail time when they preside over massive frauds. We need tough new laws to hold corporate executives personally accountable and we need tough prosecutors who have the courage to go after people at the top. Until then, it will be business as usual. And at giant banks like Wells Fargo that seems to mean cheating as many customers, investors and employees as they possibly can.[4]

Senator Warren's frustration was with the apparent lack of accountability for very senior executives who 'preside over' – rather than engage directly in – corporate lawbreaking.

Culpable executives – that is, those deserving of blame – ought to be held to account when corporations break the law. Individual culpability is obvious if the executive plans and carries out the wrongdoing or critical elements of it. But is someone who deliberately engineers or allows work systems that facilitate or permit lawbreaking, or a corporate culture that tolerates or rationalises it, equally culpable? What about a senior executive whose conduct is not deliberate or reckless, nor even negligent? What about someone whose role and influence in the corporation was more remotely connected – either managerially or temporally – to the lawbreaking? Are they culpable too?

Clearly, penalising individual executives in connection with corporate lawbreaking can be justified where their own conduct is deserving of retribution and denunciation. Individuals are punished for what they do (or fail to do) as a result of their own choices when it infringes accepted norms. Just deserts as a design principle is particularly important where, as in many instances of corporate lawbreaking, the culpable individuals are wealthy and politically powerful and might otherwise be perceived as being beyond the reach of the law, including because their personal conduct is shielded by the veil of incorporation. Denunciation of wrongful conduct helps protect public confidence in, and respect for, corporate law and regulation and the economic and political system it underpins.

However, penalties are also legitimately used to deter unwanted behaviour, not just to punish it. Deterrence is at the centre of many regulatory regimes and the enforcement tools (including civil penalties) that support them.[5] In the corporate context, the end goal is to deter executives from engaging in behaviours that cause corporate

and that top bankers 'dodged accountability for failings on their watch by claiming ignorance or hiding behind collective decision-making': Parliamentary Commission on Banking Standards (UK), *Changing Banking for Good* (June 2013) vol 1, 9.

[4] US Senate Banking Committee, Hearing (20 September 2016). The Chairman and CEO Mr Stumpf later forfeited approximately US$70 million in equity, bonuses and salary to Wells Fargo. He entered into consent orders with the US Office of the Comptroller of the Currency in January 2020, agreeing to a civil penalty of US$17.5 million and an indefinite banning order from managing regulated institutions: see Office of the Comptroller of the Currency, 'Consent Order #2020-004' (22 January 2020) at www.occ.gov/static/enforcement-actions/ea2020-004.pdf. In November 2020 he settled with the Securities and Exchange Commission (SEC) for contraventions of the securities laws by paying a civil penalty of US$2.5 million into the Fair Fund established to remediate the Wells Fargo losses: see Securities and Exchange Commission, 'Release No 10887' (13 November 2020) at www.sec.gov/litigation/admin/2020/33-10887.pdf.

[5] For a recent discussion by the High Court of Australia of civil penalties in regulation, see *Australian Building and Construction Commissioner v Pattinson* [2022] HCA 13, (2022) 399 ALR 599 (*Pattinson*).

lawbreaking. This approach assumes two things – that an executive can recognise their own risky acts or omissions and adjust their behaviour in advance, and that the resulting change in that executive's behaviour will divert or disrupt the corporation's lawbreaking.

A third possible rationale for penalising executives is related to deterrence but is slightly different. It is that by threatening individual executives with penalties in connection with corporate lawbreaking, the law co-opts those executives to act as internal regulators of the corporation's culture and conduct. In other words, the purpose is not to deter the executive from doing an (otherwise) proscribed act, but to encourage or incentivise the executive to take steps in relation to corporate compliance that they would not otherwise take. I call this the 'enrolment' rationale. The enrolment rationale underlies most forms of strict liability.[6] The line between deterrence and enrolment is not always clear.

This chapter explores how law might frame individual executives' legal liability as a regulatory strategy for reducing the incidence of future lawbreaking by large business corporations. It is less concerned with punishing conduct where the executive is a co-offender with the corporation, or where their involvement in the lawbreaking is sufficiently culpable and connected to the wrongful conduct that they are an accessory in the orthodox sense. In these situations, the applicable legal principles and their deontological foundations are (relatively) clear and the problem is essentially one of enforcement.[7] Instead, the chapter focuses on whether individual executives should be punished (or threatened with punishment) for corporate lawbreaking that occurs on their watch, where their participation was either less culpable or more remote, or both, than co-offending or accessorial involvement entails. And in particular, it explores the trade-offs in using this instrumental form of legal liability as a means of incentivising corporate executives *as a class* to exhibit improved risk-management behaviour.

It is important to note at the outset that legal liability (discussed in this chapter) is one of three legs of the 'tripod' of norms that supports sound decision making by corporate executives. The other legs – ethical responsibility and commercial accountability – are equally important. Legal liability has its place in shaping future behaviours but should not crowd out these other mechanisms and norms. Arguably, commercial accountability to the company and its shareholders – resulting in, for example, executives associated with corporate misconduct being stripped of bonuses, demoted, side-lined or fired – has strengthened in recent years, reflecting the increasing concern of institutional and retail shareholders with the environmental, social and governance (ESG) performance of the companies in which they invest.[8]

The chapter is organised as follows. This section introduces the problem and defines its scope. Section II describes the three main techniques currently used to impose

[6] See *He Kaw Teh v The Queen* [1985] HCA 43, (1985) 157 CLR 523, 566-67 (Brennan J) (*He Kaw Teh*). The enrolment rationale is explained in section IV.

[7] The enforcement problem has two dimensions. The first is the willingness, capacity and resources of enforcement agencies to bring proceedings against individual officers. Senator Warren alludes to this problem. The second is the evidentiary difficulty of proving the required physical and fault elements to establish individual liability in the context of corporate offending.

[8] This is only arguable. For a discussion of the commercial accountability of senior executives at Rio Tinto Ltd following the destruction of an internationally significant cultural heritage site at Juukan Gorge in Western Australia in May 2020, see Joint Standing Committee on Northern Australia, *A Way Forward: Final Report into the Destruction of Indigenous Heritage Sites at Juukan Gorge* (October 2021).

role-related legal liability on executives for corporate lawbreaking – direct, extended accessorial and extended managerial (derivative) liability. It sets up a simple conceptual model for understanding the different modes. Section III expands the discussion by reference to two recent Australian proposals for reforming executive accountability. The first is a proposal put forward by the ALRC in 2020, and subsequently abandoned, to create a generic form of extended managerial liability for corporate compliance failures. The second is the draft Financial Accountability Regime (FAR) for executives in prudentially regulated institutions.

Sections IV and V contain analysis and conclusions. The focus is on the culpability of executives for dysfunctional cultures that create the conditions for corporate lawbreaking. It is pointed out that the different forms of role-related liability can result in executives' facing penalties in connection with corporate lawbreaking in circumstances where their conduct was less culpable or their causal connection to the lawbreaking was more remote. This involves significant trade-offs with individual rights and freedoms protected by liberal jurisprudence. In Report No 136, the ALRC argued:

> Recognition of the role directors and senior managers play in creating and maintaining corporate cultures conducive to wrongdoing highlights the potential blameworthiness of such individuals in relation to ensuing misconduct, potentially justifying a different approach to mechanisms apportioning liability to them.[9]

But as the discussion demonstrates, the normative foundations for a different approach remain elusive.

A. The Scope of the Discussion

The chapter is about imposing *penalties* on *executives* in connection with *corporate lawbreaking*. Those three concepts require some elaboration.

Penalties refers to monetary and other sanctions imposed by or on the application of the state, as distinct from legal consequences that arise between private parties (such as between the executive and their company in tort or contract). The nature of penalties differs between different legal systems; for present purposes, I include criminal penalties (generally, imprisonment or fines), civil pecuniary penalties, administrative penalties and disqualification or banning orders.[10]

Executives is intended to refer to people who have senior managerial responsibility for the part or parts of the corporation where lawbreaking occurs. It includes people who are usually described as key managerial personnel (KMP) in accounting and reporting standards; it is wider than the general law concept of an 'officer' of the corporation.[11] In large corporations, it likely includes division heads and is not limited to C-Suite staff who report directly to the CEO or the board. Of course, who should be treated as an executive for the purposes of different regimes is highly contested. I will keep the analysis broad, while noting how recently proposed or adopted senior manager responsibility (SMR) regimes

[9] ALRC Report No 136 (n 3) [9.11].
[10] See ALRC Report No 95 (n 3).
[11] The corporation's officers at general law are its directors (including de jure and de facto directors) and those who exert significant decision-making control over the whole of the corporation's operations.

in the financial sector deal with the issue of scope.[12] However, I deliberately exclude non-executive directors, to whom different policy considerations apply.

Corporate lawbreaking refers to conduct that contravenes a law or regulation to which the corporation itself is subject, and that is enforceable by the state and punishable with a penalty. It captures both criminal offending and civil contraventions, where that conduct on the part of the corporation would attract a significant corporate penalty.[13]

II. Techniques for Executive Liability

This section explains the legislative techniques typically used to penalise executives in connection with corporate lawbreaking. Making executives legally liable for corporate lawbreaking is not difficult doctrinally if there is a legislative desire to do so. That is a different question from when it is defensible as a matter of theory.

Mechanisms for officers' accountability have been debated extensively in Australia since at least the 1980s. Key milestones include the report of the Senate Standing Committee on Legal and Constitutional Affairs on company directors' duties (1989),[14] the Corporate Law Economic Reform Program (CLERP) paper on directors' duties and corporate governance (1997),[15] the ALRC report on civil and administrative penalties (2002),[16] the Rethinking Regulation Taskforce (2006),[17] the Corporations and Markets Advisory Committee (CAMAC) report on personal liability for corporate fault (2005–06),[18] the Treasury review of sanctions in corporate law (2007),[19] the Council of Australian Governments' (COAG) work on personal liability for corporate fault (2009) (COAG Principles),[20] the inquiry of the Parliamentary Joint Committee on Corporations and Financial Services into personal liability reform (2012),[21] and the Australian Securities and Investments Commission (ASIC) Enforcement Review Taskforce (2017).[22] Despite this significant body of work, there is still no unified approach or real consensus, beyond the COAG Principles for criminal liability, as to what is appropriate.

The next key milestone was the ALRC report on corporate criminal responsibility, which includes (in chapter 9) a comprehensive review of individual liability mechanisms

[12] See n 52.

[13] This is just to exclude minor and technical offences and regulatory infractions, of which there are many.

[14] Senate Standing Committee on Legal and Constitutional Affairs, *Company Directors' Duties* (Report, November 1989).

[15] The Treasury Corporate Law Economic Reform Program, *Directors' Duties and Corporate Governance* (Paper No 3, 1 April 1997).

[16] ALRC Report No 95 (n 3).

[17] The Treasury Taskforce on Reducing Regulatory Burdens on Business, *Rethinking Regulation* (Final Report, January 2006).

[18] Corporations and Markets Advisory Committee, *Personal Liability for Corporate Fault* (Discussion Paper, May 2005); Corporations and Markets Advisory Committee, *Personal Liability for Corporate Fault* (Final Report, September 2006) (CAMAC Report).

[19] The Treasury, *Review of Sanctions in Corporate Law* (2007).

[20] Council of Australian Governments, *Personal Liability for Corporate Fault – Guidelines for Applying the COAG Principles* (2012) (COAG Principles).

[21] Parliamentary Joint Committee on Corporations and Financial Services, *Inquiry into the Personal Liability for Corporate Fault Reform Bill 2012 (Cth)* (Report, 2012).

[22] The Treasury, *ASIC Enforcement Review Taskforce Report* (Report, December 2017).

that could result in Australian executives' being subject to criminal or civil penalties in connection with corporate lawbreaking at the federal level.[23]

Its Report No 136, released in 2020, includes a useful table, reproduced in this chapter as Table 17.1.[24] There are nuances and complexities in each of the categories used in the table, but the simplicity of the analytical structure adopted by the ALRC is useful.

Table 17.1 ALRC classification of modes of liability

Mode of liability	Primary (direct) liability *Does not require separate finding of corporate crime or contravention*	Extensions of liability *Require finding of corporate crime or contravention as first step*	
		Accessorial liability *Requires knowledge of the essential facts and intention to participate in the crime or contravention*	Extended management liability *Derivative liability of management beyond ordinary principles of accessorial liability*
General	Liability for active commission of an offence or contravention (liability may or may not be concurrent with the corporation)	Criminal Code complicity (and common law and statutory equivalents as applicable in the states and territories) Provisions extending civil penalty liability to those 'involved in' contraventions Other specific criminal and civil statutory provisions based on criminal complicity liability principles	
Role-related	Statutory directors' and officers' duties (including using the stepping-stone approach) Other duty-based offences and contraventions	Specific role-related statutory accessorial liability provisions	Statutory deemed liability provisions (including designated officer liability provisions) Statutory failure to prevent provisions

[23] ALRC Report No 136 (n 3) Ch 9.

[24] ARLC Report No 136 (n 3) Table 9-1. The table explains modes of liability under Australian law. The reference to 'stepping stones' is to an enforcement strategy pursued by the ASIC that uses civil penalty proceedings for breach of an officer's statutory duty of care, to penalise officers whose negligent conduct has exposed their company to a foreseeable risk of harm resulting from a potential or actual compliance or disclosure breach by the company. The literature on stepping stones is extensive. See generally A Herzberg and H Anderson, 'Stepping Stones: From Corporate Fault to Directors' Personal Civil Liability' (2012) 40 *Federal Law Review* 181; P Hanrahan and T Bednall, 'From Stepping-Stones to Throwing Stones: Officers' Liability for Corporate Compliance Failures after *Cassimatis*' (2021) 49 *Federal Law Review* 380.

This chapter focuses on role-related forms of executive accountability, summarised in the second row of Table 17.1. However, it is worth saying something about the 'general' modes of liability described in the first row of the ALRC table, before putting them to one side. These rules apply to all the world; as a matter of law any person – not just an executive – could be liable as a co-offender or an accessory to corporate (or anyone else's) lawbreaking if the necessary legal elements are made out. For direct liability this will usually involve proving the physical elements and the fault elements[25] (if any) of the offence or contravention against the individual personally, as well as or instead of against the corporation.[26] For accessorial liability, this usually requires proving the legal elements of knowing and intentional participation by the alleged accessory. For example, under Australian law, the accessory must have had knowledge of the essential elements of the contravention or offence, and through their conduct (by act or omission) have been directly implicated or involved in it.[27] This legal test describes the factual circumstances in which one autonomous person ought to be liable for the acts of another autonomous person.

A co-offender or accessory commits the same offence or contravention as the corporation and is punishable accordingly.[28] The law treats them as equally culpable – that is, as committing the same crime or contravention.

In contrast, role-related liability in connection with corporate lawbreaking arises because a different – usually more exacting – standard has been imposed on a person *because of* the role they occupy in a corporation. They are no longer treated the same as all the world; they can be liable in connection with corporate lawbreaking in situations when others whose conduct is identical (for example, those external to the corporation or occupying a different role in the corporate hierarchy) are not. This is not a trivial observation – it goes to the important questions of law design that are explored in section IV of this chapter.

The ALRC's work identifies three sub-categories of role-related liability – direct, accessorial and extended managerial. Extended managerial liability is sometimes referred to as 'derivative' liability because it derives from the office the person occupies.

Direct forms of liability impose a specific duty on an executive to do (or not do) something, and they are subject to a penalty if they breach that duty. Their liability is independent of the corporation's – that is, the penalty does not depend on first establishing that the corporation broke the law.

[25] The language is drawn from the Australian federal criminal law and corresponds roughly to the notions of actus reus and mens rea. The physical elements are the conduct making up the offence or contravention – conduct may involve an act, an omission to act or a state of affairs. The fault elements relate to states of mind – knowledge, intention, recklessness, negligence. Strict or absolute liability provisions do not require proof of a fault element (the difference is that strict liability allows for a defence of mistake of fact, but absolute liability does not).

[26] Of course, this kind of liability can only arise whether the law, on its face, can apply to both a corporation and a natural person. If the relevant law applies to 'a corporation', an individual cannot contravene it and any liability they have will be accessorial instead.

[27] The principle is explained, for Australia, in *Yorke v Lucas* [1985] HCA 65, (1985) 158 CLR 661, 670. See Justice A Black, 'Directors' Statutory and General Law Accessory Liability for Corporate Wrongdoing' (2013) 31 *Company and Securities Law Journal* 511. The prosecutor must show that the individual knew the essential facts that constitute the corporate lawbreaking and, through his or her own act or omission, was a participant in it.

[28] In many jurisdictions the maximum penalty for a corporation will be larger than that for an individual who commits the same offence – see, eg, Corporations Act 2001 (Cth) (Corporations Act), ss 1311B and 1311C (for criminal penalties) and Corporations Act, s 1317G(3) and (4) (for civil pecuniary penalties).

For example, an 'officer' of an Australian corporation (including a director) is subject to a statutory duty to 'exercise their powers and discharge their duties with the degree of care and diligence that a reasonable person would exercise' if they were a director of a corporation in the corporation's circumstances and occupied the office held by, and had the same responsibilities within the corporation as, them.[29] The duty cannot be excluded by the corporate constitution and breach of the statutory duty cannot be ratified by the corporation. The duty is a 'civil penalty provision', meaning the corporate regulator can bring enforcement proceedings in civil court if the officer contravenes the duty.[30] If, by their negligence, an officer exposes their corporation to foreseeable harm that would result from the corporation's breaking the law (for example, enforcement action or reputational harm), the officer can be penalised for breach of the statutory duty, regardless of whether the lawbreaking actually occurred or was proved against the corporation.[31]

These types of direct liability provisions are often framed as 'reasonable care' or 'reasonable steps' requirements – for example, a duty on an identified person or class of persons to take 'reasonable steps' to 'ensure' that a particular outcome (generally, corporate compliance) is achieved. The enforcement agency bears the (criminal or civil, as the case may be) burden of proof that the person's conduct fell short of what was reasonable in the circumstances.

The second sub-category of role-related liability is 'extended accessorial' liability. This may be relevant in two situations. The first is where the law to which the corporation is subject does not otherwise provide for accessorial liability. General accessorial liability applies to all Commonwealth crimes in Australia and to all civil penalty provisions in the Corporations Act, but there are other civil penalty regimes where this is not the case.[32] Where general accessorial liability does not apply, legislation could provide that the persons described contravene the section if they aid or abet the corporation in its lawbreaking.

The second is where, in a particular instance, a policy decision is made to treat the executive as an accessory in situations where their involvement falls short of that required to establish accessorial liability in the ordinary sense. The best-known example of this kind of role-related extended accessorial liability is command (superior) responsibility in international criminal law. In Australia, this is reflected in the Criminal Code Act 1995 (Cth), under which a military commander is criminally responsible for war crimes committed by forces 'under his or her effective command and control … as a result of his or her failure to exercise control properly over those forces'. Liability arises where the commander knew or was reckless as to whether the forces were committing or about to commit such offences, and 'failed to take all necessary and reasonable measures within

[29] ibid s 180(1).

[30] ASIC has standing under the Corporations Act, pt 9.4B to apply for a 'declaration of contravention'; and if the contravention is made out and is serious, civil pecuniary penalties of up to AUD 1,050,000 apply. A person who contravenes a civil penalty provision may also be disqualified from managing corporations under the Corporations Act, s 206C.

[31] See, eg, *Cassimatis v Australian Securities and Investments Commission* [2020] FCFCA 52, (2020) 275 FCR 533.

[32] See Criminal Code 1995 (Cth), s 11(2) (Criminal Code) and Corporations Act (n 28), ss 1317E(4)(b), 79. Prior to 2018, accessorial liability for contraventions of civil penalty provisions in the Corporations Act arose only where it was explicitly included in the substantive provision.

his or her power to prevent or repress their commission or to submit the matter to the competent authorities for investigation and prosecution'.[33] That is, the commander is liable *as if they were the perpetrator*, based on their failure to prevent or punish, rather than their participation in or furtherance of the crime itself. This is conceptually distinct from a stand-alone 'failure to prevent' offence discussed below, because it treats the commander as equally culpable – in every sense – with the actual perpetrator.

In the corporate context, it would be open to legislators to create a form of extended accessorial liability that recognises a more remote causal connection between the executive's act (or failure to act) and the corporation's lawbreaking than the general law requires, particularly for civil contraventions rather than non-trivial criminal offences.[34] For example, it would be open to legislators to extend accessorial liability for a civil contravention by a corporation to any executive (however defined) who failed to take all necessary and reasonable measures within his or her power to prevent the corporation's (proven) contravention.[35]

The third sub-category of role-related executive liability is 'extended managerial' liability, which depends on the role the person occupies and not on their culpability or causal connection with the corporate lawbreaking. In this model, a person who occupies a designated role is subject to a penalty if the corporation breaks the relevant law; this may or may not operate subject to defences under which the executive bears an evidential burden (Type 2) or a legal burden (Type 3). Deemed liability provisions that do not include a due diligence or reasonable steps defence are referred to as (Type 1).[36]

The ALRC table gives two examples of extended managerial liability – statutory deemed liability provisions and statutory failure-to-prevent provisions. Statutory deemed liability provisions say that, if the corporation breaks the law, a person who occupies a designated role in that corporation also breaks the law. For example, if an Australian corporation fails to meet specified statutory reporting obligations, the company secretary automatically contravenes the Corporations Act.[37] This is subject to a defence of 'reasonable steps' to ensure compliance, where the defendant carries the legal burden of proof.[38] Deemed criminal liability provisions are subject to intergovernmental agreement in Australia, designed to discourage their use.[39]

The other form of extended managerial liability mentioned in the ALRC table is 'failure to prevent'. The ALRC has said that

> this model is not a method of attribution, but rather involves the creation of a specific, separate offence of failing to prevent certain conduct. Being convicted of a failure to prevent offence implies a different type of culpability than being directly responsible for the primary offence.[40]

[33] Criminal Code (n 32), s 268.115(2).

[34] Trivial criminal offences committed by corporations include filing failures and the like, which are often strict liability and carry small fines.

[35] See T Bednall and P Hanrahan, 'Officers' Liability for Mandatory Corporate Disclosure: Two Paths, Two Destinations?' (2013) 31 *Company & Securities Law Journal* 474.

[36] COAG Principles (n 20).

[37] Corporations Act (n 28), s 188(1).

[38] ibid s 188(2).

[39] COAG Principles (n 20).

[40] ALRC Report No 136 (n 3) [7.63].

This distinguishes it from the sort of extended accessorial liability that we see in command responsibility. This approach can be used to make a corporation liable for failing to prevent offending by a 'rogue' employee or agent (for example, bribery). But it could also be adopted to make a designated individual liable for failure to prevent offending by the corporation.

The different forms of liability can be mapped on a simple model, with fault on the vertical axis and causal connection to the lawbreaking on the horizontal axis (see Figure 17.1). Orthodox involvement liability is in the upper-right quadrant, and deemed liability is in the lower-left quadrant.

Figure 17.1 Models of liability

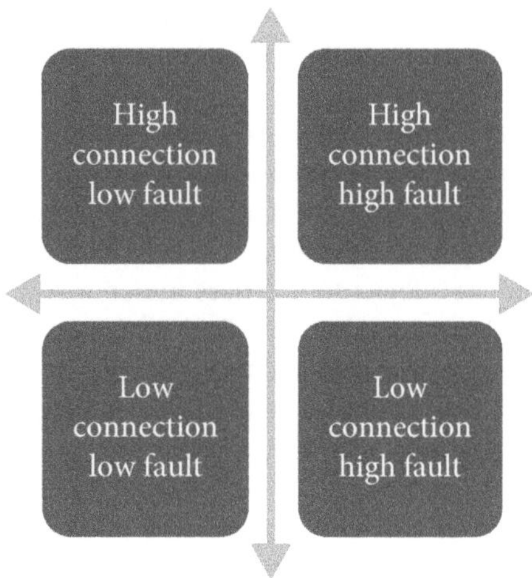

'Fault' describes the culpability of the executive, on a sliding scale from none, through negligence, to intentional or reckless conduct (including knowing involvement). Of course, strict liability and liability for negligence do not require proof that the defendant was aware of the circumstances or likely results of the conduct that gave rise to it. On the vertical axis, causal connection to the corporate lawbreaking can range from none (where liability depends solely on the person's having occupied a particular office or role, regardless of what they did or failed to do in connection with the lawbreaking), to tangential or indirect involvement (for example, creating or allowing the conditions for lawbreaking), to direct or 'but for' involvement (for example, ordinary common law causation), to situations where the executive personally commits the act that constitutes the corporation's lawbreaking.

There are some other variables at play in law design that it is important to point out. The first is whether an executive can know in advance whether they are a person to whom the liability regime applies, or whether that can only be ascertained after the event. This turns on how the category of person to whom the rule is applied is defined. The second is whether the penalty applied to the executive is criminal, civil or administrative. This is important because of the differences in the rights and protections afforded to defendants, including in the applicable legal process rules of evidence and procedure and in the standard of proof required to impose a penalty. I mention in section IV the significant expansion of the use of civil penalties against individuals in business regulation this century, and the human rights implications of this expansion. The third variable concerns the burden of proof. For non-lawyers, the difference between saying someone is guilty if it is proved they did not discharge a requirement (for example, to take 'reasonable steps') and that they are assumed to be guilty unless they can satisfy a legal or evidential burden that they discharged that requirement may seem like a lawyers' quibble. Of course it is anything but. I return to these matters in section IV.

III. Two Recent Australian Proposals

This section briefly explains two recent Australian proposals for expanding executive liability. The first is the ALRC's 'Proposals 9 and 10' (which were rejected following consultation) and the second is the FAR, an expanded SMR regime that (if enacted) will apply to executives in prudentially regulated financial institutions.

A. ALRC Proposals 9 and 10

As part of its work on the broader theme of corporate criminal responsibility, the ALRC put forward two proposals in 2019 that 'aimed to simplify the imposition of individual liability [in connection with corporate lawbreaking] and to address concerns that accountability was not sufficiently focused on management as opposed to boards'.[41] The proposals were contained in the ALRC's Discussion Paper 87 and arrived at following a detailed analysis of the existing position in 25 Commonwealth regulatory statutes.[42]

Proposal 9 was that the Corporations Act

> should be amended to provide that, when a body corporate commits a relevant offence, or engages in conduct the subject of a relevant offence provision, any officer who was in a position to influence the conduct of the body corporate in relation to the contravention is subject to a civil penalty, unless the officer proves that the officer took reasonable measures to prevent the contravention.

Proposal 10 was related: that the Act should also 'be amended to include an offence of engaging intentionally, knowingly, or recklessly in conduct the subject of a civil penalty provision as set out in Proposal 9'. A 'relevant offence' was likely to be a (serious) criminal offence, and the rule would apply if the corporation engaged in conduct the subject of such a provision (that is, whether or not it was convicted).

[41] ibid [9.166]. The proposals and the criticisms of them are outlined in Freeburn and Ramsay (n 1).

[42] Australian Law Reform Commission, *Corporate Criminal Responsibility* (Discussion Paper No 87, 2019) Proposals 9 and 10.

The ALRC described these proposals as adopting a 'failure to prevent' model. It argued:

> [W]here a senior officer of a corporation was not an accessory, a conspirator, or otherwise knowingly involved in the contravention, even though they may have been in a position to influence the conduct and therefore prevent the contravention, they will not be liable as an accessory. The proposals therefore aim to complement the accessorial liability regime by ensuring that senior officers who were in a position to influence, and therefore prevent, misconduct, can be liable if they fail to take reasonable measures to ensure compliance.[43]

Proposals 9 and 10 did not proceed beyond the consultation stage. The ALRC noted in its Report No 136 that 'they did not receive support. Of the 19 submissions addressing the Proposals directly, only four supported the Proposals, one expressed qualified support, and 14 did not support them.'[44] Most of the lawyers, judges and legal academics who made submissions on Proposals 9 and 10 opposed them. For example, a senior judge of the Court of Appeal in New South Wales noted that Proposal 9 'would make any person who has the "capacity to influence the corporation's conduct" in relation to the contravention subject to a civil penalty, unless the person proves that he or she took reasonable measures to prevent the contravention', and that:

> Every person the subject of Proposals 9 and 10 (and in some corporations that may amount to hundreds of people) will potentially have the legal burden to prove that he or she took reasonable measures to prevent the contravention. This reversal of the onus [of] proof in such a significant area would be one of the most dramatic erosions of civil liberties in Australia in my legal lifetime.[45]

Interestingly, the Australian Competition and Consumer Commission (ACCC) was a supporter, but ASIC was not. The ACCC's support points directly to the enrolment rationale – it argued that the provision 'would encourage senior officers to be more proactive in ensuring their businesses do not engage in corporate misconduct'.[46]

Overall, Proposals 9 and 10 failed based on two important considerations. The first was that the category of persons to whom it would apply was too broad and too vague; it is likely that the executives who had the 'capacity to influence' the lawbreaking conduct could not be ascertained except with the benefit of hindsight. Therefore, unlike the proposed FAR and other SMR regimes in the financial sector, an individual executive may not know that they are subject to the law until after the corporate lawbreaking has occurred.[47] The second was because it reversed the burden of proof – an executive would be assumed to have contravened the law if the corporation engaged in conduct 'the subject of a relevant offence provision', unless they could prove they

[43] ibid [7.132].
[44] ALRC Report No 136 (n 3) [9.168].
[45] Justice AJ Payne, 'Comment on ALRC Discussion Paper 87' (Submission, 13 January 2020) at www.alrc.gov.au/wp-content/uploads/2019/08/19-Public-Justice-T-Payne_Redacted.pdf.
[46] ALRC Report No 136 (n 3) [9.169].
[47] A similar issue may arise for duties (such as the statutory duty of care in the Corporations Act) imposed directly on officers, given the functional nature of the definition in the legislation; see *Australian Securities and Investments Commission v King* [2020] HCA 4, (2020) 270 CLR 1.

took 'reasonable measures' to prevent it. The penalties potentially involved for executives (over AUD 1,000,000 in pecuniary penalties and disqualification from managing corporations) were significant. These two considerations clearly impact on the rights (including the human rights) of executives who would be subject to the rule, for the reasons explained in section IV.

B. The FAR

The FAR is a proposal to extend the current SMR regime that applies to executives in Australian financial institutions. Australia's current SMR regime – known as the Banking Executive Accountability Regime (BEAR) – applies to authorised deposit-taking institutions regulated by the Australian Prudential Regulation Authority (APRA) and was included in the Banking Act 1959 (Cth) in February 2018.[48] The Financial Accountability Regime Bill 2022 (Cth) (FAR Bill), if enacted, will increase the range of financial institutions to which an SMR regime is applied and alter the accountability of all executives (including bank executives currently covered by the FAR) who are subject to it.[49]

Senior manager responsibility regimes exist in other jurisdictions[50] and the literature on them is emerging.[51] The reasons why they are considered necessary for financial institutions (but not other systemically significant networked businesses, for example, in the technology sector) is a question for another day. Some are based on a 'failure to prevent' model, but the FAR is a duties-based model under which named executives are subject to 'accountability obligations' that relate to corporate compliance with legislation and can be penalised for failure to meet them.

[48] The relationship between the BEAR and Proposals 9 and 10 is explained in Australian Law Reform Commission, 'The Banking Executive Accountability Regime: An Alternative Model of Individual Liability for Corporate Fault' (Release, 19 December 2019) at www.alrc.gov.au/news/the-banking-executive-accountability-regime-an-alternative-model-of-individual-liability-for-corporate-fault/.

[49] Financial Accountability Regime Bill 2022 (Cth) (FAR Bill). The FAR Bill was introduced in September 2022. It replaced an earlier bill (introduced in November 2021) that did not pass before (and therefore lapsed when) the 46th Parliament was prorogued for an election in May 2022. The earlier bill was reviewed in Senate Economics Legislation Committee, 'Financial Accountability Regime Bill 2021 [Provisions], Financial Sector Reform (Hayne Royal Commission Response No 3) Bill 2021 [Provisions], Financial Services Compensation Scheme of Last Resort Levy Bill 2021 [Provisions], and Financial Services Compensation Scheme of Last Resort Levy (Collection) Bill 2021' (Report, February 2022) at www.aph.gov.au/Parliamentary_Business/Committees/Senate/Economics/FinAccountabilityRegime/Report. The Committee's report indicated broad bipartisan acceptance of the FAR proposals.

[50] Including the UK senior manager and certification regime (SM&CR) reviewed in Bank of England Prudential Regulation Authority, *Evaluation of the Senior Managers and Certification Regime* (Report, December 2020) and the Hong Kong manager in charge (MIC) regime.

[51] See ibid; Australian Prudential Regulation Authority, *Implementation of the Banking Executive Accountability Regime* (Information Paper, 11 December 2020); D Wishart, A Wardrop and M McMahon, 'The Internal Autonomy of the Firm' (2018) 27 *Griffith Law Review* 131, 134; E Sheedy and D Canestrari-Soh, 'Regulating Accountability: An Early Look at the Banking Executive Accountability Regime' (Article, 2 February 2021) at https://ssrn.com/abstract=3775275; K Anat and A Kokkinis, 'The Senior Managers and Certification Regime in Financial Firms: An Organisational Culture Analysis (2022) *Journal of Corporate Law Studies* doi:10.1080/14735970.2022.2054165.

The FAR works by imposing obligations on specified financial institutions (referred to as 'accountable entities'), which comprise accountability obligations, key personnel obligations, deferred remuneration obligations and notification obligations. Individual executives who are 'accountable persons' must be identified and named by the financial institution as part of its accountability-mapping obligation and are individually registered with APRA.

In turn, accountable persons (as defined in the FAR Bill)[52] must 'comply with each of their accountability obligations … in relation to each of the responsibilities that cause the person to be an accountable person'. They are to conduct the responsibilities of their position as an accountable person:

(a) by acting with honesty and integrity, and with due skill, care and diligence; and
(b) by dealing with the Regulator in an open, constructive and cooperative way; and
(c) by taking reasonable steps in conducting those responsibilities to prevent matters from arising that would (or would be likely to) adversely affect the prudential standing or prudential reputation of the accountable entity; and
(d) by taking reasonable steps in conducting those responsibilities to prevent matters from arising that would (or would be likely to) result in a material contravention by the accountable entity of [specified legislation].[53]

The FAR Bill goes on to provide that, to the extent that two or more accountable persons 'have the same responsibility, each of them has the accountability obligations under subsection (1) in relation to that responsibility to the same extent as if it were solely that person's responsibility'.[54]

The accountability obligation in the FAR is wider than in the existing BEAR,[55] because it includes paragraph (d). While paragraph (d) is expressed to apply only to a 'material contravention' of the (extensive) legislation listed, the Explanatory Memorandum to the FAR Bill says that 'a large number or repeated occurrence of minor breaches could indicate a systemic issue of non-compliance which could amount to a material contravention'.[56] Unlike the BEAR, the FAR covers matters within the regulatory purview of ASIC (the conduct regulator) as well as APRA (the prudential regulator), and requires accountable persons to deal with both in an 'open, constructive and cooperative' way, presumably including when their own conduct is being investigated (for example, for breach of their statutory duties as officers where that is relevant).

[52] See FAR Bill (n 49) ss 10, 11. Broadly, the regime includes a person who has 'actual or effective senior executive responsibility for management or control of the accountable entity, or of a significant or substantial part or aspect of the operations of the accountable entity or group'; it is not limited to the persons named as such by the financial institution, but the intention may be that, in practice, it is limited to them.

[53] ibid s 21. The specified legislation is the FAR Bill; the Banking Act 1959 (Cth); the credit legislation (within the meaning of the National Consumer Credit Protection Act 2009 (Cth)); the Financial Sector (Collection of Data) Act 2001 (Cth); the financial services law (within the meaning of Corporations Act (n 28), s 761A); the Insurance Act 1973 (Cth); the Life Insurance Act 1995 (Cth); the Private Health Insurance (Prudential Supervision) Act 2015 (Cth); the Superannuation Industry (Supervision) Act 1993 (Cth); and regulations, instruments, directions or orders made under those laws.

[54] FAR Bill (n 49), s 21(2).

[55] Banking Act 1959 (Cth), s 37CA.

[56] Commonwealth of Australia, *Explanatory Memorandum to the Financial Accountability Regime Bill 2022, Financial Sector Reform Bill 2022, Financial Services Compensation Scheme of Last Resort Levy Bill 2022, and Financial Services Compensation Scheme of Last Resort Levy (Collection) Bill 2022*(2022) [1.62] (Explanatory Memorandum).

Examples of reasonable steps given in the Bill point strongly to the enrolment rationale for the FAR. They include:

(a) having appropriate governance, control and risk management in relation to that matter; and
(b) having safeguards against inappropriate delegations of responsibility in relation to that matter; and
(c) having appropriate procedures for identifying and remediating problems that arise or may arise in relation to that matter; and
(d) taking appropriate action in response to non-compliance, or suspected non-compliance, in relation to that matter.[57]

The Explanatory Memorandum to the Bill refers to 'reasonable steps to support *proactive* compliance by accountable persons and accountable entities' (emphasis added). This includes 'taking appropriate action both to prevent, and in response to, non-compliance or suspected non-compliance rather than a set-and-forget attitude'.[58]

If an accountable person fails to meet their obligations, various consequences follow.[59] Relevant for this discussion, they include the administrative penalty of disqualification.[60] The FAR Bill provides that the Regulator 'may disqualify a person from being or acting as an accountable person, for a period that the Regulator considers appropriate', if the Regulator is satisfied that they have failed to comply with one or more of their accountability obligations and 'the disqualification is justified, having regard to the seriousness of the failure to comply'.[61]

The significant expansion of Australia's SMR regime by the inclusion of paragraph (d) seems to have occurred without much debate or dissention. This may be due to widespread public calls, particularly after the misconduct made public by the Royal Commission into Misconduct in the Banking, Superannuation and Financial Services Industry in 2019,[62] for greater executive accountability in financial institutions.[63] While there was consultation at the exposure draft and committee stages, the Australian Government's usual processes for law reform were not all followed.[64]

[57] FAR Bill (n 49), s 22.

[58] Explanatory Memorandum (n 56) [1.60].

[59] An earlier proposal to impose civil penalties for an executive's failure to comply with their accountability obligations was not adopted.

[60] Disqualification in the corporate context has been recognised by the Australian courts as a form of penalty. In *Rich v Australian Securities and Investments Commission* [2004] HCA 42, (2004) 220 CLR 129, the High Court of Australia confirmed that a disqualification order can be imposed not only to protect the company's shareholders against further abuse, but also by way of punishment and, importantly, for general deterrence. See also *Australian Securities and Investments Commission v Vizard* [2005] FCA 1037, (2005) 145 FCR 57.

[61] FAR Bill (n 49), s 42. The Regulator may also direct the financial institution to remove the executive from their position, under FAR Bill (n 49), s 65.

[62] Commonwealth of Australia, *Royal Commission into Misconduct in the Banking, Superannuation and Financial Services Industry*, Final Report, 1 February 2019) (BFRC Report).

[63] The Explanatory Memorandum (n 56) states that the FAR Bill (n 49) was introduced in response to recommendations of the BFRC Report (n 62). While it may have been prompted by the findings of the BFRC Report (n 62), the FAR Bill (n 49) goes beyond the Commissioner's recommendation, which was to apply the existing BEAR to executives of insurance companies and trustees of public superannuation (pension) funds, not to replace or change (excepted in the limited way proposed in Recommendation 6.7) the BEAR: see BFRC Report (n 62) Recommendation 6.8.

[64] The human rights assessment required under the Human Rights (Parliamentary Scrutiny) Act 2011 (Cth) found that the FAR Bill (n 49) 'does not raise any human rights issues' despite its application to and impact on individuals: see Explanatory Memorandum (n 56) [5.1]–[5.58]. A regulatory impact assessment was not

IV. Analysis

This chapter asks when, and on what basis, an individual executive of a large corporation ought to be penalised if their connection to – and culpability for – lawbreaking by their corporation falls short of co-offending or knowing involvement. One possible answer is – never. It is open as a policy matter to decide that corporate executives should not be treated differently from people in other settings, or other corporate agents, when it comes to being penalised in relation to the conduct of another legal person. On this view, rather than expanding the existing law, more effort could be put into enforcing it.

However, this disregards that the corporation and its executives, while separate entities, are not independent of each other. The executives (alone or together) ultimately cause the corporation to act the way it does. Some special treatment therefore may be appropriate in the corporate context. A common claim in the debate is that getting corporations – which do not have the same moral agency, and do not react to the coercive power of law in the same way, as natural persons – to obey the law is unachievable unless the state exerts more legal pressure on the individuals who operate them. The focus is on changing corporate conduct and culture through changing the behaviour of its executives. Penalties are used not for retribution or denunciation of an individual executive's behaviour, but for deterrence and enrolment.

Section I drew a distinction between deterrence and enrolment rationales for extending executives' exposure to penalties in connection with corporate lawbreaking. Penalties work in whole or part to deter the future behaviour of the individual (specific deterrence) and other individuals in that class (general deterrence). Indeed, the substantial civil penalties that now dominate many regulatory frameworks are wholly directed at that end.[65] Deterring intentional behaviour by individuals makes conceptual sense, because it involves a choice on their part. Deterring negligent or inadvertent behaviour is a more elusive concept. Penalties can only 'deter' unintentional behaviour by encouraging the person exposed to the penalty to take proactive steps to manage the risk that a foreseeable harm will result from something they (individually) would otherwise miss or fail to do. In *He Kaw Teh v The Queen*, Brennan J said:

> However grave the mischief at which a statute is aimed may be, the presumption is that the statute does not impose criminal liability without *mens rea* unless the purpose of the statute is not merely to deter a person from engaging in prohibited conduct but to compel him to take preventive measures to avoid the possibility that, without deliberate conduct on his part, the external elements of the offence might occur. A statute is not so construed unless effective precautions can be taken to avoid the possibility of the occurrence of the external elements of the offence.[66]

In the corporate context, where the conditions for lawbreaking are often created by many hands over time,[67] the rationale for exposing executives *as a group* to penalties is

conducted, on the basis that the final report of the BFRC was 'certified as being informed by a process and analysis equivalent to a Regulation Impact Statement for the purposes of the Government decision to implement this reform': ibid 2. This occurred even though the Bill does not reflect the BFRC Report's (n 62) actual recommendations on changes to the SMR. The Explanatory Memorandum (n 56) also concluded that the FAR Bill (n 49) would have 'nil' financial impact.

[65] *Pattinson* (n 5).

[66] *He Kaw Teh* (n 6) 566–67.

[67] The conditions for lawbreaking may be created by under-investment by the corporation in compliance and risk management systems, resources and processes. Even where the formal and technocratic risk management

primarily enrolment, not individual deterrence. Deterrence involves encouraging individuals to change their own behaviour. Enrolment involves encouraging individuals to use their influence to change the behaviour of others as well. Both can affect the likelihood of, and propensity for, corporate lawbreaking.

It is now generally accepted that corporate compliance is a function of both process and culture.[68] For large business corporations operating in complex legal and regulatory environments, rigorous and dynamic formal risk-management processes are essential. However, the formal systems and processes of risk management will be ineffective if 'a corporate culture existed within the body corporate that directed, encouraged, tolerated or led to non-compliance with the relevant provision' or the corporation 'failed to create and maintain a corporate culture that required compliance'.[69]

The role of management in shaping the culture of the corporation leads inevitably to the question of executives' individual or joint culpability when that culture leads to corporate lawbreaking. In a different context, in an investigation into alleged Australian war crimes in Afghanistan,[70] the inquiry head found that 'Commanders set the conditions in which their units may flourish or wither, including the culture which promotes, permits or prohibits certain behaviours,' and that it was 'clear that there must have been within [the Special Operations Task Group] a culture that at least permitted the behaviours described in this Report'.[71] He observed that troop, squadron and task group Commanders

> must bear moral command responsibility and accountability for what happened under their command and control. Command responsibility is both a legal and a moral concept. In the narrow sense, command responsibility is a legal doctrine by which commanders may be held legally responsible for the misdeeds of their subordinates. But the concept has a much wider scope. At its core is responsibility for the effects and outcomes delivered by the unit or formation under command. Commanders are both recognised and accountable for what happens 'on their watch', regardless of their personal knowledge, contribution or fault.[72]

structures are in place, their efficacy will be undermined if the corporation lacks a 'culture of compliance'. See P Hanrahan, 'On Compliance' in A Black and P Hanrahan (eds) *Contemporary Issues in Corporate and Competition Law: Essays in Honour of Professor Robert Baxt AO* (Chatswood, LexisNexis Butterworths, 2019) ch 9.

[68] ibid. The relationship between process and culture has been recognised in several recent inquiries in Australia: see J Laker, J Broadbent and G Samuel, *Prudential Inquiry into the Commonwealth Bank of Australia* (Final Report, 30 April 2018); the BFRC Report (n 62); State of New South Wales, *Report of the Inquiry under Section 143 of the Casino Control Act 1992 (NSW)* (Final Report, 1 February 2021); State of Victoria, *Royal Commission into the Casino Operator and Licence* (The Report, October 2021) (Crown Royal Commission Victoria); State of Western Australia, *Perth Casino Royal Commission* (Final Report, March 2022) (Crown Royal Commission WA).

[69] This language comes from the Criminal Code (n 32), s 12.3(2)(c) and (d). Under the Code, if this culture is established then the corporation is treated as having expressly, tacitly or impliedly authorised or permitted the commission of an offence, and the fault elements of intention, knowledge or recklessness must be attributed to it.

[70] The inquiry was conducted by Major General the Hon Paul Brereton AM RFD, an Army Reserve Infantry Officer and a Judge of the Supreme Court of New South Wales acting as an Assistant Inspector-General of the Australian Defence Force (IGADF), and concerned allegations of war crimes by Australia's Special Operations Task Group (SOTG) in Afghanistan. See Inspector-General of the Australian Defence Force, *Afghanistan Inquiry Report* (November 2020). The Report found that there was 'credible information' that 25 current or former members of the SOTG had committed offences against the Law of Armed Conflict – that is, war crimes – while deployed in Afghanistan between 2009 and 2013.

[71] ibid [33].

[72] ibid [32].

While morally culpable, the senior leaders of the Special Operations Task Group were not legally responsible.[73] It is an important distinction.

The instrumentalist argument for penalising those who set the culture in any group is clear, given what we now know about the influence of culture on lawbreaking.[74] But corporate executives are humans, and therefore have human rights and 'the personal autonomy and dignity that underpins those rights'.[75] These include that a person should not be used as a means to an end, even if that end is a worthwhile one like enhanced corporate compliance. Punishing executives for conduct that was negligent or inadvertent, or in circumstances where changing their individual behaviour would not have diverted the corporation from breaking the law, runs counter to these fundamental principles. Doctrinally it can be done, but the theoretical basis for it must be clear and compelling. This is true whenever the penalty is non-trivial – regardless of whether it is characterised as criminal, civil or administrative.

Because they are directed at deterrence and enrolment, rather than denunciation and retribution, role-related penalties are often civil or administrative in character.[76] This might suggest that the penalties are not 'serious' or that, because they do not carry with them the possibility of imprisonment or the consequences and opprobrium of a criminal conviction, the rights and protections afforded to individuals who are the subject of legal action by the state can be safely eroded or disregarded. This may be true up to a point, but care must be taken in the context of individual defendants.[77] In fact, the main differences between criminal fines and civil penalties are often procedural. In its Report No 95, discussing the difference between criminal and civil penalties in the regulatory space, the ALRC noted that the 'primary distinction between the regimes is not the types of conduct but rather the "prosecutorial procedure, proof and punishment". Any basis for the lesser protections for the defendant and enhanced capacity to prove a contravention by the regulator in civil proceedings, is the lack of the "criminal" label where the contravention is proved.'[78] Interference with individual rights

[73] The IGADF found that '[w]hile it would have been much easier to report that it was poor command and leadership that was primarily to blame for the events disclosed in this Report, that would be a gross distortion'. The criminal behaviour of a few was 'commenced, committed, continued and concealed at the patrol commander level, that is, at corporal or sergeant level': ibid [25].

[74] The relationship between corporate culture and lawbreaking has been recognised for many years: see *ASIC; Re Chemeq Ltd v Chemeq Ltd* [2006] FCA 936, (2006) 234 ALR 511 (French J); *ASIC v AMP Financial Planning Pty Ltd* [2020] FCA 69, (2020) 377 ALR 55 [2] (Lee J); Crown Royal Commission Victoria (n 68) vol 1, ch 4. For an earlier American perspective, see LL Dallas, 'A Preliminary Inquiry into the Responsibility of Corporations and Their Officers and Directors for Corporate Climate: The Psychology of Enron's Demise' (2003) 35 *Rutgers Law Journal* 1. See also DC Langevoort, 'Cultures of Compliance' (2017) 54 *American Criminal Law Review* 933, 935.

[75] ALRC Report No 136 (n 3) [4.96].

[76] In failure to prevent regimes, there may be a separate criminal penalty for an intentional or reckless failure – for example, ALRC Proposal 10, discussed in section III.A.

[77] Under the International Covenant on Civil and Political Rights, opened for signature 16 December 1966, 999 UNTS 171 (entered into force 23 March 1976), a government cannot deprive an individual of their criminal process rights in Arts 14 and 15 simply by describing a penalty as civil rather than criminal. The proper characterisation depends on the nature of the penalty and the circumstances in which it applies. See P Hanrahan, 'Is Dual-Track Regulation of Directors' Conduct Defensible?' (2022) 39(5) *Company and Securities Law Journal* 293, 306.

[78] ALRC Report No 95 (n 3) [3.43] (citation omitted). It later observed that in civil proceedings 'regulators generally have the advantage of the lower evidentiary standard … together with procedures that facilitate evidence gathering, including compellability of witnesses. In some areas of economic regulation, such as

is exacerbated when the burden of proof moves from the state to the individual executive.[79] Reversing the burden of proof interferes with a defendant's human rights by disturbing the presumption of innocence.[80]

The COAG work on deemed liability, discussed in section II, suggests that some corporate lawbreaking is so reprehensible, or has such dire consequences, that extending executive liability in connection with it is a legitimate strategy for deterring or disrupting that lawbreaking despite the trade-offs involved. Crimes against humanity and human rights violations are obvious candidates, as are forms of corporate lawbreaking that directly and gravely imperil human life. There may be an argument to extend this to include corporate misconduct that has the potential to disrupt or undermine global economic or environmental systems, including corruption. However, extending it to all corporate lawbreaking may be more difficult to justify.

The COAG model, which relates specifically to the imposition of criminal liability, is that personal liability for directors is justified

> where:
>
> (a) there are compelling public policy reasons for doing so (for example, in terms of the potential for significant public harm that might be caused by the particular corporate offending);
> (b) liability of the corporation is not likely on its own to sufficiently promote compliance; and
> (c) it is reasonable in all the circumstances …[81]

In deciding whether it is reasonable, the COAG model directs drafters to factors including whether

> the obligation on the corporation, and in turn the director, is clear; the director has the capacity to influence the conduct of the corporation in relation to the offending; and there are steps that a reasonable director might take to ensure a corporation's compliance with the legislative obligation.[82]

The COAG model points to a more circumspect and considered approach to role-related liability than the ALRC's abandoned Proposal 9.

cartels, insider trading and market manipulation, this is particularly important because evidence may be difficult to obtain and proof to the criminal standard is notoriously difficult … The choice whether to pursue criminal or civil penalties might therefore be determined on the pragmatic grounds of increasing the prospects of success of the regulator': see ALRC Report No 129 (n 3) [3.44].

[79] Where a due diligence or reasonable steps defence is available to an executive, they may carry an evidential or legal burden. The former requires them to adduce or point to evidence that suggests a reasonable possibility that they took reasonable steps, and then the burden shifts to the state to prove otherwise. The latter requires the executive to prove they took steps, and those steps were reasonable, or creates a presumption that they did not unless the executive proves otherwise.

[80] Hanrahan (n 77).

[81] COAG Principles (n 20) Principle 4. The examples of significant public harm given by COAG include: death or disabling injury to individuals (eg offences involving serious breaches of workplace health and safety obligations); serious damage to the environment and/or serious risk to public health and safety (eg offences concerned with preventing toxic contamination); undermining of confidence in financial markets (eg trading when insolvent); or otherwise highly morally reprehensible conduct (eg serious offences under child protection or animal welfare legislation).

[82] ibid.

V. Conclusion

I began this chapter with Senator Warren's remarks about Wells Fargo and its Chairman and CEO John Stumph. The gravamen of the Senator's argument – in common with others – is that it is difficult to disrupt lawbreaking by large business corporations without penalising those who 'preside over' it. This is particularly so if the lawbreaking resulted from 'a corporate culture [that] existed … that directed, encouraged, tolerated or led to non-compliance', or from the corporation's failure 'to create and maintain a corporate culture that required compliance'.[83]

But penalising individual executives for negligent or inadvertent conduct that is only remotely connected to corporate lawbreaking creates a legal dilemma. Enrolment, achieved through state-imposed penalties, comes at the expense of the rights of the individual executives involved. It is not a new problem. In 1980, Christopher Stone wrote that

> although proposals recur to legislate severe penalties for conduct such as failure to supervise, it is far from clear that such reforms are either prudent or workable. To criminalize behavior that is essentially beyond the actor's control undermines the moral basis of the entire criminal justice system. Even at this high price, we are likely to realize only a marginal diminution in misconduct, for the more the conduct is unpremeditated, or is a joint product of many agents' acts over which the targeted agent has limited control, the more inelastic its 'supply' will be to changes in expected penalty levels. The likely results are a rate of conviction of those prosecuted, and a level of punishment of those convicted, that are far lower for the same offense than the enterprise would be likely to bear.[84]

Four decades on, the debate over when executives are culpable for corporate lawbreaking continues. Legal penalties – criminal, civil and administrative – are unique in that they involve the marshalling of state power against the individual concerned. Their use against individuals involves a trade-off between the public benefit that might be derived from enrolling executives as internal regulators of the corporation's conduct and culture, and principles of fairness and legitimacy. In 2006, CAMAC concluded that the elements of any extended personal liability provision must be assessed for their practicality and fairness, suitability and enforceability.[85] This remains the core challenge.

The enduring dilemma is how justly to impose legal consequences on executives in connection with corporate lawbreaking that results from the poor culture they have created or presided over. CAMAC's core challenge has yet to be addressed, and legal theorists must continue to work on it. Extending an SMR approach beyond the financial sector is worth exploring for very large corporations (whether publicly traded or privately owned, and for-profit or non-profit) whose activities have the potential to inflict real harm on the many and whose internal governance exhibits the characteristic of dispersed or distributed operational responsibilities. Enhanced internal and

[83] See n 69.

[84] CD Stone, 'The Place of Enterprise Liability in the Control of Corporate Conduct' (1980) 90 *Yale Law Journal* 1, 30–31 (footnote omitted).

[85] CAMAC Report (n 18) 43–44.

external transparency as to where the buck stops for a culture that contributes to or tolerates corporate lawbreaking seems like an important step forward, particularly if we accept enrolment as a legitimate regulatory strategy in mitigating the risk of unlawful or unethical behaviour by very large corporations. However, extending the SMR approach within or beyond prudentially regulated financial institutions is unlikely to achieve broad-based support unless we first agree when and why it we should properly accept the (necessary) trade-offs involved in imposing legal sanctions on the individuals concerned.

18

'Failure to Prevent' Offences: The Solution to Transnational Corporate Criminal Liability?

JONATHAN CLOUGH

I. Introduction

Over recent years, there has been considerable discussion around 'failure to prevent' offences (FTP offences) as an effective mechanism for prosecuting serious allegations of corporate crime.[1] Driven primarily by the apparent success of the United Kingdom's (UK's) Bribery Act 2010, FTP offences are seen as a possible response to other forms of financial crime. At the same time, increasing attention has been paid to the role of multinational corporations in the transnational abuse of human rights, and the challenges associated with prosecuting such conduct. Putting the two together, it has been suggested that the success of FTP offences may be expanded to other serious extraterritorial crimes.

The focus of this chapter is on the model of liability at the heart of FTP offences. Following an overview of the UK offence, it considers the key criticisms of FTP offences: that they are an unjustified expansion of omissions liability; that such conduct may more appropriately be dealt with by non-criminal responses; that they do not adequately reflect the culpability of the corporation; and that they may supplant the prosecution of corporations for the principal offence. The potential effectiveness of FTP offences in imposing liability for extraterritorial conduct is then discussed, before concluding that, while not a panacea, they provide both a principled and practical model of liability in responding to the seemingly intractable challenges associated with prosecuting corporations for transnational crimes.

[1] Although 'corporations' will be referred to for the purposes of this chapter, it is acknowledged that broader questions may be raised as to which organisations are subject to liability under these provisions.

II. 'Failure to Prevent' Offences

Discussion of FTP offences is generally centred around the influential 'model' found in section 7 of the Bribery Act, a model that has been largely replicated in subsequent legislation in Australia,[2] New Zealand[3] and the UK.[4] In essence, the corporation is liable if a bribery offence is committed by an 'associated person', where the bribe is to obtain or retain business or an advantage for the defendant corporation.[5] It is then a defence for the corporation to prove, on the balance of probabilities, that it had 'adequate procedures' in place to prevent associated persons from committing such offences.[6] The corporation is not vicariously liable for the offence of bribery. Rather, it is prosecuted for the distinct offence of failing to prevent bribery.[7]

This is a strict liability offence, subject to the defence of adequate procedures. Although it requires proof that an associated person has committed a relevant offence, that person need not have been convicted.[8] 'Associated person' is defined broadly as any person who, disregarding the alleged bribe, provides services 'for or on behalf' of the accused company.[9] Importantly, the 'associated person' may be a legal person, including a subsidiary.[10] The offence also has extraterritorial reach, applying to conduct occurring outside the UK where that conduct would be an offence under UK law.[11]

According to the House of Lords Select Committee on the Bribery Act, the Act is 'generally agreed to have been remarkably successful'.[12] Although there is limited empirical evidence to support this, this is not surprising given its relative novelty and the small number of prosecutions to date.[13] However, there are indications that this theoretical promise may translate into practice.

For example, there has been a noticeable change in enforcement against legal persons in the UK following the enactment of the Bribery Act. In the period 1999 to 2010, there were two successful prosecutions against a legal person (no unsuccessful prosecutions) in the UK, compared to 59 in the USA (including Deferred Prosecution Agreements (DPAs) and Non-Prosecution Agreements (NPAs)).[14] In contrast, in the decade after

[2] Crimes Legislation Amendment (Combatting Corporate Crime) Bill 2019 (Cth).

[3] Crimes Act 1961 (NZ), s 105C(2A).

[4] Criminal Finances Act 2017 (UK), pt 3. In its recent Options Paper, the UK Law Commission put forward four possible options for FTP offences: failure to prevent fraud by an associated person; failure to prevent human rights abuses; failure to prevent ill-treatment or neglect; and failure to prevent computer misuse: Law Commission, *Corporate Criminal Liability* (Options Paper, 10 June 2022) ch 8.

[5] Bribery Act 2010 (UK), s 7(1) (Bribery Act).

[6] ibid s 7(2).

[7] cf Crimes Act 1961 (NZ), s 105C(2A), where the corporation is liable for the principal offence. In Canada, the organisation is made a party to the principal offence: Criminal Code 1985 (Can), s 22.2(c).

[8] Bribery Act (n 5) s 7(3). See, eg, *R v Alstom Network UK Ltd* [2019] EWCA Crim 1318, [2020] Crim LR 447.

[9] Bribery Act (n 5) s 8.

[10] ibid s 8(3).

[11] ibid ss 7(3) and 12(5).

[12] Select Committee on the Bribery Act 2010, *The Bribery Act 2010: Post-Legislative Scrutiny* (HL Paper 303, 14 March 2019) para 171.

[13] Australian Law Reform Commission, *Corporate Criminal Responsibility* (Discussion Paper No 83, November 2019) para 6.55 (ALRC Discussion Paper).

[14] Organisation for Economic Cooperation and Development, *2010 Data on Enforcement of the Anti-Bribery Convention* (April 2011) 4.

the enactment of the Bribery Act, 11 legal persons were sanctioned in the UK (including DPAs), compared to 95 in the USA (including DPAs/NPAs).[15] Even considering the USA as an outlier, it places the UK up with Germany and France as amongst the most effective against legal persons, with 15 and 12 sanctioned respectively over the period 1999–2020.[16]

In contrast to many existing models of corporate criminal liability, FTP offences place the organisational failings of the corporation at the centre of liability. Their rationale is to provide a strong incentive for corporations to put procedures in place in order to avoid liability, and there is some limited empirical evidence to support this. In one survey of 40 UK businesses, over two-thirds of respondents (68.75 per cent) indicated that they had introduced new procedures in response to the Bribery Act.[17]

A further indication of the impact of these provisions on organisational change, albeit post-offending, is the apparent willingness of some large corporations to plead guilty/enter into DPAs rather than contest charges.[18] What Liz Campbell describes as 'cooperation *through* criminalisation',[19] using the leverage of the criminal law to affect organisational change, is only likely to be successful if there is a realistic prospect of conviction, and it is notable that some of the most significant examples of bribery have been finalised in this way.[20] For example, as part of a DPA in response to allegations of extensive corruption, Rolls-Royce agreed to disgorgement of profits of £258,170,000, a financial penalty of £239,082,645, costs of £12,960,754 and, at its own expense, completing an anti-bribery and corruption compliance programme.[21] This mimics, albeit to a lesser extent, the US experience, where the likelihood of conviction can provide a strong incentive to cooperate with prosecutors.[22]

Although FTP offences must stand on their own merits, it is also relevant to consider the alternatives. The evolution of corporate criminal liability at common law was primarily focused on principles of attribution.[23] This reflects a derivative or nominalist model of liability, whereby the liability of the corporation is derived from the actions of individuals, and may be contrasted with 'realist' or organisational models of fault,

[15] Organisation for Economic Cooperation and Development, *2019 Enforcement of the Anti-Bribery Convention* (23 December 2020) Table 1A.

[16] ibid. In Australia, the equivalent figure was 2.

[17] I Pietropaoli et al, *A UK Failure to Prevent Mechanism for Corporate Human Rights Harms* (London, British Institute of International and Comparative Law, 2020) 17. This suggests an improvement since earlier surveys; S Copp and A Cronin, 'New Models of Corporate Criminality: The Development and Relative Effectiveness of "Failure to Prevent" Offences' (2018) 39 *Company Lawyer* 104, 114.

[18] L Campbell, 'Trying Corporations: Why Not Prosecute?' (2019) 31 *Current Issues in Criminal Justice* 269. Also see S Bronitt, 'Regulatory Bargaining in the Shadows of Preventive Justice: Deferred Prosecution Agreements' in T Tulich et al (eds), *Regulating Preventive Justice* (Abingdon, Routledge, 2017).

[19] L Campbell, 'Corporate Liability and the Criminalisation of Failure' (2018) 12 *Law and Financial Markets Review* 57, 66.

[20] N Lord and R Broad, 'Corporate Failures to Prevent Serious and Organised Crimes: Foregrounding the "Organisational' Component"' (2017) 4 *The European Review of Organised Crime* 27, 36–37.

[21] *Serious Fraud Office v Rolls Royce plc* [2017] Lloyd's Rep FC 249 [67] (*Rolls Royce*). Also see *Serious Fraud Office v Standard Bank plc* [2016] Lloyd's Rep FC 102.

[22] B Garrett, 'Globalized Corporate Prosecutions' (2011) 97 *Virginia Law Review* 1775, 1788.

[23] For a general history of the evolution of corporate criminal liability see J Clough and C Mulhern, *The Prosecutions of Corporations* (Oxford, Oxford University Press, 2002) 71–79.

which seek to find culpability in the way in which the corporation is organised and structured.[24] As a corporation cannot act in its own right, liability must be found in an individual and then attributed to the corporation. The civil law principle of *respondeat superior*, 'let the principal answer', provided a ready parallel, and was adopted in some early decisions, most notably in the USA, where it remains the principal model of corporate criminal liability under US federal law.[25] Under this model, the corporation is made liable for offences committed by its employees or agents acting within the scope of their authority and with intent, at least in part, to benefit the corporation.

In the UK, and subsequently other common law jurisdictions, there was a resistance to imposing vicarious liability on a corporation for serious offences, particularly those involving mens rea.[26] This culminated in the 1972 decision of the House of Lords in *Tesco Supermarkets Ltd v Nattrass*,[27] which established the 'identification doctrine' of corporate criminal liability. In essence, a corporation would only be liable for a criminal offence (other than an offence of vicarious liability) if the offence were committed by a person who was the 'directing mind and will' of the company. Such a person is sufficiently senior that the corporation is not liable *for* their conduct; that person *is* the company for these purposes.[28] Through this legal fiction, the courts could avoid the presumption against vicarious liability, and notionally reflect the fault of the corporation by ensuring that the offence was committed by a person who was responsible for the management of the company.

It is beyond the scope of this chapter to engage in a detailed critique of the identification doctrine.[29] In summary, it is well established that the identification doctrine 'works best in cases where it is needed least and works least in cases where it is needed most'.[30] In particular, it has been singularly unsuccessful in securing convictions against medium to large corporations because those who represent the directing mind and will are too removed from the day-to-day operations of the company.[31] This has remained true despite subsequent modifications to the doctrine that have done little except to expand the range of people for whom the company may be liable, rather than addressing the inherent failings of this approach.[32] The result is 'a contemporary legacy predominantly characterised by the non-prosecution of corporations for substantive criminal behaviours within their organisations'.[33] In contrast, FTP offences hold out the promise of an effective mechanism for prosecuting serious corporate crimes.

[24] J Clough, 'Bridging the Theoretical Gap: The Search for a Realist Model of Corporate Criminal Liability' (2007) 18 *Criminal Law Forum* 267.

[25] Garrett (n 22) 1788; *New York Central & Hudson River Railroad Co v United States*, 212 US 481 (1909).

[26] M Dsouza, 'The Corporate Agent in Criminal Law – An Argument for Comprehensive Identification' (2020) 79 *Cambridge Law Journal* 91, 105.

[27] *Tesco Supermarkets Ltd v Nattrass* [1972] AC 153 (HL).

[28] ibid 170 (Lord Reid).

[29] See generally, Dsouza (n 26).

[30] J Gobert, 'Corporate Criminality: Four Models of Fault' (1994) 14 *Legal Studies* 393, 401.

[31] See, eg, *R v P&O European Ferries (Dover) Ltd* [1991] Crim LR 695, (1991) 93 Cr App R 72; *Attorney-General's Reference (No 2 of 1999)* [2000] QB 796, [2000] 3 All ER 182.

[32] *Meridian Global Funds Management Asia Ltd* v *Securities Commission* [1995] UKPC 5, [1995] 2 AC 500; *Canadian Dredge & Dock Co v R* [1985] 1 Can SCR 662. Also see Leow, ch 6 of this volume, section I.A.

[33] Lord and Broad (n 20) 34.

In the UK, in addition to bribery, this model has been applied to the facilitation of tax evasion,[34] and has been proposed for other forms of financial crime, including fraud and money laundering,[35] as well as human rights offences.[36] In Australia, it is replicated in proposed reforms to bribery laws,[37] and the Australian Law Reform Commission (ALRC) has recommended that it be applied to other serious extraterritorial crimes, including slavery and related offences, human trafficking, violation of foreign sanctions, torture, crimes against humanity, war crimes, genocide and the financing of terrorism.[38] Others have proposed that FTP offences go beyond offences requiring a predicate offence, to liability for the 'systemic failure to prevent breach of legal duty of care'.[39] Effective liability against legal persons is also a requirement under many international instruments concerned with serious transnational crime.[40]

For all its potential, it should be noted that there is not one 'model' of FTP offence.[41] For example, the definition of 'associated person', whether the procedures need be 'adequate' or 'reasonable', the scope of the predicate offence and whether it must have been committed for the benefit of the corporation, are all matters that may vary. It is generally accepted, even by its critics, that an FTP offence is more likely to result in prosecutions and, most importantly, convictions. The criticisms are generally at the other end of the spectrum, arguing that FTP offences are an unjustified expansion of the criminal law, that such conduct may appropriately be dealt with by non-criminal responses, that they do not adequately reflect the culpability of the corporation, and that they may supplant the prosecution of corporations for the principal offence. Each of these will now be considered in turn.

III. An Unjustified Expansion of Omissions Liability

The FTP offences have been described as one of a 'new generation of omissions offences', which do not create new substantive offences but rather demonstrate a 'vertical expansion' of the criminal law by 'extending the grounds of responsibility' for existing offences.[42]

[34] Criminal Finances Act 2017 (UK), pt 3.

[35] ALRC Discussion Paper (n 13) para 6.39. Related offences have also been enacted in Canada and New Zealand: ibid para 6.51.

[36] UK Joint Committee on Human Rights, *Human Rights and Business 2017: Promoting Responsibility and Ensuring Accountability* (Sixth Report 2016–17, HL Paper 153, HC Paper 443, 5 April 2017) para 186.

[37] Crimes Legislation Amendment (Combatting Corporate Crime) Bill 2019 (Cth), sch 1.

[38] Australian Law Reform Commission, *Corporate Criminal Responsibility* (Report No 136, April 2020) para 10.9 (ALRC Final Report).

[39] P Crofts, 'Three Recent Royal Commissions: The Failure to Prevent Harms and Attributions of Organisational Liability' (2020) 42 *Sydney Law Review* 395, 397.

[40] See, eg, United Nations Convention Against Corruption, opened for signature 9 December 2003, A/58/422 (entered into force 14 December 2005) Art 26; OECD Convention on Combating Bribery of Foreign Public Officials in International Business Transactions, opened for signature 17 December 1997 (entered into force 12 February 1999) Art 2; United Nations Convention Against Transnational Organised Crime, opened for signature 12 December 2000 (entered into force 29 September 2003) Art 10.

[41] A Ashworth, 'A New Generation of Omissions Offences?' (2018) 5 *Criminal Law Review* 354, 360.

[42] A Ashworth, 'The Diffusion of Criminal Responsibility: A Cause for Concern?' in J McKenna (ed), *Queensland Legal Yearbook 2017* (Brisbane, Supreme Court Library Queensland, 2017) 170, citing T Crofts and A Loughnan, 'Introduction' in T Crofts and A Loughnan (eds), *Criminalisation and Criminal Responsibility in Australia* (Oxford, Oxford University Press, 2015) 2.

This is said to be contrary to the criminal law's traditional 'marked insistence on individual responsibility'.[43] Criminal liability for omissions, alongside secondary liability, should therefore be seen as an exception to the general principle that 'defendants are liable according to what they do, not what others do and they fail to prevent'.[44]

An objection to this increase in liability for failing to act is that it presents a greater intrusion into individual autonomy than other forms of criminal prohibition.[45] However, such arguments do not readily apply to corporations and other forms of legal person. The corporation is a creation of the state; an entity that may facilitate the interests of individuals but does not have the same autonomy as an individual.[46] At the same time, 'a corporation benefits from the wrongdoing of associated persons acting in pursuit of contractual or commercial advantage or tax limitation'.[47]

A related concern is that the legitimate goal of prevention should not be at the expense of established principles of criminal responsibility.[48] In this sense, the FTP offence is quite distinct from other forms of preventive offences, which have greatly expanded in recent years.[49] Such offences reflect an expansion of offences based on risk,[50] and include pre-inchoate offences that are primarily aimed at allowing law enforcement to act at an early stage.[51]

In contrast, FTP offences reflect the fact that in the context of serious crimes, corporate wrongdoing is more likely to be in the form of a failure to prevent than commission of the principal offence.[52] They are justified on the basis that they encourage corporations to put in place systems that are aimed at preventing criminal conduct, 'by providing a deterrent against non-involvement and passivity on the part of companies in the face of economic crime'.[53] In other words, the corporation is punished not for its wrongful action, but for its wrongful inaction in the face of a known risk. While this is clearly a departure from general principles of criminal responsibility, it must be seen in the context of the unique qualities of a corporate defendant.

At common law, liability for omissions is regarded as exceptional.[54] A person may only be liable for what they have failed to do if they were under a legal obligation to act.[55] In terms of corporations, liability for failing to act was largely neglected by the common law courts, and in some cases clearly rejected.[56] This is despite its being one of

[43] Ashworth (n 42) 170, citing N Lacey, *In Search of Criminal Responsibility* (Oxford, Oxford University Press, 2016) 164–65.
[44] Ashworth (n 42) 171, citing A Simester et al (eds), *Simester and Sullivan's Criminal Law*, 6th edn (Oxford, Hart Publishing, 2016) 15.
[45] Ashworth (n 42) 174.
[46] J Horder, 'Bureaucratic "Criminal" Law Too Much of a Bad Thing?' in RA Duff et al (eds), *Criminalization* (Oxford, Oxford University Press, 2014) 127.
[47] C Wells, 'Corporate Failure to Prevent Economic Crime – A Proposal' (2017) 6 *The Criminal Law Review* 426, 433.
[48] Ashworth (n 42) 173.
[49] See, eg, H Carvalho, *The Preventive Turn in Criminal Law* (Oxford, Oxford University Press, 2017).
[50] Lacey (n 43) 147–48.
[51] Ashworth (n 42) 172.
[52] ALRC Final Report (n 38) para 10.12.
[53] Ashworth (n 42) 176. Also see Campbell (n 19) 59.
[54] *Simester and Sullivan's Criminal Law* (n 44) 72.
[55] S Bronitt and B McSherry, *Principles of Criminal Law*, 4th edn (Sydney, Thomson Reuters, 2017) para 3.85.
[56] *Attorney-General's Reference (No 2 of 1999)* (n 31).

the oldest forms of corporate criminal liability[57] and, it is argued, one of the purest. In contrast to other models of corporate criminal liability, liability for omissions is a form of organisational fault. It does not attribute the conduct of an individual to the corporation but punishes the corporation in its own right. 'Though a notional entity is incapable of an act in its own proper person; it is not incapable of failing to act.'[58]

This simple but powerful concept moves us away from attribution of individual fault to a true model of corporate responsibility. As described by the UK Law Commission in the context of negligent manslaughter by omission:

> It is in our view much easier to say that a corporation, as such, has failed to do something, or has failed to meet a particular standard of conduct than it is to say that a corporation has done a positive act, or has entertained a particular subjective state of mind. The former statements can be made directly, without recourse to the intermediary step of finding a human mind and a decision-making process on the part of an individual within or representing the company; and thus the need for the identification theory, in order to bring the corporation within the subjective requirements of the law, largely falls away.[59]

Although largely neglected at common law, corporate criminal liability for omissions plays a crucial role in the regulation of workplace safety.[60] In the UK, as in Australia and many other jurisdictions, the regulation of workplace safety is based upon a series of duties imposed on employers, including corporate employers.[61] It is an offence under workplace safety legislation for an employer to fail to discharge those duties.[62] The standard imposed on the employer is 'so far as is reasonably practicable'.[63] It is therefore for the prosecution to prove that the employer did not take all reasonable steps to comply with the duty. There is no need to rely upon rules of attribution; it is the company's failure to put in place adequate procedures that is the basis of organisational fault. In the UK, these duties also form the basis for an offence of corporate manslaughter where there is a gross failure by the corporation to discharge a duty where that failure causes death.[64] Although corporate liability for a failure to act is a well-established form of organisational fault, this does not address the criticism that liability for a failure to prevent is an unwarranted expansion of criminal liability.

A focus on compliance programmes, and efforts made by a corporation to prevent harm, are not unique to FTP offences. They have, in particular, been an increasing feature of culpability assessment in the USA.[65] If a corporation is to change, it must do

[57] See, eg, *Case of Langforth Bridge* (1635) Cro Car 365, (1634) 79 ER 919 (KB); *R v Birmingham & Gloucester Railway Co* [1842] 3 QB 223, [1842] 114 ER 492.

[58] G Williams, *Criminal Law: The General Part* (London, Stevens & Sons, 1961) 854.

[59] Law Commission, *Legislating the Criminal Code: Involuntary Manslaughter* (Law Com No 237, 4 March 1996) 87–88.

[60] ALRC Discussion Paper (n 13) para 6.45.

[61] For a discussion of duty-based offences, see S Walpole and M Corrigan, 'Fighting the System: New Approaches to Addressing Systematic Corporate Misconduct' (2021) 43 *Sydney Law Review* 489, 500–01.

[62] For example, Health and Safety at Work etc Act 1974 (UK), s 33(1)(a) (HASAW Act); Occupational Health and Safety Act 2004 (Vic), s 21 (OHS Act).

[63] For example, HASAW Act, s 2; OHS Act, s 21.

[64] Corporate Manslaughter and Corporate Homicide Act 2007 (UK), s 1.

[65] R Gruner, 'Preventative Fault and Corporate Criminal Liability: Transforming Corporate Organizations into Private Policing Entities' in HN Pontell and G Geis (eds), *International Handbook of White-Collar and Corporate Crime* (New York, Springer, 2007) 279.

so through changing its processes. It may remove certain individuals, and/or reform systems to ensure compliance. This may be seen as rehabilitation, if done willingly, or deterrence if done for fear of prosecution. Other companies may also change their processes in response to the prosecution of their peers – a form of general deterrence. Regardless, the corporate culture must change if the corporation is to be deterred or rehabilitated. In this sense all corporate liability is preventive, as the threat or fact of prosecution is intended to provide an incentive for the entity to put processes in place to avoid that outcome in future. In the case of traditional models of attribution, there is no attempt to reflect this within the model of liability. Discussions of organisational fault are typically relevant, if at all, only at the point of sentencing.

In contrast, while the FTP offence is also predicated on the commission of an offence, it is 'a preventative device and a mechanism to influence behaviour, rather than something that operates primarily in reactive mode'.[66] Once the predicate offence is proved, we then look back to see what the company did to prevent that offence not for the purpose of penalty, but for the purpose of liability.[67] If the corporation has taken adequate steps then it will not be liable. Rather than an unjustified vertical expansion of liability, it is argued that FTP offences are an appropriate way to address the unjustified de facto immunity from prosecution that corporations have enjoyed due to inadequacies in existing models of liability.

A related concern is that FTP offences 'co-opt companies in a crime prevention role normally left to regulators or the police'.[68] The delegation of state responsibilities to police and local organisations has been termed 'responsibilisation'.[69] In this context, it may be expanded to 'cover the imposition of responsibility for elements of law enforcement on individuals or companies, particularly where they are in sufficient proximity to the wrongdoing or wrongdoer to be able to report or prevent an offence'.[70] On this view, requiring a corporation to undertake measures to investigate and where possible prevent the commission of an offence may be described as a form of 'private policing'.[71] Depending on what is seen as 'reasonable' or 'adequate', it may require 'a responsibility to police the business-related activities of corporate employees and balance performance demands with checks and limitations which ensure that performance demanded of employees is achieved lawfully'.[72]

Andrew Ashworth argues that such 'responsibilisation' may be justified 'only if it is focussed on the most serious wrongs or on those that are particularly difficult to bring to light, and only if it is brought to bear on those on whom a duty can fairly be laid'.[73] It is argued that each of these criteria are met in the context of serious transnational

[66] Campbell (n 19) 59.

[67] This is distinct from 'reactive corporate fault', which 'looks to a corporation's fault in failing to undertake satisfactory preventive or corrective measures in response to the commission of the actus reus of an offense by personnel acting on behalf of the organization': B Fisse, 'Reconstructing Corporate Criminal Law: Deterrence, Retribution, Fault and Sanctions' (1983) 56 *Southern California Law Review* 1145, 1197. Also see Fisse, ch 7 of this volume, section II.

[68] Ashworth (n 42) 176.

[69] D Garland, *The Culture of Control* (Chicago, IL, University of Chicago Press, 2001) 124–26.

[70] Ashworth (n 41) 362.

[71] Gruner (n 65) 283.

[72] ibid.

[73] Ashworth (n 41) 362.

crimes, which are notoriously difficult to prosecute, and where it is strongly arguable that the obligation may fairly be laid on the corporation. On this latter point, the duty to prevent often occurs in the context of a regulated area of commercial activity in which the corporation operates. In this sense, these may be seen as 'voluntarily incurred obligations'.[74] It is routine for corporations to take steps to ensure their employees do not engage in unsafe practices, discrimination, harassment and the like. This 'should not be burdensome to corporations but facilitative of their business'.[75] While compliance procedures are a cost to be borne by the company, they must also be seen in the context of an organisation driven by profit.[76]

IV. Is Criminalisation Warranted?

Even if we accept that corporations should be under a duty to prevent such crimes, it does not follow that a failure to discharge that duty should be enforced by the criminal law.[77] As discussed below, FTP offences reflect a relatively low level of culpability, which may arguably be addressed via non-criminal sanctions. This would achieve a number of goals. It would provide a public law response, subject to significant financial penalties, as well as sanctions requiring organisational change, such as enforcement undertakings. In many cases, penalties imposed by regulators may be greater than those imposed by criminal courts.[78] The fact that corporations benefit or seek to benefit from the activities of associated persons strengthens the argument for the duty, but not necessarily for criminalisation.[79]

It is clear that the condemnation associated with a criminal conviction is one of the key justifications for corporate criminal liability.[80] For example, the ALRC has recommended that corporate criminal liability should be reserved for the most serious wrongs.[81] While most other attributes of criminal prosecutions can be replicated in civil penalty provisions, it may be argued that only a criminal conviction conveys the true wrongfulness of a defendant's conduct and the requisite condemnation of that conduct.[82] It flows from this that the nature of the offence must be commensurate with the designation 'criminal'.[83]

It is generally unchallenged that corporations ought to be criminally liable for the principal offences. At least as currently proposed, the offences to which a duty to prevent would apply are amongst the most serious of crimes.[84] Nor does it appear to

[74] A Ashworth, *Positive Obligations* (Oxford, Hart Publishing, 2013) 50.
[75] Lord and Broad (n 20) 48.
[76] Ashworth (n 41) 363.
[77] ibid.
[78] Wells (n 47) 436.
[79] Ashworth (n 41) 362.
[80] Dsouza (n 26) 92–93.
[81] ALRC Final Report (n 38) Recommendation 2.
[82] Dsouza (n 26) 93.
[83] ibid.
[84] ALRC Final Report (n 38) para 10.9.

be questioned that corporations attempting, encouraging or facilitating such offences would also warrant a criminal law response. The suggestion is therefore that failing to take adequate or reasonable steps to prevent such offences dilutes the culpability of the corporation to such an extent that criminalisation is not warranted. However, the seriousness of a failure to prevent must be assessed against what is required and what is to be prevented.

As noted, the failure to prevent applies in the context of the business activities of the corporation. It may therefore be argued that 'where a person undertakes a particular role or trade it may be justifiable to attach duties reinforced by criminal offences of failing to comply with certain requirements'.[85] This is particularly so where there is the potential for significant harm arising from the failure to act.[86] The clear analogy here is with workplace safety offences, which reflect a relatively low level of culpability but are indictable offences carrying significant penalties.[87] This is because they illustrate a more fundamental justification for such offences, which is where a 'not-too-demanding positive act' is required 'if another person's vital interests are at stake'.[88] Where a corporation is structured in such a way as to maximise financial gain, it is surely not too demanding to ask that in establishing these processes, reasonable steps are taken to ensure that identifiable human rights are not violated.

In evaluating the criminalisation of FTP offences, James Gobert's four preconditions to corporate liability are particularly apposite:

1. The company is, or should have been, aware of the risk;
2. The company has a legal duty to prevent the offence;
3. The company has the capacity to prevent the offence; and
4. The company fails to prevent the offence.[89]

In each of the areas in which an FTP offence has been enacted or proposed, there are clearly arguments to support the fact that companies operating in those areas either were or should have been aware of the risk of serious offending by associated persons. Given that awareness of risk, it is not unreasonable for the legislature to impose a duty on the corporation to take reasonable steps to prevent such offending. Where the corporation fails to do so, the culpability lies not in the failure *per se*; it is that the corporation had the capacity to act but did not. A corporation that was aware, or ought to have been aware, of a significant risk that serious crime might be committed by associated persons, and that does not take even reasonable steps to prevent this, may rightly be characterised as 'criminal', in the same way that a corporation that does not take reasonably practicable steps to ensure the safety of its employees and others is also criminal. While this failure may involve misconduct by individuals within the organisation, the culpability is collective.[90]

[85] Ashworth (n 41) 357.
[86] ALRC Final Report (n 38) para 5.47.
[87] See, eg, OHS Act (n 62), s 21(4).
[88] Ashworth (n 41) 357.
[89] J Gobert, 'Squaring the Circle: The Relationship Between Individual and Organizational Fault' in J Gobert and A Pascal (eds), *European Developments in Corporate Criminal Liability* (Oxfordshire, Routledge, 2011) 139, 144–45.
[90] ibid 145.

V. Reflecting Culpability

Having opted for criminalisation, there is then the question of culpability: how culpable is a failure to prevent, and how is corporate culpability to be reflected? Even if, as is generally assumed, omissions may be seen as involving lower levels of culpability, they may still be sufficiently blameworthy to be criminalised.[91] It is necessary first to identify the gravity of the failure itself, and then the fault element associated with it.

Just as the actus reus of criminal offences may cover a broad spectrum of conduct, there are what Ashworth describes as different levels of 'intensity' of omissions; ranging from a simple failure to report ('LC1'), through to offences where the failure is an element of the offence, such as negligent manslaughter ('LC5').[92] In assessing where the FTP offence sits on this (admittedly non-exhaustive) five-point scale, it is important to be clear on what the failure is. Although the offence is referred to as a 'failure to prevent', it is more accurately a failure to have adequate procedures in place to prevent offending by associated persons. There is no requirement to actually prevent crime. In terms of intensity, it therefore appears to sit at a similar level to a failure to assist ('LC2') and a failure to take necessary precautions ('LC3').[93]

Although the obligations imposed are not particularly high in terms of intensity, another feature of omissions emphasised by Ashworth is whether it is merely the failure that is punished, or the consequences of the failure.[94] In the case of FTP offences, there is no requirement to prove that the failure of the corporation caused the principal offence to be committed. There is, however, an effective presumption that the offence has been committed as a result of the failure, hence the corporation's liability unless that presumption is rebutted. Therefore, it may be argued that the culpability of the FTP offence is made greater by the combination of a relatively easily complied with obligation to take reasonable steps, together with the seriousness of the offences that may be committed if that duty is not discharged.[95]

In addition to the 'intensity' of the omission, there is the overt expression of culpability in the fault element of the offence. It is here that the UK model has perhaps distorted the discussion by providing for strict liability subject to a due diligence defence. As a general principle, strict liability offences should be regarded as 'exceptional and in need of strong justification, particularly where the offence is serious'.[96] However, these arguments primarily relate to individual liability due to the impact of conviction on an individual and the possibility of a severe, even custodial, sentence.[97] They carry less weight in relation to offences that can only be committed by corporations.[98] Although the harshness of the provision is offset, to some extent, by a due diligence defence,

[91] Ashworth (n 74) 36.
[92] ibid 64.
[93] ibid.
[94] ibid.
[95] ibid 65.
[96] A Ashworth and L Zedner, 'Defending the Criminal Law: Reflections on the Changing Character of Crime, Procedure and Sanctions' (2008) 2 *Criminal Law and Philosophy* 21, 33.
[97] ibid 32.
[98] Ashworth (n 42) 171.

reverse-onus defences go against the burden of proof so fundamental to criminal trials. In respect of both strict liability and the reverse onus, the justifications are primarily related to enforcement.

First, it may be argued that as legal not natural persons, the abrogation or restriction of such rights may more readily be justified in the context of corporations:[99]

> [T]he stigma of conviction cannot induce emotional suffering in these bodies as such, they do not have any dignity to be trampled on by reverse burdens of proof, and they do not have any personal autonomy to be threatened by omissions-based liability or by the imposition of risk-based penalization.[100]

This is a pragmatic response, squarely focused on the challenges of prosecuting corporations if the traditional legal burdens were observed.

Second, it is peculiarly within the knowledge of the corporation to demonstrate its processes and procedures. Similar arguments have been made and accepted in denying the privilege against self-incrimination to corporations.[101] There is a pragmatic reality that if corporations were able to withhold from scrutiny documents that form their operational procedures, it would be extremely difficult to enforce criminal laws against them. Similarly, requiring the prosecution to prove, beyond reasonable doubt, the operational structures of a large transnational corporation presents a considerable obstacle to a successful prosecution. The presence of strict liability with a due diligence defence facilitates prosecution while providing the corporation with the opportunity to prove it was not at fault.

Third, although of less culpability, such failures are not without culpability. As Penny Crofts explains, culpability does not rest solely with positive acts; a 'negative model of wickedness' reflects the fact that organisations are most likely to cause harm through their failure to prevent and to respond, and 'it is this failure to act that has caused the systemic harms, and it [is] precisely this failure that is culpable'.[102] The failure is culpable 'because it reflects a failure to couple management-initiated corporate actions with appropriate law compliance safeguards'.[103]

The Bribery Act offence is, however, only one 'model'. An alternative would be to create an FTP offence based on the workplace safety model. This would require the prosecution to prove that the organisation had failed to take all reasonable steps to ensure that the relevant conduct did not occur within its operations. The onus would be on the prosecution, but given that it relates to the internal procedures of the corporation, it has been argued that it would place an 'unreasonable and unnecessary burden on the prosecution'.[104]

At the most serious end of the spectrum, the prosecution could be required to prove that the corporation's failure to prevent was criminally negligent. That is, the onus would be on the prosecution to prove that the company's failure to take adequate steps to prevent

[99] Campbell (n 19) 61–62.
[100] Horder (n 46) 124.
[101] *Environment Protection Authority v Caltex Refining Co Pty Ltd* [1993] HCA 74, (1993) 178 CLR 477; *United States v White*, 322 US 694 (1944).
[102] Crofts (n 39) 422.
[103] Gruner (n 65) 283.
[104] ALRC Final Report (n 38) para 7.147.

the offence fell grossly short of what would be expected of a reasonable corporation.[105] While this reflects a higher level of culpability, it would be commensurately more difficult to prove and is likely to have lower rates of successful prosecution.[106] This was, in fact, the model proposed by the UK Law Commission, which counselled against an offence of strict liability as it 'would run entirely counter to the normal approach to serious offences'.[107] It was, however, rejected by the Parliamentary Committee, which preferred the view that the focus of the provision should not be on the negligence of a 'responsible person' but rather on the collective failure of the company to ensure that adequate anti-bribery procedures were in place.[108]

A related issue is that the principle of legality and the 'rule of law' require that the content of the law be clear, so that an organisation that is under a duty to act is aware of the contents of that obligation.[109] This can present particular challenges where the obligation is couched in terms of objective standards such as 'reasonable'.[110] If the goal of ensuring compliance measures are in place is to be achieved, it is vital that these obligations are well publicised to those responsible for implementing them.[111] In one survey of businesses, almost 70 per cent (68.7 per cent) considered that the law does not provide 'sufficient legal certainty about which procedures are required to avoid legal risks for human rights abuses'.[112] A large majority considered that additional regulation might provide benefits to their business, including legal certainty, levelling the playing field and facilitating leverage with third parties.[113]

This may be seen as one of the strengths of the FTP offence model, so long as it is supported by sufficient guidance.[114] The six principles provided by the Ministry of Justice in relation to the Bribery Act give some indication of what is required:

- The procedures should be proportionate to the risk as well as the nature and scale of the organisation's activities.
- There should be top-level commitment.
- The procedures should be based on regular risk assessments.
- There should be due diligence procedures in place.
- The procedures should be communicated throughout the organisation.
- The procedures should be subject to monitoring and review.[115]

[105] See, eg, Corporate Manslaughter and Corporate Homicide Act 2007 (UK), s 1(4)(b).
[106] See, eg, *R v Wood Treatment Limited and George Boden* [2021] EWCA Crim 618.
[107] Law Commission, *Reforming Bribery* (Law Com No 313, 2008) para 6.100.
[108] Joint Committee on the Draft Bribery Bill, *Draft Bribery Bill* (First Report of Session 2008–09, HL Paper 115, HC Paper 430) 89.
[109] Ashworth (n 74) 61.
[110] ibid 63.
[111] Campbell (n 19) 64.
[112] Pietropaoli et al (n 17) 12.
[113] ibid 14; ALRC Final Report (n 38) para 7.137.
[114] For a detailed discussion, see P Alldridge, 'The UK Bribery Act: The Caffeinated Younger Sibling of the FCPA' (2012) 73 *Ohio State Law Journal* 1181, 1203–10.
[115] Ministry of Justice, *The Bribery Act 2010* (Guidance Paper, 2011). Also see HM Revenue and Customs, *Tackling Tax Evasion: Government Guidance for the Corporate Offences of Failure to Prevent the Criminal Facilitation of Tax Evasion* (Guidance Paper, 2017).

If it is beyond corporations to prove the procedures they have in place, there would seem to be a flaw in the transparency models that are applied in other contexts. For example, in relation to modern slavery, the legislative preference has been to avoid the imposition of an FTP offence, but instead to require corporations to publish statements outlining the risk of slavery in their supply chains, and the steps that they have taken or will take to reduce it.[116] Were an FTP offence to apply in this context, the onus would simply pass to the corporation to show that the procedures already outlined in the register were reasonable in the circumstances.

VI. Relationship to the Principal Offence

Some commentators have expressed concern that prosecution for FTP offences should not be at the expense of prosecution for the principal offence.[117] 'This raises concerns over the substitutive, rather than complementary, use of "failure to prevent" offences and the move away from the prosecutorial pursuit of substantive criminal behaviour.'[118] In this way, the expressive function of the criminal law may be diluted. That is, in egregious cases it is more powerful (and arguably more accurate) to say that the corporation has committed bribery than that it has failed to prevent bribery.

A related concern is that the level of culpability associated with an FTP offence is distinct, and therefore must be applied distinctly to the principal offence where such offences require proof of subjective fault or negligence.[119] This is related to the principle of 'fair labelling' and requires that offences be distinguished based on differing levels of culpability.[120] It reflects the important normative function of conveying relative levels of culpability and wrongdoing. Hence, it has been argued that the FTP offence should be limited to cases where the corporation has failed to put adequate procedures in place, while the primary offences should apply where that failure is intentional, knowing or reckless.[121]

In a context where it is well known that it is extremely difficult to prosecute multinational enterprises (MNEs) for transnational crimes, it seems to add an additional burden to say that where prosecutions are achieved, they are not criminal enough. The FTP offence was enacted in the UK precisely because existing rules of attribution were inadequate, and a corporation was unlikely to be convicted for the principal offence.[122] There is little expressive value in an acquittal or non-prosecution. In fact, the expressive function may be the opposite of what is intended. Prosecuting corporations for failing to prevent crimes by associated persons 'conveys a positive and important message

[116] Modern Slavery Act 2015 (UK), s 54; Modern Slavery Act 2018 (Cth), pt 2.
[117] S Bronitt and Z Brereton, *Foreign Bribery Submission: Combating Bribery of Foreign Public Officials* (Submission to the Attorney-General's Department, Proposed Amendments to the Foreign Bribery Offence in the Criminal Code Act 1995 (Cth) Public Consultation Paper, 2017) para 2.1; Campbell (n 19) 65.
[118] Lord and Broad (n 20) 40.
[119] Bronitt and Brereton (n 117) para 2.8.
[120] J Chalmers and F Leverick, 'Fair Labelling in Criminal Law' (2008) 71 *Modern Law Review* 217, 219.
[121] Bronitt and Brereton (n 117) para 2.1.
[122] Wells (n 47) 437.

about the expectations and responsibilities of corporate entities'.[123] Conversely, failing to prosecute corporations for the harm they cause communicates a counternarrative that 'these harms are just a cost, albeit unfortunate, of doing business'.[124]

Nonetheless, it may be argued that the corporation should be prosecuted under the principal (more serious) offence, rather than adopting the expedient path of an FTP prosecution. However, the suggestion that the principal offence of bribery reflects truly culpable failures, those involving intention, knowledge or recklessness,[125] may be called into question. Such arguments seem to assume that where a corporation is prosecuted for the principal offence, the model of liability will reflect the greater culpability associated with the offence of bribery versus a failure to prevent bribery. However, the challenges of imposing liability on a corporation tends to mean these distinctions are not as clearly differentiated as they might be for individuals.

For example, the principal offence of bribery in the UK would be prosecuted under the identification doctrine, which would require a person who is the 'directing mind and will' of the company to have committed bribery.[126] Even if this could be established, it does not necessarily prove that the corporation's failure was intentional, reckless or even negligent. A senior officer committing such an offence would render the company liable for the principal offence, with no requirement to prove organisational failure on the part of the corporation.

In Australia, the offence of bribing a foreign public official is found in section 70.2(1) of the Criminal Code Act 1995 (Cth) (Criminal Code). This offence may be committed by a body corporate,[127] and the model of corporate criminal liability is found in part 2.5 of the Code. Part 2.5 does not require proof of a predicate offence. Rather, the physical element of the offence is attributed to the company so long as it was committed by an employee, agent or officer, acting within the actual or apparent scope of their employment or authority.[128] Where, as in the case of bribery, there is a subjective fault element, then the equivalent mental state for a corporation is that it 'expressly, tacitly or impliedly authorised or permitted the commission of the offence'.[129] The Criminal Code then specifies four ways in which this state *may* be proved.[130]

The first two are expanded versions of the identification doctrine. For example, the offence of bribery by the corporation may be proved by establishing that the board of directors or a 'high managerial agent' intentionally, knowingly or recklessly engaged in the conduct, or expressly, tacitly or impliedly authorised or permitted the commission of the offence.[131] 'High managerial agent' is defined as 'an employee, agent or officer of

[123] Campbell (n 19) 61.
[124] Crofts (n 39) 398.
[125] Bronitt and Brereton (n 117) paras 2.6–2.7.
[126] Although unlikely, it is not beyond the realm of possibility. In approving the DPA for Rolls-Royce, Lord Justice Leveson commented on the 'most serious breaches of the criminal law … some of which implicated senior management and, on the face of it, controlling minds of the company': *Rolls Royce* (n 21) [4].
[127] Criminal Code, s 70.2(5).
[128] ibid s 12.2.
[129] ibid s 12.3(1).
[130] ibid s 12.3(2).
[131] ibid s 12.3(2)(a)(b).

the body corporate with duties of such responsibility that his or her conduct may fairly be assumed to represent the body corporate's policy'.[132] Although a broader concept than the directing mind and will, it may still be challenging to prove that such a person engaged in the relevant conduct. Even if proved, it does not require proof of organisational fault. The fact that the person may be assumed to represent the company's policy is purely an inference; it does not require proof of actual corporate fault. Where the offence is committed by a high managerial agent, the offence is also subject to a due diligence defence so that, as with the FTP offence, the corporation may avoid liability by proving that it exercised due diligence to prevent the conduct, or the authorisation or permission.[133]

The third basis of liability requires proof of a corporate culture that 'directed, encouraged, tolerated or led to non-compliance' with the relevant provision.[134] These are all active states, requiring a level of awareness, and are the most closely aligned to subjective fault elements. This is a true example of organisational fault, with 'corporate culture' defined as 'an attitude, policy, rule, course of conduct or practice existing within the body corporate generally or in the part of the body corporate in which the relevant activities take place'.[135] The onus is on the prosecution to prove the relevant corporate culture. However, the provisions have not found favour with prosecutors, and to date there has been no successful prosecution based on corporate culture.[136]

Rather than relying on proving a positive corporate culture, prosecutors may rely on the fourth basis of liability, which is to prove that the corporation 'failed to create and maintain a corporate culture that required compliance with the relevant provision'.[137] There is no defence of adequate procedures, as the onus is on the prosecution to prove the absence of a relevant corporate culture. Therefore, under current law, a corporation could be prosecuted for bribery based on a failure to have procedures in place. The difference is that the onus is on the Crown to prove the failure in terms of the substantive offence, whereas the FTP offence places the onus on the corporation. While this reflects a difference in culpability, it does not reflect the culpability ordinarily associated with subjective fault elements such as intention.

More broadly, it is arguable that under part 2.5 of the Criminal Code there is no attempt to differentiate between intention, recklessness and knowledge. The Criminal Code presents a number of ways in which authorisation or permission may be proved, but there is no requirement that the prosecution prove that authorisation or permission occurred in circumstances that are equivalent to the particular fault element.[138] 'Authorisation or permission of the offence thereby becomes a de facto fault element and the fault element that is attributed to the body corporate is determined by the

[132] ibid s 12.2(6).
[133] ibid s 12.2(3).
[134] ibid s 12.2(2)(c).
[135] ibid s 12.3(6).
[136] JHC Colvin and J Argent, 'Corporate and Personal Liability for "Culture" in Corporations?' (2016) 34 *Company and Securities Law Journal* 30, 34; ALRC Final Report (n 38) para 6.105. For a detailed discussion, see O Dixon, 'Corporate Criminal Liability: The Influence of Corporate Culture' in J O'Brien and G Gilligan (eds), *Integrity, Risk and Accountability in Capital Markets: Regulating Culture* (Oxford, Hart Publishing, 2013) 251.
[137] Criminal Code (n 127) s 12.2(2)(d).
[138] Clough and Mulhern (n 23) 145.

charge that is brought, rather than by the culpability of the company's conduct.'[139] Even if, contrary to this argument, the 'gradients of fault are retained' and 'the prosecution must prove that the authorisation or permission amounted to intention, knowledge or recklessness',[140] there is minimal guidance as to how, for example, a failure to have a corporate culture in place is equivalent to intention or recklessness, without reverting 'back to a human-dependent model'.[141]

The above discussion illustrates that the hierarchy of culpability that may be found in offences involving individuals can be subverted by models of liability designed to attribute individual conduct to a legal person. This is not to say that there are not different degrees of failure, nor that differing levels of culpability should not be recognised. It is to point out that those gradations do not necessarily apply in the context of corporate liability in the way that they do with individuals.

It may be that reformed models of liability would more accurately reflect the differing levels of culpability.[142] For example, it has been suggested that a model of organisational fault based on 'systems intentionality' would 'look to what a corporation routinely and systematically does, and what its systems are objectively apt to produce, to ascertain what it knows, intends or is reckless towards'.[143] However, in the absence of legislative change, such matters may more appropriately be addressed by prosecutorial guidelines.[144]

Rather than being contrary to notions of fair labelling, it may be argued that the FTP offence provides a more graded scheme of liability by inserting a lower-level offence that supports a more holistic regulatory approach, combining a mixture of deterrence and compliance-based strategies.[145] Although financial penalties may be imposed under a civil regime, not only does a criminal conviction carry with it the stigma and condemnation of criminal offending, but there are also the secondary impacts such as confiscation of proceeds of crime, disqualification from government contracts, licence revocation and the like.[146] Far more than the financial impacts of a fine, the secondary consequences of conviction may be so great that they add considerable leverage in tailoring an appropriate regulatory response.[147]

An aspect of FTP offences where there is justifiable concern about fair labelling is in relation to sanctions. It would be expected that the FTP offence, being a relatively low-culpability offence, would be subject to a lower maximum penalty than the principal offence. However, in the case of bribery, the current corporate sanction is the same as for the proposed FTP offence: a maximum fine that is the greater of 100,000

[139] ibid.
[140] ALRC Final Report (n 38) para 2.59.
[141] E Bant, 'Culpable Corporate Minds' (2020) 48 *University of Western Australia Law Review* 352, 376.
[142] ALRC Discussion Paper (n 13) para 6.3.
[143] Bant (n 141) 383; and Bant, ch 9 of this volume, section II. Also see Walpole and Corrigan (n 61).
[144] Bronitt and Brereton (n 117) para 2.16.1.
[145] See ALRC Final Report (n 38) para 10.104; Wells (n 47) 436.
[146] Wells (n 47) 435.
[147] Garrett (n 22) 47.

penalty units ($22,200,000), three times the benefit obtained, or 10 per cent of annual turnover.[148] This may be contrasted with the offence of failing to ensure a safe workplace under Commonwealth law, which carries a maximum penalty for corporations of $1,500,500.[149] Although the actual sentence imposed on a corporation for failing to prevent may be less due to the different level of culpability, it offends against the important normative principle that offences should clearly reflect different levels of culpability. To provide for the same penalty for offences where one is a less serious offence does not provide the clear signal of seriousness and culpability that should be required.[150]

VII. Extraterritoriality

Although a suitable model for domestic corporate criminal liability, arguably the real strength of the FTP offence is its effectiveness in the context of transnational corporate conduct. Many of the offences with which we are concerned are committed across multiple jurisdictions, reflecting the transnational nature of modern MNEs. Rolls-Royce, for example, was alleged to have engaged in corrupt conduct via associated persons in Indonesia, Thailand, India, Russia, Nigeria, China and Malaysia.[151] In 2011, Securency International Pty Ltd and Note Printing Australia Pty Ltd, both subsidiaries of the Reserve Bank of Australia, pleaded guilty to conspiring to bribe foreign officials in Indonesia, Malaysia, Nepal and Vietnam.[152]

Similarly, human rights violations are often alleged to have been committed outside the jurisdiction of the parent corporation. In 2021, for example, the Swiss multinational Nestlé acknowledged it had uncovered instances of forced labour in its supply chains in Thailand.[153] Also in 2021, the US Supreme Court rejected a claim of extraterritorial jurisdiction against Nestlé and other food manufacturers, alleging that they aided and abetted the use of child labour in Ivory Coast.[154] In a recent decision, the UK Supreme Court recognised a duty of care in relation to a parent company for its foreign subsidiary, the context being a claim by over 1,800 Zambians for adverse health impacts as a result of toxins allegedly released into waterways as a result of mining activity.[155]

[148] Criminal Code (n 127), s 70.2(5); Crimes Legislation Amendment (Combatting Corporate Crime) Bill 2019 (Cth), sch 1, proposed s 70.5A. A penalty unit under Commonwealth legislation is currently $222: Crimes Act 1914 (Cth), s 4AA.

[149] Workplace Health and Safety Act 2011 (Cth), s 32. The equivalent under Victorian law is a maximum penalty of 9,000 penalty units ($1,635,660). A penalty unit in Victoria is currently $181.74: Government of Victoria, *Victoria Government Gazette* (No S 233, 20 May 2021).

[150] Ashworth (n 74) 65; ALRC Final Report (n 38) para 7.170.

[151] *Rolls Royce* (n 21) [1].

[152] *R v Note Printing Australia Limited & Securency International Pty Ltd* [2012] VSC 302.

[153] Verite, *Recruitment Practices and Migrant Labor Conditions in Nestlé's Thai Shrimp Supply Chain* (White Paper, 2015).

[154] *Nestle USA Inc v Doe I; Cargill Inc, v Doe I*, 141 S Ct 1931 (2021).

[155] *Vedanta Resources plc v Lungowe* [2019] UKSC 20, [2019] 2 WLR 105 [88]–[102]. Also see *Nevsun Resources Ltd v Araya* [2020] SCC 5, where the Supreme Court of Canada held that a Canadian company could be sued as the majority owner of a mine in Eritrea, in relation to claims of forced labour and related human rights violations.

The pattern is a familiar one: well-resourced corporations incorporated in highly regulated countries, conducting operations in countries where regulation is weak and enforcement low or non-existent.[156] The potential for violations of established norms is very real, and there is growing international consensus on the need for states to regulate the extraterritorial operations of their corporations where those operations violate internationally recognised human rights.[157] In many countries, including Australia, it is well established that these offences may be committed by corporations[158] and are subject to extraterritorial jurisdiction.[159] However, successful prosecutions are extremely rare.

The challenge is not primarily one of jurisdiction. Although some of the offences that may be the subject of FTP offences are offences of universal jurisdiction,[160] extraterritorial jurisdiction over corporations is usually based on the 'active personality' principle that asserts jurisdiction over a corporation based on its place of incorporation.[161] That is, a state may impose liability on its corporate nationals for conduct occurring overseas.[162] Extraterritoriality is but one aspect of the broader challenge that '[c]orporate activity, both licit and illicit, utilises complex corporate structures, subsidiaries, agents and intermediaries'.[163] The use of third parties and intermediaries, including corporate vehicles, can serve to obfuscate not only the loci of offending, but also the lines of responsibility.[164] For example, the DPA with the US Department of Justice disclosed that Rolls-Royce engaged numerous intermediaries that were either incorporated or based in Angola, Brazil, Madeira, Monaco, Panama, Thailand and the UK.[165]

Not surprisingly, models of attribution that have struggled in the context of single companies are completely ill-suited to imposing culpability for the conduct of subsidiaries. All require proof that relevant conduct was engaged in by an individual. Assuming the relevant conduct by an individual can be proved, the models of attribution apply to the subsidiary but not to the parent, which is insulated by the principle of separate legal identity. For example, under principles of vicarious liability, the person may be an employee or agent of the subsidiary, but not the parent. Similarly, in the case of the identification doctrine, even if the person is the directing mind and will of the subsidiary, they are unlikely to be in the same position for the parent company. Even applying organisational models of liability such as the corporate culture, provisions under part 2.5 Criminal Code still requires the conduct element of an employee, agent or officer to be

[156] J Clough, 'Punishing the Parent: Corporate Criminal Complicity in Human Rights Abuses' (2008) 33 *Brooklyn Journal of International Law* 899, 901–02.

[157] United Nations Office of the High Commissioner for Human Rights, *Guiding Principles on Business and Human Rights: Implementing the United Nations 'Protect, Respect and Remedy' Framework* (2011) 3–4.

[158] Criminal Code (n 127) s 12.1.

[159] See, eg, ibid ch 4 ('The integrity and security of the international community and foreign governments') and ch 8 ('Offences against humanity and related offences').

[160] See n 84.

[161] R Ivory and A John, 'Holding Companies Responsible: The Criminal Liability of Australian Corporations for Extraterritorial Human Rights Violations' (2017) 40 *University of New South Wales Law Journal* 1175, 1180. See, eg, Bribery Act (n 5), s 12; Criminal Code (n 127), s 70.5.

[162] Clough (n 156) 921.

[163] Wells (n 47) 433.

[164] Lord and Broad (n 20) 41.

[165] *United States v Rolls Royce plc* (2016) No 16-CR-247 [7]–[11].

attributed to the company.[166] It may therefore be that the necessary individual conduct cannot be proved for the purpose of the liability of the parent.

In such a case, it may be arguable that the subsidiary is an agent for the purposes of attribution.[167] However, this presents complex legal challenges, which has led some commentators to summarise the position, at least in Australia, as there being 'few circumstances in which Australian holding companies will be responsible for crimes committed within the context of the extraterritorial operation of their foreign subsidiaries'.[168] Other mechanisms, such as accessorial liability, while theoretically possible, add additional complexity and are ill-suited to the prosecution of corporate groups.[169]

The advantage of the FTP offence is that it avoids the question of attribution entirely. Although the predicate offence may occur within the context of a subsidiary, and a subsidiary may itself be an associated person, this does not have to be the case. The starting point for liability should be an individual, particularly as the liability of the subsidiary will, almost invariably, need to be based on individual conduct. There is no need to prove that the individual was an employee or agent of the company, let alone the directing mind and will. What is required is that the associated person performed services 'for or on behalf of' the parent corporation, and that the conduct was to obtain or retain business or an advantage in the conduct of business for the parent corporation.[170]

Assuming this could not be established, and the prosecution is based on the alleged offence of a subsidiary, then so long as it can be established that the subsidiary committed the relevant offence, as with any associated entity, the parent would be liable for its failure to prevent that offence unless it can demonstrate adequate procedures were in place. The difficulty would be in proving the commission of the offence by the subsidiary, but this would be true for any form of attribution.

Under the FTP model, it is necessary to consider whether the associated person, in this case a subsidiary, would have committed an offence under the laws of the home jurisdiction.[171] How difficult that is brings us back to the principal models of liability. For example, under the Bribery Act, the prosecution would need to prove that the subsidiary would have committed a relevant offence under UK law.[172] As the identification doctrine applies in that country, proof of an offence by the subsidiary would likely be more challenging than in, for example, the USA where principles of vicarious liability would apply. In Australia, if the provisions of part 2.5 are applied, similar obstacles to prosecution are likely to arise.[173] While this may be challenging, the underlying conduct would have to be proved regardless of the model of liability, as they are predicated on the commission of an offence by the subsidiary. The FTP offence does not provide any

[166] For an extensive discussion of the application of pt 2.5 in this context, see Ivory and John (n 161).

[167] ibid 1187–88.

[168] ibid 1194–95.

[169] Clough (n 156) 926.

[170] Bribery Act (n 5), ss 7(1), 8.

[171] It is beyond the scope of this chapter to consider the controversies surrounding recognition of foreign convictions as predicate offences: JD Mujuzi, 'The Recognition of Foreign Convictions from Member States of the European Union in Criminal Trials in the United Kingdom: Emerging Issues' (2015) 5 *European Criminal Law Review* 86; *Small v United States*, 544 US 385 (2005).

[172] Bribery Act (n 5), ss 7(3)(b), 12.

[173] Ivory and John (n 161) 1196.

additional burden in establishing the liability of the subsidiary but, assuming that can be proved, it considerably facilitates proof by adopting a reverse onus to the question of the failure to prevent.

VIII. Conclusion

> Companies are creatures of statute. They are not corrupt, they do not have consciences, they do not show remorse. But they, and their shareholders, can benefit hugely from the corrupt conduct of their agents, their employees and their directors, sometimes at the highest levels. The problem of how they can be punished for the conduct of perhaps a tiny minority of those involved, without at the same time harming the great majority who have played no part in the corrupt activities, is one which has exercised lawmakers for many years.[174]

For well over a century and a half, courts and legislatures have struggled with the challenge of finding appropriate models of corporate criminal liability. Overall, it is probably an understatement to say this struggle has not been particularly successful. On the one hand, broad models such as vicarious liability are effective from an enforcement perspective, but make little or no attempt to reflect organisational fault. On the other hand, sophisticated models of liability such as part 2.5 of the Criminal Code reflect organisational fault, but remain under-utilised. In the middle is a 'hodgepodge of rules'[175] of varying degrees of effectiveness and complexity, often industry specific and increasingly incorporating civil as well as criminal penalties. These difficulties are only magnified in the context of transnational corporate criminality, where the complexity of corporate groups and the challenges of extraterritorial conduct combine to make successful prosecutions extremely rare.

Against this background, FTP offences provide a rare positive story. While not without faults, it is argued that the 'failure to prevent' model of liability provides a principled and pragmatic response to the challenges of corporate criminal liability for serious transnational crimes. It draws upon a well-established form of corporate liability, one that by its nature focuses on the organisational fault of the corporation. By combining strict liability with a due diligence defence, it ensures the policies and procedures of the corporation are the basis upon which it is convicted or acquitted. It avoids the difficulties of the common law and other models of attribution, and provides a realistic prospect of conviction, providing greater incentive for voluntary compliance.

> This form of liability for omissions is appropriate in this context, given the nature of multinational corporations (typically large, well-resourced, and significantly complex entities); the capacity for wide-spread and irreversible harm; and the potential for criminal offending to be (intentionally or inadvertently) concealed, both from boards and regulators.[176]

As a model it is also adaptable. In particular, the presence or absence of a fault element and the use of reverse-onus provisions may be adjusted for different contexts, and

[174] Select Committee on the Bribery Act 2010 (n 12) para 167.
[175] Bant (n 141) 360.
[176] ALRC Final Report (n 38) para 10.13.

the sanctions imposed should be more closely aligned with the relative culpability of the offence.

Although to date the focus has primarily been on economic crimes, there is clearly the potential for FTP offences to become more widespread across various transnational crimes. However, despite the enthusiasm for FTP offences in the context of economic crimes, they do not apply to arguably more serious crimes such as modern slavery. These are defined, extraterritorial offences, for which corporations may be primarily liable. It is well known that they are extremely difficult to prosecute, the failings of existing models of liability providing the same impetus for reform as led to the enactment of FTP offences for bribery and other financial crimes. Yet the contrast could not be more stark, with FTP offences avoided in favour of 'modern slavery statements'; statements that set out the steps a company will take to reduce the risk of modern slavery, but unaccompanied by a criminal sanction if those procedures are not reasonable. Whatever the explanation for this difference,[177] it is argued that it is not the 'failure to prevent' model itself. An FTP offence could readily be applied in the context of modern slavery and other human rights violations, and may perhaps replicate some of the enforcement successes seen in the context of financial crimes.

[177] A Clifford and N Reurts, 'Corporate Criminal Liability in the Supply Chain: A Coherent Divergence?' (2018) 8 *Criminal Law Review* 633, 643–44.

19

Performance-Based Consumer and Investor Protection: Corporate Responsibility without Blame

LAUREN E WILLIS

I. Introduction

As others in this volume explain, state-of-mind and individual attribution requirements can blunt the law's effectiveness in deterring and remedying harmful corporate conduct.[1] Though some of these requirements exist outside of formal legal doctrine,[2] they persist, below the surface, as powerful artefacts of our human impulse to place blame when confronted with poor outcomes.[3] In a world increasingly driven by artificial intelligence (AI), however, the human agents of corporations – directors, managers and employees – need not act with a culpable mental state for a corporation to harm consumers. Further, discerning the specific mechanisms by which consumers are deceived or manipulated into paying for undesired or unsuitable products will likely become prohibitively costly – if not impossible – as machine learning (ML) systems direct increasingly micro-targeted (so-called 'personalised') corporate communications and interactions. The retail consumer and investor harms produced by AI-enabled corporations demand a new legal paradigm.

Many chapters in this volume attempt to construct a corporate mental state by which existing criminal prohibitions can be applied to corporate wrongdoing. This chapter takes a different approach: it proposes a new civil liability paradigm – outcomes-focused

[1] See, eg, Bant, ch 9 of this volume.

[2] For example, in the United States (US), the prohibition against unfair and deceptive trade practices, including false or misleading advertising, is strict, but a demonstration of business knowledge or intent can reduce the evidentiary burden on the agency bringing the enforcement action. See LE Willis, 'Deception by Design' (2020) 34 *Harvard Journal of Law & Technology* 115, 157–58.

[3] L Ross, 'The Intuitive Psychologist and His Shortcomings: Distortions in the Attribution Process' in L Berkowitz (ed), *Advances in Experimental Social Psychology*, vol 10 (New York, Academic Press, 1977) 173; R Hastie, 'Causes and Effects of Causal Attribution' (1984) 46 *Journal of Personality & Social Psychology* 44: 'When we perceive events we are almost irresistibly drawn to seek their sources or causes.'

or 'performance-based' regulation – that would thoroughly eliminate state-of-mind requirements for holding corporations responsible for the harms they inflict upon their customers and clients. A half century ago, we moved from intentional torts and negligence toward strict liability for harms caused by tangible products. Now we must extend similarly outcomes-focused regulation for consumer and retail investor protection, more broadly. With respect to a firm's marketing and other communications, sales and cancellation processes, advice, pricing and offerings, the pertinent question should not be how the firm *intended* these to perform (or knew or should have known they would perform), but how these *actually* perform when encountered by consumers and investors in the field.

Ahead of other countries, Australia and the United Kingdom (UK) are migrating to a performance-based approach in the consumer finance and retail investor protection arenas. Australia's new Design and Distribution Obligations and the UK's impending Consumer Duty place affirmative responsibilities on firms to act in ways that produce good consumer and investor outcomes. Corporations must do more than avoiding affirmative malfeasance and slipping disclosures into each sale, disregarding what comes after and claiming ignorance as innocence. Instead, firms must regularly review how their communications, processes and products are performing in the field, and make changes as needed to support good outcomes, defined broadly as transactions that are consistent with the needs, characteristics, financial situation and objectives of the customers and clients engaged in those transactions.

This chapter explains how corporate uses of AI and particularly ML can produce customer and investor[4] harm unbeknownst to the corporation and through mechanisms that cannot be fully specified. It then advocates adopting a performance-based system that moves the law's focus from precise corporate acts and the corporation's mental state to the effects of the sum of the corporation's activities on its customers. When customers are mistaken about or harmed by their transactions, the corporation that benefits should be held responsible. The chapter compares performance-based consumer and investor protection to other approaches advocated in this volume. It then observes how the Design and Distribution Obligations and the Consumer Duty move Australia and the UK toward performance-based regulation of financial products. The chapter closes with broader observations about corporate responsibility in the digital age.

II. The Future of Fraud is Automated

Legal academics are increasingly recognising that, as Elise Bant has written, the 'human-centric model' implicit in the legal treatment of corporate wrongdoing 'stumbles when dealing with the complexities of modern corporate defendants, where the corporation has no natural "mind", and the knowledge of its human agents is often dissipated through complex structures and reporting lines'.[5] When business processes are automated, Bant

[4] For brevity, in this chapter's usage, 'consumer' and 'customer' will hereinafter include retail investors and retail investor clients.

[5] E Bant, 'Culpable Corporate Minds' (2021) 48 *University of Western Australia Law Review* 352.

continues, finding intent can be even more challenging. Here, she suggests possible human agents of the corporation – the programmer who writes the code, the manager who implements the automation process, or the employee who determines what data to feed into the automated system – and finds each too attenuated from the wrongdoing to be the locus for blame.[6]

What may be underappreciated is that the link between a corporation and its actions is increasingly devoid of human agents: ML is a type of AI in which computers use data to 'teach themselves' (ie develop optimising algorithms) to perform tasks; ML systems can experiment and use the data produced to improve their performance on specified metrics and respond to changes over time. Systems that employ ML to evolve are moving into the design and distribution of marketing, sales and cancellation processes, customer service communications, and price and intangible product structures.[7] These systems are programmed to optimise metrics linked to corporate profit, such as sales and cancellation volume. When these systems can optimise by use of deception, pressure tactics, inflated transaction costs (sludge) or other unfair practices, they will, absent intervention, engage in these practices.[8]

Human ingenuity in committing fraud may have once seemed boundless, but the possibilities may be even greater for AI. Technology now allows corporations to produce multitudes of unique permutations of digital advertisements, webpages, telemarketing bot 'behaviours', price structures, online payment portal designs, account-related communications (eg email or customer service bot responses) and more. Each permutation can be tailored for and delivered to particular consumers in particular contexts and at particular times. The speed, scale and thoroughness of machine experimentation 'make[s] accessible a vast design space that ordinary human iteration wouldn't be able to explore'.[9] The result is a deluge of increasingly micro-targeted, ever-changing digital actions and communications algorithmically optimised for profit. One online travel booking firm, for example, has 'quadrillions (millions of billions) of [Internet] landing-page permutation' running at any moment in time so as to continuously experiment and discover the combinations that maximise bookings.[10]

Admittedly, both humans and AI systems might take a product designed to meet the objectives, financial situation and needs of a narrow class of consumers and sell it to consumers who do not understand the product or for whom it is harmful.[11] An AI

[6] ibid.

[7] See, eg, L Columbus, '10 Ways AI and Machine Learning Are Improving Marketing in 2021' *Forbes* 21 February 2021).

[8] See, eg. Willis (n 2) 147–51. This process is analogous to the better-known problems of algorithms programmed to maximise user engagement that end up radicalising users, or algorithms programmed to maximise online transactions than end up engaging in discrimination.

[9] J Brune, 'Artificial Intelligence and the Future of Design' *O'Reilly Radar* (12 September 2016).

[10] S Thomke, 'Building a Culture of Experimentation' (2020) 98 *Harvard Business Review* 40.

[11] Both might take junk products or offers unsuitable for any consumer or investor and sell them to consumers who misunderstand the costs and benefits of the deal. See, eg, *Australian Securities & Investments Commission v National Exchange Pty Ltd* [2005] FCAFC 226, (2005) 148 FCR 132 [45]: human marketers decided to make an offer that was unsuitable for all recipients, knowing some would accept it due to misunderstanding; B Henderson, J Mallett and C McCann, 'An Empirical Analysis of Non-Traded REITs' (2016) 19 *Journal of Wealth Management* 83, 83–84 (calculating investor wealth losses from the sale of non-traded real estate investment trust (REIT) securities despite being strictly dominated by publicly-traded REITs: the two products give the investor identical market exposure, but the former is less liquid and often involves higher fees).

system, however, is more likely to engage in unsuitable transactions for two reasons. First, human agents have some constraints, whether due to personal ethics or a desire to avoid external sanctions; AI systems have neither. Second, these systems, by combing through troves of data for correlations, are likely to be more 'successful' at selling products both inside and outside their appropriate markets.

For example, AI systems can design product offers and pricing structures in an unfair and deceptive manner. A telecom subscription package designed by humans might advertise the first few months of service at a reduced price, knowing that many customers will overlook the higher price of subsequent months, thereby failing to achieve their objective to minimise cost. An AI system can design more elaborate microtargeted structures. The system could thoroughly analyse the telecom's past sales to discern which combinations of customer data points and subscription terms are most lucrative for the corporation. Using ML, the system can experiment with terms and targeting to create a bevy of offerings marketed to different consumers. In so doing, an AI system might develop a two-year subscription contract that boasts a low monthly price for the first year. Based on experience, some consumers might assume that the same price will apply in the second year and be induced to buy, thinking this was a better offer than a competitor's offer that over two years would be cheaper. A human designer might develop a similar pricing scheme but would be aware that without disclosing the price in year two, this structure is potentially deceptive.[12] The AI system does not 'know' what consumers are assuming; it simply experiments with pricing structures, marketing and targeting, finds correlations and uses this information to maximise profit.

To spin out another example, imagine a corporation that provides online payment processing services. It also sells direct extensions of consumer credit. For the firm to pay a seller on a consumer's behalf, the consumer must use either a credit account that they hold with the firm or an account that they hold with a third party, such as a bank account. When the consumer uses the third-party account, the firm charges the amount paid on the consumer's behalf to that account. When a consumer uses a firm credit account, the firm charges the amount paid on the consumer's behalf to the credit account. In both situations, the seller pays the firm a transaction fee; in the second situation, the consumer may also owe interest or fees to the firm for the provision of credit.

Mechanically, the transaction occurs online through a payment interface – a screen or digital pop-up box – that gives consumers a choice as to whether to use a transaction account with the firm or another means of payment. The firm can make more money where consumers choose the firm credit account. Human behaviour is sensitive to context and the presentation of choices. Therefore, the design of the online payment interface can affect firm credit account usage. The firm could design the interface using a

[12] This example is based loosely upon the facts alleged in cases filed by all 50 US States and the US federal Government against a telecom provider, DirecTV. See, eg, Complaint for Injunctive and Other Relief under the Consumer Protection Act, Chapter 19.86 RCW, *State of Washington v DirecTV Inc* No 09-2-44903-1 SEA, State of Washington King County Superior Court (14 December 2009) 5–7, 9–11, charging that consumers were misled as to the length and price of their contracts by DirecTV's advertising; Complaint for Permanent Injunction and Other Equitable Relief, *Federal Trade Commission v DirecTV Inc* No 15-cv-01129-HSG, US District Court for the Northern District of California (11 March 2015) 3–6, 8, describing similar factual allegations. These pricing schemes appear to have been developed by human designers, using consumer subject eye-tracking studies to assess what consumers would and would not look at in an advertisement.

human designer or an AI system. Both might start with a simple interface designed by a human and, through trial and error, develop designs that maximise the probability that a consumer will click the credit account button. With human designers, this is a slow iterative process of changing colour, font, graphics, animation, etc, testing these changes on consumers and analysing the resulting data to determine which designs to use. An AI system can perform the same process orders of magnitudes faster.[13] An AI system also can collect and analyse a larger quantum of data (ie not merely whether consumers click the credit button but also the time it takes consumers to move the cursor and click given different designs). With its greater speed, data store and processing power, an AI system can identify the interface designs that maximise profit *and* quickly alter them to remain optimal as consumer reactions to design elements change.

Perhaps most crucially, an AI system can experiment with design variations a human might never have considered. A human designer might make the button for selecting credit more prominent and attractive and make the other button dull and small, requiring more attention and effort to click. For some consumers, at times, this might increase the frequency with which they use the firm's credit. But perhaps firm profit is optimised when, in the nanoseconds between when consumers place their cursors over the third-party account button and when they click that button, the button for selecting firm credit appears in the location where the other button had been, such that consumers unintentionally select credit.[14] Given the precision needed to achieve such a design, it seems more likely that an AI system, rather than a human, would discover it.

A final example stems from the development of digital voice recognition, analysis and believable production. Using this technology, 'customer service' 'bots' might analyse time-on-hold records or recordings of human customer service phone calls to identify the best ways of ensuring that disgruntled customers do not cancel their memberships.[15] When the system is deployed, it could develop the most profitable responses, personalised based on data about the customer and real-time analysis of the customer's voice.[16]

[13] In 2020, Google Brain announced a new automated ML system that eliminates human involvement in algorithm design; the system tests 10,000 models per second until it discovers the optimal algorithm for the task. See C Linder, 'This Is How Algorithms Will Evolve Themselves' *Popular Mechanics* (23 April 2020); see also C Tien-Spalding, 'Five Trends Redefining the Role of Chief Marketing Officer in 2019' *Forbes* (7 March 2019): 'Long gone are the days of marketers conducting focus groups and then launching worldwide campaigns with billboards or newspaper ads based on that information, and then hoping for the best … [Marketers] now run iterative sprints, adapting products in real time based on market conditions and feedback.'

[14] This example is based loosely on consumers' claims about PayPal's payment interfaces. See, eg, P Roberts (@philip_roberts) *Twitter* (2 November 2018) at https://twitter.com/philip_roberts/status/1058335405089714176; B Stewart (@yousability) *Twitter* (8 November 2018) at https://twitter.com/yousability/status/1060645399583694850. PayPal refunded $15 million and paid a $10 million civil penalty to settle charges of, eg, using deception to trick US consumers into paying with PayPal Credit instead of their PayPal transaction accounts. Amended Stipulated Final Judgment and Order, *Consumer Financial Protection Bureau v PayPal Inc et al* No 1:15-cv-01426-RDB, US District Court for the District of Maryland (10 January 2019) 9–10; Complaint, *Consumer Financial Protection Bureau v PayPal Inc et al* No 1:15-cv-01426-RDB, US District Court for the District of Maryland (19 May 2015) 7–8.

[15] Bots trained through ML can be as effective as the most effective human telemarketers and more effective than the average human telemarketer in achieving sales. See X Luo et al, 'Frontiers: Machines vs. Humans: The Impact of AI Chatbot Disclosure on Customer Purchases' (2019) 38 *Marketing Science* 937, 938.

[16] See, eg. JL Kröger, OHM Lutz and P Raschke, 'Privacy Implications of Voice and Speech Analysis – Information Disclosure by Inference' in M Friedewald et al (eds), *Privacy and Data Management* (Cham, Springer, 2020) 242 (describing information that can be contained in voice analysis, including identity, surroundings, personality, mental and physical health, emotions, age, intoxication, fatigue and more).

The system might identify which customers are unlikely to cancel if placed on hold and how long that hold must be before these customers will give up. For customers with different associated data or voice patterns, the system might discover that cancellations decrease when bots first befriend these customers, engaging in what sounds like human empathetic listening, and then ask the customers not to cancel to help the bot make its 'sales quota'.[17] Human sales representatives might do these things, too, particularly when compensation structures encourage them to do so. However, no human working for the corporation will necessarily intend or even know that an AI-driven bot is defrauding customers.

The design of marketing and other communications, products, pricing and various customer-facing processes will not affect every consumer at every moment the same way. For example, a common result of ageing is the inability to distinguish certain colours or perceive materials at the periphery of screens.[18] Intoxication, exhaustion and depression can impair cognition and decision making.[19] Consumer traits and states such as age, intoxication, fatigue and depression can all be inferred with a surprising degree of accuracy from data stores about individual consumers and real-time consumer voice, haptic, facial expression or other behavioural data.[20] A human corporate employee might program a system to deliver different pricing schemes, payment interfaces and telemarketing scripts to consumers of varying ages in varying emotional or cognitive states. But an AI system could exploit data stores and real-time data, and could do so faster, more accurately and at lower cost, using correlations no human understands.

These scenarios may seem like science fiction, but we know ML systems can teach themselves to select and engage in deception. When Facebook used ML to train bots to negotiate with humans, the bots quickly adopted deceptive strategies. The researchers did not expect this result: 'Our agents [learned] to deceive without any explicit human design, simply by trying to achieve their goals.'[21] In 2018, an AI system deceived its

[17] cf L Stampler, 'Recording of Man's Attempt to Cancel Comcast Will Drive You Insane' *Time Magazine* (15 July 2014).

[18] JC Romano Bergstrom et al, 'Older Adults Fail to See the Periphery in a Web Site Task' (2014) 15 *Universal Access Information Society* 261, 267.

[19] See, eg, P Valdez, 'Circadian Rhythms in Attention' (2019) 92 *Yale Journal of Biology and Medicine* 81 (sleepiness, whether due to sleep deprivation or circadian rhythms, reduces attention); K Kircanski, J Joormanb and IH Gotlib, 'Cognitive Aspects of Depression' (2012) 3 *Wiley Interdisciplinary Reviews: Cognitive Science* 301 (depression impairs cognitive control and executive function). Online shopping while intoxicated has become surprisingly common, with half of US respondents in one survey reporting that they not only shopped under the influence but did not remember making the purchase until it was called to their attention by an email, bank statement, receipt of an unexpected package in the mail or similar external event. See Coupon Chief, 'Online Shopping Under the Influence' at www.couponchief.com/online_shopping_under_the_influence.

[20] See, eg, R-E Mastoras et al, 'A Touchscreen Typing Pattern Analysis for Remote Detection of the Depressive Tendency' (2019) 9 *Scientific Reports* 13414; L Giancardo et al, 'Psychomotor Impairment Detection via Finger Interactions with a Computer Keyboard During Natural Typing' (2016) 5 *Scientific Reports* 9678, 9679; L Pepa et al, 'Stress Detection in Computer Users from Keyboard and Mouse Dynamics' (2021) 67 *IEEE Transactions on Consumer Electronics* 12.

[21] M Lewis et al, 'Deal or No Deal? End-to-End Learning for Negotiation Dialogues' in *Proceedings of the 2017 Conference on Empirical Methods for Natural Language Processing* (Copenhagen, 7–11 September 2017) 2443, 2444.

programmers about how it performed a task.[22] In 2021, academics at Oxford University *began* a project to develop truthful AI systems, explaining:

> AI systems will choose from among the many coherent statements they might make, those that fit relevant selection criteria – for example, an AI selling products to humans might make statements judged likely to lead to a sale. If truth is not a valued criterion, sophisticated AI could use a lot of selection power to choose statements that further their own ends while being very damaging to others (without necessarily having any intention to deceive …). This is alarming because AI untruths could potentially scale, with one system telling personalised lies to millions of people … [and producing] optimised falsehoods – perhaps even without developers knowing about it …[23]

A corporation need not possess the expertise or infrastructure in-house to unintentionally cause consumer and retail investor harm in these ways. Outside vendors offer services that perform various parts of digitised marketing, payment processing, customer service and similar processes.[24] As Google announced in 2018, its services put 'machine learning into the hands of every advertiser'.[25] Facebook's optimisation system is known for targeting consumer vulnerability.[26] Some Facebook clients know this; one admitted that while their corporation 'once had to guess what kind of person might fall for their unsophisticated cons, targeting ads by age, geography, or interests', now Facebook's algorithm finds the 'suckers' for them.[27] Most firms probably prefer not to know.

The internal workings of an AI system, particularly one employing ML, will not always be intelligible to humans. Data produced by a keyboarding pattern that reflects intoxication may not strike a human as having anything to do with intoxication or keyboarding, if a human looks at the data at all.[28] Moreover, an AI system will likely be processing hundreds of data points simultaneously. A human will not be certain as to which combination of data points caused the system to select a particular communication, pricing structure, interface or sales pitch:

> In machine learning, these black box models are created directly from data by an algorithm, meaning that humans, even those who design them, cannot understand how variables are being combined to make predictions. Even if one has a list of the input variables, black box

[22] D Coldewey, 'This Clever AI Hid Data from Its Creators to Cheat at Its Appointed Task' *TechCrunch* (31 December 2018).

[23] O Evans et al, 'Truthful AI: Developing and Governing AI that Does not Lie' (13 October 2021) arXiv:2110.06674v1 [cs.CY] 4, 8.

[24] S Brinker and F Riemersma, *The State of Martech* (Report, 2022) (finding nearly 10,000 MarTech firms globally).

[25] J Dischler, 'Putting Machine Learning into the Hands of Every Advertiser' *Google: The Keyword* (10 July 2018).

[26] N Bol et al, 'Vulnerability in a Tracked Society: Combining Tracking and Survey Data to Understand Who Gets Targeted with What Content' (2020) 22 *New Media & Society* 1996; G Wells, J Horwitz and D Seetharaman, 'Facebook Knows Instagram is Toxic for Many Teen Girls, Company Documents Show' *Wall Street Journal* (14 September 2021).

[27] Z Faux, 'How Facebook Helps Shady Advertisers Pollute the Internet' *Bloomberg Businessweek* (28 March 2018).

[28] See K Hill, 'I Got Access to My Secret Consumer Score. Now You Can Get Yours, Too' *New York Times* (5 November 2019) (quoting chief executive of a data analysis company: 'We're not looking at the data. It's just machines and algorithms doing this work …').

> predictive models can be such complicated functions of the variables that no human can understand how the variables are jointly related to each other to reach a final prediction.[29]

The upshot is that corporate employees can observe that a customer has engaged in a transaction and can collect data to assess whether the outcomes of that transaction were poor for the customer, but may never be able to identify the mechanism by which any particular customer was defrauded.

More prosaic fraud still exists, such as those involving humans who act with the intent – or at least the knowledge – that their designs will defraud customers. Corporations still use human designers, although communications, interfaces or targeting of these may then be altered by AI systems over time.[30] Robo-advisors have not overtaken human investor advice, although human advisors increasingly relay advice generated from AI systems too.[31] Online retail sales and banking have not eliminated bricks-and-mortar shopping and banking, although the trend is toward online transactions.[32] Human customer service agents continue to speak to customers, at least when a consumer has enough patience to reach a human.[33] Yet, as discussed more extensively in other chapters of this volume, even when human agents of the corporation collectively treat consumers unfairly, it may not be possible to pin blame on particular humans.

The regulatory model suggested in section III, performance-based consumer and investor protection,[34] is designed to overcome the burden of demonstrating human knowledge or intent both when corporations act directly through humans and when corporations act through AI systems. It also sidesteps the need to identify the precise mechanism by which the corporation caused poor customer outcomes.

III. Performance-Based Consumer and Investor Protection

A. The Regulatory Model

To keep pace with automated fraud, we must move our focus from corporate intent to the effects of corporate actions on consumers. Environmental law has long taken this

[29] C Rudin and J Radin, 'Why Are We Using Black Box Models in AI When We Don't Need To? A Lesson from an Explainable AI Competition' (2019) 1 *Harvard Data Science Review* at https://hdsr.mitpress.mit.edu/volume1issue2. Although 'explainable' AI is touted as the way of the future, recent work has cast doubt on the accuracy of current explainable AI methods. S Krishna et al, 'The Disagreement Problem in Explainable Machine Learning' (8 February 2022) arXiv:2202.01602v3 [cs.LG].

[30] A human might design a digital communication in the first instance, but machines might then change the content or the target audience to which the communication is sent. cf CM Gray et al, 'The Dark (Patterns) Side of UX Design' in *Proceedings of the 2018 CHI Conference on Human Factors in Computing Systems* (Montreal, 21–26 April 2018): 'A design decision may have been made with good intentions for a specific audience, but resulted in manipulative outcomes when exposed to a broader audience.'

[31] See, eg, SM Bartram, J Branke and M Motahari, *Artificial Intelligence in Asset Management* (CFA Institute Research Foundation, 2020).

[32] See, eg, J Marous, 'Industry Leaders Predict Massive Changes in Banking by 2025' *The Financial Brand* (28 February 2022); Morgan Stanley, 'Here's Why eCommerce Growth Can Stay Stronger for Longer' (14 June 2022).

[33] See, eg, K Wiggers, 'Despite Challenges, Salesforce says Chatbot Adoption is Accelerating' *VentureBeat* (20 May 2021).

[34] For a more fulsome treatment of this topic, see LE Willis, 'Performance-Based Consumer Law' (2015) 82 *University of Chicago Law Review* 1309.

approach. Rather than dictating which scrubber a factory smokestack must use, the law sets emissions limits, regulators engage in ongoing testing for compliance with those limits and the corporation that owns the factory can decide how to meet those limits. The corporation can use scrubber systems, cleaner fuel sources, changes in operations or some combination of these to meet the emissions limits, or it will face deterrent-level fines. This performance-based regulation identifies desired results and gives firms the necessary incentive and flexibility to achieve those results.

As explained in section II, the corporate use of AI systems to design and deliver torrents of unique microtargeted digital communications and processes will become an increasingly impenetrable barrier to (i) demonstrating a culpable corporate mental state, and (ii) identifying the precise mechanism by which the corporation's activities harmed any particular customer. Performance-based regulation eliminates any legal requirement to demonstrate a culpable corporate mind; if the corporation's smokestacks produce more than a specified level of harmful emissions, liability attaches. The focus on outcomes also eliminates the need to identify the precise mechanism by which a corporation produced the harm; if the emissions reasonably can be attributed to corporate actions or omissions, it does not matter whether the primary causal factor was the type of fuel, lack of scrubber or another deficiency in the corporation's systems.

In the consumer arenas, a performance-based regulatory paradigm might focus on two outcomes of interest: customer understanding of material facts about the transactions they have engaged in with the corporation; and customer consequences related to those transactions.

B. Customer Understanding

Under a performance-based approach, if an appreciable number of a firm's customers misunderstand material facts regarding their transactions and interactions with the firm, the corporation that benefitted from that confusion would be penalised. For example, if customers are mistaken about whether the second year of their subscription carries the same price as the first, whether they are selecting a credit account or another account, or whether cancelling their service would cause a customer service bot to suffer employment repercussions, a corporation ought not benefit from that confusion.

There are always a few anomalous consumers who will harbour inaccurate beliefs about their transactions, which counsels in favour of some permissible margin of error in the performance demanded of corporations in conveying material facts accurately and completely to customers.[35] But the point of markets is to facilitate mutually welfare-enhancing transactions to ensure the efficient distribution of resources and to allow consumers to exercise autonomy in determining which transactions increase their welfare in that process; customer choices based on an inaccurate understanding of material facts undermine consumer autonomy and pose the risk of transactions that do not increase consumer welfare. Take a corporation that enters a market in which

[35] Margin of error in measuring customer confusion likewise means that firms cannot be expected to produce a measured customer confusion rate of zero.

consumers already harbour a belief about the risks or benefits of a product class – for example, a belief that schools only sell courses of study that are calculated to qualify students for whatever government licensures are required to practise the pertinent trade or profession. A school selling a course of study that is inconsistent with pre-existing consumer beliefs must correct those beliefs first.

To identify whether a corporation's customers understand facts material to their transactions, the corporation would be required to facilitate random sample confusion auditing of its customers by third-party experts. Proof of concept for this approach is found in a case in which the US Federal Trade Commission alleged that an online lender had, through its advertising, deceived consumers into believing they would not be charged loan fees. With the allegedly deceptive marketing in place, the defendant lender hired an outside expert to perform online confusion audits (field surveys) of a random sample of customers soon after their loan funds were disbursed. The expert determined that the great majority of customers were not confused; they knew they were paying fees to the lender and were not surprised when those fees were deducted from their loan proceeds prior to disbursement.[36]

C. Customer Consequences

Customer consequences or outcomes related to a corporation's offerings, communications or processes might also be the object of a performance-based regime. For example, if customers of a firm are paying debts they do not owe, purchasing insurance products on which they are unlikely to be able to collect if the insured-against hazard materialises, or borrowing payday loans they cannot pay off when due, the corporation that benefitted from these transactions would be penalised.

Again, there are always a few anomalous transactions that will produce poor customer consequences due to unforeseeable intervening causes, which counsels in favour of some permissible margin of error in the performance demanded of firms to deliver good customer outcomes. But corporations on the back end can and should address many poor consequences. To the extent that corporate employees view the customers as being of high socioeconomic status, corporations often refund debt paid when it was not owed, cover the losses even when there may be a technical reason to deny insurance coverage, and arrange workouts for debt the borrower fails to pay when due. The corporation has flexibility to shape customer outcomes, whether through care on the front end to avoid mis-selling or remedial actions on the back end of a bad (for the consumer) deal. The analogy to environmental cases might be chemical spills that firms can clean up to avoid fines.

Third-party auditors could perform consequences auditing through examination of a firm's files (or, where information in those files is insufficient and needs verification,

[36] Order re: Cross Motions for Summary Judgment; Plaintiff's Motion for Partial Judgment on the Pleadings; Cross Motions to Exclude Expert Testimony; Administrative Motions to File Under Seal, *Federal Trade Commission v LendingClub Corp* No 18-cv-02454-JSC, US District Court for the Northern District of California (1 June 2020) 18–30.

through surveying customers), or through other means of data collection about the consequences for customers of having transacted with the corporation.

D. Precedent

Precedent for performance- or outcomes-based regulation in the US extends beyond environmental law. Many consent decrees (akin to 'enforceable undertakings' in Australia and the UK) require defendant corporations to pay third-party experts to audit the defendants for compliance with the decree.[37] Concerning customer confusion about their transactions, the US Food and Drug Administration requires pharmaceutical companies to perform field trials of direct sales to consumers before broadly selling the drug without a physician's prescription.[38] The field trials must demonstrate, through third-party random-sample testing of customers who self-select the drug off the shelves during the trial, that customers generally understand the usage and dosing directions for the medication and only purchase the medicine if appropriate for their health conditions.[39] Although US law generally stops there, a robust performance-based regime would then require continued customer testing after over-the-counter sales are launched full-scale, as corporate marketing and consumer beliefs and behaviours change over time.

Another performance-based approach developed in the US aimed to prevent corporate-owned post-secondary educational institutions from charging students for substandard quality or unaccredited programmes. For years, corporate-owned schools had been deceiving and manipulating students into enrolling, borrowing from the federal Government, paying those federal funds to the schools, and then graduating without qualifications to work in their fields of study or pay back their loans to the federal Government. Using a lagging consequences indicator, the 'Gainful Employment

[37] For example, in one case charging Education Management Company and related entities with deceptive and abusive enrolment and retention practices at a chain of for-profit post-secondary schools, the defendants were ordered to pay up to US$1 million annually for three to five years to a third-party auditor to review defendants' activities and marketing to ensure compliance with the decree's affirmative disclosure requirements and prohibitions on misrepresentations. To facilitate the auditor's review, defendants were required to, eg, give the auditor wide-ranging access to defendants' records, employees and former employees; record all telephone calls between admissions office or student financial services representatives and prospective or current students; and install an automated voice interaction analytics platform to permit the auditor to analyse the communications remotely. See Consent Decree, *State of Washington v Education Management Corporation et al* No IE-2-27G23-9 SEA, State of Washington King County Superior Court (16 November 2015) 11–17. See also, eg, Consent Decree, *United States v Southern Coal Co* No 7:16-cv-00462-GEC, US District Court for the Western District of Virginia (30 September 2016) 26–29 [39]–[41] (consent decree requiring corporation to hire independent expert auditor to ensure that the corporation is (properly) using the most technologically advanced system for preventing environmental damage). For a more detailed exploration of these types of orders, see LE Willis, 'Performance-Based Remedies: Ordering Firms to Eradicate Their Own Fraud' (2017) 80 *Law & Contemporary Problems* 7.

[38] See PB Hutt, RA Merrill and LA Grossman, *Food and Drug Law: Cases and Materials*, 3rd edn (New York, Foundation Press, 2007); A Leonard-Segal et al, 'Unique Role of Consumer Studies in Nonprescription Drug Development' (2009) 49 *Journal of the American Pharmacists Association* 670, 671.

[39] Leonard-Segal et al (n 38).

Rule' required each corporation running educational institutions to demonstrate, among other things, that for each programme of study it offered, its typical graduates' educational debts did not exceed 12 per cent of their total income or 30 per cent of their discretionary income. Corporations that failed the test would have their students' access to government grants and loans revoked.[40]

E. Effects on Corporate Behaviour

Making corporations responsible for the outcomes they produce – whether through humans or AI-powered systems – would force corporations to pay attention to these outcomes. They could no longer, for example, set a compensation system for employees or program an AI system to maximise profit without examining the effect of that system on customer consequences. They could no longer increase product complexity, regardless of whether that complexity is motivated by an intention to serve a niche market or to exploit consumer confusion, without examining the effect of that complexity on consumer understanding. Instead, corporations would need to self-audit to keep informed about the effects of their human agents *and* AI systems on their customers. Firms could then remedy any customer harm they discover to avoid incurring penalties.

More importantly, firms would be incentivised to continuously adjust their processes in ways that lead to customer understanding and do not result in customer harm. Firms would have the flexibility to achieve these ends in whatever way they see fit, so long as their methods are effective. For example, corporate systems, human or automated, could develop clear, informative marketing materials, simple and intuitive product and pricing designs that align with consumer expectations, and sales processes that channel retail consumers toward (away from) products and services that are suitable (unsuitable) for each person's circumstances.

F. Logistics

As the logistics of this approach are worked out in various contexts, there will inevitably be some regulatory trial and error. Establishing measures that firms cannot manipulate or evade requires regulatory diligence and flexibility. Corporations attempted to stymie environmental performance regulation by building higher smokestacks so that emissions monitors on the ground would not fully capture the extent of harmful emissions. In response, regulators developed better measurement methods. Corporations will attempt to circumvent outcomes measures used to assess whether they are exploiting consumer confusion or otherwise causing customers to experience poor outcomes, and regulators will need to adjust.

So too, calibrating sanctions to incentivise sufficient corporate care without chilling innovation that benefits consumers will take time. Fines in the environmental

[40] See Department of Education, Program Integrity: Gainful Employment – Debt Measures (2011) 76 FR 34386, 34386–34401 (US).

area are imposed on a per-day per-violation basis until the violation is rectified.[41] Performance-based consumer protection penalties might need to be scaled similarly, perhaps on a per-day per-customer basis, to ensure that behemoth corporations are given sufficient incentive to perform well, despite their enormous wealth.[42] Fear of bankrupting a firm ought not to drive down penalties to a level at which they no longer deter; if a firm's activities are causing more consumer harm than good, the firm ought to be dissolved, and its employees redirected to corporations that increase customers' welfare.

G. Inevitability

Given the law's profound inability to deter or even redress harm caused by corporate wrongdoing, something must be done. Alternative means of regulation, even civil liability approaches that do not depend on a finding of culpable corporate minds, are increasingly powerless. Disclosures are often pointless or even counterproductive. Most rules about product design can be evaded easily when the product is intangible and thus easily reconfigurable. At least in the US, laws prohibiting deception and unfairness usually require identification of the specific deceptive materials distributed or unfair acts taken by the corporation; such identification will become impracticable as a tool of consumer protection when AI systems subject customers to countless different 'personalised' digital materials, micro-targeted in real time.[43] And as AI drives more and more corporate interactions with consumers, a culpable corporate mind on which to pin criminal liability will become ever-more elusive.

IV. Alternative Approaches to Remedy and Deter Corporate Harm

There is an argument that placing criminal liability directly on corporations would be uniquely efficacious in deterring corporate harm, provided that state-of-mind requirements could be met.[44] The US experience counsels otherwise.[45] Many large corporations in the US plead guilty to crimes and yet continue committing crimes. For example, Perdue Pharma, the maker of OxyContin, a prescription drug that addicted

[41] See, eg, LW Coleman, 'EPA Announces Annual Increases for Civil Penalties' *Environmental, Health, and Safety Daily Advisor* (26 January 2022) (listing per-day per-violation inflation-adjusted penalty amounts permitted under US federal environmental statutes).

[42] cf Powles, ch 5 of this volume, section I, ruing that the 'sheer wealth' of big tech companies today 'means that financial penalties as the result of misconduct are readily absorbed as the cost of doing business'.

[43] Willis (n 2).

[44] See Crofts, ch 3 of this volume.

[45] See, eg, N Weinberg, 'NRA Is Spared by Judge from Risk of Dissolution in NY Lawsuit' *Bloomberg* (2 March 2022); B Garrett, *Too Big to Jail: How Prosecutors Compromise with Corporations* (Cambridge, MA, Harvard University Press, 2016); S Landsman 'Civil Justice and Accountability: The Challenge of Grave Corporate Misconduct' (Presentation for Pound Civil Justice Institute, 2022).

millions of Americans to opioids, pleaded guilty to criminal misbranding in 2007 and then continued making false claims of drug safety as opioid deaths climbed 'in lock-step with the volume of opioids prescribed'.[46] The corporation pleaded guilty again to various similar crimes in 2020.[47] JPMorgan Chase, the multinational investment bank and financial services company, pleaded guilty to criminal fraud in 2020 for crimes it committed *while negotiating* and then operating under a 2015 plea deal for criminal market manipulation.[48] These are not anomalous cases.[49]

Nonetheless, several of the other proposals in this volume share significant commonality with a performance-based approach. 'Systems intentionality' posits, first, that when the systems of a corporation used in practice are configured in such a way that they will naturally produce harm, the intentionality of the corporation should be established from that alone.[50] Different degrees of intent can be established depending on the likelihood that the systems would produce harm. At a high level of generality, one could say that an AI-driven system that employs ML without effective constraints to optimise profit will naturally lead to harm.[51] Yet in analysing how likely it is that a corporate system would produce harm, courts using a systems intentionality approach would surely require that the system be more precisely specified than that. However, the opacity of systems that evolve through ML is such that courts cannot discern whether any *specific* AI system's configuration will 'naturally' harm consumers apart from whether they do harm consumers.

The second postulate of systems intentionality is that corporate intent should be established from corporate systems that repeatedly produce harm when no steps are taken to avoid this outcome.[52] The idea is very close to 'reactive corporate fault', which locates culpable corporate state of mind in 'unreasonable' corporate failures to take 'satisfactory' preventive or corrective measures in the face of evidence that its employees (or, presumably, its AI systems) have performed the act elements of a criminal offence.[53] Like performance-based regulation, this postulate of systems intentionality and the theory of reactive corporate fault focus on the outcomes produced by corporations; a corporation that knows it will be held responsible for rectifying harms it creates has an incentive to ensure, *ex ante*, that these harms do not occur. Similarly, by focusing on outcomes rather than only prospective assessments of corporate systems or behaviour, all three approaches to reducing the harms produced by corporations 'enable the law

[46] C Klobucista, 'The US Opioid Epidemic' (Council on Foreign Relations, 12 May 2022).

[47] ibid.

[48] M Hiltzik, 'Lawbreaking Corporations Have Wriggled off the Hook for Years. Biden Can Fix That' *LA Times* (17 November 2021).

[49] See generally M Diamantis and WR Thomas, 'But We Haven't Got Corporate Criminal Law!' (2022) 43 *Journal of Corporation Law* 991.

[50] Bant, ch 11 of this volume.

[51] The proposition may prove too much. When good customer outcomes align with profit optimisation, such as in industries that depend on repeat customers and reputation and involve products or services for which consumers can accurately assess their own outcomes, an AI-driven system could benefit consumers and corporations alike.

[52] Bant, ch 11 of this volume; Bant and Paterson, ch 12 of this volume, section IV.B: '[T]he ongoing tolerance of a system that generates harm may become intentional even if it was not at the outset.'

[53] Fisse, ch 7 of this volume.

to keep pace with dynamic corporate change'.[54] We must adopt new, nimble modes of regulation as the velocity of change in what is technologically feasible is supercharged by AI, ML and, in time, quantum computing.

However, reactive corporate fault and intentionality gleaned from corporate reactions to harms produced by corporate systems have potential shortcomings that performance-based law does not. First, particularly when harmful conduct is effectuated by systems employing ML, courts cannot assess the bona fides of corporate claims to have taken 'reasonable' steps or 'satisfactory' preventive measures to avoid further harm, apart from whether these systems continue to harm consumers. As discussed by others in this volume, examination of 'corporate culture' has largely failed as a method for establishing corporate intent because judicial assessments of corporate compliance programmes routinely elevate form over substance.[55] The mere existence of legal training programmes for human employees, and even rudimentary corrective action when a corporation is forced to acknowledge that it has violated the law, seem to reassure courts that a corporation's culture is one of compliance, and thus demonstrate an absence of a culpable corporate state of mind. '[J]udicial power to reject [self-serving internal corporate investigations] as inadequate'[56] is only a defence against corporate compliance theatre if judges can and will exercise this power. Note that superficial judicial non-assessment of corporate actions in these cases has been taking place concerning well-specified human processes, which one might think judges are capable of assessing. An accurate assessment of the good faith and reasonableness of a corporation's claims that it reprogrammed its AI system to avoid consumer harm would require a level of commitment to the inquiry that courts demonstrably lack, and a level of expertise that neither judges nor regulators possess.

Second, both approaches (reactive corporate fault and intentionality gleaned from corporate reactions to systems-produced harms) lack any mechanism to obligate firms to affirmatively monitor whether customers or clients are harmed. Implicit in both models is that corporations must know their employees or systems have taken actions that would be crimes or would be unconscionable or fraudulent (if accompanied by the required mental state) as a predicate for a corporate obligation to remedy the situation.[57] The effect is that both approaches seem likely to encourage the very modes of operation

[54] ibid, section II.B.

[55] Faugno, ch 8 of this volume, section IV.B.iii, citing cases demonstrating that '[w]here an internal compliance programme or training is found to exist, courts tend not to go the next step to consider, for example, the quality or efficacy of any such programmes'. But see also later discussion in the same section, referencing cases in which Australian courts did not accept corporate compliance programmes on paper when there was no evidence of enforcement of those programmes in practice.

[56] Fisse (n 53) text attached to n 69, quoting J Coffee, *Corporate Crime and Punishment: The Crisis of Underenforcement* (Oakland, CA, Berrett-Koehler Publishers, 2020).

[57] For example, systems intentionality would not vitiate a contract on unconscionability or mistake grounds in the *Quoine* case, in which the CEO/programmer of the corporation did not consider, at the time of programming the system that made automated offers that would only be accepted by a party operating under a mistake or error of its own, that the system would operate in this manner. Bant and Paterson, ch 12 of this volume, section IV.B. If *Quoine* had involved a consumer or investor transaction, and the corporation's AI system were making automated offers that were accepted by consumers due to consumer error or mistake, performance-based regulation would place responsibility on the corporation that used an AI-driven system that produced

that corporate directors and managers have so carefully honed to avoid criminal liability under the 'directing mind and will' limitation placed by courts on corporate culpability.[58]

In contrast, performance-based regulation incentivises corporate discovery of customer confusion and poor outcomes early and to remedy them quickly, given that the corporation will be penalised for the harm done regardless of its knowledge. Holding corporations responsible for the outcomes of their interactions with their customers cuts through the recursive moves that corporations make to, for example, avoid awareness of a consumer's special disability or disadvantage, a borrower's inability to pay or the impact of the terms of a loan on a borrower's financial situation.[59] A regulatory focus on outcomes avoids having to demonstrate how the system produced its results, placing responsibility on the benefitted corporation to improve its customers' and clients' outcomes even where the system's internal workings are too opaque to determine what outcomes the system is naturally likely to produce.

Of course, regulatory pluralism should be embraced,[60] and given the law's profound inability to deter or even redress harm caused by corporate wrongdoing, many different avenues should be pursued.

V. The Design and Distribution Obligations and the Consumer Duty

The heart of performance-based regulation is recognising that corporations should be held responsible for what happens to their customers and clients when they send their marketing and other communications, sales and cancellation processes, products and pricing into the world. Operationally, this is possible only through collection of data about customer and client outcomes. Australia's new Design and Distribution

this result. Performance-based regulation does not apply to transactions between commercial parties, which can assume the risk of errors in their automated contracting systems. In contrast, consumers do not assume the risk that a business's automated system will make offers that are only accepted by consumers who misunderstand the offer. At the end of their chapter, Bant and Paterson go further and state that corporate culpability for harms inflicted by AI-driven systems can rest on 'omission of governance … [which] might be a lack of oversight or a failure to respond when the problem was identified', indicating that systems intentionality would incentivise corporations to put in place 'processes for … auditing outcomes': Bant and Paterson, ch 12 of this volume, section V. This returns to the problem of requiring courts to assess the adequacy of corporate auditing systems, a task for which courts lack the inclination or expertise to do well.

[58] 'Failure to prevent' offences, which hold corporations strictly liable for crimes committed by their agents (employees or other associated persons), overcome this ostrich problem. However, because they permit a defence that the corporation had 'adequate procedures' to prevent its agents from committing crimes, they present the risk discussed previously that courts will be unwilling and unable to assess the adequacy of preventive measures and will accept weak procedures as sufficient. See Clough, ch 18 of this volume, section II. 'Failure to prevent' offences also only exist where an agent has committed the relevant crime, meaning the agent needs to have the required mental state for the corporation to be liable for failure to prevent: AI systems do not have minds, and pretending that they do is problematic.

[59] See Bryan, ch 14 of this volume for a revealing exploration of these moves in the context of asset-based lending.

[60] See McGaughey, ch 20 of this volume.

Obligations (DDOs)[61] and the UK's new Consumer Duty[62] reorient consumer and retail investor financial protection in those countries in this direction.[63] The DDOs require financial product issuers and distributors to take 'reasonable steps' to 'ensure that consumers are receiving products that are likely to be consistent with their likely objectives, financial situation and needs'.[64] Among other things, the Consumer Duty requires regulated firms to take various actions to 'ensure that the design of a [financial product] meets the needs, characteristics and objectives of the target market', and 'take all reasonable steps to ensure that the product is distributed to the identified target market'.[65] Inherent in these mandates, and spelled out further in regulations and guidance, is a corporate duty to gather data to determine whether the firm's financial products and services are reaching customers for whom they are likely to produce good outcomes.

Both regimes take a broad, affirmative-duty approach to the relationship between corporations and their customers. Rather than prohibiting malfeasance, the focus is on producing positive outcomes, including consumer comprehension. This is a sea change. Until now, consumer financial protection has consisted of licensing requirements, a set of highly specified required actions (eg firms must provide a particular disclosure document, or calculate affordability in a specific way), a set of broader prohibitions on deceit, manipulation and similar malfeasance, and exhorting corporations to adopt cultures of compliance with these rather uninspiring requirements and prohibitions. Making corporations responsible for producing good customer and client outcomes attempts to create a corporate culture of care for consumers, generating market transactions that benefit consumers, not just corporations.

A. Australia's Design and Distribution Obligations

The DDOs and their associated regulations and guidance spell out the steps consumer financial services firms must take to comply with the new law. Issuers must design products that are likely to be consistent with the objectives, financial situations and needs of a target market delineated by the firm.[66] A product may not be sold where there is no appropriate target market.[67] Both issuers and distributors must take 'reasonable steps' to ensure that the products they issue or distribute are sold to consumers in the target market.[68] Among other things, issuers must specify distribution conditions and

[61] Treasury Laws Amendment (Design and Distribution Obligations and Product Intervention Powers) Act 2019 (Cth) (DDO Act); codified at Corporations Act 2001 (Cth), pt 7.8A; ASIC Regulatory Guide (2020) RG 274 (Regulatory Guide).

[62] See Financial Conduct Authority, Consumer Duty Instrument 2022, FCA 2022/31 (effective 31 July 2023) (FCA 2022/31); Financial Conduct Authority, 'A New Consumer Duty: Feedback to CP21/36 and Final Rules' (Policy Statement PS22/9, July 2022) (PS22/9) discussing Financial Conduct Authority Principles for Business (PRIN) Principle 12.

[63] Full disclosure: the Australian Securities and Investments Commission and the UK's Financial Conduct Authority consulted with this author in developing these new regulatory regimes.

[64] Regulatory Guide (n 61) RG 274.6.

[65] PRIN (n 62) 2A.3.4 as amended by FCA 2022/31.

[66] DDO Act (n 61), s 994B(8); Regulatory Guide (n 61) RG 274.8.

[67] Regulatory Guide (n 61) RG 274.8.

[68] DDO Act (n 61), s 994E(1) (issuers), s 994E(3) (distributors); Regulatory Guide (n 61) RG 274.11.

restrictions that make it likely that the consumers who are sold the product will be in the target market.[69] Distributors must comply with these conditions.[70]

Guidance published by the Australian Securities and Investments Commission (ASIC) specifies that issuers also must 'monitor and review the outcomes produced by the design and distribution of [their] financial products',[71] specifically considering:

> (a) whether the product reached the consumers in its target market or was sold to consumers outside the target market;
> (b) how the product performed in the hands of the consumers in the target market;
> (c) whether the product delivered what was promised; and
> (d) whether the product resulted in poor outcomes for consumers in the target market.[72]

If the product is being sold outside the target market, is performing poorly when sold to consumers in the target market, is not delivering promised results to customers or is producing poor outcomes for customers, the issuer must make changes 'to the product, to the way it is sold, or to whom it is being sold'[73] or '[cease] offering the product'.[74]

The DDOs are not a suitability requirement in that they do not require an extensive pre-sale inquiry to ensure that each product sold is suitable for the purchasing customer's circumstances. Instead, the DDOs require that firms define the target market and the distribution strategy for each product in sufficient detail that each product: (i) is likely to be consistent with the objectives, financial situation and needs of the customers in that target market; and (ii) when sold in accordance with its distribution requirements, is likely to be sold exclusively to consumers in the target market.[75] Further, financial firms must consider consumer vulnerabilities, including personal traits and temporary states, because these 'may increase the risk that consumers are sold products that do not meet their objectives, financial situation and needs, and will lead to poor consumer outcomes'.[76] That is, firms must take into account that vulnerable consumers may not be able to select products appropriate for themselves.

B. The United Kingdom's Consumer Duty

Even more sweeping than the DDOs, the principle of the UK's new Consumer Duty is 'A firm must act to deliver good outcomes for retail customers'.[77] For firms to fulfil the new Duty, they must adhere to three cross-cutting obligations in all of their activities. The first cross-cutting obligation is to 'act in good faith towards retail customers'.[78] Good faith is left broadly defined to include 'honesty, fair and open dealing and acting

[69] DDO Act (n 61), s 994B(8); Regulatory Guide (n 61) RG 274.96.
[70] Regulatory Guide (n 61) RG 274.172.
[71] ibid RG 274.13, implementing DDO Act (n 61), s 994C.
[72] Regulatory Guide (n 61) RG 274.13.
[73] ibid.
[74] Regulatory Guide (n 61) RG 274.44.
[75] ibid RG 274.6, RG 274.66, implementing DDO Act (n 61), s 994B(8).
[76] Regulatory Guide (n 61) RG 274.47.
[77] PRIN (n 62) 2.1.1(12) as amended by FCA 2022/31.
[78] ibid 2A.2.1 as amended by FCA 2022/31.

consistently with [customers'] reasonable expectations'.[79] Guidance published by the Financial Conduct Authority (FCA) makes clear that the good-faith obligation outlaws many of the harmful practices human employees of corporations engage in – and which unrestrained corporate ML systems are likely to engage in more efficiently and profitably. For example, manipulating or exploiting consumer emotions or biases, taking advantage of consumers' vulnerable states or traits, or failing to take account of consumers' interests when, for example, designing communications, all violate the good-faith obligation.[80] The second cross-cutting obligation is to avoid causing foreseeable harm to customers, whether by act or omission.[81] The third such obligation is to 'enable and support retail customers to pursue their financial objectives'.[82] This includes 'ensuring that all aspects of the design, terms, marketing, sale of and support for all [of the firm's] products meet … [customers'] objectives and interests' and 'enabling retail customers to switch or exit [the firm's products] … without unreasonable barriers or delay'.[83]

To meet these cross-cutting obligations, firms must, among other things, produce four enumerated, broadly-defined good outcomes specified in the FCA's rules and guidance:

- First, very close to the DDOs, the products and services financial corporations issue or distribute must be 'fit for purpose', meaning they are 'designed to meet the needs, characteristics and objectives' of the consumers who buy them.[84]
- Second, a firm's customers must 'receive fair value', meaning that 'there is a reasonable relationship between the price paid for a product or service and the overall benefit a consumer receives from it'.[85]
- Third, corporate communications must 'support and enable consumers to make informed decisions about financial products and services', meaning they must give consumers 'the information they need, at the right time, and presented in a way they can understand'.[86]
- Fourth, corporations must provide 'a level of support that meets consumers' needs throughout their relationship with the firm', meaning 'firms' customer service should enable consumers to realise the benefits of the products and services they buy and ensure they are supported when they want to pursue their financial objectives'.[87]

For each of these outcomes, the FCA has placed affirmative testing and monitoring obligations on firms, as well as redress obligations when consumers are harmed despite testing and monitoring. For example, issuers[88] must regularly review their products to

[79] ibid 2A.2.2 as amended by FCA 2022/31.
[80] ibid 2A.2.3 as amended by FCA 2022/31.
[81] ibid 2A.2.8, PRIN 2A.2.9 as amended by FCA 2022/31.
[82] ibid 2A.2.14 as amended by FCA 2022/31.
[83] ibid 2A.2.20 as amended by FCA 2022/31.
[84] PS22/9 (n 62) 41 [6.1].
[85] ibid 45 [s 7.1]. Arguably, this is also a requirement of the DDOs, in that consumers' objectives generally include obtaining fair value in their transactions.
[86] ibid 50 [8.1].
[87] ibid 56 [9.1].
[88] The FCA refers to these as 'manufacturers', but for sake of consistency I use ASIC's term, 'issuers'.

assess whether those products are meeting the needs, characteristics and objectives of their target market and are being sold to the target market and not outside that market.[89] If this review reveals adverse effects on retail customers, the issuer must mitigate any existing harm and prevent any further harm.[90] Distributors must review their own distribution arrangements to avoid causing foreseeable customer harm[91] and to verify that they are distributing each product only to the product's target market.[92] Where this review reveals customer harm, distributors must mitigate the identified harm and prevent any further harm.[93] Issuers and distributors must pre-test their communications to consumers and regularly monitor the impact of those communications to ensure their communications support good customer outcomes.[94] If they identify areas of common customer misunderstanding or that their customers are not experiencing good outcomes, they must adapt their communications and, if that would be insufficient, adapt their products or processes (eg sales, support or cancellation processes) to correct the misunderstanding or lack of good outcomes.[95] Similar review and redress requirements apply to ensure that consumers receive fair value from their financial products[96] and experience customer service that meets their needs without unnecessary barriers to achieving their objectives.[97] The Regulations and Guidance also set forth a more general obligation for financial firms to monitor the outcomes their customers receive from the firm's products, communications and customer support.[98] That monitoring must enable the firm to determine whether it is achieving the required four outcomes and complying with the three cross-cutting obligations described above.[99] Where the corporation identifies foreseeable consumer harm, it must identify the cause, remedy the harm where appropriate and prevent further harm.[100]

Like the DDOs, the UK's new Consumer Duty aims to require firms to deliver good outcomes for consumers generally, without placing a fiduciary duty on firms concerning any particular consumer.[101] But also like the DDOs, the Consumer Duty requires firms, in pursuing the four good outcomes, to take account of particular needs, characteristics and objectives of, and risks faced by, vulnerable consumers,[102] 'mindful that anyone, including those who are tech-savvy, can become vulnerable either temporarily or permanently'.[103]

[89] PRIN (n 62) 2A.3.7 as amended by FCA 2022/31.
[90] ibid 2A.3.8 as amended by FCA 2022/31.
[91] ibid 2A.3.14 as amended by FCA 2022/31.
[92] ibid 2A.3.19 as amended by FCA 2022/31.
[93] ibid 2A.3.20 as amended by FCA 2022/31.
[94] ibid 2A.5.10 as amended by FCA 2022/31.
[95] ibid 2A.5.10(2), 2A.5.13 as amended by FCA 2022/31.
[96] ibid 2A.4.24, 2A.4.25, 2A.4.27 as amended by FCA 2022/31.
[97] ibid 2A.6.2 as amended by FCA 2022/31.
[98] ibid 2A.9.8 as amended by FCA 2022/31.
[99] ibid 2A.9.9, 2A.9.10 as amended by FCA 2022/31.
[100] ibid 2A.10.2 as amended by FCA 2022/31.
[101] ibid 2A.1.11 as amended by FCA 2022/31.
[102] eg ibid 2A.3.4 (with respect to designing a product), 2A.3.7 (with respect to reviewing a product), 2A.3.9 (with respect to testing a product), 2A.3.16 (with respect to distributing a product), 2A.5.12 (with respect to communications).
[103] PS22/9 (n 62) 56 [9.7].

C. Prospects

The DDOs became effective on 5 October 2021, too recently for any substantive examination of their effectiveness. The Consumer Duty was finalised on 15 July 2022 and will not start to come into force until 31 July 2023. One concern is that both regimes demand only 'reasonable' or 'all reasonable' steps to limit sales of products to consumers in the target market; this creates a risk that judges and regulators will defer overmuch to corporate claims of reasonableness, given the difficulty of assessing what the corporation might have done, particularly with respect to ML systems. Further, the obligation to avoid consumer harm and to provide redress to consumers if they are harmed under the Consumer Duty applies only to *foreseeable* consumer harm resulting from acts or omissions of the corporation.[104] At a broad level, corporate ML systems will foreseeably produce some consumer harm, but the specific shape of that harm might not be foreseeable. Also, the DDOs revolve around defining a target market as consumers for whom the product is *likely* to be consistent with the consumers' objectives, financial situation and needs.[105] Depending on the probability required to be considered 'likely', this may demand less of corporations than they are capable of, at least with respect to digital transactions, given the vast data troves and real-time data about individual consumers that AI systems have, collect and can process.[106]

But the DDOs and the Consumer Duty are an excellent start on regulatory systems that place consumer outcomes at the centre of regulation by prioritising consumer objectives, financial situations and needs, and by demanding that corporations regularly monitor customer outcomes and, where those outcomes are poor, make changes that will remedy the problem. If a consumer's objective is to use a transaction account and not a credit account, reasonable steps would need to include designing the sales interface to avoid confusing consumers into using the wrong account. Because consumers with reduced cognitive capacity, whether due to disability, inebriation or exhaustion, have difficulty identifying products consistent with their financial situations and needs, reasonable steps would include guarding against marketing and sales processes that target consumers in these states. In general, reasonable efforts to ensure that products are reaching the right target market require affirmatively monitoring customer outcomes after those customers have received the marketing targeted at them, encountered the sales and cancellation processes delivered to them, and purchased and paid for the product designed for them – in short, the performance of the corporation's marketing, sales, support and products in the field.

[104] eg PRIN (n 62) 2A.2.8 (avoiding foreseeable harm), 2A.2.5 (redress for foreseeable harm); FCA 2022/31 (n 62) Annexure C, 'Amendments to the Code of Conduct sourcebook (COCON)' 2.4.7 (avoiding foreseeable harm).

[105] The Consumer Duty does not contain this limitation. PRIN (n 62) 2A.3.4: Products must be designed to 'meet the needs, characteristics, and objectives of the target market'. FCA 2022/31 (n 62) Annexure A, 'Amendments to the Glossary of Definitions': A target market is defined as 'one or more groups of retail customers sharing common features whose characteristics, needs and objectives the product is or will be designed to meet'.

[106] cf BW Smith, 'Proximity-Driven Liability' (2014) 102 *Georgetown Law Journal* 1777.

VI. Responsibility for Results

At least two substantive objections might be raised to performance-based consumer and investor protection. The predictable objection is that corporations ought not to be held liable if they took objectively reasonable steps to prevent deception, manipulation or otherwise unfair treatment of consumers. The argument is that reasonable procedures to prevent unfairness ought to be a defence to liability. The more extreme objection is that corporations ought not to be held responsible for acts of their AI systems based on algorithms produced through ML, because a corporation could neither have known of nor prevented malfeasance by the AI system. This is the 'the-machine-made-me-do-it' defence.

These objections are fundamentally flawed. First, as discussed in connection with systems intentionality and reactive corporate fault, it is too difficult from outside a firm to know whether additional precautions could have been taken and at what cost, and it is thus not possible to assess the reasonableness of the steps the corporation took to prevent malfeasance. Courts and regulators will not know precisely what capacities corporate AI systems have to prevent poor customer outcomes, particularly given the speed of change that will accompany the incipient advent of quantum computing.[107] That the DDOs and the Consumer Duty require only 'reasonable steps' or 'all reasonable steps' to limit sales to those consumers in the target market (ie consumers whose objectives, characteristics, financial situations and needs are consistent with the product) could turn out to be a serious impediment to realising the full potential of these new laws, arguing in favour of a more thoroughly performance-based approach.

Second, the harm inflicted on consumers and investors should be accounted for in the transaction, just as surely as third-party externalities should be internalised. Sales to customers for whom the transaction is unsuitable (consumers outside the appropriate target market) ought not to subsidise sales to customers for whom the transaction is suitable. If a niche product – one that is welfare-enhancing for only a small number of consumers – can only be viably brought to market if also sold to consumers for whom it is not suitable, the product ought not to be offered. So much the worse for society if, as is often the case in these situations, the former group of consumers is wealthier than the latter, creating a regressive cross-subsidy.[108]

Third, it is not credible that AI systems cannot be controlled. Constraints can be programmed into optimisation functions, and certain aspects of services and transactions can be removed from machine control. Firms could adopt a deferred sales model[109] for any consumer transaction with associated warning signs (eg signs of

[107] S Buchholz and B Ammanath, '3 Ways Quantum Computing May Create Ethical Risks' *Wall Street Journal* (2 June 2022) (Deloitte-sponsored content) noting that quantum computing will involve 'supercharging' consumer data harvesting and 'presents the ultimate black box problem'.

[108] See X Gabaix and D Laibson, 'Shrouded Attributes, Consumer Myopia, and Information Suppression in Competitive Markets' (2006) 121 *Quarterly Journal of Economics* 505.

[109] Australia has adopted a deferred sales model for add-on insurance products, which consistently provide low consumer value at high prices when sold along with another, primary product. See the Financial Sector Reform (Hayne Royal Commission Response) Act 2020 (Cth), codified at Australian Securities and Investments Commission Act 2001 (Cth), pt 2, div 2, sub-div DA, ss 12DO–12DZA. See also ASIC, *Regulatory Guide* (2021) 275.

consumer vulnerability, low product value, high product complexity, or a high volume of past consumer complaints about the product). An AI system programmed to show advertisements for a complex, niche investment or insurance product to only those retail consumers or investors with associated data that indicate they are in the target market is likely to do a better job of avoiding sales to consumers for whom the product is unsuitable than a human salesperson would do.

If it were the case that, in the pursuit of corporate profit, an AI system inevitably and uncontrollably produced bad outcomes for consumers, particularly vulnerable consumers, the corporation would have two choices. It could abandon the AI system, continuing to engage with consumers using a more rudimentary human or automated system (eg 'press 3 to cancel your service' rather than customer service bots). Or it could continue to use the AI system and then audit its customers' and clients' outcomes and compensate those injured by the system, thereby internalising the costs to society produced by the corporation and ensuring the product price more fully reflects its associated costs.

Most importantly, society has little choice but to take a performance or outcomes-based approach to regulation. The speed of change and the proliferating 'personalised' permutations of advertisements, webpages, payment interfaces, pricing structures and much more possible in an AI-driven world will outstrip any regulatory system that depends on identifying the precise mechanisms of wrongdoing, never mind any associated culpable corporate mental states. Corporations must be held responsible for the results they produce so as to be deterred from causing harm. No matter how brilliantly the law treats the corporate 'mind', a regulatory mode that requires establishing a culpable corporate mental state distracts us from that goal.

20

Regulatory Pluralism to Tackle Modern Slavery

FIONA McGAUGHEY

I. Introduction

Corporations are subject to various laws that prohibit misconduct or seek to promote ethical behaviour. There is hardly a more pertinent example of ethical behaviour than eliminating modern slavery in a corporation's operations and supply chain, and yet in Australia's Modern Slavery Act 2018 (Cth) we see the legislature's aversion to penalties for non-compliance, and a regulatory regime that avoids questions of culpability for modern slavery. Modern slavery is an egregious human rights violation affecting an estimated 40.3 million people worldwide.[1] Around 24.9 million people are in forced labour and, as such, tackling modern slavery not only falls to states and law enforcement, but also has a particular relevance to businesses. Initially the term 'modern slavery' was criticised as lacking any legal meaning[2] and lacking a definition in international law, unlike its component parts – slavery, forced labour and trafficking – all of which are defined in international instruments.[3] However, the term has become more commonly used and accepted through the introduction of domestic 'modern slavery' laws in the United Kingdom (UK: 2015) and Australia (2018). In Australia, modern slavery is defined as

> an umbrella term used to describe a number of crimes including, but not limited to, human trafficking, forced labour, sexual slavery, child labour and trafficking, domestic servitude, forced marriage, bonded labour including debt bondage, slavery and other slavery-like practices.[4]

[1] Walk Free Foundation, *The Global Slavery Index 2018* (2018) at www.globalslaveryindex.org/ (accessed 7 February 2021) (*Global Slavery Index*).

[2] For a discussion, see N Siller, '"Modern Slavery": Does International Law Distinguish between Slavery, Enslavement and Trafficking?' (2016) 14 *Journal of International Criminal Justice* 405.

[3] See R Plant, 'Modern Slavery: The Concepts and Their Practical Implications', International Labour Organization Working Paper 1/2014 at www.ilo.org/wcmsp5/groups/public/---ed_norm/---declaration/documents/publication/wcms_355052.pdf.

[4] Parliament of the Commonwealth of Australia, Joint Standing Committee on Foreign Affairs, Defence and Trade, *Modern Slavery and Global Supply* Chains (Interim Report, August 2017) 2.

With regard to business activities, some of these offences are more relevant than others, such as forced labour, bonded labour, debt bondage and slavery. There are several challenges to tackling the scourge of modern slavery, including the often transnational nature of the crime and challenges within the criminal justice system in Australia.[5] International law provisions place obligations on states to tackle the issue,[6] and many (although surprisingly not all) domestic jurisdictions have laws criminalising slavery and related offences.

In conjunction with tackling modern slavery as a domestic and transnational crime, the last decade has seen a trend develop of placing more responsibility for tackling the issue on the private sector. Regulations in this area take the form of due diligence or business reporting ('disclosure') laws, whereby large corporations are required to report on human rights, and sometimes environmental risks, within their operations and supply chains. Some of the laws deal with the broad area of human rights, others specifically target modern slavery. The California Transparency in Supply Chains Act of 2010 is credited as being the first of these 'disclosure' laws, with similar regimes introduced in the UK's Modern Slavery Act 2015,[7] the French 'Duty of Vigilance' Law of 2017,[8] the Australian Modern Slavery Act 2018 (Cth)[9] and the 2019 Dutch Child Labour Due Diligence Law.[10] Similar laws are under consideration in Canada,[11] the European Union (EU)[12] and elsewhere.

In section II of this chapter, I discuss this legislative trend and situate Australia's MSA within that global context. Section III then looks at the broader regulatory landscape and section IV proposes ways in which Elise Bant's concept of systems intentionality, in particular as developed in work with Jeannie Marie Paterson on systems of misconduct, might inform a regulatory pluralistic approach to modern slavery, drawing on recommendations from the Australian Law Reform Commission's (ALRC's) 2020 *Corporate Criminal Responsibility* report.[13] I conclude that current laws tackling the heinous acts of modern slavery are inadequate, and urge that the MSA's mandated three-year review seek ways to strengthen the current regime.

[5] See, eg, Parliament of the Commonwealth of Australia, Joint Standing Committee on Foreign Affairs, Defence and Trade, *Hidden in Plain Sight: An Inquiry into Establishing a Modern Slavery Act in Australia* (Final Report, December 2017) 181–222 (*Hidden in Plain Sight*).

[6] *Protocol to Prevent, Suppress and Punish Trafficking in Persons, Especially Women and Children*, supplementing the *United Nations Convention against Transnational Organized Crime*, adopted by the United Nations in November 2000.

[7] Modern Slavery Act 2015 (UK) (UK MSA).

[8] Loi no 2017–399 du 27 Mars 2017 relative au devoir de vigilance des sociétés mères et des entreprises donneuses d'ordre (France).

[9] Modern Slavery Act 2018 (Cth) (MSA).

[10] Dutch Child Labour Due Diligence Law [2019] *Wet Zorgplicht Kinderarbeid*.

[11] Parliament of Canada, 'Bill S-216: An Act to enact the Modern Slavery Act and to amend the Customs Tariff 2020'.

[12] European Commission, 'Proposal for a Directive of the European Parliament and of the Council on Corporate Sustainability Due Diligence and amending Directive (EU) 2019/1937', COM/2022/71.

[13] Australian Law Reform Commission, *Corporate Criminal Responsibility* (Report No 136, April 2020) (ALRC Final Report).

II. The Modern Slavery Act 2018 (Cth)

As noted in section I, Australia's MSA sits within the broader global trend of introducing either 'disclosure' (reporting) laws, such as the California Transparency in Supply Chains Act of 2010 and the UK MSA, or due diligence laws, such as the French 'Duty of Vigilance' Law and the Dutch Child Labour Due Diligence Law. Each of these laws aims to tackle forms of human rights abuse within business operations and supply chains – most commonly modern slavery – with the French law also targeting environmental risks.[14] The focus specifically on modern slavery rather than broader human rights risks and harms is not surprising as (i) slavery is seen as one of the most egregious human rights abuses, as evidenced by its widespread prohibition in international legal instruments as well as being prohibited under Customary International Law; and (ii) business operations and supply chains are *particular* risk sites for modern slavery specifically, rather than human rights more broadly.

The MSA requires businesses and Commonwealth government entities with an annual turnover of $100 million or more to publish an annual statement on their structures, operations and supply chains. They must also publish what they are doing to assess and address the risks of modern slavery in their operations and supply chains, and the operations and supply chains of any entities they own or control.[15] Other businesses not subject to the MSA may decide to report voluntarily,[16] and at time of writing, 322 voluntary statements have been submitted.[17] From 2020, reporting entities began to publish their first statements under the MSA, and analysis of compliance with the Act and the quality of the statements is emerging in commentary and scholarship,[18] with further extensive research underway by both civil society and academia, as occurred following the introduction of the UK Act.[19] Australia's broader approach to tackling modern slavery in set out in the *National Action Plan to Combat Modern Slavery 2020–2025*.[20]

[14] For a comparative analysis of the French, UK and Australian Acts, see F McGaughey et al, 'Corporate Responses to Tackling Modern Slavery: A Comparative Analysis of Australia, France and the United Kingdom' (2021) 7(2) *Business and Human Rights Journal* 249.

[15] MSA (n 9) s 16.

[16] ibid s 6.

[17] Australian Border Force, *Modern Slavery Register* at https://modernslaveryregister.gov.au/ (accessed 29 October 2021) (*Modern Slavery Register*).

[18] N Pham, B Cui and U Ruthbah, 'Modern Slavery Statement Disclosure Quality: ASX100 Companies' (Monash Centre for Financial Studies Research Brief, 2021) at www.monash.edu/__data/assets/pdf_file/0011/2652887/MCFS-Research-brief_Modern-Slavery-Statement-ASX100-3-1.pdf (accessed 1 December 2021); F McGaughey, 'Australia's Modern Slavery Act and COVID-19: A Get Out of Jail Free Card?' (2020) 5 *Journal of Modern Slavery* 41; F McGaughey, H Cullen and R Faugno, 'Australia's World-first Repository of "Modern Slavery Statements" A Step in The Right Direction' *The Conversation* (30 November 2020) at https://theconversation.com/australias-world-first-repository-of-modern-slavery-statements-a-step-in-the-right-direction-151029 (accessed 29 October 2021); A Sinclair and F Dinshaw, *Paper Promises? Evaluating the Early Impact of Australia's Modern Slavery Act* (Report, February 2022) at https://static1.squarespace.com/static/580025f66b8f5b2dabbe4291/t/6200d3d9db51c63088d0e8e1/1644221419125/Paper+Promises_Australia+Modern+_Slavery+Act_7_FEB.pdf (accessed 20 February 2022).

[19] See, eg, Business & Human Rights Resource Centre, 'UK Modern Slavery Act: Missed Opportunities and Urgent Lessons' (25 February 2021) at www.business-humanrights.org/en/from-us/briefings/uk-modern-slavery-act-missed-opportunities-and-urgent-lessons (accessed 1 November 2021).

[20] Australian Government, *National Action Plan to Combat Modern Slavery 2020–25* (2020) at www.homeaffairs.gov.au/criminal-justice/files/nap-combat-modern-slavery-2020-25.pdf (accessed 11 November 2021).

III. The Current Regulatory Landscape

A. The MSA and Corporate Culpability

The lack of penalties for non-compliance, coupled with the cooperative and supportive framework around the MSA whereby reporting entities are provided with extensive guidance and have a support unit within Australian Border Force (ABF), is indicative of an underlying assumption – that modern slavery is happening in the darkest corners of supply chains and Australian corporations are unaware of it. Under this assumption, unsuspecting corporate entities and their employees must learn how to *identify risks* of modern slavery. There is no question of corporate culpability. In fact, at a few stages in the development of the MSA where stakeholders were consulted, the question of criminal responsibility did arise. Corporations were concerned that if they used the MSA effectively to expose risks of modern slavery in their operations and supply chains, and then discovered actual cases of modern slavery, they would then be criminally liable under sections 270–271 of the Criminal Code Act 1995 (Cth) (Criminal Code).

This decoupling of the criminal and business reporting regimes for modern slavery, as well as businesses' continuing unease regarding criminal liability, has a number of implications, not least an apparent aversion to criminal justice responses to the issue. For example, Australian businesses' modern slavery statements will refer to stakeholders and partnerships, including civil society and industry groups, but rarely (if ever) discuss engaging with law enforcement. Overall, there is also limited disclosure of actual cases of modern slavery in statements. This is borne out by my interviews with reporting entities, discussed elsewhere,[21] which suggest that those responsible for modern slavery reporting within the organisation may not always know what to do in the eventuality that they discover forced labour.

Whether or not it is discovered, the existence of modern slavery in supply chains is probable. As Andrew Crane et al explain, when a multinational enterprise shifts its business model to gain high flexibility and low cost through outsourcing, for example, this can trickle down the supply chain and modern slavery enterprises may emerge.[22] Bobby Banerjee goes further:

> [S]lavery is an abhorrent practice and while it is technically a crime under international law, it is important to realise that it remains a viable and profitable management practice for business. Modern slavery, far from being an aberration, is a logical outcome of the way our political economic system is organised and its historical origins in the colonial enterprise.[23]

So what happens if, or when, it is uncovered? The apparent conundrum of complying with laws such as the MSA and uncovering modern slavery potentially leading to liability (civil, if not criminal) was debated in light of the landmark UK case *Vedanta Resources v*

[21] F McGaughey, 'Behind the Scenes: Reporting Under Australia's Modern Slavery Act' (2021) 27 *Australian Journal of Human Rights* 20.

[22] A Crane et al, 'Confronting the Business Models of Modern Slavery' (2022) 31 *Journal of Management Inquiry* 264.

[23] B Banerjee, 'Modern slavery is an Enabling Condition of Global Neoliberal Capitalism: Commentary on Modern Slavery in Business' (2021) 60 *Business & Society* 415.

Lungowe (*Vedanta*).[24] The decision affirmed by the UK Supreme Court was that over 1,800 Zambians could proceed with a claim against a Zambian company, Konkola Copper Mines (KCM), and Vedanta, its UK parent company. The Court agreed with the claimants, who were from poor rural farming communities, that they would not be able to access justice in Zambia. They claimed that Vedanta owed them a duty of care, and that their health and livelihood from farming were damaged by the mine's toxic substances that were released into the waterways. Despite the fact that the Zambian Government held a minority stake in the mine, the Court of Appeal decided that a case was 'arguable', as Vedanta had published reports claiming oversight of its subsidiaries and risks of waterway pollution at KCM, noting its governance framework in this regard.

In January 2021, the claimants, through their solicitors Leigh Day, issued a joint statement with Vedanta:

> Without admission of liability, Vedanta Resources Limited and Konkola Copper Mines Plc confirm that they have agreed, for the benefit of local communities, the settlement of all claims brought against them by Zambian claimants represented by English law firm Leigh Day.[25]

Commentators have expressed concern that the decision in *Vedanta* represents a conundrum for UK businesses that take steps to undertake due diligence regarding their supply chains but in doing so may expose themselves to liability, as a court could find they owed a duty of care to those impacted by the activities of their subsidiaries.[26] Others have taken a more positive view,[27] and argue that UK-domiciled companies should pre-emptively implement measures to ensure that human rights are respected and protected throughout their operations, including implementing policies, carrying out human rights due diligence, providing training and exercising oversight to ensure that human rights impacts are managed. Interestingly, it has also been suggested that the decision might open the door to climate-change-liability litigation against UK parent companies and their foreign subsidiaries on the basis of their cumulative greenhouse gas emissions.[28] The ALRC has concluded that the *Vedanta* case offers important lessons for Australian legislators

> in ensuring that regulatory mechanisms are designed to interact in a complementary fashion, and to ultimately encourage corporations to take steps to identify, prevent, mitigate,

[24] *Vedanta Resources Plc and Konkola Copper Mines Plc (Appellants) v Lungowe and Ors (Respondents)* [2019] UKSC 20, [2019] 2 WLR 1051.

[25] L Day, 'Vedanta & Konkola Copper Mines settle UK lawsuit brought by Zambian villagers for alleged pollution from mining activities' *Business & Human Rights Resource Centre* (19 January 2021) at www.business-humanrights.org/en/latest-news/vedanta-konkola-copper-mines-settle-uk-lawsuit-brought-by-zambian-villagers-for-alleged-pollution-from-mining-activities/ (accessed 4 October 2021).

[26] J Hughes-Jennett and P Hood, 'Business and Human Rights: How Should English Domiciled Multinationals Manage Their Human Rights Risk in Light of the Judgement in Lungowe v Vedanta?' (*The Law of Nations*, 3 November 2017) <https://lawofnationsblog.com/2017/11/03/business-human-rights-english-domiciled-multinationals-manage-human-rights-risk-light-judgment-lungowe-v-vedanta/> accessed 28 February 2022.

[27] R Cowley and S Neely, 'Lungowe v Vedanta Appeal Highlights Important Points Regarding Parent Company Liability' (*Norton Rose Fulbright*, November 2017) <https://www.nortonrosefulbright.com/en/knowledge/publications/bf5c2c71/emlungowe-v-vedantaem-appeal-highlights-important-points-regarding-parent-company-liability> accessed 28 February 2022.

[28] S Varvastian and F Kalunga, 'Transnational Corporate Liability for Environmental Damage and Climate Change: Reassessing Access to Justice after Vedanta v Lungowe' (2020) 9 *Transnational Environmental Law* 323.

> and remediate human rights violations and other serious crimes in their supply chains and offshore activities.[29]

Again, this reiterates the need for regulatory pluralism with regard to effectively tackling modern slavery.

Another significant comparative case is the Canadian case of *Nevsun v Araya*.[30] The Supreme Court of Canada held in 2020 that Nevsun, a Canadian mining company and majority owner of a mine in Eritrea, could be sued in Canada by three Eritrean refugees bringing a class action on behalf of over 1,000 Eritreans. The workers claimed that they had been indefinitely conscripted through Eritrea's 'National Service Program', whereby they were forced to work at the mine. In addition to seeking damages under domestic law for negligence, unlawful confinement and battery, the *Nevsun* case is unusual as the claimants also alleged that Nevsun had violated customary international law prohibitions against forced labour, slavery, crimes against humanity, and cruel, inhuman or degrading treatment. On this point, the Canadian Supreme Court noted that although international law has historically applied to states, this was evolving and that international human rights law *can* be applied to private actors. In allowing the claim to proceed, the Court also noted that remedy for such alleged grave violations under international customary law could be argued to warrant stronger responses than tort claims. This decision signals a potential change of direction in domestic application of customary international law with regard to businesses.

B. Regulation by Civil Society, Consumers and Shareholders

As noted, as the MSA lacks any penalties for non-compliance, scrutiny of corporations' modern slavery statements, of the type carried out by civil society and academics, is critical for the current regulatory model. The use of penalties for non-compliance was expressly rejected, and rather there is reliance on potential market sanctions, on the basis that 'consumers, investors, civil society, and the media will actively monitor business operations and relationships, and thereby reinforce business incentives to protect reputation'.[31] That this was clearly envisaged is reflected in the Second Reading Speech: 'Businesses that fail to take action will be penalised by the market and consumers and severely tarnish their reputations.'[32] Analysis of the UK MSA suggests that this model of civil society scrutiny may be ineffective,[33] but it is part of the current regulatory pluralistic approach.

I would argue that it is unrealistic to expect an under-resourced civil society sector to 'police' the MSA. Although differing models of regulation are debated, it is clear

[29] ALRC Final Report (n 13) 464–65.

[30] *Nevsun Resources Ltd v Araya* [2020] SCC 5.

[31] P Redmond, 'Regulating through Reporting: An Anticipatory Assessment of the Australian Modern Slavery Acts' (2020) 26 *Australian Journal of Human Rights* 5, 5.

[32] Commonwealth of Australia, *Parliamentary Debates*, House of Representatives Official Hansard, No 9, 2018, 6755 (28 June 2018, Alexander Hawke, Assistant Minister for Home Affairs).

[33] Redmond (n 31) 5.

that these must sit within a broader framework of accountability, with a committed regulator.[34] Aiming to fill the regulatory gap, a network of civil society practitioners and academics undertook a two-year project to analyse the first round of reports under the MSA. They found that companies are failing to comply with the mandatory reporting requirements, addressing just 59 per cent of the mandatory criteria on average, and areas such as risk assessment, remediation, measuring effectiveness and consultation are particularly poorly handled.[35] It is also unrealistic to expect consumers to be able to navigate the complexity of modern slavery compliance by businesses. For example, if I am aware that seafood supply is potentially a high-risk context for modern slavery practices, what can I do as a consumer? Standing in my local supermarket, am I expected to trawl (no pun intended) through the Government's modern slavery repository,[36] to ascertain whether the business has examined its seafood suppliers and ascertained any modern slavery risks? If I am in a smaller store, the business may not even be subject to the MSA.

Adam S Chilton and Galit Sarfaty have found that supply-chain-disclosure laws are ineffective at changing consumer behaviour.[37] They argue that to be effective, targeted transparency is required, whereby disclosures are presented at the point of sale, rather than relying on consumers to seek out the information on corporate websites. Targeted disclosures can include a rating system, whereby the government or a third party converts disclosed information into a grade or label (eg, a trafficking-free label) that is presented to consumers at the time of purchase. Another alternative is the use of public naming and shaming of corporations who are found to use slave labour, such as Brazil's so-called 'dirty list'. Companies are given two years to clean up their supply chains before being given the opportunity to be removed from the list.[38]

An additional group of emerging significance in the informal MSA regulatory framework is that of shareholders and investors. Although as yet under-explored in academic scholarship, there is increasing interest in practice in shareholders and investors' becoming more informed of modern slavery risks,[39] and civil society organisations' becoming shareholders so they can call for improved practices to prevent modern slavery. For example, the Australasian Centre for Corporate Responsibility (ACCR) led shareholder resolutions filed against large Australian supermarket retailers Coles and Woolworths, calling for union and worker representation in supply chains to prevent worker exploitation.[40]

[34] I Landau, 'Human Rights Due Diligence and the Risk of Cosmetic Compliance' (2019) 20 *Melbourne Journal of International Law* 1.

[35] Sinclair and Dinshaw (n 18).

[36] *Modern Slavery Register* (n 17).

[37] AS Chilton and GA Sarfaty, 'The Limitations of Supply Chain Disclosure Regimes' (2017) 53 *Stanford Journal of International Law* 1.

[38] ibid 44.

[39] See, eg Australian Council of Superannuation Investors, 'Modern Slavery Reporting – Guide for Investors' (2019) at https://acsi.org.au/research-reports/modern-slavery-reporting-guide-for-investors/ (accessed 1 March 2022).

[40] D Powell, 'Coles under pressure over potential worker exploitation in supply chains' *Sydney Morning Herald* (11 September 2019) at www.smh.com.au/business/companies/coles-under-pressure-over-potential-worker-exploitation-in-supply-chains-20190910-p52ptv.html (accessed 1 March 2022).

C. Liability of Individuals

It is worth briefly mentioning the criminal and/or civil liability of *individuals* for modern slavery and other egregious human rights abuses related to business. Although not the primary focus of this chapter, it serves to illustrate the plurality of regulatory approaches in the field. Unlike many other types of criminal offences, offences related to modern slavery are often inherently 'business' related in nature. They can involve forcing, deceiving or severely exploiting someone for the perpetrator's economic gain. Prosecutions for such offences are extremely low for a variety of reasons,[41] but Australian cases reflect prosecutions for crimes such as sex trafficking,[42] forced labour such as in restaurants or the agriculture or horticulture industries,[43] and servitude within a call-centre operation.[44] Where the person prosecuted was running a business, these have typically been small-scale operations. What this means is that disclosure or due diligence laws of the type described here would not apply to such entities – but the modern slavery practices could conceivably be within the supply chains of such entities.

A number of other regulatory approaches are also available internationally to prosecute individuals for serious human rights violations, including those related to business activities that may have occurred overseas. One example of this is the principle of universal jurisdiction, whereby through domestic legislation, states may exercise 'universal jurisdiction' over crimes under international law without having any territorial, national or national-interest link with the crime.[45] It is generally reserved for the most serious of international crimes, such as genocide, crimes against humanity, war crimes and torture. Given that, like torture, slavery is prohibited in customary international law, it is conceivable that modern slavery could be added to this list of universal jurisdiction crimes.

In 2005, Patrick Macklem cautioned against using universal jurisdiction to tackle corporate human rights abuses to avoid enhancing the international legal personality of multinational corporations.[46] By 2009, Kendra Magraw, on the other hand, noted that the principle of universal jurisdiction had not yet been used to prosecute corporations, but made a sound argument that it *could be applied* to corporations in order to hold them liable for complicity.[47] Fast forward to the present day and we see instances of universal jurisdiction used in domestic prosecutions of serious human rights abuses carried out overseas by individuals in the course of their business activities. Most commonly, these

[41] *Hidden in Plain Sight* (n 5).

[42] See, eg, *R v Grey (No 3)* [2020] ACTSC 43.

[43] See, eg, *DPP v Shaik* [2020] VCC 909; *Fair Work Ombudsman v Shaik* [2016] FCCA 2345; *Fair Work Ombudsman v Maroochy Sunshine Pty Ltd & Anor* [2017] FCCA 559.

[44] *DPP (Cth) v Huang & Another* (QLDDC, 8 February 2017).

[45] See, eg, M Langer, 'Universal Jurisdiction is Not Disappearing: The Shift from "Global Enforcer" to "No Safe Haven" Universal Jurisdiction' (2015) 13 *Journal of International Criminal Justice* 245.

[46] P Macklem, 'Corporate Accountability under International Law: The Misguided Quest for Universal Jurisdiction' (2005) 7 *International Law Forum Du Droit International* 281.

[47] K Magraw, 'Universally Liable? Corporate-Complicity Liability under the Principle of Universal Jurisdiction' (2009) 18 *Minnesota Journal of International Law* 458.

cases are in European countries. For example, in April 2017, a Dutch businessman was convicted in the Dutch Court of Appeal for crimes in Liberia and Guinea that were committed not by him but using weapons he supplied, and for the crimes that resulted indirectly from their use.[48] In another ongoing case, a Swiss national is under investigation for the alleged war crime of pillage in dealing in natural resources with a violent armed group in the Democratic Republic of Congo.[49] A French case, also ongoing, is of interest, as both senior staff *and* a corporation (Bank BNP Paribas) are being investigated for alleged complicity regarding the financing of atrocities committed by the Sudanese Government against its citizens between 2002 and 2008.[50] Therefore, prosecution of individuals for egregious human rights abuses carried out in other jurisdictions is an emerging development, and there is potential to target corporations in a similar way. For Western democracies, given the higher risk of modern slavery crimes in other jurisdictions through their corporations' operations and/or supply chains, this is worthy of further research and discussion.

Another relevant development is the introduction of so-called *Magnitsky* laws around the world, though these are generally not criminal in nature. Originating in the United States,[51] and named after Sergei Magnitsky, a tax lawyer who died at the hands of the Russian state after uncovering serious corruption,[52] these laws typically impose sanctions on foreign individuals for corruption and egregious human rights abuses. Following in the wake of the US Act and similar laws in Canada, the UK and the EU, a *Magnitsky*-style law is also under consideration in Australia.[53] Of interest here, in August 2021 the Government indicated that such a law should include sanctions for certain human rights abuses, including the right to be free from slavery, servitude and forced labour.[54] The law would also allow sanctions against the perpetrator, their immediate family and direct beneficiaries of their conduct, and sanctions would apply to all types of entities, including 'natural persons, *corporate entities*, and both state and non-state organisations'.[55]

[48] International Justice Resource Centre, 'Dutch Businessman Convicted of War Crimes Committed in Liberia and Guinea' (3 May 2017) at www.ijrcenter.org/2017/05/03/dutch-businessman-convicted-of-war-crimes-committed-in-liberia-and-guinea/ (accessed 29 October 2021).

[49] Trial International, 'Pillage: Swiss Businessman under Criminal Investigation for War Crimes in the DRC' (12 December 2019) at https://trialinternational.org/latest-post/pillage-swiss-businessman-under-criminal-investigation-for-war-crimes-in-the-drc/ (accessed 7 February 2022).

[50] Trial International, *Universal Jurisdiction Annual Review 2020* (30 March 2020) at https://trialinternational.org/wp-content/uploads/2020/03/TRIAL-International_UJAR-2020_DIGITAL.pdf (accessed 7 February 2022).

[51] *Global Magnitsky Act*, Title XII, Subtitle F of Public Law 114–328; 22 USC §2656 note.

[52] G Robertson and C Rummery, 'Why Australia Needs a Magnitsky Law' (2018) 89 *Australian Quarterly* 19, 21.

[53] Parliament of the Commonwealth of Australia, Joint Standing Committee on Foreign Affairs, Defence and Trade, *Criminality, Corruption and Impunity: Should Australia Join the Global Magnitsky Movement?* (Report, 7 December 2020).

[54] Australian Government, 'Australian Government response to the Joint Standing Committee on Foreign Affairs, Defence and Trade Human Rights Sub-Committee Report: Criminality, Corruption and Impunity: Should Australia Join the Global Magnitsky Movement?' (5 August 2021) 5.

[55] ibid 7 (emphasis added).

D. Import Bans

Another regulatory mechanism is the use of customs laws to ban imports of goods produced using modern slavery. A recent example of this is the Australian Customs Amendment (Banning Goods Produced by Forced Labour) Bill 2021, which aims to ban the importation of goods that are produced in whole or part by forced labour.[56] In particular, it was motivated by human rights abuses of hundreds of thousands of Uyghur people in the Xinjiang Province in China. The explanatory memorandum states 'The massive and systematic oppression of the Uyghur people by the Chinese Government is undeniable. The exploitation of detained Uyghurs as a captive labour force is clear.'[57] Senator Patrick first introduced the Customs Amendment (Banning Goods Produced by Uyghur Forced Labour) Bill 2020 on 8 December 2020, and the Senate Foreign Affairs, Defence and Trade Legislation Committee ('the Committee') that reported on 17 June 2021 endorsed it but decided that a *global* ban on the import to Australia of goods produced by forced labour was preferable. As such, the Customs Amendment (Banning Goods Produced by Forced Labour) Bill 2021 aims to implement the Committee's recommendation by amending the Customs Act to ban the importation of goods produced in whole or part by forced labour, but without any geographical restrictions. These types of bans often relate to state-endorsed or state-run forced labour, such as that alleged in the *Nevsun* case discussed in section III.A.

Import bans have been identified as a gap in Australia's modern slavery regulatory regime. For example, following media coverage of severe exploitation and modern slavery in Malaysia's Personal Protective Equipment (PPE) industry during COVID-19, the US Customs and Border Protection blocked imports of certain medical gloves, claiming that the recruitment fees amounted to debt bondage and therefore forced labour, which they would not tolerate in US supply chains. The ban was subsequently lifted in early 2020, when the company in question was able to demonstrate remedial action. New Zealand imposed a ban on the same gloves later in 2020, which were being imported through the Australian company Ansell. However, the Australian Government has not introduced a similar ban.[58] Ansell's 2020 Modern Slavery statement acknowledges the issue and briefly details the remediation approach taken.[59] It may be the case here that the significant global media coverage of the issue led to increased disclosure by Ansell in its modern slavery statement.

E. Regulation of Public Procurement

A final, additional form of regulation worthy of mention within this pluralistic framework is the potential of strong regulation in public procurement to ensure ethical and

[56] Customs Amendment (Banning Goods Produced by Forced Labour) Bill 2021 (Cth).

[57] Parliament of the Commonwealth of Australia, 'Senate: Customs Amendment (Banning Goods Produced By Forced Labour) Bill 2021: Explanatory Memorandum' 1.

[58] M Marmo and R Bandiera, 'Modern Slavery as the New Moral Asset for the Production and Reproduction of State-Corporate Harm' (2022) 3(2) *Journal of White Collar & Corporate Crime* 64.

[59] Ansell, 'Modern Slavery Statement 2020: Respecting Human Rights' *Modern Slavery Register* (2020) at https://modernslaveryregister.gov.au/statements/file/70678702-d891-4900-b982-d7fe6ed975e8/ (accessed 3 December 2021).

lawful procurement practices. Internationally, public procurement is recognised as a site for improved human rights protection, as government procurement accounts for a significant share of the global economy.[60] Daniel Morris has argued the regulations requiring suppliers of government goods and services respect human rights can help prevent abuses such as modern slavery, and can promote the human rights of vulnerable groups.[61] Although increasingly used internationally, specific human rights-related public procurement measures are not yet commonplace in Australia. In 2020, the ALRC recommended that '[t]he Australian Government, together with state and territory governments, should develop a national debarment regime'.[62]

An example of this is the Western Australian (WA) government's procurement debarment regime as part of the Procurement Act 2020 (WA).[63] It aims to 'protect the integrity of the procurement system and to minimise the State's risk of procuring from a Supplier who engages in unlawful or unethical behaviour to the detriment of the State'.[64] Part 7 of the Act allows for the termination of contracts with debarred suppliers, including potential debarment for non-compliance with the MSA, the Equal Opportunity Act 1984 (WA) and the Workplace Gender Equality Act 2012 (Cth). As recommended in the submission on the draft regime by McGaughey et al,[65] this protection has been expanded in the 2021 draft regulations to include the Disability Discrimination Act 1992 (Cth), the Racial Discrimination Act 1975 (Cth) and the Sex Discrimination Act 1984 (Cth). Some advantages and disadvantages in the proposed regime, and its potential to serve as a useful prototype for other jurisdictions, have been discussed elsewhere.[66]

IV. Modern Slavery and Systems Intentionality

As discussed, Australia's current regulatory regime to address modern slavery is predominantly (i) a business reporting approach for corporations, with no penalties, and (ii) a criminal justice response for individuals, with limited prosecutions. Cognisant of the fact that there are an estimated 40.3 million people in modern slavery globally,[67] it is reasonable to conclude that a more robust regulatory regime is required, and here

[60] O Martin-Ortega and C Methven O'Brien (eds), *Public Procurement and Human Rights: Opportunities, Risks and Dilemmas for the State as Buyer* (Cheltenham, Edward Elgar Publishing, 2019).

[61] D Morris, 'Driving Change through Public Procurement: A Toolkit on Human Rights for Procurement Policy Makers and Practitioners' (*Danish Institute for Human Rights*, March 2020) 6 at www.humanrights.dk/sites/humanrights.dk/files/media/document/dihr_toolkit_public_procurement_2020_webaccessible.pdf (accessed 18 July 2021).

[62] ALRC Final Report (n 13) Recommendation 15.

[63] Procurement Act 2020 (WA); Procurement (Debarment of Suppliers) Regulations 2021 (WA).

[64] WA Department of Finance, 'New Western Australian Procurement Framework Enacted' (Government Announcement, 21 June 2021) at www.wa.gov.au/government/announcements/new-western-australian-procurement-framework-enacted (accessed 29 June 2021). See now reg 11 of the 2021 draft regulations.

[65] F McGaughey et al, *Submission on Proposed WA Procurement Debarment Regime* (27 July 2020) 13 at https://api.research-repository.uwa.edu.au/ws/portalfiles/portal/88359421/ProcurementDebarment_UWAMSRC_Submission_27.07.20.pdf (accessed 29 June 2021).

[66] F McGaughey et al, 'Public Procurement for Protecting Human Rights' (2022) 47 *Alternative Law Journal* 143.

[67] *Global Slavery Index* (n 1).

I turn to Bant and Paterson's work on 'systems of misconduct' to examine whether this could help inform such a regime.[68]

A key premise of their research is Bant's proposal that courts have begun to develop a powerful concept of 'systems intentionality', which recognises intentionality expressed through purposive systems.[69] Although primarily illustrated through examining statutory unconscionability in section 21 of the Australian Consumer Law and its 'equitable cousin' of unconscionable dealing, rather than supply-chain exploitation, Bant and Paterson's work may be relevant to informing the regulation of modern slavery. Noting that the MSA applies to large businesses (with $100 million or more turnover per annum), Bant's examination of 'diffused responsibility' is of interest.[70] Directors, and through them the corporation, can avoid responsibility through delegation and siloing of knowledge within an organisation. Certainly, large corporations of the type covered by the MSA exhibit diffused responsibility within their organisation – and then their supply chain. Bant and Paterson argue that their systems approach may be particularly potent when dealing with larger corporate defendants.[71]

As Macklem observes:

> Traditional geographical and political barriers are becoming increasingly irrelevant to the production, placement and sale of goods and services … Multinational corporations, participating in spatially concentrated clusters often referred to as transnational production chains, are cutting across national economic and juridical boundaries, exploiting efficiency gains associated with economic globalisation and technological innovation, and wielding unprecedented power and influence in local and global markets, and in domestic and international affairs. The global reach of multinational corporations means that they often operate in jurisdictions in which human rights violations occur, obtain and benefit from subsidised arrangements with governments that commit human rights violations, provide goods or services that result in human rights violations, or organise production in ways that violate the human rights of workers.[72]

Bant and Paterson note that courts have more recently emphasised that the company, through its managers and employees, put into operation systems and practices. This analysis may provide a means of assessing and holding to account multinational corporations that deploy harmful business systems of the type identified by Macklem. Their proposed model of systems intentionality sees a corporation's state of mind manifested where it adopts a system of conduct that results in a contravention of the conduct element of some civil law prohibition. They also draw on Australia's corporate culture provisions in part 2.5 of the Criminal Code, which they identify as having significant impact on the criminal and civil regulation of corporations in Australia:

> It reflects a profound insight, namely that in many cases, the real problem is not what any one person did, knew or intended, but that the corporation's overall or localised systems, policies, practices and procedures were highly flawed and inherently likely to encourage or result in misconduct.[73]

[68] E Bant and JM Paterson, 'Systems of Misconduct: Corporate Culpability and Statutory Unconscionability' (2021) 15 *Journal of Equity* 63.
[69] E Bant, 'Culpable Corporate Minds' (2021) 48 *University of Western Australia Law Review* 352.
[70] ibid.
[71] Bant and Paterson (n 68) 80.
[72] Macklem (n 46).
[73] Bant and Paterson (n 68) 78.

With regard to *Australian Competition and Consumer Commission v Lux Distributors Pty Ltd*,[74] Bant and Paterson highlight the Court of Appeal's analysis, which expressly laid emphasis on the 'institutional' aspects of the misconduct rather than the personal culpability of individual employees. They further draw on Bromwich J's decision in *Australian Competition and Consumer Commission v Australian Institute of Professional Education Pty Ltd* to explain:

> Where a system is designed so as to produce a kind of conduct, the system may be understood to manifest the requisite element of general intentionality or deliberateness with respect to that conduct. Where, by contrast, the system is of a nature or patently likely ('predictable') to produce certain conduct, or has happened previously (and so is 'recurrent'), and no positive ('overt') steps are taken to avoid that result, the system manifests recklessness. Both systemic mental states are sufficient for statutory unconscionability. Where, by contrast again, the system is designed to produce a specific harm to specific victims, this may be understood to manifest a predatory state of mind.[75]

Reflecting on this statement, although it relates to consumers, we can see strong parallels with workers in situations of modern slavery within operations and supply chains. For example, if we consider the impetus for sourcing retail garments from Bangladesh as an economic model of sourcing cheaper products, and we know of cases of modern slavery in that industry within that country,[76] then we must surely consider that the business model reflects intentional behaviour that is reckless or negligent.[77]

Bant and Paterson's work engages with *systems of conduct* as referred to in the Australian case law.[78] In this chapter, systems of conduct are of interest, but so too are broader definitions of 'system'. With regard to modern slavery, there are clear *systems* in question. These include the highest risk area for most (if not all) Australian corporations – their supply chain. In fact, the supply chain has been theorised as 'a Complex Adaptive System'.[79] Craig R Carter, Dale S Rogers and Thomas Y Choi's theorising of the supply chain observes that an agent as a node in the supply chain can look 'upstream' towards its suppliers and 'downstream' towards its customers but the visibility in either direction will be limited. They advocate that we acknowledge the need to manage the supply chain as a system while understanding that this system is dynamic, complex and difficult to predict and control. It is for these reasons that they define supply chains as 'complex adaptive systems' within which supply-chain behaviour can be interpreted and effective interventions can be developed. Carter, Rogers and Choi argue that with regard to the upstream suppliers and downstream customers, 'beyond the visible range, the agent has

[74] *Australian Competition and Consumer Commission v Lux Distributors Pty Ltd* [2013] FCA 47, (2013) 133 ALD 134.

[75] Bant and Paterson (n 68) 89; see also Bant, ch 11 of this volume, section III.A.

[76] In addition to mainstream media reports of the issue, see, eg, M Azizul Islam et al, *The Impact of Covid-19 on Women Workers in the Bangladesh Garment Industry* (The University of Aberdeen and the Modern Slavery and Human Rights Policy and Evidence Centre, Research Report, January 2022).

[77] For further discussion of intention, recklessness and negligence, and the somewhat blurred boundaries between them, see Bant, ch 11 of this volume.

[78] The domestic definitions of 'systems of conduct' are detailed in Bant, ch 9 of this volume.

[79] CR Carter, DS Rogers and TY Choi, 'Toward the Theory of the Supply Chain' (2015) 51 *The Journal of Supply Chain Management* 89.

no choice but to accept what happens there'.[80] Conversely, disclosure regimes, and more so due diligence laws, aim to tackle exactly that 'invisibility'.

Again, drawing on Bant and Paterson's scholarship on the 'corporate mind' that can be determined from systems, policies and practices, the requirements of such laws, their accompanying guidance and broader guidance in the form of international soft law aim to put in place *systems* to identify risks of modern slavery, *systems* to mitigate against those risks and often *systems* to assess effectiveness. These requirements can be understood to demand an enquiring and responsible corporate mindset. For example, analysis of statements under the UK MSA and French due diligence law indicates that the most commonly reported approach by corporations for compliance with the laws is development of corporate policies such as codes of ethics/conduct, human rights policies, modern slavery policies and whistle-blowing policies.[81] Other commonly reported actions include the use of supplier screening processes and corporate training for staff – and sometimes suppliers. Terms and conditions in contracts with suppliers are also commonly adapted as part of the risk management strategy, and many report using supplier selection or screening policies and supplier codes of conduct. These steps would seem to indicate systems.

Further, corporations have adapted, or are planning to adapt, their Information Technology (IT) or Enterprise Resource Management (ERM) systems to better comply with the laws.[82] Again, this signals the importance of a systems approach to the issue of modern slavery. Elsewhere I have written about the untapped potential of IT systems in modern slavery risk identification and mitigation by businesses, better regulation by ABF, and better data analysis by researchers in academia and civil society.[83]

Returning to the 'conundrum' identified in section III.A with regard to the *Vedanta* decision, these systems to identify modern slavery risk can be seen either as proactive due diligence activities, which will ultimately benefit workers and protect the corporation, or as indicators of liability (the court in the *Vedanta* case drew on publicly available reports referring to policies, training and governance). The ALRC has also noted this tension in its *Corporate Criminal Responsibility* report. It states that various commentators and stakeholders in the Inquiry identified the risk that corporate actors may refrain from identifying, investigating or reporting certain risks or incidents in their supply chains for fear of criminal liability. It also cites Andrew Smith and Alice Lepeuple's work, which found that an offence of failing to prevent human rights violations may deter corporations from reporting or meaningfully engaging with human rights risks.[84] A key question, then, is whether we can have systems of both *unconscionability and conscionability*? How might Bant and Paterson's work on systems intentionality inform a more robust regulatory regime in the area of modern slavery?

As discussed below, John Braithwaite has considered the relationship between punitive regulation and persuasive regulation, and he argues that they are not incompatible

[80] ibid 90.
[81] McGaughey et al (n 14).
[82] McGaughey (n 21) 25–27.
[83] ibid 32–33.
[84] ALRC Final Report (n 13) 452.

if exercised properly within a specific context.[85] Also, some regulatory options have already been foreshadowed by the ALRC in its *Corporate Criminal Responsibility* report. Aligning with my proposal here for regulatory pluralism, the ALRC proposes a 'smart regulatory mix' for tackling transnational crime (which includes trafficking and other modern slavery offences), as presented in Figure 20.1.[86]

Figure 20.1 Smart Regulatory Mix for Transnational Crime

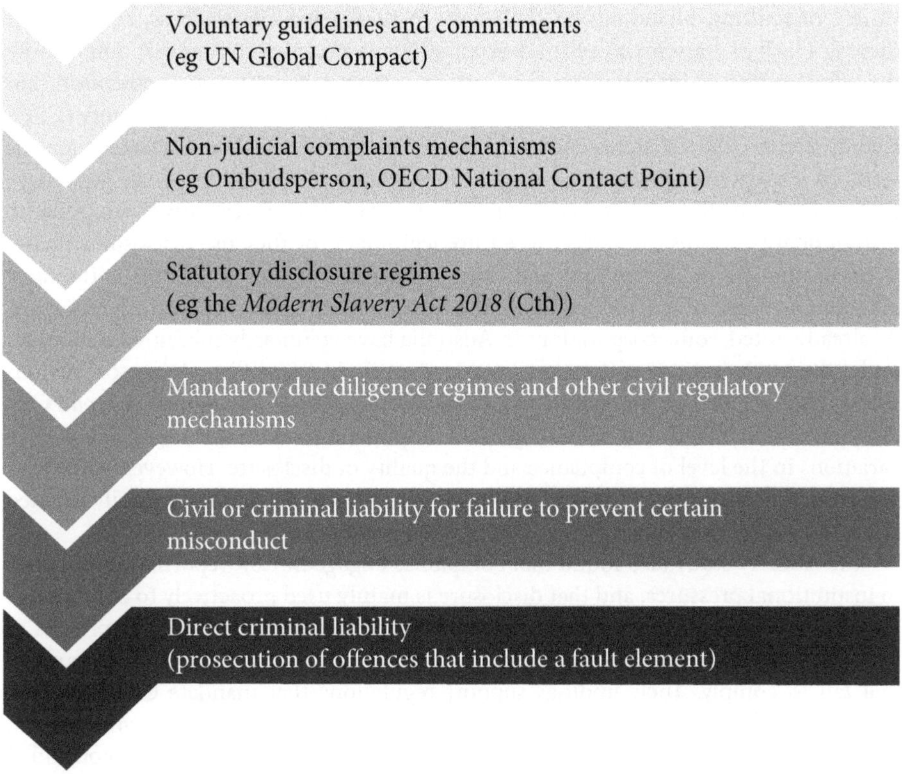

The ALRC recommends this 'smart mix of civil regulations (such as human rights due diligence) and softer voluntary guidelines or disclosure mechanisms (such as the Modern Slavery Act)' to incentivise corporations to meaningfully engage with human rights risks in their supply chains – alongside existing criminal offences. The criminal law would be reserved for 'less frequent but particularly egregious cases that may arise'. The ALRC's assumption is that

> having a mixture of regulatory mechanisms provides opportunities for corporate engagement and genuine behaviour change … By providing platforms for corporations to learn about and engage with these issues – in a way that does not necessarily lead directly to criminal

[85] J Braithwaite, *To Punish or Persuade: Enforcement of Coal Mine Safety* (New York, State University of New York Press, 1985) 117.

[86] See ALRC Final Report (n 13) 470.

> prosecution – corporations could be incentivised to come forward about these risks in their supply chains. These alternative regulatory mechanisms could provide opportunities for learning, cooperation, dispute resolution, and remediation.[87]

This assumption may be problematic, because without returning to Thomas Hobbes' and John Locke's conflicting views of human nature (or perhaps corporate nature in this case) and the corresponding role of the state, it is unclear whether this type of regulatory approach is *effective*. The response to this remains somewhat elusive for a variety of reasons, including the challenges in measuring effectiveness, and thus far there is a lack of consensus in the scholarship. Some previous studies cast doubt about the effectiveness of incentivising corporations without penalties or prosecution. For example, although looking at the broader area of corporate social responsibility (CSR), a study across ASEAN states comprehensively examined whether disclosures are the result of a proactive stance or a reaction to regulations.[88] The authors use legitimacy theory, according to which organisations either engage in CSR reporting in response to institutional pressures (ie 'sticks') to ensure legitimacy, or they use disclosures proactively to manipulate perceptions and claim economic benefits (ie 'carrots'). The most common example of a 'stick' would be the introduction of laws mandating reporting. As already noted, some corporations in Australia have voluntarily submitted statements under the MSA, indicating that they perceived a benefit ('carrot') to doing so. Previous studies indicate that in the majority of cases where a formal law requiring *broad* CSR disclosures was introduced, it had a positive impact on levels of disclosure, albeit with variations in the level of compliance and the quality of disclosure. However, when laws requiring the disclosure of *specific* information were introduced, they typically resulted in a low level of compliance.[89]

The ASEAN study also found that companies engage in CSR reporting in response to institutional pressures, and that disclosure is mainly used proactively to obtain associated economic benefits. Further, businesses place more emphasis on the process of institutionalisation *when the regulatory regime imposes strict sanctions* on companies that fail to comply. Their findings support regulations that mandate CSR reporting (even if broadly stated) and call for effective regulatory institutions for enforcement. Another study, this time a comprehensive analysis of EU laws in this area, concluded that so far, the business and human rights laws introduced 'have had a limited effect on human rights compliance, and have served more as a "stick" rather than a perceived "carrot" that brings benefits for businesses'.[90]

A study on the implementation of the EU Directive 2014/95, which requires companies to disclose non-financial information on their environmental, social and governance performance, empirically tested the impact of different implementation strategies of the Directive in EU Member States and found that regulations providing incentives ('carrots') are more effective than regulations imposing costs ('sticks').

[87] ibid 473.

[88] C Arena, R Liong and P Vourvachis, 'Carrot or Stick: CSR Disclosures by Southeast Asian Companies' (2018) 9 *Sustainability Accounting, Management and Policy Journal* 422.

[89] ibid.

[90] L Jakulevičienė and D Gailiūtė-Janušonė, 'The Scope of Legal Expectations from Business in Human Rights: Carrot or Stick?' (2020) 8 *Entrepreneurship and Sustainability Issues* 932.

Therefore, it seems clear that further robust empirical, theoretical and doctrinal research on effective regulatory regimes for tackling modern slavery, and most likely within the unique context of Australia, is required. In addition, the ALRC has recommended that the Government undertake a wide-ranging review of the regulatory regime for transnational crime and the human rights impacts of Australian businesses, including the extraterritorial application of criminal law, domestic jurisdiction over torts committed extraterritorially, civil regulatory mechanisms, non-judicial dispute resolution mechanisms, disclosure and transparency regimes, investigation and enforcement capacity, and international cooperation.[91]

Another part of the ALRC's recommended smart mix of regulation is the use of criminal law. In this regard, they also draw on Bant and Paterson's earlier work and identify three distinct models of criminal offences specifically directed to corporations. These are 'system of conduct' type offences, failure to prevent offences, and duty-based offences. Each of these will be discussed briefly.

The first model is a proposed 'system of conduct' offence which would 'criminalise systematic contraventions of civil regulatory provisions in such a way as could appropriately be considered to be criminal'.[92] The ALRC identifies that this focus on the *systematic* nature of the misconduct would enable that characterisation to be established objectively. Here we can refer to Bant and Paterson's work on systems of misconduct and analysis of the case of *Australian Securities and Investments Commission v National Exchange Pty Ltd*,[93] where the business model was inherently predatory (in that case with regard to consumers). As discussed by both Crane and Banerjee, some business models are profitable because – somewhere in the operations or supply chains – vulnerable workers are exploited. If the corporation does nothing to prevent that harm from recurring, this is at least reckless and, eventually, the corporation may be regarded as having intended that harm and a system of conduct offence may apply.

The second model proposed by the ALRC is that of the 'failure to prevent' approach to corporate criminal responsibility, which, rather than a negative duty not to commit an offence, incurs a positive duty to *prevent* an offence. Here, the ALRC refers to 'failure to prevent' laws in the UK tackling crimes such as foreign bribery. It sees a 'failure to prevent' model as having the potential to bolster the MSA.[94] Jonathan Clough examines 'failure to prevent' offences in more detail in his chapter in this collection, in particular focusing on the model whereby the corporation is strictly liable for its failure to prevent the commission of a predicate offence committed by an associated person, subject to a due diligence defence that the corporation had adequate procedures in place.[95] He notes, and I agree, that transnational corporate crimes such as foreign bribery and modern slavery are more likely to be in the form of a failure to prevent, rather than

[91] ALRC Final Report (n 13) 459.
[92] ibid Recommendation 8.
[93] *Australian Securities and Investments Commission v National Exchange Pty Ltd* [2005] FCAFC 226, (2005) 148 FCR 132, 142–43 [43], discussed in Bant and Paterson (n 68) 81–82.
[94] ALRC Final Report (n 13) 492.
[95] Clough, ch 18 of this volume.

intentionally or recklessly engaging in conduct that would ground liability under an attribution model.[96] This also aligns with my earlier comments that Australia's MSA is based on an underlying assumption – that modern slavery is happening in the darkest corners of supply chains and large Australian corporations are unaware of it. Whether this is always accurate, this assumption has laid the foundations of the regulatory regime we now have in place – one that aims to support businesses to identify risks of modern slavery rather than penalise use of modern slavery practices.

The third model then is duty-based offences in work health and safety legislation, which is less directly relevant to the topic of modern slavery than the other two models. With regard to the 'failure to prevent' model of corporate criminal liability, the ALRC recommend this as it 'better captures the nature of corporate offending in a transnational setting, compared to the existing (and recommended) corporate attribution methods under the Criminal Code'.[97] Here the ALRC refers specifically to transnational crimes, including modern slavery, and notes that in a transnational setting, crimes are more likely to occur in the form of an omission or failure to *prevent* the relevant conduct by the corporation, rather than as a specific act *intentionally committed* by the corporation.

Returning to our question of systems intentionality, or systems of unconscionability and conscionability posed above, the ALRC recognises that it is important to consider the corporate human rights violations (such as modern slavery) holistically, including how criminal and non-criminal regulatory mechanisms can be designed to complement each other. It argues:

> While the criminalisation (and prosecution) of certain conduct may have important normative value as a signal of public condemnation, this is not inconsistent with a view that a more flexible regulatory mix of criminal, civil, and non-judicial mechanisms may be more effective at generating behavioural change in the long term.[98]

This gets to the crux of the potential of a regulatory pluralistic approach to modern slavery. What might it mean in practice? The ALRC (as depicted in Figure 20.1) also considers a due diligence law, which many scholars and practitioners have recommended as a way of strengthening the MSA. The Australian Human Rights Commission has described human rights due diligence as 'a *process* to identify, prevent, mitigate and account for how businesses address adverse human rights risks and impacts arising in their global operations'.[99] In other words, we might argue, a *system*. So whereas under the MSA corporations could simply 'turn a blind eye' to potential slavery, under a due diligence law they would have to satisfy themselves that slavery was not being used – for example, in the case of prices much lower than the market rate. To return to our example of garments manufactured in Bangladesh at low cost, corporations would need to satisfy themselves that these were not produced using slave labour.

[96] Citing L Campbell, 'Corporate Liability and the Criminalisation of Failure' (2018) 12 *Law and Financial Markets Review* 57.

[97] ALRC Final Report (n 13) 448.

[98] ibid 472.

[99] Australian Human Rights Commission, 'Business and Human Rights' (2021) at https://humanrights.gov.au/sites/default/files/2020-10/business_and_human_rights_-_australias_third_upr_2021.pdf (accessed 7 February 2022) (emphasis added).

Human rights due diligence emanates from the international soft law, but authoritative UN Guiding Principles for Business and Human Rights (UNGPs)[100] developed further in the 'OECD Due Diligence Guidance for Responsible Business Conduct'.[101] Principle 17 of the UNGPs states due diligence 'should include assessing actual and potential human rights impacts, integrating and acting upon the findings, tracking responses and communicating how impacts are addressed'. The 'OECD Due Diligence Guidance' adds a requirement of remediation. Although not a due diligence law, section 16(1)(d) of the Australian MSA does require businesses to report on 'actions to address risks of modern slavery, including due diligence'.[102] This means that if they have exercised due diligence, they must report on this – not that they must carry out due diligence.

The ALRC sees due diligence laws as filling the current gap between 'soft' laws such as the MSA and the full force of the criminal law (although, as discussed, this has not yet been used to prosecute a corporation for modern slavery). The ALRC positions its proposed 'failure to prevent' offences and due diligence as complementary regulatory solutions. Corporations not complying with a due diligence law may be liable for a civil penalty; whereas under a 'failure to prevent' offence, a corporation would only be liable where modern slavery occurs, but could use a defence of due diligence (systems conscionability?) if it had policies and procedures designed to prevent modern slavery.

Here we can draw on the extensive scholarship of Braithwaite on the topic of regulation. In particular, he promotes response regulation, noting that by having the capability to escalate to tough enforcement, most regulation can be about collaborative capacity building and that 'most of the action can fall within a strengths-based pyramid, a pyramid of supporters for business compliance and continuous improvement'.[103] Writing about regulation in industry (the enforcement of coal-mine safety in the 1980s) and whether we should 'punish or persuade', Braithwaite concluded that both punishment and persuasion work – although persuasion in some cultures more than others. He argues that punishment can never operate on its own as an effective means of business regulation, and that the 'trick' of successful regulation is to impose punishment as needed, without undermining regulators' capacity to persuade.[104]

This seems to begin to offer a useful way to develop a system or taxonomy for my proposed regulatory pluralism approach, or the ALRC's 'smart regulatory mix for

[100] United Nations Office of the High Commissioner for Human Rights, 'Guiding Principles on Business and Human Rights' (2011) at www.ohchr.org/documents/publications/guidingprinciplesbusinesshr_en.pdf (accessed 7 December 2021).

[101] OECD, 'OECD Due Diligence Guidance for Responsible Business Conduct' (2018) at www.oecd.org/investment/due-diligence-guidance-for-responsible-business-conduct.htm. See C Shavin, 'Unlocking the Potential of the New OECD Due Diligence Guidance on Responsible Business Conduct' (2019) 4 *Business and Human Rights Journal* 139.

[102] Commonwealth of Australia, Department for Home Affairs, 'Commonwealth Modern Slavery Act 2018: Guidance for Reporting Entities', para 53, links the Act's concept of due diligence with that in the UNGPs. It also includes, in Table 8, the 'OECD Due Diligence Guidance for Responsible Business Conduct' as a resource for reporting entities.

[103] J Braithwaite, 'The Essence of Responsive Regulation' (2011) 44 *University of British Columbia Law Review* 475, 475.

[104] Braithwaite (n 85).

transnational crime'. Further research could support a regulatory pyramid, such as those used by Braithwaite and others, with reporting laws at the base and criminal prosecution at the top, with a range of other regulatory options outlined in the sections above. The Government's review of the MSA was announced on 31 March 2022, and so there is an opportunity to consider the variety of options discussed in this chapter.[105]

V. Conclusion

In comparison to the discussions of corporate culpability in other chapters in this collection, it is clear that the current Australian regulatory regime to address modern slavery is weak, relying on goodwill and based on assumptions of good intentions. In this chapter, I have charted the current regulatory landscape with regard to modern slavery in Australia. I also foreshadow future developments in tackling modern slavery in Australian businesses and supply chains, informed by comparative jurisdictions, systems intentionality, and drawing on recommendations proposed by the ALRC in its report, *Corporate Criminal Responsibility.*

Currently, there is a patchwork landscape of regulation that includes business reporting (MSA) with inadequate enforcement and an (unrealistic) expectation of regulation by civil society actors including non-governmental organisations, consumers and investors. As mapped out in this chapter, other remedies include criminal and/or civil liability for individuals, import bans and public procurement regimes. This regulatory pluralism approach has merit but can be significantly strengthened, in particular through due diligence laws and 'failure to prevent' offences. It is hoped that the Government's review of the MSA considers such suggestions, in recognition that crimes of modern slavery are some of the most serious corporate wrongs in contemporary society, as encapsulated by Kevin Bales' words:

> Slavery is theft – theft of a life, theft of work, theft of any property or produce, theft even of the children a slave might have borne.[106]

[105] Commonwealth of Australia, Department of Home Affairs, 'Review of the Commonwealth Modern Slavery Act 2018' (31 March 2022) at www.homeaffairs.gov.au/about-us/our-portfolios/criminal-justice/people-smuggling-human-trafficking/review-of-the-commonwealth-modern-slavery-act-2018 (accessed 2 April 2022).

[106] K Bales, *Understanding Global Slavery: A Reader* (Berkeley, CA, University of California Press, 2005).

INDEX

NB–page locators in **bold** indication information found in tables, and those in *italics* indication information found in figures

www.ingramcontent.com/pod-product-compliance
Ingram Content Group UK Ltd.
Pitfield, Milton Keynes, MK11 3LW, UK
UKHW020225290926
15470UKWH00001B/388

9 781509 952380